Praise for *The Divided*

"Patel and Rushefsky for s[u]ccess]ful observers of healthcare policy in America. *The Divided State of American Healthcare* continues their excellent work. It provides a comprehensive examination of some of the major themes in American thought that affect healthcare policy. They make it clear that religious and political beliefs, for example, often substitute for scientific findings in the minds of far too many citizens, especially in "red states." Those states suffer accordingly.

Ever since Shakespeare assured us that "the truth will out," advocates of self-government and education have been optimistic. Today, though, the efforts of one of America's two major political parties have become fervently re-oriented toward ensuring that the truth will not "out"; rather it will be *stamped* out—even with regard to healthcare.

Patel and Rushefsky here—albeit tactfully—take their place among those seeking to preserve the search for truth, not suppress it."

Max J. Skidmore, *University of Missouri Curators' Distinguished Professor Emeritus, USA*

"Although there are studies which explore how polarized politics in America have impacted the social, and moral policies of state governments, the question that scholars have pondered for many years is whether or not the healthcare of the American people has also been conditioned by the polarized and tribal character of contemporary American politics. That question has finally been answered by Kant Patel and Mark Rushefsky in *The Divided State of American Healthcare: Red States Sing the Blues*. A cutting edge and empirically based volume consisting of nine clearly written chapters, the authors demonstrate with impressive bodies of evidence that a state's politics and political values have direct bearing on the healthcare of those who reside within its borders. A very helpful volume for courses related to public policy, state and local government, or political parties."

Gary L. Rose, *Professor of Politics, Scholar in Residence, Sacred Heart University, USA*

"Few issues have had a longer political road to travel than healthcare. This is particularly true with the nation's increased polarization and "red" state politics. Now, Patel and Rushefsky return to the topic for which they're nationally recognized to assess how residents in GOP-controlled states have lost out in the decade since the Affordable Care Act. Accessible and engaging, their book is a must-read for anyone interested in healthcare, federalism, and public management."
Brian Calfano, *Professor of Journalism, University of Cincinnati, USA*

"When it comes to healthcare, do different people living in different states have different odds of getting good care and living longer? In this new book, Patel and Rushefsky dig into the data to demonstrate the distinctive results that flow from America's political system. It's a central part of the culture wars that have broken out between the states, and their analysis helps the reader understand where this comes from—and why it matters to twenty-first century governance."
Donald F. Kettl, *Professor Emeritus and Former Dean, School of Public Policy, University of Maryland, USA*

"Long well-known in the field of HealthCare policy, Professors Kant Patel and Mark Rushefsky's newest book provides a comprehensive understanding of key U.S. health policy issues surrounding the Democratic (Blue State) and Republican (Red State) responses to current healthcare issues. Each main chapter investigates differing party responses, including policy preferences, to contemporary healthcare challenges, such as Medicaid, Reproductive Rights, and the COVID-19 Pandemic. This book stands out as the definitive history of how Democrats and Republicans approach the American healthcare system. While each offers a unique mix of public and private programs, Rushefsky and Patel painstakingly retrace the various policy preferences of key healthcare actors. They offer a play-by-play breakdown of each party's approach and the differences between the two, which, in turn, will ultimately shape America's healthcare policy."
Ken Rutherford, *Professor, Political Science, James Madison University; Co-Founder of the Landmine Survivors Network, co-recipient of the 1997 Nobel Peace Prize as part of the global international campaign to ban landmines*

THE DIVIDED STATE OF AMERICAN HEALTHCARE

Political polarization among 'red' and 'blue' states in the United States is reflected in major divides that exist along social, economic, educational, geographic, and demographic lines, but nowhere is polarization and political divide more evident than in the field of American healthcare. This book examines the healthcare divide between the red and blue states.

In this book, authors Kant Patel and Mark Rushefsky analyze how political polarization at the state level has impacted state health policymaking, policy outputs, and policy outcomes and led red and blue states to create vastly different healthcare and health policies. And, as state governments enjoy a considerable amount of authority and discretionary power, the authors further examine how polarization has influenced the implementation of national health policies by the red and blue states. The book begins with an exploration of the origins and evolution of political polarization and the factors that have contributed to it at the national level. This is followed by an analysis of how political polarization separates red and blue states and how they differ from each other in political, economic, demographic, and racial dimensions. It then considers how the health profiles of red and blue states differ in health indicators such as the uninsured or underinsured population, healthcare spending, and healthcare access. The book analyzes how political polarization has produced vastly different sets of health policies on issues including the Affordable Care Act (ACA), Medicaid, reproductive rights, and the COVID-19 pandemic. The book concludes with a critical examination of proposed solutions to political polarization and the dangers of our current deeply divided political climate.

Written in an accessible and jargon-free style, *The Divided State of American Healthcare* is vital reading for undergraduate and graduate courses on health policy, public policy, political science, and public health. It will also be of keen interest to healthcare professionals in the public and private sectors.

Kant Patel is an Emeritus Professor of Political Science at Missouri State University, USA. He has co-authored seven books (with Mark Rushefsky) and published numerous peer-reviewed articles in academic journals on topics of healthcare policy and American politics. He is retired and enjoys reading suspense/mystery novels, cheering for his favorite sports teams, and especially rooting for his Alma Mater, the University of Houston.

Mark Rushefsky is an Emeritus Professor of Political Science at Missouri State University, USA. He has co-authored seven books (with Kant Patel), authored books on cancer policy and public policy in the United States, and published several articles in academic journals on the topics of health policy, environmental policy, and American politics. He is retired and enjoys spending his time in the company of his wife, children, and grandchildren, playing with his cat and his dog, and cheering for his beloved Yankees, Knicks, and his adopted Kansas City Chiefs.

THE DIVIDED STATE OF AMERICAN HEALTHCARE

Red States Sing the Blues

Kant Patel and Mark Rushefsky

NEW YORK AND LONDON

Designed cover image: © wildpixel – Getty Images

First published 2025
by Routledge
605 Third Avenue, New York, NY 10158

and by Routledge
4 Park Square, Milton Park, Abingdon, Oxon, OX14 4RN

Routledge is an imprint of the Taylor & Francis Group, an informa business

© 2025 Kant Patel and Mark Rushefsky

The right of Kant Patel and Mark Rushefsky to be identified as authors of this work has been asserted in accordance with sections 77 and 78 of the Copyright, Designs and Patents Act 1988.

All rights reserved. No part of this book may be reprinted or reproduced or utilised in any form or by any electronic, mechanical, or other means, now known or hereafter invented, including photocopying and recording, or in any information storage or retrieval system, without permission in writing from the publishers.

Every effort has been made to contact copyright-holders. Please advise the publisher of any errors or omissions, and these will be corrected in subsequent editions.

Trademark notice: Product or corporate names may be trademarks or registered trademarks, and are used only for identification and explanation without intent to infringe.

ISBN: 978-1-032-67113-0 (hbk)
ISBN: 978-1-032-67111-6 (pbk)
ISBN: 978-1-032-67114-7 (ebk)

DOI: 10.4324/9781032671147

Typeset in Sabon
by SPi Technologies India Pvt Ltd (Straive)

This book is dedicated to
My teachers for instilling in me a love for learning.
Kant Patel

To my wife, Cindy, 55+ years of marriage. She has had health issues for the last several years. And she has shown during this time what she always was, a strong person. She is my hero.
Mark Rushefsky

CONTENTS

List of Figures xii
List of Tables xiii
Acknowledgments xxiv
Foreword by Thomas Patterson xxv

1 Political Polarization in America   1

   Political Discourse and Political Divide 2
   What Is Political Polarization? 3
   Origins of Political Polarization 4
   Evolution of Political Polarization 6
   Political Polarization of the Elites 14
   Partisan and Ideological Polarization of the Judiciary 18
   Polarization of the American Electorate 24
   Public Opinion and Polarization of the
      American Electorate 29
   Causes of Political Polarization 30
   Political Rhetoric, Violence, and Talk of Civil War 35
   Consequences of Political Polarization 38
   Polarization and Public Policy at the National Level 41
   Polarization and Public Policy at the State Level 42
   Do Red And Blue States Adopt Different Public Policies? 43
   Typology of Red, Blue, and Purple States 43
   Bibliography 46

2 Profiles of Red and Blue States in America   63

The Evolution of the American Federal System 63
American Federalism as A Double-Edged Sword 65
Changing Politics of American Federalism 67
Profiles of Red and Blue States 69
Political Polarization within the Red and Blue States 138
Political Polarization: Red and Blue State Divide 148
Bibliography 150

3 Health Profile of Red and Blue States   160

Healthcare Financing 160
Health Status Indicators 165
Healthcare Indicators 200
Ranking the States 213
Polarization and Healthcare Politics and Policy 215
Bibliography 217

4 Red and Blue State Divide Over Affordable Care Act   222

Political Divide over the Adoption of the ACA 223
The Empire Strikes Back: Attacking the ACA 229
Legal Challenges to Aca by Red States 232
Implementation of the Aca by Red and Blue States 240
Public Opinion and the Affordable Care Act 256
Polarization and the Politics of the Aca 261
Bibliography 265

5 Medicaid: Red and Blue State Divide   270

Transformation of Medicaid 271
Structure of Medicaid 273
Expanding Medicaid 292
Work Requirements 300
Churning and the Great Unwinding 305
Polarization and the Politics of Medicaid 316
Bibliography 318

6 Reproductive Rights in Red and Blue States   324

The Context of Debate and Action over
  Reproductive Rights 326
The Struggle for Reproductive Rights in America 332

*The Supreme Court and Reproductive
  Rights, 1960s–1980s 334*
Post Roe V. Wade Developments 335
Dobbs V. Jackson Women's Health Organization 2022 351
*Post-Dobbs Decision: Reproductive Rights in Red
  and Blue States 354*
Medication Abortion 374
Religious Divide over Abortion 383
Bibliography 387

7   Red and Blue States' Response to the Covid-19 Pandemic   400

The Impact of the Pandemic 402
Partisan Controversy over the Origin of the Pandemic 406
Federalism and the Pandemic 408
The Policy Toolkit and Partisanship 409
Presidential Administrations Address the Pandemic 412
The Importance of Partisanship 416
Mitigation 424
Masking 427
Lawsuits over Federal Mandates 433
Vaccines 434
Public Health and Partisanship 441
Polarization and the Politics of Covid-19 444
Bibliography 448

8   Political Polarization and America's Divided Healthcare   459

*Political Polarization and the Crisis of American
  Democracy 460*
Are There Solutions to Political Polarization? 469
Polarization and Divided State of American Healthcare 480
Concluding Thoughts 485
Bibliography 487

Index   497

FIGURES

3.1	Rate of Violent Crime Offenses Per 100,000 People, 1991–2022	185
4.1	Public Approval Rating of ACA, 2011–2022	257
4.2	Favorability/Unfavorability Rating of ACA by Political Party (2022–2023)	259
7.1	New Covid Hospital Admissions by Week. From Centers for Disease Control and Prevention (2024a)	403
7.2	Covid-19 Deaths by Week	404

TABLES

2.1 Annual Estimated Resident Population by State (July 1, 2023). Adapted from "Annual Estimate of the Resident Population for the United States, Regions, States, District of Columbia, and Puerto Rico: April 1, 2020 to July 1, 2023." U.S. Census Bureau; https://www.census.gov/   72

2.2 Urbanization by State (2020). Adapted from: Lopez, Adriana. 2021. "Most Urbanized States 2021." https://www.porch.com and Rakich, Nathaniel. 2020. "How Urban or Rural is Your State?" https://www.FiveThirtyEight.com   73

2.3 Net Domestic Migration by State (June 1, 2020 to June 1, 2022). Adapted from: "State Population Totals and Components of Change."2022. https://census.gov   75

2.4 Share of Foreign-Born Population (2021) and Net International Migration Per 1,000 Inhabitants by State (2018–2019). Adapted from: "Immigration and Border Security." 2022. https://usafacts.org; "Sate Population Totals and Componenets of Change." 2022. https://www.census.gov   78

2.5 Percent of Racial/Ethnic Adult Population by State (2021). Adapted from: "Adult Population by Race and Ethnicity in the United States." 2022. https://datacenter.kidscount.org   81

2.6 Racial/Ethnic Diversity Index by State (2020). Adapted from: "Racial and Ethnic Diversity Index by State 2020." 2021. https://www.census.gov   83

2.7 Age Distribution by State (2021). Adapted from: "Population Distribution by Age 2021." 2021. https://www.kff.org 85

2.8 Median Age by State (2022). Adapted from "Median Age in the United States in 2022, by State." 2023. https://www.statista.com/statistics/208048/median-age-of-population-in-the-usa-by-state/ 87

2.9 Male to Female Ratio by State (2022). Adapted from: American Community Survey, "Age and Sex." 2024. (Table S0101); https://data.census.gov/ 88

2.10 Median Per Pupil Public School Expenditures by State (2019). Adapted from: "How Much Money Do Schools Spend on Eduction?" 2022. https://usafacts.org/ 90

2.11 Estimated Average Annual Salary of Teachers at Public Primary and Secondary Schools, 2021–2022. Adapted from "Estimated Average Annual Salary of Teachers at Public Primary and Secondary Schools 2021–2022." 2023. National Cener foir Educational Statistics; https://nces.ed.gov/ 91

2.12 Share of Residents With Less Than a High School Diploma by States (2021). Adapted from: "Which States are the Most Educated?" 2022. https://usafacts.org/ 92

2.13 Share of Residents 25 and Older with a Bachelor's Degree or Higher by State (2021). Adapted from: "Which States are the Most Educated?" 2022 https://usafacts.org/ 93

2.14 States Ranked by Level of Education and Public Schools (2021). Adapted from: McCann, Adam. 2021. "States with thee Best and Worst School Systems." https://wallethub.com/ and McCann. Adam. 2022. "Most and Least Educated States in America." https://wallethub.com/ 95

2.15 States Ranked by the Quality of Higher Education (2021). Adapted from: "Education Rankings: Measuring How Well States are Educating Their Students." 2021. https://www.usnews.com/ 97

2.16 Real Personal Per Capita Income by State (2020). Source: DePietro, Andrew. 2021. "U. S. Per Capita Income by State in 2021." https://www.forbes.com/ 100

2.17 Median Household Income by State (2022). Adapted from: Carlin, Doug. 2023. "US Median Household Income by State (Report 2023)." https://usabynumbers.com/ 101

2.18 Unemployment Rate Seasonally Adjusted by State (December 2022). Adapted from: Bureau of Labor

	Statistics. 2022. "Unemployment Rate by States, Seasonally Adjusted." https://www.bls.gov/	103
2.19	Poverty Rate and Median Household Income by State (2022). Adapted from "SAIPE State and County Estimates for 2022." December 2023. https://www.census.gov/data/datasets/2022/demo/saipe/2022-state-and-county.html	104
2.20	Tax Rate and Ranking by State (2022). Adapted from: Kiernan, John. S. 2022a. "States With the Hihest and the Lowest Tax Rate". https://wallethub.com/	105
2.21	Cost of Living Index by States (2022). Adapted from: "Cost of Living Index by State 2022." 2022. https://worldpopulationreview.com/	107
2.22	Constant Dollar Gross Domestic Product (2023). Adapted from Berau of Economic Analysis. 2024. "Level and Percent Change From Preceeding Period." Period." https://www.bea.gov/data/gdp/gdp-state/	108
2.23	Level of Dependence on the Federal Government by State (2020–2021). Adapted from: Kiernan, John S. 2022. "Most and Least Federally Dependent States." https://wallethub.com/	110
2.24	Ranking of States' Economy (2024). Adapted from McCann, Adam. 2024. "Best and the Worst State Economies in 2024." https://wallethub.com	111
2.25	Share of Women in Population (2021) and State Legislatures by State (2022). Adapted from: "U.S. Share of Women in State Legislatures 2022, by State." 2023. https://www.statista.com/ and "Population Distribution by Sex." 2021. https://www.kff.org/	114
2.26	Share of Non-White Representatives in State Legislatures by State (2020). Adapted from: Renuka Rayasam. Et al. 2020. "Why State Legislatures are still Very White -- and Very Male." https://www.politico.com/ and National Conference of State Legislatures. 2020. "State legislature Demographics." https://ncsl.org/	116
2.27	State Supreme Court Diversity (2022). Sources: Powers, Amanda., and Alicia Bannon. 2022. "State Supreme Court Diversity -- May 2022 Update." https://www.brennancenter.org/ and "Population Distribution by Sex: 2021. http://www.kff.org/	118
2.28	Registration and Voter Turnout by State (2020). Adapted from: "Voting and Regirstration by State." 2020. https://census.gov/	121

2.29	Most Difficult to Least Difficult Sates to Vote (2021). Adapted from: Morris, Kathy. 2022. "The Most Diifficult States to Vote (and the Least)." https://www.zippia.com	124
2.30	Rating of States on Conservative Policies (2021). Adapted from: Center for Legislative Accountabklity. 2021. "State Ranking of Conservative Policies." 2021. https://ratings.conservative.org	127
2.31	Religious Affiliation by State (2021). Adapted from: Public Religious Research Institute. 2021a. "Religious Affiliation by State." 2021. https://ava.prri.org/	130
2.32	White Evangelical Protestants by State (2021). Adapted from: "White Evangelical Protestants by State." 2021. https://ava.prri.org/	132
2.33	Frequency of Church Attendance by State (2021). Adapted from: "Frequnecy of Church Attendance 2021." 2021. https://ava.prri.org/	133
2.34	Divorce Rates by State (2021). Adapted from: U.S. Center for Disease Control and Prevention. 2022. "Divorce Rates by State: 1990, 1995, and 1999-2021." https://cdc.gov/	135
2.35	Teen Pregnancy Rate (2023), Teen Birth Rate (2020) and Percent of Babies Born to Unmarried Mothers (2020). Adapted from: "Teen Pregnancy Rate by State." 2023. https://worldpopulationreview.com/; Teen Birth Rate by State 2020." 2020a. https://www.cdc.gov/; "Percent of Babies Born to Unmarried Mothers 2020b." https://cdc.gov/	136
2.36	Happiest States in America (2022). Adapted from: McCann, Adam. 2022b. "Happiest States in the US." https://wallethub.com	139
2.37	Presidential Election Results by State (2020). Adapted from: "Presidential Electin Rsults." 2020. https://nbcnews.com; https://www.fec.gov	141
3.1	State Health Spending Per Person (2019). Source: Adapted with permission from Johnson et al (2022)	161
3.2	State Spending by Payee. Source: Adapted with permission from Johnson et al (2022)	163
3.3	Ranking of How Well States Control Costs. Source: Adapted with permission from McCann (2022). Online at https://wallethub.com	165
3.4	Life Expectancy by State (2020). Source: Adapted fromArias et al (2022). Online at www.cdc.gov	168
3.5	Life Expectancy by State (2018). Source: Adapted from Arias et al (2021). Online at www.cdc.gov	169

3.6	Crude Death Rates per 100,000 (2020). Adapted from Centers for Disease Control and Prevention (2020). Online at www.cdc.gov	170
3.7	The 15 Leading Causes of Death in the U.S. (2019). Adapted from Xu et al (2021)	171
3.8	Heart Disease Mortality Rate by State (2020). Adapted from National Center for Health Statistics (2022b) and Kaiser Family Foundation (2023). Online at https://www.kff.org/statedata	172
3.9	Adjusted Death Rates and Rank for Deaths by Cancer (2020b). Adapted from National Center for Health Statistics (2022a) and Centers for Disease Control and Prevention (2022b)	173
3.10	Age-Adjusted Accidental Mortality Rates by State. Adapted from National Center for Health Statistics (2022c)	174
3.11	Obesity Prevalence by State (2021). Adapted from Centers for Disease Control (2022c). Online at www.cdc.gov	175
3.12	Percentage of Adults Who Report Engaging in Physical Activity (2021). Adapted from Kaiser Family Foundation (2023). Online at www.kff.org	176
3.13	Share of Adults Told They Had Chronic Lung Disease. Adapted from Kaiser Family Foundation (2023). Online at www.kff.org	177
3.14	Percentage of Adults Reporting Mental Illness in the Past Year (2019–2020). Adapted from Kaiser Family Foundation (2023). Online at www.kff.org	178
3.15	Age-Adjusted Suicide Rate (2020). Adapted from Kaiser Family Foundation (2023). Online at www.kff.org	180
3.16	Adults Reporting Unmet Need for Mental Health Treatment (2019–2020). Adapted from Kaiser Family Foundation (2023). Online at www.kff.org	181
3.17	Share of Adults with any Mental Illness in Past Year Covered by Medicaid (2018–2019). Adapted from Kaiser Family Foundation (2023). Online at www.kff.org	182
3.18	Mental Health Workforce Availability (2020). Online at www.mhanational.org	183
3.19	Overall Ranking of States on Mental Health Policy (2020). Online at www.mhanational.org	184
3.20	Estimated Gun Ownership by State. Online at cbsnews.com/pictures/gun-ownership-rates-by-state	187

3.21	Gun-Friendliness of States. Online at https://www.criminalattorneycincinnati.com/comparing-gun-control-measures-to-gun-related-homicides-by-state	188
3.22	Maternal Mortality by State. Online at https://www.kff.org	190
3.23	Rating States on Prenatal and Maternal Care. Online at https://www.valuepenguin.com/	192
3.24	Health Insurance Coverage for Children (2021). Online at https://www.kff.org/statedata	193
3.25	Low Birthweight Babies (2020). Online at www.aecf.org	195
3.26	States with Laws Protecting Children from Firearms. Online at https://www.kff.org	196
3.27	Teen Birth Rate by State (2020). Online at www.CDC.gov	198
3.28	Sex Education Programs by State. Online at www.guttmacher.org	199
3.29	Ranking States on Child Health (2020). Online at www.wallethub.com	200
3.30	State Uninsurance Rates (2021). Online at https://www.kff.org/statedata	202
3.31	The Underinsured. Adapted from Schoen et al (2014)	204
3.32	Income and Insurance Costs (2019). Online at https://quotewizard.com	205
3.33	Medical Debt (2018–2021). Adapted from Consumer Financial Protection Bureau (2022)	207
3.34	Primary Care and Specialist Providers Per Capita. Adapted from Kaiser Family Foundation (2023). Online at https://www.kff.org/statedata	208
3.35	Prevalence Rate of Dentists (2021). Adapted from Kaiser Family Foundation (2023). Online at https://www.kff.org/statedata	209
3.36	Percentage of Adults Not Having Personal Provider. Online at https://www.kff.org/statedata	210
3.37	Adults Not Seeking Care Because of Cost. Online at https://www.kff.org/statedata	211
3.38	Overall Ranking of State Healthcare Systems. Online at www.commonwealth.org	212
4.1	Uninsured Rate and Population, 2008–2021. Adapted from Bureau of the Census. Online at www.census.gov	225
4.2	Overall Public Opinion on the Affordable Care Act (2010). Adapted from Kaiser Family Foundation (2010). Online at www.kff.org	227
4.3	Partisan Divide Over ACA (2010). Adapted from Kaiser Family Foundation (2010). Online at www.kff.org	227

4.4	ACA Court Cases. Adapted with permission from Gluck, Regan, and Turret (2020)	233
4.5	NFIB v Sebelius. Kaiser Family Foundation (2023a). Online at https://www.kff.org/statedata	235
4.6	Burrell v. Hobby Lobby Stores. Carter (2014); Office of Attorney General (California) (2014)	236
4.7	King v. Burrell. Online at https://www.scotusblog.com/case-files/cases/king-v-burwell/	238
4.8	California v. Texas. Adapted from Musumeci (2020)	240
4.9	The Trifecta of Power. Adapted with permission from Apple (N.D.). Online at https://www.spokesman.com/stories/2020/jun/25/control-house-and-senate-19/	242
4.10	Oppositional Measures (2010–2013). Adapted from Kaiser Family Foundation (2013). Online at https://www.kff.org/wp-content/uploads/sites/3/2015/03/state-legislation-opt-out-pdf	246
4.11	State Decisions on Exchanges. Adapted from Kaiser Family Foundation (2024). Online at www.kff.org. Centers for Medicare and Medicaid Services (2023). Online at https://www.cms.gov	248
4.12	Red State Marketplace Enrollment Trends, 2014–2023. Adapted from Kaiser Family Foundation (2023a). Online at https://www.kff.org/statedata	250
4.13	Blue State Marketplace Enrollment Trends, 2014–2023. Adapted from Kaiser Family Foundation (2023a). Online at https://www.kff.org/statedata	251
4.14	Red State Uninsurance Rates, 2029–2021. Adapted from Kaiser Family Foundation (2023a). Online at https://www.kff.org/statedata	252
4.15	Blue State Uninsurance Rates, 2029–2021. Adapted from Kaiser Family Foundation (2023a). Online at https://www.kff.org/statedata	255
4.16	Percentage of Republicans and Democrats Saying It Is Important to Keep Provision in ACA (2019). Adapted from Kirzinger et al (2022)	258
5.1	Medicaid Groups. Adapted from Mitchell (2023)	274
5.2	Mandatory and Optional Medicaid Benefits. Adapted from Centers for Medicare and Medicaid Services (N.D-1). Online at www.cms.gov	275
5.3	Medicaid and CHIP Income Eligibility Levels for Selected Groups (Red States). Adapted from Centers for Medicaid and Medicare Services (2022). Online at cms.gov	276

5.4	Medicaid and CHIP Income Eligibility Levels for Selected Groups (Blue States). Online at cms.gov	277
5.5	Medicaid Income Eligibility Levels For Other Adults (2023). Adapted from Kaiser Family Foundation (2023a). Online at www.kff.org	279
5.6	Percentage of State Population Covered by Medicaid (2021). Adapted from Rudowitz et al (2023). Online at www.kff.org	280
5.7	Percent of Births Covered by Medicaid (2020). Adapted with permission from March of Dimes (2020). Online at https://www.marchofdimes.org/peristats/data?reg=99&top=11&stop=154&lev=1&slev=1&obj=18	281
5.8	Income Eligibility Levels for Pregnant Women in Medicaid (2020). Adapted with permission from Clark (2020). Online at www.ccf.georgetown.edu	282
5.9	Extending Postpartum Coverage. Adapted with permission from National Academy of State Health Policy (2023). Online at https://nashp.org/state-tracker/view-each-states-efforts-to-extend-medicaid-postpartum-coverage/	284
5.10	Timeliness of Prenatal and Postpartum Care (2019). Adapted with permission from Clark (2023). Online at www.ccf.georgetown.edu	285
5.11	Medicaid Per Capita Expenditures (2019). Adapted from Centers for Medicare and Medicaid Services (N.D.-b) Online at www.cms.gov	286
5.12	Medicaid as Share of States' Total Budgets and State-Funded Budgets (2020). Adapted from MACPAC (2022). Online at www.macpac.gov	287
5.13	FMAP Payments. Adapted from MACPAC (2022). Online at www.macpac.gov	288
5.14	Percentage of State Population Covered by Medicaid (2021). Adapted from Rudowitz et al (2023). Online at www.kff.org	290
5.15	Medicaid Low Income Coverage (2023). Adapted from Kaiser Family Foundation (2023b). Online at www.kff.org	291
5.16	Expansion and Non-Expansion States (2023). Adapted from Coleman and Federman (2022). Online at www.commonwealthfund.org and Kaiser Family Foundation (2023c). Online at www.kff.org	295

5.17	Work Requirement Waivers. Adapted from Kaiser Family Foundation (2023e). Online at www.kff.org	298
5.18	Structure of Medicaid Population and Expenditures. Adapted from Rudowitz et al (2023). Online at www.kff.org	303
5.19	Medicaid Enrollment Changes (2017–2018). Adapted with permission from Ruff and Fishman (2019). Online at www.familiesusa.org	307
5.20	Continuous Eligibility Policies (2019). Adapted from Brooks, Roygardner, and Artiga (2019). Online at www.kff.org	308
5.21	Medicaid Renewal Time(2023). Adapted from Centers for Medicaid and Medicare Services (2023). Online at www.cms.gov	310
5.22	Unwinding Metrics. Adapted from Tolbert, Moreno, and Rudowitz (2023). Online at www.kff.org	311
5.23	States Use of Unwinding Metrics. Adapted from Tolbert, Moreno, and Rudowitz 2023. Online at www.kff.org	312
5.24	Disenrollment and Renewal Rates (December 2023). Adapted from Kaiser Family Foundation (2023f). Online at www.kff.org	313
5.25	Reasons for Terminations. Adapted from Kaiser Family Foundation (2023f). Online at www.kff.org	315
5.26	Rating State Medicaid Programs. Adapted with permission from McCann (2021). Online at https://wallethub.com/edu/states-with-the-most-and-least-medicaid-coverage/71573	317
6.1	Number of Abortion Clinics by State 2017–2020. Adapted from "Number of Abortion Clinics by State, 2017–2020." 2021. Online at https://data.guttmacher.org/	339
6.2	Percent of Women Ages 15–44 who live in Counties Without An Abortion Provider 2019. Adapted from: Jennifer Welsh. 2021. "A Verywell Report: Abortion Access Ranked by State." 2021. Online at https://verywellhealth.com	340
6.3	Percentage of Legal Abortions Obtained by Our of State Residents 2020. Adapted from:" Percentage of Legal Abortions Obtained by Out of State Residents " 2020. Online at https://www.kff.org/	342
6.4	Percent Change in Abortion Rate by State 2017–2020. Adapted from: "Percent Change in Abortion Rate by State, 2017–2020" 2021. Online at https://data.guttmacher.org	345

6.5	Abortion Per 1,000 Women Aged 15 to 44 by State: July 1, 2020. Adapted from: Ranji, Usha; Kren Diep; and Alina Salganicoff. 2023. "Key Facts on Abortion in the United States." Online at https://www.kff.org	346
6.6	States' Reproductive Rights: Index Score, Ranking and Grade 2015. Adapted from: Institute for Women's Policy Research. 2015. Chapter 5: "Reproductive Rights," pp. 167–193 in The Status of Women in the States, 2015 Report. Online at https://statusofwomendata.org/	347
6.7	States' Reproductive Rights Index: Index Score, Ranking, and Grade 2022. Adapted from: Manson, Nicole C. et al. 2022 "IWPR Reprodctive Rights Index: A State-by-State Analysis and Ranking." Online at https://iwpr.org/	348
6.8	States' Grades on Reproductive Health and Rights 2022. Adapted from: "The State of Reproductive Health and Rights: A 50-State Report Card." 2022. Online at https://www.populationinstitute.org/	350
6.9	Abortion Laws By State As of July 17, 2024. Adapted from: "Interactive Map: US Abortion Policies and Acess After Roe." Online at https://states.guttmacher.org/policies	356
6.10	Abortion Policies from Most Restrictive to Most Protective by State, As of December 20, 2023. Adapted from: "Interactive map: US Abortion Policies and Access After Roe." 2023. Online at https://states.guttmacher.org/	358
6.11	Mandatory Waiting Periods and Counseling by State as of August 2023. Adapted from: "Counseling and Waiting Period for Abortion." 2023. Online at https://www.guttmacher.org/	359
6.12	Monthly Abortions by State April 2022 and June 2023. Adapted from: "Change in Number of Abortions by State." 2023. Online at https://societyfp.org/research/wecount/	370
6.13	Estimated Number and Percent of Abortion Provided to Out of State Residents. Adapted from: "Monthly Abortion Provision Study." 2023. Online at https://www.guttmacher.org/	375
7.1	Total Coronavirus Cases (January 2024). Source: Worldometer (2024b). Online at https://www.worldometers.info/coronavirus/	402
7.2	Percentage Supporting Policies to Control the Spread of the Coronavirus by Party. Source: Adapted with permission from Baum et al (2020).	

	Online at https://www.covidstates.org/reports/public-support-for-covid-19-measures	410
7.3	COVID-19 Metrics by State (through May 2023). Adapted with permissions from "Tracking U.S. COVId-19 Cases, Deaths and Other Metrics by State." (2023). Online at https://www.washingtonpost.com/graphics/2020/national/coronavirus-us-cases-deaths/?itid=sn_coronavirus_1/&state=US	417
7.4	Days of High ICU Stress Due to COVID-19 (2022). Adapted with permission from Radley, Baumgartner, and Collins 2022. Online at https://www.commonwealthfund.org/sites/default/files/202206/Radley_2022_State_Scorecard_Appendices.pdf#page=24	418
7.5	Prevalence of Long Covid Among Adults (2022). Adapted from Ford et al (2024). Online at https://www.cdc.gov/mmwr/volumes/73/wr/mm7306a4.htm	419
7.6	COVID-19 Impact on Health Care System (Red States) (2022). Adapted with permission from Radley et al (2022). Online at https://www.commonwealthfund.org/sites/default/files/2022-06/Radley_2022_State_Scorecard_Appendices.pdf#page=24	421
7.7	COVID-19 Impact on Health Care System (Blue States) (2022). Adapted with permission from Radley et al (2022). Online at https://www.commonwealthfund.org/sites/default/files/2022-06/Radley_2022_State_Scorecard_Appendices.pdf#page=24	422
7.8	State Vaccination Rates (2022). Adapted from USAFacts (2024). Online at https://usafacts.org/visualizations/covid-vaccine-tracker-states/	437
7.9	State Bans on School Mask and COVID-19 Vaccination Mandates. Adapted with Permission from National Academy for State Health Policy (2024). Online at https://nashp.org/state-tracker/states-address-school-vaccine-mandates-and-mask-mandates/	442

ACKNOWLEDGMENTS

We would like to thank the following people for making this book possible. Laura Varley, senior publisher at Routledge, has worked with us ever since we began writing for Routledge. She has been an enthusiastic advocate for the projects we have suggested. Lauren Powell is the editorial assistant for this book and kept us on the straight and narrow. We would also like to express appreciation to the copy editor for finding errors that we missed and making the book better. And we would like to thank Tom Patterson of Harvard University for being a really nice guy and agreeing to write the Foreword.

FOREWORD

Polarization has impacted the politics of every Western democracy, but none more so than the United States and in no policy area more fully than healthcare.

The distinctive nature of American healthcare policy owes partly to the country's deeply ingrained individualistic culture, which accentuates personal responsibility and has a restricted view of the government's responsibility for providing economic security. The United States trails nearly every Western democracy in social welfare spending.[1] America's distinctive brand of social welfare policy also owes to its constitutional framework, which vests authority over health policy largely to the states. This arrangement allowed stakeholders such as insurance companies, pharmaceutical firms, hospitals, and medical associations to influence the shape of healthcare policy, most notably in helping to thwart efforts by Harry Truman and Bill Clinton to expand the federal government's role in healthcare. Lyndon Johnson, who guided Medicare and Medicaid through Congress in 1965, and Barack Obama, who oversaw the passage of the Affordable Care Act in 2010, overcame that resistance but only in part. The states' constitutional authority over health policy and health-related interests limited the scope of their efforts and largely dictated the mechanisms through which health insurance would be expanded. The United States remains the most advanced Western democracy yet to institute a universal healthcare system.

Political polarization has made U.S. healthcare policy, always a complex and difficult political issue, into a maddeningly complex and difficult one. This book shows why. It takes the study of polarization to the state level, which, remarkably, has received relatively little attention from scholars. Compared with the hundreds of excellent studies of polarization at the national level, there are only a handful of such studies at the state level.[2] Even references to red (Republican) states, blue (Democratic), and purple (competitive) states take place largely in the context of congressional and presidential politics.

This focus stems partly from a media system preoccupied with what happens in the nation's capital. That trend began decades ago with the start of network television news and intensified with the advent of cable TV news, which has a nearly insatiable appetite for Washington policymakers.[3] Over this same period, there's been a shift in power from the states to the nation as the federal government has through grants-in-aid intruded in policy areas once almost totally within control of the states. More recently, polarization has accelerated the "nationalization" of politics – the issues that have come to define the national partisan divide have worked their way down to the lowest levels of American government, including school board elections.[4]

Healthcare policy has been caught up in the nationalization of politics. America's response to the COVID-19 pandemic differed markedly from how it responded to the polio epidemic of the early 1950s and the Spanish Flu outbreak of 1918. Back then, the states were largely on the same page. Not so for COVID-19. Democratic governors were typically faster to mandate social distancing, mask-wearing, and business and school closures than Republican governors.[5] The priority in most blue states was public health whereas keeping businesses open was the priority in red states. In most countries, these priorities were properly seen as linked – judicious public health measures were the best way to limit economic damage.

That linkage was not the policy guide in many American states. Some Democratic governors went too far in closing schools and businesses and some Republican governors went too far in relaxing public health standards. The result is that the United States ranked near the bottom among Western democracies for deaths per capita from COVID-19 and had equally unnecessary declines in school attendance and business activity. Moreover, the red-blue divide on the coronavirus did not end when the pandemic ended. Some red states, for example, are in the process of rolling back vaccine requirements.[6] Why a state would choose a policy option that serves to protect both public health and the economy is mystifying outside the context of polarization-driven policymaking.

As the example shows, and this book explains in detail, our understanding of the COVID-19 pandemic and other healthcare policy issues, including abortion and Medicaid expansion, is incomplete when we fail to look beyond Washington, D.C., to what is happening in states and localities.

Every chapter of the book is packed with evidence and insights, and I could have picked any chapter to illustrate the richness of what you'll encounter in the coming pages. Chapter 4, for example, examines the political divide on the Affordable Care Act. The national component of that landmark legislation is well-known: its origins in the Republican Party when the GOP was still marketplace-oriented,[7] the strict partisan divide that surfaced when President Obama and congressional Democrats championed it, the unsuccessful GOP effort to get the Supreme Court to kill it, the stripping out of the individual mandate in 2017 after Republicans gained control of all three branches of the federal government.

But, as Chapter 4 reveals, that is not even half the story. The rest is told through the actions of the states. The most familiar part of that story is the refusal of some states to expand Medicaid coverage to individuals with incomes up to 138% of the federal poverty line. After the Supreme Court in 2012 made Medicaid expansion optional, some states – all of them Republican – rejected expansion even though it was entirely funded by the federal government for the first three years. That action led to variations in the states' healthcare access and coverage. Beyond this, the states design and operate the health insurance plans available to individuals and small businesses, resulting in variations in the availability and affordability of health insurance coverage. States also have a role in regulating health insurance markets and overseeing insurance plans offered within their borders. While the ACA established certain minimum standards for health insurance coverage, states have the authority to impose additional regulations and requirements on insurance plans sold within their jurisdictions. This includes regulations related to benefit design, provider networks, and premium rates. America's patchwork healthcare system has no equivalent among Western democracies.

Nuggets of information like that populate every chapter. Indeed, each chapter could stand by itself as a much-needed monograph on an area of health policy. Although the study of state and local politics and policy is enjoying a resurgence in political science, it's an area that we know far less about than national politics which, as it has become more polarized, has attracted ever more scholarly attention. But, as each chapter of this book reveals, the tendency to overlook what's happening at the state and local levels is to miss a huge share of America's public policies.

The federal nature of our governing system is one of the threads that connects the book's chapters. The other is party polarization, which is arguably the defining feature of contemporary American politics. My research has focused more on politics than policy and includes work on the impact of party polarization.[8] Given my background, I wasn't expecting to learn much new about partisan polarization from reading the book. I was wrong and wrong from the start. The book's first chapter is a masterful meta-analysis of recent research on polarization. But it's more than that. The chapter takes us back in the nation's history to the roots of our divide, some of which, like nativism, go back more than a century.

In reading the book, you'll gain an understanding of the nation's crazy quilt of healthcare policy, but you'll also acquire a fuller understanding of the threat that polarization poses to our country. It leads to policy gridlock – a familiar story for anyone who has followed Congress during the past decade. But it's also true of states where the Democratic and Republican parties are closely matched. These states deadlock even over common-sense responses to health policy problems like access to care, cost containment, and quality improvement, much less over inflammatory issues like transgender transition. Each side has the power to prevent the other side from enacting policy and lacks interest in finding common ground. Policy gridlock has only one beneficiary – the special interests that have a vested stake in the status quo.

Accountability disappears with polarization. For many on each side of the partisan divide, the test of accountability is the party label of those in power. Our tolerance for bad governance is monumental when our party is in power, as is our unwillingness to give appropriate credit when the other party succeeds. This tendency is reinforced by partisan and social media, which act as tribal echo chambers in which all that is good originates with our side.[9] The impact is more substantial than might be imagined – for example, Democrats are more likely than similarly situated Republicans to enroll in a health insurance program.[10] If there is an area that deserves more attention than it receives in this exceptional book, it would be the role of national and local media in deepening the partisan divide over healthcare policy and virtually every other salient issue.

Polarization also contributes to discontinuous healthcare policy. Rather than comprehensive lasting initiatives, what we often get are piecemeal policies subject to reversal if there is a change in party control, as when Republicans in 2017 killed the individual insurance mandate. This fluidity has disrupted healthcare delivery and created uncertainty for healthcare providers, insurers, and patients. Kentucky is a case in point. In the first years after the ACA's implementation, Kentucky's Democratic governor set up a state exchange, which was voided in favor of the federal exchange when a Republican governor took office, who then later switched back when the federal exchange proved less successful.

To be fair, the parties have long had different views of healthcare policy with Democrats more inclined toward government intervention to ensure healthcare access and Republicans more inclined toward market-based solutions and limited government involvement. But polarization has made that divide virtually unbridgeable. Our public health challenges, including the opioid epidemic, mental health crisis, and pandemic preparedness, are major challenges. They won't go away on their own. If that's plain as day, so, too, is the role of polarization in their persistence. By highlighting the consequences, this book underscores the urgency of finding solutions that make the health of Americans a priority.

Thomas E. Patterson, Bradlee Professor of Government and Press
John F. Kennedy School of Government at Harvard University

Notes

1. OECD data, 2022.
2. See, for example, Raymond J. La Raja and Brian F. Schaffner, "Ideological Polarization in State Legislatures," in Raymond J. La Raja and Brian F. Schaffner, eds., Campaign Finance and Political Polarization (Ann Arbor: MI: University of Michigan Press, 2015): 87–107.
3. Daniel Sutter, "News Media Incentives, Coverage of Government, and the Growth of Government," *The Independent Review*, 8 (2004): 549–567.
4. Daniel J. Hopkins, *The Increasingly United States: How and Why American Political Behavior Nationalized* (Chicago: University of Chicago Press, 2018).
5. Christopher Adolph, Kenya Amano, Bree Bang-Jensen, Nancy Fullman, and John Wilkerson, "Pandemic Politics: Timing State-Level Social Distancing Responses to COVID-19," *Journal of Health Politics, Policy and Law*, August 2020, pp. 1–17.
6. National Academy for State Health Policy, "State Efforts to Limit or Enforce COVID-19 Vaccine Mandates," April 19, 2024. https://nashp.org/state-tracker/state-efforts-to-ban-or-enforce-covid-19-vaccine-mandates-and-passports/.
7. Jakob Hacker, "The Road to Somewhere: Why Health Reform Happened, or Why Political Scientists Who Write about Public Policy Shouldn't Assume They Know How to Shape It," *Perspectives on Politics* 8 (2010): 281–323.
8. See, for example, Thomas E. Patterson, *How America Lost Its Mind: The Assault on Reason that's Crippling Our Democracy* (Norman, OK: University of Oklahoma Press, 2018).
9. Amy Chau, *Political Tribes: Group Instinct and the Fate of Nations* (New York: Penguin, 2018).
10. Amy E. Lerman, Meredith L. Sadin, and Samuel Trachtman, "Policy Uptake as Political Behavior: Evidence from the Affordable Care Act," *American Political Science Review* 111 (2017): 755–770.

1
POLITICAL POLARIZATION IN AMERICA

Political polarization has come to define American politics over the last 50 years and has intensified in recent years dividing the country into two nations. One nation is made up of Republican-dominated and politically conservative red states and the second nation is made up of Democratic-dominated and politically liberal blue states. It has led former chief justice of the New Hampshire Supreme Court, John T. Broderick (2022), to remark that "What disturbs me most is my nagging belief that we have already become 'two nations under God' and that without a shot being fired we might need to make that a physical reality: one nation blue and the other red."

The impact of political polarization is evident in red and blue states moving in very different directions in many public policy areas. For example, the social safety net, i.e., a collection of programs designed to protect financially vulnerable population groups, looks very different in different states. Blue states provide more generous benefits in their state-directed programs while red states enjoy more generous benefits in federally directed programs. In short, the federal government has played a role in partially offsetting the benefit differential between the red and blue states (Watson and Godman 2024).

However, of all the various policy arenas, nowhere is the impact of political polarization more evident than in health policy. Red and blue states have shifted their health policies in recent decades in conservative and liberal directions, respectively. The impact of state health policies on population health has become clearer. The shift in health policy in red and blue states has led to a growing disparity in healthcare of residents of red and blue states (Montez 2024).

This book examines how political polarization has led the red and blue states to move in very different directions concerning health policies dealing with the Affordable Care Act (ACA), Medicaid, reproductive rights, and the response to the COVID-19 pandemic. The red and blue states have moved in opposite directions dividing American healthcare into two separate and unrecognizable nations—one red and one blue—with significant consequences for the health of Americans. To understand the divided state of American healthcare, we first need to examine the origins, evolution, nature, and various facets or dimensions of political polarization in American politics. Second, we need to understand how the demographics, socioeconomic, political, and religious environment as well as healthcare status and indicators of the red and blue states differ.

Political Discourse and Political Divide

In today's American political discourse, red states refer to states that consistently vote Republican while blue states are ones that consistently vote for Democrats. Purple states are considered competitive states that often tend to switch between Republicans and Democrats between different election cycles. The origins of using the color-coded scheme to represent American states can be traced back to the election of 1976 when NBC used a color-coded electoral map for the first time as part of its election coverage. However, individual news outlets decided which colors to assign to candidates and their political parties. It was not until the election of 2000 between Al Gore and George W. Bush that the use of the terms "red states" and "blue states" became common among various news outlets including television and print media. States whose voters predominantly voted for the Republican Party came to be referred to as red states and states whose voters predominantly voted for the Democratic Party came to be called blue states. Since that time, the "red states" and "blue states" have come to represent much more than just color-coded electoral map schemes. Today, the use of this terminology has become embedded in any discourse on American politics to symbolize political polarization of American politics along the partisan, ideological, and electorate divide.

What is Political Polarization?

Broadly speaking, political polarization can be defined as the divergence of political beliefs and attitudes away from the political center (moderate) toward ideological extremes on a continuum (Fiorina, And Abrams 2008; DiMaggio, Evans, Bryson 1996). In the context of American politics, the "left" is associated with liberals who advocate social and economic policies designed to create a broad social safety net. In contrast, the "right" is associated with conservatives who advocate social and economic policies that emphasize traditional social values, and less government regulation of the economy. In ideological polarization, citizens and members of different political parties become so entrenched in their own set of political values and political beliefs that it creates a divide between those who hold different values and political beliefs. Such ideological polarization is often reflected in diametrically opposite policy positions held by citizens and members of political parties. Ideological polarization is not necessarily limited to differences in issue/policy positions but may also exhibit itself in economic, social/cultural, geographic, and demographic divides.

Ideological polarization (difference between policy positions) is often distinguished from affective polarization which represents the phenomenon of animosity or hostility between political parties. It is a psychological state of mind in which Democrats and Republicans view the other party's members as hypocritical, selfish, close-minded, etc. and thus refuse to socialize with members of the other party creating intense partisan animosity (Iyengar et al. 2019). Affective polarization deals with the extent to which the electorate dislikes and distrusts members of other parties and politics comes to be seen as a binary choice between "us" vs. "Them." Partisan polarization, in American two-party politics, is tied to partisan identities (Carmines, Wagner, Ensley, and Wagner 2012; Layman, Horowitz, and Menasce 2006).

Scholars of American politics have also identified two levels of political polarization—elite polarization and mass polarization. Elite polarization refers to polarization among political elites such as party activists, party organizers, and elected public officials such as a member of Congress. For example, scholars have attempted to analyze partisan polarization in Congress and other legislative bodies through analysis of roll call voting to measure trends in party-line voting. Mass polarization focuses on ideological polarization among the public, i.e., the electorate, to examine the extent to which they are divided over public policy issues such as abortion, gun control, climate change, and the like. Partisan polarization among the electorate focuses on the extent to which the electorate or the public identifies with a political party based on racial, gender, socioeconomic, and demographic characteristics such as age and education. This is frequently referred to as partisan sorting. Partisan polarization among the electorate is often measured by relying on data derived from public opinion polls and election surveys.

Origins of Political Polarization

The increase in the frequency of divided government post-World War II can be viewed as an early warning signal of coming polarization in American politics. A divided government refers to a situation in which one party controls the presidency while the other party controls one or both houses of Congress. Under a unified government, one party controls the presidency as well as both houses of Congress.

Before World War II, a unified government was the norm. However, post-World War II divided government has become the norm. Between 1901 and 1947, the United States had a unified government 87 percent of the time and a divided government only 13 percent of the time. However, post-World War II, the situation was dramatically reversed. Between 1947 and 2022, we had a unified government only 37 percent of the time and a divided government 63 percent of the time. In other words, since the end of World War II, a divided government has become the norm in American politics.

Policymaking becomes more problematic during a period of divided government since the president's party's policy agenda may differ significantly from the political party that controls one or both houses of Congress. Some have tended to blame the divided government for policy gridlock within Congress and between the executive and legislative branches of government (Galderisi, Herzberg, and McNamara 1996). According to Badger (2010), a divided government causes gridlock because political parties are less likely to compromise through bargaining and negotiations. However, the American public favors a divided government as an additional method of checks and balances. In a poll conducted of 1,500 registered voters between August 8 2020 and August 9, 2020, 41 percent favored the divided government, 33 percent favored the unified government, and 26 percent were unsure (Roper 2020).

Some have traced the origins of political polarization to the 1960s and 1970s to the Johnson administration following the assassination of John F.

Kennedy when the Democratic Party turned away from traditional liberalism. The passage of the Civil Rights Act of 1964, the turbulent 1968 Democratic Party Convention in Chicago, and the institutionalization of identity politics shattered the existing political consensus and put political divisions into a widening trajectory (Klein 2020; Pierson 2015; Frymer 2011). The 1970s witnessed the realignment of the two major political parties leading to a shift in political ideology that started the United States on the path toward political polarization. This was the beginning of the disappearance of the Northeast-centered moderate/liberal Republicans which coincided with the disappearance of the moderate/conservative Democrats from the South. For example, in 1974, the combined Congressional delegation from New England favored Democrats 15 to 10, but by 2012, the Democratic advantage had increased to 20 to 2. Similarly, the Congressional delegation from the South favored Democrats 92 to 42 Republicans in 1974, but by 2012, it changed in favor of Republicans by 107 Republicans to 47 Democrats ("The Origins of Today's Political Polarization" 2018). Southern states that used to vote strictly for Democrats started to shift toward Republicans. The Democratic Party's increasingly more liberal position on a variety of social issues such as civil rights, voting rights, school integration, busing, affirmative action, abortion, and the like shifted southern states toward the Republican Party. Richard Nixon won the presidency in 1968 by employing the "Southern strategy" appealing to Southern whites by criticizing affirmative action and other policies and programs advocated by the Democrats (Greenblatt 2021). Political parties resorted themselves to the changes that took place in the 1960s (Milbank 2022).

Michael Tomasky (2019) argues that political discord has always been the "default setting" for much of the history of the United States; i.e., America has always been a polarized country. However, he suggests that what sets the current state of political polarization apart from other times in history is that the Democratic and Republican parties have become entrenched in their polarization and representation of specific geographical regions. He traces the origin of current political polarization to the early 1980s to the Reagan presidency and points to a series of events such as the firing of striking air-traffic controllers, the repeal of the fairness doctrine, and the contentious Senate confirmation hearing of Reagan's Supreme Court nominee Robert Bork. According to Tomasky (2019), the fracturing of American politics was inflamed further in the 1990s with the Republican capture of the U.S. House of Representatives for the first time in 40 years, Newt Gingrich becoming the Speaker of the House, the "contract with America" and the "Gingrich Revolution," Newt Gingrich's toxic attacks against basic norms and norms of American politics, the impeachment of President Bill Clinton by the House, and the Supreme Court's role in stopping the 2000 presidential election recount vote in Florida.

Most scholars and journalists have traced the origins and increased political polarization of American politics to the mid-1990s when the election of 1994 ushered in a period of divided government (1995–2001) in which the Democratic Party controlled the White House (Bill Clinton) and the Republican Party controlled both houses of Congress. For example, Kornacki (2018) traces the origins of political polarization in American politics to the early 1990s and the bare-knuckle brawls between President Bill Clinton and Speaker of the House Newt Gingrich that brought about major policy shifts and had far-reaching political consequences (Greenblatt 2021; Mondak and Donna-Gene 2009; Olson and Green 2009; Gelman et al. 2008). Newt Gingrich advised Republicans to go negative and to treat opponents as enemies. He referred to Democrats as "sick," "radicals," and "un-Americans," igniting a new era of incivility in Congress (Hornaday 2021). The rise of Newt Gingrich in the 1990s also coincided with the rise of conservative talk shows, Fox News, followed by the advent of social media (Milbank 2022). By the mid-1990s, political polarization has become the defining characteristic of contemporary American politics.

Mugambi Jouet (2019) argues that the United States is more polarized compared to most other Western countries due to its unique history, culture, religion, race, politics, and political and legal institutions. Forces of polarization include anti-intellectualism, Christian fundamentalism, market fundamentalism that fosters suspicion of government, and racial resentment.

Regardless of when political polarization started, one thing is clear. Polarization did not start with one specific event but it was a culmination of many events over several decades to make America a divided nation. Politics became toxic with endless conflicts without any middle ground and characterized by personal attacks, hatred of the opposition, resentment, tribal, sectarian, and nativism.

Evolution of Political Polarization

Greenblatt (2021) argues that America has become a **"49 percent nation,"** meaning that both parties enjoy support that is close to a majority but neither party can enjoy stable majority control for long. Under such conditions, politics has become clannish and, consequently, both parties are engaged in endless feuds where there is no middle ground. Lee (2016) argues that the growing ideological gulf between the two parties has led to a situation in which the two parties compete for control of Congress on an even footing resulting in **"insecure majorities."** This, in turn, has changed the incentive and strategies of political parties that make for contentious partisanship since each side engages in actions that promote a positive image of their party while undercutting that of the opposition leaving little room for compromise and bipartisanship. American politics has become **"calcified"** leading to hardening and rigidity among Americans because they have become firmly rooted in their place and have become harder to move from their predispositions. Growing calcification is the natural growth of growing polarization (Sides, Tausanovitch, and Vavreck 2022).

The Tribalism

Of the two identities—party affiliation and political ideology—which one do Americans give higher priority? Does party identity trump political ideology or does ideology trump party identification? Barber and Pope (2017) conclude that to most Americans group loyalty and social identity are more important than any professed ideology in influencing their opinions. Another term for social identity is tribalism (Adler 2017). Some other synonyms for tribe include clique and pack. A democracy requires that different political groups view each other as valid, equal, and legitimate, even though they may disagree on specific issues. The absence of such conditions results in tribalism and conflict (Gibian 2012). Humans are a social species and tribal by nature, who need a sense of belonging and the capacity for empathy and compassion. However, tribal humans also have a dark side, at times exhibiting belligerence, hostility, and a capacity for destruction (Levine 2018). Andrew Sullivan (2017), in a thought-provoking essay, argues that tribalism is a default human experience and healthy tribalism can exist in civil society in benign ways because it provides individuals a sense of belonging, to their neighborhood and community. However, benign and healthy tribalism can become dangerous when they calcify into something bigger and more intense, turning tribes into enemies. Such forms of tribalism can destabilize democracy. He further argues that over the last few decades, the complex divides of party, ideology, geography, class, religion, and race have mutated into two coherent tribes (the Democratic and Republican parties), fighting not just to advance their own interests but to condemn and defeat each other at any cost. One tribe (the Democratic Party) contains mostly racial minorities, lives on the coast and in the cities, is less tolerant of religion, and is globalist in its outlook, while the other tribe (the Republican Party) is disproportionately white, lives in rural areas, values traditional faith and religion, and is nationalist in its outlook. The incomprehension and hatred of each other have been further fueled by the arrival of partisan and ideologically based talk radio, Fox News, MSNBC, and the Internet—making bargaining, compromises, and coalition-building between opposing tribes impossible. Under such conditions, politics becomes a zero-sum game where the goal of each side is to obliterate the other side. One of the great attractions of such tribalism is that one does not have to think for oneself since one's opinion on any subject is based on what side of the tribe one belongs to (Sullivan 2017). In political tribalism, loyalty to the political tribe becomes more important than anything else because social identity becomes rooted in emotions. Everything in politics comes to be viewed as "us v. them," (Chong 2020; Stalder 2018; Chua and Rubenfeld 2018; Fallows 2017). Under the influences of tribalism, a group enters the divisive mindset in which their relationship with other tribes becomes confrontational and closes the mind to understanding others' points of view. The Trump presidency magnified the political divisions and tribal mindset in American politics by disregarding the rule of law, operating outside the constraints of a democratic system, and creating a cult of personality (Shapiro and Fogel 2019).

Sectarianism

The term "sectarianism" traditionally has referred to group conflict centered around religious differences, especially within the same faith; i.e., sectarianism is a conflict between sects. Originally the use of this concept was limited to the study of sectarian conflict in the Middle East. In recent years, a more inclusive understanding of the concept of sectarianism has helped expand the meaning of the term to apply it to communal, identity-based divisions of all types and not just focused on religious beliefs, making it applicable to a variety of different settings. Thus, the term political sectarianism can be applied to a society like the United States that is driven by identity-based divisions mobilized for political ends. Political sectarianism relies on scapegoating "others" for political purposes (Mabon 2021; Mabon and Ardovini 2016; Ardovini 2016).

Finkel et al. (2020) have argued that antagonism between the left and right has become so intense that terms such as polarization and tribalism no longer capture the level of partisan hostility, and thus they use the term—political sectarianism—to describe the current political divide. Political sectarianism refers to a tendency of a political group to identify itself as moral and other political groups as immoral. They argue that political sectarianism consists of three ingredients. One is othering, i.e., the tendency to view opposing partisans as alien to oneself. The second is aversion, i.e., the tendency to dislike and distrust opposing partisans. The third ingredient is moralization, i.e., the tendency to view opposing partisans as immoral and evil. All three ingredients together have created a poisonous cocktail of political sectarianism. It reflects differences in beliefs/values and divides people around race, religion, region, education, occupation, and geography and feeds cultural wars. It has created a toxic political environment in which each side sees oneself as good and the other side as evil and an existential threat (Calvert 2022; Edsall 2020;). The three characteristics—othering, aversion, and moralization—make up the key components of "negative partisanship" whereby people support their political party based on their own social identity rather than ideology or policy (Masaru 2021).

In contrast to "tribalism," the core of which is kinship in which members of the tribal group feel a familiar bond with one another, the core of "sectarianism" is religion and faith in which members of the group feel a sense of moral correctness and superiority of one's sect against other sects. Thus, sectarianism has a strong moral component, and American political sects are bonded by their faith that their side is morally superior to others. Without any incentives for politicians to avoid polarizing language and policies, today, politicians and political elites are more likely to push ideologically more extreme ideas and language. Political sectarianism incentivizes politicians to adopt anti-democratic tactics and legitimizes willingness to inflict collateral damage in pursuit of electoral and political goals. In such a situation, political stakes become so high that the violation of democratic principles and violence in pursuit of political goals become more acceptable (Finkel et al. 2020; Merrefield 2020; Edsall 2020). In recent years, it has become common for conservative websites and political leaders to use violent rhetoric and demonize political opponents. The elevated level of political polarization increases the chances of violent rhetoric spreading to both sides of the political spectrum. The likelihood of violence increases with the magnification of extremism (Byman 20212). This coincides with increased political polarization in the United States, including among the public, members of Congress, and political parties.

An analysis of 1,040 terrorist attacks and plots in the United States between January 1, 1994, and December 31, 2021, by the Center for Strategic and International Studies (CSIS) revealed three major trends. One, there was a significant increase in the number and percentage of domestic terrorist incidents at demonstrations between 2020 and 2021. Second, the major target of domestic terrorists from all sides of the political spectrum has been U.S. law enforcement agencies. Third, white supremacists, anti-government militias, and like-minded extremist groups such as the Three Percenters, Proud Boys, Patriot Prayer, and Oath Keepers conducted 49 percent of attacks and plots. The percentage of attacks and plots conducted by anarchists, and anti-fascists, also increased in 2021. Political violence has escalated particularly in metropolitan areas (Doxsee et al. 2022).

The insurrection and the physical attack on the U.S. Capitol on January 6, 2021, by a mob of Trump supporters that included individuals from most extreme right-wing militia groups such as Proud Boys, Oath Keepers, Three Percenters, along with followers of conspiracy groups such as QAnon, which resulted in violence and death of five individuals provide a perfect example of the consequence of political sectarianism. The attack occurred when a joint session of Congress was meeting to officially certify the electoral votes cast by the states declaring Joe Biden, a Democrat, to be the winner of the presidential election against Donald Trump, a Republican.

Masaru (2021) has argued that quantitative evidence shows a deterioration in American democracy, and this could be attributed to the presidency of Donald Trump who used authoritarian actions and rhetoric to further inflame political sectarianism and negative partisanship. Even after his defeat in the 2020 presidential election, Trump has continued to exacerbate the conflict with his claim that the election was "stolen" from him and his "stop the steal" campaign.

It should come as no surprise that Democrats and Republicans viewed the 2020 general election in moralistic and good-versus-evil terms. For example, a nationwide poll of 2,500 randomly selected adults by the non-profit and nonpartisan Public Religion Research Institute found that 78 percent of Democratic respondents thought that the Republican Party has been overtaken by racists while 81 percent of Republican respondents thought that the Democratic Party has been overtaken by socialists (Merrifield 2020).

Political sectarianism has become a growing threat to American democracy. Political sectarianism in American politics has come to symbolize two hostile identity groups that clash with one another because each side sees the other side as alien and immoral. Partisanship has become a mega-identity that divides the two parties not just over policy differences in areas such as healthcare, reproduction, voting, and civil rights, guns, pandemic but has also produced a broader clash between white, Christian conservatives on the one side and secular, multiracial, liberals on the other side. Both political parties have further sorted themselves along racial, religious, socioeconomic, demographic, and geographic lines (Cohn 2021).

The Return of Nativism

Nativism is defined as an intense opposition toward minorities due to their foreign connection. It is often race-based and anti-immigrant. It is correlated to racism due to fear or resentment of "other," "outsider," or non-white foreigners. In recent years, the term "nativism" has been associated with the rise of the right-wing population in the United States and Europe. Betz (2019) argues that there are three faces of nativism—economic, welfare chauvinism, and symbolic. Economic nativism relies on the notion that jobs should be reserved for native citizens. Welfare chauvinism rests on the idea that when it comes to social benefits, the highest priority should be given to native citizens over immigrants. Symbolic nativism advances the notion that the government should defend the cultural identity of the country, i.e., defending the cultural national identity of the country. Nativism advocates a preference for "native-born" over foreigners. Since nativism is associated with anti-immigrants, especially non-white immigrants, it is also invariably interlinked with white nationalism (Serwer 2019; Amaya 2018). The notion of national identity is also strongly associated with attitudes toward immigrants in the United States (Hill 2022a, 2022b).

Nativism has raised its ugly face in American politics frequently throughout its history from the American Revolution to the Civil War to Anti-Catholicism during the 1940s and 1950s to modern xenophobia in which anti-Catholic sentiments have been replaced by anti-Muslim sentiments. It is impossible to separate the rise of nativism and anti-immigrant sentiments from the country's history of immigration (Ritter 2021; Schrag 2010). In recent years nativism has been directed at Asian and Latino immigrants (Mallapragada 2021; Sanchez 1997).

During the 1940s and 1850s, there was resentment against German, Catholic, and Irish immigrants. During the 1870s and the 1880s, resentment was directed against Chinese and Asian immigrants. From the 1890s to the 1920s, and especially during World War I, Southern and Eastern Europeans had become the victims of such resentment. The more recent form of nativism, from the 1990s to the present, is reflected in the resentment of Mexicans, Hispanics, and other non-white immigrants (Nassir 2013).

The notion of nativism was prominent in America during World War I and the 1920s. During this time, the notions of welcoming immigrants and their assimilation into American society and America as a melting pot quickly dissipated. It was replaced by nativism as a force for patriotism, national unity and conformity, total allegiance, anti-immigration attitudes especially directed at German Americans and political radicals, and the idea of America for Americans. Nativism did not diminish at the end of World War I. Congress overwrote President Wilson's veto, in early 1921, of legislation limiting immigration based on nationality. The 1924 National Origins Act led to a sharp decrease in the volume of European and Asian newcomers to the United States. President Calvin Coolidge declared that America must be kept American ("Nativism – World War I and the 1920s" n.d.)

Trump capitalized on white fear of loss of status using the tactic of "white victimology." This had appealed to a great many white supremacists, Trumpists, and many Republicans who advanced the "great replacement" conspiracy theory rooted in the belief that white people are in danger of being replaced by back and brown people. The fear of losing of white way of life, and the belief that the election was stolen from them and somehow they were cheated, made them more susceptible to rejecting democratic norms (DeVega 2022a; Keller and Kirkpatrick 2022). A poll conducted by the Southern Poverty Law Center and Tulchin Research in April of 2022 found that seven out of ten Republicans believed in the idea of the "great replacement" theory (Carless 2022).

Sides, Tesler, and Vavreck (2019) have argued that Donald Trump's victory in the 2016 presidential election was the result of changes that had taken place in the Democratic and Republican coalitions driven by racial and ethnic identities. The 2016 presidential campaign represented a crisis of identity and what it means to be an American and what America should be. During the campaign and later as a president, Trump exacerbated and magnified the existing divisions by hammering away on issues of race, immigration, and religion. He exploited the dormant nativism in American society and tribalism of American politics by calling Mexican immigrants, rapists, and criminals, African American countries as "shitholes," and Muslims as terrorists. He articulated all three facets of nativism—economic, symbolic, and welfare chauvinism—and pushed for an "America First" policy in both domestic and international arenas (Mansfield et al. 2021; Lynch 2019; Shapiro and Fogel 2019; Young, Ziemer, and Jackson 2019).

A cultural backlash against modernity, globalization, and immigration embodied by nativist impulses and right-wing populism combined with the belief among many Americans that the American political system was broken powered Trump's rise to the presidency (Bricker et al. 2019; Young, Ziemer, and Jackson 2019). Nativist sentiments played a key role in support for a specific political party. Davis et al. (2019) in their research found a strong positive relationship between nativist sentiments and support for political parties with a nativist platform. Republican governors of red states such as Texas, Florida, and Arizona took Trump's hard-line immigration policy further by sending migrants to sanctuary cities in blue states such as Delaware and Massachusetts (Haberman and Bender 2022).

The four years (1917 to 1921) of the Trump administration's anti-immigration, anti-Muslim policies, divisive and hate-filled rhetoric used by President Trump, and his "Big Lie" about the 2020 election being rigged and stolen from him empowered right-wing white nationalists and militia groups which ultimately culminated into the January 6, 2021 insurrection, with an attack on the U.S. Capitol and violence following his loss to the Democratic nominee, Joe Biden.

The tribal nature of American politics has created an environment in which the two major tribes—the Democratic Party and the ideological Left and the Republican Party and the ideological Right—view each other as a clear and present danger to American democracy. However, the extremist partisan and ideological drift is more pronounced in the Republican Party. Despite all the evidence to the contrary, millions of Republicans and Trump supporters continue to believe that the 2020 presidential election was stolen. In fact, according to the Washington Post (2022) analysis, of the 569 Republican nominees on the ballot for the 2022 election for the U.S. House and the Senate and many state-wide offices, 299 (53 percent) have been election deniers who have refused to accept Joe Biden's victory in the 2020 presidential election or questioned the outcome of the election. Kamarck and Eisen (2022a, 2022b), identified 341 Republican candidates running on a platform of election denial. This number is higher than the one by the *Washington Post* because it also includes state legislative candidates. According to their post-2022 election analysis, 224 election denials (66 percent) won their races. Many of them were incumbents running in deep red districts. Among the 97 candidates for state legislative offices, 70 (72 percent) won their races. Another such analysis by the University of Virginia's Center for Politics, of 552 Republican election candidates in 2022, found that of the 368 candidates ranging from those who accepted the 2020 election results with reservations to those who fully denied the election results, 221 won their election (60 percent). Of the 199 candidates who fully denied the 2020 election results, 138 of them won (59 percent), nor did they have any trouble raising campaign funds (Whaley 2022).

Thus, while many election-denier candidates running for high offices at the state level who were endorsed by Trump lost, some election deniers did win. Some saw the defeat of some of the prominent election deniers as a victory for democracy while others saw it as a return to normalcy (Douthat 2022). Some of the major election deniers included Ohio Republican U.S. Senate candidate J. D. Vance (won), Georgia Republican candidate Herschel Walker (lost), Republican candidate for Governor of Arizona, Kari Lake (lost), Pennsylvania Republican candidate for governor, Doug Mastriano (lost), and many others who have espoused nativist themes in their campaigns (Nichols 2022; Hill 2022a, 2022b; Graham 2022; Cramer 2022; Nichols 2021). It is premature to jump to any conclusion based on the results of one election cycle whether the results of the 2022 elections represent a victory for democracy or a temporary, short-term deviation. On December 3rd, 2022, Donald Trump on his social media platform, Truth Social, called for the termination of the U.S. Constitution to overturn the 2020 election results and demanded that he be installed as the president (Legaspi 2022). Millions of his supporters still believe his "Big Lie."

During the Great Depression and World War II, Americans came together to help one another and made sacrifices for the "common good." However, in the toxic political environment of today, Americans no longer seem to believe in and are willing to sacrifice for the common good. This is exemplified by the hostility directed at mask-wearing and vaccination to prevent the spread of a pandemic (House 2021). Political polarization has paralyzed the American political system (Jenkins 2022).

Political Polarization of the Elites

We need to think of polarization as not one specific thing but as a multidimensional concept (Park 2018). In this section, we analyze the partisan and ideological polarization of the elites. Elites refer to the party leaders, legislators, and activists at the federal and state levels. We have focused our discussion here on elite-level polarization in the Congress of the United States.

Elite Partisan Polarization

The Framers of the U.S. Constitution were very skeptical of political parties and viewed them as something to be avoided. James Madison viewed them as nothing but factions that engaged in mischief. George Washington, Alexander Hamilton, John Adams, and Thomas Jefferson believed that well-educated and well-informed citizens would find them useless. They saw political parties as a negative instrument that would ignite uncontrolled political passion and thus unsuitable to act as a filter for mass expression of public opinion. However, political parties became inevitable to organize elections, legitimize opposition, and ensure a peaceful transfer of power (White and Kerbel 2022).

The reality is that partisan divide has existed from the very beginning of the formation of the first party system demonstrated by the fact that Thomas Jefferson and his party, the Democratic-Republican Party, opposed John Adams and Alexander Hamilton's Federalist Party. Political parties engaged in vicious attacks not only on opponents but also on their wives, and their ancestors (Katz 2015).

Over the last several decades, Democratic and Republican political elites have become much more polarized. By the mid-1990s partisanship had become resurgent, especially at the elite level, i.e., elite polarization (Brewer 2005). This is especially evident in the Congress of the United States. The contemporary partisan divide can be traced to the presidencies of John F. Kennedy and Lyndon Johnson which emphasized the role of the federal government in addressing the social ills of American society. Republican presidential candidates offered a starkly contrasting alternative in the form of the candidacy of Berry Goldwater in 1964 and Richard Nixon in 1968 (Katz 2015). Partisanship reasserted itself in Congress during the 1970s and the 1980s and had increased dramatically by the end of the 1980s. The increased partisan or elite polarization was reflected in a variety of trends.

The percentage of the party-line vote where the majority of one-party votes together against the majority of the other party increased substantially in Congress. So did the party unity score—the percentage of votes in which a member votes with the member of his/her fellow party members. Parties were becoming more internally cohesive in their voting behavior and growing further apart from each other (Fleisher and Bond 1996; Jacobson 2000).

The partisan polarization is reflected in increased partisan differences in congressional voting behavior (voting along party lines) and low-level or lack of party competition in congressional districts (McCarthy, Poole, and Rosenthal 2009). The polarization of the Democratic and Republican parties has been at its highest since the end of the Civil War and partisan conflict has grown sharper and unrelenting (Hare and Poole 2014). In the 112th Congress (2011–2012), 91 percent of the Democrats and 93.5 percent of the Republicans voted with their fellow party members on roll calls, leaving very little room for compromise and coalition-building (Campbell 2016).

From 1949 to 1979, members of different political parties often agreed and voted the same way and cross-party agreements were common. However, since 1977, congressmen of different parties have become less likely to agree with each other on roll call votes and more likely to agree with the members of their own party. There has been a steady divergence between same-party and cross-party agreement rates (Khazatsky 2021). However, individual voters often underestimate the extent to which legislators from their own party vote the party line (Dancey and Sheagley 2018).

Political parties in Congress have assumed an "uncompromising mindset" marked by mutual distrust (Gutmann and Thompson 2010). The unwillingness of the two main political parties to compromise on virtually most issues has led to major gridlock in Washington. The gridlock in Washington is the by-product of partisan polarization (Kuo 2018; 2015). Voters' perception of elite polarization, in turn, can affect their party identity and identity strength (Harrison 2016; Katz 2015; Davis, Frost, and Cohen 2011). Others have argued that party elites, particularly elected representatives, have experienced significant party polarization in the sense that liberals and conservatives have mostly sorted themselves into Democrats and Republicans, respectively (Benkler, Faris, and Roberts 2018).

Elite Ideological Polarization

There have been several attempts by scholars to describe and analyze ideological labels and political philosophies that underlie American politics and debates over policy issues and their appeals to various groups (Pew Research Center 2021; Wolf 2021; Classen, Tucker, and Smith 2015; Wenz 2009; Frank 2004). In our discussion of ideological polarization, we confine ourselves to a traditional framework that aligns American political ideologies with the left-right (liberal-conservative) political continuum since most Americans identify themselves as liberal, moderate, or conservative, even though there are sub-strains within each.

The increase in partisan polarization is also associated with an increase in ideological polarization between the two political parties. Democrats and Republicans are ideologically further apart today than in the past (Hibbing, Hays, and Deol 2017.) Since the 1970s, the ideological distance between the Democratic and Republican parties has increased significantly. Political parties have become more cohesive due to ideological sorting and the realignment of each party's coalition base. Democrats have moved further to the left and the Republicans have moved further to the right on the liberal-conservative axis in Congress.

Since the 1970s the distance between the Democratic and Republican parties in both chambers of Congress, especially in the House of Representatives, increased significantly. The average distance between the average Democrat and the average Republican in the House of Representatives almost doubled between 1977 and 1979. Similarly, the distance between the average Democrat and the average Republican in the United States Senate also increased by 50 percent during the same years. However, the rightward shift of the Republican Party was much greater than the leftward shift of the Democratic Party. For example, over 80 percent of the increase in the size of the ideological divide in the Senate and over 70 percent of the increase in the Senate were the result of the rightward shift in the location of the average Republican on the ideological spectrum. During the same period, the proportion of political "moderates" declined dramatically, and it was much steeper for Republicans (Abramowitz 2013).

Since 1945 Republican congressmen have become more conservative and Democratic congressmen have become more liberal (Khazatsky 2021; Kuo 2015). The number of policy issues over which the two parties battle publicly has increased dramatically. Regardless of what measure is used to measure ideological polarization, the Democratic and Republican parties have become more ideologically polarized (Brewer 2005).

The ideological polarization is reflected in the fact that from 2005 to 2012, every Democrat in Congress was ideologically to the left of every Republican. Also, in 2013, only one percent of Republicans in the House and four percent of the Senate were moderate while the corresponding numbers for Democrats were 13 percent in the House and 9 percent in the Senate (Altschuler 2017). Both political parties have moved away from the ideological center. Since the 1970s, the Republican and Democratic caucuses in Congress have become more homogeneous and have moved further apart (Farina 2015). Thomsen (2014) attributes the increased ideological polarization of parties to an ideological shift in the electorate in which the electoral bases of the two parties changed from being more diverse to more uniform; however, political parties have experienced an **"asymmetric polarization"** in that the Republican Party has moved further to the ideological right than the Democratic Party has moved to the ideological left (Fishkin and Pozen 2018; Thomsen 2014).

In the past, the "center" was made up of pragmatic conservative Democrats mainly from the southern states and moderate Republicans from the Midwest and the Northeast. Over the years, the "center" or the "middle" made up of the political moderates has declined considerably or has disappeared completely like in the Republican Party (Ehrenhalt 2022). According to a survey conducted by the Pew Research Center (2022a), the number of members of Congress who can be labeled as "moderate" declined from 160 in 1971 to about two dozen in 2020. Between the 92nd Congress of 1971–1972 and the current 117th Congress (2021–2022), both parties in both the House and the Senate have shifted further away from the center, but Republicans more so. Partisan-ideological sorting is also related to the expansion of cable and satellite programming and the fragmentation of media along ideological lines (Davis and Dunaway 2016).

During the 1950s the two major political parties agreed on certain major political issues such as anti-communism in foreign affairs. There was also a broad agreement on the nature of the American political system and often fashioned compromises that kept changes within established boundaries. However, bargaining and compromises have become uncommon with increased ideological polarization in Congress (Higgs 2018). The United States is now more ideologically polarized than at any other time in history and data suggests that Democrats and Republicans are more likely to vote in opposition to one another indicating a growing divergence in each party's position on a variety of policy issues (Bateman, Clinton, and Lapinski 2017). However, it should be noted that even within highly polarized political parties, one can find ideological factions that create their own sub-brands of party politics (Clarke 2020).

Partisan and Ideological Polarization of the Judiciary

The partisan and ideological polarization not only is confined to the Congress and the electorate but has also permeated the American judiciary in recent years, especially at the highest level of courts.

It is a fact that partisanship affects the selection and nomination of justices at both the state and federal levels. Governors and presidents who nominate judges, legislators who confirm judges, and/or voters who vote on judicial candidates are more apt to support or oppose judges based on their partisan affiliation. Given the partisan nature of the judicial selection mechanism and the fact that political parties have different sets of values and ideologies that drive the selection process, one should not be too surprised to discover that partisan and ideological polarization can also be reflected in judicial decision-making. This, in turn, may lead the public to view judges and judicial decisions through a partisan lens (Hasen 2019).

It is a fallacy and a myth, often perpetuated by the judges themselves, that judges merely apply the law to a given set of facts in making their decisions. For example, the United States Chief Justice Robert famously proclaimed that the court did not have Trump judges, Obama judges, Bush judges, or Clinton judges. Using the baseball analogy, he stated that judges are like home plate empires in baseball. They simply call balls and strikes neutrally. What he failed to mention is that in baseball different home plate umpires have different interpretations of what constitutes the strike zone and call balls and strikes differently. Going as far back as the 1940s, research and scholarship had begun to challenge the view that judges simply interpret the law and do not make policies. More contemporary research has shown that ideology measured via partisanship is one of the most crucial factors that shape judicial decision-making. Thus, justices on the Supreme Court and judges throughout the American judiciary make policy with their decisions (Bonica and Sen 2021). Hyperpartisanship has permeated every part of the American political system including the federal judiciary (Greenblatt 2023). Consequently, public respect for the Supreme Court has plummeted (Jenkinson 2023).

State Judiciary

In 2021, 39 states used some form of popular election for selecting, retaining, or both for state supreme court and major trial courts. These elections take on four forms. First is a partisan election in which candidates are listed by their party affiliation. Second is semi-partisan elections in which nominations are made through party primaries or conventions but on the general election ballot nominees' party is not identified. The third is nonpartisan elections in which political parties do not play any role and the ballot does not list candidates' party affiliation. The fourth format takes the form of a referendum in which voters are asked whether the incumbent should be retained in office for another term (Kritzer 2021). Research has shown the existence of a partisan pattern in states using both nonpartisan and semi-partisan elections. Partisanship has increased in all four forms of judicial elections in the last several decades with the sharpest increase registered in nonpartisan elections. Since 2012, increased partisan polarization has been demonstrated in several state supreme court selections using three of the election formats. State supreme courts have not been immune from increased partisanship associated with increased political polarization (Kritzer 2021; Bonneau and Cann 2015).

Court-packing is already happening at the state level. For example, in several states such as Florida and Iowa, Republican legislatures have changed the rules for judicial nominating commissions to give governors more control. Ideological polarization is reflected in the fact that some Republican state legislatures, such as ones in Georgia and Arizona, have added seats to the state supreme courts to create conservative majorities. In states where the majority on the Supreme Court is up for grabs or where courts have issued high-profile controversial decisions (e.g., gerrymandering, abortion), interest groups and political action committees are spending millions of dollars in state supreme court races to support their respective candidates/nominees. The 2019–2020 election cycle saw a record of $97 million in such spending and it is only going to escalate (Corriher 2022).

Federal Judiciary

Starting in the 1960s scholars had begun to discover robust partisan differences between Democratic and Republican judges in federal district courts (Rowland and Carp 1996). A study by Manning, Sennewald, and Carp

(2013) analyzed 60,201 federal district court decisions from 1996 to 2011 and found an ideological gap between Democratic and Republican judges with Democratic judges consistently handing down more liberal decisions. The problem of the ideological polarization of the federal judiciary was exacerbated during the Trump presidency since he appointed more partisan and conservative justices to the federal bench. During his four years in office, Trump was successful in appointing three justices to the Supreme Court, 54 judges on the circuit appeals court, and 174 to the district courts. Judges appointed by Trump are significantly more conservative than judges appointed by other Republican presidents in the past and he has had a significant impact on the ideological orientation of the federal judiciary and has altered the decision-making pattern of the federal courts (Gerstein and Cheney 2024; Rubin 2022a; Manning, Carp, and Holmes 2020).

The polarization of the federal judiciary is not limited to the lower level of courts. According to Liptak (2014), three changes have contributed to the increased polarization of the Supreme Court. Presidents have become more sensitive to the ideology of potential nominees than they did in the past. Second, Presidents have become more skilled at finding nominees who reliably vote according to that ideology. Third, party affiliation has become the best predictor of justices' views.

There was a time when Supreme Court nominations were noncontentious, and nominees were often confirmed on a voice vote. Also, many confirmation votes were bipartisan. The last time a Supreme Court nominee received more than 70 votes in the Senate was 20 years ago when Chief Justice John Roberts, Jr. was confirmed. Since that time bipartisanship has declined as partisanship concerning both nomination and confirmation has increased (Joyner 2022). The refusal of Republicans in the Senate to even consider Democratic President Obama's nomination of Merrick Garland for almost seven months before the 2016 presidential election highlighted the partisan politics surrounding the Supreme Court appointments (Hulse 2018). Republicans in the Senate had no qualms about rushing in to approve outgoing Republican President Trump's nomination of Amy Barrett to the Supreme Court a week before the 2020 presidential election raising questions about the legitimacy of the Supreme Court (Dorman 2022).

One of the important consequences of partisan polarization in the nomination and confirmation of Supreme Court justices is ideological polarization of the court itself. One of the important questions is to what extent ideological polarization of the court affects judicial decisions and policy outcomes (Clark 2009). Supreme Court often divides along party lines in highly contested cases. Thus, polarization can be reflected in decisions the justices make on issues such as abortion, voting rights, and affirmative action (Hasen 2019). Current research suggests that ideological polarization of the Supreme Court has produced highly ideological and partisan judicial decisions by the court. Some have suggested that polarization has turned the Supreme Court into a partisan judicial body (Devins and Baum 2017).

One indicator of the ideological polarization of the Supreme Court is the margins by which the court's decisions are made. Unanimous decisions generally indicate less ideological polarization while decisions by narrow margins are often viewed as political. From 1801 to 1940, less than two percent of the Supreme Court's total rulings were decided by 5-4 margins. Since then, more than 16 percent of the Supreme Court's rulings have been decided by a "minimum winning coalition" (Kuhn 2012). During the late 1930s and early 1940s, over 70 percent of the court's opinions were unanimous but this dropped off afterward (Feldman 2022).

Until Justice Ruth Ginsberg died in September 2020, the Supreme Court had enjoyed a 5-4 conservative majority which often led to split 5-4 decisions by the courts. President Trump during his one term in office was able to fill three seats on the court with very conservative justices which created a conservative supermajority on the Supreme Court. The Supreme Court's 2021 term had the highest percentage of 6-3 decisions in all cases that went to the oral arguments since the 1937 term (Feldman 2022). Even before establishing the supermajority of six conservative justices, the 5-4 conservative majority handed down a series of conservative decisions. In 2010, in *Citizens United*, a 5-4 conservative majority overturned any limits on campaign funding by corporations. In 2013, five conservative justices in *Shelby County v. Holder* gutted the key enforcement provision of the Voting Rights Act that required prior federal government approval of voting changes in states with a history of voting discrimination. In 2014, in McCutcheon v. FEC, a 5-4 conservative majority outlawed any limits on how much money an individual could give to candidates of campaign committees in any election cycle. In 2019, in the case of *Moore v. Harper*, the Supreme Court ruled that the federal court would no longer review cases of partisan gerrymandering (Heuvel 2022; Sherman 2022a).

A recent study also documented a 35 percent increase in the rate of rulings in favor of religion in orally argued cases which translated to an 81 percent success rate under Chief Justice Robert's court. The court has ruled in favor of religious organizations including mainstream Christian organizations more frequently than in the past. Also, what is different about the current court compared to previous courts is that most rulings have benefited mainstream Christian organizations. In contrast, under the Warren court, all the rulings in favor of religion tended to favor minority or dissenting practitioners (Epstein and Posner 2021).

An updated study by Rothchild (2022) concluded that the politicization of religious freedom has infiltrated every level of the federal judiciary and argues that between 2015 and 2020, federal judges' partisan affiliation had become strongly correlated to their votes on the court. During this time, judges appointed by Democrats sided with religion ten percent of the time, compared to 49 percent for ones appointed by Republicans and 72 percent for ones appointed by President Trump.

In one of the most controversial decisions, in January of 2022, in *Dobbs v. Jackson's Women's Health Organization*, a 5-4 conservative majority ignored a 50-year precedent and overturned the 1973 *Roe v. Wade* that had granted women a constitutional right to abortion, leaving individual states to set policy. This has led Republican-controlled states to severely restrict or eliminate abortion rights while Democratic-controlled states have moved to strengthen and expand abortion rights (Brownstein 2020).

The increased partisanship associated with the nomination and confirmation of the Supreme Court justices combined with partisan, ideologically driven court rulings raises questions about the impartiality of decisions rendered by the court and the Supreme Court's legitimacy in the minds of the American public (Hulse 2018). In the Supreme Court's 2021 term, in 14 cases (20 percent of the court's docket), the ruling was split 6-3 along partisan and ideological lines that included divisive decisions on abortion, guns, religion, and the environment (Wolf 2022).

The line between partisanship and ideology is narrow and can often get blurred. In a series of cases, the Supreme Court has ruled in a way that might be considered against their partisan interests. For example, the Supreme Court denied almost all court challenges by Trump against claims of election fraud in the 2020 election; the Supreme Court has also rejected Trump's attempts to prevent the House Ways and Means Committee from obtaining his tax returns, refused South Carolina's Republican Senator Lindsay Graham's efforts to avoid testifying before a special Georgia grand jury investigating 2020 election interference, cleared way for a New York grand jury to obtain Trump's financial records, among others. However, the conservative majority on the Supreme Court has consistently shown ideological hostility toward voting rights, reproductive rights, limits on campaign funding, and protecting religious rights of mainline religions against challenges by minorities. Thus, it is reasonable to conclude that the current Supreme Court is driven more by ideology than partisanship (Marcus).

In a recently completed term (October 2023 to June/July 2024), a fractured Supreme Court with a conservative majority has remade America. It took on several major legal disputes and played a major role in reshaping American society and democracy. The range of legal disputes the Supreme Court dealt with included the power of administrative agencies, homelessness, voting rights, public corruption, abortion, and presidential immunity. In sweeping rulings, it erased a fundamental precedent requiring courts to defer to agency expertise, gave states the power to remove homeless encampments from public lands, removed voting rights protections, made it difficult to prosecute public officials for corruption, eliminated constitutionally guaranteed abortion rights, and granted the president broad immunity from criminal prosecution for actions undertaken related to presidential powers. In almost all these cases, the court was divided 6-3 along partisan and ideological lines (Liptak 2024). In granting the president broad immunity from criminal prosecution, the Supreme Court has paved the way for creating a lawless presidency unencumbered by constitutional checks and balances (Shaw 2024 Howe 2024; Gerstein and Cheney 2024). This led Ruth Marcus to call the Supreme Court a "dishonorable court" (2024).

A Gallup poll conducted in September of 2021 found that the approval of the job the Supreme Court was doing had reached a new low while disapproval had reached a new high with 53 percent of respondents disapproving of the way the Supreme Court was handling its job while only 40 percent approved. The poll was conducted shortly after the Supreme Court allowed the Texas abortion ban as soon as six weeks into the pregnancy to take effect. The poll also found a significant decline in the number of Americans who trust the federal judiciary (Aldridge 2021). In a nationwide survey conducted by Pew Research Center (2022b) in August 2022, 49 percent expressed an unfavorable view while 48 percent expressed a favorable view of the Supreme Court. The opinions were divided along partisan lines with more Democrats expressing an unfavorable opinion compared to the Republicans.

The negative views and public criticism of the Supreme Court have forced conservative justices like Roberts, Alito, and Barrett to attempt to defend the legitimacy of the court in their public comments while liberal justices Sotomayor and Kagan have warned that Supreme Court could forfeit its legitimacy and lose public's trust if the court comes to be viewed by the public as ideologically outcome-oriented political branch of the government (Biskupic 2022; Hurley 2022; Rubin 2022b; Sherman 2022b). Such a public discourse by the Supreme Court justices itself is rare and further exemplifies the partisan and ideological polarization of the Supreme Court. Some of the ideas suggested to address the Supreme Court's crisis of legitimacy include expanding the size of the court by adding more justices, placing an age limit on justices, and imposing term limits (Eisen and Matsuki 2022).

An abundance of legal scholars have recently raised alarm that the current Supreme Court has been rapidly accumulating and consolidating more power at the expense of other parts of the government and referred to the current court as "The Imperial Court" (Liptak 2022; Lemley 2022; Tucker and Lindquist 2022; Liptak 2020). Concerns over the partisan and ideological nature of the Supreme Court, the danger of an "Imperial Court," and corruption scandals associated with some of the justices on the court due to the lack of any enforceable code of ethics have caused President Biden (who has decided not to seek re-election in 2024) to propose three major proposals to reform the Supreme Court. One is a proposed constitutional amendment called "No One Is Above the Law Amendment" that will state that the Constitution does not confer any immunity from federal prosecution, indictment, trial, conviction, or sentencing by virtue of previously serving as president. The second proposed reform would impose an 18-year term limit on Justices. The third proposed reform would have Congress pass a binding, enforceable code of conduct that would apply to all federal judges ("Fact Sheet: President Biden Announces Bold Plan to Reform the Supreme Court and Ensure No President is Above the Law" 2024). Unfortunately, the chances of these reform proposals becoming a reality are slim. The first would require a Constitutional Amendment passed by a two-thirds majority in both houses of Congress and ratified by three-fifths of the states. The passage of the other two reform proposals is unlikely in the current divided Congress operating in an environment of partisan and ideological polarization.

Polarization of the American Electorate

Earlier we discussed partisan and ideological elite polarization in American politics. Here we examine whether similar partisan and ideological polarization has occurred in the American electorate.

Partisan Polarization

During the 1970s several scholars noted a decline in partisanship among the electorate in American politics. The title of David Brody's (1971) book, *The Party is Over*, symbolized this presumed decline in partisanship. Similarly, Nie, Verba, and Petrocik (1976) concluded that the decline of partisanship during the 1960s and the 1970s represented the most dramatic shift in the American electorate.

However, by the 1980s partisanship was on the upswing. New research showed that partisanship was very much a factor in elections from 1980 to 1996 and the influence of party identification on Americans' voting choice had increased tremendously (Bartels 2000, 1998). By the 1990s, mass partisanship had started to rebound and partisanship had become more pervasive within the American electorate (Brewer 2005), and the relationship between party identification and ideology had become much stronger (Abramowitz 2006).

In recent decades party loyalty has increased significantly among the American electorate. The partisanship, ideology, and opinions of American voters have become internally more consistent, and partisan identity has become a strong predictor of voting behavior (Jacobson 2013). This is reflected in increased party-line voting in the 2020 elections in which more than 96 percent of voters opted to vote for candidates of their own party. American voting behavior has become very consistent with only about seven percent of Americans regularly switching parties (Hobbes 2020). In the 1970s, partisanship explained less than 30 percent of the variation in voting choice while today it explains 70 percent (Edsall 2022). Partisanship's impact is limited to not only voting behavior but also economic behavior and public discourse (Strickler 2018; McConnell et al. 2018).

As the partisanship divide has deepened, ticket spitting by voters has declined to its lowest levels in decades (Hobbes 2020). Widespread ticket-splitting has become a thing of the past (Galston 2020). Today, Americans are more likely to prefer a single party's candidates up and down the ballot. The share of the U.S. House districts that delivered a split outcome, i.e., simultaneously supporting candidates of the opposite party in presidential and Congressional voting, has declined from 33 percent in 1980 to 20 percent in 2000, and just four percent in 2020. Straight party-line voting has risen even in state and local elections (Hopkins 2022). The 2022 elections saw a slight increase in split-ticket voting especially in state-wide races for governor and U.S. Senate due to the poor quality of some of the Senate candidates. However, split-ticket voting has not returned to levels common between the 1960s and the 1990s (Greenblatt 2022).

In summary, the mass public has become more clearly sorted and voters have aligned their partisanship and ideology; i.e., Democrats are more likely to be liberal and Republicans are more likely to be conservative.

Today, the Democratic and Republican parties are made up of nonoverlapping coalitions of voters who want to move the country in opposite directions. This has divided the country into two camps turning national elections into existential all-or-nothing events (White and Kerbel 2022). In 1952, only 50 percent of voters said that they saw a big difference between the Democratic and Republican parties. By 1984, it was up to 62 percent; in 2004, 76 percent; and by 2020, 90 percent. American voters have become firmly entrenched in their predispositions. Thus, on the one hand, American politics has become so calcified that almost nothing matters. On the other hand, since neither political party enjoys a clear majority, elections are so close that everything matters (Klein 2022a).

Ideological Polarization

Increased elite ideological polarization strongly correlates with increased ideological polarization of the American electorate. Wood and Jordan (2011) define electoral ideological polarization as a condition in which Americans align themselves to a set of liberal and conservative poles on a left-right continuum. Quirk (2011) has argued that increased partisan voting and ideological polarization in Congress (elite polarization) reflect the increased partisan and ideological polarization of the American electorate. According to Cohn (2014), voters of both political parties have become more ideologically homogeneous than in the past. Ninety-nine percent of politically engaged Republican voters are more conservative than the median Democratic voter. Similarly, 98 percent of Democratic voters are more liberal than the median Republican voters. In 2004, the percentages were 88 percent and 84 percent, respectively.

In the twenty-first century, partisanship returned in a form more ideological and more issue-based along liberal-conservative lines than it has been in more than 30 years. This can be seen in the strength of partisan voting, in the relationship between partisanship and ideology, and the strength of the relationship between partisanship and self-reported liberal-conservative ideology to the public's opinions and attitudes about economic, social, racial, and religious issues (Bafumi and Shapiro 2009). Recent research has outlined important changes in partisanship among political elites in the United States. Conflict among political elites has increased in many policy issue areas. Similar changes have taken place among the general electorate. Mass partisanship has rebounded significantly and has become more pervasive within the electorate, especially in racial, social, and economic equality issue areas (Brewer 2005).

The Pew Research Center (2014) conducted a major political survey of 10,000 adult Americans between January and March of 2014. The results of the study found that not only have Americans become more ideological but also that such ideological polarization is also reflected in their personal lives and lifestyles (Doherty 2014). The share of Americans who expressed consistently conservative or liberal opinions had doubled between the 1990s and 2010 from 10 percent to 21 percent. Compared to the past, Americans' ideological thinking has become much more closely aligned with their partisanship. Consequently, the ideological overlap between the two parties has diminished considerably. In 2014, 92 percent of Republicans were to the right of the median Democrat, and 94 percent of Democrats were to the left of the median Republican. According to a Pew Research Center (2017) survey, since 1994, more Americans have moved to the left or right on the ideological continuum. In 2004 almost half of Americans had a mix of conservative and liberal positions but by 2017 that number had dropped down to about a third of Americans. Correspondingly, the proportion of Americans with ideologically consistent values has increased over this time. Such a shift is especially pronounced among politically engaged Americans. The shift in political values also has become more strongly associated with partisanship.Davis and Dunaway (2016) attribute partisan and ideological sorting of the American electorate to the growth and availability of the partisan media and the growth of elite polarization in Congress and state legislatures. The media fragmentation and market penetration of cable, satellite, and Internet technologies have expanded media choice allowing audiences to engage in selective exposure to partisan and ideological media sources. Elite polarization has helped clarify political parties' ideological positions on a variety of issues for the American electorate allowing them to form a more consistent ideological position aligned with their partisanship. In short, the ideological divide among the political elites has helped heightened homogeneity in voters' ideology within political parties (Saeki 2019). According to a Pew Research Center (2017) survey which tracked ten political values since 1994, the average percentage point gap between Republicans and Republican-leaning independents and Democrats and Democratic-leaning independents had increased to 36 percentage points by 2017 from 15 percentage points in 1994. Political polarization within the American electorate has resulted in the increased divergence of social and economic policies at the state level with Republican and Democratic-controlled states moving in opposite directions (Abramowitz 2013).

Affective Polarization

The notion of partisanship has become increasingly intertwined with the concept of social identity. Current literature in political psychology conceives partisanship as a social category like religion, race, or gender. Accordingly, partisan affiliation consists mainly of identification with a social group in which political parties function as a social group in and of themselves, and identifying with a political party constitutes a deeper emotional attachment and not just political attachment with one's party's policy agenda and issue positions. This is different from a traditional view of partisanship in which partisanship revolves around different issue positions and ideological orientations (Busby et al. 2021; Rothchild et al. 2019). Today, party identity should be understood as a social identity whereby partisans behave like sports fans, who feel emotionally invested in the welfare of their own party and prefer to spend their time with other members of the party. This can be referred to as the social polarization of the electorate.

Strong emotional attachment to one's party generates anti-deliberative attitudes about disagreement on issues creating partisan bias, activism, and anger (Mason 2015). Increased partisan animosity also spills out of the political realm to private interpersonal relationships (Orr and Huber 2020). Recent surveys have shown that partisan animosity has grown substantially in recent decades.

Ideological polarization (difference between policy positions) is often distinguished from affective polarization which represents the phenomenon of animosity or hostility between political parties (Iyengar et al. 2019). Using nationally representative survey data (Miller, Johnston, and Conover 2015) demonstrated that stronger partisan identities are associated with a greater sense of partisan hostility—specifically, party rivalry and anger. Ideological identities or issue preferences play a much lesser role compared to partisan identities. Partisan hostility mediates the impact of partisan identities on political attitudes and actions. Consequently, strong partisan identifiers hold the most hostile and uncivil attitudes and are the most likely to participate in elections.

A survey by the Pew Research Center (2016) found that partisans' views of the opposing party were more negative than at any point in nearly a quarter of a century and more than half of Democrats (55 percent) say the Republican Party makes them "afraid," while 49 percent of Republicans say the same about the Democratic Party. Furthermore, 70 percent of Democrats say that Republicans are more closed-minded than other Americans. And nearly as many Democrats, 67 percent, say the people in their party are more open-minded than other Americans.

A poll conducted in May 2022 by the University of Chicago's Institute of Politics found that partisans view each other with hostility and skepticism. For example, about three-quarters of both Republicans and Democrats viewed members of the other party as bullies, dishonest, and spreading misinformation (Bump 2022a; Institute of Politics 2022). Democratic and Republican partisans dislike each other far more than in the past and ideological differences between the electorate strongly influence feelings toward the opposition party and its candidates. When voters are affectively polarized, they tend to dislike other parties and view politics as high-stake competition and electoral outcomes as highly consequential. Affective polarization also increases over time and with age and is related to an increase in voters' partisan strength (Phillip 2022; Ward and Tavits 2019; Webster 2018; Webster and Abramowitz 2017).

The affective polarization has led to an increase in **"negative voting."** For example, in the 2020 presidential election, almost one-third of American voters cast a ballot "against" a candidate rather than "for" a candidate. The predictive probability of casting a negative vote increases greatly among voters for whom the "hate" for the other party's candidate outweighs "love" for their own party's candidate (Garzia and Ferreira da Silva 2022). The tendency to support a candidate or a political party based largely on the "dislike" for the other side is referred to as **negative partisanship**. Voters vote for a party not based on the party's platform/policy agenda or a candidate but due to their dislike or disdain toward the opposition party.

Public Opinion and Polarization of the American Electorate

Public opinion polls consistently show that Americans view just about everything related to politics—elections, policy issues, political institutions, etc.—through partisan and ideological lenses. In a poll by the *Wall Street Journal* following the Supreme Court's decision overturning the *Roe v. Wade* decision, 92 percent of Democrats said abortion should be legal in all or most cases compared to only 27 percent of Republicans saying abortion should be legal in all or most cases (Lucey 2022). In a poll conducted by ABC News/Ipsos during February 5–6, 2021 of a nationally representative probability sample of 508 adults over the age of 18, it was found that 67 percent of all Americans approved and 32 percent disapproved of the way President Biden handled the response to the COVID-19 pandemic. However, when broken down by party affiliation, the approval rating was 96 percent among Democrats, 67 percent among Independents but only 33 percent among Republicans. Similarly, in the same poll, 56 percent of Americans strongly supported the Senate convicting former President Trump on second impeachment charges while 43 percent opposed it. However, when responses were broken down by party affiliation, nine out of ten Democrats supported conviction while eight out of ten Republicans opposed conviction ("American Public Approves Administration's First Steps on Coronavirus" 2021).

In another poll conducted by USA Today/Suffolk University of 1,000 registered voters between December 16, 2021 and December 20, 2021, an overwhelming margin of 70 to 26 percent said that it was time for Trump to concede the election after the Electoral College had voted, but 57 percent of Republicans said he should not concede. Seventy-one percent of Republicans indicated that they would support, and the other 16 percent indicated that they would consider supporting Trump if he was the nominee of the Republican Party in 2024. Only ten percent indicated that they would not support Trump (Page and Elbeshbishi 2020).

In an NBC/Wall Street Journal poll conducted from January 10, 2021 to January 13, 2021, among 1,000 registered voters, 73 percent of Americans expressed the belief that the country will remain divided during the next four years of the Biden presidency. Broken down by party affiliation, 59 percent of Democrats, 64 percent of Independents, and 93 percent of Republicans believed that the country would remain divided (Murray 2021). In another poll conducted by USA Today/Suffolk University between December 16, 2020 and December 20, 2020, 79 percent of Democrats said that dismantling Trump's legacy would be a good thing while 72 percent of Republicans said it would be a bad thing. In the same poll, 96 percent of Democrats stated that Biden was legitimately elected to the presidency while 78 percent of Republicans said that he was not elected legitimately (Page and Elbeshbishi 2020).

Causes of Political Polarization

Scholars and journalists have attributed the causes of political polarization to a variety of factors. Some of these factors include an increase in divided government; primaries; safe districts created by Congressional redistricting and gerrymandering; Electoral College system which has produced presidential victors who lost the popular vote, generating more political animus, (e.g., George W. Bush in 2000 and Donald Trump in 2016); a revolution in communication technology with the rise of the social media platforms; regional/sectional realignment of political parties; divisive social issues resulting in "cultural wars" on issues such as abortion and same-sex marriage; new institutional norms producing abrasive adversarial and slash-and-burn tactics in both houses of Congress; and income inequality (Klein 2020; Kakutani 2018; Lukianoff and Haidt 2018; Berman 2016; Rosen 2016; Davis and Dunaway 2016; Sides and Hopkins 2015; Cohn 2014; Jacobson 2013; Sasse 2019; Bishop 2008; Cummings 2008; Teixeira 2008; Nivola and Brady 2006; Nivola 2005).

Divided Governments and Partisan Polarization

The frequency of divided governments has increased significantly since post-World War II. Before it, unified governments was the norm. During unified government, it is easier for the party in control to pass its policy agenda in Congress. During the period of divided government, more conflicts arise between the two political parties. Divided governments can have a moderating influence since presidents may have to bargain and compromise with the opposition party to achieve their policy goals. However, partisan polarization during a divided government can lead political parties to view politics as a zero-sum game making compromises and bargaining difficult leading to gridlock (Cohen 2011).

Electoral College

According to the U.S. Constitution, each state is accorded electoral votes equal to the number of senators and house representatives it has in Congress. The number of representatives a state has is supposed to be proportionate to its population in the most recent decennial census. However, due to increasing urbanization and population mobility, population distribution among the states has become skewed over time and so have the electoral votes. The winner-take-all method for awarding electoral votes of individual states gives states with smaller populations disproportionately higher weight so that the per capita voting power per electoral vote is significantly greater than that of states with a bigger population. Consequently, the Electoral College has become a less accurate reflection of the popular vote over time. Under such circumstances, the winner of the majority of the Electoral College vote becomes president over the winner of the popular vote (Webster 2007). The Electoral College overrepresents small and medium-sized states. Thus, at times, Electoral College acts operate under the counter-majoritarian principle. Republican presidential candidates have won the popular vote only once since 1992 (in 2004) but have won the presidency half of that time span (West 2022). For example, in the 2016 presidential election, the Republican candidate Donald Trump won the majority of the Electoral College votes and thus the presidency even though the Democratic candidate Hillary Clinton received almost three million more popular votes nationwide than Trump.

Redistricting and Gerrymandering

Congressional districts are redrawn every ten years after the decennial census to reflect population changes. In most states, this is done by state legislatures while in some other states, it is done by bipartisan or independent commissions. When a political party that controls the state legislature redraws the districts to its own advantage by weakening the support base of the opposition party, it is referred to as gerrymandering a district. Partisan redistricting and gerrymandering have produced more safe congressional districts and fewer competitive districts. Politically competitive districts have declined significantly over time. Congressional districts are increasingly gerrymandered for the sole purpose of gaining partisan advantage. Safe districts encourage candidates to appeal primarily to their base without trying to reach voters across party lines. Legislatures everywhere have become deeply partisan due to gerrymandering (Leonhardt 2022; Ehrenhalt 2021; Frymer 2011; McCarthy, Pool, and Rosenthal 2009; Epstein and Graham 2007; Nivola 2005).

Primaries

One of the major consequences of partisan redistricting and gerrymandering is a significant increase in the number of "safe" congressional districts where there is any lack of party competition, one party dominates, and its nominee is assured of winning the election. What this means is that in a "safe district," the election that matters is the primary election and not the general election. This leads to increased political polarization because primary voters pull candidates to further right or left on the ideological continuum (Epstein and Graham 2007). The threat of a primary challenge drives candidates to take ideological positions closer to the primary voters than the general election voters. This creates an incentive to demonize political opponents and embrace extreme political positions (Cummings 2008). Candidates are often forced to protect their flanks by moving away from the political center. Others have argued that closed primaries give parties more control and enable ideologically extreme voters unequal say which leads to increased polarization (Pildes 2011). Furthermore, extreme candidates can win the party's nomination in the primary due to the influence of financial contributors (the donor class). Candidates in primaries are often more responsive to the donor class than the primary or general electorate (Kujala 2020).

The Role of the Mass Media

The mass media of communication have undergone dramatic changes since the 1980s and 1990s. The Fairness Doctrine, introduced in 1949 by the Federal Communication Commission, required media companies to present both liberal and conservative sides when discussing prominent issues. In 1987, the Fairness Doctrine was repealed allowing media companies to be as biased or one-sided as they wanted to be. The 1990s and 2000s witnessed tremendous growth in Internet use and social media. The Internet and other social media platforms not only made it possible for individuals to post whatever they want to post without any fact-check but also made it possible for users to connect with others with similar views and opinions, allowing them to live in their own echo chambers and be continuously reinforced of their opinions. Social platforms such as Facebook have become a major source of political news for many individuals. A 2016 Per Research Center (2016) study found that about 37 percent of Americans had learned about the 2016 election from Facebook (Khazatsky 2021).

The changing media landscape of 24/7 cable news, talk shows, and social media platforms such as Facebook, Instagram, Twitter, and mass access to the Internet allows people to pick the news they want and unite to hate those on the other side. Before the emergence of new social media platforms, publishing one's views about politics and social issues, or expressing discontent with the way things were, was a tedious process requiring one to write a letter to the local newspaper where the editor acted as a gatekeeper to check the content for facts, rhetoric, and civility before publishing it or rejecting it altogether. The digital revolution, in effect, has given everyone their own printing press and a distribution network regardless of whether the published content has any facts, relevance, or value. Today, one can sit at a computer, select a social media platform, and publish his or her opinions without any gatekeeper. The gatekeeping function of the media has changed dramatically with the advent of social media platforms (Jenkinson 2021a).

Today, the mass media environment incentivizes gatekeeping practices that lead to a bias toward reporting content that focuses on partisan conflict and ideological extremity. A recent content analysis of 46,218 cable and broadcast television news transcripts from the years 2005 to 2013 found that ideologically extreme members of Congress get to speak more often than moderates on both cable and broadcast networks. Overrepresentation of political conflict and drama in news coverage to attract viewers and boost advertising revenue fits the business model. The 24/7 cable news networks often follow the partisan advocacy model of journalism. For example, Fox News and MSNBC cater to partisan audiences (Padgett, Dunaway, and Darr 2019). Partisan media polarize the electorate by making extreme citizens more extreme. Even though a narrow segment of the public watches partisan media programs, partisan media's effects extend much more broadly throughout the political arena (Van Bavel et al. 2021; Martin and Yurukoglu 2017; Levendusky and Malhotra 2016; Levendusky 2013). In the current media environment, the gatekeeping function vastly overrepresents extreme partisans on both sides of the partisan divide (Padgett, Dunaway, and Darr 2019).

Consequently, extremely conservative or liberal politicians receive far more airtime on cable and broadcast media compared to their moderate counterparts. Furthermore, social media allows politicians to bypass reporters and editors because they can tweet or post whatever they want. Since news companies operate on a business model in which they want to boost advertisement revenue, they are more inclined to cover/report conflict and drama created by extremist politicians (Darr, Padgett, and Dunaway 2021). A noisy minority gets more news coverage (Graham 2021).

Without a meaningful gatekeeping function, social media platforms also make it easier to promote false claims, news/stories, and conspiracy theories. For example, false claims about the 2020 elections spread on platforms like Facebook and Twitter. Fabricated or highly misleading news is often referred to as fake news. There is a great deal of evidence that often lay people are instrumental in spreading such false material. This has less to do with ignorance but more to do with partisan affiliation to discredit political opponents. Partisan individuals and groups share news articles that are consistent with their partisanship even when they may be aware that the information is from a dubious source and may not be true. Partisanship and self-reported animosity toward the opposing party are strongly related to fake news sharing (Osmundsen, Petersen, and Bor 2021). According to a poll by the Pearson Institute/AP-NORC (2021) conducted in September of 2021, 95 percent of respondents stated that spread of misinformation was a major problem and over 90 percent blamed the social media and users for the spread of misinformation.

Vaidhyanathan (2018) describes Facebook as an anti-social media and argues that Facebook disconnects individuals and undermines democracy. He described Facebook as "the pleasure machine," "the attention machine," "the politics machine," and "the disinformation machine" that feeds people's worst appetite and undermines people's ability to think collectively about societal problems. Others have argued that social media like Facebook contributes to partisan animosity. Facebook's Mark Zuckerberg has frequently dismissed criticism that Facebook stokes divisiveness (Barrett, Hendrix, and Sims 2021). Pablo Barbera, a research scientist at the company, has not only denied that Facebook contributes to political polarization but also argued that political polarization could be a good thing. He points to increased polarization as a positive force that has contributed to major social movements resulting in major changes such as voting rights and extension of voting rights (Mac and Silverman 2021). Facebook's algorithm shapes conservative and liberal bubbles (Jingnan and Bond 2023). However, such assertions run contrary to scholars and experts on social media platforms who have concluded that the use of social media contributes to partisan animosity and helps intensify political sectarianism. They have concluded that social media may not be the main driver of polarization but at the least, it has been a key facilitator (Barrett, Hendrix, and Sims 2021).

The cable news networks have become not just silos and echo chambers, but giant megaphones listened to by their faithful followers and social media that amplifies the voices of small but loud minorities (Jenkinson 2021c). George Saunders (2008), one of the greatest fiction writers, has similarly argued that the media environment has turned American politics into a competition in which the loudest voices garner the most attention and set the agenda for everyone. The person with the megaphone may not be the smartest person, the most experienced, or even the most articulate but he/she can drown out the other voices by degrading national discourse through dumbed-down language. He argues that it is such a **"braindead megaphone"** that has made American politics awful (Klein 2022b). As the proliferation of conspiracy theories demonstrates, Americans have shown a lack of capacity for critical thinking to distinguish facts and truth from nonsense published online (Jenkinson 2021a). The mass media stifles deliberative democracy as a marketplace of ideas (Baym 2023).

Political Rhetoric, Violence, and Talk of Civil War

American democracy survived Trump but barely. The violent January 6, 2021, insurrection he incited shook the democratic system and weakened the democratic institution leading some to predict America's coming age of instability where constitutional crises and political violence could become the norm in American politics. Others have warned of the coming crisis in which America could slide toward competitive authoritarianism (Levitsky and Way 2022; Leonhardt 2022; Tharoor 2022). Still, others warn of America moving in the direction of separatism and disintegration with talks of some states succeeding from the Union (Rivlin and Rivlin 2022; Brown 2022; French 2020; Jenkinson 2020). Ken Kalfus' (2022) dystopian new novel presents an even darker picture in which America's ongoing political strife descends into outright civil war whereby many Americans flee the country and establish "mini enclaves" in foreign lands. During Donald Trump's presidential campaign and presidency, political discourse in the United States became even more hateful and divisive, especially against racial, ethnic, and religious minorities. Threats against individuals and groups signaled out and demonized by Trump increased significantly. While Trump did not invent racist and nativist hate speech, he publicly expressed support for violent, extremist right-wing groups making it a part of mainstream politics (Nacos, Shapiro, and Bloch-Elkon 2020).

On January 6, 2021, President Trump told his followers to fight like hell and urged them to march on the Capitol which resulted in violence including the deaths of law enforcement officers. Increased polarization is associated with an increase in violent rhetoric on both the right and the left of the ideological spectrum. When political leaders use incendiary rhetoric, it does not just fade away. Instead, rhetoric is instantly magnified by millions of followers/supporters when it is retweeted and shared with others on social media platforms. For example, when President Trump tweeted out the phrase "Chinese virus" when COVID-19 began to spread, it resulted in not only increased use of the term on social media but also increased tweets expressing anti-Asian sentiments that ultimately led to violence against

Asian Americans (Byman 2021). Similarly, after the FBI's court-approved search of former President Trump's residence in Palm Beach, Florida, pro-Trump influencers, media figures, and even some Republican candidates used the language of violence to rally opposition and threats against the FBI increased (Feuer 2022). The Department of Homeland Security has stated that domestic violent extremism is one of the most important threats facing the United States (Dallek 2022).

While it is difficult to establish a causal link between violent rhetoric and subsequent individual or group acts of violence, plenty of research suggests that incendiary rhetoric can make political violence more likely (Byman 2021). President Trump's anti-Muslim and anti-Hispanic rhetoric made it more acceptable for others to denigrate and attack other groups. Anti-Muslim conversations grew on Facebook and other social media sites in 2016. Anti-Muslim tweets also increased among Trump followers, and it was followed by a 32 percent increase in hate crimes against Muslims and to a lesser extent against Hispanics. Hateful speech can stir negative emotions toward the target of the hate speech (Byman 2021). After Elon Musk, who calls himself a "free speech absolutist," bought Twitter (now called X), racial slurs against black Americans increased to 3,876 per day compared to 1,282 per day before Musk became the owner. Slurs against gay men jumped from 2,506 pre-Musk to 3,964 average per day post-Musk ownership. Similarly, antisemitic posts referring to Jews or Judaism soared more than 61 percent in two weeks after Musk acquired Twitter (Frenkel and Conger 2022).

In a USA Today/Suffolk University poll conducted December 7–11, 2022, 74 percent expressed concern about the rise in hate speech and the rise of antisemitism and white nationalism and 52 percent stated that social media companies have a responsibility to restrict hateful or inaccurate posts. Thirty-four percent gave Elton Musk a favorable rating while 42 percent rated him unfavorably. However, the opinions were divided along partisan and ideological lines reflecting the political polarization. In the poll, liberals and moderates overwhelmingly supported restricting hate speech online while conservatives opposed it by a 2-1 margin. Democrats expressed more alarm about hate speech than did the Republicans. Similarly, 60 percent of Republicans in the poll viewed Musk favorably compared to only seven percent of Democrats (Page 2022).

Hateful rhetoric is often connected to real-world violence. According to a Washington Post analysis of data collected by the CSIS, domestic terrorism incidence by white supremacists, anti-Muslim, and anti-government extremists have reached new heights in the United States. Most victims of such attacks have been blacks, Asians, Jews, immigrants, and LBGTQ individuals (Harrow, Tran, and Hawkins 2021). MAGA Republicans such as Fox News Host Tucker Carlson, House Republican Rep. Elise Stefanik, NY, and Republican Senator Ron Johnson, among others, have fanned racial hatred by promulgating **"replacement theory"** about minorities replacing whites (Rubin 2022c). In May of 2022, an 18-year-old white male, Payton Grendon, traveled from Conklin, NY, to Buffalo, NY, and opened fire in Topps grocery store in a black neighborhood killing 10 people and injuring three others. Eleven of the victims were blacks. In a manifesto the shooter had posted online, he identified himself as a fascist, white supremacist, and antisemite and expressed fear that white people were being replaced by non-whites which he compared to white genocide (Levenson et al. 2022). In October 2022, an intruder broke into the home of Speaker Nancy Pelosi's home in San Francisco shouting "Where is Nancy" (who was in Washington, DC) and assaulted her husband with a hammer before being taken into custody.

The toxic violent language used in political speeches, conspiracy theories, and misinformation on social media pose a great threat to democracy. According to statistics from the Capitol Police and the federal law enforcement department that protects members of Congress, there were more than 9,625 threats against members of Congress reported in 2021. Threats against the members of Congress increased more than tenfold in five years after Trump was elected president in 2016 (Edmondson 2022). The assassination attempt on the former president and current Republican nominee for president, Donald Trump, on July 13, 2024, at a campaign rally in Pennsylvania underscores not just the threat of but also the presence of actual political violence in American democracy.

By 2016 political polarization had reached its worst since the Civil War (Paisley 2016). The rise in political violence has given rise to talk about the possibility of a civil war breaking out in the United States (Burris 2022; Fisher 2022; Alfaro and Scott; Garrett and Becker 2022; Gale and West 2021). Others have argued that America is not on the verge of a civil war (Norman 2022; Woodlief 2021). The reality is that the United States has a complicated relationship with the idea of political violence. The country itself was born out of violent struggle and has witnessed political violence throughout its history. Political violence has been persistent in American society and only the targets of political violence have varied over time. Consequently, the condemnation of violent political speech often rings hollow because the language of political violence has become deeply ingrained in American politics (Homans 2024; Suri 2024).

In a poll conducted in November 2021 by the Public Religion Research Institute, four in ten respondents stated that the 2016 election was stolen from Donald Trump and that violence might be justified to save the country (Blake 2021). In a poll conducted in January 2022 by the Washington Post and the University of Maryland, 34 percent of Americans expressed the sentiment that sometimes violence against the government is justified (Cole 2022). In another poll conducted in September of 2022 by CBS News, 64 percent expressed the belief that violence in the United States will increase over the next few years and 54 percent stated the United States will be less of a democracy for the next generation (Durkee 2022). In a Yahoo News and You-Gov poll conducted in June of 2022, half of Americans said that American democracy was already lost (DeVega 2022b).

In a September 2021 national survey conducted by pollster Zogby, 46 percent of Americans believed that a future civil war was likely while 43 percent thought it was unlikely (Gale and West 2021). In an August 2022 poll by the Economist and YouGov, 14 percent said that a civil war was likely in the next decade while 35 percent said it was not very likely or not likely at all (Orth 2022; Bump 2022b).

Consequences of Political Polarization

Political polarization is associated with negative as well as positive consequences. Overall, there are more negative consequences of political polarization than positive ones.

Negative Consequences

Corrosion of Confidence in American Democracy

An *Ipsos/Reuters poll* (2022) published in September 2022 found that almost two-thirds of Americans believe that President Trump's MAGA movement is a threat to America's democratic foundations. In a New York Times/Siena College poll conducted in October 2022, 45 percent of Americans regarded Trump as a major threat to American democracy (Blake 2022; Corasaniti et al).

In an NPR/Ipsos poll conducted in January of 2022, 64 percent of Americans believed that American democracy was in crisis and at risk of failing (Rose and Baker 2022). Misinformation was one of the driving forces behind the public's eroding confidence in American democracy (Sanchez, Middlemass, and Rodriguez 2022). In the Associated Press-NORC Center for Public Affairs Research poll conducted in October of 2022, only nine percent of Americans thought that democracy was working extremely well or very well while 52 percent said it was not working well (Fields and Cassidy 2022).

The hyper-polarization has eroded the foundations of American democracy. The "Big Lie" about elections being rigged and stolen, the spread of misinformation, and conspiracy theories have shaken Americans' trust and faith in American democracy. Democratic norms require that competing political parties and candidates accept the results of free and fair elections. However, when partisans see opponents as an existential threat to the country, it weakens the democratic norms because winning at any cost becomes the main goal. Under such conditions, politics becomes an all-out war of "us" against "them" and the casualty is the American democracy (Drutman 2021).

Diminishing Trust in Institutions and Leaders

Another negative consequence of polarization is America's declining trust in national institutions and leaders. According to an NBC News poll, only 27 percent of Americans expressed confidence in national institutions down from 50 percent in 1979. Americans have reported a significant loss of trust in institutions such as the police, Supreme Court, presidency, criminal justice system, television news, and Congress. Congress's approval rating stood at seven percent. Yet, ironically, incumbent members of Congress are re-elected at the rate of 95 percent due to gerrymandering and safe districts (Jenkinson 2022).

During the COVID-19 pandemic, polarization was demonstrated in the partisan divide over vaccines and mandates. A poll in September of 2022 from the Kaiser Family Foundation found that the public's trust in the Center for Disease Control and Prevention (CDC) and the nation's top doctors like Anthony Fauci, the National Institutes of Health's top infectious disease doctor, and Deborah Birx, the White House Coronavirus coordinator, has dropped considerably. The drop in confidence in the CDC was especially more pronounced among Republicans. For example, overall public confidence in CDC had dropped 16 points since April 2020 but Republican confidence had dropped 30 points since April compared to only a 12 percent drop among Democrats. Similarly, since April, the public's overall favorability rating of Doctor Fauci had dropped ten percent, but among Republicans it has dropped 30 percent, while among Democrats his favorability increased by six percent. Poll also revealed a significant partisan divide about reliable sources of information (Florko 2020).

Legislative Gridlock

Partisan and ideological polarization makes members of Congress less willing to compromise and build consensus, resulting in legislative gridlock. Gridlock can be defined as the share of significant issues on the country's policy agenda that are left in limbo, i.e., unresolved at the close of each Congress. Using this definition as a measuring stick, legislative gridlock between the 1940s and 1990s increased a great deal (Epstein and Graham 2007).

Polarization during a period of divided government tends to produce even more policy gridlock than during a period of unified government. Increased policy differences dramatically reduce the number of policy issues political parties are willing to compromise on further hindering policymaking. One of the most important consequences of polarization is Congress' reduced capacity to legislate (Newport 2019; Mansbridge and Martin 2013).

Loss of Congressional Power and Expansion of Presidential Power

Legislative gridlock produced by increased polarized politics has also resulted in a change in the balance of power between the legislative and executive branches of government. Legislative stalemate due to polarization and the divided government has led presidents to use measures such as executive orders and issuance of new government rules and regulations to accomplish their policy goals. The decreased legislative capacity had led to the expansion of presidential power at the cost of a reduction in Congressional powers (Dionne, Jr. 2022; Carmines and Fowler 2017; Mansbridge and Martin 2013).

Dehumanization of Political Process

Political polarization has contributed to the debasement of political discourse that uses dehumanizing language and rhetoric and demonizes political opponents. Partisans on both sides of the aisles often demonize their opponents sometimes openly and blatantly but also more frequently in subtle ways. Lack of civility has become common not just among political elites but also among their followers. Social media has further contributed to this development. Negative partisanship and affective polarization have contributed to the dehumanization of not just political opponents and public discourse but also the political process itself which eventually is more corrosive to Democratic values (Cassese 2021; Lupu 2015).

Positive Consequences

Clarify Choices for Voters

One of the positive consequences of polarization is that it could help clarify voters' choices and create a stronger attachment to one's party. A strong emotional attachment to one's partisan and ideological reference group can have a positive impact on individuals by giving them meaning and purpose from their solidarity with their own in-group against the out-group. Presented with a clear set of policy choices by political parties due to ideological polarization, voters may become less confused with the myriads of choices presented to them. Political parties' clear position on a given issue can provide an important cue to voters about how to vote. Simplified choices may help voters better understand the stakes involved in an election (Simas, and Ozer 2021; Newport 2019; Lupu 2015; Epstein and Graham 2007).

Increase Voter Turnout

Partisan and ideological polarization may motivate more voters to turn out to vote and thus increase voter participation and turnout. Political parties becoming further apart may make it easier for voters to distinguish among the electoral choices they face. In a competitive political environment, where election outcomes may be decided by a few thousand votes, which party can mobilize and turn out its supporters can make a difference in a win or a loss. For example, the elections of 2016, 2020, and 2022 saw a significantly larger voter turnout (Lupu 2015).

More Ideological Voting

Ideological polarization can also lead to consistent ideological voting by members of Congress as well as by the electorate concerning policy issues (Lupu 2015). Anti-majoritarian tools such as presidential veto and Senate filibuster often inhibit majority rule and hinder policymaking resulting in gridlock. Political parties that are cohesive, distinct, and programmatic can offer a corrective countermeasure to the failure of policymaking in Congress (Mansbridge and Martin 2013).

Polarization and Public Policy at the National Level

While there is a plethora of scholarly and journalistic literature written on political polarization, including partisan, ideological, and electorate polarization, there is surprisingly not a great deal of research on how partisan and ideological polarization at the national level, especially in Congress, influences public policymaking on different issues. What are the implications of current political polarization for public policy outcomes (Hare and Poole 2014)? Does partisan and ideological polarization affect social polarization, policy consistency, and policy predictability (McCarty 2018; Mason 2015; Garner and Palmer 2011)?

Some literature has looked at the effect of political polarization at the national level on policies such as income inequality (Kwon 2015; Dettrey and Campbell 2013), environment and climate change (Johnson and

Schwadel 2019; Farrell 2016; Antonio and Brulle 2011), immigration (Johnston et al. 2015; Bresler 2010), public health (Greer and Singer 2017), civil and voting rights (Bateman, Clinton, and Lapinski 2017), and other social policies (Flores and Barclay 2016; Mason 2015). Few other studies have examined the relationship between health insurance (Beaussier and Raillard 2014), decentralization of health policy (Weissert and Uttermark 2017), public opinion (Utz, Hollingshaus and Dien 2010), health issues (Fowler and Gollust 2015), and welfare (Jacobs 2002).

Polarization and Public Policy at the State Level

Examination of data regarding unified state governments since 1993 demonstrates that the number of unified governments has increased dramatically over the last several decades. In the early 1990s, an average of 20 states had unified government but that jumped to 36 by 2016. Polarization within legislative chambers and across states closely mirrors polarization trends at the national level. What is left unexplored is how polarization across states affects policymaking and policy outputs of the state governments (Jordan and Bowling 2016).

There is a dearth of literature dealing with if and how political polarization impacts states' public policies. Given increased partisan, ideological, and electoral polarization combined with the rise of tribalism, sectarianism, and nativism in the country, we would expect Republican- and Democratic-controlled states to adopt different public policies on a range of issues (Wines 2023). There have been few studies that have examined the broad question of partisan and ideological polarization in state legislatures, party competition, and conflict, and how polarization might impact state legislative policymaking (National Conference of State Legislatures 2018; Jordan and Bowling 2016; La Raja, Raymond, and Schaffner 2015; Fiorina, Abrams, and Pope 2008). Some studies have looked at the relationship between partisanship, ideology, public opinion, and state public policy (Gray et al. 2004; Erickson, Wright, and McIver 1994; 1989; Wright, Erickson, and McIver 1987). Few studies have looked at the relationship between political and/or economic polarization on immigration policy (Ybarra Sanchez, and Sanchez 2016), interstate highways (Nall 2015), and federalism (Schragger 2019; Pickerill and Bowling 2014).

In the parlance of current American politics, political polarization across states has been discussed in terms of red and blue states. Red states refer to states where the Republican Party controls most levers of power (governorships, control of state legislatures) while blue states refer to states where the Democratic Party controls most levers of power.

Do Red and Blue States Adopt Different Public Policies?

While the exploration of political polarization has focused on the national level, there has been much less exploration of this phenomenon at the state level. This lack of exploration of state-level political polarization has left several questions unanswered. One is how polarization at the state level might impact state policymaking. Second, how state-level polarization might impact the policy outputs and outcomes of individual states? Third, since state governments enjoy a considerable amount of authority, and discretionary power in a federal system, how polarization might impact the implementation of national public policies by the state governments? The lead role states play in making and implementing public policies gives them opportunities to make partisan and ideological policy choices.

There is limited systematic scholarly research addressing the question of whether polarization leads red and blue states to adopt different health policies. Research that does exist has focused on how red and blue states have responded differently to the passage of the ACA, its implementation, and expansion of the Medicaid and CHIP programs under the ACA (Pacheco, Haselswerdt, and Michener 2020; Beland, Rocco; and Waddan 2020; Singer 2016; Grogan and Rigby 2009). In recent years, few journalists have noted how red and blue states have moved further apart on health policy (Armour 2018), and how red and blue states have not experienced the same coronavirus pandemic and have responded differently to measures designed to contain the spread of the virus, like vaccines, mask-wearing, social distancing, and the like (Brownstein 2020; Derysh 2020; McCarthy 2020).

Typology of Red, Blue, and Purple States

The red states (Republican) refer to states that have traditionally voted in favor of Republican candidates. These are states in which the Republican Party has controlled the executive and legislative branches of government over a sustained period. The term Red Wall is often used to refer to states where the Republican Party regularly wins the majority of votes in elections. Presidential election results from 1992 to 2016 show that an overwhelming majority of the time Republican candidates won the state. Between 1995 and 2020, in 21 of these states, Republicans at some points have enjoyed what is referred to as a **"trifecta"**; i.e., they have held governorships and majority in both houses of the state legislature.

Twenty-four states red states include:

Alabama
Alaska
Arizona
Arkansas
Georgia
Idaho
Indiana
Kansas
Kentucky
Louisiana
Mississippi
Missouri
Montana
Nebraska
North Carolina
North Dakota
Oklahoma
South Carolina
South Dakota
Tennessee
Texas
Utah
West Virginia
Wyoming

The blue states (Democratic) refer to states that have consistently voted for Democratic candidates for president regularly over some time. In blue states, the Democratic Party also controls state governing institutions such as governorship and state legislatures. Between 1992 and 2015, the overwhelming majority of times, the Democratic presidential candidate won these states. In these states, between 1995 and 2020, Democrats also at some point enjoyed the "trifecta" of controlling the governorships and both houses of state legislatures. The term Blue Wall is used to describe blue states. In addition, Washington, DC has been reliably democratic in its voting. The 17 blue states include:

California
Connecticut

Delaware
Hawaii
Illinois
Main
Maryland
Massachusetts
Michigan
New Jersey
New Mexico
New York
Oregon
Pennsylvania
Rhode Island
Vermont
Washington

The term purple states are considered the swing states. These are states that often swing back and forth in their support of Republican and Democratic candidates. Several of these states have experienced "divided government" at the state level. The nine states that are considered purple states include

Colorado
Florida
Iowa
Minnesota
Ohio
Nevada
New Hampshire
Virginia
Wisconsin

It is important to note that the division of states into blue, red, and purple states is based on long-term trends in voting patterns in presidential, Congressional, and state elections. However, on a short-term basis, the division of states into these categories based on the voting pattern is not permanent but dynamic and often in a state of flux. For example, in recent elections states such as Florida and Ohio have shown a tendency to lean more Republican while Colorado has tended to move more toward the Democrats. In Florida, Republicans have enjoyed a trifecta control of government for the last several election cycles. In the 2016 presidential election, the Republican presidential candidate, Donald Trump, won states such as Pennsylvania and Michigan that have traditionally tended to vote Democratic. In the 2020 presidential election, the same two states swung back in the Democratic column when they voted for the Democratic candidate, Joe Biden. Over the last two decades, much of the West had turned blue except Texas (Barabak 2023).

This book examines the healthcare divide between the red and blue states. The political polarization across states is reflected in how blue and red states have responded very differently to health policy and healthcare. The red and blue states also present very different political, cultural, and socioeconomic profiles. Political polarization among the red and blue states is reflected in the major divides that exist along social, economic, educational, geographic, and demographic lines. But nowhere is the polarization and political divide more evident than in the field of healthcare. In this book, we analyze how political polarization at the state level has impacted state health policymaking, policy outputs, and policy outcomes and led red and blue states to create vastly different healthcare and health policies. Since state governments enjoy a considerable amount of authority and discretionary power in a federal system, we also examine how polarization has influenced the implementation of national health policies by the red and blue states.

Bibliography

Abramowitz, Alan I. 2013. "The Electoral Roots of America's Dysfunctional Government." *Presidential Studies Quarterly* 43, no. 4 (December): 709–731.

Abramowitz, Alan I., and Kyle L. Saunders. 2006. "Exploring the Basis of Partisanship in the American Electorate: Social Identity v. Ideology." *Political Research Quarterly* 59, no. 2 (June): 175–197.

Adler, Jerry. 2017. "In 2017, the Tug of Tribalism Grew Stronger." Online at www.yahoo.com/news/2017-tug-tribalism-grew-stronger-100004695.html

Aldridge, Bailey. 2021. "Public Approval of Supreme Court Hits a New Low in US, Gallup Poll Finds." https://www.mcclatchydc.com/

Altschuler, Glenn C. 2017. "Partisanship, Polarization and the Future of American Politics." Online at www.huffingtonpost.com

Amaya, Hector. 2018. "White Nationalism and Publicness in the United States." *Javnost/The Public* 25, no. 4 (October): 365–378.

"American Public Approves Administration's First Steps on Coronavirus." 2021. February 7. https://www.ipsos.com/

Antonio, Robert J., and Robert J. Brulle. 2011. "The Unbearable Lightness of Politics: Climate Change Denial and Political Polarization." *Sociological Quarterly* 52, no. 2 (Spring): 195–2020.

Ardovini, Lucia. 2016. "The Politicisation of Sectarianism in Egypt: 'Creating an Enemy' The State v. The Ikhwan." *Global Discourse* 6, no. 4 (October): 579–600.

Armour, Stephanie. 2018. "Red and Blue States Move Further Apart on Health Policy." *Wall Street Journal*, February 28. https://www.wsj.com/

Badger, Emily. 2010. "Divided Government Usually Means Gridlock." Miller-McCune, *Idea Lobby*. Online at www.miller.mccune.com/

Bafumi, Joseph., and Robert Y. Shapiro. 2009. "A New Partisan Voter." *Journal of Politics* 71 no. 1 (January): 1–24.

Barabak, Mark Z. 2023. "Over Two Decades, Much of the West has Turned Blue. Why hasn't Texas?" https://www.governing.com/

Barber, Michael., and Jeremy C. Pope. 2017. "Does Party Trump Ideology? Disentangling Party and Ideology in America." Brigham Young University Scholar Archives. Online at https://drive.google.com/file/d/0B6-zXaKeceR4dXJnMGhpblRFNjQ/preview

Barrett, Paul; Justin Hendrix; and Grant Sims. 2021. "How Tech Platforms Fuel U.S. Political Polarization and What Government can do About it." https://www.brokkings.edu

Bartels, Larry M. 2000. "Partisanship and Voting Behavior, 1952–1996." *American Journal of Political Science* 44 no 1 (January): 35–50.

Bartels, Larry M. 1998. "Electoral Continuity and Change, 1868–1996." *Electoral Studies* 17 no. 3 (September): 301–326.

Bateman, David A.; Joshua D. Clinton; and John S. Lapinski. 2017. "A House Divided? Roll Calls, Polarization, and Policy Differences in the U.S. House, 1877–2011." *American Journal of Political Science* 61, no. 3 (July): 698–714.

Baym, Geoffrey. 2023. "How Medi Stifles Deliberative Democracy." https://daily.jstor.org/

Beaussier, Anne-Laure, and Sarah-Louise Raillard. 2014. "American Health Insurance: In the Context of Partisan Polarization." *Revue française de science politique* (English Edition), 64 no. 3: 1–22.

Beland, Daniel; Philp Rocco; and Alex Waddan. 2020. "The Affordable Care Act in the States: Fragmented Politics, Unstable Policy." *Journal of Health Politics, Policy, and Law* 45, no. 4 (August): 647–660.

Benkler, Yochai; Robert Faris; and Hal Roberts. 2018. *Network Propaganda: Manipulation, Disinformation, and Radicalization in American Politics*. Offord Scholarship Online. Polarization in American Politics - Oxford Scholarship (universitypressscholarship.com)

Berman, Russell. 2016. "What is the Answer to Political Polarization in the U. S.?" Online at www.theatlantic.com/

Betz, Hans-Georg. 2019. "Facets of Nativism: A Heuristic Exploration." *Patterns of Prejudice* 53, no. 2 (March): 111–135.

Biskupic, Joan. 2022. "Analysis: Supreme Court Justices Respond to Public Criticism with Distance and Denial." https://www.cnn.com

Bishop, Bill. 2008. *The Big Sort: Why the Clustering of Like-Minded America Is Tearing Us Apart*. New York. Houghton Mifflin Harcourt.

Blake, Aaron. 2022. "Democrats' Failure to Make 2022 About the Threat to Democracy." https://www.nytimes.com

Blake, Aaron. 2021. "Nearly 4 in 10 Who Say Election was Stolen from Trump Say Violence Might be Needed to Save America." https://www.washingtonpost.com

Bonica, Adam., and Maya Sen. 2021. "Estimating Judicial Ideology." *Journal of Economic Perspectives* 35, no. 1 (Winter): 97–118.

Bonneau, Chris W., and Damon M. Cann 2015. *Voters' Verdicts: Citizens, Campaigns, and Institutions in State Supreme Court Elections.* Charlottesville: University of Virginia Press.

Bresler, Robert J. 2010. "Perils of Political Polarization." *USA Today* (July): 13.

Brewer, Mark D. 2005. "The Rise of Partisanship and the Expansion of Partisan Conflict within the American Electorate." *Political Research Quarterly* 58, no. 2 (June); 219–229.

Bricker, Darrell; Christine Lipsmeyer; Guy Whitten; and Clifford Young. 2019. "Immigration, Nativism, and Changing Politics: Special Issue Introduction." *Social Science Quarterly* 100, no. 2 (April): 409–411.

Broder, David S. 1971. *The Party is Over*. New York: Harper and Row.

Broderick, John. 2022. "Former Chief Justice: Is the United States Headed Toward a Two-Nation Solution?" https://www.msn.com

Brown, Jon. 2022. "Secession Movements Gain Traction in US Amid Deepening Political Rift 'A Long-Standing Problem'" https://www.yahoo.com

Brownstein, Ronald. 2020. "Red and Blue America Aren't Experiencing the Same Pandemic." March 20. https://www.theatlantic.com

Bump, Philip. 2022a. "A New Measure of the Bleak, Alarming Partisan Divide in America." https://www.washingtonpost.com

Bump, Philip. 2022b. "Most Trump Voters See Civil War as Somewhat Likely Within a Decade." https://www.washingtonpost.com

Burris, Sarah K. 2022. "Lincoln Project's Rick Wilson Warns a Civil War is Coming – If it Isn't Here Already." https://www.rawstory.com

Busby, Ethan C.; Adam J Howat; Jacob Rothschild; and Richard M. Shafranek. 2021. *Partisan Next Door: Stereotypes of Party Supporters and Consequences for Polarization in America*. Cambridge, MAA: Cambridge University Press.

Byman, Daniel L. 2021. "How Hateful Rhetoric Connects to Real-World Violence." https://www.brookings.edu/

Calvert, Drew. 2022. "The Political Divide in America Goes Beyond Polarization and Tribalism." https://insight.kellogg.northwestern.edu/

Campbell, James E. 2016. *Polarized: Making Sense of a Divided America*. Princeton, NJ: Princeton University Press.

Carless, Will. 2022. "Month Before Buffalo Shooting, Poll Finds, 7 out of 10 Republicans Believed in "great replacement" ideas." https://www.usatoday.com

Carmines, Edward G., and Matthew Fowler. 2017. "The Temptation of Executive Authority: How Increased Polarization and the Decline in Legislative Capacity Have Contributed to Expansion of Presidential Power." *Indiana Journal of Global Legal Studies* 24, no. 2 (Summer): 369–398.

Carmines, Edward G; M. J. Ensley; and M. W. Wagner. 2012. "Who Fits the Left-Right Divide? Partisan Polarization in the American Electorate." *American Behavioral Scientist* 56, no. 12 (October): 1631–1653.

Chong, Shiao. 2020. "Political Tribalism." https://www.thebanner.org
Chua, Amy., and Jed Rubenfeld. 2018. "The Threat of Tribalism." https://www.theatlantic.org
Clark, Tom S. 2009. "Measuring Ideological Polarization on the United States Supreme Court." *Political Research Quarterly* 62, no. 1 (March): 146–157.
Clarke, Andrew J. 2020. "Party-Sub Brands and American Party Factions." *American Journal of Political Science* 64, no. 3 (July): 452–470.
Classen, Christopher; Patrick Tucker; and Steven S. Smith. 2015. "Ideological Labels in America." *Political Behavior* 37, no. 2 (June): 253–278.
Cohen, Jeffrey E. 2011. "Presidents, Polarization, and Divided Government." *Presidential Studies Quarterly* 41, no 3 (September): 504–520.
Cohn, Nate. 2021. "Why Political Sectarianism is a Growing Threat to American Democracy." https://www.nytimes.com
Cohn, Nate. 2014. "Polarization is Dividing American Society, Not Just Politics." Online at www.nytimes.com/
Cole, Devan. 2022. "34% of Americans Say Violence Against Government Sometimes Justified, New Poll Finds." https://www.cnn.com
Corriher, Billy. 2022. "State Supreme Court Races: Big Issues, Big Money." https://www.governing.com
Cramer, Ruby. 2022. "On Kari Lake's Campaign for Arizona Governor, the Mic is Always Hot." https://www.washingtonpost.com
Cummings, Stephen D. 2008. *Red States, Blue States, and the Coming Sharecropper Society*. New York: Algora Publishing.
Dallek, Matthew. 2022. "The Fading Line Between Rhetorical Extremism and Political Violence." https://www.newyorktimes.com
Dancey, Logan., and Geoffrey Sheagley. 2018. "Partisanship and Perception of Party-Line Voting in Congress." *Political Research Quarterly* 71 no. 1 (March): 32–45.
Darr, Joshua P; Jeremy Padgett; and Johanna Dunaway. 2021. "46,218 News Transcripts Show Ideologically Extreme Politicians get More Airtime." https://www.governong.com
Davis, Nichols T.; Kirby Goidel; Christine L. Lipsmeyer; Guy D. Whitten; and Clifford Young. 2019. "The Political Consequences of Nativism: The Impact of the Nativist Sentiments on Party Support." *Social Science Quarterly* 100 no. 2 (April): 466–475.
Davis, Nicholas T., and Johanna L. Dunaway. 2016. "Party Polarization, Media Choice, and Mass Partisan-Ideological Sorting." *Public Opinion Quarterly*, 80, Special Issue: 272–297.
Derysh, Igor. 2020. "Study: Republican Governors 'Slower' to Adopt Coronavirus Restrictions, Causing 'Significant' Harm." April 1. https://www.salon.com
Dettrey, Bryan J., and James E. Campbell. 2013. "Has Growing Inequality Polarized the American Electorate? Class, Party, and Ideological Polarization." *Social Science Quarterly* 94, no. 4 (December): 1062–1083.
DeVega, Chauncey. 2022a. "We Regret to Inform You that Donald Trump is Cashing in on White America's Death Wish." https://www.msn.com

DeVega, Chauncey. 2022b. "Is American Democracy Already Lost? Half of Us Think So – But the Future Remains Unwritten." https://www.salon.com

Devins, Neal., and Lawrence Baum. 2017. "Split Definitive: How Party Polarization Turned the Supreme Court into a Partisan Court." *Supreme Court Review* 2016, no 1: 301–365.

DiMaggio, Paul; John Evans; and Bethany Bryson. 1996. "Have American Social Attitudes Become More Polarized?" *American Journal of Sociology* 102, no. 3 (November): 690–755.

Dionne, Jr. E. J. 2022. "Divided Government Demands Creativity. Here are 3 Ways to Get Things Done." https://washingtonpost.com

Doherty, Carroll. 2014. "7 Things to Know about Polarization in America." Online at www.pewresearch.org/.Farina, Cynthia R. 2015. "Congressional Polarization: Terminal Constitutional Dysfunction?" *Columbia Law Review*, 115, no. 7: 1689–1738.

Dorman, John L. 2022. "Ex-Senator Al Franklin Says Senate GOP 'Destroyed' the legitimacy of the Supreme Court: They have Stolen Two Seats." https://www.yahoo.com

Douthat, Ross. 2022. "Did the Midterms Save American Democracy?" https://www.nytimes.com

Doxsee, Catrina; Seth G. Jones; Jared Thompson; Grace Hwang; and Kateryna Halstead. 2022. "Pushed to Extremes: Domestic Terrorism Amid Polarization and Protest." https://www.csis.org

Drutman, Lee. 2021. "Why the Two-Party System is Wrecking American Democracy: Other Democracies are Polarized, But the U.S. is Unique." https://fivethirtyeight.com

Durkee, Alison. 2022. "Most Americans Think the U.S. Will have More Political Violence and be Less of a Democracy, Poll Finds." https://www.msn.com

Edmondson, Catie. 2022. "Pelosi Attack Highlights Rising Fears of Political Violence." https://www.nytimes.com

Edsall, Thomas B. 2022. "The Left-Right Divide Might Help Democrats Avoid a Total Wipeout." https://www.nytimes.com

Edsall, Thomas B. 2020. "America, We Have a Problem." https://www.nytimes.com

Ehrenhalt, Alan. 2022. "The 'Missing Middle' in American Life: Can we Get it Back?" https://www.governing.com

Ehrenhalt, Alan. 2021. "What Painted Us So Indelibly Red and Blue?" https://www.governing.com

Eisen, Norman., and Sasha Matsuki. 2022. "Term Limits—A Way to Tackle the Supreme Court's Legitimacy." https://www.brookings.edu

Epstein, Diana., and John D. Graham. 2007. *Polarized Politics and Policy Consequences*. Occasional Papers. Santa Monica, CA: Rand Corporation.

Epstein, Lee., and Eric A. Posner. 2021. "The Robert Court and the Transformation of Constitutional Protections for Religions: A Statistical Portrait." *Supreme Court Review* vol. 2021 (April): 315–347.

Erickson, Robert S.; Gereald C. Wright; and John P. McIver. 1994. *State House Democracy: Public Opinion and Policy in American States*. Cambridge, MA: Cambridge University Press.

Erickson, Robert S.; Gerald C. Wright; and John P. McIver. 1989. "Political Parties, Public Opinion, and State Policy in the United States." *American Political Science Review* 83, no 3 (September): 729–750.

"Fact Sheet: President Biden Announces Bold Plan to Reform the Supreme Court and Ensure No President is Above the Law." 2024. https://www.whitehouse.gov/

Farina, Cynthia R. 2015. "Congressional Polarization: Terminal Constitutional Dysfunctional?" *Columbia Law Review* 115, no. 7 (March): 1689–1738.

Fallows, James. 2017. "A Nation of Tribes, and Members of Tribes." https://www.theatlantic.org

Farrell, Justin. 2016. "Corporate Funding and Ideological Polarization About Climate Change." *Proceedings of the National Academy of Sciences of the United States of America*. 113, no. 1 (January): 92–97.

Feldman, Adam. 2022. "The Most Powerful Supermajority." https://www.empiricalscotus.com

Feuer, Alan. 2022. "The F.B.I. Search Ignited the Language of Violence and Civil War on the Far Right." https://www.newyorktimes.com

Fields, Gary., and Christina A. Cassidy. 2022. "Many Remain Critical of US Democracy: AP-NORC Poll." https://www.apnews.com

Finkel, Eli J. et al. 2020. "Political Sectarianism in America." *Science Magazine* 370, no. 6516 (October 30): 532–536.

Fiorina, Morris P., and Samuel J. Abrams. 2008. "Political Polarization in the American Public." *Annual Review of Political Science* 11, no. 1 (June): 563–588.

Fiorina, Morris P; Samuel A. Abrams; and Jeremy C. Pope. 2008. "Polarization in the American Public: Misconceptions and Misreadings." *Journal of Politics* 70 no. 2 (April): 556–560.

Fisher, Marc. 2022. "Is the United States Headed for Civil War?" https://www.washingtonpost.com

Fishkin, Joseph., and David E. Pozen. 2018. "Asymmetric Constitutional Hardball." *Columbia Law Review* 118, no. 3 (April): 915–982.

Fleisher, Richard., and John R. Bond. 1996. "The President in a More Partisan Legislative Arena." *Political Research Quarterly* 49 no. 4 (December): 729–748.

Florko, Nicholas. 2020. "Public Trust in CDC, Fauci, and Other Top Health is Officials Evaporating, Poll Finds." https://statnews.com

Flores, Andrew R., and Scott Barclay. 2016. "Backlash, Consensus, Legitimacy or Polarization: The Effects of the Same-Sex Marriage Policy on Mass Attitudes." *Political Research Quarterly* 69, no. 1 (March): 43–56.

Fowler, Erika F., and Sarah E. Gollust. 2015. "The Content and Effect of Politicized Health Controversies." *Annals of the American Academy of Political and Social Science* 658 (March): 155–171.

Frank, Thomas. 2004. *What's the Matter with Kansas?* New York: Metropolitan Books.

French, David. 2020. *Divided We Fall: America's Secession Threat and How to Restore Our Nation*. New York: St. Martin's Press.

Frenkel, Sheera., and Kate Conger. 2022. "Hate Speech Rise on Twitter Use Unprecedented, Researchers Find." https://www.nytimes.com/

Frymer, Paul. 2011. "Debating the Causes of Polarization in America." *California Law Review* 99, no. 2 (April): 335–349.

Galderisi, Peter, Roberta Q. Herzberg, and Peter McNamara, eds. 1996. *Divided Government: Change, Uncertainty, and the Constitutional Order.* New York: Rowman and Littlefield.

Gale, William G., and Darrell M. West. 2021. "Is the US Headed for Another Civil War?" https://www.brookings.edu

Galston, William A. 2020. "Hold Your Fire: Dueling Democrats." https://www.brookings.edu

Garrett, Major., and David Becker. 2022. *The Big Truth: Upholding Democracy in the Age of "The Big Lie."* New York: Diversion Publishing Group.

Garner, Andrew., and Harvey Palmer. 2011. "Polarization and Issue Consistency Over Time." *Political Behavior* 33, no. 2 (June): 225–246.

Garzia, Diego., and Frederico Ferreira da Silva. 2022. "The Electoral Consequences of Affective Polarization? Negative voting in the 2020 US Presidential Election." *American Politics Research* 50, no. 3 (May): 303–311.

Gelman, Andrew; David Park; Boris Schor; Josephy Bafumi; and Jeronimo Cortina. 2008. *Red State, Blue State, Rich State, Poor State: Why America Votes the Way They Do.* Princeton, NJ: Princeton University Press.

Gerstein, Josh., and Kyle Cheney. 2024. "Trump is Immune from Prosecution for Some Acts in Federal Election Case." https://www.politico.com/

Gibian, T. C. 2012. "Political Tribalism in the USA" https://www.dailykos.com/stories/2012/4/3/1079564/-Political-Tribalism-in-the-USA

Graham, David A. 2021. "The Noisy Minority." https://www/theatlantic.com

Gray, Virginia.; Davd Lowery; Matthew Fellowes; and Andrea McAtee. 2004. "Public Opinion, Public Policy, and Organized Interests in the American States." *Political Research Quarterly* 57, no 3 (September): 411–420.

Greer, Scott L., and Singer, Philip M. 2017. "Addressing Zika in the United States: Polarization, Fragmentation, and Public Health." *American Journal of Public Health* 107, no 6 (June): 861–862.

Greenblatt, Alan. 2023. "Exploring the Dangers of a Purely Partisan Judiciary." https://www.governing.com/

Greenblatt, Alan, 2022. "How Big a Comeback Did Ticket Splitting Make this Year?" https://www.governing.com

Greenblatt, Alan. 2021. "It Took Decades for America to Become Divided." https://www.governing.com

Grogan, Colleen M., and Elizabeth Rigby. 2009. "Federalism, Partisan Politics, and Shifting Support for State Flexibility: The Case of the U.S. State Children's Health Insurance Program." *Publius* 39, no 1 (Winter); 47–69.

Gutmann, Amy and Dennis Thompson. 2010. "The Mindset of Political Compromise." *Perspectives on Politics*, 8, no. 4: 1125–1143.

Haberman, Maggie., and Michael C. Bender. 2022. "The Origin of the G.O.P. Tactic of ending Migrants to Blue States." https://www.nytimes.com

Hare, Christopher., and Keith T. Poole. 2014. "The Polarization of Contemporary American Politics." *Polity*, 43, no. 3: 411–429.

Harrison, Brian F. 2016. "Bully Partisan or Partisan Bully?" *Social Science Quarterly* 97, no. 2 (June): 418–438.

Harrow, Robert O; Andrew B. Tran; and Derek Hawkins. 2021. "The Rise of Domestic Extremism in America." https://www.washingtonpost.com
Hasen, Richard L. 2019. "Polarization and the Judiciary." *Annual Review of Political Science* 22, no. 1 (May): 261–276.
Heuvel, Katrina V. 2022. "The Supreme Court's Majority Reconvenes its Assault on Democracy." https://www.washingtonpost.com
Hibbing, Matthew V., Matthew Hays, and Raman Deol. 2017. "Nostalgia Isn't What It Used to Be: Partisan Polarization in Views on the Past." *Social Science Quarterly*, 98, no. 1: 230–243.
Higgs, Robert. 2018. "Ideology and Political Divisiveness." *The Independent Review* 22, no. 4 (Spring): 638–640.
Hill, Amanda. 2022a. "Exploring the Relationship Between National Identity and Attitudes Towards Immigrants in the United States." *National Identities* (published online May 30). https://doi.org/10.1080/14608944.2022.2079118
Hill, Jemela. 2022b. "Herschel Walker's Candidacy is Just Insulting." https://www.theatlantic.com
Hobbes, Michael. 2020. "Partisanship is Making Americans Vote for Things They Don't Actually Want." https://www.huffpost.com
Homans, Charles. 2024. "How Americans Justify Political Violence." https://www.nytimes.com/
Hornaday, Ann. 2021. "A New Era of Incivility in Congress Brings 'The Birth of Nation' Full Circle." https://www.washingtonpost.com
House, Silas. 2021. "Some Americans No Longer Believe in the Common Good: They Now Are Thinking Only of Themselves." https://www.theatlantic.com
Howe, Amy. 2024. "Justices Rule Trump Has Some Immunity from Prosecution." https://www.scotusblog.com/
Hulse, Carl. 2018. "Political Polarization Takes Hold of the Supreme Court." https://www.nytimes.com
Hurley, Lawrence. 2022. "Justices Join Debate on Supreme Court's Legitimacy After Abortion Ruling." https://www.nbcnews.com
Institute of Politics. 2022. "Our Precarious Democracy: Extreme Polarization and Alienation in Our Politics." https://uchicagopolitics.opalstacked.com/
Ipsos/Reuters Poll. 2022. "Americans Think President Biden's Speech will Further Divide the Country." https://www.ipsos.com/
Iyengar, Shanto; Yphtach Lelkes; Matthew Levendusky; Neil Malhotra; and Sean J. Westwood. 2019. "The Origins and Consequences of Affective Polarization in the United States." *Annual Review of Political Science* 22, no. 1 (May): 129–146.
Jacobs, Hacker S. 2002. *The Divided Welfare States*. Cambridge, MASS: Cambridge University Press.
Jacobson, Gary C. 2000. "Party Polarization in National Politics: The Electoral Connection." in John R. Bond and Richard Fleisher, eds. *Polarized Politics: Congress and the President in Partisan Era.* pp. 9–30. Washington, D.C.: CQ Press.
Jacobson, Gary C. 2013. "Partisan Polarization in American Politics: A Background Paper." *Presidential Studies Quarterly*, 43, no. 4: 688–706.
Jenkinson, Clay S. 2023. "Anatomy of the Supreme Court as an Institution in Crisis." https://www.governing.com/

Jenkinson, Clay S. 2022. "Americans Diminishing Trust in Their Institutions." https://www.governing.com

Jenkinson, Clay S. 2021a. "Gutenberg to Zuckerberg: A Tale of Two Revolutions." https://www.governing.com

Jenkinson, Clay S. 2021c. "How America's Three Constitutions Define the Nation." https://www.governing.com

Jenkinson, Clay S. 2020. "Is It Time for Texas and California to Leave the Union?" https://www.governing.com

Jingnan, Huo., and Shannon Bond. 2023. "New Study Shows How Facebook's Algorithm Shapes Conservative and Liberal Bubbles." https://www.npr.org/

Johnson, Erik W., and Philip Schwadel. 2019. "Political Polarization and Long-Term Change in Public Support for Environmental Spending." *Social Forces* 98, no. 2 (November): 913–939.

Johnston, Christopher D; Benjamin J; Newman, and Yamil Velez. 2015. "Ethnic Change, Personality, and Polarization over Immigration in the American Public." *Public Opinion Quarterly* 79, no. 3 (Fall): 662–686.

Jordan, Soren., and Cynthia J. Bowling. 2016. "The State of Polarization in the States." *State and Local Government Review* 48, no. 4 (December Special Issue): 220–226.

Jouet, Mugambi. 2019. *Exceptional America: What Divides Americans from the World and Each Other*. Oakland, CA: University of California Press.

Joyner, James. 2022. "Supreme Court Confirmation and Political Polarization." https://www.outsidethebeltway.com

Katz, Allan. 2015. "The Great American Partisan Divide: The Formation and the Cure." *Horizons: Journal of International Relations and Sustainable Development* no. 5 (Autumn): 222–235.

Kakutani, Michiko. 2018. *The Death of Truth: Notes on Falsehood in the Age of Trump*. New York: Tm Dugan Books.

Kalfus, Ken. 2022. *2 A.M. in Little America*. Minneapolis, MN: Milkweed Editions.

Kamarck, Elaine., and Norman Eisen. 2022a. "Democracy on the Ballot – How Many Election Deniers are on the Ballot in November and What is Their Likelihood of Success?" https://www.brookings.edu

Kamarck, Elaine., and Norman Eisen. 2022b. "Democracy On the ballot—Hobbs Finishes off Election Denier (For Now)." https://www.brookings.edu

Keller, Michael H., and David D. Kirkpatrick. 2022. "Their America is Vanishing. Like Trump, They Insist They Were Cheated." https://www.nytimes.com

Khazatsky, Andrei. 2021. "The Rise of Political Polarization and Partisanship in the U.S." https://www.theuniverse.com/

Klein, Ezra. 2022a. "Three Theories that Explain This Strange Moment." https://www.nytimes.com

Klein, Ezra. 2022b. "George Saunders on the 'Braindead Megaphone' That Makes Our Politics So Awful." The Ezra Klein Show Podcast. https://www.nytimes.com/

Klein, Ezra. 2020. *Why We're Polarized*. New York: Simon and Schuster.

Kornacki, Steve. 2018. *The Red and the Blue: The 1990s and the Birth of Political Tribalism*. New York: Ecco Imprint; HarperCollins Publishers.

Kritzer, Herbert M. 2021. "Polarization and Partisanship in State Supreme Court Elections." *Judicature* 105, no. 3 (Fall-Winter): 65–75.

Kuhn, David P. 2012. "The Incredible Polarization and Politicization of the Supreme Court." https://www/theatlantic.com

Kujala, Jordan. 2020. "Donors, Primary Elections, and Polarization in the United States." *American Journal of Political Science* 64, no. 3 (July): 587–602.

Kuo, Didi. 2018. "The Paradox of Party Polarization." *The American Interest*. https://www.the-american-interest.com/

Kuo, Didi. 2015. "Polarization and Partisanship." *The American Interest* 11, no. 2: (October)

Kwon, Roy. 2015. "Does Radical Partisan Politics Affect National Income Distribution? Congressional Polarization and Income Inequality in the United States, 1913–2008." *Social Science Quarterly* 96, no. 1 (March): 49–64.

La, Raja, Raymond J., and Brian F. Schaffner. 2015. "Ideological Polarization in State Legislatures." pp. 87–107 in La Raja, Raymond J., and Brian F. Schaffner, *Campaign Finance and Political Polarization*. Ann Arbor: University of Michigan Press.

Layman, Geoffrey C; Thomas M. Horowitz; and Juliana Menasce. 2006. "Party Polarization in American Politics: Characteristics, Causes, and Consequences." *Annual Review of Political Science* 9, no. 1 (June): 83–110.

Lee, Frances E. 2016. *Insecure Majorities: Congress and the Perpetual Campaign*. Chicago: University of Chicago Press.

Legaspi, Althea. 2022. "Trump Demands America Rip Up the Constitution, Make Him President." https://www.rollingstone.com/

Lemley, Mrak A. 2022. "The Imperial Supreme Court." *Harvard Law Review* 136, no 1 (November): 97–188.

Leonhardt, David. 2022. "'A Crisis Coming': The Twin Threats to American Democracy." https://www.yahoo.com

Levendusky, Matthew S., and Neil Malhotra. 2016. "Does Media Coverage of Partisan Polarization Affect Political Attitudes?" *Political Communication* 33, no. 2 (April - June): 283–301.

Levendusky, Matthew S. 2013. "Why Do Partisan Media Polarize Viewers" *American Journal of Political Science* 57, no. 3 (July): 611–623.

Levenson, Eric; Sarah Jorgensen; Polo Sandoval; and Samantha Beech. 2022. "Mass Shooting at a Buffalo Supermarket was a Racist Hate Crime, Police Say." https://www.cnn.com

Levine, Saul. 2018. "Belonging is Our Blessing, Tribalism is Our Burden." Online at www.psychologytoday.com

Levitsky, Steven., and Lucan Way. 2022. "America's Coming Age of Instability." https://www.foreignaffairs.com

Liptak, Adam. 2024. "In a Volatile Term, a Fractured Supreme Court Remade America." https://www.nytimes.com/

Liptak, Adam. 2022. "An 'Imperial Supreme Court' Asserts Its Power, Alarming Scholars." https://www.nytimes.com

Liptak, Adam. 2020. "Missing from Supreme Court's Election Cases: Reasons for Its Rulings." https://www.nytimes.com

Liptak, Adam. 2014. "The Polarized Court." https://www.nytimes.com

Lucey, Catherine. 2022. "Support for Legalized Abortion Grows Since Dobbs Ruling, WSJ Poll Shows." https://www.wsj.com

Lukianoff, Greg., and Jonathan Haidt. 2018. *The Coddling of the American Mind: How Good Intentions and Bad Ideas are Setting Up a Generation for Failure.* New York: Penguin Books.

Lupu, Noam. 2015. "Party Polarization and Mass Partisanship: A Comparative Perspective." *Political Behavior* 37, no. 2 (June); 331–356.

Lynch, Frederick R. 2019. "How Did this Man Get Elected? Perspectives on American Politics, Populism and Donald Trump." *Society* 56, no. 3 (June): 290–294.

Mabon, Simon. 2021. "Afterword: Sectarianism Beyond Middle-East." *Religion, State, & Society* 49, no. 2 (February): 174–180.

Mabon, Simon., and Lucia Ardovini. 2016. "People Sects, and States: Interrogating Sectarianism in the Contemporary Middle East." *Global Discourse* 6, no. 4 (October): 551–560.

Mac, Ryan., and Craig Silverman. 2021. "Polarization is Good for America, Actually, Says Facebook Executive." https://www.buzzfeednews.com

Mallapragada, Madhavi. 2021. "Asian American as Racial Contagion." *Cultural Studies* 35, no. 2–3 (May): 279–290.

Manning, Kenneth L; M.A. Sennewald; and Robert A. Carp, 2013. "Partisanship and Polarization in the Federal District Courts." Conference Paper Presented at the *Southern Political Science Association Annual Meeting.* Orlando; FL. January 3–5.

Manning, Kenneth L.; Robert A. Carp; Lisa M. Holmes. 2020. "The Decision Making Ideology of Federal Judges Appointed by President Trump." https://www.politico.com/

Mansbridge, Jane., and Cathie J. Martin. eds. 2013. *Negotiating Agreement in Politics.* Task Force Report. Washington, D.C. American Political Science Association.

Mansfield, Erin; Ryan W. Miller; Bart Jensen; and Terry Collins. 2021. "The Far-Right's Effort to Normalize Nativism: Pushing America First." https://www.usatoday.com

Marcus, Ruth. 2024. "God Save Us From this Dishonorable Court." https://www.washingtonpost.com/

Martin, Gregory J., and Ali Yurukoglu. 2017. "Bias in Cable News: Persuasion and Polarization." *American Economic Review* 107, no. 9 (September): 2565–2599.

Masaru, Nishikawa. 2021. "Presidency of Donald Trump and American Democracy: Populist Messages, Political Sectarianism, and Negative Partisanship." *Asia-Pacific Review* 28, no. 1: 80–97.

Mason, Lilliana. 2015. "'I respectfully Disagree': The Differential Effects of Partisan Sorting on Social and Issue Polarization." *American Journal of Political Science* 59, no. 76yu (January): 128–145.

McCarty, Nolan. 2018. "Pivotal Politics, Partisan Polarization, and Policy Predictability." *Journal of Politics* 80, no. 3 (May): 1076–1081.

McCarthy, Tom. 2020. "Disunited States of America: Responses to Coronavirus Shaped by Hyper-Partisan Politics." March 29. https://www.thegaurdian.com

McCarthy, Nolan, Keith T. Poole, and Howard Rosenthal. 2009. "Does Gerrymandering Cause Polarization?" *American Journal of Political Science*, 53, no. 3: 666–680.

McConnell, Christopher; Yotam Margalit; Neil Malhotra; and Matthew Lavendusky. 2018. "The Economic Consequences of Partisanship in a Polarized Era." *American Journal of Political Science* 62, no. 1 (January): 5–18.

Merrefield, Clark. 2020. "Political Sectarianism in America and 3 Things Driving the "Ascendance of Political Hatred"". https://www.journalistsresource.org

Milbank, Dana. 2022. "The GOP is Sick. It Did not Start with Trump—and Won't End with Him." https://www.washingtonpost.com

Miller, Patrick R., and Pamela Johnston. 2015. "Red and Blue States of Mind: Partisan Hostility and Voting in the United States." *Political Research Quarterly* 68, no 2 (March): 225–239.

Mondak, Jeffrey J., and Mitchell Donna-Gene. 2009. *Fault Lines: Why the Republicans Lost Congress*. New York: Routledge.

Montez, Jennifer K. 2024. "10 Ways to Better Understand How Shifting State Policy Context Affects Americans' Health." https://www.milbank.org/

Murray, Mark. 2021. "NBC News Poll: Biden Takes Helm of a Polarized, Pessimistic, and pained Nation." January 19. https://www.nbcnews.com

Nacos, Brigitte L; Robert Y. Shapiro; and Yaeli Bloch-Elkon. 2020. "Donald Trump: Aggressive Rhetoric and Political Violence." *Perspectives on Terrorism*. 14, no. 5 (October): 2–25.

Nall, Clayton. 2015. "The Political Consequences of Spatial Policies: How Interstate Highways Facilitated Geographic Polarization." *Journal of Politics* 77, no. 2 (April): 394–406.

Nassir, Ameera. 2013. "Nativism in America Today." https://www.soapboxie.com

National Conference of State Legislatures. 2018. *State Legislative Policy Making in an Age of Political Polarization*. Washington, D.C.: National Conference of State Legislatures.

"Nativism – World War I and the 1920s" n.d. World War I and the 1920s - Nativism (americanforeignrelations.com)

Newport, Frank. 2019. "The Impact of Increased Political Polarization." https://www.gallup.com

Nichols, Tom. 2022. "Clowns and Charlatans." https://www.theatlantic.com

Nichols, Tom. 2021. "The Moral Collapse of J. D. Vance." https://www.theatlantic.com

Nie, Norman H; Sidney Verba; and John R. Petrocik. 1976. *The Changing American Voter*. Cambridge, MA: Harvard University Press.

Nivola, Pietro S. 2005. *Thinking About Political Polarization*. Policy Brief #139. Washington, DC: The Brookings Institution. Online at www.brookings.edu/

Nivola, Pietro S., and David W. Brady. Editors. 2006. **Red and Blue Nation?** Washington, D.C.: Brookings Institution Press, 2006.

Norman, Erin. 2022. "No, America is Not on the Verge of a New Civil War." https://www.governing.com

Olson, Laura., and John C. Green. 2009. *Beyond Red States, Blue State: Electoral Gap in the Twenty-First Century American Electorate.* New York: Pearson.

Orr, Lilla V., and Gregory A. Huber. 2020. "The Policy Basis of Measured Partisan Animosity in the United States." *American Journal of Political Science* 64, no. 3 (July): 569–586.

Orth, Taylor. 2022. "Two in Five Americans Say a Civil War is at Least Somewhat Likely in the Next Decade." https://today.yougov.com/

Osmundsen, Mathia; Michael B. Petersen; and Alexander Bor. 2021. "How Partisan Polarization Drives the Spread of Fake News." https://www/brooking.edu

Quirk, Paul J. 2011. "Polarized Populism: Masses, Elites, and Partisan Conflict." *Forum*, 9, no. 1: 1–16.

Pacheco, Julianna; Jake Haselswerdt; and Jamila Michener. 2020. "The Affordable Care Act and Polarization in the United States." *Journal of Social Sciences* 6, no. 2 (July): 114–130.

Padgett, Jeremy; Johanna L. Dunaway; and Joshua P. Darr. 2019. "As Seen on TV? How Gatekeeping Makes the U.S. House Seem More Extreme." *Journal of Communication* 69, no. 6 (December): 696–719.

Page, Susan. 2022. "Paging Elton Musk: Poll Shows Americans Back Twitter Safeguards Amid Worry Over Hate Speech." https://www.usatoday.com

Page, Susan., and Sarah Elbeshbishi. 2020. "Exclusive: As Trump Leaves Office, 50% Americans See Him as Failed President." https://www.usatoday.com

Paisley, Laura. 2016. "Political Polarization at Its Worst Since the Civil War." https://news.usc.edu

Park, Barum. 2018. "How Are We Apart? Continuity and Change in the Structure of Ideological Disagreement in the American Public, 1980—2012." *Social Forces* 96, no. 4 (June): 1757–1784.

Pearson Institute/AP-NORC. 2021. "The American Public Views the Spread of Misinformation as a Major Problem." https://apnorc.org/

Pew Research Center. 2022a. "The Polarization in Today's Congress has Roots that Go back Decades." https://www.perresearch.org

Pew Research Center. 2022b. "Positive View of Supreme Court Declines Sharply Following Abortion Ruling." https://www.pewresearch.org

Pew Research Center. 2021. "Beyond Red and Blue: The Political Typology." https://www.pewresearch.org/

Pew Research Center. 2017. "The Shift in the American Public's Political Values." https://www.pewresearch.org

Pew Research Center. 2016. "Partisanship and Political Animosity in 2016." https://www.oewresearch.org

Pew Research Center. 2014. "Political Polarization in the American Public." https://www.pewresearch.org

Phillip, Joseph. 2022. "Affective Polarization: Our Time, Through the Generations, and During the Lifespan." *Political Behavior* 44, no. 3 (September): 1483–1508.

Pickerill, Mitchell J., and Cynthia J. Bowling. 2014. "Polarized Parties, Politics, and Policies: Fragmented Federalism in 2013–2014." *Publius* 44, no. 3 (Summer): 369–398.

Pierson, James. 2015. *Shattered Consensus: The Rise and Decline of America's Postwar Political Order*. New York: Encounter Books.

Pildes, Richard H. 2011. "Why the Center Does not Hold: The Causes of Hyperpolarized Democracy in America." *California Law Review* 99, no. 2 (April): 335–349.

Ritter, Luke. 2021. *Inventing America's First Immigration Crisis: Political Nativism in the Antebellum West*. New York: Fordham University Press.

Rivlin, Alice M., and Allan Rivlin. 2022. *Divided We Fall: Why Consensus Matters*. Washington, D.C.: Brookings Institution.

Roper, Willem. 2020. "Americans Prefer Divided Government." https://www.statista.com/chart/23506/divided-vs-unified-government/

Rose, Joel., and Liz Baker. 2022. "5 in 10 Americans Say U.S. is in Crisis as 'Big Lie' Takes Toot." https://npr.org

Rosen, Mark D. 2016. "Can Congress Play a Role in Remedying Dysfunctional Political Partisanship?" *Indiana Law Review*, 50, 265–279.

Rothchild, Jacob E; Adam J. Howat; Richard M. Shafranek; and Ethan C. Busby. 2019. "Pigeonholing Partisans: Stereotypes of Party Supporters and Partisan Polarization." *Political Behavior* 41, no. 2 (June): 423–443.

Rothchild, Zalman. 2022. "Free Exercise Partnership." *Cornell Law Review* vol. 107 (August): 1067–1135.

Rubin, Jennifer. 2022a. "We Now Have Two Federal Judiciaries." https://www.washingtonpost.com

Rubin, Jennifer. 2022b. "Roberts Joins the Chorus of Supreme Court Whining." https://www.wachintonpost.com

Rubin, Jennifer. 2022c. "Don't Let MAGA Republicans Off the Hook by Enabling Violence." https://www.wahingtonpost.com

Saeki, Manabu. 2019. "Anatomy of Party Sorting: Partisan Polarization of Voters and Party Switching." *Politics and Policy* 47, no. 4 (August): 699–747.

Sanchez, Gabriel R.; Keesha Middlemass; and Aila Rodriguez. 2022. "Misinformation is Eroding the Public's Confidence in Democracy." https://www.brokkings.edu

Sanchez, George J. 1997. "Face the Nation: Race, Immigration, and the Rise of Nativism in Late Twentieth Century America." *International Migration Review* 31, no. 4 (Winter): 1009–1030.

Sasse, Ben. 2019. *Them: Why We Hate Each Other--and How to Heal*. New York: St. Martin's Press.

Saunders, George. 2008. *The Braindead Megaphone*. New York: Bloomsbury.

Schrag, Peter. 2010.. *Not Fit for Our Society: Immigration and Nativism in America*. Berkley, CA: University of California Press.

Schragger, Richard C. 2019. "Federalism, Metropolitanism, and the Problem of States." *Virginia Law Review* 105, no. 8 (December): 1537–1604.

Serwer, Adam. 2019. "White Nationalism's Deep American Roots." https://www.theatalantic.com

Shapiro, Daniel L., and Mikhaila Fogel. 2019. "Tribalism in the Trump Era: The Societal Resilience Index." *Negotiation Journal* 35, no. 1 (January): 235–241.

Shaw, Kate. 2024. "The Supreme Court Creates a Lawless Presidency." https://www.nytimes.com/

Sherman, Mark. 2022a. "Justices Mull Latest Challenge to Landmark Voting Rights Law." https://www.pbs.org

Sherman, Mark. 2022b. "Justice Kagan Cautions Supreme Court can Forfeit Legitimacy." https://www.yahoo.com

Sides, John; Chris Tausanovitch; and Lynn Vavreck. 2022. *The Bitter End: The 2020 Presidential Campaign and the Challenge to American Democracy*. Oxford: Princeton University Press.

Sides, John., and Daniel J. Hopkins., editors. 2015. *Political Polarization in American Politics*. New York: Bloomsbury Publishing Inc.

Sides, John; Michael Tesler, and Lynn Vavreck. 2019. *Identity Crisis: The 2016 Presidential Campaign and the Battle for the Meaning of America*. Second Edition. Princeton: Princeton University Press.

Simas, Elizabeth N., and Adam L. Ozer. 2021. "Polarization, Candidate Positioning, and Political Participation in the U.S." *Electoral Studies* 73, no. 2 (October): 102370.

Singer, Phillip M. 2016. "States of Reform: Polarization, Long-term Services and Supports, and Medicaid Waivers." *State and Local Government Review* 48, no. 4 (December): 246–258.

Stalder, Daniel R. 2018. "Tribalism in Politics." https://www.psychologytoday.com/

Strickler, Ryan. 2018. "Deliberate with the Enemy? Polarization, Social Identity, and Attitudes Toward Disagreement." *Political Research Quarterly* 71, no 1 (March): 3–18.

Sullivan, Andrew. 2017. "America wasn't Built for Humans." https://nymag.com/

Suri, Jeremi. 2024. "How the Attempted Assassination of Donald Trump Fits into American Violent History." https://time.com/

Teixeira, Ruy A. Editor. 2008. **Red, Blue, and Purple America: The Future of Election Demographics**. Washington, D.C.: Brookings Institution Press.

Tharoor, Ishaan. 2022. "U.S. Democracy Slides Toward 'Competitive Authoritarianism'" https://www.washingtonpost.com

"The Origins of Today's Political Polarization." 2018. https://www.redstate.com/

Thomsen, Danielle M. 2014. "Ideological Moderates Won't Run: How Party Fit Matters for Partisan Polarization in Congress." *Journal of Politics* 76, no. 3: 786–797.

Tomasky, Michael. 2019. *If We Can Keep It: How the Republic Collapsed and How It Might be Saved*. New York: Lighthouse Publishing Corporation.

Tucker, Lisa., and Stepfanie A. Lindquist. 2022. "How the Supreme Court is Erasing Consequential Decisions in the Lower Courts." https://www.nytimes.com

Utz, Rebecca; Michael Hollingshaus; and Peter Dien. 2010. "Public Opinion and Health Care." *Contexts* 9, no. 2 (Spring): 66–67.

Van Bavel, Jay J; Steve Rathje; Elizabeth Harris; Claire Robertson; and Anni Sternisko. 2021. "How Social Media Shapes Polarization." *Trends in Cognitive Sciences* 25, no. 11 (November): 913–916.

Ward, Dalston G., and Margit Tavits. 2019. "How Partisan Affect Shapes Citizens' Perception of the Political World." *Electoral Studies* 60 (August): 102045.

Watson, Tara, and Gabriela Godman. 2024. "The Social Safety Net Looks Different in Every State." https://www.brookings.edu/

White, John K., and Matthew R. Kerbel. 2022. *American Political Parties: Why They Formed, How They Function, and Where They are Headed*. Lawrence: University of Kansas.

Wines, Michael. 2023. "In State Legislatures, Old Rivalries are Reheated by National Politics." https://www.nytimes.com/

Webster, Gregory D. 2007. "The Electoral College Exacerbates the Red-Blue Divide and Disenfranchises Ethnic Minorities." *American Psychologist* 62, no. 7 (October): 701–715.

Webster, Steven W. 2018. "It's Personal: The Big Five Personality Traits and Negative Partisan Affect in Polarized U.S. Politics." *American Behavioral Scientist* 62, no. 1 (January): 127–145.

Webster, Steven W., and Alan I. Abramowitz. 2017. "The Ideological Foundations of Affective Polarization in the U.S. Electorate." *American Political Research* 45, no. 4 (July): 621–0647.

Weissert, Carol S., and Matthew J. Uttermark. 2017. "Glass Half Full: Decentralization in Health Policy." *State and Local Government Review* 49, no. 3 (September): 199–214.

West, Darrell M. 2022. "Trump is Not the Only Threat to Democracy." https://www.brookings.edu/

Wenz, Peter S. 2009. *Beyond Red and Blue: How Twelve Political Philosophies Shape American Debates*. Cambridge, MAS: MIT Press.

Whaley, Sarah O. 2022. "No, Big Lie Hasn't Gone Away: Tracking How Election Deniers Performed in 2022." https://centerforpolitics.org

Wolf, Richard. 2022. "The Supreme Court's New Term Could be Historic. Remember that Legitimacy Works Both ways." https://www.usatoday.com

Wolf, Zachary W. 2021. "There are Nine Political Types in US. Which are You?" https://www.cnn.com

Wood, Dan B. and Soren Jordan. 2011. *Electoral Polarization: Definition, Measurement, and Evaluation* (August 9). Online at SSRN: https://ssrn.com/

Woodlief, Tony. 2021. "Is America in 'a Cold Civil War'? Not at all." https://www.governing.com

Wright, Gerald C.; Robert S. Erickson; and John P. McIver. 1987. "Public Opinion and Policy Liberalism in American States." *American Journal of Political Science* 31, no. 4 (November): 980–1001.

Vaidhyanathan, Siva. 2018. *Antisocial Media: How Facebook Disconnects Us and Undermines Democracy*. Cambridge, Mass: Oxford University Press.

Ybarra, Vickie D; Lisa M. Sanchez; and Gabriel R. Sanchez. 2016. "Anti-Immigration Anxiety in State Policy: The Great Recession and Punitive Immigration Policy in the American States, 2005–2012." *State Politics & Policy Quarterly* 16, no. 3 (September): 313–339.

Young, Clifford; Katie Ziemer; and Chris Jackson. 2019. "Explaining Trump's Popular Support: Validation of a Nativism Index." *Social Science Quarterly* 100, no. 2 (April): 412–418.

2
PROFILES OF RED AND BLUE STATES IN AMERICA

Following the Declaration of Independence on July 4, 1776, 13 former colonies became independent states. The first task they were confronted with was to create a national government and establish itself as a nation-state within the community of nations. The term "states" was used for the first time in the Declaration of Independence to claim independence for the colonies and sovereign rights under the law of nations. The newly established independent states quickly realized they would have to unite and establish a national government for mutual defense and survival. The major question confronting the states was how much sovereignty each state would give up to the national government.

The Evolution of the American Federal System

The Articles of Confederation

The first effort to create a national government resulted in the adoption of the Articles of Confederation which went into effect in 1781. States were unwilling to create a strong national government having witnessed how the concentration of all powers and authority in the British monarchy had resulted in the tyranny and injustices against which they had rebelled and declared themselves free. Consequently, the Articles of Confederation specified that each state was an independent sovereign with all the rights and powers except those specifically delegated to the national government. Thus, states viewed the Articles of Confederation as a compact between 13 free and independent states for the main purpose of mutual defense. States surrendered only some of their sovereign rights but retained all others (Bellia et al. 2020).

The result was the creation of a nation-state with a very weak national government and strong, powerful state governments. Even though the national government was responsible for the common defense, Congress lacked the power to raise revenue and create an army making it solely dependent on states to voluntarily contribute revenue and manpower for the army which many states often failed to do. By 1785, it had become clear that the first effort at forming a union under the Articles of Confederation was unworkable and Congress passed a resolution calling for a Constitutional Convention to meet in Philadelphia in May of 1787 to revise the Articles of Confederation.

The New Constitution and Federal System of Government

Instead of revising the Articles of Confederation, the Constitutional Convention ended up scrapping the Articles of Confederation altogether and adopting a new constitution creating a federal system of government that went into effect in 1789. Under the new Constitution, state governments surrendered several important sovereign rights and powers to the national government they had retained under the Articles. The Constitution created a stronger national government than was the case under the Articles. At the same time, the Constitution did not engage in wholesale abrogation of state sovereignty, and the national government it created was stronger but not all-powerful.

The Constitution created a federal system of government without explicitly stating so. A federal system of government is one in which the powers and authority of the government are divided between the national government (Central government) and the state governments (subnational governments). In contrast, in a unitary form of government, all the powers and authority of the government are given to the national government making it all-powerful. The U.S. Constitution spells out certain powers that belong to both the national and state governments (e.g., power to tax, collect revenue), powers that belong to the national government (e.g., raise and support an army, national defense, regulate interstate commerce), powers that are specifically denied to the national government (e.g., grant title of nobility), and power specifically denied to the state governments (enter into treaty or alliance with foreign powers, coin money). The 10th Amendment to the Constitution states that all the leftover or residual powers, i.e., powers not delegated to the national government, not prohibited by it to the states, are reserved to the states or the people.

American Federalism as a Double-Edged Sword

Benefits of American Federalism

American federalism has been heralded as a great laboratory of democracy and as an example of American exceptionalism because of the uniqueness of the American political system. Perhaps the uniqueness attributed to the American political system has been overblown a bit (Krislov 2001). One of the advantages claimed about American federalism is that it allows 50 states the freedom and flexibility to innovate and experiment with public policies/programs to address public problems. Successful policy experiments can lead to the diffusion of policy/program on both the vertical and horizontal planes. Successful public policy can also diffuse upward; i.e., successful state policy can lead Congress to adopt a similar policy nationwide. This might be called "bottom-up" policy diffusion. Garlick's (2022) analysis found a positive correlation between bills introduced in the 50 state legislatures in 22 policy areas and the number of Congressional bills introduced in the next Session. Similarly, policy diffusion can take place on a horizontal plane where states adopt policies or programs that have been successful in other states.

However, often it is not clear, nor is there a clear understanding, as to what are successful experiments, i.e., policy or program. It is very difficult to determine which policy innovations are "effective" because there is a lack of consensus about what a "good" policy is, and a great deal of disagreement exists over most major policy options. Furthermore, state legislatures rarely, if ever, delegate full authority to state agencies to design policy experiments and policy implementation may deviate from the intentions of the experiment designers. Consequently, policy diffusion, i.e., policy emulation by other states, may take place not because the policy or program is effective but because it is politically popular.

What is clear is that states do experiment, innovate, and tinker with their policies. They also alter their policies to improve performance. A variety of factors influence policy innovation and diffusion. For example, research suggests that policy innovation and diffusion are more likely to occur among states that are like one another (Bricker and LaCombe 2010). More professionalized states are faster to adopt policy innovation than less professionalized states (Mallison 2021). The saliency and complexity of an innovative policy also condition the speed of the adoption of policy innovation (Menon and Mallison 2022). Finally, research also indicates that states with higher broadband subscriptions are more innovative and the growth of information flow due to digital communication has led states to become more innovative (LaCombe, Tolbert, and Mossberger 2022). The federal government can also play a supportive role in innovation adoption. However, there are times when states adopt policy innovation that explicitly defies federal law. The state government's adoption of medical marijuana laws is one such example (Hannah and Mallison 2018).

Dangers of American Federalism

As discussed above, decentralization of power and authority in the American federal system provides multiple levels of government freedom and flexibility to address their problems in their unique ways. However, the same features can often become a hindrance by creating conditions for unequal treatment and in the process reduce equality and democratic accountability (Grumbach and Michener 2022). For example, some have argued that Americans suffered more and died at a higher rate from the COVID-19 pandemic because of its decentralized system of federalism. President Trump deferred to the states to respond to the pandemic and leadership at the state level varied considerably. State governments did not prove themselves to be good laboratories in dealing with the pandemic. States' policy responses to the pandemic were influenced more by partisan and ideological considerations than scientific evidence. States did plenty of experimenting but very little learning (Kettl 2021). Chapter 7 provides a detailed analysis of the different policy responses to the pandemic and policy outcomes in the red and blue states.

One can argue that partisan and ideological polarization has led states to practice a partisan form of federalism creating more tensions in intergovernmental relations. Partisan federalism has seen states turn down federal grants that are at odds with partisan goals, file legal challenges in courts to stop federal policy actions by states controlled by the political party that is out of power at the national level, attempt to use the doctrine of nullification to declare federal laws null and void within their jurisdictions, and create inequalitties in programs such as Medicaid, Affordable Care Act (ACA), reproductive rights, and pandemic response. Political polarization has turned contemporary American federalism into laboratories against democracy (Grumbach 2022; Makhlouf 2020).

Contemporary American federalism has become risky and dangerous for American democracy because it pits red states versus blue states and blue cities against red states. David French (2020), a conservative thinker, has argued that contemporary American federalism is an unhealthy one and warns that political polarization and tribalism, if left unchecked, can lead to dangerous consequences for the country. This polarization and tribalism are reflected in policy debates and actions in areas such as the environment (Karapin et al., 2020), immigration (Pratheepan, Su, and

Villazor 2019), and marijuana legalization, to name a few (Trachtman 2022; Huberfeld 2021; Hannah and Mallison 2018), in which red and blue states have followed a very different path. American federalism has entered a new phase that can become a threat to democracy itself (West 2022; "A House Divided" 2013).

Changing Politics of American Federalism

For a federal system to be effective, the national (federal) government must possess vigorous national authority while at the same time ensuring that states also have vigorous power and authority to guard against too powerful a national government that can destroy liberty. The first ten Amendments to the Constitution, known as the Bill of Rights, is designed to restrain the authority of the national government by creating a national government of limited powers (Lacroix 2010). To some extent, the balance of power between the federal and state governments must remain indeterminate, dynamic, and in a state of flux. The balance of political power between the federal and state governments is constantly challenged by economic, technological, social, and political changes taking place in the country over time. Thus, over its history, American federalism has undergone several short-term cycles of centralization of power in the national government versus decentralization of power to the state government. This is often reflected in the zigzag in the national policy agenda during the Democratic and Republican administrations with Democrats generally favoring centralization while Republicans favoring decentralization and devolution of power and authority to the state governments (Conlan 2014). This frequently results in policy instability and uncertainty.

Scholars of American federalism have described this changing relationship between the federal and state governments by a variety of names. The term "**dual federalism**" is used to describe conditions in which there is a clear delineation of powers, authority, and functions between the national and state governments whereby both levels of government operate separately and independently. Dual federalism is also referred to as "**layer cake federalism.**" Dual federalism was the characteristic feature of American federalism from the founding of the American Republic to about the 1930s. From about the 1930s to the 1950s, the changing nature of the national-state relationship has been referred to as "**cooperative federalism**" or "**marble cake federalism**" symbolizing the sharing and intermingling of functions and responsibilities between national, state, and local governments. The federal government used grant-in-aid programs to lure more cooperation from the state government to achieve national policy goals. This new relationship was reflected in Franklin Roosevelt's New

Deal programs. The term **"creative federalism"** or **"picket fence federalism"** is used to describe Lyndon Johnson's Great Society programs under which the federal government assumed more powers by bypassing state governments to exercise direct control over state programs.

The trend toward decentralization and devolution of authority back to the state governments started with the Regan administration and it has been often called the **"new federalism."** This trend continued for much of the 1980s. Starting in the late nineteenth century, the federal government used mandates, preemption, and other regulatory tools to force the state governments to implement national policy objectives in areas such as civil rights, environmental protection, occupation safety, and the like. This period has been described as **"coercive federalism."** The Trump administration (2016–2020) inflamed political polarization to new heights and ushered in a new dimension to the vertical power sharing between the national and state governments. Under the Trump administration, policy differences between the national and state governments generated a more vindictive response, i.e., retaliation from the federal government against states whereby the federal government has used its powers to punish states. Goelzhauser and Konisky (2020) refer to such retaliatory behavior by the national government as **"Punitive federalism."** The Trump administration took punitive actions against some states in policy areas such as environment, immigration, COVID-19, and disaster relief based on states' political allegiance. Examples include the Trump administration withholding federal grant money to "sanctuary" jurisdiction, threatening California with withholding further assistance when the state was ravaged by wildfires, and withholding billions of dollars in funds Congress had allocated for relief after Puerto Rico had suffered a series of devastating earthquakes. Such punitive actions were essentially directed against blue states, i.e., states governed by Democrats.

States have followed the national pattern of increasing partisan and ideological polarization. Partisan and ideological polarization at the state level has produced a sharp divide between the red and blue states over important public policies. In recent years, the number of states controlled by one political party has increased creating homogeneity within red and blue states. Consequently, red and blue states have formed and acted as a block over a wide range of public policy issues. This is referred to as **"block party federalism."** This has created a new form of political sectionalism and a sharp divide between the national and dissident state governments over important public policy questions (Greve 2018). One good example of block party federalism is the controversy surrounding states policies regarding lesbian, gay, bisexual, and transgender (LGBT) communities. Some of the red states have passed anti-LGBT laws such as Georgia's law that allows the banning of transgender girls from participating in girls' sports. In response, blue states like California, Washington, New York, and others have restricted their state employees from official travel to states that have passed anti-LGBT laws (Carroll 2022).

While red and blue states are taking different paths in several policy areas, nowhere the divergence in state policies is more evident than in the field of healthcare. State governments are responsible for funding and coordinating public health functions, financing, and delivery of many personal health services. They are also responsible for regulating providers of medical care and technology, the health insurance industry. In addition, they also engage in state rate setting, licensing, cost control, and a host of other functions and activities. However, it is also clear that there has been increased involvement by the federal government in health policies previously dominated by state governments. The intergovernmental relations in health policy have vacillated between forces of centralization versus decentralization. State governments have sometimes used their experience and expertise in designing and implementing health policies while at other times they have frequently resisted federal health policy actions by going to court. The federal government on its part has used federal grants (financial incentives) as carrots and mandates and pre-emption as sticks to influence and shape state health policy decisions and actions (Weissert and Uttermark 2017).

Overall, contemporary American federalism and the changing political dynamics have been characterized by three major trends – conflict between forces of centralization and decentralization in policymaking; the influence of political polarization on policymaking and administration; and incremental delegitimation and erosion of public trust in the national government. Contemporary American federalism must be understood in the context of these trends (Konisky and Nolette 2022; Conlan 2017).

Profiles of Red and Blue States

In the remainder of this chapter, we explore the differences between the red and blue states within the context of American federalism. Red and blue states can be thought of as economic, political, and cultural categories. The difference between the red and blue states makes up more than just differences of opinions on questions of public policy. They are different in their demographics, economies, politics, and their commitment to democracy and culture.

Over the last 30 years or so, many states have switched their political party allegiance. For example, in the 1980s states such as New Jersey and Connecticut voted solidly for Ronald Reagan. Today, they vote

Democratic. Similarly, in the 1980s, West Virginia was a Democratic stronghold; today, it is a Republican stronghold (Ehrenhalt 2021). Thus, an individual state's political affiliation is often dynamic and may change over time. What we can say for sure is that, over the years, political polarization has led to a shrinking of the number of purple states (competitive states) as more states have become closely aligned with one of the two major political parties. Also, the number of blue states has declined while the number of red states has increased. In 2012, blue states outnumbered red states 20 to 12 (Saad 2013). Today, red states outnumber blue states. There is little doubt that there is a growing divide between the red and blue states and there are some fundamental demographic, economic, political, racial/ethnic, and cultural changes taking place that will have major political and policy consequences (Green 2020; Kotkin and Cox 2020). The red and blue states reflect two competing visions of America (Miller and Sinclair 2022). The states of California and Texas represent the opposites of the liberal-conservative axis and competing visions of America.

How many red, blue, and purple states there are at any given point in time largely depends on the method used to classify states. Our classification of American states is based on long-term trends in state voting patterns in presidential elections as well as long-term control of the governorship and state legislatures rather than relying on a voting pattern in one or two election cycles. However, it is important to understand that long-term trends are not permanent and calcified, and temporary changes are constantly taking place that over some time may become more permanent. For example, purple states such as Florida in recent years have been trending red while Colorado has been trending blue.

Since our primary focus is on political polarization and how red and blue states are moving in different directions when it comes to public policies, and more specifically health policies, we have excluded nine purple states, Colorado, Florida, Iowa, Minnesota, Ohio, Nevada, New Hampshire, Virginia, and Wisconsin, along with the District of Columbia, Puerto Rico, and U.S territories from all the tables and our analysis.

Demographics

The United States decennial census is mandated by Article 1, Section 2 of the U.S. Constitution. The decennial census is two censuses, jointly called the Census of Population and Housing, undertaken every ten years. Originally it was set up to apportion the House of Representative seats in Congress among states based on their population. However, the Census does much more than that. It provides a valuable profile of changes and trends taking place in American society as a whole and at the individual state level. In between the ten-year censuses, the U.S. Census Bureau issues estimates based on surveys and statistical models, specifically the American Community Survey.

Population Characteristics

The first Census conducted in 1790 placed the U.S. population at 3.9 million. The 2020 Census placed the population of the United States at 331.9 million people. Between 2010 and 2020, the U.S. population grew more diverse and older ("How is the Population Changing and Growing" 2022; "Our Changing Population: United States" 2022). The demographic changes varied across states. Some states are more populous than others and some states gained while others lost population. Table 2.1 provides the annual estimated resident population and state population as a percent of the total U.S. population for the red and blue states.

Seven of the top ten most populated states (excluding purple states of Florida and Ohio) are blue states – California, New York, Pennsylvania, Illinois, Michigan, New Jersey, and Washington – while three of the top ten populated states are Texas, Georgia, and North Carolina. Among the top ten least populated states, five are red states – Wyoming, Alaska, North Dakota, South Dakota, and Montana – while the other five are blue states of Vermont, Delaware, Rhode Island, Maine, and Hawaii. The most populous state is California with a population of 38.9 million accounting for almost 11.6 percent of the total U.S. population. The least populous state is Wyoming with a population of 584,057 thousand making up less than half a percent of the total U.S. population.

Overall, the 24 red states make up about 37.4 percent while the 17 blue states make up about 41.6 percent of the total U.S. population with purple states, the District of Columbia and Puerto Rico, making up the remaining 21 percent. Table 2.2 provides additional confirmation of this.

The urban population has increased significantly over the years and today accounts for over 80 percent of the total U.S. population. Even though urban land makes up a small fraction of the total land area in the United States, urban land use has grown significantly accounting for high population density. Urban land use and urban growth vary considerably across states (Lopez 2021). It is also important to note that "urban" areas include cities as well as suburbs and a great deal of the urban population growth is happening in suburbs. The United States is increasingly becoming a suburban nation (Renn 2021). While cities have been strongholds of Democrats, they have made significant inroads into the suburban areas which previously used to be Republican strongholds.

TABLE 2.1 Annual Estimated Resident Population by State (July 1, 2023)

Red States	Population	% of Total US Population	Blue States	Population	% of Total US Population
Texas	3,05,03,301	9.1%	California	3,89,65,193	11.6%
Georgia	1,10,29,227	3.3%	New York	1,95,71,216	5.8%
North Carolina	1,08,35,491	3.2%	Pennsylvania	1,29,61,683	3.9%
Arizona	74,31,344	2.2%	Illinois	1,25,49,689	3.7%
Tennessee	71,26,489	2.1%	Michigan	1,00,37,261	3.0%
Indiana	68,26,199	2.0%	New Jersey	92,90,841	2.8%
Missouri	61,96,156	1.9%	Washington	78,12,880	2.3%
South Carolina	53,73,555	1.6%	Massachusetts	70,01,399	2.1%
Alabama	51,08,468	1.5%	Maryland	61,80,253	1.8%
Louisiana	45,73,749	1.4%	Oregon	42,33,358	1.3%
Kentucky	45,26,154	1.4%	Connecticut	36,17,176	1.1%
Oklahoma	40,53,824	1.2%	New Mexico	21,14,371	0.6%
Utah	34,17,734	1.0%	Hawaii	14,35,138	0.4%
Arkansas	30,67,732	0.9%	Maine	13,95,722	0.4%
Kansas	29,40,546	0.9%	Rhode Island	10,95,962	0.3%
Mississippi	29,39,680	0.9%	Delaware	10,31,890	0.3%
Nebraska	19,78,379	0.6%	Vermont	6,47,464	0.2%
Idaho	19,64,726	0.5%			
West Virginia	17,70,071	0.5%			
Montana	11,32,812	0.3%			
South Dakota	9,19,318	0.3%			
North Dakota	7,83,926	0.2%			
Alaska	7,33,406	0.2%			
Wyoming	5,84,057	0.2%			
Total Red States	12,58,16,344	37.4%	Total Bue States	13,99,41,496	41.6%
Red State Average	52,42,347			82,31,852	
Total USA	33,49,14,895				

Adapted from: "Annual Estimate of the Resident Population for the United States, Regions, States, District of Columbia, and Puerto Rico: April 1, 2020 to July 1, 2023." U.S. Census Bureau; https://www.census.gov/

Note: The nine purple states, District of Columbia, and Peurto Rico make up the remaining 21 percent of the US population.

TABLE 2.2 Urbanization by State (2020)

Red States	Urbanization Index	Urban Land Area % of Total	Blue States	Urbanization Index	Urban Land Area % of Total
Arizona	11.30	2.0	New York	12.56	9.7
Texas	11.17	3.5	New Jersey	12.24	40.1
Utah	10.96	1.2	California	12.19	5.3
Georgia	10.55	9.7	Massachusetts	11.84	38.8
Indiana	10.41	7.2	Rhode Island	11.72	39.0
North Carolina	10.32	9.9	Maryland	11.71	21.1
Missouri	10.20	3.1	Illinois	11.62	7.2
Nebraska	10.20	0.7	Connecticut	11.41	38.0
Tennessee	10.20	7.3	Pennsylvania	11.15	10.7
Louisiana	10.18	4.7	Washington	11.12	3.7
Kansas	10.12	1.2	Hawaii	11.09	6.2
South Carolina	10.11	8.3	Delaware	11.01	22.0
Kentucky	9.79	3.7	Michigan	10.81	6.5
Alabama	9.61	4.5	Oregon	10.71	1.2
Idaho	9.59	0.6	New Mexico	9.90	0.7
Oklahoma	9.34	1.9	Maine	9.04	1.2
Arkansas	9.26	2.2	Vermont	8.84	1.7
West Virginia	9.11	2.7			
North Dakota	9.05	0.3			
Mississippi	8.91	2.4			
Alaska	8.74	0.0			
South Dakota	8.73	0.3			
Montana	8.47	0.2			
Wyoming	8.26	0.2			
Average	9.79	3.2		11.11	14.8

Adapted from: Lopez, Adriana. 2021. "Most Urbanized States 2021." https://www.porch.com and Rakich, Nathaniel. 2020. "How Urban or Rural is Your State?" https://www.FiveThirtyEight.com

Note: Urbanization index is calculated as natural logarithm of the average number of people within a five-mile radius of a given resident.

In 2020, about 82.6 percent of the total US population lived in cities or urban areas.

Table 2.2 provides data on the level of urbanization and urban land area as a percent of the total for the red and blue states. In 2020, about 82.6 percent of the total U.S. population lived in cities or urban areas. The overall average urbanization index for red states is 9.79 compared to 11.11 for blue states. The average urban land area as a percent of the total is 3.3 percent for red states and 14.8 percent for blue states. This again indicates that, overall, the blue states are more urbanized and have more urban land areas compared to the red states. Of the top ten states with the highest urbanization index, eight are blue states – New York, New Jersey, California, Massachusetts, Rhode Island, Maryland, Illinois, and Connecticut – while two are red states of Arizona and Texas. With few exceptions, a state with high urbanization and population density tends to be blue states that vote Democratic while many red states, where rural and small towns dominate the landscape, tend to vote Republican (Rakich 2020). The 2020 Census also revealed that, for the first time in history, rural America lost population, even though the loss was minimal, amounting to –0.6 percent (Johnson 2022). Sociologists Carr and Kefalas (2010) attribute the loss of the rural population to the exodus of young people from America's countryside. We examine this urban-rural-suburban divide in more detail later in the chapter.

Population Shifts: Domestic Migration

The country's total population is projected to grow 14 percent by 2050 driven by immigration even though the growth rate of the U.S. population has declined continuously since the first census in 1790 largely driven by international migration. The reduced population growth rate seems to have been amplified by COVID-19 deaths and related restrictions on immigration. Despite this, in 2021, population gains from international migration were greater than gains from a natural (birth) increase (Smith 2022).

Domestic migration and immigration account for varying rates of population gains and losses by various states. Factors that often account for the gain or loss of population could be state's tax and regulatory policies, labor and energy costs, cost of living, economic growth or decline in concerns about "quality of life". Table 2.3 provides data on the net gain or loss of population and rate per 1,000 by red and blue states. In 2021, population gains from international migration were greater than gains from the natural (birth) increase.

What the data in Table 2.3 reveals is that between June 1, 2020, and June 1, 2022, among the red and blue states, a total of 16 states lost population. Ten of the 16 states that lost population were blue states while six

TABLE 2.3 Net Domestic Migration by State (June 1, 2020 to June 1, 2022)

Red States	Total	Rate Per 1,000	Blue States	Total	Rate Per 1,000
Texas	1,70,307	5.77	Maine	15,473	11.28
Arizona	93,026	12.78	Delaware	12,207	12.17
North Carolina	88,673	8.40	Oregon	8,080	1.90
South Carolina	64,833	12.49	Connecticut	5,134	1.42
Tennessee	61,390	8.80	Vermont	4,589	7.11
Georgia	50,632	4.69	Rhode Island	890	6.21
Idaho	48,876	25.71	Washington	−29	0.00
Utah	32,200	9.65	New Mexico	−2,186	−1.03
Oklahoma	24,687	6.19	Pennsylvania	−3,194	−0.25
Alabama	22,136	4.39	Michigan	−7,893	−0.79
Montana	19,240	17.42	Hawaii	−12,603	−8.74
Arkansas	16,016	5.29	Maryland	−19,871	−3.22
Missouri	14,861	2.41	New Jersey	−27,766	−3.00
Indiana	14,280	2.10	Massachusetts	−46,187	−6.61
Kentucky	10,022	2.22	Illinois	−1,22,460	−9.66
South Dakota	5,564	6.21	New York	−3,52,185	−17.75
West Virginia	2,343	1.31	California	−3,67,299	−9.36
Wyoming	1,252	2.16			
Nebraska	−3,313	−1.69			
Alaska	−3,879	−5.29			
Mississippi	−4,246	−1.44			
Kansas	−5,241	−1.79			
North Dakota	−6,460	−8.34			
Louisiana	−30,312	−6.56			

Adapted from: "State Population Totals and Components of Change." 2022. https://census.gov

were red states. Of the ten blue states that lost population, California, New York, Illinois, and Massachusetts topped the list. Among the red states, Louisiana topped the list. However, overall, the loss of population by red states was much smaller than by the blue states. The states that gained the most population were the red states of Texas, Arizona, North Carolina, Georgia, Tennessee, South Carolina, and North Carolina. Among the red states, Idaho, Montana, Arizona, South Carolina, and Utah had the highest growth rates. Among the blue states, Delaware and Maine experienced the highest growth rates. Among the blue states, California lost the most population while among red states Texas gained the most population. However, the state of Florida which has been trending red experienced the most population gain. Despite its natural beauty, California's population loss can be attributed to factors such as exorbitant housing costs, high taxes, and problems of crime and homelessness. Many large corporations have moved their headquarters out of California to low-tax states such as Texas (Olsen 2023). Neither the state of Texas nor Florida has a state income tax and Florida does not tax pension. Such factors, combined with low cost of living, warmer climate, etc., make states such as Florida, Arizona, North Carolina, and South Carolina also very attractive for retirees. In 2023, Texas and Florida were the top two growth states ("U-Haul Migration Trends: Texas, Florid Top Growth States Again in 2023" 2024). Americans are also segregating themselves by their politics with conservatives moving to red states while liberals moving to blue states creating a geographic divide (Riccardi 2023).

There is an exodus of people from the blue states to the red states and it is likely to continue shortly. Texas and Florida which make up about 15 percent of the population accounted for 70 percent of the population growth of two states. Red states with lower taxes and more affordable housing like Florida, Texas, North Carolina, South Carolina, Tennessee, and Arizona attracted the most newcomers. The population shifts from the Northeast and Midwest to the Sun Belt states have been happening for several decades but it has accelerated in recent years ("Opinions: Red and Blue States – Americans Vote with Their U-Hauls" 2023; "The Blue State Exodus Continues" 2022; Louis 2022; Koutsobinas 2021).

The loss of population by the blue states and the gain of the population by the red states also translated to some shift in political power. After the 2020 census, six states – Texas (two seats), Colorado, Florida, Montana, North Carolina, and Oregon (one seat each) – gained seats in the House of Representatives while seven states will lose one seat each. Of these seven states, five are blue states – California, Illinois, Michigan, New York, and Pennsylvania. The other two are Ohio and West Virginia (U.S. Census Bureau 2021).

Trends in Immigration

Immigration involves people from other countries coming to reside or settle in the United States. The share of the immigrant population has almost tripled since 1970. In 2021, 13.6 percent of the population in the United States was foreign-born. The U.S. Census Bureau defines a foreign-born individual as someone who was not a U.S. citizen at birth, and thus the estimate of the immigrant population includes authorized and unauthorized immigrants ("Immigration and Border Security" 2022). Table 2.4 provides data on the share of the foreign-born population and net gains or losses by state.

Some of the top states with the largest share of the foreign-born population are California, New Jersey, New Mexico, Hawaii, Massachusetts, Texas, Maryland, Connecticut, Rhode Island, and Washington. Except for Texas, all others are blue states. California is the leader with 27 percent of its population being foreign-born. Florida was fourth concerning share of foreign-born population and first for net gain per 1,000. The states of Rhode Island, New Jersey, Michigan, and Maine were the leaders concerning the net gain in the foreign-born population. Overall, red states on average had only a six percent share of the foreign-born population compared to blue states' average of 12.8 percent. This seems to suggest that perhaps blue states are more welcoming of immigrants from other countries than red states or immigrants immigrate to blue states because they perceive them to be more welcoming.

The issue of immigration has always been a difficult subject in America. States such as California are welcoming of immigrants, including unauthorized immigrants, while states such as Texas and Florida view the influx of immigrants as a five-alarm fire. In February of 2023, the Florida legislature passed a bill expanding Governor DeSantis' program to fly migrants to blue states (Edelman 2023). In Texas Governor Abbott plans to wall off Texas from Mexico and the state has doled out $830 million in contracts to build over 30 miles of border barriers (Miller 2023). He also wants to deny undocumented kids a public education. Abbott's policy agenda includes not only bussing migrants to sanctuary cuties in the blue states but also building its own border wall and forcing out undocumented children from public schools (Lee 2023b).

The sonnet "The New Colossus" written by Emma Lazarus for the pedestal on which the Statue of Liberty stands says, "Give me your tired, your poor, your huddled masses yearning to breathe free.... I lift my lamp beside the golden door." Unfortunately, these famous words have never really represented an American consensus. In American history, immigrants have been viewed by some in a negative light. The Irish immigrants were often portrayed as lazy, drunk, and feckless. The Chinese were often portrayed as representing the "yellow peril." Later, Italians, Polich, Mexicans, and recent immigrants from Latin America have been viewed apprehensively. It was President Trump who called for a national ban on "Muslims" from other countries. Thus, throughout American history, there have been many attempts to slam shut the "golden door" (Jenkinson 2023).

TABLE 2.4 Share of Foreign-Born Population (2021) and Net International Migration Per 1,000 Inhabitants by State (2018–2019)

Red States	% Foreign Born[a]	Net International Migration[b]	Blue States	% Foreign Born[a]	Net International Migration[b]
Texas	17.0	2.2	California	27.0	1.9
Arizona	13.0	1.1	New Jersey	23.0	2.4
Georgia	10.0	1.4	New Mexico	22.0	0.7
Utah	8.3	1.7	Hawaii	19.0	3.5
North Carolina	8.2	1.4	Massachusetts	18.0	4.1
Alaska	8.1	0.9	Maryland	16.0	2.5
Nebraska	7.4	1.7	Connecticut	15.0	3.5
Kansas	6.9	1.4	Rhode Island	15.0	3.5
Idaho	6.1	0.1	Washington	15.0	3.2
Oklahoma	5.8	1.1	Illinois	14.0	1.5
Indiana	5.6	2.1	Delaware	10.0	0.1
Tennessee	5.3	1.4	Oregon	9.7	0.8
South Carolina	5.2	1.1	New York	9.1	2.4
Arkansas	4.7	0.1	Pennsylvania	7.2	1.5
North Dakota	4.4	1.3	Michigan	6.8	1.3
Louisiana	4.3	0.7	Vermont	4.2	0.6
Missouri	4.1	0.9	Maine	4.1	0.6
Kentucky	4.0	0.2			
Alabama	3.5	0.6			
South Dakota	3.5	0.5			
Wyoming	3.4	0.9			
Montana	2.2	0.3			
Mississippi	2.1	0.5			
West Virginia	−0.1	−0.1			
Average	6.0	1.0		13.8	2.0
USA average	14.0	1.8			

Adapted from:

[a] "Immigration and Border Security." 2022. https://usafacts.org.
[b] "State Population Totals and Components of Change." 2022. https://www.census.gov

Accordingly, some states have welcomed immigrants with open arms while others have tried to shut their doors on immigrants. Many red states have often banded together to block new immigration to the United States (Hernandez 2022). Governors of Texas and Florida have bussed or flown migrants from their states to discard them in blue states (Edelman 2023). In contrast, blue states, counties, and cities have welcomed immigrants by adopting "sanctuary policies." A sanctuary policy can cover a variety of measures adopted by a jurisdiction that attempt to limit federal immigration enforcement efforts, prohibiting local police from inquiring about immigration status and refusing to honor a request from federal immigration authorities to hold criminal aliens until those officials can assume custody. Today there are approximately 600 sanctuary jurisdictions of varying sizes across the United States. States with the most sanctuary jurisdictions (cities and counties) are California, Colorado, Connecticut, Illinois, Massachusetts, New Jersey, New Mexico, New York, Oregon, Vermont, and Washington (Vaughan and Griffith 2021). All are blue states except for Colorado – a purple state that in recent years has been trending blue. California has built a large safety net for undocumented immigrants (Miranda 2022).

Racial/Ethnic Diversity

William Frey (2018) argues that there has been a racial diversity explosion in the United States that is reshaping America. He explains how rapidly growing "new minorities" made up of Hispanics, Asians, and multiracial Americans along with blacks and other groups are transforming the nation's demographic and political landscape. His basic message is that a multiracial, young America is emerging in both cities and suburbs that will reshape American politics and institutions.

The 2020 census confirms this diversity explosion taking place in the United States. There has been a rapid and significant growth of racial and ethnic groups, especially among those who identify themselves as Hispanic, Aian American, and two or more races throughout much of the country. Between 2010 and 2020, there was an absolute decline in the white population. Black Americans are continuing to return to the South which is a reversal of the past migration of blacks from the South to the Northeast and west coast (Frey 2022; Frey 2021a).

According to the 2020 census, Latinos or Hispanics make up about 18.7 percent of the population, while blacks make up 12.1 percent and Asian Americans 6.1 percent. Latino/Hispanics and Asian Americans are the fastest-growing racial and ethnic groups nationally. Between 2010 and 2020, the Latino/Hispanic population grew by 23 percent while the Asian American population grew by 35.6 percent. Large metropolitan areas have been the destination for black, Latino/Hispanic, and Asian American immigrants. In contrast, the white population declined and is projected to continue because of more deaths and fewer births among the aging white population (Frey 2021a, 2021b, 2021c). While the white population remains the largest racial or ethnic group in the United States, the white population declined by 8.6 percent between 2010 and 2020. However, some states are far more racially diverse than others (Hubbard 2021). Table 2.5 provides data on the racial/ethnic share of the population broken down by red and blue states.

The states with the largest share of blacks are the red states of Mississippi, Louisiana, Georgia, Alabama, South Carolina, and North Carolina. Among blue states, Maryland and Delaware have the largest share of the black population. The blue states of New Mexico and California and the red states of Texas and Arizona have the largest share of the Latino/Hispanic population. The blue state of Hawaii has the largest percent of Asians at 39 percent. States with a large share of the Asian population include California, Washington, Maryland, New Jersey, and New York among the blue states and Alaska among the red states. States with the largest share of the white population making up 80 percent or more of the total population are the red states of West Virginia, Montana, Wyoming, North Dakota, Kentucky, South Dakota, Idaho, Missouri, Nebraska, and Indiana. Among the blue states, the states of Maine and Vermont have the highest percentage of white people at 94 and 93 percent, respectively. On average, red states have a higher share of the white and black population while blue states have a higher share of the Larino/Hispanic population.

Red and blue states vary concerning racial and ethnic diversity because some states promote diversity more than others. The most diverse states include California, Texas, Hawaii, New Jersey, New York, New Mexico, Maryland, Florida, Nevada, and Illinois. The only red state is the state of Texas while two other states – Nevada and Florida – are purple states ("Most Diverse States" 2023).

The U.S. Census has rated states by their diversity index. The diversity index is the chance that two people chosen randomly will be from two different racial and ethnic groups. Table 2.6 provides the racial/ethnic diversity index by state.

The ten most diverse states include the blue states of Hawaii, California, Maryland, New Jersey, New York, New Mexico, and Illinois and the red states of Texas, Georgia, and Arizona. The ten least diverse states include the two blue states of Maine and Vermont and eight red states of West Virginia, Montana, Wyoming, North Dakota, Kentucky, South Dakota, Idaho, and Utah. The overall combined average of red states' diversity index is 46.6 percent compared to blue states' 53.8 percent. Thus, overall,

TABLE 2.5 Percent of Racial/Ethnic Adult Population by State (2021)

Red States	Percent Whites	Percent Blacks	Percent Hispanic/Latino	Percent Asian	Percent Other		Blue States	Percent Whites	Percent Blacks	Percent Hispanic/Latino	Percent Asian	Percent Other
West Virginia	92	4	2	1	1		Maine	94	1	2	1	2
Montana	88	1	4	1	6		Vermont	93	1	2	2	2
North Dakota	86	3	4	2	5		Michigan	77	13	5	3	2
Kentucky	85	8	3	2	2		Oregon	77	2	12	5	4
Wyoming	85	1	9	1	4		Pennsylvania	77	10	7	4	2
South Dakota	84	2	4	2	8		Rhode Island	74	6	15	3	2
Idaho	83	1	11	2	3		Massachusetts	73	7	11	7	2
Missouri	81	11	4	2	2		Washington	69	4	11	10	6
Nebraska	81	5	10	3	1		Connecticut	69	10	15	5	2
Indiana	80	9	6	3	1		Delaware	64	21	8	4	3
Utah	79	1	13	3	4		Illinois	63	14	16	6	1
Kansas	78	6	11	3	2		New York	57	14	18	9	2
Tennessee	76	16	5	2	1		New Jersey	56	13	20	10	1
Arkansas	74	15	7	2	2		Maryland	51	30	8	7	4
Oklahoma	68	7	10	2	5		New Mexico	40	2	47	2	9
Alabama	68	27	4	2	0		California	38	6	37	16	3
South Carolina	66	25	5	2	2		Hawaii	24	2	9	39	26[b]
North Carolina	65	21	8	3	3							
Alaska	63	3	7	7	16[a]							

(Continued)

TABLE 2.5 (Continued)

Red States	Percent Whites	Percent Blacks	Percent Hispanic/ Latino	Percent Asian	Percent Other	Blue States	Percent Whites	Percent Blacks	Percent Hispanic/ Latino	Percent Asian	Percent Other
Louisiana	60	31	5	2	2						
Arizona	58	5	29	4	4						
Mississippi	58	36	3	1	2						
Georgia	54	31	9	5	1						
Texas	44	12	37	5	2						
					63						
Average	73	12	9	3	3		64	9	14	8	2

Adapted from: "Adult Population by Race and Ethnicity in the United States." 2022. https://datacenter.kidscount.org

Notes:

[a] Includes 14% American-Indian and Alaska Natives.
[b] Includes 17% multi-racial groups and 9% Hawaiian Natives and Pacific Islanders.

TABLE 2.6 Racial/Ethnic Diversity Index by State (2020)

Red States	Diversity Index	Blue States	Diversity Index
Texas	67.0	Hawaii	76.0
Georgia	64.1	California	69.7
Alaska	62.0	Maryland	67.3
Arizona	62.8	New Jersey	65.8
Oklahoma	59.0	New York	65.8
Louisiana	58.6	New Mexico	63.0
North Carolina	57.9	Illinois	60.3
Mississippi	55.9	Delaware	59.6
South Carolina	54.6	Washington	55.9
Alabama	51.0	Connecticut	55.7
Arkansas	51.1	Massachusetts	51.6
Tennessee	46.6	Rhode Island	49.4
Kansas	45.4	Oregon	46.1
Indiana	41.3	Michigan	45.2
Missouri	40.8	Pennsylvania	44.0
Nebraska	40.8	Vermont	20.2
Utah	40.7	Maine	18.5
Idaho	35.9		
South Dakota	35.6		
Kentucky	32.8		
North Dakota	32.6		
Wyoming	32.4		
Montana	30.1		
West Virginia	20.2		
Average	46.6		53.8

Adapted from: "Racial and Ethnic Diversity Index by State 2020." 2021. https://www.census.gov

Note: The diversity index is the chance that two people chosen randomly will be from different racial and ethnic groups.

blue states are racially and ethnically more diverse compared to the red states.

The political significance of this is that ideological changes within the Democratic Party have varied along racial and ethnic lines. The Democratic Party is now a coalition of white liberals and non-white voters, especially, blacks, Asian Americans, and Hispanics/Latinos. However, the Latino/Hispanic situation is more complex in that Catholic Hispanics are more likely to identify with Democrats than Hispanic evangelicals. The share of Hispanic evangelicals as a percent of the total Hispanic vote is increasing rapidly. In contrast, the Republican Party is now largely a party of white people concentrated in small towns and rural areas (Galston 2023). For example, in the 2020 presidential elections, of the total votes Donald Trump received, non-Hispanic white Americans made up about 85 percent of the votes (Bacon 2022). Today's Republican Party receives its sustenance largely from the right-wing conservative populism associated with the white working class (Gest 2018).

Age and Gender Distribution

Younger populations typically result from high fertility and birth rates while an aging population goes together with a declining population because of higher death rates and lower birth rates. A population's age can affect political, social, and cultural aspects.

As can be observed from Table 2.7, among the red states, states of Utah, Texas, South Dakota, Alaska, and Idaho rank among the top in the share of the population under the age of 18. Among the blue states, New Mexico, California, Illinois, Maryland, and Washington have the largest share of the population under the age of 18. The state of Utah, at 30 percent, has the highest share of children under the age of 18 and the highest share of the population between 19 and 25 years of age. Utah also has the smallest number of elderly populations at 11.7 percent. Thus, overall Utah is the youngest state in the Union. On average, red states have a larger share of children and young adults.

When it comes to population over the age of 65, the top blue states with the largest share of the elderly population are Maine, Vermont, Hawaii, Delaware, and Pennsylvania while the top red states include states of West Virginia, South Carolina, Montana, Arizona, and Wyoming. Overall, on average, blue states have more population over the age of 65.

Another way to examine the oldest and the youngest states is to look at the median age of the population. Table 2.8 provides the median age for the year 2022 for the red and blue states.

The top five states with the highest median age population include the blue states of Main, Vermont, Delaware, Connecticut, and Pennsylvania and the red states of West Virginia, South Carolina, Montana, Alabama, and Kentucky. The youngest red states include Utah, Texas, Alaska, North Dakota, and Oklahoma while blue states include California, Washington, Illinois, New Mexico, and Maryland. Overall, on average, red states have a younger population than blue states.

Table 2.9 provides data on the male-to-female ratio broken down by state. The male-to-female ratio indicates the number of males per 100 females in the population. Male-to-female ratios are affected by factors such

TABLE 2.7 Age Distribution by State (2021)

Red States	Children 0–18 years (Percent)	Young Adults 19-5 years (Percent)	Adults 26-4 (Percent)	Elderly 65+ (Percent)	Blue States	Children 0-8 years (Percent)	Young Adults 19-5 years (Percent)	Adults 26-4 (Percent)	Elderly 65+ (Percent)
Alabama	23.6	8.7	50.1	17.7	California	23.6	8.7	52.3	15.3
Alaska	26.4	8.5	51.5	13.7	Connecticut	21.6	8.3	52.0	18.0
Arizona	23.6	8.8	49.0	18.6	Delaware	21.8	7.8	50.3	20.1
Arkansas	24.6	8.7	49.2	17.4	Hawaii	22.6	7.1	49.9	20.4
Georgia	25.0	8.6	51.4	14.9	Illinois	23.5	8.5	51.5	16.6
Idaho	26.1	8.6	48.6	16.7	Maine	19.0	6.8	52.4	21.8
Indiana	24.6	8.9	50.1	16.4	Maryland	23.4	7.8	52.4	16.4
Kansas	25.4	9.1	48.8	16.6	Massachusetts	21.0	8.2	53.3	17.6
Kentucky	23.7	8.7	50.4	17.2	Michigan	22.6	8.8	50.4	18.2
Louisiana	24.8	8.9	49.6	16.7	New Jersey	23.0	7.9	52.3	16.8
Mississippi	25.2	9.0	48.9	17.1	New Mexico	24.1	8.4	48.9	18.7
Missouri	23.9	8.3	50.2	17.6	New York	21.9	8.1	52.5	17.5
Montana	22.2	8.9	49.1	19.8	Oregon	21.1	8.2	51.9	18.7
Nebraska	26.0	8.8	48.8	16.4	Pennsylvania	21.9	7.7	51.3	19.0
North Carolina	23.4	8.3	51.1	17.3	Rhode Island	20.5	8.5	52.7	18.3
North Dakota	25.3	9.8	48.9	16.0	Vermont	19.3	8.2	51.6	20.9
Oklahoma	25.6	9.0	49.0	16.3	Washington	22.8	8.2	52.7	16.3

(Continued)

TABLE 2.7 (Continued)

Red States	Children 0–18 years (Percent)	Young Adults 19-5 years (Percent)	Adults 26-4 (Percent)	Elderly 65+ (Percent)	Blue States	Children 0-8 years (Percent)	Young Adults 19-5 years (Percent)	Adults 26-4 (Percent)	Elderly 65+ (Percent)
South Carolina	23.0	8.2	50.0	18.9					
South Dakota	26.0	9.0	47.6	17.5					
Tennessee	23.2	8.5	51.2	17.1					
Texas	26.8	9.1	50.8	13.3					
Utah	30.0	10.8	47.6	11.7					
West Virginia	21.2	8.3	49.6	20.0					
Wyoming	24.0	8.5	49.4	18.1					
Average	24.7	8.8	49.6	16.8		21.9	8.1	51.6	18.3
USA	23.5	8.5	51.1	16.9					

Adapted from: "Population Distribution by Age 2021." 2021. https://www.kff.org

TABLE 2.8 Median Age by State (2022)

Red States	Overall Median Age	Blue States	Overall Median Age
West Virginia	42.9	Maine	45.1
South Carolina	40.5	Vermont	43.2
Montana	40.2	Delaware	41.5
Alabama	39.6	Connecticut	40.9
Kentucky	39.4	Pennsylvania	40.9
North Carolina	39.2	Hawaii	40.8
Tennessee	39.2	Rhode Island	40.7
Missouri	39.1	Oregon	40.5
Wyoming	39.1	New Jersey	40.4
Arkansas	38.9	Michigan	40.3
Mississippi	38.9	Massachusetts	40.3
Arizona	38.8	New York	40.0
South Dakota	38.5	Maryland	39.7
Indiana	38.2	New Mexico	39.4
Louisiana	38.2	Illinois	39.1
Georgia	37.6	Washington	38.4
Kansas	37.6	California	37.9
Idaho	37.5		
Nebraska	37.4		
Oklahoma	37.1		
North Dakota	36.2		
Alaska	35.9		
Texas	35.6		
Utah	32.1		
Average	38.2		40.5
USA	39.0		

Adapted from: "Median Age in the United States in 2022, by State." 2023. https://www.sratista.com/

as birth, death, immigration, and migration rates. States with the highest male-to-female ratio include the red states of Alaska, North Dakota, Wyoming, South Dakota, Utah, Montana, and Idaho and the blue states of Hawaii and California. Alaska has the highest male-to-female ratio (109.2) while Delaware has the lowest male-to-female ratio at 93.6.

Education

Education is an investment in the future. Investment in education leads to better-educated students who go further in school. A better-educated

TABLE 2.9 Male to Female Ratio by State (2022)

Red States	Ratio	Blue States	Ratio
Alaska	109.2	Hawaii	100.6
North Dakota	104.9	Washington	100.1
Wyoming	103.9	California	98.9
South Dakota	101.5	Oregon	98.3
Utah	101.4	New Mexico	98.0
Montana	101.2	Vermont	97.6
Idaho	100.6	Michigan	97.0
Nebraska	99.5	Illinois	96.6
Kansas	99.4	Pennsylvania	96.1
Arizona	98.8	Maine	96.0
Texas	98.7	New Jersey	95.5
Oklahoma	98.2	Connecticut	95.2
West Virginia	97.8	Rhode Island	94.7
Indiana	97.2	New York	94.4
Kentucky	97.0	Massachusetts	94.3
Arkansas	96.4	Maryland	94.0
Missouri	96.3	Delaware	93.6
Louisiana	95.4		
Tennessee	95.3		
Georgia	94.7		
North Carolina	94.7		
South Carolina	94.1		
Mississippi	93.9		
Alabama	93.6		
Average	98.4%		96.5%

Adapted from: American Community Survey, "Age and Sex." 2024. (Table S0101); https://data.census.gov/

Note: Male to female ratio indicates the number of males per 100 females in the population.

workforce is more innovative. For millions of Americans, education is the ticket to a better future because education opens doors to career opportunities and higher earnings. The higher the level of education achievement, the higher the income potential and the lower the chance of being unemployed (McCann 2022a, 2022b).

The quality of public education is also crucial to one's aspiration and potential for success. For millions of American families, public education is the only option since most parents cannot afford to place their children in exclusive or private schools. Public education is largely a matter for state governments that allocate funding for public education and local school boards that administer states' educational policies (McCann 2021). However, the federal government often has involved itself in the educational field. Under the No Child Left Behind Act, President George W. Bush's administration put in place annual testing requirements for states that show significant disparities in achievement gaps among different racial/ethnic and income groups. Similarly, the Obama administration pushed states to adopt more rigorous academic standards and tests, new teacher evaluation, and a pay system based in part on student test scores and improvement models of "failing" schools. Congress in 2015 replaced the No Child Left Behind Act with the Every Student Succeeds Act which kept the testing requirements but rolled back some of the federal involvement in K-12 education. The Act required states to publish school-level per pupil expenditures data every fiscal year.

In this section, we examine the red and blue states' commitment to education with respect to their per pupil public school expenditures, average K-12 public school teacher pay, the share of residents with less than high school education, the share of residents with a bachelor's degree or higher, and how they rank concerning their education system and the quality of education. Spending on education is one indicator of states' commitment to investing in education. However, it is also important to note that other factors such as the cost of living can also influence states' spending per pupil and teacher pay. Table 2.10 provides data on the median per pupil public school expenditures by red and blue states.

As can be seen from the table, spending on K-12 education varies considerably by state. The state of New York tops the list with a median per pupil expenditure of $26,360, while Utah is at the bottom of the list at $7,810. The top three New York, New Jersey, and Connecticut, the three blue states, spend over $20,000. Among the top ten states with the highest median per pupil expenditures are New York, Connecticut, New Jersey, Alaska, Rhode Island, Massachusetts, Wyoming, Hawaii, Delaware, and Pennsylvania. Of the top ten, only two – Alaska and Wyoming – are red states while the other eight are blue states. The bottom ten are all red states of Utah, Idaho, Arizona, Mississippi, Oklahoma, Texas, Tennessee, Arkansas, Indiana, and Alabama. Overall, the blue states spend considerably more per pupil than the red states.

Teachers' salary is another indicator of the state's commitment to education because higher salaries attract better and more qualified teachers which often can translate to better student success and educational attainment. Table 2.11 provides data for the annual average salary of teachers in public primary and secondary schools.

New York is at the top of the list for an average teacher salary of $92,222. In contrast, Mississippi is at the bottom with an average annual

TABLE 2.10 Median Per Pupil Public School Expenditures by State (2019)

Red States	Per Pupil Expenditures	Blue States	Per Pupil Expenditures
South Dakota	NA	New York	$26,360
Alaska	$19,920	Connecticut	$20,740
Wyoming	$17,020	New Jersey	$20,250
North Dakota	$14,610	Rhode Island	$17,230
Nebraska	$13,490	Massachusetts	$17,140
Montana	$12,620	Hawaii	$16,280
West Virginia	$12,110	Delaware	$15,410
Louisiana	$11,720	Pennsylvania	$15,270
Kansas	$11,670	Illinois	$15,130
Georgia	$11,470	Maryland	$15,100
Kentucky	$11,420	Vermont	$15,020
South Carolina	$11,020	Maine	$14,690
Missouri	$10,420	Washington	$14,220
North Carolina	$10,220	California	$13,030
Alabama	$10,140	Oregon	$12,440
Indiana	$10,090	Michigan	$10,830
Arkansas	$10,060	New Mexico	$10,580
Tennessee	$9,810		
Texas	$9,790		
Oklahoma	$9,450		
Mississippi	$9,260		
Arizona	$8,560		
Idaho	$8,010		
Utah	$7,810		
Average	$11,334		$15,865

Adapted from: "How Much Money Do Schools Spend on Education?" 2022. https://usafacts.org/

salary of $47,162. The top ten states with the highest average salary are New York, Massachusetts, California, Washington, Connecticut, Alaska, New Jersey, Rhode Island, Maryland, and Illinois. Of these, only Alaska represents a red state while the other nine are blue states. Of the 17 blue states, ten pay over $70,000, while out of a total of 24 red states, only Alaska pays over $70,000.

The bottom ten states that pay teachers the least are all red states of Mississippi, South Dakota, West Virginia, Louisiana, Missouri, Arkansas, Montana, South Carolina, Tennessee, and North Carolina. The overall average salary blue states pay their teachers is $73,576 compared to $55,304 paid by the red states.

TABLE 2.11 Estimated Average Annual Salary of Teachers at Public Primary and Secondary Schools, 2021–2022

Red States	Average Salary	Blue States	Average Salary
Alaska	$73,722	New York	$92,222
Georgia	$61,249	Massachusetts	$88,903
Wyoming	$60,820	California	$87,275
Texas	$58,887	Washington	$81,586
Utah	$58,619	Connecticut	$81,185
Nebraska	$57,420	New Jersey	$79,045
Alabama	$55,834	Rhode Island	$76,852
North Dakota	$55,769	Maryland	$75,766
Kansas	$54,815	Illinois	$72,301
Oklahoma	$54,804	Pennsylvania	$72,248
Arizona	$54,580	Oregon	$69,671
Kentucky	$54,574	Hawaii	$67,000
Idaho	$54,232	Delaware	$65,647
Indiana	$54,126	Michigan	$65,198
North Carolina	$53,644	Vermont	$62,866
Tennessee	$53,619	Maine	$58,757
South Carolina	$53,393	New Mexico	$54,272
Montana	$52,628		
Arkansas	$52,486		
Missouri	$52,481		
Louisiana	$52,376		
West Virginia	$50,315		
South Dakota	$49,761		
Mississippi	$47,162		
Average	$55,304		$73,576
National average	$66,397		

Adapted from: "Estimated Average Annual Salary of Teachers at Public Primary and Secondary Schools 2021-022." 2023.
National Center for Educational Statistics. 2023. https://nces.ed.gov/

The national average for the overall teacher salary in 2021–2022 was $66,397. Twenty-three of the 24 red states pay their teachers far below the national average compared to five of the 17 blue states – New Mexico, Maine, Vermont, Michigan, and Delaware.

Next, we examine states' share of residents with less than a high school diploma and the share of residents with a bachelor's or higher degree. Both are an indicator of how educated state residents are. A highly educated workforce is often the driver of economic growth and innovation. Tables 2.12 and 2.13 provide these data.

TABLE 2.12 Share of Residents with Less Than a High School Diploma by States (2021)

Red States	Percent with Less Than High School Diploma	Blue States	Percent with Less Than High School Diploma
Texas	14.6	California	15.5
Mississippi	13.6	New Mexico	12.5
Louisiana	13.3	New York	12.0
Alabama	12.1	Rhode Island	10.9
Kentucky	12.1	Illinois	9.9
Arkansas	11.3	New Jersey	9.0
Oklahoma	11.3	Connecticut	8.9
West Virginia	11.1	Maryland	8.9
Arizona	11.0	Massachusetts	8.9
Georgia	11.0	Delaware	8.7
South Carolina	10.4	Oregon	8.1
North Carolina	10.3	Pennsylvania	8.1
Tennessee	10.3	Michigan	8.0
Indiana	9.3	Washington	7.7
Idaho	8.8	Hawaii	7.0
Missouri	8.5	Maine	5.5
Kansas	8.1	Vermont	5.5
Nebraska	7.8		
South Dakota	6.9		
Utah	6.8		
Alaska	6.7		
Wyoming	6.4		
North Dakota	6.3		
Montana	5.6		
Average	9.7		9.1

Adapted from: "Which States Are the Most Educated?" 2022. https://usafacts.org/

Of the top ten states with the largest share of residents with less than a high school diploma, seven are red states – Texas, Mississippi, Louisiana, Alabama, Kentucky, Oklahoma, and Arkansas – while three are blue states – California, New Mexico, and New York. Among the bottom ten states, six are red states of Montana, North Dakota, Wyoming, Alaska, Utah, and South Dakota, while four are blue states of Vermont, Maine, Hawaii, and Washington. Of the 17 blue states, in only four states 10 percent or more of their residents are without a high school diploma compared to 13 of the 24 red states. Overall, blue states have a smaller share of residents without a high school diploma.

TABLE 2.13 Share of Residents 25 and Older with a Bachelor's Degree or Higher by State (2021)

Red States	Percent with Bachelor's Degree	Blue States	Percent with Bachelor's Degree
Utah	36.8	Massachusetts	46.6
Kansas	35.4	Vermont	44.4
North Carolina	34.9	New Jersey	43.1
Montana	34.8	Maryland	42.5
Georgia	34.6	Connecticut	42.1
Nebraska	34.4	New York	39.9
Texas	33.1	Washington	39.0
Alaska	32.8	Illinois	37.1
Arizona	32.4	Oregon	36.6
Missouri	31.7	Rhode Island	36.5
North Dakota	31.7	California	36.2
South Dakota	31.7	Maine	36.0
South Carolina	31.5	Delaware	35.6
Idaho	30.7	Hawaii	35.3
Tennessee	30.5	Pennsylvania	34.5
Wyoming	29.2	Michigan	31.7
Indiana	28.9	New Mexico	30.1
Oklahoma	27.9		
Alabama	27.4		
Kentucky	27.0		
Louisiana	26.4		
Arkansas	25.3		
Mississippi	24.8		
West Virginia	24.1		
Average	30.7		38.0

Adapted from: "Which States Are the Most Educated?" 2022. https://usafacts.org/

When it comes to the share of residents with bachelor's degrees or higher, the blue states win hands down. The top ten states with the largest share of residents with a bachelor's degree or higher are the blue states of Massachusetts, Vermont, Maryland, New Jersey, Connecticut, New York, Washington, Michigan, Illinois, and Oregon. All the bottom ten states are red states comprising West Virginia, Mississippi, Arkansas, Louisiana, Kentucky, Alabama, Oklahoma, Indiana, Wyoming, and Tennessee. On average, 38 percent of blue states residents have a bachelor's degree or higher compared to 30 percent of residents of red states.

Table 2.14 provides a ranking of states by the level of education and the quality of their public schools. The ranking is created by wallethub.com using 32 metrics based on quality and safety.

Massachusetts ranks at the top for educational attainment followed by Maryland, Vermont, Connecticut, and New Jersey, all three blue states. At the bottom of the rankings are West Virginia, Mississippi, Louisiana, Arkansas, Alaska, Alabama, and Kentucky, all red states. Blue states rank considerably better than the red states indicating that the blue states are more educated than the red states.

When it comes to the ranking on quality of public schools, Massachusetts again emerges at the top followed by blue states of Connecticut, New Jersey, Maryland, and Delaware with only one red state – Nebraska – cracking the top ten rankings. Ten states at the bottom of the ranking include the blue states of New Mexico and California and the red states of Louisiana, Arizona, Alaska, Alabama, Oklahoma, Mississippi, West Virginia, and South Carolina. Here again, blue states fare much better than red states when it comes to the quality of public schools.

Finally, in Table 2.15, we examine the ranking of red and blue states by the quality of higher education and Pre-K-12 as measured by the *U.S. News and World Report*. The higher education ranking is measured utilizing educational attainment, two- and four-year college graduation rate, cost of in-state tuition and fees, and college debt at graduation. The Pre-K-12 ranking is based on the measurement of college readiness, public high school graduation rate, math and reading scores, and preschool enrolment.

On the quality of higher education ranking, the top ten states included states of Florida, Washington, California, Wyoming, Colorado, Utah, North Carolina, South Dakota, Nevada, and Nebraska. Of the top ten states, two are blue states – Washington and California; four are red states – Wyoming, Utah, North Carolina, and South Dakota; and four are purple states – Colorado, Nevada, and Nebraska. What the data suggests is that the red states, on average, have done better than the blue states.

What our analysis demonstrates is that blue states spend more on public education, have a smaller share of the population with less than a high school diploma, have a higher share of the population with a bachelor's degree or higher, and have better quality public schools than red states. The quality of higher education is the only area where there is not a significant difference between the red and blue states. The red states do slightly better in this area.

According to David Brooks (2022), Americans are sorting themselves out by education into two separate camps. People without college degrees have flocked to the Republican Party while people with college degrees

TABLE 2.14 States Ranked by Level of Education and Public Schools (2021)

Red States	Education Level Attainment		Public Schools		Blue States	Education Level Attainment		Public Schools	
	Total Score[a]	State Rank[b]	Total Score[c]	State Ranking[b]		Total Score[a]	State Rank[b]	Total Score[c]	State Ranking[b]
Utah	63.2	11	55.9	16	Massachusetts	81.8	1	73.1	1
Nebraska	55.1	18	57.8	8	Maryland	78.5	2	60.2	6
Montana	55.0	19	50.3	27	Connecticut	72.7	3	67.5	2
Kansas	52.6	23	47.5	29	Vermont	69.7	5	57.4	10
North Dakota	52.0	24	55.3	17	New Jersey	69.2	6	64.4	3
Wyoming	50.9	27	53.0	23	Washington	63.3	10	51.3	26
Alaska	50.4	28	36.4	47	Illinois	58.3	12	56.3	15
North Carolina	49.7	29	46.0	33	New York	57.4	13	56.4	14
Missouri	47.7	32	45.9	35	Oregon	57.2	14	41.0	41
Georgia	46.8	33	46.2	32	Rhode Island	56.6	15	57.2	11
South Dakota	45.9	34	52.4	25	Delaware	55.9	16	58.0	7
Idaho	44.7	36	45.2	36	Hawaii	55.4	17	43.1	39
Arizona	44.5	37	35.1	48	Maine	54.1	21	56.9	13
Indiana	43.0	38	55.3	22	Michigan	51.7	25	45.9	34
Texas	39.1	39	49.9	28	California	51.4	26	42.4	40
South Carolina	39.0	40	39.0	42	Pennsylvania	49.2	30	52.9	24
Tennessee	38.8	41	46.9	31	New Mexico	38.0	42	25.3	50

(Continued)

TABLE 2.14 (Continued)

Red States	Education Level Attainment		Public Schools		Blue States	Education Level Attainment		Public Schools	
	Total Score[a]	State Rank[b]	Total Score[c]	State Ranking[b]		Total Score[a]	State Rank[b]	Total Score[c]	State Ranking[b]
Oklahoma	36.2	44	37.2	45					
Kentucky	35.4	45	54.2	19					
Alabama	33.1	46	37.0	46					
Arkansas	31.0	47	43.8	37					
Louisiana	25.8	48	33.4	49					
Mississippi	25.4	49	38.2	44					
West Virginia	23.2	50	38.5	43					
Average score	42.9	35	45.9	32.6		60.0	15	53.5	20

Adapted from: McCann, Adam. 2021. "States with the Best and Worst School Systems." https://wallethub.com/ and McCann. Adam. 2022. "Most and Least Educated States in America." https://wallethub.com/

Notes:

[a] Total score is calculated on a 100-point scale using 18 metrics along two dimensions – educational attainment and quality of education.
[b] States are ranked from 1 = best to 50 = worst.
[c] Total score is calculated on a scale of 100 points using 32 metrics based on two dimensions – quality and safety.

TABLE 2.15 States Ranked by the Quality of Higher Education (2021)

Red States	Higher Education	Blue States	Higher Education
Louisiana	48	Pennsylvania	50
West Virginia	47	Rhode Island	49
South Carolina	45	Vermont	44
Arkansas	41	Connecticut	43
Alabama	39	Michigan	42
Kentucky	38	Maine	40
Mississippi	37	Illinois	32
Alaska	36	New Jersey	27
Indiana	34	Massachusetts	25
Arizona	33	New Mexico	24
Texas	31	Oregon	23
Idaho	30	Hawaii	21
Tennessee	29	Delaware	20
Oklahoma	28	New York	14
Missouri	26	Maryland	12
Montana	22	California	3
Georgia	19	Washington	2
North Dakota	16		
Kansas	13		
Nebraska	10		
South Dakota	8		
North Carolina	7		
Utah	6		
Wyoming	4		
Average	27		28

Adapted from: "Education Rankings: Measuring How Well States Are Educating Their Students." 2021. https://www.usnews.com/

have flocked to the Democratic Party. This has been especially true between non-college and college-educated whites with non-college-educated whites gravitating heavily toward the Republican Party. The difference between the two groups goes beyond politics. Americans with a college education and those without a college education not only have different ideas about the role of government but also live different lifestyles and have different views about patriotism, faith, corporal punishment, and gender and racial equality. American politics which has long been characterized by a lack of class consciousness may be moving in the direction of class consciousness. In the 2012 presidential election, the states that voted for Obama, on average, had higher high school and college education rates than the states that supported Republican Mitt Romney (Dhillon 2014). This pattern strengthened further in the 2016 and 2020 presidential elections. Later in the chapter, we examine how electoral polarization was reflected in the 2020 presidential election.

Public education has often become the political battlefield between the red and blue states. Conservatives in red states have made public education their political target. Republican officials have cast higher education and college professors as the culprit for the nation's problems. Republican Richard Nixon was the first president to declare that "professors are the enemy." J.D. Vance, the Republican candidate for the U.S. Senate in the 2022 election, gave a keynote address titled, "The Professors are the Enemy," at the National Conservative Conference in November of 2022. When Scott Walker was the governor of Wisconsin, with the cooperation of a conservative legislature, he stripped faculty members and other public employees of their collective bargaining rights and slashed higher education budgets. Republicans are in a better position to influence public colleges and higher education since they control more than 60 percent of all legislative chambers across the country. They enjoy "trifecta" in 23 states compared to only 14 states for Democrats. Trifecta refers to a condition in which the same party controls both chambers of the state legislature and the governorship (Fischer 2022).

In Texas, Governor Abbott wants to overturn an earlier Supreme Court decision requiring states to provide free education for all its children (Crosby 2022). He also wants to enact private school vouchers and expand eligibility for "education savings accounts" allowing parents to use public funding for private school tuition, like the ones adopted by other Republican-led states (Wallace 2023). He also recently signed into law a "critical race theory" bill limiting the teaching of current events and prohibiting students from receiving credits for civic activities that include political activism and lobbying elected officials on a particular issue. Governors in Idaho and Tennessee have signed similar bills into law. More than a dozen other red states are considering similar legislation (McGee 2021). Red states have targeted black history lessons, while blue states have embraced them (Natanson 2023).

In Arkansas, the Republican Governor Sarah Huckabee Sanders signed an executive order prohibiting public schools from teaching critical race theory. She also banned the word "Latinx," a gender-neutral alternative to Latina or Latino, from state documents (Astor 2023). Republican Governor DeSantis of Florida, a state that is trending red, has taken on a fight with the education establishment requiring mandated courses in Western civilization, elimination of diversity programs, and weakening protections of faculty tenure (Saul, Mazzei, and Gabriel. 2023).

Banning books in public schools has also become common in several red states in the war on public education. Republican-controlled states including Florida, Georgia, Tennessee, and Texas are now pushing statewide rules that make it easier for critics to remove books they dislike from school libraries in every community. The torrent of laws has been approved in Republican-controlled states since 2021 to limit how teachers can discuss race, gender, or sexual orientation (Mumma 2023; Price 2023; Meckler and Natanson 2023; Gabriel 2023; Brownstein 2022b; Skolnik 2022; Gowen 2022).

Economy

Discussion of the U.S. economy mostly focuses on the national economy as one economy, However, economic differences between American states can be significant and very striking. It has been suggested that while the United States is one nation with a single currency, red and blue states constitute two different economies (Klement 2018). Not only do red and blue states experience different economies, but these two economies are also diverging faster (Muro and Whiten 2019). The divergence between the economies of the red and blue states is astounding (Rennenkampff 2020). Blue states' economy is powered by finance, trade, and knowledge while red states' economy is driven by energy extraction and agriculture (Worstall 2015). Republican-led red states are in the deep South, Midwest, and mountainous Northwest while the Democratic-led blue states are in the Northeast and the west coast (Sager 2014). Consequently, voters in red and blue states live and experience different economies (Edsall 2019). Furthermore, within red and blue states, local economic context influences voters' priorities (Cummings 2008).

Paul Chiariello (2020) analyzed eight economic indicators – GDP per capita, median income, high school graduation, college graduation, unemployment overall poverty, child poverty, and homelessness – in the red and blue states and concluded that of the eight indicators blue states performed better in all but one indicator. Red states did better with the problem of homelessness. To analyze how red and blue states' economies differ, we use personal per capita income, median household income, unemployment rate, rate of poverty, tax rate, cost of living, GDP, and level of dependence on the federal government.

Per Capita Income

Table 2.16 provides data on the red and blue states concerning per capita income.

TABLE 2.16 Real Personal Per Capita Income by State (2020)

Red States		Blue States	
	Real Personal Per Capita Income[a]		Real Personal Per Capita Income[a]
Wyoming	$60,463	Connecticut	$68,533
North Dakota	$60,286	Massachusetts	$65,853
South Dakota	$58,414	New York	$60,936
Nebraska	$55,891	New Jersey	$59,594
Alaska	$55,470	California	$57,347
Kansas	$54,773	Pennsylvania	$57,030
Montana	$52,054	Maryland	$56,578
Indiana	$50,624	Illinois	$56,482
Missouri	$50,404	Washington	$56,385
Tennessee	$49,955	Rhode Island	$53,859
Texas	$49,945	Vermont	$53,726
Louisiana	$49,483	Delaware	$51,689
North Carolina	$49,396	Michigan	$51,071
Georgia	$49,392	Maine	$50,516
Utah	$49,388	Oregon	$49,485
Oklahoma	$49,254	Hawaii	$47,234
Idaho	$48,216	New Mexico	$45,637
Arkansas	$47,765		
Kentucky	$47,551		
South Carolina	$47,252		
Alabama	$46,963		
West Virginia	$46,130		
Arizona	$45,193		
Mississippi	$43,284		
Average	$50,731		$55,409

Adapted from: DePietro, Andrew. 2021. "U. S. Per Capita Income by State in 2021." https://www.forbes.com/

Note:

[a] Real personal per capita income is income per person adjusted for state price level differences and National inflation according to Bureau of Economic Analysis.

The state of Connecticut ranks number one with a personal per capita income of $57,347. The top ten states include seven blue states Connecticut, Massachusetts, New York, New Jersey, California, Pennsylvania, and Maryland and three red states – Wyoming, North Dakota, and South Dakota. The bottom ten states include eight red states of Idaho, Arkansas, Kentucky, South Carolina, Alabama, West Virginia, Arizona, and Mississippi and two blue states of Hawaii and New Mexico. On average,

TABLE 2.17 Median Household Income by State (2022)

Red States	Median Household Income	Blue States	Median Household Income
Utah	$87,649	Maryland	$97,332
Alaska	$79,253	New Jersey	$88,559
North Dakota	$64,894	Washington	$87,648
Wyoming	$64,049	Massachusetts	$86,566
Texas	$61,874	Hawaii	$82,199
Nebraska	$61,439	California	$81,575
Kansas	$59,597	Connecticut	$78,109
Arizona	$58,945	New York	$72,920
Georgia	$58,700	Delaware	$70,821
South Dakota	$58,275	Rhode Island	$68,882
Indiana	$56,303	Illinois	$67,404
Idaho	$55,785	Oregon	$62,818
Missouri	$55,461	Vermont	$61,973
Montana	$54,970	Pennsylvania	$61,744
North Carolina	$54,602	Maine	$57,918
Tennessee	$53,320	Michigan	$57,144
South Carolina	$53,199	New Mexico	$49,754
Oklahoma	$52,919		
Kentucky	$50,589		
Alabama	$50,536		
Arkansas	$49,597		
Louisiana	$49,469		
West Virginia	$46,711		
Mississippi	$45,081		
Average	$57,634		$72,550

Adapted from: Carlin, Doug. 2023. "US Median Household Income by State (Report 2023)." https://usabynumbers.com/

Note: The term "median household income" or "median income" refers to the average yearly wage of all adults living in a given household, regardless of their relationship to each other.

residents in blue states make $5,000 more in personal income per capita than the residents of red states.

Median Household Income

Another way to compare the income is to look at the median household income in red and blue states. Table 2.17 provides this information.

When we compare the median household income of residents in red and blue states, the difference between the two becomes even more glaring. Of the top ten states, eight are blue states while only two are red states. The blue states include Maryland, New Jersey, Washington, Massachusetts, Hawaii, California, Connecticut, and New York. The two red states are Utah and Alaska. The bottom ten states with the smallest median household income include nine red states – Tennessee, South Carolina, Oklahoma, Kentucky, Alabama, Arkansas, Louisiana, West Virginia, and Mississippi – and one blue state – New Mexico. The average median household income of blue states is almost $15,000 higher than that of the red states.

Unemployment

Another indicator of the state's economy is the unemployment rate. Table 2.18 provides unemployment rates in the red and blue states.

The red states enjoy a clear advantage over the blue states when it comes to the unemployment rate. Of the top ten states with the lowest unemployment rates, nine are red states – Utah, North Dakota, South Dakota, Nebraska, Alabama, Missouri, Montana, Idaho, and Georgia. The only blue state among the top ten is Vermont. The top ten states with the highest unemployment rates include the blue states of Illinois, Oregon, Delaware, Michigan, New York, Connecticut, Washington, and California and two red states of Alaska and West Virginia.

One of the major reasons why red states have performed better than red states in recent years is the impact of the COVID-19 pandemic. Republican-led red states recovered faster economically than the Democratic-led blue states because blue states were more aggressive in fighting the pandemic by imposing stricter social distancing, leading to closing public schools, restaurants, and the like than their Republican counterparts. Thus, the blue states paid an economic price for putting public health ahead of the economy. Also, during the pandemic, workers and employers moved from the coasts to the middle of the country and states like Texas and Florida due to lower taxes and cost of living. Remote work also made it possible for workers to move to red states for financial reasons such as cheaper housing and better weather (Mitchell 2022; Csiszar 2022; Weissmann 2020; Krishan 2020).

Poverty

Table 2.19 compares the estimated poverty rate, i.e., the share of the population that lives below the poverty line and the median household income for the red and blue states. Poverty can occur due to several factors such as unemployment, inability to own property, limited access to education that

TABLE 2.18 Unemployment Rate Seasonally Adjusted by State (December 2022)

Red States	Percent Unemployed	Ranking	Blue States	Percent Unemployed	Ranking
Alaska	4.3	44	Illinois	4.7	49
West Virginia	4.1	39	Oregon	4.5	48
Arizona	4.0	35	Delaware	4.4	47
Kentucky	4.0	35	Michigan	4.3	44
Mississippi	4.0	35	New York	4.3	44
North Carolina	3.9	31	Connecticut	4.2	41
Texas	3.9	31	Washington	4.2	41
Wyoming	3.7	29	California	4.1	39
Arkansas	3.6	28	Maryland	4.0	35
Louisiana	3.5	25	Pennsylvania	3.9	31
Tennessee	3.5	25	Maine	3.8	30
Oklahoma	3.4	23	New Mexico	3.8	31
South Carolina	3.3	20	Rhode Island	3.5	25
Indiana	3.1	16	New Jersey	3.4	23
Georgia	3.0	14	Massachusetts	3.3	20
Idaho	2.9	12	Hawaii	3.2	18
Kansas	2.9	12	Vermont	2.6	6
Alabama	2.8	9			
Missouri	2.8	9			
Montana	2.8	9			
Nebraska	2.6	6			
North Dakota	2.3	2			
South Dakota	2.3	2			
Utah	2.2	1			
Average	3.3	21		3.9	34

Adapted from: Bureau of Labor Statistics. 2023. "Unemployment Rate by States, Seasonally Adjusted." https://www.bls.gov/

Note: Rates shown are a percentage of the labor force. Purple states are excluded.

limits job opportunities, and systemic discrimination in hiring due to race, gender, and disability, among others.

As can be observed from the data, red states in general have some of the worst poverty rates while the blue states have much lower poverty rates. Among the top ten states with the highest poverty rates, eight are red states of Mississippi, Louisiana, West Virginia, Arkansas, Kentucky, Alabama,

TABLE 2.19 Poverty Rate and Median Household Income by State (2022)

Red States	Percent Poverty All Ages	Median Household Income	Blue States	Percent Poverty All Ages	Median Household Income
Mississippi	19.2%	$52,788	New Mexico	17.3%	$59,842
Louisiana	18.6%	$55,458	New York	14.2%	$79,463
West Virginia	17.4%	$54,097	Michigan	13.3%	$66,926
Arkansas	16.3%	$55,505	California	12.2%	$91,517
Kentucky	16.3%	$59,246	Oregon	12.0%	$75,638
Alabama	16.2%	$59,703	Illinois	11.9%	$76,744
Oklahoma	15.6%	$59,632	Pennsylvania	11.8%	$71,789
South Carolina	14.0%	$64,227	Rhode Island	11.2%	$80,873
Texas	14.0%	$72,279	Maine	10.9%	$69,485
Tennessee	13.3%	$65,231	Massachusetts	10.4%	$94,538
Missouri	13.1%	$64,783	Vermont	10.2%	$74,555
Georgia	12.9%	$72,742	Delaware	10.0%	$81,933
North Carolina	12.8%	$67,516	Hawaii	10.0%	$93,683
Arizona	12.5%	$74,355	Washington	10.0%	$91,255
Indiana	12.5%	$66,768	Connecticut	9.8%	$88,182
South Dakota	12.4%	$70,597	Maryland	9.8%	$94,957
Kansas	11.9%	$68,827	New Jersey	9.7%	$96,341
Montana	11.8%	$67,915			
North Dakota	11.2%	$73,240			
Wyoming	11.2%	$71,275			
Nebraska	11.1%	$69,828			
Alaska	10.8%	$88,072			
Idaho	10.5%	$72,634			
Utah	8.3%	$88,531			
Average	13.5%	$67,302		11.5%	$81,630
National	12.6%	$74,755			

Adapted from: "SAIPE State and County Estimates for 2022." December 2023. https://www.census.gov/data/datasets/2022/demo/saipe/2022-state-and-county.html

Oklahoma, and South Carolina and two blue states of New Mexico and New York. Among the top ten states with the lowest poverty rates, eight are the blue states of New Jersey, Maryland, Connecticut, Washington, Hawaii, Delaware, Vermont, and Massachusetts and two red states of Utah and Idaho. The average poverty rate for blue states is 11.5 percent compared to 13.5 percent for red states. Similarly, the median household income in blue states is much higher than in the red states. The median household income in nine blue states is over $80,000 compared to only two red states of Utah and Alaska.

TABLE 2.20 Tax Rate and Ranking by State (2022)

Red States	Percent Tax Rate[a]	Rank[b]	Blue States	Percent Tax Rate[a]	Rank[b]
Alaska	5.8	1	Delaware	6.3	2
Montana	7.1	3	California	9.0	11
Wyoming	8.1	4	Oregon	9.0	12
Utah	8.3	7	New Mexico	10.5	19
Idaho	8.4	8	Hawaii	10.7	23
Tennessee	8.7	10	Massachusetts	10.9	25
South Carolina	9.1	13	Maryland	11.5	31
Alabama	9.1	14	Vermont	11.6	32
Arizona	9.5	15	Maine	11.8	33
West Virginia	9.7	16	Washington	12.0	36
North Dakota	10.0	17	Michigan	12.2	37
Georgia	10.6	20	Rhode Island	12.7	39
North Carolina	10.6	21	New Jersey	12.8	41
Louisiana	10.6	22	Pennsylvania	14.0	47
South Dakota	11.2	26	New York	14.1	48
Missouri	11.3	27	Connecticut	14.9	49
Arkansas	11.3	29	Illinois	15.0	50
Oklahoma	11.4	30			
Indiana	11.8	34			
Mississippi	12.0	35			
Kentucky	12.5	38			
Texas	12.8	40			
Nebraska	13.3	45			
Kansas	13.4	46			
Average	10.3	22		11.7	31

Adapted from: Kiernan, John. S. 2022a. "States with the Highest and the Lowest Tax Rate". https://wallethub.com/

Notes:

[a] Effective total state and local tax rates on median U.S. households taking into account real estate, vehicle property, income, and sale/excise taxes.
[b] Number 1 ranking means the lowest tax rate and 50 ranking means the highest tax rate.

Taxes

Next, in Table 2.20, we examine the effective state and local tax rates on median households that consider real estate, vehicle, property, income, and sales/excise taxes.

Alaska has the lowest tax rate while Illinois has the highest tax rate. In general, blue states have a much higher tax rate than the red states, The top five states with the highest tax rates include the blue states of Illinois, Connecticut, New York, and Pennsylvania and one red state of Kansas. Among the top five states with the lowest tax rates are four red states – Alaska, Montana, Wyoming, and Utah – and one red state – Delaware. Red states average around 10.3 percent tax rate compared to 11.7 percent for blue states.

Cost of Living

Another indicator of the economy is the cos of living index. The cost of living index is designed to compare the cost of basic expenses in different states. The cost of living index includes expenses such as food, shelter, transportation, energy, clothing, healthcare, and childcare. It also allows us to track how much the costs of basic expenses rise over a period. The costs of consumer goods and services vary between different states. Another way to interpret what a cost-of-living index represents is to think of it in terms of consumers' purchasing power. How many goods and services a given sum of the money, let's say $100, could buy in a given location? The cost of living can impact a person's choice of work and needed salary as well as where to live. Table 2.21 compares red and blue states' cost of living index. The average cost of living in the United States is used as the baseline set at 100 and states are measured against the baseline.

It is clear from the data presented in the table that red states in general have a much lower cost of living index compared to the blue states. The top ten states with the lowest cost of living index are all red. Conversely, the top ten states with the highest cost of living index, except for Alaska, are blue states. The average cost of living index of red states is 94.5 compared to 121 for blue states. It is certainly more expensive to live in blue states than in red states. However, it should be noted that, as we discussed earlier, the per capita income in blue states tends to be much higher in blue states compared to the red states.

A recent analysis by the Council for Community and Economic Research (2024) found similar results. According to this research of the ten least expensive states to live in, nine were red states -- Mississippi, Oklahoma, Kansas, Alabama, Georgia, Missouri, Indiana, West Virginia, and Tennessee – and one purple state – Iowa. In contrast, of the ten most expensive states to live in, eight were blue states – Hawaii, Massachusetts, California, New York, Maryland, Oregon, New Jersey, and Maine plus the District of Columbia. The only red state in the top ten most expensive states to live in was Alaska. However, according to another analysis, some of the richest states are blue states while some of the poorest states are red states (Ciotti 2023).

TABLE 2.21 Cost of Living Index by States (2022)

Red States	Index	Ranking	Blue States	Index	Ranking
Mississippi	83.3	1	New Mexico	91.0	12
Kansas	86.5	2	Michigan	91.3	13
Alabama	87.9	3	Illinois	94.3	20
Oklahoma	87.9	3	Pennsylvania	102.5	32
Georgia	88.8	5	Delaware	107.9	36
Tennessee	89.0	6	Washington	111.8	38
Missouri	89.8	7	Maine	115.0	39
West Virginia	90.5	9	New Jersey	115.2	40
Indiana	90.6	10	Vermont	117.0	41
Arkansas	90.9	11	Rhode Island	117.2	42
Texas	92.1	15	Connecticut	121.6	43
Louisiana	93.0	16	Maryland	124.0	44
Kentucky	93.1	17	Oregon	130.1	46
South Carolina	93.6	18	Massachusetts	135.0	47
Nebraska	93.7	19	California	142.2	48
Wyoming	94.3	20	New York	148.2	49
North Carolina	95.7	22	Hawaii	193.3	50
North Dakota	96.2	24			
Utah	99.0	25			
Montana	100.7	28			
South Dakota	101.0	29			
Idaho	102.1	31			
Arizona	103.2	33			
Alaska	127.1	45			
Average	94.5	17		121.0	38

Adapted from: "Cost of Living Index by State 2022." 2022. https://worldpopulationreview.com/

Note: The average cost of living in the United States is used as the baseline set at 100. States are measured against this baseline.

Productivity

Gross domestic product (GDP) tells us something about the economic health of a state. It represents the value of all goods and services produced over a specific time within a state's borders. Changes in GDP are most frequently used to measure overall economic health. Table 2.22 compares the GDP of the red and blue states and how states rank overall. The figures shown are in millions of dollars and not adjusted for inflation.

Overall, the blue states are more productive compared to the red states. Of the ten top-ranked states with the highest GDP, seven are blue states

TABLE 2.22 Constant Dollar Gross Domestic Product (2023)

Red States	Current Dollar GDP (Million $)	Overall Ranking	Blue States	Current Dollar GDP (Million $)	Overall Ranking
Texas	$25,63,508	2	California	$38,62,171	1
Georgia	$8,05,397	6	New York	$21,52,262	3
North Carolina	$7,66,919	9	Illinois	$10,82,968	4
Tennessee	$5,23,240	12	Pennsylvania	$9,65,067	5
Arizona	$5,08,244	14	Washington	$8,01,515	7
Indiana	$4,97,036	15	New Jersey	$7,99,305	8
Missouri	$4,22,396	16	Massachusetts	$7,33,860	10
South Carolina	$3,22,259	18	Michigan	$6,58,992	11
Louisiana	$3,09,601	20	Maryland	$5,12,289	13
Alabama	$3,00,152	21	Connecticut	$3,40,181	17
Kentucky	$2,77,747	22	Oregon	$3,16,461	19
Utah	$2,72,586	23	New Mexico	$1,30,202	29
Oklahoma	$2,54,134	24	Hawaii	$1,08,023	31
Kansas	$2,26,012	25	Delaware	$93,595	33
Nebraska	$1,78,421	26	Maine	$91,081	34
Arkansas	$1,76,240	27	Rhode Island	$77,322	35
Mississippi	$1,48,401	28	Vermont	$43,130	41
Idaho	$1,18,791	40			
West Virginia	$99,511	32			
North Dakota	$74,113	36			
South Dakota	$72,421	37			
Montana	$70,560	38			
Alaska	$67,337	39			
Wyoming	$50,172	40			
Totals	$91,05,198			$1,27,68,424	
Average	$3,79,383	24		$7,51,083	18

Adapted from: Bureau of Economic Analysis. 2024. "Level and Percent Change from Preceding Period." https://www.bea.gov/data/gdp/gdp-state/

and four are red states. Blue states include states of California, New York, Illinois, Pennsylvania, Washington, New Jersey, and Massachusetts. The three red states are Texas, Georgia, and North Carolina. Among the blue states, California has the highest GDP. Among the red states, Texas has the highest GDP.

Among the top ten states with the lowest GDP, six are red states and four are blue states. The state with the lowest GDP among the blue states is Vermont while among the red states is Wyoming. Overall, the average GDP of red states is $349,177 compared to blue states' average of $697,107 which indicates that, in general, blue states have higher GDPs and healthier economies.

Dependence on Federal Government

The federal government provides a great deal of financial assistance to the state and local governments via federal grants to help finance programs that the federal government views as critical (e.g., healthcare, education, crime) to achieve federal policy goals. This is often called an intergovernmental transfer of funds. This has become an important source of revenue for state governments. Since most federal grants are distributed to states based on a formula that considers factors such as population count, demographics, and economic characteristics such as per capita income, poverty, housing, and the like, poorer states tend to receive more federal grant money. Another way to think of federal grants and intergovernmental transfers of funds is to look at which states are financially more dependent on the federal government for federal funds.

In 2022, the federal government's total spending amounted to 6.48 trillion dollars. Of the total spending, 1.21 trillion dollars involved the transfer of federal funds to states in the form of grants and contracts. This amounted to almost 19 percent of the total federal spending. State-levied taxes make up most of each state's revenue and budget, but a significant portion of the state's revenue also comes from the federal government in the form of federal grants. In FY 2017, 22.9 percent of state revenues came from the federal government. This had increased to 33 percent in FY 2022 partly due to added federal assistance provided to states to deal with the COVID-19 pandemic ("How Much Does the Government Spend and Where Does the Money Go?" 2023; Cammenga 2020).

Table 2.23 ranks the overall level of dependency on the federal government by the red and blue states. The total dependency score is based on a 100-point scale where 100 represents the highest level of dependency and a lower score represents lower dependency. The ranking is based on a scale of 1 to 50 where #1 represents the highest dependency and 50 represents the least dependency.

A clear picture emerges from the data in the table. Of the top ten states most dependent on the federal government, nine are red states, and one is the blue state of New Mexico. In fact, among the top 20 states most dependent on the federal government, 16 are red states and 4 are blue states.

TABLE 2.23 Level of Dependence on the Federal Government by State (2020–2021)

Red States	Total Score[a]	Overall Rank[b]	Blue States	Total Score	Overall Rank[b]
Alaska	93.2	1			
Mississippi	84.9	2	New Mexico	75.1	6
Kentucky	79.5	3	Maine	57.5	13
West Virginia	78.1	4	Pennsylvania	47.2	16
Montana	75.9	5	Vermont	45.7	18
Arizona	69.9	7	Maryland	41.7	21
Louisiana	69.5	8	Michigan	41.5	22
Indiana	68.2	9	Oregon	39.3	25
Alabama	66.9	10	Hawaii	38.0	26
South Carolina	62.9	11	New York	37.7	27
Wyoming	60.4	12	Rhode Island	36.5	30
Tennessee	52.7	14	Connecticut	35.9	31
Missouri	47.4	15	California	26.9	41
Oklahoma	46.4	17	Massachusetts	21.2	43
South Dakota	45.7	19	Illinois	20.6	45
Idaho	44.5	20	Washington	19.9	46
North Dakota	41.3	23	New Jersey	13.2	49
Arkansas	40.2	24	Delaware	12.3	50
Georgia	37.6	28			
North Carolina	36.9	29			
Texas	33.7	37			
Nebraska	28.2	40			
Utah	15.5	47			
Kansas	13.5	48			
Average	53.8	18		35.9	30

Adapted from: Kiernan, John S. 2022b. "Most and Least Federally Dependent States." https://wallethub.com/

Notes:

[a] Total score is based on a 100-point scale with a score of 100 representing the highest level of federal dependency.

[b] States' ranking ranges from 1 to 50 where #1 ranking represents highest and 50 represents the lowest level of federal dependency.

Among the ten states least dependent on the federal government, six are blue states and four are red states. Blue states are much less dependent while the red states are heavily dependent on the federal government. Other studies have found similar results (Manzanetti 2021).

Ironically, the Republican-led red states which are recipients of the most federal dollars are often the same ones who complain and criticize the

TABLE 2.24 Ranking of States' Economy (2024)

Red States	Total Score	Blue States	Total Score
Utah	62.00	Washington	71.10
Texas	60.08	Massachusetts	61.52
North Carolina	55.08	California	59.63
Arizona	53.69	Maryland	52.92
Idaho	52.46	Michigan	46.52
Georgia	50.24	Oregon	45.39
Tennessee	49.20	New Mexico	45.10
North Dakota	47.62	Delaware	45.05
Nebraska	46.52	New Jersey	44.29
Kansas	46.21	New York	44.06
Wyoming	45.62	Vermont	43.33
South Carolina	45.25	Connecticut	42.74
Montana	43.96	Pennsylvania	42.43
Oklahoma	42.73	Illinois	38.50
Alabama	42.70	Maine	36.26
Missouri	41.16	Rhode Island	35.32
Alaska	40.29	Hawaii	29.79
Indiana	39.07		
South Dakota	36.41		
Kentucky	35.18		
Louisiana	32.60		
Arkansas	31.77		
West Virginia	31.13		
Mississippi	26.67		
Average	44.08		46.05

Adapted from: McCann, Adam. 2024. "Best and the Worst State Economies in 2024." https://wallethub.com

Note: Total score is based on three factors: economic activity, economic health, and innovation potential utilizing 28 key indicators.

federal government the most. Contrary to Republican contention, red states are often the "takers" and blue states are the "givers."

Overall Economy and Fiscal Stability

Table 2.24 provides a ranking of states based on their economy as measured by *wallethub.com* in 2024. Ranking on the economy is based on three major factors – economic activity, economic health, and innovation potential – using 28 key indicators.

Some of the top ten states with the highest scores on their economy are the six red states of Utah, Texas, North Carolina, Arizona, Idaho, and

Georgia and the four blue states of Washington, Massachusetts, California, and Maryland. The bottom ten states with the lowest score on the economy include six red states – South Dakota, Kentucky, Louisiana, Arkansas, West Virginia, and Mississippi – and four blue states of Illinois, Maine, Rhode Island, and Hawaii. The combined average score of blue states is 46 compared to 44 for red states. These data should be examined in the context of the COVID-19 pandemic (2019–2023) since red and blue states were impacted differently because blue states imposed more mandatory restrictions than red states, which affected their economies differently.

In summary, the blue states are wealthier, have higher per capita and median household incomes, less poverty, are more productive, and have higher tax rates while the red states have lower unemployment, lower tax rates, and lower cost of living, but are less productive and more dependent on federal financial assistance. Voters in the red and blue states do indeed live in two different economies.

Politics

The political environment of a state consists of several elements. One, which party controls the levers of government such as the governorships and legislatures because it impacts the adoption and implementation of the party's policy agenda. It also can impact the composition of the state's judiciary and especially the state's Supreme Court. Second, does the composition of political institutions such as state legislatures and the Supreme Court reflect the population at large? Political institutions that are more reflective of the population at large are more likely to be responsive to the needs of their varied constituents. Third, ease or difficulty voters face in registering to vote and exercising their right to vote. This can influence the overall voter turnout. Fourth, which party controls the levers of government can influence the conservative, moderate, or liberal direction of the states' policies. The red and blue states differ considerably when it comes to state politics.

Partisan Composition of State Legislatures

As we discussed in Chapter 1, based on long-term voting patterns, we classified 50 American states into 24 red states, 17 blue states, and 9 purple states. However, short-term fluctuations are often inevitable as voters' moods change resulting in a different voting pattern. For example, two traditionally red states – Arizona and Georgia – voted for Biden for president in 2020 and both states in recent years have elected Democrats for the

U.S. Senate. Whether, over the long run, these two states change from red to blue remains to be seen.

There are 1,973 state senators and 5,413 state House representatives made up of 50 state legislatures. This amounts to a total of 7,386 state legislators. Nebraska is the only state that has a unicameral legislature while the other 49 states have a bicameral legislature. As of January 30, 2023 (excluding vacant seats and legislators with no or other party affiliations), of the total of 7,386 state legislators, Republicans controlled 55 percent while Democrats controlled 44 percent of all state legislative seats ("Partisan Composition of State Legislatures" 2023; "State Partisan Composition" 2022).

As of February 16, 2023, Republicans enjoyed trifecta control in 22 states while Democrats enjoyed trifecta control in 17 states, and 11 states had a divvied government. As a result of the 2022 elections, the trifecta status changed in six states. Four states – Maryland, Massachusetts, Michigan, and Minnesota – changed from divided government to a Democratic trifecta. In Nevada, the Democratic trifecta became divided government, while in Arizona, the Republican trifecta became divided government ("Election Results, 2022: State Government Trifectas 2022"). Trifecta describes a condition in which one political party holds the position of governorship and enjoys majorities in both houses of state legislatures. When a political party enjoys trifecta control of the government, it is much easier for the party in control to adopt and implement its policy agenda. Eleven states had divided government where neither party holds trifecta control; i.e., one party controls the governorship while the other party controls one or both chambers of the legislature. Divided government makes policy adoption and implementation more problematic due to inherent conflict that arises over two parties' different agendas and priorities ("Partisan Composition of State Legislatures" 2023; "State Partisan Composition" 2022).

Gender and Racial/Ethnic Composition of State Legislatures

Next, we examine the makeup of individual state legislatures and the Supreme Court to see how representative they are of women and the nonwhite population at large. Table 2.25 provides a breakdown of individual state legislatures by gender.

As can be observed from the table, among all 24 red and 17 blue states, there are only four states – Wyoming, North Dakota, South Dakota, and Montana – in which women constitute less than 50 percent of the population. Both the red and blue states on average have a 51 percent female population. Overall, in all red and blue states, women are

TABLE 2.25 Share of Women in Population (2021) and State Legislatures by State (2022)

Red States	Women in Population	Women in Legislature	Difference	Blue States	Women in Population	Women in Legislature	Difference
West Virginia	51%	12%	-39%	Pennsylvania	51%	31%	-20%
Tennessee	51%	14%	-37%	Massachusetts	51%	32%	-19%
South Carolina	52%	15%	-37%	New York	51%	34%	-17%
Mississippi	52%	15%	-37%	New Jersey	51%	35%	-16%
Alabama	51%	17%	-34%	Hawaii	51%	36%	-15%
Louisiana	52%	19%	-33%	Connecticut	51%	37%	-14%
Oklahoma	51%	20%	-31%	Delaware	52%	39%	-13%
Arkansas	51%	23%	-28%	Michigan	51%	41%	-10%
Wyoming	49%	22%	-27%	Illinois	51%	41%	-10%
North Dakota	49%	25%	-24%	Maryland	52%	42%	-10%
Utah	50%	26%	-24%	California	50%	42%	-8%
Indiana	51%	27%	-24%	Oregon	50%	42%	-8%
North Carolina	52%	29%	-23%	Maine	51%	44%	-7%
Missouri	51%	29%	-22%	Rhode Island	51%	44%	-7%
Kentucky	51%	29%	-22%	New Mexico	51%	45%	-6%
Texas	51%	30%	-21%	Vermont	50%	45%	-5%
Kansas	51%	30%	-21%	Washington	50%	46%	-4%
South Dakota	49%	29%	-20%				
Idaho	50%	31%	-19%				
Alaska	52%	33%	-19%				
Montana	49%	32%	-17%				
Georgia	52%	35%	-17%				
Nebraska	50%	37%	-13%				
Arizona	51%	48%	-3%				
Average	51%	26%	-25%	Average	51%	40%	-11%

Adapted from: "U.S. Share of Women in State Legislatures 2022 by State." 2023. https://www.statista.com/ and "Population Distribution by Sex." 2021. https://www.kff.org/

underrepresented in state legislatures compared to their numbers in the population. However, significant differences emerge between red and blue states for the underrepresentation of women in the state legislatures. Of the 24 red states, women are underrepresented in 18 state legislatures by a margin ranging from 20 to 39 percent. Among blue states, there is only one state – Pennsylvania – where women are underrepresented by a margin of 20 percent. On the other side of the coin, there are 11 states where women are underrepresented by less than 10 percent, and only one of them – Arizona – is a red state. On overall averages, women hold 40 percent of seats in blue state legislatures compared to 26 percent in red states. Thus, women are underrepresented by a margin of 25 percent in red states compared to 11 percent in blue states.

Table 2.26 presents data related to the share of the non-white population compared to the share of non-white persons in state legislatures broken down by state to see if there are any major differences between the red and blue states when it comes to the representation of non-whites.

Again, like women, non-whites are underrepresented in state legislatures compared to their population in both the red and blue states. Overall, blue states have a larger non-white population and a larger percentage of non-whites in state legislatures. Blue states combined have an average of 37 percent non-white population and 23 percent non-whites in state legislatures. Red states have an average of 28 average non-white populations and 14 percent non-whites in state legislatures. However, of the 11 states with a 10 percent or less difference between non-white population and non-whites in state legislatures, seven are red states and four are blue states. On overall average, non-whites are underrepresented in both red and blue states by a margin of 14 percent.

Over the several hundred years of history of state legislatures, women and racial/ethnic minorities have been excluded and underrepresented. Since the 1970s, the number of women of color elected to state legislatures has increased more rapidly than men of color or white women (Reingold 2019). To be sure both women and minorities have made gains in representation in state legislatures. In 2012, there were 23.7 percent women in state legislatures and by 2021 their share of seats in state legislatures has increased to 30.6 percent. After the additional gains they made in the 2022 elections, they will make up around 32.3 percent of the state legislatures (Greenblat 2022; Smith 2021a; Povich 2021).

Since 2015, 25 states have seen an increase in the percentage of black lawmakers, though they continue to be underrepresented. Similarly, two of the largest immigrant groups in America – Asian Americans and Latinos – are heavily underrepresented in state legislatures. Racial minorities have made some gains in state legislatures but their gains have been smaller than

TABLE 2.26 Share of Non-White Representatives in State Legislatures by State (2020)

Red States	% Non-White Population	% in State Legislature	% Difference	Blue States	% Non-White Population	% in State Legislature	% Difference
Oklahoma	34	7	-27	Delaware	38	14	-24
Alaska	39	13	-26	Oregon	24	1	-23
Texas	58	36	-22	New Mexico	63	42	-21
Georgia	47	29	-18	Washington	31	11	-20
Nebraska	21	4	-17	California	63	46	-17
Arkansas	28	12	-16	New Jersey	45	28	-17
Utah	22	6	-16	Connecticut	33	17	-16
Louisiana	41	26	-15	Michigan	25	19	-16
Kansas	24	9	-15	Rhode Island	28	13	-15
Idaho	18	3	-15	Massachusetts	28	14	-14
North Dakota	16	1	-15	Pennsylvania	24	10	-14
Mississippi	43	29	-14	New York	44	32	-12
North Carolina	37	23	-14	Maryland	49	38	-11
South Dakota	18	5	-13	Illinois	39	29	-10
Wyoming	16	4	-12	Hawaii	78	71	-7
Alabama	34	23	-11	Maine	7	3	-4
Indiana	21	10	-11	Vermont	7	3	-4
South Carolina	36	26	-10				
Tennessee	26	16	-10				
Missouri	21	13	-8				
Arizona	45	38	-7				
Kentucky	15	7	-7				
West Virginia	8	2	-6				
Montana	14	9	-5				
Average	28	14	-14		37	23	-14

Adapted from: Renuka Rayasam et al. 2020. "Why State Legislatures are still Very White -- and Very Male." https://www.politico.com/ and National Conference of State Legislatures. 2020. "State Legislature Demographics." https://ncsl.org/

Note: The 2020 data do not include legislators who were newly elected in 2020 and took office in 2021.

women. Even though the share of non-white Americans has grown, there is a striking lack of diversity in the state legislatures when it comes to persons of color (Rayasam et al. 2021; Smith 2021b; Smith 2020; Phillips 2016; Morrison 2016).

Gender and Racial/Ethnic Composition of States' Supreme Courts

The underrepresentation of non-whites in state legislatures is also reflected in their representation on the state supreme courts. In contrast, women fare much better when it comes to their representation on states' supreme courts. Table 2.27 provides data for the percentage of non-white and women on states' supreme court relative to their numbers in the population.

There is no significant difference between red and blue states when it comes to the representation of women on the state supreme courts. However, blue states perform slightly better than red states. Women justices are represented in higher numbers compared to the share of their population in the three red states of Wyoming, Tennessee, and Arkansas compared to the nine blue states of Washington, New Mexico, Hawaii, California, Maryland, Michigan, New York, Oregon, and Rhode Island.

Significant differences emerged between red and blue states when we compared the representation of non-white persons on the state supreme courts relative to their share in the states' population. In 2022, 15 out of 24 red states had zero non-white persons on their supreme court even though the share of the non-white population in these states ranged from 10 to 41 percent. The worst state was Alaska which has a non-white population of 41 percent but had no non-white person on its supreme court. In comparison, blue states performed much better. Among the blue states, states of Michigan and Pennsylvania had zero representation of non-white persons even though their share of the non-white population was 26 and 25 percent, respectively. States of California, New York, Washington, Massachusetts, Oregon, and Maine had a higher share of non-white persons on their Supreme Court relative to their number in the population.

Registration and Voter Turnout

Registration and voter turnout provide some indication of the level of citizens' participation in a democracy. However, rules and regulations governing registration and voting can impact voter turnout and citizens' right to vote. Restrictive laws can negatively impact registration and voter turnout and vice versa. For the election of U.S. Senators and Representatives, Article 1, Section 4, of the U.S. Constitution leaves it up to the states to

TABLE 2.27 State Supreme Court Diversity (2022)

Red States

	Percent Non-White Population	Percent Justices of Color	# of Justices	Percent Women Population	Percent Women Justices
Alabama	36	0	9	51	22
Alaska	41	0	5	52	40
Arizona	40	29	7	51	29
Arkansas	30	0	7	51	57
Georgia	48	22	9	52	44
Idaho	18	0	5	50	40
Indiana	23	0	5	51	20
Kansas	24	0	7	50	43
Kentucky	18	0	7	51	43
Louisiana	43	14	7	52	14
Mississippi	44	11	9	52	11
Missouri	23	29	7	51	43
Montana	15	0	7	49	43
Nebraska	22	0	7	50	29
North Carolina	38	29	7	52	43
North Dakota	17	0	5	49	20

Blue States

	Percent Non-White Population	Percent Justices of Color	# of Justices	Percent Women Population	Percent Women Justices
California	59	71	7	50	57
Connecticut	34	43	7	51	29
Delaware	40	20	5	52	40
Hawaii	77	40	5	51	80
Illinois	39	14	7	51	43
Maine	9	14	7	51	29
Maryland	51	43	7	52	57
Massachusetts	30	43	7	51	43
Michigan	26	0	7	51	57
New Jersey	45	29	7	51	29
New Mexico	49	40	5	51	80
New York	45	57	7	51	57
Oregon	25	29	7	50	57
Pennsylvania	25	0	7	51	43
Rhode Island	29	20	5	51	60
Vermont	10	20	5	50	40

						Washington	33	50	8	50	88
Oklahoma	36	21	14	51	21						
South Carolina	37	20	5	52	20						
South Dakota	19	0	5	49	40						
Tennessee	28	0	5	51	60						
Texas	50	17	18	51	39						
Utah	21	0	5	50	20						
West Virginia	10	0	5	51	40						
Wyoming	15	0	5	49	60						
Average	29	8	172	51	49		37	31	110	51	52

Adapted from: Powers, Amanda., and Alicia Bannon. 2022. "State Supreme Court Diversity – May 2022 Update." https://www.brennancenter.org/ and "Population Distribution by Sex." 2021. http://www.kff.org/

Note: Percentages may not add to 100 due to rounding.

determine the times, place, and the manner of holding elections. States also regulate rules governing elections for state and local offices. Thus, lacking any national standards, voters' experiences with registration and voting can vary from state to state. In essence, voting rights are impacted by what state voters live in. Table 2.28 provides a breakdown, by state, of the percentage of people who were registered to vote and who voted in the 2020 election. Due to the pandemic, most states before the 2020 elections had made it easier to vote by easing rules regarding absentee and mail-in-voting and expanding early voting, resulting in a record-breaking nationwide turnout for the presidential election. However, as can be observed from Table 2.28, both the registration and voter turnout varied considerably by state.

Among the red states, voter registration varied from a low of 62 percent in Arkansas to a high of 80.4 percent in Mississippi. Among the blue states, registration varied from a low of 68.6 percent in New Mexico to a high of 84.6 percent in New Jersey. Overall, voter registration was higher in blue states compared to the red states. A similar pattern emerges when we look at voter turnout. Voter turnout in red states ranged from a low of 54 percent in Arkansas to a high of 73.5 percent in Montana. Among the blue states, it ranged from a low of 62.6 percent in New Mexico to a high of 78.3 percent in New Jersey. Among blue states, in six states voter turnout was 70 percent or higher while the same was the case for only three red states. Overall average voter turnout among red states was 2.6 percent below the national average of 66.8 percent, while among the blue states, it was 1.8 percent higher than the national average.

In the 2020 presidential elections, more than 159 million people voted, the highest voter turnout in a century. Election officials in many states attributed the record turnout to relaxed voting rules adopted during the pandemic and advocated keeping the same rules for future elections. However, starting in 2021, some states maintained and further expanded rules making it easier for people to vote while other states began to retrench and adopt more restrictions on voting rights (Brennan Center for Justice 2021; Viebeck 2021a; Voting Rights Lab 2021; Boschma and Schouten 2021; Boschma 2021).

Overall, many blue states moved to expand voting rights while several red states passed restricting and making it more difficult for people to vote. The "big lie" propagated by Trump about the 2020 election being rigged and accepted by the Republican Party and Republican voters led many red states to pass laws limiting voting. However, it should be noted that not all red states adopted strictly restrictive laws. Some have adopted a mixed bag of restrictions and expansions. For example, Indiana placed new limits on drop boxes but expanded options for voter ID requirements and early

TABLE 2.28 Registration and Voter Turnout by State (2020)

Red States	Percent Registered[a]	Percent Voted[b]	Difference[c]	Blue States	Percent Registered[a]	Percent Voted[b]	Difference
Mississippi	80.4	70.3	-10.1	New Jersey	84.6	78.3	-6.3
Montana	77.5	73.5	-4.0	Oregon	79.9	74.1	-5.8
North Dakota	77.3	67.1	-10.2	Maryland	78.6	73.6	-5.0
Arizona	76.4	71.9	-4.5	Washington	78.4	71.5	-6.9
Kentucky	75.9	68.5	-7.4	Maine	77.4	71.3	-6.1
Missouri	75.7	66.8	-8.9	Pennsylvania	76.3	70.2	-6.1
Tennessee	74.3	66.4	-7.9	Delaware	75.1	67.7	-7.4
Alaska	74.2	63.8	-10.4	Illinois	74.4	68.4	-6.0
Texas	71.8	63.9	-7.9	Rhode Island	74.1	66.3	-7.8
Nebraska	70.9	65.2	-5.7	Michigan	73.8	66.9	-6.9
Kansas	70.8	65.7	-5.1	Connecticut	73.3	66.6	-6.7
Georgia	70.7	66.1	-4.6	Vermont	73.0	68.4	-4.6
South Carolina	70.0	63.4	-6.6	Massachusetts	72.4	66.3	-6.1
North Carolina	69.8	64.7	-5.1	New York	70.5	64.7	-5.8
Idaho	69.3	64.9	-4.4	California	69.4	65.1	-4.3
Indiana	69.3	61.0	-8.3	Hawaii	68.7	64.3	-4.4
Louisiana	69.3	61.9	-7.4	New Mexico	68.6	62.6	-6.0
Wyoming	69.3	65.5	-3.8				
Alabama	68.0	60.5	-7.5				

(Continued)

TABLE 2.28 (Continued)

Red States	Percent Registered[a]	Percent Voted[b]	Difference[c]	Blue States	Percent Registered[a]	Percent Voted[b]	Difference
South Dakota	67.4	58.5	-8.9				
Utah	67.4	63.5	-3.9				
Oklahoma	67.3	58.3	-9.0				
West Virginia	67.3	56.1	-11.2				
Arkansas	62.0	54.0	-8.0				
Average	71.3	64.2	-7.1		74.6	68.6	-6.0
US	72.7	66.8	-5.9				

Adapted from: "Voting and Registration by State." 2020. https://census.gov/

Notes:

[a] Percent of eligible voters who registered to vote in 2020 Federal Elections.
[b] Percent of eligible voters who voted in 2020 Presidential Elections.
[c] Difference between percent registered and percent voted.

voting opportunities. Louisiana extended the early voting period and removed some hurdles to registering people with felony convictions while providing new instructions for voter purges (Swasey 2021).

Blue states, states such as California, Connecticut, Delaware, Hawaii, Illinois, Maine, Maryland, New Jersey, New Mexico, New York, Oregon, and Vermont, have undertaken measures to expand voting rights ranging from making it easier to register, restoring voting rights to felons, expanding time and places for ballot drop-offs, early voting, mail voting, eliminating the requirement of "excuse" for mail voting, providing greater access to people with disabilities, establishing a process to "cure" signature errors on ballot envelopes, to improving language accessibility for ballots, among others.

Blue states have sought to bolster voter protections while red states have sought to weaken voter protections. The red states such as Arizona, Arkansas, Georgia, Kansas Montana, Texas, Wyoming, and others have passed laws designed to restrict access to voting by adopting measures such as curtailing ballot drop box usage, shortening the timeline for requesting absentee ballot, restricting third-party groups from mailing, or returning ballots to imposing tougher voter ID requirements, and imposing earlier registration deadline. Florida, where Republicans currently enjoy a trifecta control, has launched a full-frontal attack on voting rights. Thus, after the 2020 elections, red and blue states have moved in opposite directions on how millions of Americans can cast their ballots creating a widening difference in ballot access depending on where voters live creating a new fault line in American politics (Alexander 2023; Alas 2021; Swasey 2021; Viebeck 2021b; Voting Rights Lab 2021).

Ease or Difficulty of Voting

Lower or high voter turnout is not a result of an accident. Several factors such as income, education, the competitiveness of elections, and other factors influence voter turnout. Some of these factors are beyond policymakers' control. However, another major factor that impacts voter turnout is whether a state makes it easier or difficult for citizens to vote. This is a factor that state policymakers do control. Policymakers in some states make it difficult for their citizens to vote for political reasons (like gerrymandering) to disenfranchise or discourage certain socioeconomic or demographic groups from voting because these groups tend to vote for the "other" party. Thus, voting experience varies from state to state.

One of the analyses ranked states on ease or difficulty of voting based on four factors – early voting, voter ID requirements, registration requirements, and felon voting rights. The result of this analysis is shown in

TABLE 2.29 Most Difficult to Least Difficult Sates to Vote (2021)

Red States	Ranking	Blue States	Ranking
Mississippi	1	New Mexico	11
Alabama	2	Delaware	13
Georgia	3	Connecticut	23
Kansas	3	Michigan	23
Missouri	3	Pennsylvania	23
Tennessee	3	Rhode Island	23
Arkansas	9	Hawaii	31
Kentucky	9	Massachusetts	35
South Carolina	9	New Jersey	35
Arizona	13	New York	35
Idaho	13	California	41
Indiana	13	Maryland	41
Louisiana	13	Illinois	46
Montana	13	Maine	46
North Carolina	13	Oregon	46
South Dakota	13	Vermont	46
Texas	13	Washington	46
Utah	23		
West Virginia	23		
Nebraska	31		
Oklahoma	31		
Alaska	35		
North Dakota	41		
Wyoming	41		
Average	15		33

Adapted from: Morris, Kathy. 2022. "The Most Difficult States to Vote (and the Least)." https://www.zippia.com

Note: Each state is ranked based on ease or difficulty of early voting, registration, voter id requirements, and felon voting rights.

Table 2.29. The ranking is from most difficult to least difficult state to vote. Many states ended up tied in their rankings. The ranking of purple states is not included in the table for our analysis.

Of the ten states that make it most difficult to vote, nine are red states – Mississippi, Alabama, Georgia, Kansas, Missouri, Tennessee, Arkansas, Kentucky, and South Carolina – and one blue state New Mexico. The top nine red states are in the South and the Midwest. Conversely, among the top nine states that make it easier to vote, seven are blue states – Washington, Vermont, Oregon, Maine, Illinois, Maryland, and California – and two red states – Wyoming and North Dakota. Red states of Alaska and blue states of New York, New Jersey, and Massachusetts were tied for the tenth spot (Morris 2022).

Another analysis examined 25 laws related to voting and assigned a score of 1 for a law that makes voting easier and/or more accessible and a 0 if such a law is absent. Thus, for example, a law that allows no-excuse absentee voting is assigned a score of 1 while a 0 score is assigned if an excuse is required. A state's score could range from 0 to 25. In this analysis, the score ranged from 5 to 18. The higher the score, the easier it was to vote in that state. According to the result, states with some of the highest scores, i.e., easiest to vote in, were blue states of California, Oregon, Hawaii, Illinois, Maryland, Washington, New Mexico, and Vermont while the ones with the lowest score, i.e., most difficult to vote, were Mississippi, South Carolina, Utah, Texas, Alabama, Tennessee, Louisiana, and blue states of Delaware, Michigan, New York, and Pennsylvania ("Voting Ease by State: October 1, 2020." 2020). Other analyses have produced more or less similar results (Schraufnagel, Pomante II, and Li 2022 and 2020; Rao, Salam, and Adolphe 2020; Shendruk 2019; Ingraham 2018).

Political Ideology

At the national level, the ideological pendulum in American politics has swung back and forth between liberal and conservative visions of American society. From the 1930s to 1980, from Roosevelt's New Deal to Kennedy's New Frontier to Johnson's Great Society programs reflected the Democratic Party-led liberal vision of American society. The election of Ronald Reagan in 1980 signaled the end of a liberal mandate that saw the government as a solver of problems and ushered in the ascendency of conservative ideology that viewed government as the problem. Since then, American politics has experienced a sustained conflict between liberalism and conservatism for dominance (Lassiter 2011; Fraser and Gerstle 1990). The ideological polarization is the result of the Democratic Party becoming more liberal while the Republican Party becoming more conservative. This has been the case with both the elites and the electorate. To be sure, the Democratic "left" and the Republican "right" are not monolithic but carry within themselves several ideological strains. The Pew Research Center (2021) has identified four ideological sub-groups within the Democratic Party consisting of the progressive left, the establishment liberals, Democratic mainstays (moderates), and the outsider left. The four ideological sub-groups in the Republican Party include the faith and flag Conservatives, committed conservatives, populist right, and ambivalent right. However, overall, the Liberal Democrats and

Conservative Republicans view issues of race and race relations, the role and size of the national government, economic policies, and views on foreign policy very differently (Miller and Sinclair 2022; Balz, Clement, and Guskin 2021; Noel 2016).

Elite, partisan, and ideological polarization is also reflected at the state level. America is divided along ideological lines between the Republican-led red and Democratic-led blue states and it is demonstrated in very different sets of public policies adopted by these states in areas such as economy, education, voting rights, reproductive rights, immigration, and healthcare. The red states are moving social policy sharply to the right while the blue states are moving in the opposite direction. Red state policies are advancing conservative cultural priorities to satisfy one of its strongest electoral support groups made up of predominantly white evangelical Christians. Red states have been at the forefront of rolling back the "rights" revolution, restricting abortion rights, opposing immigration, and restricting discussion of race, gender, and sexual orientation issues in public education (Brownstein 2022c).

The Center for Legislative Accountability (CLA), an initiative of the Conservative Political Action Conference (CPAC), provides a conservative Congressional scorecard and a state rating program that ranks states across different policy areas. It annually reviews thousands of pieces of legislation passed by state legislatures over 186 policy issue areas from which it selects a sample of several thousand top roll-call votes to evaluate each member on a score of zero to 100 where a score of 100 represents a voting record that is perfectly aligned with conservative principles. The score for each state legislative chamber is based on the average score of all lawmakers within each chamber. A legislature's overall score is calculated by averaging each state's two legislative chambers' scores together ("About the Center for Legislative Accountability" 2023). Table 2.30 provides its rating of states' conservative policies in which a higher score represents more conservative policies.

The top ten states with the highest rating on conservative policies include the red states of Alabama, Indiana, Tennessee, South Dakota, Arkansas, Idaho, Wyoming, West Virginia, Kentucky, and Mississippi. In contrast, the top ten states with the least conservative policies are the blue states of Massachusetts, Hawaii, Rhode Island, California, Vermont, New York, Maryland, New Jersey, Connecticut, and Oregon. In fact, of the 24 red states, only one, Alaska, received a score of less than 50. Among the blue states, only two states – Pennsylvania and Michigan – received a score higher than 50. The rating and ranking of states on conservative policies provide a clear picture of the ideological polarization of state legislatures in red versus blue states.

TABLE 2.30 Rating of States on Conservative Policies (2021)

Red States	Overall Score	Overall Ranking	Blue States	Overall Score	Overall Ranking
Alabama	74	1	Michigan	58	25
Indiana	73	3	Pennsylvania	54	28
Tennessee	73	2	Maine	40	34
South Dakota	72	4	Washington	39	35
Arkansas	71	5	Illinois	37	36
Idaho	70	7	Delaware	36	38
Wyoming	70	8	New Mexico	36	37
West Virginia	69	10	Oregon	32	41
Kentucky	68	14	Connecticut	30	42
Mississippi	68	13	New Jersey	27	43
Oklahoma	68	11	Maryland	26	46
North Carolina	66	15	New York	26	44
Georgia	65	16	Vermont	26	44
North Dakota	65	17	California	24	47
Kansas	64	18	Rhode Island	20	48
Utah	64	19	Hawaii	19	49
Nebraska	61	22	Massachusetts	15	50
Louisiana	61	20			
Missouri	61	21			
Montana	59	24			
Texas	58	26			
South Carolina	54	27			
Arizona	53	29			
Alaska	46	31			
Average	62	15		32	40
U.S. Congress	42				

Adapted from: Center for Legislative Accountability. 2021. "State Ranking of Conservative Policies." 2021. http://ratings.conervative.org/

Notes:

Rating scale is based on scores where higher score represents more conservative policies. Nebraska has a unicameral legislature.

Religion and Cultural Wars

Socialization is a process through which individuals acquire and inculcate certain values and beliefs. These values and beliefs, in turn, can influence political views and beliefs. Political socialization is a process through which individuals learn and acquire political values and beliefs which, in turn, can influence individuals' positions on a variety of public policy questions. Many institutions act as agents of socialization. These include institutions such as family, schools, peers, work associates, and religious institutions such as a church. Socialization is a lifelong process in which different societal institutions can exercise varying degrees of influence at different stages in one's life. For example, research has demonstrated the important role a family plays in creating and establishing one's partisan identity. Children at a young age tend to take on the same party identification as their parents (Lyons 2017).

Similarly, individuals' religious affiliation and church attendance can shape not only their religious beliefs but also their political orientation. For example, research shows that more religious people tend to vote Republican while less religious people tend to vote Democratic. Similarly, protestants are more likely to be Republicans while Catholics and Jews are more likely to be Democrats. The alignment of more religious voters (especially white evangelical protestants) with the Republican Party perhaps is a function of the fact that the Republican Party has shifted toward a conservative position on many social issues over the last several decades. At the same time, beginning in the 1980s with the Regan presidency, religious elites saw an opportunity to expand their influence by entering politics and mobilizing their followers. Thus, a mutually beneficial alliance was forged. The meteoric rise of what came to be known as the "Christian Right" started around the mid-1990s (coincided with the beginning of political polarization) and rose to prominence in the Republican Party. It became a social movement that mobilized evangelical protestants and other orthodox Christians into conservative political actions on a variety of social issues such as abortion, gay rights, and prayers in schools. The movement preached "family values" and "religious freedom" agenda and organized itself through the "Tea Party" to take over the Republican Party from "within" (Djupe, Neiheisel, and Conger 2018).

There is little doubt today that religion matters in American political life. It has come to matter so much in politics that religion can be considered political tribalism. In recent years, the discussion in American politics has focused on what can be called the "God Gap," referring to the tendency of "religious" Americans to vote Republican and non-religious to vote Democratic. In other words, religion has become an expression of political tribalism with churchgoers in the Republican column and secular Americans solidly in the Democratic column. However, it is important to note that while religion can be considered a form of political tribalism among many Americans, it does not include a wide swath of Americans (Campbell 2021).

According to the Public Religion Research Institute (PRRI), a non-profit, non-partisan organization, seven in ten Americans identify as Christian.

Religiously unaffiliated Americans, those who do not claim any specific religious affiliation, comprise about 17 percent of the population while those who identify themselves as atheist or agnostic comprise 3 percent each. The remaining 7 percent constitute non-Christian groups such as Jewish, Muslim, Buddhist, and Hindu. Over the last few decades, there has been a rise in the number of religiously unaffiliated Americans. Young Americans are more religiously diverse. While in both Republican and Democratic parties Christians constitute a majority, there is a big difference between white Christians and Christians of color. Two-thirds (68 percent) of Republicans identify themselves as white and Christian compared to 39 percent of Democrats ("The 2020 Census of American Religion" 2021).

However, there is considerable variation among states concerning religious affiliation and church attendance (religiosity). In this section, we explore the role religion has played in political polarization between the red and blue states. Table 2.31 provides a breakdown of religious affiliation by red and blue states. The data for the purple states are excluded from our analysis.

A few observations stand out. One, in all the red states and most blue states, Protestants constitute either a majority or the largest plurality. Only in five blue states – Connecticut, Rhode Island, New Jersey, Massachusetts, and New York – Catholics constitute the largest plurality. Second, in all the red states, protestants outnumber Catholics. Out of 24 red states, in 19 states, Protestants make up 50 percent or more of the population. In contrast, among the 17 blue states, only in the state of Maryland Protestants make up at least 50 percent of the population. Protestants-dominated states do tend to be more pro-Republican. Third, blue states have more religious diversity compared to red states and they tend to be more pro-Democratic. Fourth, in many red and blue states, people with no religious affiliation outnumber people with a Catholic affiliation.

As we mentioned earlier, evangelical protestants, especially white evangelical protestants, have been strongly aligned with the Republican Party and have helped push the Republican Party further to the ideological right often bordering on extremism. Table 2.32 provides a breakdown of white evangelical Protestants by state.

Again, the red states outnumber the blue states by a wide margin when it comes to the share of white evangelical protestants. Twenty of the 24 red states have more evangelical protestants than any of the blue states. The combined average of white evangelical protestants in red states is 27 percent compared to 11 percent for the blue states. Among the red states, the top ten states with a white evangelical protestant population making up 30 or more percent are all located in the South and the Midwest except for the state of Wyoming. They are also politically very conservative.

TABLE 2.31 Religious Affiliation by State (2021)

Red States	Percent Protestant	Percent Catholic	Percent None	Percent Other	Blue States	Percent Protestant	Percent Catholic	Percent None	Percent Other
Mississippi	81	7	10	2	Maryland	50	20	19	11
Alabama	77	7	11	5	Michigan	47	21	24	8
Arkansas	72	10	13	5	Delaware	46	21	25	8
Tennessee	72	6	16	6	Pennsylvania	45	28	19	8
South Carolina	67	13	16	4	Maine	43	26	28	3
Georgia	65	9	16	10	Hawaii	42	21	26	11
North Carolina	65	10	18	7	Illinois	42	29	22	7
Kentucky	63	12	19	6	New Mexico	40	27	21	12
West Virginia	63	9	21	7	Washington	39	16	33	12
Oklahoma	62	15	17	6	Vermont	37	19	32	12
South Dakota	60	20	18	12	Oregon	36	14	37	13
Indiana	57	16	21	6	California	32	29	27	12
Missouri	57	16	29	7	Connecticut	32	39	22	7
Louisiana	54	27	14	5	Rhode Island	30	44	21	5
North Dakota	54	21	16	9	New Jersey	27	38	18	17
Kansas	53	16	24	7	Massachusetts	25	37	22	16
Texas	51	25	18	6	New York	25	34	22	19
Wyoming	51	9	22	22[c]					
Nebraska	50	29	17	4					
Montana	49	13	29	9					

Alaska	41	15	28	16			
Arizona	33	27	25	15			
Idaho	33	16	27	24[a]			
Utah	11	10	20	61[b]			
Average	56	15	19	6	36	27	25	11

Adapted from: Public Religious Research Institute. 2021a. "Religious Affiliation by State." 2021. https://ava.prri.org/

Notes:

[a] Includes 20% Mormon.
[b] Include 56% Mormons.
[c] Includes 13% Mormons.

TABLE 2.32 White Evangelical Protestants by State (2021)

Red States	Percent White Evangelical Protestant	Blue States	Percent White Evangelical Protestant
Tennessee	43	Michigan	18
West Virginia	40	Pennsylvania	18
Alabama	39	Maine	17
Arkansas	39	Oregon	17
Kentucky	39	New Mexico	16
Mississippi	37	Washington	16
Oklahoma	33	Illinois	13
South Carolina	33	Vermont	13
Wyoming	32	Delaware	11
North Carolina	30	California	9
Indiana	29	Maryland	9
South Dakota	29	Rhode Island	8
Missouri	27	Connecticut	7
Georgia	26	Hawaii	6
Kansas	26	Massachusetts	6
Montana	26	New Jersey	5
North Dakota	24	New York	5
Louisiana	20		
Nebraska	20		
Texas	19		
Idaho	16		
Alaska	15		
Arizona	12		
Utah	4		
Average	27		11

Adapted from: "White Evangelical Protestants by State." 2021. https://ava.prri.org/

The frequency of church attendance is often used as a measure of a person's religiosity despite some of its limitations. One, self-reported measure of church attendance can produce overestimation due to inherent bias and difficulty in verifying such self-reported church attendance. Second, self-reported frequency of church attendance may not necessarily reflect how "religious" a person is since people attend church services for a variety of reasons other than pure spiritual enhancement. Table 2.33 provides data on the frequency of church attendance in the red and blue states.

The frequency of church attendance is much higher among the red states compared to the blue states. In 19 of the red states, 30 percent or more

TABLE 2.33 Frequency of Church Attendance by State (2021)

Red States	Percent Once a Week	Percent Once-twice a month	Percent Seldom or never	Blue States	Percent Once a week	Percent once-twice a month	Percent seldom or never
Utah	52	12	35	Illinois	28	22	50
Mississippi	45	21	34	Maryland	26	25	49
Idaho	40	12	48	Michigan	26	23	51
Arkansas	37	22	40	Pennsylvania	26	23	51
Tennessee	37	19	44	California	24	24	53
Alabama	36	25	39	Delaware	24	20	55
South Dakota	36	26	38	New Mexico	24	26	50
Nebraska	34	17	49	New Jersey	21	22	58
North Dakota	34	28	38	New York	21	21	58
Georgia	33	25	42	Connecticut	20	24	56
Indiana	33	18	50	Hawaii	20	6	74
Louisiana	33	22	45	Maine	19	15	67
Montana	33	12	54	Oregon	19	14	67
Kansas	32	21	47	Vermont	19	9	72
North Carolina	32	25	43	Washington	19	11	70
South Carolina	32	23	45	Massachusetts	14	20	66
Texas	32	24	44	Rhode Island	13	19	68
Missouri	31	18	51				
Kentucky	30	23	46				
Oklahoma	29	24	46				
West Virginia	27	18	55				
Wyoming	26	10	64				
Alaska	24	10	66				
Arizona	23	17	60				
Average	33	20	47		21	19	60
National	27	21	52				

Adapted from: "Frequency of Church Attendance 2021." 2021. https://ava.prri.org/

individuals report attending church services at least once a week while such is not the case in any of the blue states. The combined average weekly church attendance among the red states is 33 percent, which is 6 percent higher than the national average and 12 percent higher than the blue states.

The combined average weekly church attendance among the blue states is 21 percent, which is 6 percent lower than the national average. In fact, among the blue states, in 16 of the 17 states, 50 percent of more report seldom or never attending church services. The only exception is Maryland in which 49 percent report seldom or never attending church services. Thus, if one were to take the frequency of church attendance as a measurement of religiosity, red states are more religious than blue states. The most religious states are red states located in the South and the Midwest while the least religious states are most of the blue states located on the east and west coasts.

The religious and conservative red states are the ones that advocate family values and a pro-family agenda that disapproves of divorce, and children born out of wedlock, and advocates for the sanctity of marriage. Ironically, red states often do not practice what they preach because there is a significant disconnect between advocacy and behavior. Table 2.34 provides a breakdown of divorce rates by state.

As can be observed from the data, some of the highest divorce rates are to be found among the same red states that have large white evangelical populations and report frequent church attendance. The top ten states with a divorce rate of 3.0 or higher per 1,000 residents age 15 or older are all red states. All 17 blue states have a divorce rate that is lower than the top ten red states with the highest divorce rate. The combined average divorce rate among the red states is 2.9 compared to 2.2 per 1,000 among the blue states.

Table 2.35 provides data on teen pregnancy, teen birth rate, and percent of babies born to unmarried mothers by state. The combined average teen pregnancy rate among red states is 21 compared to 12.5 for blue states per 1,000 females aged 15–19.

Again, some of the same red states that have the highest divorce rates also have the highest rates of teen pregnancy rates and teen birth rates. Most of them are in the South and the Midwest. Of the top ten states with the highest teen pregnancy rates, nine are red states and one blue state. The top ten states with the highest teen birth rates are red states. The average teen pregnancy rate for the red states is 21 compared to 12.5 for the blue states. Similarly, the average teen birth rate for red states is 19.7 compared to 11.5 for blue states. The one area where there is not a significant difference between the red and blue states is the percentage of babies born to unmarried mothers. The overall average for red states is 40.8 compared to 39.7 for blue states.

What the data suggests is family values divide between the red and blue states. The blue states and liberal strongholds on the east and the west coast that vote Democratic have the lowest divorce rates, teen pregnancy

TABLE 2.34 Divorce Rates by State (2021)

Red States	Divorce Rate	Blue States	Divorce Rate
Indiana	NA	California	NA
Oklahoma	3.8	Hawaii	NA
Wyoming	3.7	New Mexico	NA
Alabama	3.6	Washington	2.9
Arkansas	3.6	Maine	2.7
Idaho	3.4	Oregon	2.7
Kentucky	3.3	Rhode Island	2.7
Mississippi	3.3	Delaware	2.6
Tennessee	3.3	Connecticut	2.5
Utah	3.3	Pennsylvania	2.4
North Carolina	3.2	Michigan	2.3
Alaska	3.1	Vermont	2.3
Missouri	2.9	New Jersey	2.2
North Dakota	2.9	New York	2.2
West Virginia	2.9	Maryland	1.6
Arizona	2.7	Illinois	1.3
Nebraska	2.6	Massachusetts	1.0
Montana	2.5		
South Dakota	2.5		
South Carolina	2.4		
Georgia	2.2		
Louisiana	2.2		
Kansas	1.9		
Texas	1.4		
Average	2,.9		2.2

Adapted from: U.S. Center for Disease Control and Prevention. 2022. "Divorce Rates by State: 1990, 1995, and 1999-021." https://cdc.gov/

Notes: Rates are per 1,000 residents age 15 or older. NA = Not available.

rates, and teen birth rates. While most Republican-led red states rank high on the "religiosity" scale as measured by the frequency of church attendance, and celebrated by conservatives as the heartland of family values, they also tend to have higher rates of divorce, teen pregnancy, and teen births. The "blue families" model emphasizes the importance of both males and females in the workplace and egalitarian gender roles while the "red families" model, associated most closely with the "Bible Belt," the mountain west and rural America, rejects the new family norms of the "blue families" (Cahn et al., 2012; "Red Families Vs. Blue Families" 2010; "Family Values in Red States Vs. Blue states" 2010). The red and blue family values, public schools, public libraries, reproductive rights, LBGTQ

TABLE 2.35 Teen Pregnancy Rate (2023), Teen Birth Rate (2020), and Percent of Babies Born to Unmarried Mothers (2020)

Red States	Percent Teen Pregnancy Rate[a]	Percent Teen Birth Rate[b]	% of Babies Born to Unmarried Mothers[c]	Blue States	Teen Pregnancy Rate	Teen Birth Rate	% of Babies Born to Unmarried Mothers[c]
Arkansas	30.0	27.8	46.8	New Mexico	24.4	21.9	53.2
Mississippi	29.1	27.9	55.8	Hawaii	15.7	13.0	39.3
Louisiana	27.8	25.7	54.5	Michigan	15.1	13.5	41.2
Oklahoma	27.4	25.0	44.4	Delaware	14.9	14.6	48.1
Alabama	25.6	24.8	48.4	Illinois	14.6	13.6	40.5
West Virginia	25.2	22.5	46.8	Maryland	13.9	13.1	40.8
Kentucky	24.9	23.8	43.1	Pennsylvania	13.3	12.6	40.9
Texas	24.0	22.4	41.7	Washington	12.7	11.3	31.6
Tennessee	23.7	23.3	44.6	California	12.4	11.0	38.6
South Carolina	21.6	19.3	46.6	Oregon	12.1	10.1	36.7
Indiana	20.3	18.7	43.6	New York	11.4	10.0	38.1
Missouri	20.3	18.8	41.1	New Jersey	10.0	9.2	33.9
Georgia	19.7	18.2	46.3	Rhode Island	10.0	9.4	44.7
Wyoming	19.4	18.1	34.1	Maine	9.1	10.6	38.4
Kansas	19.2	18.1	36.8	Connecticut	7.7	7.6	38.1
South Dakota	19.2	18.7	36.0	Vermont	7.6	7.0	38.9
Arizona	18.5	16.6	45.2	Massachusetts	6.9	6.1	33.0

Alaska	18.3	17.7	36.5
North Carolina	18.2	17.3	41.9
Montana	16.3	13.2	33.9
North Dakota	15.6	13.7	32.8
Nebraska	15.3	15.1	33.4
Idaho	14.9	14.6	27.7
Utah	12.0	10.8	19.3
Average	21.0	19.7	40.8
	12.5	11.5	39.7

Notes: Number of Pregnancy and Birth Rates are per 1,000 females aged 15–19.

Adapted from:

a "Teen Pregnancy Rate by State." 2023. https://worldpopulationreview.com/
b "Teen Birth Rate by State 2020." 2020a. https://www.cdc.gov/
c "Percent of Babies Born to Unmarried Mothers 2020b." https://cdc.gov/

rights, immigration, and race/ethnicity have become the new frontier in the cultural war between the red and blue states.

Happiness: A State of Mind or a Place?

Research has found that good economic, emotional, and physical health are important ingredients to individual's well-balanced and happy life. To determine which states exhibit the best combination of these ingredients, Wallethub.com examined the 50 states across three dimensions – emotional and physical well-being, work environment, and community and environment – using 30 different metrics. The overall score was calculated using the weighted average across all metrics to rank order states overall and on each of the three dimensions. The results are displayed for only the red and blue states and not the purple states in Table 2.36.

Some of the top happiest states include the blue states of Hawaii, Maryland, New Jersey, California, Illinois, and Connecticut and the red states of Utah, Idaho, and Nebraska. Among the ten states that ranked the lowest on the happiness scale, nine are red states and one is blue state of New Mexico. Most of the nine red states are again found mostly in the South and the Midwest. The combined average ranking of red states is 32 compared to 19 for blue states indicating the blue states rank much higher on the happiness scale compared to the red states. A similar contrast emerges when we look at ranking on three specific dimensions. The combined average ranking on dimensions of the emotional and physical well-being of red states is 33 compared to 18 for blue states. Overall, the blue states also rank higher on the dimensions of work environment and community and environment, though the contrast is not as dramatic.

Political Polarization Within the Red and Blue States

Our analysis in this chapter has focused on the polarization of American states into red and blue states. The 2020 presidential election outcome demonstrates this. Table 2.37 provides the 2020 presidential election results by state.

All 17 blue states voted for Biden, the Democratic nominee. Of the 24 red states, Trump, the Republican nominee, won 22 states. Biden won two red states – Arizona and Georgia – by a slim margin of 0.3 percent. North Carolina, another red state was competitive but Trump managed to win by a margin of 1.3 percent. Among the blue states, one competitive state was Pennsylvania, which Biden won by a margin of 1.2 percent. Twenty-one of the 24 red states and 15 of the 17 blue states were not competitive. In the

TABLE 2.36 Happiest States in America (2022)

Red States

	Ranking	Overall Score	Emotional Physical Well-Being	Work Environment	Community Environment
Utah	4	62.41	29	1	1
Idaho	6	61.60	25	3	2
Nebraska	9	58.19	13	7	22
South Dakota	12	57.60	15	10	15
North Dakota	13	57.37	19	9	10
Georgia	19	54.78	16	32	14
North Carolina	20	53.65	14	25	40
Wyoming	25	52.40	36	31	3
Montana	29	51.34	41	4	13
Arizona	31	50.22	28	29	33
Kansas	32	49.90	31	23	26
South Carolina	33	49.62	32	38	11
Texas	36	47.74	17	39	50
Indiana	37	47.41	37	22	30
Alaska	40	46.27	24	37	49
Missouri	41	45.38	40	27	35
Tennessee	43	43.35	44	26	42
Oklahoma	44	40.69	46	44	12
Mississippi	45	39.58	43	50	38
Alabama	46	39.32	45	40	46
Kentucky	47	38.36	49	45	25
Arkansas	48	38.23	47	46	31

Blue States

	Ranking	Overall Score	Emotional Physical Well-Being	Work Environment	Community Environment
Hawaii	1	66.31	1	17	7
Maryland	2	62.60	4	24	4
New Jersey	5	61.71	2	28	19
California	7	59.97	12	14	5
Illinois	8	58.59	3	33	34
Connecticut	10	58.15	7	21	28
Massachusetts	14	57.12	6	15	41
Delaware	17	55.16	11	41	18
Washington	22	53.53	33	5	8
New York	23	53.36	8	42	45
Maine	24	52.67	22	19	35
Oregon	26	52.11	30	12	23
Pennsylvania	27	51.87	26	34	21
Rhode Island	28	51.55	23	18	43
Vermont	34	48.46	34	11	44
Michigan	39	46.51	38	35	24
New Mexico	42	43.64	42	47	17

(Continued)

TABLE 2.36 (Continued)

			Red States						Blue States			
				Emotional							Emotional			
	Ranking	Overall Score	Physical Well-Being	Work Environment	Community Environment		Ranking	Overall Score	Physical Well-Being	Work Environment	Community Environment
Louisiana	49	34.81	48	49	39						
West Virginia	50	33.83	50	48	32						
Average	32	48.08	33	29	26		19	54.88	18	24	24

Adapted from: McCann, Adam. 2022b. "Happiest States in the US." https://wallethub.com

Notes: Fifty states were compared across three dimensions -- physical and emotional well-being, work environment, and community environment. Thirty metrics were used to evaluate the three dimensions using a 100-point scale for each metrics to arrive at overall score where a score of 100 represents maximum happiness.

States were then ranked from 1 to 50.

TABLE 2.37 Presidential Election Results by State (2020)

Red States	Percent Trump	Percent Biden	Blue States	Percent Biden	Percent Trump
Wyoming	69.9	26.6	Vermont	66.1	30.7
West Virginia	68.6	29.7	Massachusetts	65.6	32.1
Mississippi	67.5	41.0	Maryland	65.4	32.2
Oklahoma	65.4	32.3	Hawaii	63.7	34.3
North Dakota	65.1	31.8	California	63.5	34.3
Idaho	63.8	33.1	New York	60.9	37.7
Arkansas	62.4	34.8	Rhode Island	59.4	38.6
Kentucky	62.1	36.2	Connecticut	59.2	39.2
Alabama	62.0	36.6	Delaware	58.7	39.8
South Dakota	61.8	35.6	Washington	58.0	38.6
Tennessee	60.7	37.5	Illinois	57.5	40.6
Louisiana	58.5	39.9	New Jersey	57.1	41.3
Nebraska	58.2	39.2	Oregon	56.5	40.4
Utah	58.1	37.6	New Mexico	54.3	43.5
Indiana	57.0	41.0	Maine	53.1	44.0
Montana	56.9	40.5	Michigan	50.6	47.8
Missouri	56.8	41.4	Pennsylvania	50.0	48.8
Kansas	56.1	41.5			
South Carolina	55.1	43.4			
Alaska	52.8	42.8			
Texas	52.1	46.5			
North Carolina	49.9	48.6			
Georgia	**49.2**	**49.5**			
Arizona	**49.1**	**49.4**			
Average	59.1	39.0		58.8	39.0

Adapted from: "Presidential Election Results." 2020. https://nbcnews.com; https://www.fec.gov

Note: Percent may not add to 100 due to rounding and votes cast for other candidates.

reddest of red states, Trump garnered more than 60 percent of the vote. Biden did the same among the bluest of the blue states.

However, what is also noteworthy is the fact that the red and blue states are politically polarized from within and divided by geography, socioeconomic status (SES), and demographics. For example, within blue states, rural areas and small towns heavily vote Republican while within red states, cities and metropolitan areas and in recent years suburbs (which in the past used to vote Republican) vote Democratic. An analysis of the voting pattern in the 2020 presidential election provides insight into the political polarization within the red and blue states.

Political Polarization and the Presidential Election of 2020

The political polarization within the red and blue states was on display during the presidential campaign and the post-election analysis of voting patterns in the 2020 presidential election. It highlighted the political divide along fault lines of geography, economy, race, education, gender, age, and religion.

Geographic Divide

Over the years, the rural areas of the country have become more Republican while urban areas have become more Democratic leading to geographic partisan segregation. According to Hopkins (2017), the urban-rural partisan divide is fueled by a combination of cultural and racial controversies that started in the late 1980s and accelerated in the 1990s. After comparing voting trends in large and small metropolitan and rural areas, he concludes that in 1992 the urban-rural voting difference was 8 percentage points but had grown to nearly 24 points by 2016. Similarly, Gest (2018) attributes the urban-rural divide to the cultural differences and tensions over issues such as abortion, sexual orientation, immigration, race relations, and gun rights, among others. The rise in the white identity can be attributed to white working-class individuals' perception that they are marginalized. An individual's probability of identifying as a strong Democrat drops by 12 percentage points if they live in a far rural area just as a person living in a densely packed area is about 11 points more likely to identify as a strong Democrat. Thus, there is a strong association between the geography of residence and party identification (Savat 2020).

The geographic divide is reflected in the examination of the voting pattern in urban/metropolitan and large cities/suburban areas versus rural and small towns. For example, in 71 percent of America's 436 most urbanized counties (metro areas of more than 1 million in population), support for Biden increased in the 2020 election while Trump expanded his support in 54 percent of the rural counties (Hendrix 2020). While Democrats have always enjoyed more support in heavily urban areas, in the 2020 election the urban-rural divide became more extreme with a big vote swing for Democrats in densely populated counties. Trump's margin of loss worsened in 74 percent of large metropolitan areas (Metropolitan Statistical Areas (MSAs) of more than 1 million population), while in the most rural parts of the United States, only in 36 percent of the counties Trump's margin got worse compared to the 2016 election. Even in red states, urban areas moved toward Biden and the Democrats (Kanik and Scott 2020).

Biden won all the largest Sun Belt metropolitan areas ranging from Charlotte and Raleigh, North Carolina in the east coast, to Phoenix, Arizona, Denver, Colorado, and Las Vegas, Nevada in the west coast. The only exceptions were Jacksonville, Tampa, and Miami in Florida. Biden was the first Democratic presidential nominee to carry all four of the largest Texas metropolitan areas since Lyndon Johnson did it in 1964. He was also the first Democratic nominee to win Maricopa County, the heart of the Phoenix metro area, since Harry Truman did it in 1948 (Brownstein 2021).

Today, more people live in large metropolitan areas than in smaller rural counties and towns. For example, 197.9 million people lived in counties won by Biden compared to 130.3 million people who lived in rural counties won by Trump. Thus, the counties won by Biden had 67 million more people. Trump won in 2,488 counties while Biden won in only 551 counties. But small metropolitan counties have far less population than large metropolitan counties. Large metropolitan counties accounted for nearly half the population (97 million) among all counties that voted for Biden and suburban counties in large metropolitan areas accounted for an additional 72 million people in Biden-won counties (Frey 2021a, 2021b, 2021c).

Biden's victory was also helped by support in suburban counties in large metropolitan areas. Analysis shows that suburban counties and smaller metropolitan areas contributed to Biden's victory in key states of Michigan, Pennsylvania, Wisconsin, and Georgia. Traditionally, especially in presidential elections, suburban and small metropolitan areas have tended to give an advantage to Republicans (Frey 2020; Danmore, Lang, and Danielson 2020; Willis and Witte 2020). The urban-rural divide is also becoming the urban-suburban divide. In 2016, 47.2 percent of suburbs (as defined by the CDC) voted for Hillary Clinton, while in the 2020 presidential election, Biden won in 52.1 percent of suburban areas. Thus, it was the suburbs that were the inflection point carrying Democrats to victory. In 2020, the dominant fissure was suburban-rural voters (Florida, Patino, and Dottle 2020).

The urban-rural divide reflects the politics of resentment. Trump fulminated against cities throughout his presidency calling them dirty, disgusting, and rat-infested and criticized them for their anarchic jurisdictions. The residents of rural areas feel that they are underrepresented in decision-making, their way of life is disrespected, and they are not getting a fair share of tax dollars and most money goes to cities (Trujillo and Crowley

2022; Cramer 2022). Conditions in rural areas have continued to worsen due to the exodus of jobs and young people and thus rural America is getting older, poorer, and sicker (Jacobs, and Muni 2019; Carr and Kefalas 2010). The urban-rural partisan "apartheid" has tended to reinforce ideological and affective polarization.

In rural areas, there is strong resentment against cities and urban elites because they believe that coastal and urban elites look down on them. Such disdain also includes a racial element because of the high concentration of minorities and persons of color in large cities and metropolitan areas. Another element is the economy because, in most states, rural areas are struggling economically since agriculture is no longer the king while urban areas are economically flourishing. On the other side, residents of cities feel frustrated that rural voters enjoy a disproportionate share of power in both the Senate and the Electoral College (Greenblatt 2021a; Graham 2017). Despite the perception that cities grab more than their share of state support, generally, the opposite is true. Cities send more tax dollars to the state than they receive back in spending. Often this happens because large cities tend to have Democratic mayors while state legislatures (due to gerrymandering, a limited number of competitive districts) are controlled by the Republicans. For example, only three of the country's 25 largest cities have Republican mayors while a majority of state legislatures are controlled by Republicans. Given this partisan divide, state legislators have no reason to consider the interests of the urban population in policymaking but have plenty of interest in not doing so. The urban-rural divide is exacerbated by political polarization (Greenblatt 2021b).

It seems as if the United States is politically divided into two counties, one rural and one urban (Graham 2017). The urban-rural divide has also moved to not only the suburbs but also major metropolitan areas located within the "swing" or purple states creating a new battleground between liberal and Democratic-leaning urban and suburban areas and predominantly conservative Republican-leaning rural areas and small towns (Danmore, Lang, and Danielson 2020). There is an ever-widening gap in the urban-rural divide. In the 2020 presidential election, cities and suburbs moved ideologically further to the left while the rural areas swung right.

The urban-rural divide is likely to become more pronounced as Americans continue to sort themselves geographically, economically, and politically into like-minded communities. Americans are fleeing into places where political views/ideology match their own. This geographic clustering of like-minded Americans is evident in the fact that of the country's 3,143 counties, the number of super landslide counties where a presidential candidate won at least 80 percent of the vote has jumped from 6 percent in 2004 to 22 percent in 2020. Biden won 85 percent of the counties with

Whole Foods and only 32 percent of counties with Cracker Barrel. It is almost like Americans are clustering themselves in Fox News' Sean Hannity's America or MSNBC's Rache Maddow's America (Burnett 2022; Vedantam 2014; Bishop 2008).

Economic Divide

In the 2020 election, political polarization within the states was not limited to the geographic divide but it was also reflected in the economic divide. Not only the red and blue America experiencing two different economies but their economies are diverging at a rapid pace. The economy of the Republican areas contains traditional industries with lower skill requirements and lower productivity such as manufacturing and resource extraction (coal mining, fracking) while Democratic-leaning urban areas contain a large concentration of higher-skill, high-tech professionals, and digital services (Muro and Whiten 2019). In the 2020 election, 477 counties Biden won made up 70 percent of America's total economic activity while 2,584 counties Trump won made up only 29 percent of the American economy. In the 2016 election, the 2,584 counties that Trump won garnered just 36 percent of the country's economic output whereas the 472 counties Hillary Clinton won equaled almost two-thirds of the nation's aggregate economy. Between the 2016 and 2020 presidential elections, this gap widened further. Bien won almost all counties with the biggest economies in the country while Trump won thousands of small-town and rural communities with very small economies (Muro et al. 2020; Muro and Whiten 2019).

The Democratic and Republican parties speak for two very different segments of the American economy. Democrats represent voters who overwhelmingly reside in the country's diverse economy while the Republican voters overwhelmingly reside in economically struggling small towns and rural areas. Blue districts saw their economic productivity climb from $118,000 per worker in 2008 to $139,000 in 2018, while the productivity of the Republican districts remained stranded at around $110,000. Democratic districts also saw their median household income soar from $54,000 in 2008 to $61,000 in 2018, while in the Republican districts, the median household income declined from $55,000 in 2008 to $53,000 in 2018 (Muro et al. 2020).

Biden's democratic base resides in more populous, educated, and prosperous communities that are home to the lion's share of economic activity. This pattern was also evident in competitive states like Michigan and Wisconsin where Biden won in most prosperous cities while Trump held on to the state's rural areas (Austin 2020). Over two-thirds of households earning at least $150,000 per year lived in counties Biden won (Frey 2021a,

2021b, 2021c). Across the electoral map, high-income and well-educated suburbs moved further left while rural areas swung right (Hendrix 2020).

Demographic Divide

Education

Biden won counties with white-college graduates while Trump won counties with a white population without college degrees. Biden received votes from 67 percent of voters with a post-graduate degree while Trump received only 32 percent of the vote from the same group, a difference of 35 percentage points. Similarly, 56 percent of college graduates voted for Biden compared to only 42 percent who voted for Trump. Among those with some college, Biden received 49 percent of the vote compared to 50 percent who voted for Trump. However, among those with a high school diploma or less, Trump garnered 56 percent of their vote compared to 41 percent for Biden (Igielnik, Keeter, and Hartig 2021). Biden won among those with more education while Trump won among the least educated. The educational divide has become one of the most important factors in American politics.

Race

Counties won by Biden were also home to a significant share of the country's persons of color. About three-quarters of the country's black, Latino, and Hispanic population lived in counties that Biden won. So did the 86 percent of Asian Americans and nearly two-thirds of persons identifying with two or more races. Biden received 87 percent of the African American votes, 65 percent of the Hispanic votes, and 61 percent of Asian votes while Trump won among white voters by a margin of 67 percent to 41 percent for Biden ("How Groups Voted in 2020." 2020).

Only half of the country's white population lived in counties that Biden won. The population of counties that Trump won had more white and older residents while younger and more diverse populations lived in counties that Biden won (Frey 2021a, 2021b, 2021c; Galston 2020).

Whites with more anti-immigrant views or more negative views of Latinos are less likely to identify as Democrats and less likely to vote for Democratic candidates. This rightward shift looks like an earlier period of white defection from the Democratic Party in the South and highlights the enduring but shifting impact of race on American politics (Hajnal and Rivera 2014). In American politics, affluent voters tend to lean Republican while poor voters tend to lean Democratic, but at the same time, rich coastal states have been bastions of Democrats while generally lower-income states in the South and the middle part of the country strongly support Republicans. This geographic pattern is consistent with the cultural war between affluent and socially liberal cosmopolitan areas and less affluent and socially more conservative small towns and rural areas that advocate for traditional social values (Gelman 2014).

Age

Biden did considerably better among younger voters while Trump did much better among older voters. Among voters aged 18–29, Biden received 60 percent of the votes. Among voters aged 30–44, Biden won 52 percent of the vote. In contrast, among voters aged 45–64 and 65 and over, Trump won 50 and 52 percent of the votes, respectively ("How Groups Voted in 2020." 2020).

Gender

Biden did considerably better among women while Trump did slightly better among men. Biden won 55 percent of women's votes compared to Trump who won 44 percent, a margin of 11 points. Among men, Trump got 50 percent of the vote compared to Biden who received 48 of the votes (Igielnik, Keeter, and Hartig 2021).

Religious Divide

In the 2020 election, protestants constituted 56 percent of all voters. Evangelical protestants accounted for only 19 percent of all voters but they accounted for 34 percent of the Trump voters. Trump received 84 percent of white evangelical protestant votes compared to 15 percent who voted for Biden. Among white non-evangelical protestants, Trump received 57 percent of the vote compared to 43 percent for Biden. However, 91 percent of black protestants voted for Biden compared to only 9 percent for Trump (Igielnik, Keeter, and Hartig 2021).

Overall, Trump received 59 percent of the protestant vote and 50 percent of the Catholic votes while Biden received 40 percent of the protestant vote and 49 percent of the Catholic votes. However, Biden received 71 percent of the votes from those who were unaffiliated with any religion while Trump received 26 percent. Biden also received 64 percent of votes from those who listed "other" religious affiliation, compared to Trump who received 32 percent (Igielnik, Keeter, and Hartig 2021).

Finally, among those who attended church services once a month or more frequently, Trump received 59 percent of the vote compared to 40 percent for Biden. In contrast, Biden received 58 percent of votes from those who attended church services yearly or less often (Igielnik, Keeter, and Hartig 2021).

Overall, Trump performed better among protestants and those who attended church services more frequently while Biden performed much better among religiously non-affiliated voters, who had other religious affiliations and attended church services less frequently.

In an online survey conducted between September 19, 2022 and September 29, 2022 by LifeWay Research, half of the Protestant churchgoers indicated that they prefer to attend a church where people share their political views. Fifty-four percent of White and 53 percent of African American churchgoers are more likely to want a church with shared politics than Hispanic churchgoers (25%). Fifty-seven percent of evangelicals indicated that they attend politically like-minded churches. Most churchgoers believe they are among their political tribe when at church (Earls 2022).

There is a danger of religion in America becoming a new form of tribalism. Political tribalism is where loyalty to the political tribe is more important than anything else. It is about identity and is rooted in emotions, i.e., affective polarization, where "others" are seen as morally suspect and dangerous. It involves an "us vs. them" mentality in which members of the tribe would go to any length to defend the tribe's leaders. It is this mentality that views others as the enemy and helps light the match that fuels the fires of distrust, conspiracy theories, and cultural wars. It is such a mentality that explains why 60 percent of white evangelical Christians believe that the 2020 election was stolen from Trump; they supported and stood by Trump and Republican U.S. Senate candidate Herschel Walker despite their moral failures; such mentality enabled Republican candidate for governor in Pennsylvania and Representative Lauren Bobert representing the Western part of Colorado in the 2022 elections to express disdain for the separation of the church and the state; and recruit children for the cultural wars (Lee 2023a; Dias 2022a, 2022b; Glueck 2022).

Political Polarization: Red and Blue State Divide

The examination of red and blue states' profiles seems to suggest that the United States looks like made up of two nations – one nation is made up of Republican-led conservative red states and the other is made up of Democratic-led liberal states. Each represents two different visions of a social contract.

Blue states are more populous, are more urban, have more immigrants, and are racially/ethnically and religiously more diverse compared to the red states. They spend more on public education and pay higher salaries to teachers. They have a more educated population with bachelor's or graduate degrees and rank higher on educational attainment and quality of the public school system. Concerning their respective economies, blue states rank higher on per capita as well as median household incomes. They have a higher unemployment rate but lower poverty rates. Compared to the red states, they have higher tax rates and have a higher cost of living, but they are more productive concerning their GDP output. They are financially less dependent on the federal government. They enjoy higher voter registration and voter turnout in elections. They also have a higher representation of women and persons of color in the state legislatures and the state supreme court. They are less religious in the sense that more individuals identify themselves as not affiliated with any religion or identify themselves as affiliated with religions other than the mainline Christian religions. Blue states are more pro-democracy because they make it easier for voters to register and vote in elections. They are more likely to enact pro-immigration, pro-environment, anti-gun, and gun violence policies. The residents of the blue states also seem to be happier.

Red states present a sharp contrast to blue states. Red states have less population, are more rural, and less racially and ethnically diverse. They spend less on public education and teachers' salaries and have a less educated population. Their residents enjoy lower per capita income and median household incomes. They enjoy lower tax rates and lower cost of living but they are economically less productive and heavily dependent on the federal government for financial assistance. The red states are more religious but they have higher divorce, teenage pregnancy, and teen birth rates. Red states enjoy lower voter registration and voter turnout rates because they make it more difficult for their residents to register and vote in elections. Their state legislatures and supreme court are less diverse in terms of race and gender. They espouse more anti-democratic values. Red states are culturally and politically more conservative and more likely to enact anti-immigration, anti-environment, and pro-gun public policies. The residents of red states are less happy.

The red states and blue states almost seem to resemble two different countries. Red states led by Republicans are actively engaged in promoting cultural wars and war against democracy while the blue states led by Democrats are promoting a multicultural and pluralist democracy (Devega 2023). Each represents a very different vision of the United States. As Cohn (2012) has suggested, blue states look more like Scandinavia while red states look more like Guatemala. Or, as Michael Podhorzer, the chair of the Analyst Institute has suggested, it is a mistake to think of America as a single nation because we have never been a one nation. According to him, historically and geographically, the United States is more like a federated republic made up of red and blue nations (Brownstein 2022a).

Bibliography

"A House Divided." 2013. *Economist* 444, no. 9311 (September): 16–19.
"About the Center for Legislative Accountability." 2023. http://ratings.conservative.org
"Adult Population by Race and Ethnicity in the United States." 2022. https://datacenter.kidscount.org/
Alas, Horus. 2021. "Report: Republican-Led State Legislatures Pass Dozens of Restrictive Voting Laws in 2021." https://www.usnews.com/
Alexander, Ayanna. 2023. "Some-Democratic-Led States Seek to Bolster Voter Protection." https://abcnews.go.com
American Community Survey. 2024. "Age and Sex." https://data.census.com/
"Annual Estimate of the Resident Population for the United States, Regions, States, District of Columbia, and Puerto Rico: April 1, 2020 to July 1, 2023." https://www.census.gov/
Astor, Maggie. 2023. "Declaring Emergencies and Banning 'Latinx': First Acts for 9 New Governors." https://www.nytimes.com
Austin, John C. 2020. "Where Midwestern Struggle, Trumpism Lives on." https://www.brookings.edu
Bacon, Jr., Perry. 2022. "America's Problem is white People Keep Backing the Republican Party." https://www.washingtonpost.com
Balz, Dan; Scott Clement; and Emily Guskin. 2021. "Not Just Red and Blue: Large Survey Explores Factions Within Democratic and Republican Parties." https://www.washingtonpost.com
Bellia, Jr; Anthony J.; and Bradford R. Clark. 2020. "The International Law Origin of American Federalism." *Columbia Law Review* 120, no. 4 (May): 835–940.
"Best State Ranking 2021." 2022. https://usnews.com/
Bishop, Bill. 2008. The Big Sort: *Why the Clustering of Like-Minded America is Tearing Us Apart*. Boston, MASS: Houghton Mifflin.
Brennan Center for Justice. 2021. "Voting Laws Roundup: December 2021." https://www.brennancenter.org/
Bricker, Christine; and Scott LaCombe. 2010. "The Ties that Bind Us: The Influence of Perceived State Similarity on Policy Diffusion." *Political Research Quarterly* 74, no 2 (June): 377–387.
Boschma, Janie. 2021. "Fourteen States Have Enacted 22 New Laws Making It Harder to Vote." https://www.cnn.com/
Boschma, Janie; and Fredreka Schouten. 2021. "Lawmakers in 47 States have introduced Bills that Would Make it Harder to Vote. See them Here." https://www.cnn.com/
Brooks, David. 2022. "Why Aren't the Democrats Trouncing These Guys?" https://www.nytimes.com

Brownstein, Ronald. 2022a. "America is Growing Apart: Possibly for Good." https://www.theatlantic.com

Brownstein, Ronald. 2022b. "Book Bans Move to Center Stage in the Red-State Education Wars." https://www.cnn.com

Brownstein, Ronald. 2022c. "Red States are Building a Nation Within a Nation." https://www.cnn.com

Brownstein, Ronald. 2021. "'Breaking Point': Why the Red State/Blue City Conflict is Peaking over Masks." https://www.cnn.com

Bureau of Economic Analysis. 2024. "Level and Percent Change from Preceding Period." https://www.bea.gov/data/gdp/gdp-state/

Bureau of Labor Statistics. 2023. "Unemployment Rate by States, Seasonally Adjusted." https://bls.gov/

Burnett, John. 2022. "Americans are Fleeing to Places Where Political Views Match Their Own." https://www.npr.org

Cahn, Naomi; and June Carbone. 2012. *Red Families v. Blue Families: Legal Polarization and the Creation of Culture.* New York: Oxford University Press.

Cammenga, Janelle. 2020. "Which States Rely the Most on Federal Aid" https://taxfoundation.org

Campbell, David E. 2021. "Religion as Political Tribalism." *Forum* 19, no. 3 (November): 499–518.

Carlin, Doug. 2023. "US Median Household Income by State (Report 2023)." https://usabynumbers.com/

Carr, Patrick J.; and Maria J. Kefalas. 2010. *Hollowing Out the Middle: The Rural Brain Drain and What It Means for America.* Boston: Beacon Press.

Carroll, Aron E. 2022. "Blue States Want Red States to Face Consequences, But Travel Bans are Harmful." https://www.nytimes.com

Center of Legislative Accountability. 2021. "State Ranking of Conservative Policies." https://ratings.conservative.org/

Chiariello, Paul. 2020. "8 Economic Indicators—Are Red or Blue States Better?" https://appliedsentience.com/

Ciotti, Lorenzo. 2023. "What are the Richest and poorest States in USA?" https://www.financial-world.org/

Cohn, Jonathan. 2012. "E Pluribus Duo." *New Republic* (October 25): 21–23.

Council for Community and Economic Research. 2024. "The Least Expensive State to Live in the US. Plus, See the runners-up." https://www.coli.org/

Conlan, Timothy J. 2017. "The Changing Politics of American Federalism." *State & Local Government Review* 49, no. 3 (September): 170–183.

Conlan, Timothy J. 2014. "Federalism and Policy Instability: Centralization and Decentralization in Contemporary American Federalism." *Revue Francaise de science Politique* (English Edition) 64, no. 2: 27–48.

"Cost of Living Index by State 2022." 2022. https://worldpopulationreview.com/

Cramer, Katherine. 2022. *The Politics of Resentment: Rural Consciousness in Wisconsin and the Rise of Scott Walker.* Chicago: University of Chicago Press.

Crosby, Jack. 2022. "Greg Abbott Reveals G.O.P. Plan After Killing Roe v. Wade: Killing Public Education." https://www.rollingstone.com/

Csiszar, John. 2022. "States Whose Economies are Failing vs. States Whose Economies are Thriving." https://finance.yahoo.com/

Cummings, Stephen D. 2008. *Red States, Blue States, and the Coming Sharecropper Society*. New York: Algora Publishing.

Danmore, David F; Robert E. Lang; and Karen A. Danielson. 2020. *Blue Metros, Red States: The Shifting Urban-Rural Divide in America's Swing States*. Washington, D.C. Brookings Press.

DePietro, Andrew. 2021. "U.S. Per Capita Income by State in 2021." https://www.forbes.com/

Devega, Chauncey. 2023. "The is no Cultural War: Republicans are Waging a War on Democracy." https://salon.com

Dhillon, Kiran. 2014. "Blue States Barak Obama Won in 20912 are More Educated than the Red States." https://www.times.com

Dias, Elizabeth. 2022a. "'Saved by Grace': Evangelicals Find a Way Forward with Herschel Walker." https://www.nytimes.com

Dias, Elizabeth. 2022b. "The Far-Right Christian Quest for Power We are Seeing them Emboldened." https://www.nytimes.com

"Divorce Rate by State: 1990, 1995, and 1999-2021." https://cdc.gov/

Djupe, Paul A; Jacob R. Neiheisel; and Kimberly H. Conger. 2018. "Are the Politics of the Christian Right Linked to State Rates of Nonreligious? The Importance of Salient Controversy." *Political Research Quarterly* 71, no. 4 (December): 910–922.

Earls, Aaron. 2022. "Churchgoers Increasingly Prefer a Congregation that Share Their Politics." https://research.lifeway.com

Edsall, Thomas. 2019. "Red and Blue Voters Live in Different Economies." https://www.nytimes.com

Edelman, Adam. 2023. "Florida Legislature Expands Ron DeSantis' Program to Fly Migrants to Blue States." https://www.nbcnews.com

"Education Rankings: Measuring How Well States are Educating Their Students." 2021. https://www.usnews.com/

Ehrenhalt, Alan. 2021. "What Painted Us So Indelibly Red and Ble?" https://www.governong.com

"Election Results, 2022: State Government Trifectas." 2022. https://ballotpedia.org

"Family Values in Red States Vs. Blue States." 2010. https://www.npr.org

Fischer, Karin. 2022. "The Red-State Disadvantage." https://www.chronicle.com

Florida, Richard; Marie Patino; and Rachel Dottle. 2020. "How Suburbs Swung the 2020 Election." https://www.bloomberg.dom

Fraser, Steve; and Gary Gerstle. 1990. *The Rise and Fall of the New Deal Order, 1930-980*. Princeton, N.J.: Princeton University Press.

French, David A. 2020. *Divided We Fall: America's Succession Threat and How to Restore Our Nation*. New York: St. Martin's Press.

"Frequency of Church Attendance 2021." 2021. https://ava.prri.org/

Frey, William H. 2022. "A 'New Great Migration' is Bringing Black Americans Back to the South." https://www.brookings.edu

Frey, William H. 2021a. "Biden-Won Counties are home to 67 million more Americans than Trump Won Counties." https://www.brookings.edu

Frey, William H. 2021b. "America's Shrinking White Population Needs to Value Youthful Diversity." https://www/brookings.edu

Frey, William H. 2021c. "New 2020 Census Results Show Increased Diversity Countering Decade-long Declines in America's White and Youth." https://www.brookings.edu

Frey, William H. 2020. "Biden's Victory Came from the Suburbs." https://www.Brookings.edu

Frey, William. 2018. *The Diversity Explosion: How New Racial Demographics are Remaking America*. Washinton, D. C.: Brookings Institution.

Galston, William A. 2023. "The Polarization Paradox: Elected Officials and Voters Have Shifted in Opposite Directions." https://www.brookings.edu

Galston, William A. 2020. "Hold Your Fire: Dueling Democrats." https://www.brookings.edu

Garlick, Alex. 2022. "Laboratories of Politics: There is a Bottom-Up Diffusion of Policy Attention in the American Federal System." *Political Research Quarterly* (February): 1–15.

Gelman, Andrew. 2014. "How Bayesian Analysis Cracked the Red State, Blue State Problem." *Statistical Science* 29, no. 1 (February): 26–35.

Gest, Justin. 2018. *The White Working Class: What Everyone Needs to Know*. New York: Oxford University Press.

Glueck, Katie. 2022. "Mastriano's Attack on Jewish School Set Off Outcry Over Antiemetic Signalling." https://www.nytimes.com

Goelzhauser, Greg; and David M. Konisky. 2020. "The State of American Federalism 2019-020: Polarized and Punitive Intergovernmental Relations." *Publius* 50, no. 3 (July): 311–343.

Gowen, Annie. 2022. "The Culture Wars New Frontier: Public Libraries." https://www.washingtonpost.com

Graham, David A. 2017. "Red State, Blue City." *The Atlantic*, (March): 24–26. https://www.theatlantic.com

Green, Andy. 2020. "The Growing Divide: Red States vs. Blue States." *Georgetown Public Policy Review*. https://gppreview.com/

Greenblatt, Alan. 2022. "The New Faces of State Legislatures." https://www.governing.com

Greenblatt, Alan. 2021a. "It Took Decades for America to Become Divided." https://www.governing.com

Greenblatt, Alan. 2021b. "Why Cities Have More People but Less Clout." https://www.governing.com

Greve, Michael S. 2018. "Block Party Federalism." *Harvard Journal of Law and Public Policy* 42, no. 1: 279–307.

Grumbach, Jacob M. 2022. *Laboratories Against Democracy: How National Parties Transformed State Politics*. Princeton, NJ: Princeton University Press.

Grumbach, Jacob M.; and Jamila Michener. 2022. "American Federalism: Political Inequality, and Democratic Erosion." *Annals of American Academy of Political and Social Science* 699, no. 1 (March): 143–155.

Hajnal, Zoltan; and Michael U. Rivera. 2014. "Immigration, Latinos, and White Partisan Politics: The New Democratic Defection." *American Journal of Political Science* 58, no. 4 (October): 773–789.

Hannah, Lee A.; and Daniel J. Mallison. 2018. "Defiant Innovation: The Adoption of Medical Marijuana Laws in the American States." *Policy Studies Journal* 46, no. 2 (May): 402–423.

Hernandez, Kristian. 2022. "States Band Together to Block Immigration Policy." https://www.governing.com/

Hendrix, Michael. 2020. "America's Ever-Widening Urban-Rural Political Divide." https://www.governing.com

Hopkins, David A. 2017. *Red Fighting Blue: How Geography and Electoral Rules Polarize American Politics.* Cambridge: MASS: Cambridge University Press.

"Gelman." 2020. https://roppercenter.cornell.edu

"How is the Population Changing and Growing" 2022. https://www.usafacts.org

"How Groups Voted in 2020." 2020. https://ropercenter.cornell.edu/

"How Much Money Do Schools Spend on Education?" 2022. https://usafacts.org

"How Much Does the Government Spend and Where Does the Money Go?" 2023. https://www.usafacts.org

Hubbard, Kala. 2021. "The 10 States with Most Racial Diversity." https://www.usnews.com

Huberfeld, Nicole. 2021. "Health Equity, Federalism, and Cannabis Policy." *Boston University Law Review* 101, no. 3 (May): 897–913.

Igielnik, Ruth; Scott Keeter, and Hannah Hartig. 2021. "Behind Biden's 2020 Victory: An Examination of the 2020 Electorate, Based on Validated Voters." https://pewresearch.org

"Immigration and Border Security." 2022. https://usafacts.org

Ingraham, Christopher. 2018. "Low Voter Turnout is no Accident, According to Ranking of the Ease of Voting in all 50 States." https://www.washingtonpost.com

Jacob, Nicholas; and B. Kal Muni. 2019. "Place-Based Imagery and Voter Evaluation: Experimental Evidence on the Politics of Place." *Political Research Quarterly* 72, no. 2 (June): 263–277.

Jenkinson, Clay S. 2023. "On Immigration: Keeping Lady Liberty's Promise." https://www.governing.com

Johnson, Kenneth. 2022. "Rural America Lost Population Over the Last Decade for the First Time in History." Carsey School of Public Policy, University of New Hampshire. https://Carsey.unh.edu

Kanik, Alexander; and Patrick Scott. 2020. "The Urban-Rural Divide Only Deepened in the 2020 Election." https://www.citymonitor.ai

Karapin, Roger; Andreas Balthasar; Miranda A. Schreurs; and Frederic Varone. 2020. "Federalism as a Double-Edged Sword: The Slow Energy Transition in the United States." *Journal of Environment and Development* 29, no. 1 (March): 26–50.

Kettl, Donald F. 2021. "How American-Style Federalism is Dangerous to Our Health." https://www.governing.com

Kiernan, John S. 2022a. "States with the Highest and the Lowest Tax Rate." https://wallethub.com/

Kiernan, John S. 2022b. "Most and Least Federally Dependent States." https://wallethub.com/

Klement, Joachim. 2018. "Red States, Blue States: Two Economies, One Nation." https://blogs.cfaininstitute/org

Konisky, David M.; and Paul Nolette. 2022. "State of American Federalism: 2021-022: Federal Courts, State Legislatures, and the Conservative Turn in the Law." *Publius* 52, no. 3 (Summer): 353–381.

Kotkin, Joel; and Wendell Cox. 2020. "Red V. Blue: Seismic Shifts in Economic and Demographic Power are Occurring Across America." https://www.city-journal.org/

Koutsobinas, Nick. 2021. "Red States Grow as Blue States Shrink: Census." https://www.newsmax.com

Krishan, Nihal. 2020. "Red States are Outperforming Blue States Economically." https://www.washingtonexaminer.com

Krislov, Samuel. 2001. "American Federalism as American Exceptionalism." *Publius* 31, no. 1 (Winter): 9–26.

LaCombe, Scott J; Caroline Tolbert; and Karen Mossberger. 2022. "Information and Policy Innovation in U.S. States." *Political Research Quarterly* 75, no. 2 (June): 353–365.

Lacroix, Allyson L. 2010. *The Ideological Origins of American Federalism*. Cambridge, MA: Harvard University Pree.

Lee, Josephine. 2023a. "The New Children's Crusade: Recruiting for America's Cultural War." https://www.texasobserver.org/

Lee, Josephine. 2023b. "Abbott Wants to Deny Undocumented Kids a Public Education." https://www.texasobserver.org

Lopez, Adriana. 2021. "Most Urbanized States 2021." https://www.porch.com

Lassiter, Matthew D. 2011. "Political History Beyond the Red-Blue Divide." *Journal of American History* 98, no. 3 (December): 760–764.

Louis, Sarah. 2022. "The States Americans are Leaving (and Where They are Headed)." https://www.moneywise.com

"Lutji, Ben. 2020. "What is the Average Teacher Salary Salary by State, Location, and School Type." https://purify.com/

Lyons, Jeffrey. 2017. "The Family and Partisan Socialization in Red and Blue America." *Political Psychology* 38, no. 2 (April): 297–312,

Makhlouf, Medha D. 2020. "Laboratories of Exclusion: Medicaid, Federalism & Immigrants." *New York University Law Review* 95, no 6 (December): 1680–1777.

"Male to female Ratio by State." 2022. https://worldpopulationreview.com/

Mallison, Daneil J. 2021. "Policy Innovation Adoption Across the Diffusion Life Course." *Policy Studies Journal* 49, no. 2 (May): 335–358.

Manzanetti, Zoe. 2021. "Are Republican Sates More Federally Dependent?" https://www.governing.com

McCann, Adam. 2024. "Best and Worst State Economies in 2024." https://wallethub.com/

McCann, Adam. 2022a. "Most and Least Educated States in America." https://wallethub.com

McCann, Adam. 2022b. "Happiest States in the U.S." https://walethub.com/

McCann, Adam. 2021. "States with the Best and the Worst School Systems." https://wallethub.com

McGee, Kate. 2021. "Texas 'Critical Race Theory' Bill Limiting Teaching of Current Events Signed into Law." https://www.texastribune.org/

Meckler, Laura; and Hannah Natanson. 2023. "More States Scrutinizing AP Black Studies After Florida Complaints." https://www.washingtonpost.com

"Median Age in the United States in 2022, by State." 2023. https://wwwe.statista.com/

Menon, Aravind; and Daneil J. Mallison. 2022. "Policy Diffusion Speed: A Replication Study Using the State Policy Innovation and Diffusion Database." *Political Studies Review* 20, no. 4 (November): 704–716.

Miller, Justin. 2023. "'Colossal Waste of Money': Texas Nears $ Billion in Border Wall Contracts." https://www.texasobserver.org

Miller, Kenneth P.; and Andrew Sinclaire. 2022. "Red v. Blue States: Competition Visions for 2022 and 2024." https://roseinstitute.org/

Miranda, Mathew. 2022. "How California Built a Safety Net for Undocumented Immigrants." https://www.governing.org

Mitchell, Josh. 2022. "Red States are Winning the Post-Pandemic Economy." http://www.wsj.com

Morris, Kathy. 2022. "The Most Difficult States to Vote (and the least)." https://www.zippia.com/

Morrison, Aaron. 2016. "Diversity and State Legislatures: 14% of Lawmakers are Non-white, Despite Minorities Being 40% of US Population." https://www.ibtimes.com

"Most Diverse States 2023." 2023 https://worldpopulationreview.com

Mumma, Kristen S. 2023. "Politics and School Libraries: What Shapes Student's Access to Controversial Content." https://www.brookings.edu

Muro, Mark; and Jacob Whiten. 2019 "America Has Two Economies: And They're Diverging Fast." https://www.brookings.edu

Muro, Mark; Eli B. Duke; Yang You; and Robert Maxim. 2020. "Biden-Voting Counties Equal 70% of America's Economy. What Does This Mean for the Nation's Political-economic Divide?" https://www.brookings.edu

Natanson, Hannah. 2023. "As Red States Target Black History Lessons, Blue States Embrace Them." https://www.washingtonpost.com

National Center for Educational Statistics. 2023. "Estimated Average Salary of Teachers in Public Primary and Secondary Schools, 2021-022." 2023. https://nces.ed.gov/

National Conference of State Legislatures. "State Legislature Demographics." 2020. https://ncsl.org/

Noel, Hans. 2016. "Ideological Factions in the Republican and Democratic Parties." *Annal of American Academy of Political and Social Science* 667, no. 1 (September): 166–188.

Olsen, Henry. 2023. "California is in Decline. And It's Likely to Get Even Worst." https://www.washingtonpost.com/

"Opinions: Red and Blue States – Americans Vote with Their U-Hauls." 2023. Las Vegas Review-Journal Editorial Board. https://www.timesfreepress.com

"Our Changing Population: United States." 2022. https://www.usafacts.org

"Partisan Composition of State Legislatures" 2023. https://ballotpedia.org

Pew Research Center, 2021. "Beyond Red Vs. Blue: The Political Typology." https://wwwpewresearch.org

Phillips, Amber. 2016. "The Striking Lack of Diversity in State Legislatures." https://www.washingtonpost.com

"Population Distribution by Age 2021." 2021. https://www.kff.org
"Population Distribution by Sex 2021." 2021. https://www.kff.org/
Povich, Elaine S. 2021. "Women Gain Record Power in State Legislatures." https://www.pewtrusts.org
"Poverty Rate by States 2023." 2023. https://worldpopulationreview.com/
Powers, Amanda; and Alicia Bannon. 2022. "State Supreme Court Diversity – May 2022 Update." https://www.brennancenter.org/ g
Pratheepan, Gulasekaram; Rick Su; and Rose C. Villazor. 2019. "Anti-Sanctuary and Immigration Localism." *Columbia Law Review* 119, no 3 (April): 837–894.
"Presidential Election Results." 2020. https://nbcnews.com; https://www.fec.gov/
"Percent of Babies Born to Unmarried Mothers 2020." 2020. https://cdc.gov/
Price, Michelle L. 2023. "Schools Become Flashpoint for Republican Eyeing White House." https://apnews.com
Public Religious Research Institute. 2021a. "Religious Affiliation by State." https://ava.prri.org/
Public Religious Research Institute. 2021b. "White Evangelical Protestants by State." https://ava.prri.org/
Public Religious Research Institute. 2021c. "Frequency of Church Attendance by State." 2021. https://ava.prri.org/
"Racial and Ethnic Diversity Index by State 2020." 2021. https://www.census.com/
Rakich, Nathaniel. 2020. "How Urban or Rural is Your State? And What Does that Mean for the 2020 Election?" https://FiveThirtyEight.com
Rao, Ankita; Erum Salam; and Juweek Adolphe. 2020. "Which US States Make it Hardest to Vote?" https://www.theguardian.com
Rayasam, Renuka; Noland D. McCaskill; Beatrice Jin; and Allan J. Vestal. 2021. "Why State Legislatures are Still Very White – and Very Male." https://www.politico.com
"Red Families Vs. Blue Families." 2010. https://www.npr.org
Reingold, Beth. 2019. "Gender. Race/Ethnicity, and Representation in State Legislatures." *Political Science & Politics* 52, no. 3 (July): 426–429.
"Religious Affiliation by State." 2021. https://ava.prri.org/
Renn, Aron M. 2021. "We're a Suburban Nation. We Need to Get Used to It." https://www.governing.com
Rennenkampff, Marik V. 2020. "'Democrat-Run Cities' Fuel the Economy, Keep Many Red States Afloat." https://thehill.com
Riccardi, Nicholas. 2023. "Conservatives go to Red States and Liberals go to Blue as the Country Grows More Polarized." https://news.yeahoo.com/
Saad, Lydia. 2013. "In the U.S.; Blue States Outnumber Red States, 20 to 12" https://new/gallup.com
"SAIPE State and County Estimates for 2022." 2023. https://census.gov/
Savat, Sara. 2020. "The Divide Between Us: Urban-Rural Political Differences Rooted in Geography." https://source.wustl.edu
Sager, Josh. 2014. "Red America vs. Blue America: State Map Illustrates the Difference," https://theprogressivecynic.com/
Saul, Stephanie; Patricia Mazzei; and Trip Gabriel. 2023. "DeSantis Takes on Education Establishment, and Builds His Brand." https://www.nytimes.com/

Schraufnagel, Scot; Michael J. Pomante II; and Quan Li. 2022. "The Cost of Voting in the American States: 2022." *Election Law Journal* 21, no. 3 (September): 220–228.

Schraufnagel, Scot; Michael J. Pomante II; and Quan Li. 2020. "The Cost of Voting in the American States: 2020." Election Law Journal 19, no. 4 (December): 503–509.

Shendruk, Amanda. 2019. "The Difficulty of Voting in Every US State, Ranked." https://qz.com/

Skolnik, Jon. 2022. "Book Banning Fever Heats Up in Red States." https://www.salon.com/

Smith, Carl. 2022. "Which States Lost Population in 2021 and What Does it Mean?" https://www.governing.com

Smith, Carl. 2021a. "The Rise of Women in State Legislatures: A State-by-State Map." https://www.govrning.com

Smith, Carl. 2021b. "Blacks in State Legislatures: A State-by-State Map." https://www.govrening.com

Smith, Carl. 2020. "Hispanics in State Legislatures: State-by-State Map." https://www.governing.com

"State Legislature Demographics." 2020. www.ncsl.org/

"State Partisan Composition." 2022. https://www.ncsl.org/

"State Population Totals and Components of Change." 2022. https://census.gov/

"State Ranking of Conservative Policies." 2021. https://ratings.conservative.org/

Swasey, Benjamin. 2021. "Map: See Which States Have Restricted Voter Access, and Which States Have Expanded it." https://www.npr.org

"Teacher Salary by State." 2020. https://study.com/

"Tenn Birth Rate by State." 2020. https://cdc.gov/

"Teen Pregnancy Rate by State." 2023. https://worldpopulationreview.com/

"The Blue State Exodus Continues." 2022. Editorial Board, *Wall Street Journal*. https://www.wsj.com

"The 2020 Census of American Religion." 2021. https://www.prri.org

Trachtman, Samuel. 2022. "State Policy and National Representation: Marijuana Politics in American Federalism." *Legislative Studies Quarterly* (January). Published Online on January 19. https://onlinelibrary.wiley.com/doi/abs/10.1111/lsq.12370

Trujillo, Kristin L.; and Zack Crowley. 2022. "Symbolic Versus Material Concerns of Rural Consciousness in the United States." *Political Geography* 96, no. 1 (June): 102658.

"U-Haul Migration Trends: Texas, Florid Top Growth States Again in 2023" 2024. https://www.prnewwswire.com/

"Unemployment Rate by States, Seasonally Adjusted." 2022. https://bls.gov/

"US GDP by State, 2022 Rankings." 2022. https://moneytransfers.com/

U.S. Census Bureau. 2021. "2020 Apportionment Results Delivered to the President." April 26, 2021, Press Release. https://www.census.gov/

U.S. Centers for Disease Control and Prevention. 2022. "Divorce Rates by States: 1990, 1995, and 1999-021." https://cdc.gov/

U.S. Centers for Disease Control and Prevention. 2021a. "Teen Birth Rate by State 2020." https://cdc.gov/

U.S. Centers for Disease Control and Prevention. 2021b. "Percent Babies Born to Unmarried Mothers 2020." https://cdc.gov/

"U.S. Share of Women in State Legislatures 2022 by State." 2023. https://www.statista.com/

"US States Ranked by Population 2022." 2022. https://www.worldpopulationreview.com/states/

Van Dam, Andrew. 2023. "The Oldest (and the Youngest) States and the Shrinking Number of Teenagers with Licenses." https://washingtonpost.com/

Vaughan, Jessica M.; and Bryan Griffith. 2021. "Map: Sanctuary Cities, Counties, and States." Center for Immigration Studies. https://cis.org

Vedantam, Shankar. 2014. "Political Map: Does Geography Shape Your Ideology?" https://www.npr.org

Viebeck, Elise. 2021a. "States Across the Country are Dropping Barriers to Voting, Widening a Stark Geographic Divide in Ballot Access." https://www.washingtonpost.com

Viebeck, Elise. 2021b. "New Texas Voting Bill Deepens Growing Disparities in How Americans Can Cast Their Ballots." https://www.washingtonpost.com

"Voting and Registration by State." 2020. https://census.gov/

"Voting Ease by State: October 1, 2020." 2020. https://publicwise.org/

Voting Rights Lab. 2021. "A Tale of Two Democracies: How the 2021 Wave of State Voting Laws Created a New American Fault Line." https://votingrightslab.org/

Wallace, Jeremy. 2023. "How Governor Greg Abbott Plans to Enact Private School Vouchers in Texas." https://www.houstonchronicle.com/

Weissert, Carol S.; and Matthew J. Uttermark. 2017. "Glass Half Full." *State & Local Government Review* 49, no 3 (September): 199–214.

Weissmann, Jordan. 2020. "The Economy Really is Worse in Blue States. But Why?" https://slate.com

West, Darrell M. 2022. "Why Federalism Has Become Risky for American Democracy." https://www/brookings.edu

"Whaite Evangelical Protestants by State." 2021. https://ava.prri.org/

"Which States are the Most Educated?" 2022. https://usafacts.org/

Willis, Haisten; and Griff Witte. 2020. "In Neighboring Georgia Counties, Election Revealed a Growing Divide that Mirrors the Nation." https://washingtonpost.com

Worstall, Tim. 2015. "Solved: Why Poor States are Red and Rich States are Blue." https://www.forbes.com

3
HEALTH PROFILE OF RED AND BLUE STATES

In this chapter we examine how partisan and ideological polarization impacts healthcare systems of the red and blue states. We discuss the health profiles of the red and blue states to highlight the differences between the two.

We begin by examining what differences might exist in state financing of their healthcare systems. We present some data on Medicaid but leave most of that discussion to Chapter 5. But we do explore differences in health spending by red and blue states and how much states (and the federal government) support state healthcare systems. We next examine health indicators, such as maternal health, obesity, and health status. We follow that up by looking at a variety of healthcare indicators, such as rates of insurance, health insurance costs, and access to care. We then explore the infrastructure of the state healthcare system. These include the type of healthcare facilities and their distribution, workforce and issues associated with them, and factors that impact access to care. We then bring this all together by presenting a ranking of state healthcare systems.

Healthcare Financing

In this section, we examine the finances surrounding state healthcare systems, focusing on differences between red and blue states. Table 3.1 begins our journey. Are there differences in the amount that states

DOI: 10.4324/9781032671147-3

spend on healthcare depending on whether they are red or blue states? Table 3.1 presents the data. On average, the blue states spend almost $900 more per person on healthcare than do the red states. Of course, there is variation. The highest spending red state, Alaska, spent $14,500 per person on healthcare. The lowest of the red states is Utah at $7,250. For the blue states, the highest spending state was New York, at $12,480 per person. The lowest spending blue state was New Mexico, at $8,900. The red state average is less than the U.S. average, while the blue state

TABLE 3.1 State Health Spending per Person (2019)

Red States		Blue States	
Alabama	$8,650	California	$9,900
Alaska	$14,500	Connecticut	$11,570
Arizona	$8,220	Delaware	$12,200
Arkansas	$9,500	Hawaii	$9,100
Georgia	$8,340	Illinois	$9,980
Idaho	$8,530	Maine	$11,540
Indiana	$10,350	Maryland	$10,280
Kansas	$9,340	Massachusetts	$12,220
Kentucky	$9,900	Michigan	$9,740
Louisiana	$9,790	New Jersey	$11,020
Mississippi	$9,190	New Mexico	$8,900
Missouri	$9,990	New York	$12,480
Montana	$10,350	Oregon	$10,110
Nebraska	$10,440	Pennsylvania	$11,300
North Carolina	$9,100	Rhode Island	$10,930
North Dakota	$12,260	Vermont	$11,740
Oklahoma	$9,360	Washington	$9,900
South Carolina	$8,740		
South Dakota	$13,150		
Tennessee	$8,710		
Texas	$8,590		
Utah	$7,250		
West Virginia	$12,310		
Wyoming	$10,220		
Average	$9,871		$10,759
U.S. Average[a]	$10,174		

Adapted with permission from: Johnson et al. (2022).

[a] Calculated by authors.

average is higher than the overall average. So, our first table suggests that blue states spend more money to fund their healthcare system than do the red states.

Table 3.2 looks at the sources or payers of healthcare. We identify four sources: Medicare, Medicaid, private insurance, and out-of-pocket payers (OOP). Medicare is a solely federally funded program. Medicaid is a shared federal/state funded program. Private insurance may come through an employer, people paying for health insurance on their own or buying insurance on exchanges through the Affordable Care Act (ACA) (which includes federal subsidies). Out-of-pocket reflects healthcare costs directly paid by the patient or the family of the patient.

As Table 3.2 shows, Medicaid pays a lower percentage of healthcare costs in red states than in blue states and lower than the overall U.S. average. This may reflect, as we discuss in Chapter 4, more stringent Medicaid eligibility requirements than in blue states. This is despite the fact, as seen in Chapter 2, that poverty levels are higher in red states than in blue states.

Private insurance pays a slightly higher percentage of healthcare spending in blue states compared to red states. The blue state average is similar to the overall average, while the red state average is below the overall average. This may be a function of red states not embracing the ACA as much as blue states (see Chapter 4). Finally, out-of-pocket spending is higher in red states than in blue states, and higher than the overall average, perhaps reflecting policies regarding Medicaid and the ACA. Red states appear to ask their residents to directly pay more of their healthcare bill than do blue states.

Table 3.3 takes a broader look at state healthcare costs. The table shows where each state ranks in terms of how well it controls costs. The lower numbers indicate states that have pretty good control of costs and higher numbers indicate states that do not control their costs very well. The table then presents an average of the rankings. The blue states, on average, do a better job of controlling costs based on rankings. The top three states are Maryland (1), Michigan (2), and Rhode Island (3). All three are blue states. The bottom three states are Louisiana (48), Delaware (49), and Alaska (50). In this case, two of the three bottom states are red states, with only Delaware being a blue state. As we have noted, averages can tell us a lot, but there is significant in-group variation. We can conclude, based on the Table 3.3 rankings, that the blue states do a better job of controlling healthcare costs than do red states.

TABLE 3.2 State Spending by Payee

State Spending by Percent Payee

Red States	Spending by payer (% of total)				Blue States	Spending by payer (% of total)			
	Medicare	Medicaid	Private	OOP[a]		Medicare	Medicaid	Private	OOP[a]
Alabama	29	14	32	26	California	23	21	37	20
Alaska	9	18	31	42	Connecticut	22	19	34	25
Arizona	26	19	35	20	Delaware	22	16	31	31
Arkansas	26	22	28	23	Hawaii	20	17	36	28
Georgia	24	13	40	23	Illinois	22	14	39	25
Idaho	21	14	35	30	Maine	23	18	33	26
Indiana	23	17	31	30	Maryland	22	17	34	27
Kansas	22	11	40	26	Massachusetts	20	19	34	27
Kentucky	25	21	34	20	Michigan	27	16	33	24
Louisiana	26	20	30	24	New Jersey	24	15	39	22
Mississippi	28	19	27	26	New Mexico	21	25	28	25
Missouri	25	17	34	24	New York	22	25	33	20
Montana	19	14	30	37	Oregon	20	21	33	25
Nebraska	20	11	38	31	Pennsylvania	24	17	34	25
North Carolina	25	16	32	27	Rhode Island	22	22	31	26
North Dakota	15	15	33	37	Vermont	19	21	34	27
Oklahoma	24	16	32	28	Washington	18	17	35	29
South Carolina	27	14	34	24					

(Continued)

TABLE 3.2 (Continued)

State Spending by Percent Payee

Red States	Spending by payer (% of total)				Blue States	Spending by payer (% of total)			
	Medicare	Medicaid	Private	OOP[a]		Medicare	Medicaid	Private	OOP[a]
South Dakota	19	10	33	38					
Tennessee	26	16	35	23					
Texas	23	16	36	25					
Utah	17	12	48	24					
West Virginia	25	18	25	32					
Wyoming	17	11	40	31					
Average	22.6	16.3	33.2	27.8		21.8	18.8	34.0	25.4
U.S. Average[b]	22.1	17.9	34.2	26.6			18.8	34.0	25.4

Adapted with permission from: Johnson et al. (2022)

[a] OOP refers to out-of-pocket spending.
[b] Authors' calculation from source.

TABLE 3.3 Ranking of How Well States Control Costs

Red States		Blue States	
Arkansas	5	Maryland	1
Kentucky	8	Michigan	2
North Dakota	9	Rhode Island	3
Montana	10	Hawaii	11
Indiana	14	Pennsylvania	12
Kansas	16	New Jersey	18
Utah	19	New Mexico	20
Arizona	22	Vermont	21
Tennessee	23	Illinois	25
Georgia	28	Massachusetts	26
Mississippi	29	New York	33
West Virginia	30	Maine	34
Idaho	31	Connecticut	37
South Dakota	32	California	39
Missouri	35	Washington	41
Alabama	36	Delaware	49
South Carolina	38	Oregon	50
Nebraska	40		
Oklahoma	43		
Wyoming	45		
Texas	46		
North Carolina	47		
Louisiana	48		
Alaska	50		
Average	29.33		24.82

Adapted with permission from: McCann (2022). Online at https://wallethub.com

Health Status Indicators

In this section, we draw a profile of the health status/issues of populations in the red and blue states using a series of indicators.

Life Expectancy

We begin by looking at life expectancy. This is a broad indicator that is a function of other indicators that we discuss below. Life expectancy is how long a person might live starting from a particular age, such as birth or at retirement. Life expectancy is a function of several variables, including genetics, lifestyle choices, and exogenous events such as floods or tornados. Genetics is, for the most part, beyond the control of individuals. Think of the genes, BRCA1 and BRCA2, that predispose women to breast cancer.

Lifestyle choices include things like the use of drugs and alcohol, smoking, dietary habits, exercise, getting vaccinations, and so forth. Exogenous events include things like the COVID-19 pandemic and the opioid epidemic, though there are overlaps between the exogenous events and lifestyle choices. Life expectancy reflects all three of these factors. We discuss the life expectancy data first and then explore some of these other factors. Montez et al. (2020, 669) argue that "Given that life expectancy captures overall social, economic, physical and mental well-being, such trends paint a troubling portrait of life and death in the United States."

Montez et al. (2020) note that life expectancy in the United States is below that of most developed nations, particularly since the 1980s. They point out that a lot of factors that could contribute to the United States' disappointing life expectancy numbers, such as lifestyle, lack of insurance, and inequities, do not play much of a role in differentiating the United States from other developed countries. They argue that data needs to be disaggregated to the state level. There are considerable differences between the states, as we have argued in this book.

A second, related explanation, which we have also argued in this book, is a structural explanation. Here we are talking about the division of power between the federal government and the states, federalism, and the devolution of policy responsibilities to the states. A related point is that states have pre-empted policies by local governments dealing with a variety of concerns such as minimum wage, smoke ordinances, and so forth. Actions by some states in the wake of the COVID-19 pandemic fit this pattern and are discussed in Chapter 7.

The first thing we should note is that U.S. life expectancy from birth has increased over the years. In 1950, life expectancy from birth in the United States was 68.33 years. By 2019, it was 78.87 years ("U.S. Expectancy 1950–2022"). This is an increase over the 69 years of 15.4 percent.

The second thing we should note is that the United States is not a leader in life expectancy. The United States is fortieth out of 60 nations ("U.S. Life Expectancy 1950–2022", n.d.).

A third point is that in the five-year period from 2014 to 2018, U.S. life expectancy declined ("U.S. Life Expectancy 1950–2022", n.d.). One possible reason for this is the opioid epidemic. Now we turn to the theme of this book, red states and blue states.

Table 3.4 presents the data. Table 3.4 first shows life expectancy from birth in our red and blue states. The U.S. average is 77 years. The average of blue states exceeds that number, at 77.8 years. The red state average is below the U.S. average at 75.4 years. This is below the U.S. average by almost 2 percent. The second column looks at life expectancy from age 65. Again, the red state average is below the U.S. average while the blue state average is slightly above the U.S. average.

Montez et al. (2020), in their time-series analysis of states across 18 policy domains, found that if states had the more liberal policies found in blue states, life expectancy would be higher and lower if states followed more red state policies. They also found that changes in state policies had tended to move in more conservative directions and, as a result, contributed to lower life expectancy (see Table 3.5). Such policies include those related to gun control, reproductive rights (i.e., abortion), Medicaid, and paid leave.

Levey (2020), reporting on the Montez et al study (2020), also noted the importance of the opioid epidemic in declining life expectancy, especially in red states. And he also mentioned the structural weakness of the U.S. public health system and other safety net programs.

Montez et al. (2020, p. 693) conclude their article as follows: "the overarching conclusion is clear: states that have invested in their populations' social and economic well-being by enacting more liberal policies over time tend to be the same states that have made considerable gains in life expectancy."

Causes of Death

We now turn to death rates in blue and red states. Table 3.6 presents the data. The data is based on crude death rates per 100,000. This adjusts for differences in state populations. As can be seen, both the red and blue states exceed the U.S. average (2020 data). While we do not present that data in this book, it is likely that purple states have lower than average death rates.

We next move on to looking at some of the leading causes of death. Let us begin with overall U.S. data. Table 3.7 displays the 15 leading causes of death in 2019. As can be seen, the top five causes of death are heart disease, cancer, accidents, respiratory diseases, and stroke. The same pattern exists at the state level. We look at 2019 data here because 2019 is the last year before the COVID-19 pandemic (which we discuss in Chapter 7).

TABLE 3.4 Life Expectancy by State (2020)

Red States	Years Expected to Live From Birth	Years of Life Beginning at Age 65	Blue States	Years Expected to Live From Birth	Years of Life Beginning at Age 65
Alabama	73.2	16.6	California	79.0	21.0
Alaska	76.6	18.8	Connecticut	78.4	19.0
Arizona	76.3	18.5	Delaware	76.7	18.4
Arkansas	73.8	16.9	Hawaii	80.7	21.0
Georgia	75.6	17.4	Illinois	76.8	18.0
Idaho	78.4	18.8	Maine	77.8	19.0
Indiana	75.0	17.3	Maryland	76.8	18.4
Kansas	76.4	17.9	Massachusetts	79.0	18.9
Kentucky	73.5	16.9	Michigan	76.0	17.8
Louisiana	73.1	16.5	New Jersey	77.5	18.2
Mississippi	71.9	16.1	New Mexico	74.5	18.3
Missouri	75.1	17.4	New York	77.7	18.4
Montana	76.8	18.4	Oregon	78.8	19.3
Nebraska	77.7	18.3	Pennsylvania	76.8	18.1
North Carolina	76.1	18.0	Rhode Island	78.2	18.6
North Dakota	76.9	18.2	Vermont	78.8	19.5
Oklahoma	74.1	16.6	Washington	79.2	19.5
South Carolina	74.8	17.7			
South Dakota	76.7	18.3			
Tennessee	73.8	17.9			
Texas	76.5	17.7			
Utah	78.6	18.8			
West Virginia	72.8	17.0			
Wyoming	76.3	18.1			
Average	75.4	17.7		77.8	18.9
U.S. Average	77.0	18.5			

Adapted from: Arias et al. (2022). Online at www.cdc.gov

While the pattern is the same among the states, the age-adjusted death rates and the ranks differ among and between our red and blue states. Tables 3.8–3.10 present the data for the top three causes of death for our red and blue states. And they tell the same story.

TABLE 3.5 Life Expectancy by State (2018)

Red States		Blue States	
Alabama	75.1	California	80.8
Alaska	78.0	Connecticut	80.4
Arizona	75.1	Delaware	77.8
Arkansas	75.6	Hawaii	81.0
Georgia	77.2	Illinois	78.8
Idaho	79.0	Maine	78.6
Indiana	76.8	Maryland	78.5
Kansas	78.0	Massachusetts	80.1
Kentucky	75.3	Michigan	77.7
Louisiana	75.6	New Jersey	79.8
Mississippi	74.6	New Mexico	77.2
Missouri	76.6	New York	80.5
Montana	78.7	Oregon	79.7
Nebraska	79.1	Pennsylvania	78.1
North Carolina	77.6	Rhode Island	79.8
North Dakota	79.3	Vermont	79.3
Oklahoma	75.6	Washington	80.0
South Carolina	76.5		
South Dakota	78.9		
Tennessee	75.5		
Texas	78.4		
Utah	79.6		
West Virginia	74.4		
Wyoming	78.1		
Average	77.0		79.3
U.S. Average	78.7		

Adapted from: Arias et al. (2021).

Note: Online at www.cdc.gov

Table 3.8 presents data about death rates due to heart disease in 2020. The U.S. rate was 168.2 per 100,000 people. The red states, on average, exceeded that rate, at 182.5 per 100,000 people. This is 14.3 percent higher than the U.S. rate. For blue states, the rate was 155.8 per 100,000 population, 7.4 percent below the U.S. average. Another way of looking at this is to rank all the states (including purple states [not included in the table]). The red states, on average, ranked 31.2, while the blue states ranked 20.1. As with our other tables, there is variation within the two groups. But, on average, blue states have a lower death rate.

Table 3.9 looks at death rates due to cancer in 2020. The U.S. rate was 144.1 deaths per 100,000 population. The blue state rate was 1.6 percent

TABLE 3.6 Crude Death Rates per 100,000 (2020)

Red States		Blue States	
Alabama	1,316.2	California	812.4
Alaska	707.1	Connecticut	1,064.2
Arizona	1020.7	Delaware	1,122.0
Arkansas	1257.5	Hawaii	855.2
Georgia	962.4	Illinois	1,053.9
Idaho	897.8	Maine	1,165.8
Indiana	1157.6	Maryland	992.0
Kansas	1100.3	Massachusetts	989.7
Kentucky	1248.1	Michigan	1,175.0
Louisiana	1221.7	New Jersey	1,080.8
Mississippi	1354.7	New Mexico	1,130.3
Missouri	1201.1	New York	1,051.1
Montana	1113.0	Oregon	948.2
Nebraska	1009.0	Pennsylvania	1,216.8
North Carolina	1032.5	Rhode Island	1,118.0
North Dakota	1052.1	Vermont	1,036.2
Oklahoma	1201.0	Washington	820.8
South Carolina	1173.3		
South Dakota	1104.6		
Tennessee	1222.7		
Texas	852.6		
Utah	661.5		
West Virginia	1462.7		
Wyoming	1027.4		
Average	1098.2		1037.2
U.S. Average	1027.0		

Adapted from: Centers for Disease Control and Prevention (2020). Online at www.CDC.gov

lower than the overall average, at 141.8 per 100,000 population. The red state average was 5.6 percent higher than average, at 155.2 deaths per 100,000 population. The blue states' average rank was just under 19, while the red states' average was 30.8.

Table 3.10 explores accidental deaths. The U.S. average accidental death rate in 2020 was 61 deaths per 100,000 population. The red states' average was just above the nation's average, at 62.8 deaths per 100,000. Blue states' average was below the country's average at 58 deaths per 100,000. The average rank of blue states was just under 22, while the average rank of red states was just above 27.

To summarize this section, death rates from various causes, in this case cancer, heart disease, and accidents, were higher in red states than in blue

TABLE 3.7 The 15 Leading Causes of Death in the U.S. (2019)

1	Heart disease
2	Cancer
3	Accidents
4	Chronic lower respiratory diseases
5	Stroke
6	Alzheimer's disease
7	Diabetes
8	Kidney disease
9	Influenza and pneumonia
10	Suicide
11	Chronic liver disease and cirrhosis
12	Septicemia
13	Hypertension
14	Parkinson's disease
15	Pneumonitis due to solids and liquids

Adapted from: Xu et al. (2021).

states. The causes of death are a function, as mentioned above, of various circumstances, such as, for example, genetics. But there are activities or inactivities that might lead to death from one of the causes listed in Table 3.7. In this section, we examine three of those factors.

The first of these factors is obesity. Obesity is commonly defined as excess body fat and is measured using the body mass index (BMI). This is an imperfect, though commonly used, measure. Some people with large muscle mass may have a high BMI but are not obese. Waist measurements may also be used to define whether someone is obese. A BMI of 30 is commonly considered the low level for obesity. The higher the BMI, the higher the level of obesity (Cleveland Clinic 2022).

Obesity is linked to a number of health issues. Obesity can lead to diabetes, heart issues, kidney disease, and chronic inflammation, among other health issues. Obesity rates have increased over the years. In 2011, the adult obesity rate in the United States was 27.4 percent; by 2020, it was 31.9 percent (Elflein 2022). This is an increase of over 16 percent.

Another way of looking at this issue is to consider how many people are affected. According to 2016 data, an estimated over 80 million people were overweight and another 100 million were obese (Waters and Graf 2018).

The cost of obesity through diseases that it affects is immense. Again, according to 2016 data, obesity is responsible for about $1.72 trillion, nearly 10 percent of the United States' gross domestic product (Waters and Graf 2018). Given the prevalence and costs of obesity, it is instructive to compare our red and blue states. Table 3.11 presents the data.

TABLE 3.8 Heart Disease Mortality Rate by State (2020)

Red States	Rate per 100,000 Population	Rank	Blue States	Rate per 100,000 Population	Rank
Alaska	139.8	8	Hawaii	125.0	2
Nebraska	143.8	10	Massachusetts	126.0	3
Arizona	144.8	12	Oregon	134.0	6
North Dakota	147.3	15	Washington	134.6	6
Idaho	151.9	17	Connecticut	138.4	7
South Dakota	155.2	20	California	144.0	11
Utah	155.6	21	Maine	146.2	13
North Carolina	156.2	22	Rhode Island	150.5	16
Wyoming	160.4	24	New Mexico	152.7	19
Montana	162.7	25	Delaware	159.6	23
Kansas	167.0	28	New Jersey	166.3	27
South Carolina	170.9	31	Vermont	167.1	29
Texas	173.9	34	Maryland	168.3	30
Georgia	183.7	36	Illinois	171.4	32
Indiana	183.9	37	Pennsylvania	175.7	35
Missouri	196.7	39	New York	183.9	38
West Virginia	197.8	41	Michigan	205.0	44
Kentucky	204.5	43			
Tennessee	212.0	45			
Louisiana	221.5	46			
Arkansas	222.5	47			
Alabama	237.5	48			
Oklahoma	244.1	49			
Mississippi	245.6	50			
Average	182.5	31.2		155.8	20.1
U.S. Average	168.2				

Adapted from: National Center for Health Statistics (2022b) and Kaiser Family Foundation (2023). Online at https://www.kff.org/statedata

Table 3.11 presents adult obesity prevalence rates. As can be seen, the prevalence rate for the United States as a whole is 38.3 per 100,0000 people. For blue states, the rate is 31.1 compared to 36.2 for the red states. The red state rate is over 16 percent higher than the blue state rate. The red states' prevalence is higher than the United States, and the blue state prevalence is below the national average. We should expect, therefore, higher rates of chronic diseases and costs for red states than for blue states due to obesity.

TABLE 3.9 Adjusted Death Rates and Rank for Deaths by Cancer (2020b)

Red States	Adjusted Death Rates per 100,00	Rank	Blue States	Adjusted Death Rates per 100,00	Rank
Utah	119.5	1	Hawaii	123.8	2
Arizona	127.7	4	New York	128.8	5
Wyoming	136.3	12	New Mexico	129.8	6
Idaho	136.5	13	California	130.3	7
North Dakota	139.5	16	New Jersey	133.4	8
Texas	139.8	17	Connecticut	133.8	9
Montana	141.5	18	Massachusetts	135.2	10
Alaska	143.7	21	Washington	138.7	15
Georgia	147.6	26	Rhode Island	141.6	19
Nebraska	147.6	27	Maryland	142.3	20
South Dakota	148.1	29	Oregon	145.8	24
North Carolina	148.4	30	Illinois	150.9	32
Kansas	151.4	35	Delaware	151.1	33
South Carolina	153.9	37	Vermont	152.2	35
Missouri	157.9	39	Pennsylvania	153.2	36
Louisiana	159.9	41	Maine	161.5	42
Alabama	161.6	43	Michigan	157.3	
Indiana	162.7	44			
Arkansas	163.8	45			
Tennessee	164.4	46			
Oklahoma	171.1	47			
Mississippi	176	48			
West Virginia	177	49			
Kentucky	177.3	50			
Average	152.22	30.75		141.75	18.94
U.S. Average	144.1				

Adapted from: National Center for Health Statistics (2022a) and Centers for Disease Control and Prevention (2022b).

As bad as obesity is for one's health, smoking is worse. According to the Food and Drug Administration (2022), smoking is "the leading preventable cause of disease and death in the United States." Over 480,000 Americans die from smoking-related deaths each year. Smoking is implicated in heart disease, cancer, diabetes, stroke, and chronic obstructive pulmonary disease (COPD), among others (Food and Drug Administration 2022). The percentage of those who smoke is higher in the red states than in the blue states (World Population Review 2024).

TABLE 3.10 Age-Adjusted Accidental Mortality Rates by State

Red States	Rate per 100,000 Population	Rank	Blue States	Rate per 100,000 Population	Rank
Alabama	59.6	25	California	44.1	4
Alaska	65.5	31	Connecticut	63.5	30
Arizona	69.1	39	Delaware	70.9	40
Arkansas	58.0	22	Hawaii	39.4	1
Georgia	50.8	10	Illinois	53.4	17
Idaho	50.8	11	Maine	76.9	43
Indiana	66.9	33	Maryland	44.4	6
Kansas	53.4	18	Massachusetts	54.3	20
Kentucky	87.5	49	Michigan	56.8	21
Louisiana	79.4	46	New Jersey	50.3	9
Mississippi	73.0	42	New Mexico	85.5	47
Missouri	68.4	37	New York	41.7	2
Montana	61.9	27	Oregon	52.0	14
Nebraska	42.3	3	Pennsylvania	69.0	38
North Carolina	67.1	34\	Rhode Island	65.6	32
North Dakota	51.9	13	Vermont	67.1	35
Oklahoma	62.0	29	Washington	51.3	12
South Carolina	77.8	44			
South Dakota	58.5	24			
Tennessee	86.5	48			
Texas	44.2	5			
Utah	49.4	8			
West Virginia	122.2	50			
Wyoming	60.4	26			
Average	62.8	27.2		58.0	########
U.S. Rate	61.0				

Adapted from: National Center for Health Statistics (2022c).

Related to health and behavior is physical activity, or the lack of physical activity, such as aerobics and resistance training. The U.S. Department of Health and Human Services (DHHS) (2018) recommends an hour of physical activity a day for children and adolescents. For adults, the recommendation is a minimum of 150 minutes of aerobic activity a week and a minimum of two resistance exercise sessions per week. The lack of physical activity can have profound effects on a person's health.

According to the National Center for Chronic Disease Prevention and Health Promotion (NCCDPHP) (2022), a component of the Centers for

TABLE 3.11 Obesity Prevalence by State (2021)

Red States	Rate per 100,000 Population	Blue States	Rate per 100,000 Population
Alabama	39.9	California	27.6
Alaska	33.5	Connecticut	30.4
Arizona	31.3	Delaware	33.9
Arkansas	38.7	Hawaii	25.0
Georgia	33.9	Illinois	34.2
Idaho	31.6	Maine	31.9
Indiana	36.3	Maryland	34.3
Kansas	36.0	Massachusetts	27.4
Kentucky	40.3	Michigan	34.4
Louisiana	38.6	New Jersey	28.2
Mississippi	39.1	New Mexico	34.6
Missouri	37.3	New York	29.1
Montana	31.8	Oregon	30.4
Nebraska	35.9	Pennsylvania	33.3
North Carolina	36.0	Rhode Island	30.1
North Dakota	35.2	Vermont	29.0
Oklahoma	39.4	Washington	34.2
South Carolina	36.1		
South Dakota	38.4		
Tennessee	35.0		
Texas	36.1		
Utah	30.9		
West Virginia	40.6		
Wyoming	32.0		
Average	36.2		31.1
U.S. Average	38.3[a]		

Adapted from: Centers for Disease Control (2022c). Online at www.cdc.gov

[a] Authors' calculations.

Disease Control and Prevention, physical inactivity can lead to heart disease, type 2 diabetes, and cancer. Physical activity can additionally help reduce pain for people with arthritis and lower blood pressure. Physical inactivity can lead to substantial healthcare costs, about $117 billion a year by one estimate (Centers for Disease Control and Prevention 2022e).

Table 3.12 presents the data (see also Centers for Disease Control and Prevention 2022d). The table shows the percentage of adults who regularly engage in physical activity, the converse of physical inactivity. The U.S. average is 77.1 percent. The blue state average is 78.3 percent, and the red

TABLE 3.12 Percentage of Adults Who Report Engaging in Physical Activity (2021)

Red States		Blue States	
Alabama	68.0	California	81.1
Alaska	79.8	Connecticut	78.7
Arizona	78.4	Delaware	74.3
Arkansas	69.1	Hawaii	80.7
Georgia	75.7	Illinois	75.5
Idaho	78.4	Maine	74.3
Indiana	74.3	Maryland	79.3
Kansas	76.9	Massachusetts	79.8
Kentucky	70.3	Michigan	77.3
Louisiana	72.5	New Jersey	76.6
Mississippi	68.4	New Mexico	77.6
Missouri	75.2	New York	74.3
Montana	79.2	Oregon	80.8
Nebraska	76.0	Pennsylvania	77.0
North Carolina	78.3	Rhode Island	77.6
North Dakota	74.8	Vermont	83.4
Oklahoma	72.3	Washington	83.2
South Carolina	75.0		
South Dakota	76.6		
Tennessee	73.0		
Texas	76.0		
Utah	82.5		
West Virginia	70.2		
Wyoming	81.2		
Average	74.6		78.3
U.S. Average	77.1		

Adapted from: Kaiser Family Foundation (2023). Online at www.kff.org

state average is 74.6 percent. The blue state percentage is about 4 percent higher than the red state percentage. Because the data in this table (and other places) is self-reported, there is a level of uncertainty about the numbers. The CDC (2022e) reports that more than 70 percent of high school students do not get physical activity. We would argue that the prevalence numbers in Table 3.12 understate the problem.

Table 3.13 concludes our discussion of chronic diseases. It focuses on three lung diseases: chronic bronchitis, emphysema, and COPD. The table shows the percentage of a state's adult population that was told they had one of these three chronic lung diseases. The U.S. average in 2021 was 7.1 percent. The blue state average was 6.4 percent. And the red state average was 8.1 percent. Again, there is variation within the states. Hawaii has the

Health Profile of Red and Blue States   177

TABLE 3.13 Share of Adults Told They Had Chronic Lung Disease

Red States		Blue States	
	Percentage (2021)		Percentage (2021)
Alabama	10.1	California	5.1
Alaska	6.8	Connecticut	6.0
Arizona	6.7	Delaware	6.5
Arkansas	10.9	Hawaii	4.0
Georgia	7.1	Illinois	6.1
Idaho	6.6	Maine	9.3
Indiana	9.3	Maryland	5.6
Kansas	7.0	Massachusetts	6.3
Kentucky	11.4	Michigan	8.5
Louisiana	9.2	New Jersey	6.1
Mississippi	9.6	New Mexico	6.5
Missouri	9.2	New York	6.4
Montana	6.5	Oregon	6.8
Nebraska	6.2	Pennsylvania	6.9
North Carolina	7.6	Rhode Island	6.4
North Dakota	5.5	Vermont	6.9
Oklahoma	8.6	Washington	5.9
South Carolina	8.5		
South Dakota	6.2		
Tennessee	10.4		
Texas	7.2		
Utah	4.8		
West Virginia	13.3		
Wyoming	5.4		
Average	8.1		6.4
U.S. Average	7.1		

Adapted from: Kaiser Family Foundation (2023). Online at www.kff.org

lowest average at 4 percent. The red states have five states with a percentage over 10 percent. West Virginia has the highest percentage, at 13.3.

Mental Health

We next address mental health. Table 3.14 presents the data. For the 2019–2020 period, the table shows the percentage of adults reporting mental illness and serious mental illness in the past year. The red states exceeded the U.S. average for both columns and the blue states were close to the U.S. average for both columns.

While we look at access to care in a subsequent section of this chapter, we now look at access to mental healthcare. Mental health issues present

TABLE 3.14 Percentage of Adults Reporting Mental Illness in the Past Year (2019–2020)

Red States	Any	Severe	Blue States	Any	Severe
Alabama	21.2	6.2	California	20.5	4.6
Alaska	22.2	5.8	Connecticut	18.8	4.8
Arizona	23.9	6.4	Delaware	20.5	5.4
Arkansas	22.6	7.3	Hawaii	17.9	4.4
Georgia	17.5	4.8	Illinois	20.7	5.4
Idaho	24.9	6.4	Maine	21.6	6
Indiana	21.8	6.8	Maryland	17.8	4.5
Kansas	26.9	6.7	Massachusetts	21.4	5.3
Kentucky	21.9	6.4	Michigan	22.3	5.5
Louisiana	21.2	5.6	New Jersey	18.3	4.5
Mississippi	21.1	5.5	New Mexico	21.2	5.3
Missouri	21.3	6.3	New York	18.8	4.5
Montana	23.4	6.2	Oregon	27.3	7.2
Nebraska	23.4	6.3	Pennsylvania	19.7	5.1
North Carolina	19.8	5.4	Rhode Island	24.1	5.6
North Dakota	20.8	6.1	Vermont	23.7	6.1
Oklahoma	25.6	6.8	Washington	25.5	6.4
South Carolina	21.7	6.0			
South Dakota	21.3	6.4			
Tennessee	20.5	6.3			
Texas	18.0	4.8			
Utah	29.7	7.6			
West Virginia	26.1	7.0			
Wyoming	23.6	6.4			
Average	22.3	6.2		21.2	5.3
U.S. Average	20.8	5.4			

Adapted from: Kaiser Family Foundation (2023). Online at www.kff.org

their own unique challenges. One of them is that mental health is not measurable in the same way that physical health is. There are few objective measurements of a person's mental health. A person's behavior can certainly be indicative of a person's mental status. So, for example, someone's behavior can distinguish between depression and schizophrenia. And there are questionnaires that can be used to help diagnose mental health issues.

Physical health issues are, for the most part, susceptible to objective measures through a variety of tests, such as MRIs, blood tests, and EKGs. One exception is pain. There are no objective measurements of pain. Patients can tell health providers they are experiencing pain; in some cases, such as late-stage cancers, the pain is so bad that it is clearly affecting the patient. Mental health, again, for the most part, lacks these kinds of objective measurements.

The lack of objective measurement contributes to the disparity in spending between mental and physical health. The comprehensive report by Milliman Research (Melek, Davenport, and Gray 2019) shows some of these disparities. Patients with behavioral issues (mental health) are much more likely to use out-of-network services than patients with physical health issues. Behavioral health providers are paid about 20 percent less than physical health providers by insurance plans (such as preferred provider organizations).

Total spending on behavioral health is dramatically lower than on physical health. In 2017, behavioral healthcare costs equalled about 5.2 percent of total healthcare spending. By contrast, physical healthcare spending comprised the other 94.8 percent of total healthcare spending (Melek, Davenport, and Gray 2019).

Suicide is a leading cause of death. It is the taking of one's own life. Risk factors for suicide include mental health issues, exposure to family violence, chronic pain, and the presence of guns in the house. More people die from gun-related suicides than from gun-related homicides. But most people with risk factors such as these do not commit or attempt suicide. Other factors such as financial difficulties and interpersonal stressors such as bullying can add to the risk factors (National Institute of Mental Health n.d.).

Table 3.15 presents the data on suicides in red and blue states. The blue state average is below the U.S. average and the red state average is about 50 percent higher than the blue state average. The red state average is nearly 40 percent higher than the U.S. average.

Table 3.16 presents data about those with behavioral/mental health issues who did not get needed treatment. The first data column of Table 3.17 presents an overall view of those needing treatment. The blue state average was a tenth of a percent below the U.S. average, while the red state average was over half a percent higher than the U.S. average. The second data column of Table 3.16 looks at the cost of care as a problem. The red state average was nearly seven percentage points lower than the U.S. average, while the blue state average was nearly four percentage points higher. The blue state average was almost 30 percent higher than the red state average.

A major reason for this discrepancy is insurance coverage. Table 3.17 presents data regarding Medicaid coverage. While neither red nor blue states excel at Medicaid coverage, blue state coverage exceeds both the national average and the red state average. The red state average is almost three percentage points below the national average while the blue state average is nearly five percentage points higher. The difference

TABLE 3.15 Age-Adjusted Suicide Rates (2020)

Red States	Rate per 100,000 population	Blue States	Rate per 100,000 population
Alabama	15.9	California	10.0
Alaska	27.2	Connecticut	9.3
Arizona	17.6	Delaware	12.1
Arkansas	19.2	Hawaii	12.9
Georgia	13.7	Illinois	10.5
Idaho	23.2	Maine	16.3
Indiana	15.0	Maryland	9.2
Kansas	18.4	Massachusetts	8.4
Kentucky	17.7	Michigan	13.1
Louisiana	13.8	New Jersey	7.1
Mississippi	13.9	New Mexico	24.2
Missouri	18.1	New York	8.0
Montana	25.9	Oregon	18.3
Nebraska	14.9	Pennsylvania	12.6
North Carolina	13.2	Rhode Island	8.4
North Dakota	18.1	Vermont	17.9
Oklahoma	21.9	Washington	15.2
South Carolina	16.3		
South Dakota	21.1		
Tennessee	17.1		
Texas	13.3		
Utah	20.8		
West Virginia	19.5		
Wyoming	30.5		
Average	18.6		12.6
U.S. rate	13.5		

Adapted from: Kaiser Family Foundation (2023). Online at www.Kff.org

between the two is about 39 percent. As we shall see in Chapter 5, there are differences between the Medicaid programs in the red and blue states and this factors in the differences in coverage and spending between the two sets of states.

All states have agencies that have some responsibility for the mental health of their citizens. But as measured by dollars, that responsibility varies among the states. On average, blue states spend almost twice as much on mental health services per capita than red states (American Addiction Centers n.d.).

A related aspect is how much was spent per client on mental health services. The disparities between the two groups are large. Blue states

TABLE 3.16 Adults Reporting Unmet Need for Mental Health Treatment (2019–2020)

Red States			Blue States		
		Percentage of Adults with Unmet Needs			Percentage of Adults with Unmet Needs
	Percentage of Adults Reporting Unmet Needs	Who Did Not Receive Treatment Because of Cost		Percentage of Adults Reporting Unmet Needs	Who Did Not Receive Treatment Because of Cost
Alabama	9.6	45.2	California	7.1	33.3
Alaska	8.1	35.8	Connecticut	5.6	21.3
Arizona	9.7	44.4	Delaware	8.1	28.1
Arkansas	9.7	44.6	Hawaii	4.2	29.8
Georgia	6.4	39.9	Illinois	7.0	42.8
Idaho	9.4	52.7	Maine	7.7	37.4
Indiana	9.7	35.2	Maryland	7.3	27.2
Kansas	11.3	44.7	Massachusetts	8.4	18.2
Kentucky	6.3	36.2	Michigan	7.6	36.5
Louisiana	7.7	32.0	New Jersey	5.4	31.1
Mississippi	6.7	44.3	New Mexico	8.1	25.9
Missouri	7.8	42.9	New York	6.1	35.0
Montana	7.1	40.8	Oregon	10.4	32.4
Nebraska	7.8	33.1	Pennsylvania	6.8	32.8
North Carolina	6.7	51.1	Rhode Island	8.9	54.0
North Dakota	6.8	47.1	Vermont	7.9	35.5
Oklahoma	9.2	47.3	Washington	7.5	38.7
South Carolina	6.0	22.1			
South Dakota	6.8	47.1			
Tennessee	7.5	59.4			
Texas	6.4	44.4			
Utah	12.6	45.9			
West Virginia	7.1	39.5			
Wyoming	7.7	64.7			
Average	8.1	43.4		7.3	32.9
U.S. Average	7.4	39.6			

Adapted from: Kaiser Family Foundation (2023). Online at www.kff.org

TABLE 3.17 Share of Adults with any Mental Illness in Past Year Covered by Medicaid (2018–2019)

Red States	Percentage of Adults	Blue States	Percentage of Adults
Alabama	15.4	California	29.7
Alaska	23.0	Connecticut	26.5
Arizona	24.2	Delaware	25.3
Arkansas	25.9	Hawaii	26.3
Georgia	14.7	Illinois	19.8
Idaho	11.3	Maine	25.7
Indiana	20.8	Maryland	22.9
Kansas	12.1	Massachusetts	28.0
Kentucky	29.9	Michigan	29.5
Louisiana	33.4	New Jersey	21.2
Mississippi	15.7	New Mexico	31.7
Missouri	13.7	New York	28.9
Montana	29.3	Oregon	22.1
Nebraska	12.6	Pennsylvania	24.8
North Carolina	17.5	Rhode Island	25.6
North Dakota	21.4	Vermont	37.1
Oklahoma	16.0	Washington	22.8
South Carolina	16.6		
South Dakota	12.1		
Tennessee	21.1		
Texas	9.7		
Utah	7.0		
West Virginia	34.3		
Wyoming	12.6		
Average	18.8		26.3
U.S. Average	21.6		

Adapted from: Kaiser Family Foundation (2023). Online at www.kff.org

spend, on average, about 58 percent more per client than do red states (authors' calculation from American Addiction Centers n.d.).

A similar question is how many people there are per mental health provider in the states.

As Table 3.18 shows, there are dramatic differences between the two groups of states. The U.S. average is 350 individuals per mental health provider. For the red states, the average is almost 466 individuals per mental health provider. Red states have 133 percent more individuals per mental health provider than the national average. Blue states, on the other hand, have about 27 percent fewer individuals per mental provider than average.

TABLE 3.18 Mental Health Workforce Availability (2020)

Red States		Blue States	
	Individuals per Mental Health Provider		Individuals per Mental Health Provider
Alabama	850	California	240
Alaska	160	Connecticut	230
Arizona	660	Delaware	340
Arkansas	400	Hawaii	360
Georgia	640	Illinois	370
Idaho	440	Maine	190
Indiana	560	Maryland	330
Kansas	470	Massachusetts	140
Kentucky	390	Michigan	330
Louisiana	310	New Jersey	380
Mississippi	540	New Mexico	240
Missouri	460	New York	310
Montana	300	Oregon	170
Nebraska	340	Pennsylvania	420
North Carolina	360	Rhode Island	220
North Dakota	470	Vermont	200
Oklahoma	240	Washington	230
South Carolina	520		
South Dakota	500		
Tennessee	590		
Texas	760		
Utah	280		
West Virginia	670		
Wyoming	270		
Average	465.8		276.5
U.S. Average	350		

Adapted with permission from: Reinert, Fritze, and Nguyen (2022). Online at www.mhanational.org

The argument can be made that regardless of which group of states we are considering, there are an insufficient number of mental health providers. Much of this may be due to lower provider reimbursement for mental health providers. And there is evidence that there is a fair amount of out-of-network provision of mental health services (Reinert, Fritze, and Nguyen 2022).

Table 3.19 is a summary of mental health features. It is a composite ranking that is based on 15 measures, some of which are included in previous tables in this chapter. The lower the number, the less the state

TABLE 3.19 Overall Ranking of States on Mental Health Policy (2020)

Red States	Ranking	Blue States	Ranking
Kentucky	10	Pennsylvania	2
South Carolina	14	Massachusetts	3
North Carolina	15	Delaware	4
North Dakota	20	Connecticut	5
Oklahoma	22	New Jersey	6
Georgia	23	New York	7
Mississippi	24	Illinois	8
Tennessee	26	Maryland	8
Montana	30	Vermont	11
Alaska	33	Rhode Island	12
Louisiana	35	Michigan	16
South Dakota	36	Hawaii	17
Indiana	38	California	18
Missouri	39	New Mexico	21
Utah	40	Maine	25
West Virginia	41	Washington	31
Arizona	42	Oregon	49
Nebraska	43		
Texas	44		
Wyoming	44		
Idaho	46		
Alabama	47		
Arkansas	48		
Kansas	50		
Average	33.8		14.3

Adapted with permission from: Reinert, Fritze, and Nguyen (2022). Online at www.mhanational.org

population suffers from some mental illness (prevalence) and access to care is higher. Lower is better than higher. Keeping this in mind, the average ranking for blue states was just over 14 while the average ranking for red states was nearly 34. As with other tables, there is variation within the two groups. Oregon, for example, is a blue state and ranks 49th. On the other hand, Kentucky, a red state, ranks 10th.

States play an important role in mental healthcare. There is federal legislation that addresses mental healthcare, such as the Affordable Care Act (2010) and the Mental Health Parity and Addiction Equity Act (2008). The federal role in mental health is complex and includes funding of mental health services, funding of research, creating the framework through legislation, regulations, oversight for the delivery of services, and protection of those with mental health issues. States work within the federal framework and can expand services if they so choose. As with physical healthcare, states oversee medical records and treatment facilities, among other things. States can use federal dollars through programs such as the Children's Health Insurance Program (CHIP) and Medicaid, as well as their own funds (Mental Health America 2022). In addition, in 2021, Congress passed the American Rescue Plan Act to provide, among other things, funds during the COVID-19 pandemic to states and local governments to help cover mental health services. The funds must be spent by 2026.

Eight states, and perhaps more, decided to use some of their funding from the American Rescue Plan to fund mental health services. The eight states were either blue or purple states (Quinton 2021).

In any event, there is unevenness in funding and providing mental health services, with the blue states providing more of those services than the red states. And it is also clear that funding and availability of services are not adequate to meet the need.

Guns and Homicide

Our next topic in this section looks at homicides and the intersection with guns. Red states have a higher rate of homicides than blue states (World Population Review 2022). Crime, including homicides, peaked in the United States in 1991 at 9.8 homicides per 100,000 (see Figure 3.1). Indeed, crime as a whole decreased significantly from the late 1980s and early 1990s. While this is not the place to discuss why crime decreased (see the discussion in Rushefsky 2017), perceptions of crime differ dramatically from the statistics. The public believes that crime has increased, while the data show that it has, in fact, decreased. Some of the perceptual issues are driven by political and ideological polarization. In 2022, record numbers of people surveyed thought that crime had gone up both locally and nationally. Interestingly, those who support the incumbent president's party tend to think that crime rates have been steady or gone down, while those

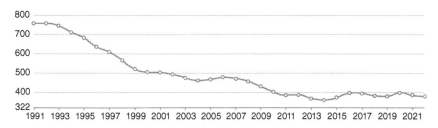

FIGURE 3.1   Rate of Violent Crime Offenses Per 100,000 People, 1991–2022.

Federal Bureau of Investigation (2022)

who oppose the incumbent president and his party tend to think that crime rates have gone up. Republicans were likely to think crime had gone up during the Obama (2009–2017) and Biden (2021–2025) administrations while Democrats were likely to think crime rates had gone up during the Trump (2017–2021) administration (Brenan 2022). For a while, increases in crime were thought to be a major campaign issue in the 2022 off-year elections that would heavily favor Republican candidates. The red wave surge that history suggested might happen in off-year elections did not occur, though Republicans regained control of the U.S. House of Representatives.

There is an argument over how to interpret the findings. Thiessen (2022) argues that the idea that red states have a murder problem is a myth pushed by Democrats. His response is that the high murder rate in red states is due to high murder rates in red states cities governed by Democrats. He points to cities such as Kansas City and St. Louis (in Missouri), Baton Rouge and New Orleans (in Louisiana), and cities in other red states with high murder rates.

Thiessen (2022) also points to studies that compared cities rather than states. A majority of cities with the highest murder rates were Democratic-led cities. And in red states with high murder rates, the number of murders in these largely red states was dwarfed by rates in large cities.

There is another element to this debate, one that involves red and blue states. That element is guns. The majority of homicides are committed with firearms, about 84 percent calculating from the U.S. average. The homicide rate among the red state average is higher than the blue state rate (Davis et al. 2022 and National Center for Health Statistics 2022e).

Table 3.20 displays data about gun ownership by state, in this case the percentage of households in a state where one or more guns are owned. The U.S. average is estimated at 44.1 percent of American households legally owning at least one gun. The red state average is over 53 percent, and the blue state average is nearly 32 percent, significantly smaller than the red state average.

Another element focusing on guns is how gun-friendly states are. In states that are gun-friendly, it is easier to legally obtain guns and there are fewer restrictions on where guns can be carried. Table 3.21 presents the data. The ranking in this table is from five to one. A state ranked "five" is extremely friendly to gun sales and ownership. A state ranked "one" is among the least friendly states.

The rankings are based on six state policies on guns: whether a gun carry permit is required, whether a purchase permit is required, whether firearm registration is required, whether open carry is allowed, whether background checks on private sales of guns are required, and whether there are restrictions on the size of the gun magazine (Joslyn Law

TABLE 3.20 Estimated Gun Ownership by State

Red States	% of Homes Where Gun Is Owned (2020)	Blue States	% of Homes Where Gun Is Owned (2020)
Alabama	55.5	California	28.3
Alaska	64.5	Connecticut	23.6
Arizona	46.3	Delaware	34.4
Arkansas	57.2	Hawaii	14.9
Georgia	49.2	Illinois	27.8
Idaho	60.1	Maine	46.8
Indiana	44.8	Maryland	30.2
Kansas	48.9	Massachusetts	14.7
Kentucky	54.6	Michigan	40.2
Louisiana	53.1	New Jersey	14.7
Mississippi	55.8	New Mexico	46.2
Missouri	48.8	New York	19.9
Montana	66.3	Oregon	50.8
Nebraska	45.7	Pennsylvania	40.7
North Carolina	45.8	Rhode Island	14.8
North Dakota	55.1	Vermont	50.5
Oklahoma	54.7	Washington	42.1
South Carolina	49.4		
South Dakota	55.3		
Tennessee	51.6		
Texas	45.7		
Utah	46.8		
West Virginia	58.5		
Wyoming	66.2		
Average	53.3		31.8
U.S. Average	44.1		

Adapted from: Learish (2022).

Note: Online at cbsnews.com/pictures/gun-ownership-rates-by-state

Firm 2023). A state rated five would likely not require carry or purchase permits, would not require gun registration, would allow guns to be carried openly, not require background checks, and have no restrictions on gun magazine size. Table 3.21 presents the data. The U.S. average is 3.9. The red state average is slightly above the U.S. average, at 4.2. The blue state average is 2.5, significantly lower than the red state average. It is clear that red states are considerably more gun-friendly than blue states. It is also clear that availability of guns is related to homicides.

TABLE 3.21 Gun-Friendliness of States

Red States	Gun-Friendliness Rating	Blue States	Gun-Friendliness Rating
Arkansas	3	California	1
Louisiana	3	Hawaii	1
Nebraska	3	Maryland	1
South Carolina	3	New Jersey	1
Alabama	4	New York	1
Georgia	4	Rhode Island	1
Indiana	4	Delaware	2
Kentucky	4	Illinois	2
Montana	4	Connecticut	3
North Carolina	4	Massachusetts	3
North Dakota	4	Michigan	3
Oklahoma	4	Oregon	3
South Dakota	4	Washington	3
Tennessee	4	New Mexico	4
Texas	4	Pennsylvania	4
Utah	4	Maine	5
Alaska	5	Vermont	5
Arizona	5		
Idaho	5		
Kansas	5		
Mississippi	5		
Missouri	5		
West Virginia	5		
Wyoming	5		
Average	4.2		2.5
U.S. Average	3.9		

Adapted from: Joslyn Law Firm (2023). Online at https://www.criminalattorneycincinnati.com/comparing-gun-control-measures-to-gun-related-homicides-by-state

Maternal Health

Maternal health focuses on the health of the prospective mother before pregnancy, during pregnancy, and in the post-partum (after pregnancy) period. In past years, pregnancy was dangerous for women, but as medical science and public health progressed as well as increased insurance coverage of pregnancy, maternal mortality rates declined. For example, in 1933, the maternal mortality rate was 619 deaths per 100,000 pregnancies. By the end of the twentieth century, the rate had declined to around nine deaths per 100,000 pregnancies (Declercq and Zephyrin 2020). The cause(s) of maternal death differ depending on the stage of the pregnancy and whether during or after the pregnancy. There are causes that are related to the quality of care and medical issues prior to pregnancy and during the pregnancy. Some of these issues can be seen in the post-partum period (Declercq and Zephyrin 2020).

While maternal mortality continued to decline in other advanced industrial nations, it began to rise in the late 1990s in the United States. In 2020, the United States had the highest maternal mortality rate among those nations, at 23.8 deaths per 100,000 live births. The next highest country was France at 8.7 deaths per 100,000 live births (Taylor et al. 2022).

A major concern about maternal mortality is racial/ethnic discrepancies. Black maternal mortality is 55 deaths per 100,000 live births versus 19 deaths per 100,000 for whites (Hispanic maternal mortality is just below the white level). The black rate is nearly three times larger than the white rate. It reflects decades of discrimination and discrepancies. However, it does not contradict the United States' first place in maternal mortality compared to other industrialized countries (Taylor et al. 2022). The problem remains.

Having established the U.S. place compared to other nations, let us consider maternal mortality among the states. Table 3.22 presents the data. As can be seen from the table, the maternal mortality rate for the blue states is below the U.S average. The red state maternal mortality rate is six points higher than the overall U.S. rate. The red state rate is 45 percent higher than the blue state rate, a sizable difference.

One important aspect of maternal mortality in the United States is that most of the deaths are preventable (Stephenson 2022). The COVID-19 pandemic played something of a role as did the age of some of the mothers (the older the mother, the more likely that there will be some issue with the pregnancy). Discrepancies based on race and/or ethnic group suggest differences in care between such groups.

Declercq and Zephyrin (2020) point out, for example, that the maternal mortality rate among black women with a college education is higher than the rate for white women who did not graduate from high school. Heart-related conditions are linked to more than a quarter of maternal deaths, while infections account for just over 13 percent, and blood-related issues account for just over 35 percent of maternal deaths (Declercq and Zephyrin 2020). Many of these causes are treatable, especially if caught early or before pregnancy begins.

There is a link between the problem of maternal mortality and other policies that we discuss in later chapters. As a result, we shall mention these briefly. Red states are more likely to have severe restrictions or bans on abortion than blue states (National Partnership for Women and Families 2022; see Chapter 6). The 2022 *Dobbs* case, which ended a federal right to

TABLE 3.22 Maternal Mortality by State

Red States	Rate per 100,000 Live Births (2018–2022)	Blue States	Rate per 100,000 Live Births (2018–2022)
Alabama	23	California	11
Alaska		Connecticut	16
Arizona	30	Delaware	
Arkansas	38	Hawaii	
Georgia	32	Illinois	18
Idaho	20	Maine	
Indiana	31	Maryland	21
Kansas	23	Massachusetts	16
Kentucky	35	Michigan	19
Louisiana	37	New Jersey	26
Mississippi	39	New Mexico	28
Missouri	24	New York	22
Montana		Oregon	17
Nebraska	25	Pennsylvania	18
North Carolina	27	Rhode Island	32
North Dakota		Vermont	
Oklahoma	30	Washington	18
South Carolina	32		
South Dakota			
Tennessee	42		
Texas	28		
Utah	16		
West Virginia	24		
Wyoming			
Average	29.3		20.2
U.S. Average	23		

Sources: Adapted from Kaiser Family Foundation (2023). Online at https://www.kff.org

abortion, has exacerbated and encouraged state bans. These states, all red states, according to the National Partnership for Women and Families (2022; referred subsequently as the National Partnership) also lag behind blue states in support for pregnant and post-partum women. Further, states that have not expanded Medicaid (see Chapter 5) have also had restrictive abortion policies. Medicaid is important because it covers 42 percent of all pregnancies (we discuss this in more detail in Chapter 5). Blue states are more likely to have paid leave laws than red states (none of which have paid leave requirements) (National Partnership 2022). In general, blue states are more supportive of women giving birth than red states. Some red states have attempted to address these issues (see Chapter 5).

We end this section by examining state rankings of maternal health (Black 2022). Table 3.23 presents the data. The ranking system is based on combining six metrics. The first metric is the percentage of women of childbirth age (18–44) with insurance coverage. The second metric is the percentage of women of childbirth age who have a primary care provider. The third metric is maternal care providers per 100,000 women of childbirth age. The fourth is the percentage of women with adequate prenatal care. These fourth metric measures access to the healthcare system for maternal care. The last two are based on quality measures. The fifth metric is the average merit-based payment incentive systems scores of OB-GYNs. This last metric is a system established by the U.S. Department of Health and Human Services that can pay bonuses to specialists depending on the quality of their work. This sixth metric is statewide maternity practices in infant nutrition and care scores for hospitals. This metric includes feeding education and support, support upon discharge, and so on.

As we can see from Table 3.23, the average ranking of blue states is about twice as high as the average ranking of red states. New Hampshire, a purple state (not shown in the table), has the number one ranking. The next highest eight states are blue states, with Rhode Island the highest of the blue states. The worst of the blue states on maternal health is New Mexico, clearly an outlier. For the red states, West Virginia has the highest score, at tenth, while Texas is last. There are clearly differences in maternal care between the two sets of states.

Children

Our last focus in this section is on the health of children. Children, it may be said, are our future and health is a particularly important aspect of care for children. Children may be covered by private insurance (most importantly, employer-based insurance) or by federal government programs such as Medicaid and the CHIP. In this section, we look at insurance coverage and other issues such as sex education, teen birth rates, rates of sexually transmitted diseases, and mental health as well as death rates.

We begin by looking at children's insurance coverage. We discuss insurance coverage in more detail in the next section, but that section covers the entire population. Here we concentrate on children. Table 3.24 presents the data. The table shows the percentage of a state's children population with insurance from an employer and through Medicaid, as well as the uninsured rate. The employer and Medicaid columns account for most of the insurance coverage, though not 100 percent. The red state average percent of those with private employer insurance is just under the U.S. average. The same is true for the percentage of children with Medicaid

TABLE 3.23 Rating States on Prenatal and Maternal Care

Red States		Blue States	
Kansas	8	Rhode Island	2
West Virginia	10	Vermont	3
Montana	11	Massachusetts	4
North Dakota	12	Connecticut	5
Indiana	21	Maryland	6
Alaska	22	Oregon	9
South Carolina	27	Pennsylvania	13
North Carolina	30	Delaware	14
South Dakota	32	Michigan	15
Kentucky	33	Maine	17
Utah	34	Washington	20
Arkansas	35	Illinois	24
Mississippi	36	New York	25
Missouri	37	New Jersey	26
Louisiana	38	California	28
Nebraska	39	Hawaii	31
Arizona	40	New Mexico	42
Oklahoma	41		
Alabama	43		
Idaho	45		
Tennessee	46		
Georgia	47		
Wyoming	48		
Texas	50		
Average	34.9		18.6

Adapted from: Black (2022). Online at https://www.valuepenguin.com/

coverage. The percentage of uninsured children is about a percent higher for red states as compared to the U.S. average.

For blue states, the percent of children with private insurance is higher than both the overall U.S. and red state average. The percentage of children covered by Medicaid in blue states is slightly higher than either the U.S. average or the red state average. There is a substantial difference between the blue state average of uninsured children and the red state/U.S. average. The blue state average is more than two percentage points below the U.S. average and more than three percentage points below the red state average.

No blue state has children's uninsured percentage higher than New Mexico's 6.9 percent. Texas has the highest rate of uninsured children among the blue and red states, at 11.8 percent, something that we will also see in the next section.

TABLE 3.24 Health Insurance Coverage for Children (2021)

Red States	Percent Insured by Employer	Percent Insured by Medicaid	Uninsured	Blue States	Percent Insured by Employer	Percent Insured by Medicaid	Uninsured
Alabama	44.5	43.6	4.3	California	46.5	42.9	3.4
Alaska	37.7	43.3	7	Connecticut	55.2	37.4	2.6
Arizona	46.5	38.4	8.4	Delaware	52.3	39.2	3.3
Arkansas	36.5	52.2	5.4	Hawaii	47.8	35.7	2.3
Georgia	46.5	39.7	6.6	Illinois	54.9	36.9	3.1
Idaho	50.3	36.0	6.4	Maine	57.2	31.0	3.4
Indiana	53.7	35.8	5.8	Maryland	51.6	36.6	4.3
Kansas	54.5	32.2	5	Massachusetts	58.2	35.3	1.0
Kentucky	43.3	47.7	3.7	Michigan	53.4	39.2	3.1
Louisiana	37.0	53.4	3.8	New Jersey	57.2	33.7	3.5
Mississippi	37.3	49.2	6.4	New Mexico	29.8	58.3	6.9
Missouri	53.7	32.7	5.7	New York	47.3	43.0	2.7
Montana	46.1	35.3	7.9	Oregon	49.7	41.7	3.3
Nebraska	57.4	28.4	5.4	Pennsylvania	52.8	37.8	4.2
North Carolina	43.9	41.2	5.4	Rhode Island	53.1	39.5	1.7
North Dakota	64.0	16.8	7.1	Vermont	48.6	45.4	
Oklahoma	38.2	46.6	7.2	Washington	50.7	39.4	3.1
South Carolina	41.5	45.8	5.2				
South Dakota	50.8	29.4	8.1				
Tennessee	47.4	40.3	4.9				
Texas	43.0	38.3	11.8				
Utah	64.4	16.7	8.1				
West Virginia	46.5	47.1	3.3				
Wyoming	57.5	23.8	10.3				
Average	47.6	38.1	6.4		51.0	39.6	3.2
U.S. Average	48.6	39.0	5.3				

Adapted from: Kaiser Family Foundation (2023). Online at https://www.kff.org/statedata

So, we start with some differences in how children get health insurance and the problem of uninsured children.

An important indicator of child health is the weight of a child at birth. Low birthweight is defined as a baby being born weighing less than 5 lbs, 8 oz. Low birthweight babies may come about because of premature delivery. There are a number of factors that might cause low birthweight babies (March of Dimes 2021). These include chronic conditions such as heart disease and diabetes, among others; taking some medications, such as those for treating high blood pressure; infections; and internal problems during pregnancy, such as with the placenta. Previous low-weight baby births are also a risk factor. The mother not gaining sufficient weight during pregnancy is a factor. Being exposed to domestic violence can lead to premature births. The age of the mother may also be a factor: teens or women over the age of 35 may have higher premature birth rates. Smoking and/or drinking during pregnancy can lead to premature births (March of Dimes 2021).

The concern about low-weight babies is threefold. First, the babies may have health issues subsequent to birth, such as breathing problems, bleeding in the brain, and weak immune systems that can lead to infections. Second, low birthweight babies may have delays in their development. Finally, low birthweight babies may experience health issues as an adult because of the low birthweight birth. These include diabetes, heart disease, developmental disorders, and obesity (March of Dimes 2021).

So, low birthweight births are a problem. How do the red and blue states compare? Table 3.25 presents the data. In 2020, the U.S. average of low birthweight babies was 8.2 percent. The red state average was slightly higher, at 8.6 percent. The blue state average was slightly lower at 7.8 percent. The lowest percentage in our set of states was Washington State, at 6.7 percent. No blue state had a percentage of low birthweight births in double-digit numbers. Nine red states had a percentage higher than 9 percent of low birthweight babies, with three states (Alabama, Louisiana, and Mississippi) at over 10 percent.

Overlapping a previous discussion about guns, we can ask whether states, and which states, have taken action to decrease the access of children to firearms. Table 3.26 presents the data. The first column asks whether a state has one or more laws that are aimed at preventing children from getting access to firearms. Such laws impose criminal liability on those possessing firearms, such as parents, who do not provide for safe storage of firearms, for those who allow children to access firearms, and so forth. The second column focuses more specifically on safe storage as well as locking devices. The third column asks whether states have laws that limit the possession, distribution, etc. of assault weapons. The issue here is

TABLE 3.25 Low Birthweight Babies (2020)

Red States	Percent of Low Birthweight Babies	Blue States	Percent of Low Birthweight Babies
Alabama	10.8	California	6.9
Alaska	6.6	Connecticut	7.8
Arizona	7.4	Delaware	8.9
Arkansas	9.6	Hawaii	8.1
Georgia	9.9	Illinois	8.3
Idaho	6.9	Maine	7.5
Indiana	8.1	Maryland	8.5
Kansas	7.2	Massachusetts	7.4
Kentucky	8.5	Michigan	8.9
Louisiana	10.9	New Jersey	7.7
Mississippi	11.8	New Mexico	8.9
Missouri	8.7	New York	8.2
Montana	7.7	Oregon	6.5
Nebraska	7.4	Pennsylvania	8.3
North Carolina	9.5	Rhode Island	7.7
North Dakota	6.9	Vermont	7.0
Oklahoma	8.4	Washington	6.7
South Carolina	9.8		
South Dakota	6.9		
Tennessee	8.9		
Texas	8.2		
Utah	7.0		
West Virginia	9.3		
Wyoming	9.7		
Average	8.6		7.8
U.S. Average	8.2		

Adapted from: Annie E. Casey Foundation (2022). Online at www.aecf.org

whether there are state laws that limit children's access to firearms and therefore limiting accidental (or deliberate) use of firearms.

The first column shows that many states have passed laws that limit children's access, though blue states are more likely to have such laws. The second and third columns really show the differences between the two sets of states. The second column focuses on whether a state has safe firearms storage laws. No red state has such a law, while 11 of the blue states have such laws. Assault weapons bans at the state level (the federal assault weapons ban was passed by Congress in 1994 and expired in

TABLE 3.26 States with Laws Protecting Children from Firearms

Red States	Child's Access to Firearms Prevention Laws	Safe Storage or Gun Lock Requirement	Assault Weapons Ban	Blue States	Child's Access to Firearms Prevention Laws	Safe Storage or Gun Lock Requirement	Assault Weapons Ban
Alabama	No	No	No	California	Yes	Yes	Yes
Alaska	No	No	No	Connecticut	Yes	Yes	Yes
Arizona	No	No	No	Delaware	Yes	Yes	Yes
Arkansas	No	No	No	Hawaii	Yes	No	Yes
Georgia	Yes	No	No	Illinois	Yes	No	Yes
Idaho	No	No	No	Maine	Yes	No	No
Indiana	Yes	No	No	Maryland	Yes	Yes	Yes
Kansas	No	No	No	Massachusetts	Yes	Yes	Yes
Kentucky	Yes	No	No	Michigan	No	Yes	No
Louisiana	No	No	No	New Jersey	Yes	No	Yes
Mississippi	No	No	No	New Mexico	Yes	No	No
Missouri	Yes	No	No	New York	Yes	Yes	Yes
Montana	Yes	No	No	Oregon	Yes	Yes	No
Nebraska	Yes	No	No	Pennsylvania	No	No	No
North Carolina	Yes	No	No	Rhode Island	Yes	No	No
North Dakota	No	No	No	Vermont	No	No	No
Oklahoma	Yes	No	No	Washington	Yes	No	Yes
South Carolina	No	No	No				
South Dakota	No	No	No				
Tennessee	Yes	No	No				
Texas	Yes	No	No				
Utah	No	No	No				
West Virginia	No	No	No				
Wyoming	No	No	No				
Number of States with Gun Laws	12	0	0		13	11	7

Adapted from: Kaiser Family Foundation (2024). Online at https:/www.kff.org

2004) show the unpopularity of such bans. No red state has such a ban, while less than half of the blue states (seven such states) have an assault weapons ban.

The last area we will examine in this section on children has to do with sex. We have already seen that births by teenage girls are more likely to lead to prematurity and low birthweights. Further, teenage girls (and boys) are not prepared for the challenges of raising children. They have not finished their own education and development into adults. Table 3.27 presents the data.

Table 3.27 looks at teen birth rates by state. The overall U.S. average was 15.7 births per 100,000 teenage girls (ages 15–19) in 2020. The blue state average was 11.4 births, and the red state average was 19.7 births. The blue state average was about 18 percent lower than the national average. The red state average was about 25 percent higher than the red state average. And the red state average was almost 53 percent higher than the blue state average.

Nine red states had teen birth rates higher than 20 per 100,000. No red state had a teen birth rate in single digits. For blue states, there were five states with teen birth rates in single digits. Only New Mexico, among blue states, had a teen birth rate in the twenties.

Teen births are obviously more of a problem in red states than in blue states, though teen pregnancy has declined over the last 20 years or so (Centers for Disease Control and Prevention 2021). Despite the decline, there are reasons to be concerned about teen pregnancy. There are costs to the teen mother, the baby, the family, and the larger society. Teen mothers are less likely to graduate from high school than female teens who do not give birth. The latter rate is almost twice as high as the former rate (Centers for Disease Control and Prevention 2021). The children of teenage mothers are also likely to have both health and economic issues:

> [they] are more likely to have lower high school achievement and to drop out of high school, have more health problems, be incarcerated at some time during adolescence, give birth as a teenager, and face unemployment as a young adult.
> *(Centers for Disease Control and Prevention 2021)*

Because the babies of teen mothers may be premature, those babies, as mentioned above, may have health problems in later life.

One reason for the relatively high rate of teenage pregnancies is the lack of adequate and accurate sex education. This is true for the blue as well as the red states. Table 3.28 presents the data. Only 11 red states mandated sex education in the schools.

TABLE 3.27 Teen Birth Rate by State (2020)

Red States		Blue States	
	Number of Births per 1,000 Females Aged 15–19		Number of Births per 1,000 Females Aged 15–19
Alabama	24.8	California	11.0
Alaska	17.7	Connecticut	7.6
Arizona	16.6	Delaware	14.6
Arkansas	27.8	Hawaii	13.0
Georgia	18.2	Illinois	13.6
Idaho	14.6	Maine	10.6
Indiana	18.7	Maryland	13.1
Kansas	18.1	Massachusetts	6.1
Kentucky	23.8	Michigan	13.5
Louisiana	25.7	New Jersey	9.2
Mississippi	27.9	New Mexico	21.9
Missouri	18.8	New York	10.0
Montana	13.2	Oregon	10.1
Nebraska	15.1	Pennsylvania	12.6
North Carolina	17.3	Rhode Island	9.4
North Dakota	13.7	Vermont	7.0
Oklahoma	25.0	Washington	11.3
South Carolina	19.3		
South Dakota	18.7		
Tennessee	23.3		
Texas	22.4		
Utah	10.8		
West Virginia	22.5		
Wyoming	18.1		
Average	19.7		11.4
U.S. Average[a]	15.7		

Adapted from: Centers for Disease Control and Prevention (2023). Online at www.CDC.gov

[a] Authors' calculation.

For the blue states, 11 states had such a mandate. The second data column asks whether the sex education material must be medically accurate. For the red states, only five states had such a mandate. For the blue states, the number is eight, better but not sufficient.

We end this section by looking at state children's healthcare systems. Table 3.29 presents the rankings of our red and blue states. The rankings employ three overall measures: access to healthcare and health of children; nutrition, physical activity, and obesity of children; and oral health of

TABLE 3.28 Sex Education Programs by State

Red States	Sex Education Mandated	Be Medically Accurate	Blue States	Sex Education Mandated	Be Medically Accurate
Alabama			California	1	1
Alaska			Connecticut		
Arizona			Delaware	1	
Arkansas			Hawaii	1	1
Georgia	1		Illinois		1
Idaho			Maine	1	1
Indiana			Maryland	1	
Kansas	1		Massachusetts		
Kentucky	1		Michigan		
Louisiana		1	New Jersey	1	1
Mississippi	1		New Mexico	1	
Missouri		1	New York		
Montana	1		Oregon	1	1
Nebraska			Pennsylvania		
North Carolina	1	1	Rhode Island	1	1
North Dakota	1		Vermont	1	
Oklahoma			Washington	1	1
South Carolina	1				
South Dakota					
Tennessee	1	1			
Texas					
Utah	1	1			
West Virginia	1				
Wyoming					
Average	11	5		11	8

Adapted from: Guttmacher Institute (2023). Online at www.guttmacher.org

children (McCann 2022). Each of these three rankings is based on a series of metrics. The metrics include the percentage of uninsured children, infant death rate, percentage of children with medical debt, children's doctors per capita, and so forth.

As Table 3.29 shows, there is a dramatic difference between the red and blue states. The average ranking of red states is 33.6 while the average ranking of blue states is 13.4. None of the red states is in the top ten, though Utah is close. Only three blue states have a ranking in the twenties or more. Hawaii is the highest ranked state and Texas is the lowest. There are clearly differences in the quality of child healthcare between our two groups of states.

TABLE 3.29 Ranking States on Child Health (2020)

Red States	Overall Rank	Blue States	Overall Rank
Utah	11	Hawaii	1
North Dakota	13	Vermont	2
South Carolina	21	New Mexico	3
Nebraska	22	Washington	3
Wyoming	23	Maryland	4
Alabama	24	Oregon	5
Montana	25	Rhode Island	6
Idaho	26	New York	8
South Dakota	29	Massachusetts	9
Missouri	30	Connecticut	12
Arizona	32	Maine	14
Louisiana	33	California	16
Indiana	35	Pennsylvania	17
Kansas	37	Illinois	20
Kentucky	38	New Jersey	28
West Virginia	39	Michigan	36
Mississippi	41	Delaware	44
North Carolina	42		
Alaska	45		
Arkansas	46		
Tennessee	47		
Oklahoma	48		
Georgia	49		
Texas	50		
Average	33.6		13.4

Adapted with permission from: McCann (2021). Online at www.wallethu.com

Healthcare Indicators

In this section, we look at indicators of access to the healthcare system. The United States has one of the best and most technologically advanced systems in the world. It is also the most expensive system, which we discuss later in this chapter. If people who need help cannot get it, perhaps for financial or geographical reasons, then it does not matter how good the quality of the system is.

Insurance

No healthcare system is free. Even those who charge nothing or very little at the point of service need money to carry on their tasks. Perhaps the money comes from taxes or insurance or from patients paying privately. But it comes from somewhere.

The U.S. healthcare system is complex, and people are covered for medical costs in a variety of ways. As we have just seen, a child may be covered through federal government programs such as Medicaid and/or CHIP. Those in their prime years may be covered by employer-provided insurance. Those in the military may be covered by Tricare. Veterans can be covered by the Veterans Health Administration. People in poverty may be covered by Medicaid. The elderly are covered by Medicare in all its complexity. But not everyone has insurance and not all insurance is adequate. We address these issues in this section.

In the absence of insurance coverage, people may not get or afford the healthcare that they need. Those without insurance or without adequate insurance may accumulate medical debt that they are unable to pay and cause havoc with a family's finances (Collins, Gunja, and Aboulafia 2020).

If we look at the United States as a whole and compare it to other westernized industrial countries, we find that the United States is the only such country without a universal system of health insurance. In 2020, there were some 30 million Americans without any health insurance and another 40 million who were underinsured (Collins, Gunja, and Aboulafia 2020; Schneider et al. 2021). The United States thus faces a paradox: it spends more than any other country on healthcare, yet its coverage is less than other high-income countries.

How does this show up in our comparison of red and blue states? Table 3.30 provides us with a picture of the uninsurance problem, presenting data about uninsurance rates in the states. The U.S. average in 2021 was 10.2 percent. The average uninsurance rate in the red states in 2021 was 11.6 percent, above the national average. For the blue states, the average uninsurance rate in 2021 was 6.7 percent, considerably less than the red state and national averages. Texas had the highest uninsurance rate of any state in the country at 20.5 percent. Only New Mexico among the blue states had an uninsurance rate in double digits.

Related to the uninsurance problem, and more complex, is the underinsurance problem. Underinsurance is when a person or family has insurance, but the insurance is not sufficient to cover their medical costs. The Commonwealth Fund (Collins, Bhupal, and Dotty 2019, 2) provides a definition of people who are underinsured:

- their out-of-pocket costs, excluding premiums, over the prior 12 months are equal to 10 percent or more of their household income; or
- their out-of-pocket costs, excluding premiums, over the prior 12 months equal to 5 percent or more of household income for individuals living

TABLE 3.30 State Uninsurance Rates (2021)

Red States	Percentage Uninsured	Blue States	Percentage Uninsured
Alabama	12.0	California	8.1
Alaska	12.1	Connecticut	6.1
Arizona	12.8	Delaware	7.0
Arkansas	11.0	Hawaii	4.4
Georgia	14.8	Illinois	8.1
Idaho	10.2	Maine	6.9
Indiana	8.8	Maryland	7.1
Kansas	11.0	Massachusetts	2.9
Kentucky	6.7	Michigan	6.2
Louisiana	8.9	New Jersey	8.4
Mississippi	14.3	New Mexico	12.1
Missouri	11.2	New York	6.2
Montana	9.9	Oregon	7.4
Nebraska	8.3	Pennsylvania	6.6
North Carolina	12.4	Rhode Island	5.1
North Dakota	9.0	Vermont	4.2
Oklahoma	16.3	Washington	7.6
South Carolina	12.2		
South Dakota	11.4		
Tennessee	12.1		
Texas	20.5		
Utah	10.2		
West Virginia	7.7		
Wyoming	14.0		
Average	11.6		6.7
U.S. Average	10.2		

Adapted from: Kaiser Family Foundation (2023). Online at https://www.kff.org/statedata

under 200 percent of the federal poverty level ($24,120 for an individual or $49,200 for a family of four); or
- their deductible constitutes 5 percent or more of household income.

To be clear about two of the terms in the quote, the premium is the monthly amount that an individual or family pays for their insurance policy regardless of the use of healthcare services. Deductibles are the amount that a person or individual pays for services before the health plan pays anything.

Being underinsured may mean that a person or family does not have the money for needed health services and the insurance policy may be inadequate and not pay for services or not pay a sufficient amount for those services for an individual or family. Thus, those services may be foregone. Further, an uninsured or underinsured person may get the needed services but not be able to pay for all the costs. The underinsured may spend a high percentage of their income on healthcare (Schoen et al. 2014). This then leads to the problem of medical debt. We address both issues in the next few paragraphs.

Let us begin by examining the extent of underinsurance. Our primary focus has been on comparing the red and blue states. Data on underinsurance by states is limited. Columns two and five of Table 3.31 present data from 2012. Several observations can be made. First, we see the usual red state/blue state divide. The red states have a higher percentage of underinsured people than the blue states. Second, the red state average is higher than the national average, while the blue state average is below the national average. Almost the entire population of the elderly have insurance coverage through Medicare. But a sizable share of Medicare beneficiaries are underinsured. Columns three and six of Table 3.31 present the data.

The national average of underinsured Medicare beneficiaries was 23.1 percent, nearly a quarter of the total number of beneficiaries. Medicare is a complex program with premiums for portions of Parts B and D and deductibles. The problem is worse for those at the low end of the income distribution. This is true for the larger population as well. The red state average was higher than the national average and the blue state average was slightly below the national average, continuing our trend.

A related point is the connection between income and health insurance costs. Table 3.32 addresses this issue. Indeed, this table shows some of the more interesting findings. The table has three columns: average household income, average premium costs and deductible costs (a measure of the cost of health insurance), and the percentage of household income devoted to health insurance costs. Average annual household income in the red states in 2019 was below the U.S. average, by nearly 7,000 dollars or over 10 percent. The blue state average was higher than the U.S. average, by a bit over $5,800 or nearly 9 percent. As we saw in Chapter 2, blue states are richer than red states. Here is where the interesting part comes. Looking at the second data columns for the red and blue states, the cost of health insurance (premiums and deductibles) is higher in the red states than in the blue states, by over $400. The cost of insurance is higher in the red states than the country as a whole. The blue state insurance costs are below the national average. It follows then that the percentage of household income spent on health insurance on average is higher in the red states than in the blue states or the national average. Residents of red states, with lower

TABLE 3.31 The Underinsured

Red States	Percent of Those Under 65 Who Are Uninsured (2012)	Percent of Medicare Recipients Underinsured (2013–2014)	Blue States	Percent of Those Under 65 Who Are Uninsured (2012)	Percent of Medicare Recipients Underinsured (2013–2014)
Alabama	14	26	California	11	20
Alaska	11	24	Connecticut	10	18
Arizona	12	25	Delaware	10	19
Arkansas	15	26	Hawaii	13	21
Georgia	12	24	Illinois	12	25
Idaho	17	25	Maine	12	24
Indiana	13	24	Maryland	9	21
Kansas	12	24	Massachusetts	10	26
Kentucky	12	30	Michigan	11	23
Louisiana	12	30	New Jersey	10	22
Mississippi	16	23	New Mexico	13	25
Missouri	11	28	New York	11	21
Montana	13	27	Oregon	15	26
Nebraska	12	24	Pennsylvania	10	26
North Carolina	14	30	Rhode Island	10	20
North Dakota	10	23	Vermont	11	21
Oklahoma	12	29	Washington	11	25
South Carolina	12	25			
South Dakota	11	28			
Tennessee	16	22			
Texas	11	27			
Utah	17	32			
West Virginia	13	30			
Wyoming	15				
Average	13	26.3		11.12	22.4
U.S. Average	12	23.1			

Sources: Adapted from Schoen et al. (2014). Schoen et al. (2016).

household income, are asked to spend more of that income on health insurance than residents of blue states or the country as a whole.

It follows, then, that medical debt can be a problem. The Consumer Financial Protection Bureau (CFPB) (2022) estimates that consumers had a medical debt totaling $88 billion in 2021. The Bureau states that this is likely an underestimate because it only looked at debt that was reported as consumer debt and in a collections phase. Nearly 60 percent of reported consumer debt was medical debt. Medical debt can have adverse consequences on a person's or family's financial well-being and physical and mental health. A person's credit card rating may be lowered because of

TABLE 3.32 Income and Insurance Costs (2019)

Red States	Average Household Income	Out-of-Pocket and Premium Costs	Percent of Income Spent on Health Care per Year	Blue States	Average Household Income	Out-of-Pocket and Premium Costs	Percent of Income Spent on Health Care per Year
Alabama	$51,734	$6,823	13.2	California	$80,440	$6,852	8.0
Alaska	$75,463	$6,576	8.7	Connecticut	$78,833	$7,816	9.9
Arizona	$62,055	$8,364	13.5	Delaware	$70,176	$7,435	10.6
Arkansas	$48,952	$7,951	15.1	Hawaii	$83,102	$6,236	7.5
Georgia	$61,980	$7,933	12.8	Illinois	$69,187	$7,396	10.7
Idaho	$60,999	$7,307	12.0	Maine	$58,924	$7,879	13.2
Indiana	$57,603	$6,729	11.7	Maryland	$86,738	$7,506	8.7
Kansas	$62,087	$7,369	11.9	Massachusetts	$85,843	$6,894	8.6
Kentucky	$52,295	$7,470	14.3	Michigan	$59,584	$6,318	10.6
Louisiana	$51,073	$7,864	15.6	New Jersey	$85,751	$8,281	9.7
Mississippi	$45,792	$7,864	17.2	New Mexico	$51,945	$6,342	12.2
Missouri	$57,409	$7,296	12.7	New York	$72,108	$6,470	9
Montana	$57,153	$7,343	12.8	Oregon	$67,058	$7,449	11.1
Nebraska	$63,229	$7,563	12.0	Pennsylvania	$63,463	$6,906	10.9
North Carolina	$57,341	$8,091	14.1	Rhode Island	$61,169	$6,906	10.9
North Dakota	$64,577	$7,195	11.1	Vermont	$63,001	$7,563	12.0
Oklahoma	$54,449	$7,312	13.4	Washington	$78,687	$5,951	7.5
South Carolina	$56,227	$7,111	12.6				
South Dakota	$59,533	$8,621	14.5				
Tennessee	$56,071	$7,966	14.2				
Texas	$64,034	$8,057	12.6				
Utah	$75,780	$6,777	8.9				
West Virginia	$48,850	$6,326	12.9				
Wyoming	$65,003	$7,732	11.9				
Average	$58,737	$7,485	12.9		$71,530	$7,043	10.1
U.S. Average	$65,712	$7,388	11.2				

Adapted with permission from: VanZint (2021). Online at Online at https://quotewizard.com

unpaid medical debt though the CFPB proposed a rule in 2024 that would eliminate medical debt as part of credit reports (Holzhauer and Avery 2024). Access to housing and employment may be adversely affected by medical debt. Medical debt, especially high levels of such debt, may lead to bankruptcy. People with high medical debt may avoid seeking needed healthcare. Mental stress from carrying high levels of medical debt may lead to physical health issues (Consumer Financial Protection Bureau 2022). So where does medical debt fit in our red states/blue states discussion?

Table 3.33 presents the data. This table provides data about the percentage of the population with medical debt. The U.S. average is 12.96 percent. The red state average is higher, at 16.59 percent. The blue state average is lower, at 10.18 percent. The difference between the red state and blue state averages is large, about 63 percent.

If we sum up the preceding paragraphs, we find that the red states have lower income, higher insurance costs, more uninsured and underinsured, and more people with medical debt than the blue states.

Access to Providers

Being able to pay for healthcare services, much of which comes from insurance, is one element of access to care. People without insurance can get some care, but likely not all the care needed. Another aspect of access to healthcare is whether facilities and providers are available for people to access.

We begin this discussion by looking at Table 3.34. This table shows the rate of active providers per 100,000 population in a state. The table contains separate columns for primary care providers and for specialists. Primary care providers include internists, family medicine practitioners, OB-GYNs, and providers for the elderly. The second column, active specialist practitioners, includes a variety of specialists, such as cardiology, surgery, oncology, and endocrinology. In both cases, the red states have fewer practitioners per 100,000 population than the U.S. average and the blue state average.

The rates per 100,000 for both types of physicians are lower than the national average for the red states. The blue state average is higher than the overall average for both primary care and specialist physicians. This is consistent with previous tables.

The same is true for dentists (see Table 3.35). In the red states, there is an average of about 54 dentists per 100,000 population. In the blue states, the average is nearly 67 dentists per 100,000 population. The U.S. average is over 62 dentists per 100,000 population.

TABLE 3.33 Medical Debt (2018–2021)

Red States	Percent of Individuals with Medical Debt	Blue States	Percent of Individuals with Medical Debt
Alabama	18.38	California	8.64
Alaska	14.07	Connecticut	10.25
Arizona	15.16	Delaware	17.37
Arkansas	18.36	Hawaii	6.91
Georgia	16.95	Illinois	13.73
Idaho	12.73	Maine	16.94
Indiana	18.19	Maryland	11.62
Kansas	17.86	Massachusetts	4.72
Kentucky	18.15	Michigan	13.84
Louisiana	21.79	New Jersey	12.66
Mississippi	17.62	New Mexico	17.94
Missouri	17.90	New York	6.13
Montana	12.16	Oregon	5.87
Nebraska	7.25	Pennsylvania	10.42
North Carolina	19.18	Rhode Island	5.60
North Dakota	6.04	Vermont	5.40
Oklahoma	21.26	Washington	5.03
South Carolina	22.87		
South Dakota	4.43		
Tennessee	19.31		
Texas	21.78		
Utah	13.54		
West Virginia	24.99		
Wyoming	18.08		
Average	16.59		10.18
U.S. Average[a]	12.96		

Adapted from: Consumer Financial Protection Bureau (2022).

[a] Authors' calculation.

The presence or lack of dentists can affect the overall health of the population. Not getting treated for dental issues can lead to a number of health issues. One is pain from infected teeth and/or gums. Poor dental health is related to cardiovascular issues such as coronary artery disease, atherosclerosis, endocarditis (inflammation of the heart valve lining), and stroke. Poor dental health is also related to pregnancy-related issues, such as low birthweight and miscarriages. Pneumonia is another health issue related to poor dental health (Cleveland Clinic 2022).

The workforce issues that underlay the last couple of tables are part of the problem of access to healthcare. There is a shortage of all kinds of

TABLE 3.34 Primary Care and Specialist Providers per Capita

Red States			Blue States		
	Primary Care Physicians per 100,000 People (2021)	Specialists per 100,000 People (2021)		Primary Care Physicians per 100,000 people (2021)	Specialists per 100,000 People (2021)
Alabama	121.80	139.88	California	144.20	139.72
Alaska	155.57	122.51	Connecticut	205.48	200.59
Arizona	124.32	141.25	Delaware	162.82	162.44
Arkansas	126.65	140.17	Hawaii	141.97	136.67
Georgia	125.24	125.24	Illinois	188.95	182.94
Idaho	99.68	77.21	Maine	191.79	190.05
Indiana	128.07	137.78	Maryland	189.88	186.25
Kansas	149.66	143.54	Massachusetts	238.67	232.72
Kentucky	128.14	159.52	Michigan	191.19	194.31
Louisiana	147.29	178.83	New Jersey	170.31	170.53
Mississippi	118.61	130.01	New Mexico	147.98	143.90
Missouri	168.02	201	New York	219.91	215.57
Montana	109.15	106.26	Oregon	148.91	145.47
Nebraska	156.84	151.18	Pennsylvania	205.98	200.50
North Carolina	138.00	160.64	Rhode Island	267.35	267.23
North Dakota	169.36	129.05	Vermont	188.80	188.34
Oklahoma	130.41	128.62	Washington	151.85	147.40
South Carolina	134.81	140.74			
South Dakota	131.86	112.29			
Tennessee	134.19	160.08			
Texas	111.62	129.93			
Utah	98.82	124.29			
West Virginia	175.71	173.92			
Wyoming	124.58	100.27			
Average	133.68	138.09		185.65	182.63
U.S. Average	155.40	178.37			

Adapted from: Kaiser Family Foundation (2023). Online at https://www.kff.org/statedata

medical personnel, including doctors and nurses. Further, the COVID-19 pandemic (see Chapter 7) exacerbated the shortages as medical personnel worked long hours during the height of the pandemic. Burnout became a problem. Retirement is also an issue as more doctors (and nurses) are retiring. As a result, there are shortages projected over the next 20 years or so. Zhang et al. (2020) provide state-by-state projections. And their results fit into our red states/blue states distinction. Fourteen states are projected to have physician surpluses by 2030. Of those 14, 11 are blue states, two are purple states, and one is a red state (Nebraska). Of the ten states with the largest projected shortage of physicians in 2030, eight are red states, one is a purple state (Florida), and one is a blue state (New Mexico). From a

TABLE 3.35 Prevalence Rate of Dentists (2021)

Red States	Number of Dentists per 100,000 (2021)[a]	Blue States	Number of Dentists per 100,000 (2021)[a]
Alabama	42.48	California	80.69
Alaska	84.15	Connecticut	74.65
Arizona	59.38	Delaware	46.61
Arkansas	42.88	Hawaii	80.43
Georgia	48.74	Illinois	70.13
Idaho	54.85	Maine	56.25
Indiana	49.14	Maryland	70.81
Kansas	51.56	Massachusetts	84.92
Kentucky	56.99	Michigan	59.32
Louisiana	49.53	New Jersey	79.03
Mississippi	44.87	New Mexico	49.68
Missouri	51.49	New York	73.82
Montana	58.76	Oregon	66.94
Nebraska	65.76	Pennsylvania	59.90
North Carolina	56.84	Rhode Island	53.89
North Dakota	54.07	Vermont	57.29
Oklahoma	50.77	Washington	72.56
South Carolina	49.26		
South Dakota	54.64		
Tennessee	47.98		
Texas	55.44		
Utah	62.22		
West Virginia	50.09		
Wyoming	54.66		
Average	54.02		66.88
U.S. Average	62.48		

Adapted from: Kaiser Family Foundation (2023). Online at https://www.kff.org/statedata

[a] Rates are authors' calculations.

healthcare workforce standpoint, the red states will be in a worse shape in 2030 than they were in 2017.

The next two tables make the access problem clearer. Table 3.36 focuses on whether people have a personal provider, effectively a medical home. Our trend of red states/blue states is evident in this table. In the United States as a whole, 13 percent of the population did not have a personal provider. For the red states, the percentage was 14.4. For the blue states, the percentage was 11.7 percent, below the national average. The red state average was 23 percent higher than the blue state average.

TABLE 3.36 Percentage of Adults Not Having Personal Provider

Red States	Percentage of Adults without Personal Provider (2021)	Blue States	Percentage of Adults without Personal Provider (2021)
Alabama	12.0	California	17.0
Alaska	19.6	Connecticut	9.5
Arizona	18.2	Delaware	12.1
Arkansas	10.8	Hawaii	8.7
Georgia	14.7	Illinois	14.8
Idaho	15.3	Maine	7.2
Indiana	11.9	Maryland	9.2
Kansas	10.7	Massachusetts	7.8
Kentucky	11.8	Michigan	8.8
Louisiana	10.8	New Jersey	12.7
Mississippi	13.1	New Mexico	22.4
Missouri	13.1	New York	12.1
Montana	16.9	Oregon	19.4
Nebraska	11.5	Pennsylvania	9.1
North Carolina	15.6	Rhode Island	7.3
North Dakota	15.1	Vermont	7.7
Oklahoma	16.0	Washington	13.0
South Carolina	11.7		
South Dakota	13.1		
Tennessee	14.1		
Texas	20.6		
Utah	16.9		
West Virginia	10.4		
Wyoming	21.1		
Average	14.4		11.7
U.S. Average	13.0		

Adapted from: Kaiser Family Foundation (2023). Online at https://www.kff.org/statedata

Not having a personal provider does not mean that a person cannot get medical care. Some people get their medical care at a community health center (CHC). CHCs charge for their services, though at a lower amount than care given in the private sector. CHCs may not charge for those who cannot pay. Emergency rooms/departments also offer care to those who do not have a regular doctor. But they can be expensive and often patients have long waits before receiving services (depending on the urgency of the health problem). Clinics in stores such as Walmart also provide a place for relatively low-cost care. But the experience of these stores is that it is expensive to do so and they are losing money. As a

TABLE 3.37 Adults Not Seeking Care Because of Cost

Red States		Blue States	
	Percent of Adults Not Seeking Care Because of Cost (2021)		Percent of Adults Not Seeking Care Because of Cost (2021)
Alabama	8.6	California	9.1
Alaska	9.7	Connecticut	6.1
Arizona	9.2	Delaware	6.3
Arkansas	8.8	Hawaii	5.0
Georgia	12.8	Illinois	9.0
Idaho	8.7	Maine	6.3
Indiana	7.7	Maryland	7.3
Kansas	8.2	Massachusetts	5.8
Kentucky	8.1	Michigan	6.8
Louisiana	9.9	New Jersey	8.3
Mississippi	12.2	New Mexico	8.3
Missouri	9.6	New York	7.6
Montana	6.5	Oregon	7.3
Nebraska	7.6	Pennsylvania	6.3
North Carolina	10.2	Rhode Island	5.6
North Dakota	5.1	Vermont	5.3
Oklahoma	12.0	Washington	7.1
South Carolina	9.0		
South Dakota	7.5		
Tennessee	10.4		
Texas	13.5		
Utah	9.4		
West Virginia	9.4		
Wyoming	8.9		
Average	9.3		6.9
U.S. Average	8.7		

Adapted from: Kaiser Family Foundation (2023). Online at Online at https://www.kff.org/statedata

result, there are fewer of these clinics, resulting in a loss of access for those in need (Williams 2024).

Another outlet for healthcare services are urgent care clinics (Meyersohn 2023). Urgent care clinics treat non-emergency issues such as ear infections or ankle injuries. People turn to such centers if they cannot get in to see their primary care physician or if they do not have one. Meyersohn (2023) notes that there is projected shortage of some 55,000 physicians over the next decade, a number consistent with Zhang et al's (2020) study. The problem with urgent care clinics combined with physician shortages is

TABLE 3.38 Overall Ranking of State Healthcare Systems

Red States	Rank	Blue States	Rank
Utah	19	Hawaii	1
Nebraska	22	Massachusetts	2
Idaho	25	Connecticut	3
Montana	28	Washington	4
North Dakota	29	Vermont	5
Alaska	30	Rhode Island	6
South Dakota	30	Maryland	7
Arizona	32	New York	10
North Carolina	34	California	11
Kansas	35	Maine	14
Indiana	37	Oregon	14
South Carolina	37	Pennsylvania	14
Louisiana	39	New Jersey	18
Tennessee	40	Illinois	22
Kentucky	41	Michigan	24
Wyoming	41	New Mexico	26
Arkansas	44	Delaware	27
Georgia	44		
Alabama	46		
Missouri	47		
Texas	48		
West Virginia	49		
Mississippi	50		
Oklahoma	50		
Average	37.38		12.24

Adapted with permission from: Radley, Baumgartner, and Collins (2022). Online at www.commonwealth.org

that intensive use of such centers can lead to fragmented care. Such centers, if not affiliated with a healthcare system, may not have complete medical records on patients (Meyersohn 2023).

A related issue is the distribution of care centers. Here we are focusing on rural and non-rural (suburban and urban areas). In general, rural areas have a decent distribution of primary care physicians. But rural hospitals face serious financial issues. Rural areas have relatively few specialist physicians and specialized medical facilities. One reason is that urban and suburban facilities pay more than rural facilities. A second, and equally important, reason is that, by definition, rural areas have fewer people and therefore fewer patients than urban and suburban areas. As we saw in Chapter 2, red states are more rural than blue states. Just under 20 percent of the nation live in rural areas. The same percentage is true for blue states. However, nearly 33 percent of the red state population lives in rural areas. It therefore follows that red states will have more of the rural healthcare issues discussed above than blue states ("Rural States Are Almost Entirely Ignored Under Current State-By-State System" n.d.). There are often not enough patients for a specialist practice to be financially viable. This can be seen in comparing the numbers of primary and specialist physicians in rural areas. The number of primary care physicians per 10,000 people in rural areas is 13.1; in urban areas, it is 31.2. That calculates to about 240 percent more primary physicians in urban areas. The contrast is even greater for specialists. There are 30 specialist physicians per 10,000 people in rural areas; in urban areas that number is 263. The urban advantage for specialist physicians is 870 percent (National Rural Health Association 2023).

Rural health is also impacted by issues centering around rural hospitals. Because of the reasons discussed above, between 2005 and 2019, about 160 rural hospitals had closed. This means that rural residents in those areas will have less access to healthcare services and will need to travel to get those services (Ollove 2020).

Cost of care remains a problem for many. Table 3.37 presents data on this issue. The question addressed is whether adults deferred seeking care because they could not afford it. As the table shows, 8.7 percent of adults in the previous year declined to seek service for this reason in the country as a whole. For red states, the percentage was 9.3 percent; for blue states, the percentage was 6.9 percent. The red state percentage was almost 35 percent higher than the blue state percentage.

Ranking the States

Periodically, the Commonwealth Fund studies 11 wealthy countries (Australia, Canada, France, Germany, the Netherlands, New Zealand, Norway, Switzerland, the United Kingdom, and the United States) and compares the quality of their healthcare systems (see Schneider et al. 2021). The 11 countries are ranked on five metrics: access to care, care process, administrative efficiency, equity, and healthcare outcomes. Each metric has several different dimensions or measures. For example, access to care includes affordability of care and timeliness of care (how soon needed care is provided). Care processes include safe care, preventive care, and coordinated care. On four of these metrics, the United States is rated 11th or last. Only on care process does the United States rank higher, at second place.

Ezekiel Emanuel (2020) asks *Which Country Has the World's Best HealthCare?* His book examines 11 countries, similar to the

Commonwealth Fund study, with a few changes: Sweden and New Zealand are replaced by the People's Republic of China and Taiwan. Emanuel's book is a comprehensive study of these 11 nations on a variety of dimensions, such as how physicians and hospitals are paid. While Emanuel ultimately does not label a specific country as the best in the world, he notes that countries differ depending on the dimension studied ("history, coverage, financing, payment, delivery, pharmaceutical regulation, and workforce" (Emanuel 2020, 351)). And he cites the United States as an underperforming country on the various dimensions. While not an explicit ranking, these two studies suggest that there is considerable room for improvement in the U.S. healthcare systems.

As we have seen, the United States is at the bottom in a comparative sense as to the quality of its healthcare system. But more than most countries, the U.S. healthcare system is divided into 50 healthcare systems, with states having important jurisdiction over healthcare quality, cost, and delivery. So how do the states rank?

While there are several different rankings of state healthcare systems, the results are pretty much the same. One of the more comprehensive rankings is from the Commonwealth Fund (Radley, Baumgartner, and Collins 2022), the same organization that ranked the nations mentioned above.

The overall ranking (see Table 3.38) is based on five dimensions: access and affordability, prevention and treatment, avoidable hospital use and cost, healthy lives, and COVID-19 (see Chapter 7). Each dimension has a series of metrics, which themselves have rankings. These are all brought together to produce a total ranking.

As with the other tables in this book, we do not include the purple states. As a result, there are some missing ranks in Table 3.38. Further, there are some states that are tied in the overall ranking, for example, Arkansas and Georgia.

As Table 3.38 shows, the blue states rank much higher than the red states, 12.24 versus 37.38. The highest-ranking red state is Utah, at 19. The lowest-ranking blue state is New Mexico, at 26. That is still higher than the red state average. Only three red states have a higher ranking than New Mexico: Idaho, Nebraska, and Utah.

The Commonwealth Fund study rankings are similar to other rankings. McCann (2022) uses three basic metrics (cost, access, and outcomes) to make his rankings. Each metric or dimension has sub-metrics that lead to scores for each dimension. For example, McCann looks at dentists per capita and finds the bottom five states are all red states. Four of the five states with the worst cancer rates are also red states.

Ziegler (2021) engages in a similar process. There are three dimensions: healthcare access, healthcare quality, and public health. Metrics under healthcare access include affordability, dental visits, and health insurance enrolment. Healthcare quality includes hospital quality, Medicare quality, and preventable admissions. For the public health dimensions, the metrics include mental health, obesity rates, and low infant mortality rates. Based on these metrics, the top five states are all blue states: California, Hawaii, Massachusetts, Connecticut, and New Jersey. The bottom five states are red states: Louisiana, West Virginia, Oklahoma, Arkansas, and Mississippi. While not completely identical, all three sets of rankings come to the same conclusion.

Polarization and Healthcare Politics and Policy

Chapter 1 set out the basic issue, that the United States is polarized in many different policy areas. That polarization, falling along party lines (Republican red states and Democratic blue states), is present in elections and in political institutions, such as legislative bodies. We argued in the first chapter that political divisions have policy consequences.

Adding to the political, policy, and ideological polarization is a fundamental feature of the American political system set up by the Constitution in 1787, that is, federalism. Federalism is the division of power between a central or national government and subgovernments, in this case states. Federalism is particularly evident in domestic policy areas such as healthcare. The federal government may set up the basic structure of healthcare in the United States, with programs such as Medicaid, CHIP, and the ACA, among others, but the implementation of such legislation is largely left up to the states.

States are the providers, financiers, administrators, and regulators of healthcare delivery in the United States. They implement federal laws, design and administer their own policies, and define and oversee local health-related activities. They also delegate and work closely with local officials and networks of private agents (Weissert and Uttermark 2017).

And that implementation can vary from state to state. The United States does not have a single healthcare system; each state has carved out its own type of healthcare system that reflects its values, or at least the values of those who get to make policy decisions, such as governors and state legislators.

Those decisions, some positive, some negative, have policy consequences. Chapter 2 laid out the federalism argument and provides a profile of states along a number of dimensions, such as economics, demography, and geography. In this chapter, we have provided a healthcare profile of the states.

It is clear from our analysis of various healthcare factors that there are differences between red states and blue states on the healthcare dimensions, just as there are in the factors discussed in Chapter 2. State rankings on child healthcare, mental healthcare, and maternal healthcare confirm the basic thesis of this chapter. Red states are different from blue states. There are health disparities between states, largely along the red and blue dimension (Montez et al. 2020; Woolf 2022).

There are some caveats to this argument. First, not all measures that we examined supported our thesis. Two related ones dealt with child abuse: the rate of child abuse per state and the rate of those who experienced a high number of adverse childhood experiences. A third measure that did not support our thesis was overdose deaths. There was little difference between the red and blue states on this measure. This is interesting because opioid drug use, the major drug in overdose deaths, was originally concentrated in red states (see Patel and Rushefsky 2020). But fentanyl has spread across the country and now afflicts all parts of the country.

A second caveat is that states differ in a number of ways discussed in Chapter 2. The demographics may be different (for example, the percentage of racial and ethnic group members in a state). The geography may differ with red states being somewhat more rural than blue states. The economies of states may differ with blue states being wealthier than red states. Educational levels may differ as well. All these can be a factor in the healthcare differences that we have seen in this chapter.

One other health policy difference between the two sets of sets focuses on policy priorities. Among the blue state priorities for 2023 were banning "flavored tobacco products, curb prescription drug prices, and expand health coverage for residents" (Beard and Roubein 2023a). Red state top priorities for 2023 included "Extending postpartum Medicaid coverage, restricting gender transition care for minors, and rolling back vaccine requirements" (Beard and Roubein 2023b).

Even given these differences, state healthcare policy decisions differ between our two groups of states (Montez et al. 2020). These differences manifest themselves in a variety of health indicators. The differences include how much states spend on healthcare. Do states expand or not expand Medicaid? Do states support the ACA or challenge or hinder it? Do states support public health efforts, such as vaccinations? Do states support or oppose abortion and all that accompanies this decision? These kinds of decisions create different healthcare systems, to the extent that the health of a person may depend on where he or she lives.

Our next chapters examine these issues.

Bibliography

American Addiction Centers. (n.d.). *Mental Health Spending by State Across the U.S.* Brentwood, TN. Online at https://rehabs.com/explore/mental-health-spending-by-state-across-the-us/
Annie E. Casey Foundation. 2022. *2022 Kids Count Data Book.* Baltimore: The Annie E. Casey Foundation.
Arias, Elizabeth et al. 2021. "U.S. State Life Tables, 2018." *National Vital Statistics Report* 70, no. 2. (March 11): 1–17.
Arias, Elizabeth et al. 2022. "U.S. State Life Tables, 2020." *National Vital Statistics Report* 71, no. 2. (August 23): 1–17. Online at www.cdc.gov
Beard, McKenzie, and Rachel Roubein. 2023a. "Three Kinds of Health Measures Blue States Are Pursing This Year." *Washington Post* (February 22).
Beard, McKenzie, and Rachel Roubein. 2023b. "Three Kinds of Health Measures Red States Are Pursing This Year." *Washington Post* (February 9).
Becker's Hospital Review. 2022. "US Primary Care Physician Workforce Per 100,000 Capita." Online at https://www.beckershospitalreview.com/
Belmonte, Adriana. 2021. "These are the Best and Worst States for Health Care." *Yahoo/Finance* (August 19). Online at www.finance.yahoo.com
Bendix, Aria, and Nigel Chiwaya. 2022. "Map: See How Much Life Expectancy Declined in Each State in 2020." *NBC News* (August 22).
Black, Michelle Lambright. 2022. *Northeast States Offer Best Access to High-Quality Prenatal, Maternal Care.* New York: ValuePenguin. Online at https://www.valuepenguin.com
Brenan, Megan. 2022. "Record-High 56% in U.S. Perceive Local Crime Has Increased." (October 28). Online at https://news.gallup.com
Center for Medicare and Medicaid Services (n.d.). *Medicaid Per Capita Expenditures.* Baltimore, MD. Online at https://medicaid.gov/state-overviews/scorecard/state-health-system-performance/index.html
Centers for Disease Control and Prevention. 2020. *Underlying Cause of Death, 2019-2020.* Atlanta: U.S. Department of Health and Human Services.
Centers for Disease Control and Prevention. 2021. *About Teen Pregnancy.* Atlanta: U.S. Department of Health and Human Services.
Centers for Disease Control and Prevention. 2022a. *Adult Obesity Prevalence Maps.* Atlanta: U.S. Department of Health and Human Services.
Centers for Disease Control and Prevention. 2022b. *Cancer Mortality by State.* Atlanta: U.S. Department of Health and Human Services.
Centers for Disease Control and Prevention. 2022c. *Adult Obesity Prevalence Maps.* Atlanta: U.S. Department of Health and Human Services.
Centers for Disease Control and Prevention. 2022d. *Adult Physical Inactivity Prevalence Maps by Race/Ethnicity.* Atlanta: U.S. Department of Health and Human Services.
Centers for Disease Control and Prevention. 2022e. *Physical Activity.* Atlanta: U.S. Department of Health and Human Services.
Centers for Disease Control and Prevention. 2023. *Teen Birth Rates by State.* Atlanta: U.S. Department of Health and Human Services.
Cleveland Clinic. n.d. "Obesity." Cleveland, OH. Online at my.clevelandclinic.org

Cleveland Clinic. 2022. "How Your Oral Health Affects Your Overall Health." Online at https://health.clevelandclinic.org

Collins, Sara R., Herman K. Bhupal, and Michelle M. Dotty. 2019. *Health Insurance Coverage Eight Years After the ACA: Fewer Uninsured Americans and Shorter Coverage Gaps, But More Uninsured.* New York: Commonwealth Fund.

Collins, Sara R., Munira Z. Gunja, and Gabriella N. Aboulafia. 2020. *U.S. Health Insurance Coverage in 2020: A Looming Crisis in Affordability.* New York: Commonwealth Fund.

Consumer Financial Protection Bureau. 2022. *Medical Debt Burden in the United States.* Washington, DC: Consumer Financial Protection Bureau.

Davis, Ari, et al. (2022). *A Year in Review: 2020 Gun Deaths in the U.S.* Baltimore: The Johns Hopkins Center for Gun Violence Solutions.

Declercq, Eugene, and Laurie Zephyrin. 2020. *Maternal Mortality in the United States: A Primer.* New York: The Commonwealth Fund. Online at https://www.commonwealthfund.org

Department of Health and Human Services. 2018. *Physical Activity Guidelines for Americans*, 2nd ed. Washington, DC: U.S. Department of Health and Human Services.

Elflein, John. 2022. "Obesity Prevalence Among U.S. Adults Aged 18 and Over 2011-2020." Available at https://www.statista.com/statistics/244620/us-obesity-prevalence-among-adults-aged-20-and-over/

Emanuel, Ezekiel J. 2020. *Which Country Has the World's Best Health Care?* New York: Public Affairs.

Federal Bureau of Investigation. 2022. "Crime Data Explorer." Online at https://crime-data-explorer.app.cloud.gov/pages/home

Food and Drug Administration (2022). *Health Effects of Tobacco Use.* MD: U.S. Department of Health and Human Services. https://www.fda.gov/tobacco-products/public-health-education/health-effects-tobacco-use

Guttmacher Institute. 2023. *Sex and HIV Education.* Washington, DC: Guttmacher Institute. Online at https://www.guttmacher.org

Holzhauer, Brett, and Dan Avery. 2024. "New Rule Would Eliminate Debt from Credit Reports." *CNBC* (August 14). Online at https://www.cnbc.com/select/medical-debt-credit-report/

Johnson, Emily K. et al (2022). "Varied Health Spending Growth Across US States Associated with Income, Price Levels, Medicaid Expansion, 2000-29." *Health Affairs* 41 (no. 8): 1088–1097.

Joslyn Law Firm (2023). *Comparing Gun Control Measures to Gun-Related Homicides by State.* Cincinnati: Joslyn Law Firm. Online at https://www.criminalattorneycincinnati.com

Kaiser Family Foundation, 2023. "State Health Facts." Online at https://www.kff.org/statedata

Kaiser Family Foundation. 2024. "States With Firearm Laws Designed to Protect Children." Online at https://www.kff.org

Kellogg, Sarah. 2023. "Missouri Senate Gives Initial Approval to Expanding Medicaid for New Mothers." *St. Louis Public Radio.* (February 21). Online at https://news.stlpublicradio.org

Learish, Jessica. 2022. "Gun Map: Ownership by State." *CBS News* (April 14). Online at https://www.cbsnews.com/pictures/gun-ownership-rates-by-state

Levey, Noam. 2020. "People Live Longer in Blue States than in Red States; New Study Points to the Impact of State Policies." *Los Angeles Times* (August 3).

March of Dimes. 2021. *Low Birthweight*. Arlington County, VA: March of Dimes. Online at https://www.marchofdimes.org/find-support/topics/birth/low-birthweight

March of Dimes. 2023. *Medicaid Coverage of Births*. Arlington County, VA: March of Dimes. Online at https://wallethub.com

McCann, Adam. 2022. "2022's Best and Worst States for Health Care." (April 13). WalletHub Online at https://wallethub.com

Melek, Steve, Stoddard Davenport, and T. J. Gray. 2019. *Addiction and Mental Health vs. Physical Health. Widening Disparities in Network Use and Provider Reimbursement*. Seattle, WA: Milliman.

Mental Health America (2022). *The Federal and State Role in Mental Health*. Alexandria, VA: Mental Health America.

Meyersohn, Nathaniel. 2023). "Why Urgent Care Centers Are Popping Up Everywhere." *CNN* (January 28). Online at https://www.cnn.com

Montez, Jennifer Kara, et al. 2020. "U.S. State Policies, Politics, and Life Expectancy." *Milbank Quarterly* 98, no, 3 (September): 668–699.

National Center for Chronic Disease Prevention and Health Promotion. (2022). *Physical Inactivity*. Atlanta: Centers for Disease Control and Prevention.

National Center for Health Statistics. 2022a. *Cancer Mortality by State*. Atlanta: Center for Disease Control and Prevention.

National Center for Health Statistics. 2022b. *Heart Disease Mortality by State*. Atlanta: Center for Disease Control and Prevention.

National Center for Health Statistics. 2022c. *Accident Mortality by State*. Atlanta: Center for Disease Control and Prevention.

National Center for Health Statistics. 2022d. *Accidents of Unintentional Injuries*. Atlanta: Center for Disease Control and Prevention.

National Center for Health Statistics. 2022e. *Assault or Homicide*. Atlanta: Center for Disease Control and Prevention.

National Institute of Mental Health. n.d. *Frequently Asked Questions about Suicide*. Bethesda, MD: National Institute of Mental Health. Online at

National Partnership for Women and Families. 2022. *Threats on All Fronts: The Links Between the Lack of Abortion Access, Health Care and Workplace Equity*. Washington, DC.

National Partnership for Women and Families. 2022 Online at https://www.nationalpartnership.org

National Popular Vote. n.d. "Rural States Are Almost Entirely Ignored Under Current State-by-State System. Online at https://www.nationalpopularvote.com/rural-states-are-almost-entirely-ignored-under-current-state-state-system

National Rural Health Association. 2023. *About Rural Health Care*. Kansas City, MO: National Rural Health Association.

Ollove, Michael. 2020. "Rural America's Health Crisis Seizes States' Attention." *Stateline* (January 31). Online at https://www.pewtrusts.org

Patel, Kant, and Mark Rushefsky. 2020. *Healthcare Politics and Policy in America.* New York: Routledge.

Quinton, Sophie. 2021. "States Have Money to Spend on Mental Health, But It May Not Last." *Stateline* (September 2). Online at https://www.pewtrusts.org

Radley, David C., Jesse C. Baumgartner, and Sara R. Collins. 2022. *2022 Scorecard on State Health Care Performance.* New York: Commonwealth Fund.

Reinert, Maddy., Danielle Fritze, and Theresa Nguyen. 2022. *The State of Mental Health in America 2023.* Alexandria, VA: Mental Health America. Online at www.mhanational.org

Rudowitz, Robin, et al. 2021. *Medicaid Financing: The Basics.* Menlo Park, CA: Kaiser Family Foundation. (May 7).

"Rural States Are Almost Entirely Ignored Under Current State-By-State System." n.d. *National Popular Vote.* Online at https://www.nationalpopularvote.com

Rushefsky, Mark E. 2017. *Public Policy in the United States: Challenges, Opportunities and Changes.* 6th ed. Routledge.

Sachs, Vanessa, and David Murphey. 2018. *The Prevalence of Adverse Childhood Experiences, Nationally, by State and by Race or Ethnicity.* Bethesda, MD: Child Trends. Online at www.childtrends.org

Schell, et al. 2020. *State-Level Estimates of Household Firearm Ownership.* Santa Monica, CA: Rand Corporation.

Schneider, Eric C., et al. 2021. *Mirror, Mirror 2021 Reflecting Poorly: Health Care in the U.S. Compared to Other High-Income Countries.* New York: Commonwealth Fund.

Schoen, Cathy, et al. 2014. *America's Underinsured: A State-by-State at Health Insurance Affordability Prior to the New Coverage Expansions.* New York: Commonwealth Fund.

Schoen, Cathy, et al. 2016. *On Medicare But at Risk: A State-Level Analysis of Beneficiaries Who Are Underinsured or Facing High Total Cost Burdens.* New York: Commonwealth Fund.

Steenland, Maria, and Laura Wherry. 2023. "Medicaid Expansion Led to Reductions in Postpartum Hospitalizations." *Health Affairs* 42, no. 1 (January): 18–25.

Stephenson, Joan. 2022. "U.S. Maternal Mortality Rate Rose Sharply During Covid Pandemic's First Year." *JAMA Health Forum* 3, no. 3 (March 8): 1–2.

Taylor, Jamila et al. 2022. *The Worsening U.S. Maternal Health Crisis in Three Graphs.* New York: The Century Foundation.

Thiessen, Marc. 2022. "The 'Red State Murder Problem?' That's Just a Democratic Myth." *Washington Post* (October 20).

USAFacts. 2021. *How Much Are Families Spending on Childcare?* Seattle: USAFacts. Online at www.usafacts.org

"U.S. Life Expectancy 1950-2022." n.d. Online at https://www.macrotrends.net/countries/USA/united-states/life-expectancy

VinZant, Nick. 2021. "States with the Most Medical Debt and Rising Health Care Costs." Online at https://quotewizard.com

Volz, Matt. 2022. "More States to Consider Extending Postpartum Medicaid Coverage Beyond Two Months." *Kaiser Health News* (December 8).

Waters, Hugh, and Marlon Graf. 2018. *America's Obesity Crisis: The Health and Economic Costs of Excess Weight.* Santa Monica, CA: Milken Institute. Online at www.milkeninstitute.org

Weissert, Carol S., and Matthew J. Uttermark. 2017. "Glass Half Full: Decentralization in Health Policy." *State and Local Government Review* 49, no. 3 (September): 199–214.

Williams, Kevin. 2024. "Why Walmart, Walgreens, and CVS Retail Health Clinic Experiment is Struggling." *CNBC* (May 28). Online at https://www.cnbc.com/2024/05/28/why-walmart-walgreens-cvs-health-clinic-experiment-is-struggling.html

Woolf, Steven H. 2022. "The Growing Influence of State Governments on Population Health in the United States." *JAMA* 327, no. 14 (April 12): 1331–1332.

World Population Review. 2022. "Murder Rate by State 2022." Online at https://worldpopulationreview.com

World Population Review. 2024. "Smoking Rates by State 2024." Online at https://worldpopulationreview.com/state-rankings/smoking-rates-by-state

World Population Review. 2023a. "Maternal Mortality Rate by State 2023. Online at https://worldpopulationreview.com/state-rankings/maternal-mortality-rate-by-state

World Population Review. 2023b. "STD Rates by State 2023." Online at https://worldpopulationreview.com

Xu, Jiaquan, et al. 2021. "Deaths: Final Data for 2019." *National Vital Statistics Reports* 70, no. 8 (July 26): 1–86.

Ziegler, Brett. 2021. "Health Care Rankings: Measuring How Well States Are Meeting Citizens' Health Care Needs." *U.S. News* (March 9). Online at https://www.usnews.com

Zhang, Xiamong, et al. 2020. "Physician Workforce in the United States of America: Forecasting Nationwide Shortages." *Human Resources for Health* 18, no. 8 (February).

4
RED AND BLUE STATE DIVIDE OVER AFFORDABLE CARE ACT

The Affordable Care Act (ACA, also known as Obamacare), established in 2010, was the largest expansion of healthcare coverage in the United States since the creation of the Medicare and Medicaid programs in 1965. Its primary goal was to make health insurance affordable, reduce the number of uninsured individuals in the country, and eliminate some of the restrictive practices of the health insurance industry (Fadden 2021). It does so by prohibiting insurance companies from canceling policies when policyholders became sick, denying coverage to individuals with preexisting conditions, placing a lifetime monetary limit on hospital stays and other health benefits deemed "essential," and establishing minimum standards for health insurance policies. The law also expanded Medicaid eligibility to include those earning up to 138% of the federal poverty level, including adults without dependents, in participating states. It subsidizes the costs of premiums to help lower-income people pay for insurance. It also made subsidies available (in the form of refundable tax credits) on the state health insurance exchanges for individuals with a household income up to 400% of the federal poverty level. Originally, the ACA imposed a penalty (tax) for people who did not purchase a health insurance plan, known as the individual mandate. The cost of insurance and healthcare for people who were unable to pay was meant to be offset in part by this mandate. However, in 2017, the tax was repealed and thus the mandate had no punitive mechanism.

As discussed in Chapter 2, under the American federal system, the powers of the government are divided between the national and state governments and some powers are shared by both the national and state governments. Thus, state governments have a considerable amount of authority and powers in certain policy areas. In addition, many federal programs and policies are implemented by state governments, giving them considerable discretion in policy implementation. While the federal government often uses the carrot (incentives) and stick (punishment) approach to encourage states to carry out federal policies, state governments can oppose federal policies that they do not like by challenging such policies in courts, delaying or selectively implementing policies, or outright refusal to implement such policies. The level of cooperation or competition between the federal and state levels of governments often depends on which party controls the levers of powers in individual states.

The ACA quickly became a symbol of political polarization involving partisan, ideological, and public opinion divides both at the national and state levels. The political divide was present from the adoption and establishment of the program at the national level to its implementation at the state level. At the national level, elite polarization was reflected in the strict party line vote in Congress where Democrats universally voted for the passage of the ACA while Republicans universally voted against it. In addition, Republicans in Congress made numerous efforts to either defund the ACA or outright repeal it without any success. At the state level, almost all Republican-controlled red states challenged the constitutionality of the ACA in courts while the Democratic-controlled blue states enthusiastically endorsed and implemented the provisions of the legislation. The red states challenged the constitutionality of the law itself as well as the various provisions of the law such as individual mandates. Subsequent rulings by federal and state courts related to these challenges also reflected the partisan and ideological divide on the courts themselves. Even after the Supreme Court upheld the constitutionality of the ACA, when it came to implementation of the ACA at the state level, most blue states were quick to embrace the ACA while the red states continued to fight and oppose the ACA. In this chapter, we analyze the political polarization surrounding the adoption, implementation, and evaluation/impact of the ACA at the state level.

Political Divide Over the Adoption of the ACA

The ACA continued the partisan divide of Democrats and Republicans on comprehensive healthcare reform. No Republicans voted for the 1993 Clinton administration Health Security Act. And we see this again in the passage of the ACA. One of the interesting elements of the debate in Congress over the ACA was that some of the legislation had Republican origins (Hacker 2010). One source was a 2006 law passed in Massachusetts. That legislation established, among other things, markets, known as connectors, where consumers could purchase health insurance policies. The legislation was pushed by the democratically controlled legislature and Democratic U.S. Senator Edward M. Kennedy. It was signed by Republican Governor Mitt Romney, hence the nickname of Romneycare. Working together, this bipartisan effort produced what was effectively an early version of the ACA (Cohn 2021; Haeder and Weimer 2015).

The other Republican origin of the ACA was the individual mandate. The idea here was that all citizens should have health insurance and, if not, should pay a penalty or tax. The concept was proposed in 1989 (Butler 1989) and contained in several Republican alternatives to the Clinton plan in 1993 ("History of the Individual Health Insurance Mandate" 2012). Newt Gingrich (R-GA), soon to be speaker of the U.S. House of Representatives, also supported the individual mandate in the early 1990s. The argument was twofold. First, the mandate was seen as part of an alternative to a single-payer plan where the federal government would be paying the healthcare bills. Second, requiring everyone to have insurance would ensure personal responsibility for one's health (Robertson and Epstein 2020). Early meetings in 2008 in the Senate Finance Committee contained both Democrats and Republicans. But by the time the bill was introduced in Congress in 2009, opposition arose, particularly among Republicans.

Support for the ACA on the part of Democrats was based on what they saw as the limitations of the American healthcare system. Not all Americans had health insurance coverage (see Table 4.1). Table 4.1 provides two sets of figures. The second column of the table is the percentage or rate of the total population lacking health insurance. The fourth column of the table shows the rate/percentage of the population under the age of 65 lacking insurance. The lower numbers in this column compared to the second reflect that virtually all those over 65 have health insurance, mostly through Medicare. In any event, the uninsurance rate in 2008 for those under 65 was over 16 percent, representing over 43 million people. 2008 was the year Obama was elected president. The uninsured numbers/percent remained high until they started declining significantly in 2014 when many of the provisions of the ACA went into effect.

Another reason for support was to limit insurance provisions that made it difficult to obtain insurance, say for someone with preexisting conditions, or to get insurance companies to cover procedures.

There were several reasons for opposition to the ACA. One was the growing conservatism of the Republican Party. While Democrats became increasingly liberal, Republicans moved much farther to the right. The partisan ideological divide grew bigger (Mann and Ornstein 2016;

TABLE 4.1 Uninsured Rate and Population, 2008–2021

	Total Population		Under 65	
	Rate	Number of people (in millions)	Rate	Number of people (in millions)
2008	14.6	43.5	16.5	43.2
2009	15.1	45.7	17.2	45.3
2010	15.5	47.2	17.7	46.8
2011	15.1	46.4	17.3	46
2012	14.8	46.6	16.9	45.2
2013	14.5	45.2	16.7	44.7
2014	11.7	36.7	13.5	36.2
2015	9.4	29.8	10.9	29.4
2016	8.6	27.3	10.0	26.9
2017	8.7	28.0	10.2	27.6
2018	8.9	28.6	10.4	28.2
2019	9.2	29.6	10.8	29.2
2020*				
2021	8.6	28.2	10.2	27.8

Adapted from: Bureau of the Census (N.D.). Online at www.census.gov.

* Information is not available.

MacDonald 2020). The polarization over the ACA can be seen in a question asked in 2014: How much should the [federal] government help provide healthcare? Overall, there was a split among the public with half saying the federal government should not play a role and nearly half saying it should. Ideologically, the differences were dramatic. Among liberals, 89 percent said that this should be a responsibility for the federal government, compared to 2 percent of conservatives who agreed with that position (Smith 2015).

A second reason, which became apparent in 2009, was opposition among Republican Party members. This can be seen in town hall meetings where members of Congress would meet directly with their constituents. A portion, the most conservative, of this public became what was known as Tea Party Republicans, evoking one of the first anti-British colonial episodes in the revolutionary period. Tea Party Republicans, who would eventually evolve into Freedom Caucus members in state legislatures and later into Donald Trump-supported MAGA (Make America Great Again) Republicans, helped convince Republican members of Congress to oppose the legislation.

Other reasons for opposition to the ACA included the increased role that the federal government would have in the healthcare system. This was combined with a lack of trust on the part of the public. Republicans were much more likely to distrust the federal government than Democrats (though levels of trust in the federal government had been declining for years) (Dalen, Waterbrook, and Alpert 2015). Ideological differences played a role, with conservatives much more likely to oppose the ACA than liberals (MacDonald 2020; Rovner 2017).

Television played a role in creating opposition to the law (MacDonald 2020). Coverage of the ACA was largely negative and the vast majority of campaign ads in the 2010–2014 period reflected this negativity (Dalen, Waterbrook, and Alpert 2015). That there were problems with implementation of the exchanges, where people would purchase insurance policies, reinforced these views, and were covered by various media.

Another reason for opposition is that the law, at least at first, created some losers, those whose insurance costs have gone up. Those who experienced this kind of loss were much more vocal than those who gained from the program (Rovner 2017).

One last element in opposition was the complexity of the law. It was difficult to understand for the average person and had a number of different parts, as noted in this chapter's introduction. The ignorance about the law combined with misperceptions and misinformation about it enhanced opposition to the ACA (Rovner 2017). One notable example of this was the claim that the law had so-called "death panels." The idea of death panels began with Elizabeth McCaughey, who had opposed many Democratic proposals for health reform. This was then picked up by former Alaskan governor and 2008 Republican vice-presidential candidate Sarah Palin (Cohn 2021).

The basic idea that was in early versions of what became the ACA was to pay physicians to consult with patients who voluntarily wanted to discuss advanced-care planning and options. Periodically, ACA recipients would meet, under the provision, with their physicians to assess the patient's health (normally an elderly patient), look at the patient's prognosis, and discuss whether the patient was interested in options such as hospice care and do not resuscitate directives. Again, the meetings would be voluntary on the patient's part, and the physician would get reimbursed for his/her efforts.

In Palin's language, such meetings became "death panels," whose purpose was to prepare the patient for death and how that would be accomplished. There was nothing in the proposals to that effect. But it played upon the mistrust of government and the concern that since proponents heralded the ACA as a way of controlling costs (affordable care), this was one of the ways to do so (Frankford 2015). While this is a somewhat

TABLE 4.2 Overall Public Opinion on the Affordable Care Act (2010)

	Percentage of Public
Favorable	46%
Unfavorable	40%
Don't Know or Refused	14%

Adapted from: Kaiser Family Foundation (2010). Online at www.kff.org.

TABLE 4.3 Partisan Divide Over ACA (2010)

	Democrats	Independents	Republicans
Favorable	77%	37%	12%
Unfavorable	12%	46%	79%
Undecided	10%	18%	9%

Adapted from: Kaiser Family Foundation (2010). Online at www.kff.org.

simplified version of what happened (see Frankford 2015 for a more extensive discussion), the phrase "death panels" had a ring to it that influenced those opposed to the law and to any similar provisions in the law after it was enacted. Such tactics likely increased opposition to the law and continued several years past enactment.

There were other reasons for opposition to the ACA, including opposition to President Obama, the first African American president, but from our standpoint these were the major ones.

Public opinion polls showed increasing opposition to the ACA. Poll results illustrated the partisan divide, and the ACA, shortly after its passage and several years into the implementation process, never had support from more than half the public as measured by public opinion surveys (Brodie et al. 2019; Kaiser Family Foundation 2010; Rovner 2017) (see Table 4.2).

As Table 4.2 demonstrates a plurality of those polled favored the ACA (46 percent) compared to those who opposed it (40 percent). But as Table 4.3 shows, there was a considerable partisan divide. Seventy-seven percent of those who identified as Democrats supported the new legislation. Republicans took the opposite position by about the same percentage: 79 percent of those identifying as Republicans opposed the legislation. The partisan divide over the ACA was clear and largely remained over the years (see further discussion of public opinion below).

The partisan divide can also be seen regionally. The regions most likely to have a favorable view of the ACA were the New England and Pacific regions (Brodie, Deane, and Cho 2011). The Pacific region includes Alaska, California, Hawaii, Oregon, and Washington states. With the exception of Alaska, these are all blue states. The New England region includes the blue states of Connecticut, Maine, Massachusetts, New Hampshire, Rhode Island, and Vermont. New Hampshire is a purple state, and the rest are blue. The East South-Central states showed the strongest unfavorability rating of all the regions. States in this region include Alabama, Kentucky, Mississippi, and Tennessee, all red states (Brodie, Deane, and Cho 2011). Brodie, Deane, and Cho's (2011, 2019) analysis shows the clear relationship between dominant party in a state and views toward the ACA: "In fact, there are sizable, statistically significant correlations between party identification and each of the opinion-related columns."

The Democrats had majorities in both houses of Congress and were able to overcome the Republican use of a filibuster in the Senate by having 60 votes to override the filibuster and then making use of the reconciliation budget process that did not require 60 votes for a companion piece of legislation. The Democratic leadership made compromises within the party to allow the ACA and the companion legislation to pass in March 2009. Again, no Republican Senator or House member voted for the ACA. That the Democrats controlled both houses of Congress and the presidency allowed the bill to be passed. That trifecta of control would end with the 2010 mid-term elections.

While the party in power, the party controlling the presidency, often suffers losses in mid-term elections (American Presidency Project 2022), the 2010 mid-terms were especially difficult for Democrats. The Republicans gained six seats in the Senate, and 63 seats in the House, giving them control of the House. This was the largest loss of House seats by one party since the 1938 mid-term elections. In addition, Republicans gained control of 15 state legislatures (Kilgore 2010). Given the importance of states in the implementation of the Affordable Care, Republican victories at the state and national levels foretold a troublesome future for the ACA.

An important part of the ACA that created opposition was its federalist nature. Significant portions of the legislation, such as the exchanges and Medicaid among others, were left to the states to implement. This can be seen as the continuation of the move toward shifting responsibilities from the federal government to the states, a process, known as devolution, that began during the Reagan administration. Given the differences between red states and blue states that we have discussed in previous chapters, implementation of the law was going to depend on where one lived. It would also affect public opinion.

The regional differences in public opinion toward the ACA noted above were related to state policy design and to the position that governors took toward the program (Pacheco and Maltby 2019). If we examine state decisions concerning health insurance exchanges (see below), the state-exchange model tended to increase favorability opinions toward the ACA. A supportive governor also helped. Lacking those two elements, public opinion in a state either declined or remained stagnant. The decision to devolve responsibility for the healthcare reform tended to increase negative opinion about the ACA (Pacheco and Maltby 2019).

The Empire Strikes Back: Attacking the ACA

With control of Congress moving back to the Republicans, the opposition to the ACA took several paths, including placing roadblocks, defunding the act, and attempts at repeal. The battle over the ACA has been labeled a ten years' war (Cohn 2021; McFadden 2021; Oberlander 2018, 2020).

The first legislative challenge to the ACA on the part of Republicans came in March 2010, shortly after the ACA was enacted. The House passed a bill simply to "replace and repeal" (Cohn 2021, 234). While there was no chance that such a bill would pass, with Republicans in the minority, it did set the theme for similar legislation when they would become a majority. These types of bills were really repeals, with no or little replacement (Cohn 2021). When the Republicans regained control of the House after the 2010 mid-term elections, more repeal and replace bills would be forthcoming.

Another policy Republicans attempted in Congress was to cut or eliminate the budget of items needed to implement the ACA. But with the Senate still in Democratic hands and Obama winning reelection in 2012, these attempts mostly failed (Cohn 2021). One exception was the risk corridor payments (Oberlander 2020)

The temporary risk corridor payments, a complex part of a complex piece of legislation, were designed to entice or attract insurance companies to participate in the exchanges. If the companies had costs that were lower than their premiums, they would have to pay some of the profit to the federal government. Conversely, if the costs were higher than their premiums, the federal government would have to pay the companies according to a formula.

The problems were twofold. First, the companies did not plan for the higher costs compared to the premiums. Second, Congress had not approved funds for the payments. In December 2014, a rider (amendment) to an appropriations bill restricted the use of other funds for paying for it. In essence, the insurance companies would be out of what they thought would be reimbursements. But in a 2020 decision, the U.S. Supreme Court, by an 8-1 decision, held that the federal government had an obligation to make the payments even if the money had not been appropriated (Keith 2020).

A second ACA program that was eliminated was the reinsurance program (Oberlander 2020). The program was designed to help stabilize premiums in policies that were not part of the ACA exchanges (state or federal). That program was allowed to expire.

Another issue, one on which supporters and opponents of the legislation would likely agree upon, is that changes needed to be made to improve the ACA. But Republicans were not interested in improving a program they strongly disliked. The few bipartisan efforts to change the bill did not pass (Oberlander 2020).

Another manifestation of Republican opposition to the ACA came in the fall of 2013. Senator Ted Cruz (R-TX) began a filibuster of the budget process. Cruz' demand was that Congress defund the ACA. While Senator Cruz failed to reach his goal, he created disruption in the operation of the federal government (Cohn 2021).

2017 was an important year for the Republicans and their opposition to the ACA. In 2016, Republicans retained control of both houses of Congress (though losing seats) and Donald Trump won the presidency. Republicans had won the trifecta. In 2017, Republicans considered a number of bills that would "repeal and replace" the ACA. The Congressional Budget Office (CBO), which evaluates or scores the impact of proposed legislation, consistently reported that upward of 20 million people would lose their coverage if the bills were passed.

One bill, the American HealthCare Act, did manage to pass the House. Because Republicans lacked 60 votes in the Senate to stop a filibuster, bill managers decided to use the budget reconciliation process which required only a majority vote. Republicans held only 51 seats. When the vote was taken to pass the American HealthCare Act through the reconciliation process, all Democrats voted against it. Three Republicans also voted against it: Susan Collins of Maine, John McCain of Arizona, and Lisa Murkowski of Alaska. The bill was defeated.

In the face of defeat, Republicans made use of another piece of legislation that was going to pass Congress: the Tax Cut and Jobs Act of 2017. This was the big tax cut that President Trump had promised during his campaign. An amendment to the bill, known as a rider, eliminated the tax penalty for consumers who did not purchase health insurance. It led to one of many ACA court cases (see below).

The Trump Administration

Donald Trump assumed the presidency in January 2017. Trump had campaigned promising to eliminate the ACA (Jost 2018). Trump made use of a variety of administrative tools allowing him to make changes in the program without congressional approval (Thompson 2020; Trachtman 2020). There were a number of ways that Trump "sabotaged" (Thompson 2020, 2) the ACA. The first way was to impede enrollment in the exchanges. This was accomplished in two ways. First, funding for navigators and advertising was cut. Advertising lets those who might purchase insurance on the exchanges know about them and obtain information. Buying insurance, whether inside the ACA exchanges or outside, is complicated. The ACA called for funding navigators who would help individuals and families select the best plan for them. The Trump administration cut funding for both of these.

Second, the administration, as well as Congress, cut subsidies to insurance companies (the reinsurance mentioned above) that would foster competition and help lower insurance costs.

Third, the Trump administration promoted alternative insurance plans. These plans, cheaper than exchange plans, were of lower quality than ACA-approved plans, covered fewer services, and paid out less. The fear was that healthy potential purchasers would move to those alternative plans and siphon off the pool for the exchanges (Jost 2018).

Fourth, the administration approved waivers to the ACA that included Medicaid work requirements and other administrative barriers (we discuss Medicaid, work requirements, and waivers in Chapter 5). The administration also encouraged waivers that might reduce coverage.

Fifth, the administration, with its anti-immigrant stance dating to the Trump election campaign, made it difficult for legal immigrants to get on Medicaid.

Sixth, the administration reduced the enrollment period to half (Trachtman 2020). Possible purchasers had less time and little help in choosing among plans.

A seventh threat was different from the previous six and involved all three branches of the federal government: a U.S. Supreme Court case based on the elimination of the tax on those who do not get insurance mentioned above. The concern was that the Court would use the case to declare the entire legislation unconstitutional, especially given the makeup of the

Court with its 6-3 conservative majority (Thompson 2020). We address court decisions next.

Under the Trump administration, the federal government reduced its role, turning over more responsibilities to state governments:

> It has transferred to the states' responsibility for ensuring that health insurers offer adequate provider networks and access to essential community providers. Recent rules allow states to alter their essential health benefit requirements, reduce transfers among insurers under the risk adjustment program, and diminish required insurer medical-loss ratios. The administration was also transferring responsibility for marketplace enrollment from the federal marketplace to private web brokers through its enhanced direct enrollment program. Increased reliance on the states or the private sector to implement the ACA risks uneven, and in some instances ineffective, enforcement and consumer protection.
>
> (Jost 2018)

Despite the efforts of the Trump administration to undermine or sabotage the ACA, it has managed to survive (Jost 2018; Thompson 2020).

Legal Challenges to Aca By Red States

> The ACA is the most challenged statute in American history. The first lawsuits were filed moments after the law was enacted on March 23, 2010 asserting that the ACA was unconstitutional. Ten years later, the ACA was still under attack, being litigated in three Supreme Court cases in 2020 for a collective total of seven Supreme Court challenges in a decade.
>
> (Gluck, Regan, and Turret 2020, 1472)

Because of the way that the ACA was crafted, the states had an important role in its implementation. States could make implementation easier or harder. And states did both. One strategy was litigation, mainly on the part of red states, to challenge the ACA (see Table 4.4).

The chief state litigation officer is the state attorney general. Attorneys general can spend a considerable amount of their time in lawsuits with the federal government, some on their own initiative and some on the federal government's initiative. Such lawsuits particularly marked the Obama administration over a variety of issues. In this section, we consider the major

TABLE 4.4 ACA Court Cases

NFIB v. Sebelius (2012)
Burrell v. Hobby Lobby Stores (2014)
KIng v. Burwell (2015)
Zubik v. Burwell (2015)
California v. Texas (2021)
Braidwood Management Inc. v. Becerra (2023)

Adapted with permission from: Gluck, Regan, and Turret (2020).

cases, ones which reached the Supreme Court. Over 70 such suits were filed against the Obama administration during its first term (Nolette 2014). The Texas Attorney General (now Governor) Gregg Abbott alone filed 24 suits. A state can be either a direct party in the suit or file an amicus curiae (friend of the court) brief in support of a particular position (Nolette 2014). The amicus curiae briefs can have a significant impact on a case with a favorably inclined judge or justice sometimes quoting directly from a brief.

National Federation of Independent Businesses (Nfib) v. Sebelius *(2012)*

The first case, as the quote beginning this section observes, was *NFIB v. Sebelius* (2012). The case revolved around two main issues. The first was whether the mandate that individuals had to purchase insurance was constitutional. If it were constitutional, what would be the basis? The main issue argued by both opponents and supporters of the ACA was whether Congress could impose the individual mandate based on Congress' constitutional power to regulate interstate commerce. The Court ruled, 5-4, that the mandate, based on the interstate commerce clause, was, indeed, unconstitutional. But in a surprising development, a slightly different Court majority voted 5-4 that the mandate was constitutional under Congress' power to levy taxes. The surprise element in these two decisions was Chief Justice John Roberts. He had originally supported the notion that the mandate was unconstitutional and wrote what was then the minority opinion. But near the end of deliberations, he changed his mind and voted to uphold the ACA, writing the majority opinion. Thus, the ACA would remain in place.

One other note is that this case, like most Supreme Court cases, moved up the line from federal circuit court judge to federal appellate court to the U.S. Supreme Court. As the cases that eventually were combined into one made their way up the ladder, decisions varied. For the most part, Republican-appointed judges voted against the ACA while

Democratic-appointed judges voted to uphold it. A couple of Republican judges did rule favorably toward the ACA. This partisan division was also seen in the Supreme Court. Apart from Roberts, Republican justices voted to declare the ACA unconstitutional, while Democratic justices voted to declare it constitutional. We will see this pattern recur in other cases.

The other major part of the ACA that became part of *NFIB v. Sebelius* had to do with Medicaid. As the ACA was drawn up, the exchanges and Medicaid would be the major vehicles for increasing the number of people with health insurance. The ACA envisioned that states would expand Medicaid to cover more people (see Chapter 5 for a discussion of Medicaid) and provided both incentives and penalties to encourage state participation. The big issue was the penalties. According to the law, states that did not expand Medicaid would lose all their Medicaid funding. Given the size and importance of Medicaid, both to its recipients and to state budgets, the Court decided by a 7-2 vote (with both conservative and liberal justices in the majority) that this penalty was unconstitutional. Instead, the Court ruled that the states could opt out of Medicaid expansion with no penalty (Gluck, Regan and Turret 2020).

Where were the states in this? Fourteen states originally challenged the law and 12 more joined them. Table 4.5 shows which states supported and opposed the ACA. Of our 24 red states, 16 challenged the ACA and eight took no position. Our blue states were a bit more mixed. Twelve supported the ACA, three challenged it, and two took no position. It is clear that the red states opposed the ACA, and the blue states supported it.

The results of *NFIB v. Sebelius* were mixed. The law itself was not declared unconstitutional, though the constitutional basis for it was different from what supporters had posed. The Medicaid provisions of the ACA showed something of an overreach, with its penalty for refusing to expand Medicaid being the loss of all federal funding. But it gave the opponents an opportunity to reject a significant portion of the ACA. We will address this in Chapter 5.

Burrell v. Hobby Lobby Stores *(2014)*

The next case, *Burrell v. Hobby Lobby Stores* (2014), was both an attack on the ACA and had wider implications. Let us begin with the ACA. One of the provisions of the ACA was that there would be a list of essential benefits, preventive healthcare benefits (Gluck, Regan and Turret 2020). The ACA did not specify what those benefits would be, leaving it to the executive branch, namely, the U.S. Department of Health and Human Services (DHHS), to develop such a list. The list included contraceptives that were approved by the Food and Drug Administration (FDA). While the

TABLE 4.5 *NFIB v Sebelius*

Red States		Blue States	
Alabama	Challenged	California	Supported
Alaska	Challenged	Connecticut	Supported
Arizona	Challenged	Delaware	Supported
Arkansas	No Position	Hawaii	Supported
Georgia	Challenged	Illinois	Supported
Idaho	Challenged	Maine	Challenged
Indiana	Challenged	Maryland	Supported
Kansas	Challenged	Massachusetts	Supported
Kentucky	No Position	Michigan	Challenged
Louisiana	Challenged	New Jersey	No Position
Mississippi	Challenged	New Mexico	Supported
Missouri	No Position	New York	Supported
Montana	No Position	Oregon	Supported
Nebraska	Challenged	Pennsylvania	Challenged
North Carolina	No Position	Rhode Island	No Position
North Dakota	Challenged	Vermont	Supported
Oklahoma	No Position	Washington	Supported
South Carolina	Challenged		
South Dakota	Challenged		
Tennessee	No Position		
Texas	Challenged		
Utah	Challenged		
West Virginia	No Position		
Wyoming	Challenged		

Online at https://www.kff.org/statedata.

ACA made no provisions for religious objections to such services, the Obama administration did. The administration made use of the Religious Freedom Restoration Act (RFRA) of 1993 which exempted some religious employers. Those left out eventually sued the administration. For-profit corporations were among those left out. The craft store, Hobby Lobby, filed suit under RFRA stating their religious objections to the rules promulgated by the Obama administration (Gluck, Regan and Turret 2020).

The Court had, in previous cases, held that for-profit corporations are persons with some civil liberties protections. In this case, the Court by a 5-4 vote ruled that closely held private corporations had freedom of religion rights under RFRA that made them exempt, if they so choose, from the contraceptive mandate of the ACA (Gluck, Regan and Turret 2020; Greenfield and Winkler 2015). The five justices in the majority were all Republican appointees and the four justices in the minority were all Democratic appointees.

TABLE 4.6 *Burrell v. Hobby Lobby Stores*

Red States		Blue States	
Alabama	Oppose	California	Support
Alaska	Oppose	Connecticut	Support
Arizona	Oppose	Delaware	Support
Arkansas		Hawaii	Support
Georgia	Oppose	Illinois	Support
Idaho	Oppose	Maine	Support
Indiana		Maryland	Support
Kansas	Oppose	Massachusetts	Support
Kentucky		Michigan	Oppose
Louisiana	Oppose	New Jersey	
Mississippi		New Mexico	Support
Missouri		New York	Support
Montana	Oppose	Oregon	Support
Nebraska	Oppose	Pennsylvania	
North Carolina		Rhode Island	Support
North Dakota	Oppose	Vermont	Support
Oklahoma		Washington	Support
South Carolina	Oppose		
South Dakota	Oppose		
Tennessee			
Texas	Oppose		
Utah	Oppose		
West Virginia	Oppose		
Wyoming			

Carter (2014); Office of Attorney General (California) (2014).

Where were the states in this? State Attorneys General filed amicus curiae briefs in support of one position or the other. The pattern is the one we have seen previously in this chapter. Table 4.6 presents the data. Fifteen of our red states submitted briefs supporting the plaintiffs (Hobby Lobby) while 15 of our blue states supported the government position.

While *Burrell v. Hobby Lobby Stores* focused on religious freedom issues, from our standpoint, the importance is that this is the first case in which the essential benefits provisions were attacked, and successfully, paving the way for future cases.

King v. Burrell *(2015)*

In the wake of the *NFIB* case, the normal path for a law would be acceptance (Gluck, Regan and Turret (2020)). Apart from the Supreme Court decision, the reelection of President Obama and Democratic gains in the

Senate in 2012 should have smoothed the way for implementation. But opponents of the law refused to accept that the ACA's constitutionality had been upheld, and held up helping implement it, especially the marketplaces or exchanges. Two of the pillars or major parts of the ACA (the individual mandate and Medicaid expansion) were upheld. The third were the marketplaces. Opponents discarded their attempts to attack the law as a whole, focusing on taking it apart piecemeal (Gluck, Regan and Turret 2020).

Here is where *King v. Burrell* (2015) comes in. The authors of the ACA assumed that states would set up exchanges for people to purchase insurance, similar to marketplaces for supplementary plans for Medicare (so-called medigap plans), Medicare Advantage Plans (Part C), and Medicare drug plans (Part D). But setting up the marketplaces was voluntary and for states that did not set up a marketplace, the federal government would do so (we discuss the exchanges later in this chapter). The right of states to refuse to set up an exchange was one that Senate Republicans pushed (Gluck, Regan and Turret 2020). The ACA is a long piece of legislation, some 2000 pages, and not as carefully written as perhaps it should have been. Opponents, looking for some way to attack the law, picked up a passage that called for subsidies for those purchasing insurance on the state-run exchanges. But a literal reading of the passage suggested that such subsidies would not be available for federally run exchanges. If that were in fact to be the case, the federal exchanges would collapse because subscribers could not afford the premiums or co-payments.

Where were the states in this case? As with the other cases we have and will discuss, the red state/blue state line held up, though a bit more mixed than in some other cases. Table 4.7 presents the data. Fifteen blue states, via amicus briefs, supported the ACA. That is, they supported the the interpretation that federally run subsidies were statutorily legal. Two blue states, Michigan and New Jersey, did not submit or participate in an amicus brief. On the red states side, seven states supported the opposition to the ACA. Interestingly, four states (Kentucky, Mississippi, North Carolina, and North Dakota) participated in amicus briefs supporting the ACA. Thirteen red states did not participate in the case. State support, a total of 19 states, favored the ACA interpretation.

The U.S. Supreme Court, by a 6-3 majority, upheld the subsidies for the federal exchanges. This was a statutory rather than constitutional issue of interpretation. The Court majority, following the arguments of ACA supporters, held that if one looked at the law as a whole, it was clear that the intent of Congress was for the subsidies to be available for federal as well as state exchanges. Thus, this important element of the ACA was upheld.

TABLE 4.7 *King v. Burrell*

Red States		Blue States	
Alabama	Challenged	California	Supported
Alaska		Connecticut	Supported
Arizona		Delaware	Supported
Arkansas		Hawaii	Supported
Georgia	Challenged	Illinois	Supported
Idaho		Maine	Supported
Indiana	Challenged	Maryland	Supported
Kansas		Massachusetts	Supported
Kentucky	Supported	Michigan	
Louisiana		New Jersey	
Mississippi	Supported	New Mexico	Supported
Missouri		New York	Supported
Montana		Oregon	Supported
Nebraska	Challenged	Pennsylvania	Supported
North Carolina	Supported	Rhode Island	Supported
North Dakota	Supported	Vermont	Supported
Oklahoma	Challenged	Washington	Supported
South Carolina	Challenged		
South Dakota			
Tennessee			
Texas			
Utah			
West Virginia	Challenged		
Wyoming			

Adapted from: SCOTSblog (n.d.); Online at https://www.scotusblog.com/case-files/cases/king-v-burwell/. Wikipedia (n.d.).

California v. Texas *(2021)*

Another critical ACA case to come before the U.S. Supreme Court was *California v. Texas* (2021). This case stems from the Tax Cut and Jobs Act of 2017 discussed above. To recall, the legislation repealed the tax penalty for an individual's failure to purchase a health insurance policy. The question raised by ACA challengers was whether the end of the mandate (no penalty for not purchasing insurance) meant that the entire ACA was unconstitutional (Gluck, Regan and Turret 2020; Musumeci 2020). To use a phrase from the case, this was a severability issue. It was as if, using a knitting analogy, someone pulled a string and the structure would fall down (Gluck, Regan and Turret 2020). This was a challenge to the entire statute.

A district judge in Texas held that the ACA was unconstitutional, a position supported by the next level of the federal judiciary, an appellate court. Both the district judge and the appellate court were decidedly Republican.

The argument made by the supporters of the ACA was that there was no severability issue. There were large portions of the ACA that did not depend on an individual mandate nor on the tax enforcement mechanism. Another argument against those who brought the suit was based on congressional intent. In 2017, Congress had made several attempts to repeal the ACA. Each one failed. The only thing that could be agreed upon, in a rider amendment, was to eliminate the tax penalty. Therefore, ACA supporters argued, congressional intent must have been limited to getting rid of the tax and nothing else (Bagley 2021).

Regardless of the merit on either side, the Court decided, on a 7-2 vote, not to hear the case because neither the plaintiffs involved, such as the state of Texas, nor anybody else were harmed by the law as it stood without the tax penalty. Further, as Bagley argues (2021), though the Court decision not to hear the case was not accompanied by a majority opinion, the majority seemed to be saying that they did not want to see any more cases challenging the ACA.

Where were the states in this case? The states, especially Texas, took a lead role in bringing the case to the judiciary. California led those states supporting the ACA. Table 4.8 presents the data. And there is a bit of a mixed picture on the challengers' side. Sixteen red states challenged the ACA, three red states defended the ACA, and four red states took no position. On the other side, all the blue states supported the ACA. Texas' argument created some disagreement among Republicans about the case (Bagley 2021). Some doubted the validity of the Texas argument, while others were concerned that if the Court did decide to invalidate the entire act, there would be no replacement available.

Braidwood Management, Inc. v. Becerra *(2022)*

Braidwood Management, Inc. v. Becerra (2022) is a case that was introduced in 2022. It raised questions about the preventive services requirements of the ACA. The idea behind these provisions is that insurance plans would offer these services without cost to patients. But, in 2022, the requirements were challenged on several grounds, including religious objections to some of the services on the list, such as "medication for HIV prevention" (Sobel et al. 2023). A district court judge in Texas, the one who ruled in the *Hobby Lobby* case that the entire ACA was unconstitutional after the tax penalty was eliminated in 2017, ruled for the plaintiffs. The federal government appealed the ruling to a federal circuit court. The circuit court has not heard the case as of this writing, but it did issue a

TABLE 4.8 *California v. Texas*

Red States		Blue States	
Alabama	Challenged	California	Defended
Alaska		Connecticut	Defended
Arizona	Challenged	Delaware	Defended
Arkansas	Challenged	Hawaii	Defended
Georgia	Challenged	Illinois	Defended
Idaho		Maine	Defended
Indiana	Challenged	Maryland	Defended
Kansas	Challenged	Massachusetts	Defended
Kentucky	Defended	Michigan	Defended
Louisiana	Challenged	New Jersey	Defended
Mississippi	Challenged	New Mexico	Defended
Missouri	Challenged	New York	Defended
Montana		Oregon	Defended
Nebraska	Challenged	Pennsylvania	Defended
North Carolina	Defended	Rhode Island	Defended
North Dakota	Challenged	Vermont	Defended
Oklahoma		Washington	Defended
South Carolina	Challenged		
South Dakota	Challenged		
Tennessee	Challenged		
Texas	Challenged		
Utah	Challenged		
West Virginia	Defended		
Wyoming			

Adapted from: Musumeci (2020).

"stay" on the district court's decision until it could be addressed by the circuit court (Sobel et al. 2023). The case has not yet attracted amicus briefs on the part of states. But it does illustrate the use of litigation to challenge much of the ACA. And it is part of the litigation strategy used to impede or eliminate the ACA. By one estimate (Gluck, Regan and Turret 2020; Sobel et al. 2023), there have been over 2,000 cases challenging some or all of the ACA.

Implementation of the ACA by Red and Blue States

Implementation is the carrying out or executing a law or plan or program. In the case of the ACA, states are major implementers. One phrase that describes the relationship of the federal government and the states where both have responsibility for implementing a program is "shared governance" (Haeder and Weimer 2015, 282). Medicare is a fully federal program, so there is very little, if any, shared governance. Medicaid is clearly a federal/state program and embodies shared governance. The nature of the enacting legislation creates the foundation by which a law is put into effect and succeeds or fails to meet its objectives.

The exchange provisions of the ACA were fairly detailed in its set of required minimum standards and operational standards (Rigby and Haselswerdt 2013). The law included federal funding to help states set up the exchanges. The impact of the standards was to push states in a liberal direction, which was acceptable to some states (i.e., blue states) but not to conservative-oriented (i.e., red) states. The Obama administration used the tools at its disposal, such as mandates, funding, and flexibility, to try to move both red and blue states to adopt their own exchanges. From the conservative state standpoint, the ACA and the exchanges were an example of "coercive federalism" (Rigby and Haselswerdt 2013, 370). This combined with generalized opposition to the Obama administration and to the ACA made it much less likely that red states would be cooperative.

Trachtman (2020) has an interesting perspective on states and public policy, particularly the ACA. He writes that state policies that might lead to dysfunctional marketplaces would tend to shed a negative light on the legislation and would help the national (Republican) party in blaming the Democrats for the failures of the law. On the other hand, state policies that result in effective markets would allow Democrats to take credit for the successes.

Three major components of the ACA that states had significant responsibility for are the exchanges, Medicaid, and the Pre-Existing Conditions Insurance Plan or PCIP (Haeder and Weimer (2015).

Of all the provisions of the Affordable Care, the exchanges or marketplaces were the ones that produced the most opposition (Béland, Rocco, and Waddan 2016). During the deliberations over the passage of the ACA, the insurance exchanges engendered very little controversy (Rigby and Haselswerdt 2013). Policy legacies are important in affecting opposition to or cooperation with a policy (Béland, Rocco, and Waddan 2016). In the case of the exchanges, the two policy legacies were the individual mandate and purchasing pools. Both had conservative origins and thus those who wrote the ACA felt that opposition to these policies in the ACA would be lessened. But no state followed the Massachusetts reform which was based on something similar to the ACA exchanges (Béland, Rocco, and Waddan 2016). This decentralized design combined with the 2010 mid-term elections (see Table 4.9) made opposition among Republicans more likely.

Apart from having a weak policy legacy, the health exchanges/marketplaces were institutionally fragmented (Béland, Rocco, and Waddan 2016). The fragmentation gave opponents lots of veto points to slow

TABLE 4.9 The Trifecta of Power

	House	Senate	Presidency
2009	D	D	D
2011	R	D	D
2013	R	D	D
2015	R	R	D
2017	R	R	R
2019	D	R	R
2021	D	D	D
2023	R	D	D

Adapted with permission from: Apple (N.D.). Online at https://www.spokesman.com/stories/2020/jun/25/control-house-and-senate-1900/.

development, adoption, and implementation. But that opposition to the exchanges manifested itself only after the ACA was passed (Béland, Rocco, and Waddan 2020).

An argument could be made that the policy legacy of the marketplaces/exchanges was somewhat stronger than suggested. Here we can turn to Medicare. Medicare recipients can make use of some combination of three marketplaces to purchase insurance. The first one is medigap policies. These are private policies offered by insurance companies that pay for services that Medicare Parts A and B (original Medicare) do not pay for or do not fully pay for. There are a range of benefits depending on which type of medigap policy is chosen and different prices depending on the choice of plans and the insurance company. A second Medicare example is Part D, which pays for some portion of a recipient's prescription medications. Again, recipients are faced with an array of choices of plans and costs. The third example is the Part C or Medicare Advantage (or MA) plans. Like the other two examples, they are administered by insurance companies. A way to think about the MA plans is that they combine many, if not most, of the elements of Medicare in one plan. Such plans are popular among recipients (because of generous benefits beyond traditional Medicare). Of course, Medicare recipients do not get their health insurance on the ACA exchanges, so the basic point of the thin legacy remains.

Some states had established their own state health exchanges but eventually decided to use the federal exchange, HealthCare.gov (Norris 2022). More recently, some states that had been part of the federal system decided to set up their own state system. These include the blue states of Maine, New Mexico, Pennsylvania, and New Jersey. The red states of Kentucky and Virginia have also made this decision (Norris 2022).

One of the more interesting stories along these lines took place in Kentucky. Under Democratic Governor Steve Beshear, Kentucky set up its own state exchange, known as Kynect. While federal exchanges were having issues in the early years, Kynect was considered one of the best working and popular state exchanges. However, as a result of the 2016 elections, Republican Matt Bevin became the new governor. During his campaign, Bevin vowed to terminate the state exchange, which he did (Phillips 2016). Beshear had created the state exchange via executive order, as opposed to via legislation, and Bevin ended it via executive order (Norris 2022).

The rollout of the federal exchange, however, was rocky and enrollment was lower than under the state exchange. In 2020, Governor Bevins decided to go back to a state-run exchange, which took place in 2021 (Norris 2022).

The Patient Protection and Affordable Care Act is a lengthy piece of legislation. At the same time, there was a fair amount of vagueness to the law, creating opportunities for states opposed to the new program to oppose all or part of it. The vagueness also created flexibility that allowed for negotiations between the federal government and the states on an individual basis. The bargaining involved four different types of items (Béland, Rocco, and Waddan 2016).

One is grants-in-aid from the federal government to the states. These are designed to encourage states to engage in certain activities. For example, the federal government offered grants to states to help establish their own state exchanges (Haeder and Weimer 2015). The amounts and terms of the grant are some of the items that are up for negotiation. States prefer to have as much control or discretion over the use of the funds as possible. The federal government can insist on tighter or looser controls.

A second tool has to do with authority. This addresses which level of government is primarily responsible for carrying out a program. The federal government can give states the main authority over a program, but only if the implementation meets federal (usually minimum) standards (Béland, Rocco, and Waddan 2016).

A third, and perhaps the most intriguing, has to do with waivers (which we discuss in Chapter 5). Waivers are changes from program requirements that allow states to carry out their preferences without changing the enacting statute. States may ask for and use waivers to get around parts of a law that the state dislikes. The result of using waivers then becomes widely varying state programs (Béland, Rocco, and Waddan 2016).

The exchanges or marketplaces became the face of the ACA, even though there is much more to the law than that (Béland, Rocco, and Waddan 2016). The exchanges were supposed to make it easier for insurance purchasers to select the plan that fit their needs. But there were issues with, especially, the federal exchanges in the early years (2013–2016 or so). The exchanges were awkward to use and sometimes just plain difficult. They required navigators, experts on insurance policies, to help distinguish between policies. States did not always cooperate here.

Navigators are people who can guide or help purchasers pick a plan that suits their needs and financial situation. Navigators perform the following functions:

> - conduct public education activities;
> - distribute fair and impartial information on health plan enrollment, premium tax credits, and free or low-cost coverage through Medicaid;
> - facilitate enrollment in qualified health plans;
> - provide referrals to other consumer assistance organizations or state agencies that address health insurance issues; and
> - provide information in a culturally and linguistically appropriate manner.
>
> (Keith, Lucia and Monahan 2013)

Insurance policies are complex legal documents that are difficult for the average person to understand. The federal government made money available to pay for navigators and assistants (for a discussion of navigators and other assistance, see Kirchoff 2014). At least 17 states had passed or were considering as of 2013 laws that effectively limited access to navigators by imposing standards that were more stringent than federal standards (Giovannelli, Lucia, and Dash 2013). With one exception (Florida, which we have labeled a purple state), the states with the most stringent standards were all red states: Georgia, Indiana, Missouri, Montana, Tennessee, and Texas. The only blue state that passed such laws was Maine (Kennedy 2014). An interesting example is the state of Missouri. In 2013, the Missouri legislature passed a law limiting the advice or discussions navigators could have with potential purchasers. The point of such limitations, which as many as 12 other states also had, was to discourage purchasing of federal ACA marketplace plans. In 2015, a federal court ruled that the state law conflicted with federal law and therefore blocked those provisions of the Missouri statute.

States had various ways of opposing or inhibiting implementation of the ACA. We have previously discussed the major court cases. States could also, as we have seen, refuse to operate their own exchanges. A third was to pass legislation or constitutional amendments that would prohibit cooperation. Most of the time, state legislatures took such action; on occasion, ballot measures were presented to the voters.

Table 4.10 focuses on three measures of opposition to the ACA. The first one is the mandates for individuals to have insurance and for employers to provide it to their employees.

Sixteen states (all red) passed a law or a constitutional amendment that said the state would not enforce the insurance mandate. Five red states have adopted legislation stating that continued compliance with the ACA would require legislative approval. Seven states made gestures toward an interstate compact that would create a healthcare program that would not be part of the ACA (Kaiser Family Foundation 2013). Additionally, four red states held elections in November 2012 (three were constitutional amendments, one a proposition) that would prohibit the mandate to purchase health insurance.

Another issue was the PCIP. The concern here were those people with previous high-risk medical conditions. The ACA, among other things, forbids qualified insurance companies from charging considerably more for premiums for high-risk patients compared to lower risk patients. Further, the ACA forbids companies from denying coverage to people with high-risk conditions. In the period before the ACA was passed, high-risk patients might be able to enroll in special state insurance pools. But the premiums for those in the high-risk pools were high, but not high enough to cover the costs. Enrollment was a fraction of the total population, and most state programs were considered failures (Haeder and Weimer 2015).

The ACA provided for preexisting conditions insurance plans as a means to bridge the period between enactment of the law in 2010 and implementation of the marketplaces/exchanges in 2014. The ACA made money available, about $5 billion, to states to set up their programs. But enrollment was small (about 8,000 people) and the costs exceeded projections. This was enough for the federal government and the states to shut the program down (Haeder and Weimer 2015).

A major variable in determining whether a state would participate in PCIP was the political party of a state's governor. Republican governors tended to oppose their states running a PCIP program and Democratic governors tended to support it (Haeder and Weimer 2015).

> Strikingly, even the implementation of the least controversial part of the ACA seems to have been driven by partisanship and polarization to a significant degree.
>
> (Haeder and Weimer 2015, 300–301)

Rigby and Haselswerdt (2013), in their quantitative analysis of ACA exchange implementation, studied, among other things, the relationship

TABLE 4.10 Oppositional Measures (2010–2013)

Red States	No Mandates or Fines	Ban on Implementing ACA w/o Legislative Approval	Interstate Health Compact	Blue States	No Mandates or Fines	Ban on Implementing ACA w/o Legislative Approval	Interstate Health Compact
Alabama	2			California			
Alaska				Connecticut			
Arizona				Delaware			
Arkansas				Hawaii			
Georgia	1		1	Illinois			
Idaho	1			Maine			
Indiana	1		1	Maryland			
Kansas	1			Massachusetts			
Kentucky				Michigan			
Louisiana	1			New Jersey			
Mississippi				New Mexico			
Missouri	1	1	1	New York			
Montana	1			Oregon			
Nebraska				Pennsylvania			
North Carolina	1			Rhode Island			
North Dakota	1		1	Vermont			
Oklahoma	2	1	1	Washington			
South Carolina	1	1					
South Dakota							
Tennessee	1		1				
Texas	1		1				
Utah	1	1					
West Virginia							
Wyoming	2	1					

1 = legislation; 2 = constitutional amendment.

Adapted from: Kaiser Family Foundation (2013). Online at https://www.kff.org/wp-content/uploads/sites/3/2015/03/state-legislation-opt-out.pdf.

between public opinion and progress toward implementing an exchange in their state. They looked at three steps of implementation. The first step was whether a state had submitted a proposal to the federal government for funds to establish an exchange. The second step was whether a state's governor had submitted an intent for the state to establish an exchange. The third step was requesting federal certification of a submitted blueprint for the exchange.

The authors found that 15 blue states had made more progress in exchange implementation than the red states, which often ended their efforts at implementing a state exchange at the first step. Their analysis suggests that partisan and ideological differences between the states statistically explain progress or opposition to setting up a state exchange.

Rigby and Haselswerdt (2013) argue that there were five outlier states, one liberal and four conservative. The party of the governor seemed to make a difference. The reasoning behind the four conservative states moving forward on implementing a state exchange was a desire to avoid federal preemption in an area (health insurance) largely the purview of the states.

Why did states oppose the ACA? The partisan and ideological makeup of a state was one of the strongest variables in explaining opposition to the ACA. Interestingly, states with the highest uninsurance rates were more likely to oppose the ACA than states with lower uninsurance rates. "Taken as a whole, our findings showed partisan politics dominating public-health need" (Mayer, Kenter, and Morris 2015, 48).

Regarding exchanges, states had three or four (depending on how one counted) choices to make. One was for states to set up their own exchanges. A second was to let the federal government set up and run exchanges. A third alternative was the state-based exchange that uses a federal platform (SBE-FP). A fourth type is the state partnership federally facilitated exchange (FFE). In this type of exchange, states perform some of the functions of the exchanges while the federal government performs other functions. The exchanges have five major functions that are performed by the federal government or by the states (Goodell 2013): determining eligibility, including eligibility for subsidies; helping people who are determined to be eligible to enroll in a plan; managing plans; assisting consumers (this is the navigator function); and overseeing plan finances. States choosing a hybrid model would then decide/negotiate with the federal government which functions it would carry out.

Table 4.11 presents the data for red and blue states. The table indicates which states picked which of the three (combining the hybrid choices) choices a state made. If a state decided on a state-based exchange, the next column indicates which year it made the decision.

TABLE 4.11 State Decisions on Exchanges

Red States	Type of Exchange	Year Approved	Blue States	Type of Exchange	Year Approved
Alabama	Federally facilitated		California	State-based	2013
Alaska	Federally facilitated		Connecticut	State-based	2012
Arizona	Federally facilitated		Delaware	Federally facilitated	
Arkansas	State-based/federal platform	2015	Hawaii	Federally facilitated	
Georgia	Federally facilitated		Illinois	Federally facilitated	
Idaho	State-based	2013	Maine	State-based	2021
Indiana	Federally facilitated		Maryland	State-based	2012
Kansas	Federally facilitated		Massachusetts	State-based	2012
Kentucky	State-based	2021	Michigan	Federally facilitated	
Louisiana	Federally facilitated		New Jersey	State-based	2020
Mississippi	Federally facilitated		New Mexico	State-based	2021
Missouri	Federally facilitated		New York	State-based	2012
Montana	Federally facilitated		Oregon	State-based/federal platform	2012
Nebraska	Federally facilitated		Pennsylvania	State-based	2020
North Carolina	Federally facilitated		Rhode Island	State-based	2012
North Dakota	Federally facilitated		Vermont	State-based	2013
Oklahoma	Federally facilitated		Washington	State-based	2012
South Carolina	Federally facilitated				
South Dakota	Federally facilitated				
Tennessee	Federally facilitated				
Texas	Federally facilitated				
Utah	Federally facilitated				
West Virginia	Federally facilitated				
Wyoming	Federally facilitated				

Adapted from: Kaiser Family Foundation (2024). Online at www.kff.org. Centers for Medicare and Medicaid Services (2023). Online at https://www.cms.gov.

The first thing that is evident from the table is that only three of the red states chose a state-based exchange. One of the three (Arkansas) chose a state-based exchange-FFE. A second observation is that of the blue states, 12 selected state-based exchanges. A third observation is that of the states choosing state-based exchanges, eight did so prior to 2014, when the exchanges first came into operation. None of the three red states eventually choosing state-based exchanges made the choice that early. There is clearly a partisan divide in exchange/marketplace choices.

Tables 4.12 and 4.13 present time series data about enrollment in the marketplaces from 2014 through 2023. One observation that can be made is the impact of the Trump administration on, especially, red state marketplace enrollment. Red state enrollment declined from 2016 to 2017. It continued that decline through 2020. Beginning in 2021, with the Biden administration in office, red state enrollment began to increase, reaching over seven million people in 2023. Texas, with its large population, was a major factor in these trends.

The story is a bit different with the blue states. Marketplace enrollment numbers are steadier compared to the red states. One can see this in the declines from 2016 to 2020. For red states, the decline was by over 700,000 people. For blue states, the decline was smaller, almost 400,000 people.

There was another set of decisions that states could make concerning the marketplaces. Note the name of the legislation: Patient Protection and Affordable Care Act. As the marketplaces were put into effect, there was some question whether they were affordable. In the late 2010s, premiums increased significantly, though most of the increase was captured by the subsidies rather than paid by consumers (Taylor et al. 2019). Nevertheless, there were people who were not eligible for subsidies and paid the full amount of the increase.

States had two ways of addressing the issue (as an aside, the marketplaces eventually stabilized, and cost increases decreased). The first was to come up with ways to provide more money for the exchanges to help cover costs. The second way was to make plans that were unqualified more available to consumers (Taylor et al. 2019).

States had several options to increase funds for the exchanges. One, which we have discussed above, dealt with reinsurance. To recall, reinsurance is partially reimbursing insurance companies that have high-cost patients. This allows the companies to lower overall premiums. As of 2019, there were two red states, Montana and North Dakota, that were planning on taking this path. The other seven states were either blue or purple states (Taylor et al. 2019).

A second path was that some states instituted an individual mandate after the federal tax penalty was eliminated in 2017. As of 2019, three blue

TABLE 4.12 Red State Marketplace Enrollment Trends, 2014–2023

	2014	2015	2016	2017	2018	2019	2020	2021	2022	2023
Alabama	97,870	1,71,641	1,95,055	1,78,414	1,70,211	1,66,141	1,60,429	1,69,119	2,19,314	2,58,327
Alaska	12,890	21,260	23,029	19,145	18,313	17,805	17,696	18,184	22,786	25,572
Arizona	1,20,071	2,05,666	2,03,066	1,96,291	1,65,758	1,60,456	1,53,020	1,54,504	1,99,706	2,35,229
Arkansas	43,446	65,684	73,648	70,404	68,100	67,413	64,360	66,094	88,226	1,00,407
Georgia	3,16,543	5,41,080	5,87,845	4,93,880	4,80,912	4,58,437	4,63,910	5,17,113	7,01,135	8,79,084
Idaho	76,061	97,079	1,01,073	1,00,082	94,507	94,430	78,431	68,832	73,359	79,927
Indiana	1,32,423	2,19,185	1,96,242	1,74,611	1,66,711	1,48,404	1,40,931	1,36,593	1,56,926	1,85,354
Kansas	57,013	96,197	1,01,555	98,780	98,238	89,993	85,837	88,627	1,07,784	1,24,473
Kentucky	82,747	1,06,330	93,666	81,155	89,569	84,620	83,837	77,821	73,935	62,562
Louisiana	1,01,778	1,86,277	2,14,148	1,43,577	1,09,855	92,948	87,748	83,159	99,626	1,20,894
Mississippi	61,494	1,04,538	1,08,672	88,483	83,649	88,542	98,892	1,10,966	1,43,014	1,83,478
Missouri	1,52,335	2,53,430	2,90,201	2,44,382	2,43,382	2,20,461	2,02,750	2,15,311	2,50,341	2,57,629
Montana	36,584	54,266	58,114	52,473	47,699	45,374	43,822	44,711	51,134	53,860
Nebraska	42,975	74,152	87,836	84,371	88,213	87,416	90,845	88,688	99,011	1,01,490
North Carolina	3,57,584	5,60,357	6,13,487	5,49,158	5,19,803	5,01,271	5,05,275	5,35,803	6,70,223	3,00,850
North Dakota	10,597	18,171	21,604	21,982	22,486	21,820	21,806	22,709	29,873	34,130
Oklahoma	69,221	1,26,115	1,45,329	1,46,286	1,40,184	1,50,759	1,58,642	1,71,551	1,89,444	2,03,157
South Carolina	1,18,324	2,10,331	2,31,849	2,30,211	2,15,983	2,14,956	2,14,030	2,30,050	3,00,392	3,82,968
South Dakota	13,104	21,393	25,999	29,622	29,652	29,069	29,331	31,375	41,339	47,591
Tennessee	1,51,352	2,31,440	2,68,867	2,34,125	2,28,646	2,21,533	2,00,445	2,12,052	2,73,680	3,48,097
Texas	7,33,757	12,05,174	13,06,208	12,27,290	11,26,838	10,87,240	11,16,293	12,91,97	18,40,947	24,10,810
Utah	84,601	1,40,612	175,637	1,97,187	1,94,118	1,94,570	2,00,261	2,07,911	2,56,932	2,95,196
West Virginia	19,856	33,421	37,284	34,045	27,409	22,599	20,066	19,381	23,037	28,325
Wyoming	11,970	21,092	23,770	24,826	24,529	24,852	24,574	26,728	34,762	38,565
Total Red States	29,04,596	47,64,891	50,08,723	47,20,780	44,54,765	42,91,109	42,63,231	32,98,574	59,46,926	72,57,975
Total U.S.	80,19,763	1,16,88,074	1,26,81,874	1,22,16,003	1,17,50,175	1,14,44,141	1,14,09,447	1,20,04,365	1,45,11,077	1,63,57,030
	36.2%	40.8%	39.5%	38.6%	40.1%	37.5%	37.4%	27.5%	41.0%	44.4%

Adapted from: Kaiser Family Foundation (2023a). Online at https://www.kff.org/statedata.

TABLE 4.13 Blue State Marketplace Enrollment Trends, 2014–2023

	2014	2015	2016	2017	2018	2019	2020	2021	2022	2023
California	14,05,102	14,12,200	15,75,340	15,56,676	15,21,524	15,13,883	15,38,819	16,25,546	17,77,442	17,39,368
Connecticut	79,192	1,09,839	1,16,019	1,11,542	1,14,134	1,11,066	1,07,833	1,04,946	1,12,633	1,08,132
Delaware	14,087	25,036	28,256	27,584	24,500	22,562	23,961	25,320	32,113	34,742
Hawaii	8,592	12,625	14,564	18,938	19,799	20,193	20,073	22,903	22,327	21,645
Illinois	2,17,492	3,49,487	3,88,179	3,56,403	3,34,979	3,12,280	2,92,945	2,91,215	3,23,427	3,42,995
Maine	44,258	74,805	84,059	79,407	75,809	70,987	62,031	59,738	66,095	63,388
Maryland	67,757	1,20,145	1,62,177	2,66,664	1,53,584	1,56,963	1,58,934	1,66,038	1,81,603	1,82,166
Massachusetts	31,695	1,40,540	2,13,883	2,66,664	2,67,260	3,01,879	3,19,612	2,94,097	2,68,023	2,32,621
Michigan	2,72,539	3,41,183	3,45,813	3,21,451	2,99,940	2,74,058	2,62,919	2,67,070	3,03,550	3,22,273
New Jersey	1,61,775	2,54,316	2,88,573	2,95,067	2,74,782	2,55,246	2,46,426	2,69,560	3,24,266	3,41,901
New Mexico	32,062	52,358	54,865	54,653	49,792	45,001	42,714	42,984	45,664	40,778
New York	3,70,451	4,08,841	2,71,964	2,42,880	2,53,102	2,71,873	2,72,948	2,15,889	2,21,895	2,14,052
Oregon	68,308	1,12,024	1,47,109	1,55,430	1,56,105	1,48,180	1,45,264	1,41,089	1,46,602	1,41,963
Pennsylvania	3,18,077	4,72,697	4,39,238	4,26,059	3,89,081	3,65,888	3,31,825	3,37,722	3,74,776	3,71,516
Rhode Island	28,485	31,337	34,570	29,456	33,021	34,533	34,634	31,174	32,345	29,626
Vermont	38,048	31,619	29,440	30,682	28,783	25,223	27,335	24,866	26,705	25,664
Washington	1,63,207	1,60,732	2,00,691	2,25,594	2,43,227	2,20,765	2,12,188	2,22,731	2,39,566	2,30,371
Total Blue States	33,21,127	41,09,784	43,94,740	44,65,150	42,39,422	41,50,580	41,00,461	41,42,888	44,99,032	44,43,201
Total U.S.	80,19,763	1,16,88,074	1,26,81,874	1,22,16,003	1,17,50,175	1,14,44,141	1,14,09,447	1,20,04,365	1,45,11,077	1,63,57,030
	41.4%	35.2%	34.7%	36.6%	36.1%	36.3%	35.9%	34.5%	31.0%	27.2%

Adapted from: Kaiser Family Foundation (2023a). Online at https://www.kff.org/statedata.

TABLE 4.14 Red State Uninsurance Rates, 2009–2021

	2009	2010	2011	2012	2013	2014	2015	2016	2017	2018	2019	2021
Alabama	20.1	21.5	20.8	20.1	20.5	18.2	15.7	14.3	14.7	15.7	14.9	15.2
Alaska	26.1	23.6	25.1	25.6	24	22.3	19.0	18.2	18.2	15.9	15.3	14.3
Arizona	23.3	22.4	22.8	23.5	23.8	18.5	14.8	13.6	13.7	14.7	15.4	14.6
Arkansas	24.8	26.1	25.7	24.9	24.4	17.8	13.6	11.8	11.6	12.3	15.4	13.4
Georgia	25.7	27.2	27.1	25.9	26.1	22.2	19.4	18.2	18.8	19.2	18.9	18.3
Idaho	23.1	25	22.2	23.4	23.4	19.3	16.6	15.3	16.4	16.4	16.0	11.9
Indiana	19.1	20.6	20.2	20.4	19.6	16.7	13.2	11.0	11.3	11.1	11.7	10.1
Kansas	17.3	19.3	18.2	17.9	17.6	15.0	13.2	12.0	12.1	12.4	13.2	13.6
Kentucky	20.7	22.1	21	19.7	21	12.5	8.2	7.2	7.4	7.9	9.0	7.9
Louisiana	25	26.1	25.9	24.7	24.8	21.6	18.3	15.4	12.5	11.8	13.0	11.1
Mississippi	24.5	26.2	25.8	25.3	25	21.7	19.2	17.8	18.3	18.7	19.5	17.7
Missouri	18.6	19	19.4	19.7	18.5	16.2	13.6	12.8	13.1	13.6	14.3	13.4
Montana	25.4	22.6	25.3	25.4	23.4	19.3	16.4	12.2	12.7	11.9	11.7	10.7
Nebraska	16.1	17.1	16.6	15.9	15.2	13.4	11.0	12.3	11.9	11.7	11.4	9.7
North Carolina	22.5	23.9	23.3	23.8	22.9	19.3	16.6	15.4	15.8	15.9	16.7	15.2
North Dakota	13.5	13.6	13.1	14.4	13.6	10.4	9.6	9.1	9.4	10.0	8.7	9.8
Oklahoma	25.8	27.1	25.9	25.9	24.7	21.5	20.2	20.0	20.3	19.7	21.7	20.4
South Carolina	23.3	24.6	23.8	24	23	20.3	16.3	14.9	16.6	15.9	16.0	15.0
South Dakota	19.6	16.8	16.8	16	17.7	13.6	15.8	12.1	13.1	13.5	13.8	12.9
Tennessee	20.6	21	21.6	20.3	20.4	17.4	15.1	13.6	13.8	14.9	14.9	14.8
Texas	31	31.6	31.1	30.6	29.9	25.7	23.3	22.8	23.7	24.0	24.5	24.4
Utah	18.8	20.3	19.6	18.5	17.8	16.2	14.1	11.6	11.9	11.6	12.2	11.4
West Virginia	20.7	21.7	23	21.5	20.5	13.5	8.1	7.5	8.8	9.4	9.9	9.4
Wyoming	21.1	20.4	21	21.6	18.1	17.1	14.3	14.9	16.5	14.9	16.7	15.6
Average Red States	21.9	22.5	22.3	22.0	21.5	17.9	15.2	13.9	14.3	14.3	14.8	13.8
Average U.S.	20.8	21.6	21.2	20.9	20.6	16.4	13.3	12.1	12.3	12.5	12.9	12.2

Adapted from: Kaiser Family Foundation (2023a). Online at https://www.kff.org/statedata.

states and the District of Columbia took this path, and another was in the process of doing so (Taylor et al. 2019).

A third path was for states to add additional subsidies to pay for premiums for those with incomes at or below 400 percent of the poverty level. Medicaid funding has been helpful with this. Three blue states have adopted this strategy as of 2019: California, Massachusetts, and Vermont (Taylor et al. 2019). To sum up, some blue states have taken measures, using additional funding, to help consumers pay for marketplace premiums.

Red states have taken the second path. In our discussion of the Trump administration's handling of the ACA, we talked about insurance plans outside the ACA. These are short-term plans that offer fewer benefits but are less costly than the exchange plans. Such plans might not cover preexisting conditions, or maternal care or the essential benefits contained in the ACA. States can offer subsidies for people purchasing these non-ACA plans. Red states have allowed such plans, which meet federal regulations, to be sold, while blue (and purple) states have tended to limit the length of such insurance policies (Taylor et al. 2019). Again, the partisan and ideological differences among our two groups of states show up in the policy decisions they make, in this case, about affordability.

Another way of looking at what happened with marketplace/exchange enrollment is to consider uninsurance rates. Before we get to that, there are a few caveats that should be mentioned. First, the purpose of the marketplaces is to provide health insurance for those who have had difficulty getting and affording insurance. This is one of the major goals of the ACA. The other major tool for providing insurance was Medicaid, which we discuss in Chapter 5. So, some of the changes in the uninsurance rates is due to Medicaid expansion. But as we shall see in Chapter 5, many of the states that opposed the ACA and the marketplaces were also hesitant to expand Medicaid.

A second caveat is that the uninsurance is impacted by the economy. The United States suffered its worst recession with the so-called Great Recession of 2007–2009. During recessions, the economy contracts, people lose jobs (the unemployment rate goes up), and they lose health insurance that came with those jobs. Economies also recover from recessions and the recovery can be quite impressive.

The point of these two caveats is that the uninsurance rate is affected by factors other than political partisanship. But we should also note that the recovery from the Great Recession does not seem to have much affected the uninsurance rates. We should also note that the uninsurance rates are for those who are under the age of 65. Those 65 and older are insured through Medicare (and in some cases by Medicaid). The data goes through the year 2021, but 2020 data was not available.

Tables 4.14 and 4.15 present the data. Our first observation, consistent with the data in Chapter 3, is that red state uninsurance rates exceed the U.S. average uninsurance rate and the blue state uninsurance rates for the entire time. Uninsurance rates begin to fall for the nation and the individual states beginning in 2014 when the exchanges were first implemented during the Obama administration. They then go up during the Trump administration. In 2021, only three of the red states had uninsurance rates below 10 percent. By contrast, only three of the blue states had uninsurance rates above 10 percent.

Another way of looking at the differences between the red and blue states is to consider the change from 2013, the year before the exchanges began, to 2021. For the red states, the uninsurance rate decreased by about 35 percent. For the blue states, the uninsurance rate decreased by about 51 percent. For the country as a whole, the decrease over this period was about 41 percent.

The ACA is, in some ways, similar to the overall American healthcare system. The way it is similar is that there is no plan that is the same for everybody. State ACA plans differ on the basis of cost and availability (Walker 2022; there are significant differences in state Medicaid programs which we discuss in the next chapter).

There are four types of plans that a person can choose. They differ on premiums and deductibles/co-payments. The cheaper the premiums, the higher the deductibles/co-payments and vice versa. On average, monthly premiums for ACA exchange plans are higher in red states than in blue states (Silva 2021).

We should note that marketplace insurance premiums rose in the early years. During the Trump administration, decisions were made that increased premiums. One, mentioned above, was the administration's canceling reimbursement to insurers for cost-sharing reductions for lower-income subscribers. Insurers then built in increases in premiums to other subscribers to cover these additional costs, resulting in increased premiums (Hollahan and Wengle 2021). Because of ACA policies, when premiums increase, premium subsidies increase, thus masking purchasers from much of the increases.

A very useful study by the Urban Institute (Holohan, Banthin and Engle 2021) sought to explain premium levels for the second tiered or silver plans in 2021. It looked at variables such as how many insurers offered policies in a marketplace, the degree of hospital concentration, and the types of insurers (commercial, Blue Cross/Blue Shield, etc.). Most interesting from our standpoint was that the researchers also included four state policy variables: "state-specific community-rating laws, Medicaid expansion to childless adults with incomes up to 138 percent of the federal

TABLE 4.15 Blue State Uninsurance Rates, 2009–2021

	2009	2010	2011	2012	2013	2014	2015	2016	2017	2018	2019	2021
California	24.7	25.5	25.3	25.0	24.1	17.5	12.1	10.5	10.2	10.2	11.0	9.9
Connecticut	12.6	13.2	12.7	13.4	13.4	9.6	8.3	6.9	7.9	7.6	8.3	7.4
Delaware	14.6	14.1	13.0	12.4	14.3	10.1	8.1	8.0	7.9	8.1	9.7	8.4
Hawaii	9.8	10.6	10.2	9.4	10.1	7.0	5.7	4.9	5.3	5.2	5.8	5.2
Illinois	19.3	20.3	19.2	19.3	18.4	14.1	10.2	9.4	9.8	10.2	10.3	10.1
Maine	14.2	15.7	15.8	15.1	16.3	13.8	11.9	11.4	11.6	11.4	11.6	8.0
Maryland	15.6	15.7	14.2	14.5	14.2	11.1	9.0	8.4	8.3	8.4	8.3	8.2
Massachusetts	6.1	6.3	5.9	5.6	5.4	4.7	4.0	3.5	3.9	3.9	4.4	3.5
Michigan	18.0	18.4	17.6	17.1	16.2	12.3	8.6	7.5	7.3	7.8	8.3	7.3
New Jersey	17.4	18.5	18.5	18.2	19.1	15.7	12.5	11.0	10.9	10.5	11.2	10.2
New Mexico	28.0	28.3	28.9	27.4	28.0	21.2	16.3	12.7	13.4	13.6	14.4	14.2
New York	16.3	16.9	16.3	15.7	15.5	12.3	10.2	8.6	8.1	7.6	7.6	7.4
Oregon	23.3	23.9	22.2	21.2	21.5	14.2	10.0	8.8	9.9	10.5	10.1	8.8
Pennsylvania	13.9	14.5	14.3	13.8	13.8	12.0	8.8	7.8	7.4	7.6	7.8	7.5
Rhode Island	15.9	17.1	16.0	16.1	16.8	10.1	7.0	6.1	6.5	5.7	6.1	6.2
Vermont	12.5	11.6	10.5	9.5	10.1	7.1	6.1	5.5	6.3	5.5	7.0	5.1
Washington	18.6	19.9	19.9	19.6	20.0	12.9	9.3	8.6	8.7	9.5	9.4	9.2
Average Blue States	16.5	17.1	16.5	16.1	16.3	12.1	9.3	8.2	8.4	8.4	8.9	8.0
Average U.S.	20.8	21.6	21.2	20.9	20.6	16.4	13.3	12.1	12.3	12.5	12.9	12.2

Adapted from: Kaiser Family Foundation (2023a). Online at https://www.kff.org/statedata.

poverty level, state reinsurance programs, and state-based Marketplaces" (Holohan, Banthin and Engle 2021, 4). Community-ratings laws require that insurers not charge more to people based on characteristics such as gender, age, health status, etc. The Medicaid provision (discussed more in Chapter 5) focuses on a group that has generally not been covered by Medicaid. The third variable, state reinsurance programs, follows from the discussion above. States reimburse insurance companies for lower premiums for low-income people. The fourth variable is whether a state had its own marketplace or relied on a federally run marketplace.

The Holohan, Banthin, and Engle (2021) study found that factors such as the level of competition and insurer experience with Medicaid led to decreases in premiums. But they also found that state policy decisions were related to lower or slower increases in premiums. In particular, states that set up their own reinsurance programs and states that expanded Medicaid saw declines or slower growth in premiums. In the case of Medicaid expansion, the changes came soon after the expansions and likely because subscribers switched from the more costly exchange plans to Medicaid, especially those who had costly medical issues.

Public Opinion And The Affordable Care Act

As noted earlier in the chapter, there was considerable dispute and unhappiness with the ACA. The fact that such an impactful piece of legislation was enacted without a single vote from the opposition party (the Republicans) indicates the disputatious nature of the law. We can see this in public opinion polls, though that changes somewhat over time.

Let us begin by looking at overall approval/disapproval of the law beginning in 2010 when it was first passed. We know, as discussed previously, that the proposed legislation led to opposition at public town hall meetings in the summer of 2009, even before it passed. Opposition organized into groups, known as the Tea Party, and then later as MAGA Republicans. In the U.S. House of Representatives and in state legislatures across the country, Republican opponents called themselves the Freedom Caucus, which was a portion of the Republican Party. Where was public opinion?

One of the first surveys, conducted in April 2010, just a month after the passage of the ACA, found that more people supported (44 percent) than opposed the law (40 percent). But for the most part, from 2011 to 2017, more people opposed than supported the law, though there was never a majority opposed to the law during this time. The big change came in February 2017, when more people favored the law than opposed it. The favorability advantage continued through 2022, reaching a high of 58 percent in October 2021

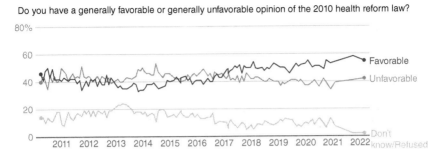

FIGURE 4.1 Public Approval Rating of ACA, 2011–2022.

Adapted from: Kirzinger, Ashley, et al. 2022. "5 Charts About Public Opinion on the Affordable Care Act." Menlo Park, CA: Kaiser Family Foundation.

(see Figure 4.1) (Kirzinger et al. 2022). This may be due to Congress and the Biden administration making the marketplaces cheaper and thus more available to purchasers in light of the Covid epidemic (see Chapter 8).

The provisions of the ACA that the public favored (important to keep in place) the most were those related to preexisting conditions. The ACA prohibits health insurance companies from denying coverage because of preexisting conditions. It also prohibits insurance companies from charging those with chronic health conditions more. It requires that health insurance companies cover pregnant women and pay for much of preventive care (though, as mentioned above, there is a U.S. Supreme Court case that is addressing this issue). The law also prohibits insurance companies from setting lifetime and annual limits on coverage. And it allows young people up to the age of 26 to stay on their parents' insurance coverage. All of these provisions were supported by a majority of those surveyed (2019 data) (Kirzinger et al. 2022).

For those who said the ACA helped them, the major reason was the ability to get and keep insurance. For those who felt that the ACA hurt them, the major reason was increases in costs (Kirzinger et al. 2022). In earlier years, prior to 2018, a major feature of the ACA that was opposed by a large number of respondents was the mandate for insurance. We shall return to that below.

The Kirzinger et al.'s (2022) study looked at the question of which parts of the ACA the public favored by political party (see Table 4.16). On all the questions, Republicans were less supportive of the ACA than Democrats, even on questions where a majority of Republican respondents favored the provision. Some examples: The first question was about the provision that forbids insurance companies from denying coverage to people with preexisting conditions.

TABLE 4.16 Percentage of Republicans and Democrats Saying It Is Important to Keep Provision in ACA (2019)

	% Republicans Supporting	% Democrats Supporting
Prohibits health insurance companies from denying coverage for people with preexisting conditions	62	88
Prohibits health insurance companies from charging sick people more	55	76
Prohibits health insurance companies from denying coverage to pregnant women	49	89
Requires health insurance companies to cover the cost of most preventive services	49	80
Prohibits health insurance companies from setting a lifetime limit	48	72
Gives states the option of expanding their Medicaid programs	36	84
Provides financial help to low-and-moderate-income Americans to help them purchase coverage	31	82
Prohibits private health insurance companies from setting an annual limit	38	67
Allows young adults to stay on their parents' insurance plans until age 26	36	68

Adapted from: Kirzinger et al. (2022).

Eighty-eight percent of Democrats approved compared to 62 percent of Republicans, a difference of 26 percent. The second question asked whether people thought it was important to keep the provision that kept health insurance companies from charging more for people with (chronic) illnesses. Fifty-five percent of Republicans approved the provisions compared to 89 percent of Democrats. Democratic respondents favored retaining the remaining six provisions. Less than a majority of Republican respondents favored keeping those six provisions.

That Republicans continued to view the Affordability Care Act unfavorably can be seen in Figure 4.2. This figure illustrates public opinion in 2022 and 2023. As can be seen in the figure, there is not much change from the first poll in this series to the last. In the May 2022 poll, 85 percent of Democratic respondents had a favorable view of the ACA, compared to 77 percent of Republican respondents who had an unfavorable view. In the last poll in this figure, May 2023, 89 percent of Democratic respondents had a favorable view of the ACA compared to 73 percent of Republican respondents who had a unfavorable view (see also Zipp 2022). The big

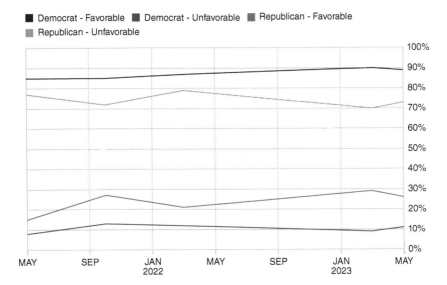

FIGURE 4.2 Favorability/Unfavorability Rating of ACA by Political Party (2022–2023).

From Kaiser Family Foundation. 2023. "KFF Health Tracking Poll: The Public's View on the ACA." (May 31) Menlo Park, CA: Kaiser Family Foundation.

change came among independent voters (not shown in the figure). In May of 2022, 54 percent had a favorable view of the ACA. One year later, 62 percent of independents had a favorable view.

The partisan nature of the differences that we have explored is at least partly related to differences in perspective on the role that government should play in providing, paying, and regulating the delivery of healthcare to the public (Roper Center for Public Opinion Research 2013). The Roper Center (2013) notes that the stark partisan division about the government's role was not always present. The Center examined public opinion in three periods, 1938, 1991, and 2013. In 1938, 83 percent of respondents supported the idea that the (federal) government should be responsible for providing care to those who could not afford it. At this time, the country was in the midst of the Great Depression and a Democrat, Franklin Roosevelt, was president, pushing his New Deal programs such as Social Security. In 1991, with a Republican president in office, George H. W. Bush, 80 percent of respondents chose the affirmative on this question. But in 2013, with the ACA enacted, and some of its most important implementation issues to be decided, and a Democratic president, Barack Obama, only 61 percent chose the affirmative. Most of the decline came from Republicans and, to a lesser extent, independents.

A figure from the Roper Center (2013) report points out the disparity in polling between Democrats and Republicans. In 2013, a question was asked whether respondents thought that it was the (federal) government's responsibility to help people pay for their healthcare versus an individual responsibility to pay for one's healthcare. Sixty-two percent of Democrats said it was the federal government's responsibility versus 25 percent of Republicans who made this choice. Interestingly, one can see the same results in the early 1990s, when the Clinton administration introduced the Health Security Act. The percentage of Democrats choosing the federal government remained in the low sixties, while the percentage of Republican respondents choosing the federal government dropped from 50 percent in 1990 (when George H.W. Bush was president) to just over 30 percent in 1994. The percentage of Republicans favoring a federal government role remained in the mid-twenties to the high thirties from 1994 to 2013.

The Gallup organization has also studied public opinion on the (federal) government's role in healthcare (Brenan 2023; Newport 2023; Newport and Dugan 2017). Their study focused on the increased differences between Republicans and Democrats on this and other policy issues. They found that the partisan differences have increased over the years. On the question of whether the government should be responsible for healthcare, in 2001, 75 percent of Democrats agreed with the statement compared to 45 percent of Republicans, a gap of 30 points. In 2016, 77% of Democrats agreed with the statement, essentially stable since 2001, compared to 24% of Republicans, a gap of 53 points (Newport and Dugan 2017). By 2023, the Democratic approval rating on this question had risen to 85%, while Republican agreement was at 30%, marginally higher than in 2017 but still a low percentage. The gap was 55 points, one of the largest gaps on issues studied by Gallup (Newport 2023). Republicans tend to prefer that the private sector run the healthcare system, rather than the government (Brenan 2023). It is clear that while a majority (largely Democratic) of the public wants the government to have the responsibility to make sure that people have healthcare, a majority (largely Republican) wants to rely on the private sector. This strong partisan divide underlies perspectives on the ACA.

The Roper Center (2013) report attributes the decline in favorability to the following:

> Opposition to the ACA's enactment, the Supreme Court's ruling against parts of it, repeated attempts to overturn and defund it in Congress, challenges to its implementation and, perhaps most important, a drumbeat of opposition by politicians and advocacy groups...

Support for the ACA has increased since 2010 (Jacobs, Mettler, and Zhu 2019). The Jacobs, Mettler, and Zhu's (2019) study differs from the massive public opinion studies that companies such as Roper and Gallup perform. In this case, the researchers conducted a panel study from 2010 to 2018. A panel study design uses the same respondents over a period of time. In the Roper Center report cited above, the respondents obviously differed in the three major time periods (1938, 1991, and 2013) and so some of the differences in results may be due to differences in the makeup of the people surveyed.

The authors argue that the 2018 mid-term elections were vital to the support of the ACA. As discussed above, the Trump administration and the Republican-led Congress had tried numerous times to repeal the ACA and failed each time (thanks to a few Republican senators). In December of 2017, Congress repealed the penalty tax on those not getting insurance. The ACA became a vital issue for supporters (i.e., Democrats) in the 2018 elections and Democrats took over the House of Representatives. The study found that, in the period between 2010 and 2018, there were important changes in the support for the ACA. The first change was the growth in support for the ACA and the decline in what they call "the most intensive opposition" (Jacobs, Mettler, and Zhu 2019, 912).

The second change was that the ACA had matured and its problems with the exchanges had receded. The result was that more people felt that the ACA had made their lives better. The authors point to three specific parts of the ACA that had this impact: allowing older children up to the age of 26 to stay on their parents' insurance, better access to prescription drugs for seniors, and increasing subsidies to purchase insurance plans on the marketplaces.

Because the ACA has had these positive effects, voters note when an elected official or candidate takes a stand that would threaten the ACA (Jacobs, Mettler, and Zhu 2019). This is similar to the public support for the Social Security program, where those who promise to cut or eliminate the program tend not to win elections. By 2024, 59 percent of those polled had a favorable view of the ACA and 39 percent of the public had an unfavorable view of the ACA (Diamond 2024). The ACA may have attained this kind of status (Jacobs, Mettler, and Zhu 2019).

Polarization and the Politics of the ACA

The Patient Protection and Affordable Care Act was one of the most contentious pieces of legislation ever to have passed Congress. No Republicans voted for the two bills that made up the ACA. This was despite a sizable contribution of Republican ideas and input. The concept of an individual mandate, that everyone had to purchase insurance or pay a penalty, was proposed by conservative policy advocates as an alternative to the kind of health policy embodied in the 1993 Health Security Act proposal by the Clinton administration. The marketplaces/exchanges, one of the major portions of the Affordable Care, was a significant feature of the Massachusetts plan passed in 2006, with the support of the Democratic legislature, a Democratic U.S. Senator (Edward Kennedy), and a Republican governor (Mitt Romney). Republicans also participated in much of the discussions in Congress leading up to passage of the ACA, though ultimately those Republicans did not support the new policy.

Historically, Democratic presidents and presidential candidates supported some form of national health insurance and, when those efforts failed, legislation to enhance coverage. There was some presidential support for health insurance expansion among Republicans, most importantly Theodore Roosevelt in his 1912 presidential campaign (which ultimately failed) and Richard Nixon, who offered two proposals in the 1970s to expand health insurance coverage. But for the most part, the campaign for a larger federal role in health insurance coverage and in healthcare in general was the purview of Democrats. So we begin with the partisan divide at the federal level.

The 2010 mid-term elections produced a divided Congress, with Republicans regaining control of the House and cutting into the Democrats' Senate majority. The ACA was one of those reasons. In 2009, the proposed legislation was a contributing factor to demonstrations at town hall meetings over the summer and the development of Tea Party Republicans. One of their major concerns was the mandate contained in the legislation to purchase legislation. This was seen, especially in the Tea Party section, as an infringement on their liberty. Republicans who might have supported the ACA were highly influenced by the intensity of the opposition. The ACA was not the only factor in the mid-terms. Tea Party Republicans, with little support among the African American community, were outraged that an African American was president. Though Obama won reelection in 2012, by 2016, the Republicans had gained control of both houses of Congress and the presidency. The ACA was in their sights.

Congressional Republicans made dozens of attempts to repeal the ACA, with one passing the House of Representatives and several attempts in the Senate failing when a few Republican senators voted against repeal. Smaller attempts led to some changes in the program. The most significant of those was the repeal of the tax in late 2017 on those who failed to purchase health insurance, the individual mandate. Some funds called for under the legislation were never appropriated. The Trump administration used its administrative powers to weaken implementation of the ACA.

As we have seen in this chapter, and explored in earlier chapters, federalism was/is an important feature of the ACA (as well as other health policies such as Medicaid and abortion). One could argue that the design of the ACA provided opportunities for red states to hinder the implementation of the legislation.

One venue for contention were the courts. Red state attorneys general filed cases and/or amicus (friend of the court) briefs challenging aspects of the ACA, even the existence of the program. While the cases that might have been fatal to the ACA failed (so far), others, such as the provision of withholding all Medicaid funding from states that did not expand the program, made significant changes to the ACA.

Red states also used administrative and legislative powers to affect implementation. The ACA gave states the power to set up their own insurance markets/exchanges or leave it to the federal government to do so. Red states, generally, chose not to set up their own exchanges. Given the opportunity to expand Medicaid and cover more people, red states chose not to expand, despite the financial incentives geared toward expansion (see Chapter 5). Some red states, such as Missouri, prohibited the use of navigators to help people seeking insurance on the federal exchanges. And so forth.

Where were the Democrats and blue states in all this? The Obama administration was clearly supportive of the ACA, though making some changes in the program. The Biden administration was also very supportive (Biden was Obama's Vice President), including using the public health emergency created by the COVID-19 pandemic to extend coverage (see Chapter 7). Blue states almost immediately created their own health insurance exchanges and tended to expand Medicaid early on.

Why the differences in response to the ACA? Some have argued that race played an important role. As we have seen earlier in this book, the two parties differ demographically. Republican supporters tend to be whiter, older, and less educated than Democratic supporters. Franz, Milner, and Brown (2021) make the argument that race is really the dividing point. They note the literature that shows that Latinos and Blacks are more supportive of the ACA than whites. The question they ask is whether white opposition is due to provisions of the ACA or whether it is due to the perception that those provisions are largely directed toward marginalized groups, such as racial minorities. The authors note that because whites make up a larger portion of the population than specific minorities, a greater percentage of minorities compared to whites benefitted from ACA. The authors also pointed out that the difference in support was greater for the ACA than it was for the Clinton administration's Health Security Act. They also suggest that racial resentment was higher with the ACA because it was identified with Obama, the first black president. There are polls that note that support for the ACA and many of its provisions was higher when referred to as the ACA and lower when referred to as Obamacare (in all fairness, this was also true in 1993–1994: the Health Security and its provisions were more supported than a similar policy known as Hillarycare). Opponents of the ACA often claimed that it would help blacks more than whites as a way of lessening support for the program.

Franz, Milner, and Brown (2021) found in their study that opponents of the ACA framed the policy debates in a way that racialized perceptions. They argue that this is similar to debates over other policies, such as affirmative action (particularly in the 2023 U.S. Supreme Court decision on affirmative action programs in higher education, *Students for Fair Admissions v. Harvard & UNC*).

2017 turned out to be a mixed year for the ACA. Congress and the Trump administration tried to cancel it. But the more it tried, the more popular it got. When Republicans in Congress addressed legislation to end the program, the CBO continually scored the various pieces of proposed legislation as moving up to 20 million people off the insurance rolls. This was especially true in 2022 as the Biden administration and the Democratically controlled Congress increased the subsidies for purchasing health insurance policies in the marketplaces. This could be seen in red states as well as blue states. And the ACA became more popular in red states (Luhby 2022).

Why would some people refuse to enroll in a program, what is called policy uptake, that benefits them? Lerman, Sadin, and Trachtman (2017) point to a study that suggests that Republicans are more likely not to participate in the ACA than Democrats. After the implementation of the ACA in 2014, uninsurance rates among Democrats declined by about 50 percent while the uninsurance rate among Republicans stayed pretty much the same (Lerman, Sadin, and Trachtman 2017) (it should be pointed out that Republicans living in red states had fewer choices, such as the lack of expansion of Medicaid and the lack of help in getting insurance, than Democrats living in blue states) The authors found that partisanship is a significant factor in the uptake decision. Controlling for a wide range of other factors, Democrats are more likely to purchase policies on the exchanges than Republicans. Further, Republicans were more likely to purchase non-ACA plans (what Democrats called "junk plans") than Democrats. The same was true when comparing conservatives and liberals. Partisanship and ideology overlap. The authors did note that when the exchanges were framed as private markets, rather than as government-run markets, Republicans were more likely to enroll in them (Lerman, Sadin, and Trachtman 2017).

A similar analysis was conducted by Reny and Sears (2020). They contrasted self-interest with symbolic politics in making decisions, such as whether to purchase health insurance on the ACA exchanges. The theoretical basis for the self-interest view is rational choice theory. Such a theory suggests that policy decisions, down to the individual level, are made largely based on how they impact the decision-maker. Symbolic politics, on the other hand, argues that "political attitudes and behaviors are motivated primarily by emotion-laden enduring predispositions such as partisanship, ideology, and racial attitudes" (Reny and Sears 2020, 2).

Reny and Sears (2020) tested attitudes toward the ACA from 2008 to 2016. They found that partisanship and ideology had a stronger influence on attitudes toward the ACA than self-interest (which the authors defined as the respondents' overall health). They then tested behavior by looking at enrollment in the exchanges. Here they found that those in poorer health were more likely to enroll than those in better health conditions. They concluded that self-interest is stronger in behavior and symbolic politics stronger in attitudes.

The data presented in this chapter is clear. There are/were deep partisan and ideological differences in how the ACA was implemented by the states (as well as presidential administrations) (MacDonald 2020). This can also be seen in decisions that individuals made about whether to participate in the program and in public opinion. Republican leaders are split as to whether to grudgingly accept the ACA or whether to continue to try to change or repeal it (Diamond 2024). The ACA lives in a different universe in red states than it does in blue states.

Bibliography

American Presidency Project. 2022. *Seats in Congress Gained/Lost by the President's Party in Mid-Term Elections*. Santa Barbara, CA: University of California. Online at https://www.presidency.ucsb.edu/node/332343/

Apple, Charles. n.d. "In Control." *The Spokesman-Review* Online at https://www.spokesman.com/stories/2020/jun/25/control-house-and-senate-1900/

Bagley, Nicholas. 2021. "*California v. Texas*—Ending the Campaign to Undo the ACA in the Courts." *The New England Journal of Medicine* 358, no. 8 (August 19): 673–675.

Béland, Daniel, Philip Rocco, and Alex Waddan. 2016. *Obamacare Wars: Federalism, State Politics, and the Affordable Care Act*. Lawrence, KS: University Press of Kansas.

Béland, Daniel, Philip Rocco, and Alex Waddan. 2020. "The Affordable Care Act in the States: Fragmented Politics, Unstable Policy." *Journal of Health Politics, Policy and Law* 45, no. 4 (August): 647–660.

Brenan, Megan. 2023. *Majority in U.S. Still Say Gov't Should Ensure Healthcare*. Washington, DC: Gallup.

Brodie, Mollyann, Claudia Deane, and Sarah Cho. 2011. "Regional Variations in Public Opinion on the Affordable Care Act." *Journal of Health Politics, Policy and Law* 36, no. 6 (December): 1097–1103.

Brodie, Mollyann, et al. 2019. "Partisanship, Polling, and the Affordable Care Act." *Public Opinion Quarterly* 83, no. 2 (Summer): 423–449.

Bureau of the Census. n.d. *Health Insurance Historical Tables: HHI Series.* Suitland, MD: Department of Commerce. Online at www.census.gov

Butler, Stuart M. 1989. *Assuring Affordable Health Care for All Americans.* Washington, DC: The Heritage Foundation.

Carter, Joe. 2014. *Explainer: The Hobby Lobby Amicus Briefs.* Grand Rapids, MI: The Acton Institute.

Centers for Medicare and Medicaid Services. 2023. "State-Based Exchanges." Online at https://www.cms.gov/cciio/resources/fact-sheets-and-faqs/state-marketplaces

Cohn, Jonathan. 2021. *The Ten Year War: Obamacare and the Unfinished Crusade for Universal Coverage.* New York: St. Martin's.

Dalen, James E., Keith Waterbrook, and Joseph S. Alpert. 2015. "Why do So Many Americans Oppose the Affordable Care Act?" *The American Journal of Medicine* 128, no. 8 (August): 807–810.

Diamond, Dan. 2024. "Obamacare Once Cost Democrats Elections. Now Biden's Hoping to Win on It." *The Washington Post* (March 30).

Frankford, David M. 2015. "The Remarkable Staying Power of 'Death Panes'." *Journal of Health Politics, Policy and Law* 40, no. 5 (October): 1087–1101.

Franz, Berkeley, Adrienne N. Milner, and R. Khari Brown. 2021. "Opposition to the Affordable Care Act Has Little to do with Health Care." *Race and Social Problems* 13 (November): 161–169.

Giovannelli, Justin, Kevin Lucia, and Sarah J. Dash. 2013. *Under Pressure: An Update on Restrictive State Insurance Marketplace Consumer Assistance Laws.* New York: Commonwealth Fund. Online at https://commonwealthfund.org/blog/2013/under-pressure-update-restrictive-state-insurance-marketplace-consumer-assistance-laws

Gluck, Abbe R., Mark Regan, and Erica Turret. 2020. "The Affordable Care Act's Litigation Decade." *Georgetown Law Journal* 108, no. 6: 1471–1534.

Goodell, Sarah. 2013. "Federally Facilitated Exchanges." *Health Affairs* (January 31). Online at https://www.healthaffairs.org/do/10.1377/hpb20130131.766527/

Greenfield, Kent and Adam Winkler. 2015. "The U.S. Supreme Court's Cultivation of Corporate Personhood." *The New Yorker* (Hune 24). Online at https://www.theatlantic.com/politics/archive/2015/06/raisins-hotels-corporate-personhood-supreme-court/396773/

Hacker, Jacob S. 2010. "The Road to Somewhere: Why Health Reform Happened: or Why Political Scientists Who Write about Public Policy Shouldn't Assume They Know How to Shape It." *Perspectives on Politics* 8, no. 3 (September): 861–876.

Haeder, Simon F., and David L. Weimer. 2015. "A Federalism Perspective on the Affordable Care Act." *Journal of Health Politics, Policy and Law* 40, no. 2 (April): 281–323.

"History of the Individual Insurance Mandate: Republican Origins of Democratic Health Care Provision." 2012. Britannica ProCon.org. Online at https://healthcarereform.procon.org/history-of-the-individual-health-insurance-mandate

Holohan, John, Jessica Banthin, and Erik Engle. 2021. *Marketplace Premiums and Participation in 2021*. Washington, DC: The Urban Institute.

Jacobs, Lawrence R., Suzanne Mettler, and Ling Zhu. 2019. "Affordable Care Act Moving to New Stage of Public Acceptance." *Journal of Health Policy, Politics and Law*. 44, no. 6 (December): 911–917.

Jones, David K. 2017. *Exchange Politics: Opposing Obamacare in Battleground States*. New York: Oxford University Press.

Jost, Timothy S. 2018. *The Affordable Care Act under the Trump Administration*. New York: The Commonwealth Fund.

Kaiser Family Foundation. 2013. "State Legislation and Actions Opting-out or Opposing Certain Health Reforms." Online at https://www.kff.org/wp-content/uploads/sites/3/2015/03/state-legislation-opt-out.pdf

Kaiser Family Foundation, 2023a. "State Health Facts." Online at https://www.kff.org/statedata

Kaiser Family Foundation. 2023b. "State Health insurance Marketplaces by Type, 2023. Online at https://www.kff.org/health-reform/state-indicator/state-health-insurance-marketplace-types/?currentTimeframe=0&sortModel=%7B%22colId%22:%22Location%22,%22sort%22:%22asc%22%7D

Kaiser Family Foundation. 2010. *Public Opinion on Health Care Issues*. (April) Menlo Park, CA: Kaiser Family Foundation.

Kaiser Family Foundation. 2023. *KFF Health Tracking Poll: The Public's View on the ACA*. (May 31) Menlo Park, CA: Kaiser Family Foundation.

Kaiser Family Foundation. 2024. *State Insurance Marketplaces by Type, 2024*. Menlo Park, CA: Kaiser Family Foundation.

Keith, Katie. 2020. "Supreme Court Rules that Insurers Are Entitled to Risk Corridor Payments: What the Court Said and What Happens Next." *Health Affairs* (April 28). Online at https://www.healthaffairs.org/do/10.1377/forefront.20200427.34146/

Keith, Katie, Kevin Lucia, and Christine Monahan. 2013. *Will New laws in States with Federally Run Health Insurance Marketplaces Hinder Outreach*. New York: Commonwealth Fund. Online at https://www.commonwealthfund.org/blog/2013/will-new-laws-states-federally-run-health-insurance-marketplaces-hinder-outreach

Kennedy, Kelly. 2014. "Study: Navigator Laws Limit Health Exchange Outreach." *USA Today* (January 14).

Kilgore, Ed. 2010. "How the Republicans Did It." *The New Republic* (November 2). Online at https://newrepublic.com/article/78903/how-the-republicans-did-it

Kirchoff, Suzanne M. 2014. *Health Insurance Exchanges: Health Insurance 'Navigators' and In-Person Assistance*. Washington, DC: Congressional Research Office.

Kirzinger, Ashley, et al. 2022. *5 Charts About Public Opinion on the Affordable Care Act*. Menlo Park, CA: Kaiser Family Foundation.

Lerman, Amy E., Meredith L. Sadin, and Samuel Trachtman. 2017. "Policy Uptake as Political Behavior: Evidence from the Affordable Care Act." *American Political Science Review* 111, no. 4 (November): 755–770.

Luhby, Tami, 2022. "Obamacare Is Proving Popular in Red States That Didn't Expand Medicaid." *CNN* (January 13). Online at https://www.cnn.com/2022/01/13/politics/obamacare-aca-red-states-medicaid/index.html

Mann, Thomas E., and Norman J. Ornstein. 2016. *It's Even Worse than It Looks: How the American Constitutional System Collided with the New Politics of Extremism*, new and expanded ed. New York: Basic Books.

Mayer, Martin, Robert Kenter, and John C. Morris. 2015. "Partisan Politics of Public-Health Need? An Empirical Analysis of State Choice During Initial Implementation of the Affordable Care Act." *Politics and the Life Sciences* 34, no. 2 (Fall): 44–51.

MacDonald, Evan. 2020. "A Polarized America: How the Partisan Divide Grew Over Decades, and Why Liberals and Conservatives Just Can't Get Along." *Cleveland.com* (September 1). Online at https://www.cleveland.com/open/2020/08/a-polarized-america-how-the-partisan-divide-grew-over-decades-and-why-liberals-and-conservatives-just-cant-get-along.html

McFadden, Alyce. 2021. "The Long, Costly Battle Over Obamacare Might Be Over." *OpenSecrets.org* (June 3 23). Online at https://www.opensecrets.org/news/2021/06/costly-battle-obamacare-over/

Musumeci, MaryBeth. 2020. Explaining *California v. Texas: A Guide to the Case Challenging the ACA*. Menlo Park, CA: Kaiser Family Foundation.

Newport, Frank. 2023. *Update: Partisan Gaps Expand Most on Government Power, Climate*. Washington, DC: Gallup.

Newport, Frank, and Andrew Dugan. 2017. *Partisan Differences Growing on a Number of Issues*. Washington, DC: Gallup.

Nolette, Paul. 2014. "State Litigation During the Obama Administration: Diverging Agendas in an Era of Polarized Politics." *Publius: Journal of Federalism* 44, no. 3 (Summer): 451–474.

Norris, Louise. 2022. "Health Insurance Marketplace by States." (August 24). Online at https://www.healthinsurance.org/health-insurance-marketplaces/

Oberlander, Jonathan. 2018. "The Republican War on Obamacare—What Has It Achieved?" *New England Journal of Medicine* no. 379 (July 30): 1–3.

Oberlander, Jonathan. 2020. "The Ten Years' War: Politics, Partisanship, and the ACA." *Health Affairs* 39, no. 3 (March): 471–478.

Office of the Attorney General of California. 2014. *On Writs of Certiorari to the United States Courts of Appeal for the Tenth and Third Circuits*. Sacramento, CA: Office of the Attorney General.

Pacheco, Julianna, and Elizabeth Maltby. 2019. "Trends in State-Level Opinions Toward the Affordable Care Act." *Journal of Health Politics, Policy and Law* 44, no. 5 (October): 737–764.

Pacheco, Julianna, Jake Haselswerdt and Jamila Michener. 2020. "The Affordable Care Act and Polarization in the United States." *RSF: The Russell Sage Foundation Journal of the Social Sciences*. 6, no. 2 (July): 114–130.

Phillips, Amber. 2016. "Kentucky, Once an Obamacare Success Story, Now Moves to Shut It Down." *Washington Post* (January 14).

Reny, Tyler T., and David O. Sears. 2020. "Symbolic Politics and Self-Interest in Post-Affordable Care Act Health Insurance Coverage." *Research and Politics* 7, no. 3: (July-September): 1–6.

Rigby, Elizabeth and Jake Haselswerdt. 2013. "Hybrid Federalism, Partisan Politics, and Early Implementation of State Health Insurance Exchanges." *Publius* 43, no. 3 (Summer): 368–391.

Robertson, Christopher, and Wendy Netter Epstein. 2020. "Conservatives Backed the Ideas Behind Obamacare, So How Did They Come to Hate it?" *The Conversation* (November 10) Online at https://theconversation.com/conservatives-backed-the-ideas-behind-obamacare-so-how-did-they-come-to-hate-it-149698

Roper Center for Public Opinion Research. 2013. *A Brief History of Public Opinion on the Government Role in Health Care*. Ithaca, NY: Cornell University. Online at https://ropercenter.cornell.edu/brief-history-public-opinion-government-role-health-care

Rovner, Judith. 2017. "Why Do So Many People Hate Obamacare So Much." *National Public Radio* (December 13) Online at https://www.npr.org/sections/health-shots/2017/12/13/570479181/why-do-so-many-people-hate-obamacare-so-much

SCOTUSblog. n.d. *King v. Burrell*. Online at https://www.scotusblog.com/case-files/cases/king-v-burwell/

Silva, Derek. 2021. "States Where Obamacare Plans Cost the Most in 2021." Online at https://www.policygenius.com/health-insurance/where-obamacare-plans-cost-the-most/

Smith, Samantha. 2015. *From the Very Start, Sharp Partisan Divisions over Obamacare*. Washington, DC: Pew Research Center.

Sobel, Laurie, et al 2023. Preventive Services Requirements: *Braidwood Management, Inc. v. Becerra*. (May 15). Menlo Park, CA: Kaiser Family Foundation.

Taylor, Jennifer, et al. 2019. *State Actions to Improve the Affordability of Health Insurance in the Individual Market*. Menlo Park, CA: Kaiser Family Foundation.

Thompson, Frank J. 2020. *Six Ways Trump Has Sabotaged the Affordable Care Act*. Washington, DC: The Brookings Institution.

Tractman, Samuel. 2020. "When State Policy Makes National Politics: The Case of 'Obamacare' Marketplace Implementation." *Journal of Health Politics, Policy and Law* 45, no. 1 (February): 111–141.

Walker, Elizabeth. (2022). "How the Affordable Care Act (ACA) Varies by State." Online at https://www.peoplekeep.com/blog/how-the-affordable-care-act-aca-varies-by-state

Zipp, Ricky. 2022. "Affordable Care Act Remains Popular Among Voters as Health Law Hits New Milestone." Online at https://pro.morningconsult.com/instant-intel/aca-obamacare-approval-survey-data

5

MEDICAID

Red and Blue State Divide

Medicaid emerged as a product of failed efforts to adopt national health insurance (NHI). President Harry Truman and the Democratic Party ran in 1948 on a platform calling for NHI. Though Truman won and the Democrats controlled both houses of Congress, the long effort to enact NHI would fail as Republicans, southern Democrats, and the American Medical Association (AMA) opposed the policy. Those who pushed for NHI decided upon an incremental strategy: to enact legislation that would protect seniors (Starr 1982).

That, too, proved difficult. Legislation in 1960, the Kerr-Mills bill, focused on impoverished seniors and gave implementation responsibility to the states. Not many states took up the challenge. Massachusetts Democratic Senator John Kennedy, in his successful run for president in 1960, supported what became known as Medicare. While unable to convince Congress to pass such legislation before his assassination in 1963, his Vice President, Lyndon Johnson, who became president, was able to do so. What helped this come about was Johnson's significant victory during the 1964 presidential elections combined with a huge Democratic victory in Congress, especially in the Senate. The result, Johnson and the Democrats were able to push through significant legislation such as the Civil Rights Act of 1964 and the Voting Rights Act of 1965. Johnson was able to implement his war on poverty programs (such as the Economic Opportunity Act of 1964) as well. When it came to healthcare, the major piece of legislation was Title XX, Medicare, of the Social Security Act (originally passed in 1935).

Where was Medicaid in all this? Opponents of Medicare, which included Republicans and interest groups such as the AMA, pushed for a program that would focus on the non-elderly poor. The chairman of the House Finance Committee, Wilbur Mills (D-AK), put together Medicare Part A (basically hospital insurance) and Medicare Part B (basically physician insurance) with Medicaid (Title XIX of the Social Security Act). Medicare's passage was celebrated as a great achievement; Medicaid was enacted quietly, with much less debate and publicity than Medicare (Katz 2010; Smith and Moore 2008; Starr 1982; Thompson 2012).

Though passed together, the two programs are considerably different. Medicare, which garnered most of the attention, operates similarly to Social Security. Both Medicare and Social Security are federally funded and operated. Eligibility for the two programs is based primarily, though not entirely, on age. Medicaid is similar to welfare policies such as SNAP (Supplemental Nutrition Assistance Program, formerly food stamps) and Temporary Assistance to Needy Families (TANF, which is considered the basic welfare program). Medicaid is jointly funded by the federal government and the states and is administered by the states. Eligibility is based on need (means-testing). Recipients of TANF and Medicaid must apply to the programs and demonstrate, on a continual basis, their eligibility. Under Medicaid, recipients (and potential recipients) are classified into different categories, such as children, parents, and so forth. These characteristics, federalism, and eligibility based on need define the nature of Medicaid.

And those characteristics also fit into our investigation of red and blue state healthcare systems. There is no single Medicaid system; rather, each state (and district and territory) has created its own system, and the differences between the red and blue states are profound. Federalism and features of Medicaid and the Social Security Act, such as section 1115 waivers, allow states to craft Medicaid policies that meet state priorities.

Transformation of Medicaid

Medicaid has evolved over the decades. Brecher and Rose (2013) use the metaphor of metamorphosis to illustrate and explain the various transformations that Medicaid has undergone since its creation in 1965. The authors argue that Medicaid at birth was a small, limited, ugly creature. However, like the caterpillar that morphs into a beautiful butterfly,

> Medicaid has since defied expectations by evolving into an enormous, complex, and, in some ways (at least to its supporters), more beautiful creature in several distinct stages.
> *(Brecher and Rose 2013, 560)*

The transformation was enabled by certain features contained within the program from the very beginning. One was the open-ended federal financing to states, which created an incentive to participate. A second feature was eligibility guidelines that gave states flexibility in addressing the needs of their citizens. The third feature was a comprehensive package of benefits that, in some ways, exceeds that of Medicare and private insurance.

Given this, the first transformation or metamorphosis was separating Medicaid from welfare programs such as TANF and SNAP. The argument was that the federal law tying the two programs limited Medicaid's ability to address other needs. In particular was a concern about prenatal and neonatal care. The belief was that offering and providing such care would result in better pregnancy outcomes and monetary savings. After lobbying by states, Congress granted states the right (and eventually the requirement) under Medicaid to offer such services for mothers and would-be mothers and children. Further, using the same reasoning, Congress required states, again under Medicaid, to cover Medicare premiums for those who are disabled or on Medicare but with low incomes (dual eligibles). The separation here was between Medicaid and the federal cash program Supplemental Security Income (SSI) (Brecher and Rose 2013).

This first transformation had several positive effects. One was that because of the separation from the cash programs, TANF and SSI, the stigma of being poor was greatly reduced. Second, Medicaid enrollment by the mid-1990s had nearly doubled. A third impact was reduced infant mortality and low birth weights. And this last effect led to the enactment of an add-on to Medicaid, the Children's Health Insurance Program or CHIP (see below) (Brecher and Rose 2013).

The second transformation or metamorphosis was a shift toward managed care. We have seen this in the private sector and in Medicare, where private plans (Medicare Advantage or Part C plans) now enroll over 50 percent of Medicare recipients. The rationale for this change was to develop plans based on capitation; that is, Medicaid (state and federal) would pay a fixed amount per recipient to a healthcare plan rather than continue paying unlimited amounts for services. This was seen as a way to coordinate services as well as to control costs. As of March 2023, 72 percent of Medicaid recipients were enrolled in managed care organizations (Hinton and Raphael 2023). Many states used their savings from managed care organizations to increase enrollment of the poor in Medicaid (Brecher and Rose 2013).

The third transformation came with the passage of the Affordable Care Act (ACA). Under the terms of the ACA, Medicaid provided a relatively inexpensive way to provide coverage for more people by raising the income limit making people eligible for Medicaid. Medicaid became one of the ways, alongside the markets/exchanges and insurance reforms, to cover more people (Brecher and Rose 2013). As we shall see below, this became controversial and marks one of the major differences between red and blue states as regards Medicaid.

One could argue that Medicaid has undergone, at least temporarily, a fourth metamorphosis. In this case, Medicaid became a vehicle to cover individuals and families who lost their jobs and their health insurance policies due to the COVID-19 pandemic (see Chapter 7). Because the pandemic at its height was temporary (2019–2023), so too was the extra coverage (see below).

Additionally, the experience with Medicaid led to the passage of a related piece of legislation creating an extended program, known now as the CHIP. CHIP, originally known as the State Children's Health Insurance Program or SCHIP, was created in 1997. The program was contained within a larger piece of legislation, the Balanced Budget Act of 1997. The architects of the bill, Senators Edward Kennedy (D-MA) and Orrin Hatch (R-UT), among others such as Congressman Henry Waxman (D-CA), were working in a changing atmosphere. Part of the atmosphere was the failure of the Clinton Health Security Act to be passed (1993–1994). Other parts of the atmosphere included attempts by Republicans to make changes to Medicaid. This included proposals to transform Medicaid into a block grant, where each state would get a specific allotment regardless of changes in the Medicaid population (Thompson 2012). The change was also related to welfare reform mentioned above, which separated the federal welfare program from Medicaid.

CHIP differed from Medicaid in several ways. For one, the income eligibility requirement was significantly higher than for Medicaid. At its peak, after the passage of the ACA, the highest income a family was allowed under Medicaid was 138 percent of the federal poverty level (FPL). For CHIP, the income eligibility level was 250 percent of the FPL. And some states allowed higher income eligibility levels, as high as 350 percent of the FPL at one point. States were moving toward covering middle-class children and not just those of the poor. A second difference is that federal payments for CHIP were higher than for Medicaid. A third difference was that CHIP allowed more flexibility to shape the program than Medicaid did (Thompson 2012).

Structure of Medicaid

Medicaid is directed at people with low income. Those who might be eligible for Medicaid consist of the categorically eligible and those who are in optional groups. Table 5.1 lists examples of the categorically eligible

TABLE 5.1 Medicaid Groups

Categorically Eligible (Mandatory)
- certain low-income families, including parents, that meet the financial requirements of the former AFDC cash assistance program;
- pregnant women with annual income at or below 133% of FPL;
- children with family income at or below 133% of FPL;
- aged, blind, or disabled individuals who receive cash assistance under the SSI program;
- children receiving foster care, adoption assistance, or kinship guardianship assistance under SSA Title IV–E;
- certain former foster care youth; individuals eligible for the Qualified Medicare Beneficiary program; and
- certain groups of legal permanent resident immigrants.

Optional Groups
- pregnant women with annual income between 133% and 185% of FPL;
- infants with family income between 133% and 185% of FPL; certain individuals who require institutional care and have incomes up to 300% of the SSI federal benefit rate;
- certain *medically needy* individuals (e.g., children, pregnant women, aged, blind, or disabled) who are otherwise eligible for Medicaid but who have incomes too high to qualify and spend down their income on medical care; and
- non-elderly adults with income at or below 133% of FPL (i.e., the ACA Medicaid expansion).

Adapted from: Mitchell (2023).

and the optionally eligible groups. The rather broad class of categorically eligible include pregnant women, children, adults, the disabled, and the elderly. Being in one of these groups does not make one automatically eligible for Medicaid coverage because there are also financial eligibility requirements. Eligibility has changed over the years and the table reflects the most recent changes as of 2022. Note that one group, the last group in the optionally eligible category, came about because of Medicaid expansion, which we discuss below. Additionally, some individuals in the children group became eligible as a function of the COVID-19 pandemic, which we also discuss below. The important point is that states get to choose who among the optional groups will get Medicaid.

We find a similar division regarding Medicaid benefits. There are mandatory benefits and optional benefits (see Table 5.2). Again, states have choices not only about which optional benefits to include but also about the shape of mandatory benefits. The result of the state discretion in groups and benefits is that each state can create the kind of Medicaid program it wants, and no two Medicaid programs are the same.

TABLE 5.2 Mandatory and Optional Medicaid Benefits

Mandatory Benefits
- Inpatient hospital services
- Outpatient hospital services
- EPSDT: Early and Periodic Screening, Diagnostic, and Treatment Services
- Nursing Facility Services
- Home health services
- Physician services
- Rural health clinic services
- Federally qualified health center services
- Laboratory and X-ray services
- Family planning services
- Nurse Midwife services
- Certified Pediatric and Family Nurse Practitioner services
- Freestanding Birth Center services (when licensed or otherwise recognized by the state)
- Transportation to medical care
- Tobacco cessation counseling for pregnant women

Adapted from: Centers for Medicare and Medicaid Services (n.d.-a). Online at www.cms.gov.

There is a third element of Medicaid that gives states discretion over the program: eligibility requirements. In the case of Medicare, the major requirement is age. In the case of Medicaid, eligibility depends on what category a person is in and financial and asset determinations. The determinations are complex and have changed/been simplified over time. In the pre-ACA period, applicants had to apply in person, fill out a considerable amount of paperwork, go through an asset test, wait for eligibility determination, and go through frequent renewal processes providing documentation of income and assets. The ACA changed this somewhat. There are several different ways to apply, such as via mail, by phone, on the computer, and in person. Now there is electronic verification of information and no asset test. Determination of eligibility is done immediately in real time. And there is automatic renewal (Brooks et al. 2018).

But the income eligibility levels, based on a percentage of the FPL, can differ by states and certainly differ between those states that expanded Medicaid and those that did not (see below). Tables 5.3 and 5.4 present the data.

There are several observations we can make comparing these two tables. First, for every category of eligibility in the tables, the blue state levels are higher than the red states. Second, an interesting observation in both tables is that the income eligibility levels go down for children as they get older. For example, the FPL for a family of four in 2022 was $27,750 (HealthCare.Gov 2023), not an especially generous level. If we look at our

TABLE 5.3 Medicaid and CHIP Income Eligibility Levels for Selected Groups (Red States)

	Children Medicaid Ages 0–1	Children Medicaid Ages 1–5	Children Medicaid Ages 6–18	Children Separate CHIP	Pregnant Women Medicaid	Pregnant Women CHIP	Adults (Medicaid) Parent/Caretaker
	% of FPL	% of FPL	% of FPL	% of FPL	% of FPL	% of FPL	% of FPL
Alabama	141%	141%	141%	312%	141%		13%
Alaska	203%	203%	203%		200%		131%
Arizona	147%	141%	133%	200%	156%		106%
Arkansas	142%	142%	142%	211%	209%		14%
Georgia	205%	149%	133%	247%	220%		30%
Idaho	142%	142%	133%	185%	133%		22%
Indiana	208%	158%	158%	250%	208%		16%
Kansas	166%	149%	133%	250%	166%		33%
Kentucky	195%	159%	159%	213%	195%	213%	21%
Louisiana	212%	212%	212%	250%	133%		19%
Mississippi	194%	143%	133%	209%	194%		20%
Missouri	196%	150%	150%	300%	196%	300%	16%
Montana	143%	143%	143%	261%	157%		24%
Nebraska	213%	213%	213%		194%		58%
North Carolina	210%	210%	133%	211%	196%		38%
North Dakota	170%	170%	170%		157%		46%
Oklahoma	205%	205%	205%		133%		36%
South Carolina	208%	208%	208%		194%		95%
South Dakota	182%	182%	182%	204%	133%		50%
Tennessee	195%	142%	133%	250%	195%		90%
Texas	198%	144%	133%	201%%	198%		13%
Utah	139%	139%	133%	200%	139%		39%
West Virginia	158%	141%	133%	300%	185%	300%	17%
Wyoming	200%	200%	200%		154%		48%
Average	182%	166%	159%	238%	174%	271%	41%

Adapted from: Centers for Medicaid and Medicare Services (2022). Online at cms.gov.

red state table, the average percentage of the FPL for children up to the age of 1 was 182% or $49,950. For children ages 6–18, the average income eligibility level was 159% or $44,122. The income level for the youngest children is over $5,000 higher than for the oldest children (see Einav and Finkelstein 2023). The same is true for the blue states. For the youngest of children, the income eligibility level is 248% of the FPL or $67,432. For the oldest group, the income eligibility level is 217% of the FPL or $60,217. The income for the youngest children in the blue states is over $7,000 higher than for the oldest children. The trend is the same for both groups.

Having said that, there are also differences between the two groups of states regarding income eligibility levels for children. The income levels are

TABLE 5.4 Medicaid and CHIP Income Eligibility Levels for Selected Groups (Blue States)

	Children Medicaid Ages 0–1	Children Medicaid Ages 1–5	Children Medicaid Ages 6–18	Children Separate CHIP	Pregnant Women Medicaid	Pregnant Women CHIP	Adults (Medicaid) Parent/ Caretaker
	% of FPL	% of FPL	% of FPL	% of FPL	% of FPL	% of FPL	% of FPL
California	261%	261%	261%		208%		109%
Connecticut	196%	196%	196%	318	258%		155%
Delaware	212%	142%	133%	212%	212%		87%
Hawaii	308%	308%	308%		191%		105%
Illinois	313%	313%	313%		208%		133%
Maine	208%	208%	208%		209%		100%
Maryland	317%	317%	317%		259%		123%
Massachusetts	200%	150%	150%	300%	200%		133%
Michigan	212%	212%	212%		195%		54%
New Jersey	194%	142%	142%	350%	194%	200	26%
New Mexico	300%	300%	240%		250%	37	
New York	218%	149%	149%	400%	218%		133%
Oregon	185%	133%	133%	300%	185%		133%
Pennsylvania	215%	157%	133%	314	215%		33%
Rhode Island	261%	261%	261%		190%	253	116%
Vermont	312%	312%	312%		208%		43%
Washington	210%	210%	210%	312	193%		133%
Average	242%	222%	216%	313%	211%	163%	101%

Adapted from: Centers for Medicaid and Medicare Services (2022). Online at www.cms.gov.

higher for blue states for virtually all the categories in the two tables. For example, for the youngest children, the blue state level is 35 percent higher than for the youngest children in red states. For the oldest group of children, ages 6–18, the blue state level is almost 30 percent higher than for the red states.

The two tables also look at children and pregnant women with coverage through the CHIP program. The first thing we should note is that the eligibility levels are higher for CHIP coverage than for regular Medicaid for both groups. For the red states, the CHIP average level is 238% of the FPL ($66,045 for a family of four), over 50 percentage points higher than the average level for the youngest children in regular Medicaid. For pregnant women in red states, the average eligibility level is 174% ($48,285 for a family of four) of the FPL for regular Medicaid recipients. This compares to the higher average of 271% ($75,203 for a family of four), almost 100 percentage points, for pregnant women on CHIP in red states. But here we should note from Table 5.3 that only three red states cover pregnant women through the CHIP program. Two of those three states, West Virginia and Missouri, have very high eligibility levels for this program.

The CHIP program for children in the blue states has an income eligibility level of 303% ($84,083 for a family of four) of the FPL. In the case of pregnant women on CHIP, the eligibility level in the blue states (211% or $58,553) is higher than in the red states (174% or $48,285). Only one of the blue states, Rhode Island, has pregnant women in the CHIP program.

We conclude, based on these two tables, that blue states have more generous Medicaid programs (at least for pregnant women and children) than red states.

The last column of these two tables focuses on adult caretakers, such as parents. First, we should note that the levels of income eligibility for caretakers in both sets of states are low. For the red states, the average income eligibility level is 41 percent of the FPL or $11,378. In blue states, the average income eligibility level is 66 percent of the FPL or $23,865. This is more than twice as much as in the red states. But, again, neither is especially generous. The levels reflect policy decisions at the state and federal levels that adults should be limited in their ability to get on Medicaid.

Table 5.5 shows how the states differed in covering adults who do not fit into the the categories mentioned above. Note first that the data is for 2023. It reflects changes made by states that expanded Medicaid (see below) so that the income eligibility level was 138% of the FPL. To some extent, the data in the table also reflects efforts to increase Medicaid coverage due to the pandemic. As the table shows, all the blue states set their standard for this group of people at the expansion percentage. But only 14 red states made the change, while 10 red states did not make such a change (see the discussion below on Medicaid expansion).

Given all this, it should come as no surprise that the red and blue states differ in the percentage of their population on Medicaid. Table 5.6 presents the data. The average for the the entire country in 2021 was nearly 21 percent. For the red states, the average was 19.6 percent. For the blue states, the average was just over 23 percent. The blue states covered more of their population through Medicaid than the red states.

Pregnancy

One of the most important areas of coverage for Medicaid and CHIP is pregnancy. We begin by looking at maternal mortality, briefly restating some of the material from Chapter 3. The United States has the highest rate of maternal mortality, which can occur up to a year after birth, among industrialized nations in the world. The U.S. rate in 2020 was 23.8 deaths per 100,000 live births (Taylor et al. 2022). The next highest country was France at 8.7 deaths per 100,000 live births. The maternal death rate is much higher among black women (55 deaths per 100,000) than for white

TABLE 5.5 Medicaid Income Eligibility Levels for Other Adults (2023)

Red States	% of Federal Poverty Level	Blue States	% of Federal Poverty Level
Alabama	0	California	138
Georgia	0	Connecticut	138
Kansas	0	Delaware	138
Mississippi	0	Hawaii	138
North Carolina	0	Illinois	138
South Carolina	0	Maine	138
South Dakota	0	Maryland	138
Tennessee	0	Massachusetts	138
Texas	0	Michigan	138
Wyoming	0	New Jersey	138
Alaska	138	New Mexico	138
Arizona	138	New York	138
Arkansas	138	Oregon	138
Idaho	138	Pennsylvania	138
Indiana	138	Rhode Island	138
Kentucky	138	Vermont	138
Louisiana	138	Washington	138
Missouri	138		
Montana	138		
Nebraska	138		
North Dakota	138		
Oklahoma	138		
Utah	138		
West Virginia	138		

Adapted from: Kaiser Family Foundation (2023a). Online at www.kff.org.

women (19 deaths per 100,000 live births) or Hispanic women (18 deaths per 100,000) (Taylor et al. 2022). Note that though the rates for white and Hispanic women are considerably lower than for black women, the rates are still considerably higher compared to other industrialized countries.

A third thing to note is that the maternal death rate has increased considerably in recent years. In 2018 the rate was 17.4 compared to 23.8 in 2020 (Taylor et al. 2022). This is an increase of almost 37 percent in just two years.

In Chapter 3, we presented some statistics that showed maternal death rates among red and blue states (see Table 3.22). We also presented a ranking of states on maternal health (see Table 3.23). Both tables showed that blue states did better than red states. In this section, we consider some Medicaid policies related to pregnancy.

TABLE 5.6 Percentage of State Population Covered by Medicaid (2021)

Red States	Percent of Population Covered	Blue States	Percent of Population Covered
Alabama	19	California	27
Alaska	26	Connecticut	23
Arizona	21	Delaware	21
Arkansas	27	Hawaii	20
Georgia	18	Illinois	20
Idaho	20	Maine	20
Indiana	20	Maryland	20
Kansas	15	Massachusetts	23
Kentucky	29	Michigan	24
Louisiana	32	New Jersey	18
Mississippi	24	New Mexico	34
Missouri	15	New York	28
Montana	20	Oregon	24
Nebraska	15	Pennsylvania	21
North Carolina	19	Rhode Island	24
North Dakota	10	Vermont	25
Oklahoma	20	Washington	21
South Carolina	20		
South Dakota	14		
Tennessee	20		
Texas	17		
Utah	11		
West Virginia	28		
Wyoming	12		
Average	19.67		23.12
U.S. Average	20.45		

Adapted from: Rudowitz et al. (2023). Online at www.kff.org.

We begin by looking at the extent of Medicaid coverage of pregnancies. Table 5.7 presents the data. Overall, Medicaid covered 42 percent of all pregnancies in the United States in 2020. For the red states, the average is nearly the same as the overall average. For the blue states, the average is 2.4% lower than the overall average. This makes sense because the red states tend to have a higher percentage of low-income people than the blue states; put another way, the blue states are richer than the red states (see Chapter 2).

The variation of coverage within the blue states is much wider than for the red states. For the red states, the variation is 38.8 percentage points. Louisiana has the highest pregnancy coverage of any state, blue or red, at

TABLE 5.7 Percent of Births Covered by Medicaid (2020)

Red States	Percent of Births	Blue States	Percent of Births
Utah	22.6	New Jersey	28.3
North Dakota	24.6	Massachusetts	31.2
South Dakota	29.4	Hawaii	34.9
Wyoming	30.0	Pennsylvania	34.9
Kansas	31.3	Connecticut	36.7
Nebraska	35.1	Washington	37.1
Idaho	35.2	Maine	38.8
Montana	38.4	Illinois	38.9
Indiana	38.5	Maryland	39.4
Alaska	39.3	Michigan	39.7
Missouri	39.7	California	39.9
North Carolina	40.9	Vermont	40.0
Arkansas	44.2	Delaware	41.1
Georgia	47.2	Oregon	42.8
Arizona	47.8	New York	46.2
West Virginia	48.2	Rhode Island	48.4
Kentucky	48.3	New Mexico	54.5
South Carolina	48.4		
Tennessee	48.9		
Alabama	50.2		
Texas	50.7		
Oklahoma	51.2		
Mississippi	60.1		
Louisiana	61.4		
Average	42.2		39.6
U.S. Average	42.0		

Adapted with permission from: March of Dimes (2020). Online at https://www.marchofdimes.org/peristats/data?reg=99&top=11&stop=154&lev=1&slev=1&obj=18.

61.4% while Utah has the lowest at 22.6%. For the blue states, the variation is much smaller, at 26.2 percentage points. The high is New Mexico, at 54.4%, while the low is New Jersey, at 28.3%.

Understanding the differences in coverage goes beyond just the percentage coverage. Pregnancy is complicated.

States have what Ranji et al. (2022, 3) label as "baselevel requirements," federal guidelevels that must be followed. For example, there are no cost-sharing requirements for pregnancy-related services. But issues such as income eligibility and benefits, which have their own baselevel requirements, may be subject to policy decisions made by states. It is these decisions that distinguish how states cover pregnancy-related issues.

TABLE 5.8 Income Eligibility Levels for Pregnant Women in Medicaid (2020)

Red States	% of Federal Poverty Level	Blue States	% of Federal Poverty Level
Idaho	138	Oregon	190
Louisiana	138	Rhode Island	195
Oklahoma	138	Hawaii	196
South Dakota	138	Washington	198
Utah	144	New Jersey	199
Alabama	146	Michigan	200
Wyoming	159	Massachusetts	205
Arizona	161	California	213
Montana	162	Illinois	213
North Dakota	162	Vermont	213
Kansas	171	Maine	214
West Virginia	190	Delaware	217
Mississippi	199	Pennsylvania	220
Nebraska	199	New York	223
South Carolina	199	New Mexico	255
Kentucky	200	Connecticut	263
Tennessee	200	Maryland	264
Missouri	201		
North Carolina	201		
Texas	203		
Alaska	205		
Arkansas	214		
Indiana	218		
Georgia	225		
Average	179.63		216.35
U.S. Average	200%		

Adapted with permission from: Clark (2020). Online at www.ccf.georgetown.edu.

Two such requirements concern income eligibility. Under federal law, all women who are pregnant and have incomes up to 138% of the FPL can get Medicaid coverage. The policy decision here is that states can cover women with higher incomes. But not all states do so. Table 5.8 presents the data. The data columns show the income eligibility percentage for pregnant women as a percent of the FPL. Federal law created a minimum level of 138%. The table shows that all of the blue states had an income eligibility level greater than 138%. Four of the red states had a 138% level and several red states had income eligibility near the 138% minimum. The average income eligibility level for the blue states was almost 36 points higher than for the red states. Another way of looking at this is that the average blue state level was 20 percentage points higher than the average red state level. The blue state income eligibility level was higher than the national average while the red state average was below the national average.

Because the maternal death rate in the United States is so high, it is important that women receive postpartum (post-childbirth) care. The standard provision of such care under Medicaid is two months. States were given the option to extend postpartum care to 12 months under the American Rescue Plan Act passed in 2021. In 2023, another piece of federal legislation, the Consolidated Appropriations Act, made the option permanent (Park et al. 2023). The federal government, as it does with other features of Medicaid, provides matching funds. Table 5.9 shows what states have done from 2018 through 2023.

Table 5.9 shows which states have approved programs for extending postpartum care from 2 to 12 months. It should be noted that all states have developed such plans, but not all states have submitted proposals or had them approved by the Centers for Medicare and Medicaid Services (CMS). Our first observation is that all the blue states have approved extensions. Our second observation is that many of the red states have such approval. Our third observation is that six red states, as of December 2022, did not have CMS approval.

Table 5.10 measures, in the case of prenatal care, the percentage of enrolled Medicaid/CHIP enrolled women who had a visit in their first trimester or within 42 days of their enrollment. The second metric, postpartum care, measures the percentage of enrolled women who had a postpartum visit within 7–84 days after delivery. The table shows that in both metrics, the red state percentages were below the national medians, while the blue state percentages were above the national medians. We should also note that the variation within the blue states (22.5% prenatal; 14.7% postpartum) was less than the variation within the red states (57.3 prenatal; 51.7% postpartum). Women in blue states were, on average, able to have maternal care earlier than those in red states.

Budget

Budget issues are an important way of looking at the importance of Medicaid and the willingness of states to provide resources for the program. One comparison is how much states spend on average on Medicaid. Table 5.11 presents the data. Note first that the table focuses on 2019 data. This was before the COVID-19 pandemic hit the country and the federal government increased its spending for programs such as Medicaid to limit the economic impact of the pandemic (which we discuss in Chapter 7).

TABLE 5.9 Extending Postpartum Coverage

Red States	Approval Of Extended Postpartum Coverage	Blue States	Approval Of Extended Postpartum Coverage
Alabama	approved	California	approved
Alaska	approved	Connecticut	approved
Arizona	approved	Delaware	approved
Arkansas	not approved	Hawaii	approved
Georgia	not approved	Illinois	approved
Idaho	not approved	Maine	approved
Indiana	approved	Maryland	approved
Kansas	approved	Massachusetts	approved
Kentucky	approved	Michigan	approved
Louisiana	approved	New Jersey	approved
Mississippi	not approved	New Mexico	approved
Missouri	not approved	New York	approved
Montana	not approved	Oregon	approved
Nebraska	not approved	Pennsylvania	approved
North Carolina	approved	Rhode Island	approved
North Dakota	approved	Vermont	approved
Oklahoma	approved	Washington	approved
South Carolina	approved		
South Dakota	approved		
Tennessee	approved		
Texas	not approved		
Utah	not approved		
West Virginia	approved		
Wyoming	approved		

Adapted with permission from: National Academy of State Health Policy (2023). Online at https://nashp.org/state-tracker/view-each-states-efforts-to-extend-medicaid-postpartum-coverage/

The COVID-19 pandemic began in 2020 and Medicaid spending was ramped up, largely by raising the income eligibility levels, so that more people could get treated for COVID. Even then, the resulting analysis in later years and early years is identical to 2019. The red states averaged $8,302 per beneficiary. This is $336 per beneficiary below the U.S. average. The blue states averaged $9,205 per beneficiary above both the U.S. and red state average. The blue state average was almost $1,000 above the red state average.

Medicaid comprised about 7.6% of the federal budget, with CHIP comprising 0.2% of the federal budget in 2021 (MACPAC 2022). The federal government funded a significant portion of state Medicaid programs.

TABLE 5.10 Timeliness of Prenatal and Postpartum Care (2019)

Red States	Timeliness of Prenatal Care (%)	Postpartum Care (%)	Blue States	Timeliness of Prenatal Care (%)	Postpartum Care (%)
Alabama	46.2	42.9	California	90.0	72.7
Alaska	n/a[a]	n/a[a]	Connecticut	90.3	81.0
Arizona	n/a[a]	n/a[a]	Delaware	85.0	72.7
Arkansas	n/a[a]	n/a[a]	Hawaii	83.2	65.7
Georgia	77.6	63.0	Illinois	63.4	66.5
Idaho	n/a[a]	n/a[a]	Maine	88.4	n/a[a]
Indiana	84.4	87.0	Maryland	88.3	81.0
Kansas	84.3	67.0	Massachusetts	83.0	77.0
Kentucky	84.2	68.3	Michigan	86.2	66.4
Louisiana	85.8	75.4	New Jersey	84.4	76.2
Mississippi	95.6	69.8	New Mexico	81.9	66.3
Missouri	92.1	52.7	New York	n/a[a]	n/a[a]
Montana	n/a[a]	n/a[a]	Oregon	n/a[a]	n/a[a]
Nebraska	n/a[a]	n/a[a]	Pennsylvania	91.7	79.3
North Carolina	n/a[a]	68.8	Rhode Island	92.1	78.8
North Dakota	66.8	n/a[a]	Vermont	69.6	65.4
Oklahoma	27.4	30.1	Washington	87.2	73.6
South Carolina	74.2	91.6			
South Dakota	35.4	32.6			
Tennessee	83.7	70.2			
Texas	n/a[a]	78.1			
Utah	90.4	76.7			
West Virginia	92.7	72.3			
Wyoming	82.2	39.9			
Average	75.2	63.9		84.31	73.04
U.S. Median	84.4	72.3			

Adapted with permission from: Clark (2023). Online at www.ccf.georgetown.edu

[a] Information is not available or not submitted.

The first thing we should note is what portion of total state budgets fund Medicaid. Table 5.12 presents the data. For the red states, Medicaid, on average, accounts for just over 25% of state budgets (2020) data. For the blue states, the figure is slightly higher at almost 27%. This includes federal funds. If we subtract out federal funding, the differences expand. The second important lesson taken from the table is how much states spend on Medicaid from their own budgets. For the red states, that percentage is just over 12 percent. For the blue states, the percentage is 14.5 percent. That is a difference of 2 percent. Another way of looking at this is

TABLE 5.11 Medicaid Per Capita Expenditures (2019)

Red States	Per Capita Expenditures	Blue States	Per Capita Expenditures
Alabama	$5,582	California	$7,443
Alaska	$10,104	Connecticut	$8,405
Arizona	$7,074	Delaware	$9,634
Arkansas	$7,928	Hawaii	$6,890
Georgia	$5,373	Illinois	$7,003
Idaho	$7,966	Maine	$10,692
Indiana	$8,999	Maryland	$9,359
Kansas	$9,944	Massachusetts	$10,288
Kentucky	$6,827	Michigan	$7,608
Louisiana	$7,005	New Jersey	$10,066
Mississippi	$7,954	New Mexico	$6,712
Missouri	$10,607	New York	$9,762
Montana	$7,708	Oregon	$9,787
Nebraska	$9,759	Pennsylvania	$12,261
North Carolina	$6,820	Rhode Island	$12,457
North Dakota	$13,811	Vermont	$9,721
Oklahoma	$7,671	Washington	$8,389
South Carolina	$5,028		
South Dakota	$8,561		
Tennessee	$7,154		
Texas	$9,084		
Utah	$10,322		
West Virginia	$7,428		
Wyoming	$9,901		
Average	$8,302		$9,205
U.S. Average	$8,638		

Adapted from: Centers for Medicare and Medicaid Services (n.d.-b) Online at www.cms.gov.

to note that blue states spend about 20 percent more of their own funds on Medicaid than red states do.

Table 5.13 tells us that the federal government gives the states funds to help pay for Medicaid services. This money is known as the federal medical assistance percentage (FMAP). It is the percentage of money the federal government gives a state for the Medicaid program. Table 5.13 presents the data. The lowest percentage is 50 percent and the highest is 83 percent. In simple terms, the FMAP is based on a state's per capita income compared to the U.S. average income (MACPAC 2022). The lower a state's per

TABLE 5.12 Medicaid as Share of States' Total Budgets and State-Funded Budgets (2020)

Red States

	Total Budget (Millions of $)	Medicaid as Share of Total Budget	State-Funded Budget (Millions of $)	Medicaid as Share of State-Funded Budget
Alabama	31,638	22.5	19,364	8.9
Alaska	11,930	19.3	7,123	9.0
Arizona	40,784	32.0	23,889	14.1
Arkansas	27,775	26.9	18,277	8.9
Georgia	60,767	20.3	42,589	8.4
Idaho	11,708	20.6	6,724	11.9
Indiana	37,656	37.3	22,755	17.3
Kansas	19,412	19.5	14,763	9.7
Kentucky	38,434	30.2	21,253	11.5
Louisiana	31,078	40.5	16,597	19.7
Mississippi	19,919	27.8	11,428	10.7
Missouri	27,310	38.5	17,584	27.0
Montana	8,302	23.6	4,955	8.7
Nebraska	12,901	17.8	9,872	10.7
North Carolina	61,655	25.9	36,343	15.2
North Dakota	7,058	17.1	5,197	9.2
Oklahoma	24,799	22.3	16,037	12.9
South Carolina	26,949	26.4	17,956	11.0
South Dakota	4,851	18.6	3,017	11.2
Tennessee	36,048	34.4	21,810	20.3
Texas	1,36,396	27.6	88,466	11.5
Utah	18,155	19.0	13,369	8.5
West Virginia	18,496	22.5	13,643	6.0
Wyoming	4,708	13.1	3,864	7.6
Average	$29,947.04	25.11	$19,036.46	12.08

Blue States

	Total Budget (Millions of $)	Medicaid as Share of Total Budget	State-Funded Budget (Millions of $)	Medicaid as Share of State-Funded Budget
California	3,57,086	27.0	2,08,090	17.0
Connecticut	34,031	24.7	27,438	16.3
Delaware	11,887	19.6	9,181	8.0
Hawaii	18,134	12.0	15,299	5.0
Illinois	77,813	30.2	59,806	17.1
Maine	10,545	30.9	6,362	18.0
Maryland	48,578	24.3	32,538	13.7
Massachusetts	63,085	29.3	46,359	20.6
Michigan	62,318	31.0	36,369	14.5
New Jersey	66,760	24.5	48,438	11.9
New Mexico	22,346	30.2	12,790	10.6
New York	1,72,981	37.1	1,12,293	21.5
Oregon	48,808	21.0	35,304	7.6
Pennsylvania	96,018	36.0	59,277	21.5
Rhode Island	11,417	22.8	6,942	14.7
Vermont	6,175	27.0	3,951	16.7
Washington	54,299	24.6	40,174	12.0
Average	$68,369.47	26.60	$44,741.82	14.51

Adapted from: MACPAC (2022). Online at www.macpac.gov.

TABLE 5.13 FMAP Payments

Red States			Blue States		
	Medicaid	CHIP		Medicaid	CHIP
	Percentages (FY 2023)	Percentages (FY 2023)		Percentages (FY 2023)	Percentages (FY 2023)
Alabama	72.43	80.70	California	50.00	65.00
Alaska	50.00	65.00	Connecticut	50.00	65.00
Arizona	69.56	78.69	Delaware	58.49	70.94
Arkansas	71.31	79.92	Hawaii	56.06	69.24
Georgia	66.02	76.21	Illinois	50.00	65.00
Idaho	70.11	79.08	Maine	63.29	74.30
Indiana	65.66	75.96	Maryland	50.00	65.00
Kansas	59.76	71.83	Massachusetts	65.00	65.00
Kentucky	72.17	80.52	Michigan	64.71	75.30
Louisiana	67.28	77.10	New Jersey	50.00	65.00
Mississippi	77.86	95.39	New Mexico	73.26	81.28
Missouri	65.81	76.07	New York	50.00	65.00
Montana	64.12	74.88	Oregon	60.36	72.22
Nebraska	57.87	70.51	Pennsylvania	52.00	66.40
North Carolina	67.71	77.40	Rhode Island	53.96	67.77
North Dakota	51.55	66.09	Vermont	55.82	69.07
Oklahoma	67.36	77.15	Washington	50.00	65.00
South Carolina	70.58	79.41			
South Dakota	56.74	69.72			
Tennessee	66.10	76.27			
Texas	59.87	71.91			
Utah	65.90	76.13			
West Virginia	74.02	81.81			
Wyoming	50.00	65.00			
Average	64.99	75.95		56.06	68.62

Adapted from: MACPAC (2022). Online at www.macpac.gov.

capita income, the higher the FMAP. Additionally, Table 5.12 shows Medicaid spending without the FMAP. The first data column shows the total state budget. Clearly, there are differences among the states. Wyoming has the lowest total budget at just over $4 billion. California has by far the largest total budget, at more than $357 billion dollars. The average blue state has a state budget with federal transfers that is 228% higher than the average red state. The second column shows the percentage of the total state budget that is devoted to Medicaid. This column reflects federal transfer payments including the FMAP. Here we can see that the total percentage is higher for the blue states than for the red states.

Now consider the third data column. It shows the total state budget without any federal transfers. This is completely state-funded. Wyoming again has the smallest state budget at $3.8 billion dollars. California still has by far the highest state budget at just over $208 billion. The average blue state budget is 235% higher than the average red state budget. Now consider the final data column for our two groups of states. The average percentage of own state funding for Medicaid on the part of red states is just over 12 percent. For the blue states, the average is just over 14.5%, two-and-a-half percent higher than the red states. This is a difference of just over 20 percent.

What do these two tables tell us? Blue states have higher budgets than red states, reflecting the greater income of blue states compared to red states. If we look at percentages of state budget dedicated to Medicaid, we can see that blue states devote more of their budget to Medicaid than red states do. The federal transfer payments, FMAP, make up for some of the differences, but it is clear that the blue states have dedicated more of their resources to Medicaid than have red states.

Enrollment

As of December 2022, enrollment in Medicaid was 92.3 million people (Corallo and Moreno 2023). In February 2020, enrollment was 81.1 million people. The 29.8% increase in enrollment was a reaction to the COVID-19 pandemic (see below and Chapter 7). Enrollment was especially notable among adults. There was a decline in enrollment from 2017 through 2019 as the Trump administration put barriers in the way of implementing Medicaid and, to a lesser extent, CHIP (Corallo and Moreno 2023).

Medicaid and CHIP covered about 18.3% of the population in 2021, and 38% of children under the age of 18 (MACPAC 2022). The next two tables explore Medicaid population coverage. Table 5.14 takes a broad look at the extent of Medicaid coverage. The U.S. average, using 2021 data, was 20.45 percent. That is, a little more than 20 percent of the national population was covered by Medicaid. For the red states, the average percentage of the state population covered by Medicaid was just under the national average, at 19.7%, less than 1 percent lower than the national average. The blue states' average was 23.1%, about 13 percent higher than the national average and almost 17 percent higher than the red states.

Table 5.15 refines our examination of differences between the red and blue states a bit. Medicaid is designed to cover low-income people and families. And, as we shall see, it does not cover everyone who is low

TABLE 5.14 Percentage of State Population Covered by Medicaid (2021)

Red States	Percent of Population Covered	Blue States	Percent of Population Covered
North Dakota	10	New Jersey	18
Utah	11	Hawaii	20
Wyoming	12	Illinois	20
South Dakota	14	Maine	20
Kansas	15	Maryland	20
Missouri	15	Delaware	21
Nebraska	15	Pennsylvania	21
Texas	17	Washington	21
Georgia	18	Connecticut	23
Alabama	19	Massachusetts	23
North Carolina	19	Michigan	24
Idaho	20	Oregon	24
Indiana	20	Rhode Island	24
Montana	20	Vermont	25
Oklahoma	20	California	27
South Carolina	20	New York	28
Tennessee	20	New Mexico	34
Arizona	21		
Mississippi	24		
Alaska	26		
Arkansas	27		
West Virginia	28		
Kentucky	29		
Louisiana	32		
Average	19.67		23.12
U.S. Average	20.45		

Adapted from: Rudowitz et al. (2023). Online at www.kff.org.

income. We begin by looking at how low-income is defined. Table 5.15 defines low income as up to 200 percent of the FPL. The first data column shows the percentage of state and national population with income at or below 200 percent of the FPL. For the United States, that percentage is 29%. That is, 29 percent of the U.S. population lives at or below 200% of the FPL. For the red states, the percentage is just over 31%. For the blue states, the percentage below is almost 26%. On average, therefore, the red states have more poverty than the blue states. This fits into our discussion in Chapter 2 of economic differences between the two sets of states. Red states are, on average, poorer than blue states.

TABLE 5.15 Medicaid Low Income Coverage (2023)

Red States	% Low Income*	% Population Covered	% Low Income Not Covered	Blue States	% Low Income*	% Population Covered	% Low Income Not Covered
Alabama	35	19	16	California	28	26	2
Alaska	24	26	-2	Connecticut	22	23	-1
Arizona	30	21	9	Delaware	25	21	4
Arkansas	38	27	11	Hawaii	23	20	3
Georgia	31	18	13	Illinois	27	20	7
Idaho	30	20	10	Maine	27	19	8
Indiana	29	20	9	Maryland	22	20	2
Kansas	29	15	14	Massachusetts	21	23	-2
Kentucky	35	29	6	Michigan	30	24	6
Louisiana	38	32	6	New Jersey	22	18	4
Mississippi	40	24	16	New Mexico	39	34	5
Missouri	29	15	14	New York	28	28	0
Montana	29	20	9	Oregon	29	24	5
Nebraska	26	15	11	Pennsylvania	26	21	5
North Carolina	31	19	12	Rhode Island	25	24	1
North Dakota	25	10	15	Vermont	24	25	-1
Oklahoma	36	20	16	Washington	23	21	2
South Carolina	33	20	13				
South Dakota	27	14	13				
Tennessee	33	20	13				
Texas	32	17	15				
Utah	24	11	13				
West Virginia	36	28	8				
Wyoming	27	12	15				
Average	31.13	19.67	11.46		25.94	23.00	2.94
U.S. Average	29	21	8				

Adapted from: Kaiser Family Foundation (2023b). Online at www.kff.org.

* Low income is defined as 200% or less of the Federal Poverty Line.

The second data column reflects the willingness and effort states and the country as a whole made to medically cover low-income people and families. On average, 21 percent of the population was covered by Medicaid and 8 percent of low-income people were not covered. For the red states, almost 20 percent of the population was covered and almost 12 percent of low-income people were not covered. For the blue states, 23 percent of the population was covered implying that nearly 3 percent of low-income people were not covered. This is a dramatic difference between the red and blue states. The percentage of the low-income population in the blue states is about five points lower than the U.S. average and nearly nine points lower than the red states. One could conclude that the red states have more poverty in their population than blue states but do less to ensure they have medical care.

As we have mentioned before, states have considerable latitude in creating their unique Medicaid programs. Two ways that this can be seen are in which groups are covered and what benefits are allowed under the program.

Expanding Medicaid

In the previous chapter, we focused on the Patient Protection and Affordable Care Act, better known as the ACA (or Obamacare by its critics). A major purpose of the ACA is to increase the number of people with insurance coverage. It did that in several ways. One was through the establishment of state/federal markets or exchanges where people could purchase insurance policies and many of them would get subsidies to lower the cost of those policies. Another way was insurance reforms that made it easier for people to obtain and keep insurance policies (see Patel and Rushefsky 2020).

The ACA provided for a third way to increase coverage: expanding Medicaid. By 2010, the year the ACA was enacted into law by Congress, Medicaid already covered a significant portion of the country: an estimated 54.6 million people, almost 18 percent of the population (Centers for Disease Control and Prevention 2010). The uninsurance rate was 15.6 percent (Kaiser Family Foundation 2023g).

The Medicaid provision related to this chapter was to raise the income eligibility level to, effectively, 138% of the FPL. Adults without children often faced, as we have seen earlier in this chapter, an income eligibility level of zero. That is, they were ineligible to enroll no matter what their income. The ACA attempted to remedy this.

As we also discussed in Chapter 4, the legislation was the subject of much litigation and several U.S. Supreme Court decisions. The first one, again discussed in Chapter 4, was *NFIB v. Sebelius* (2012). *NFIB v. Sebelius* most famously addressed the constitutionality of the ACA, which we discussed in the previous chapter. But the ACA also required that states expand Medicaid or risk losing all of its Medicaid funding. The Court ruled in *NFIB v. Sebelius* that the penalty (the stick) of not expanding Medicaid was too severe. Thus, states had the option of expanding Medicaid or not expanding Medicaid. The Court did rule that once a state agreed to expand Medicaid, it had to follow all relevant federal regulations (Jones 2013).

The Court ruling also enhanced the federal nature of healthcare politics, where states could craft their own policies. If all the states had to comply with the 138% income eligibility requirement, there would have been more uniformity in state Medicaid programs. Absent the mandate, states were free to continue crafting their own versions of Medicaid.

NFIB v. Sebelius took away the stick policy tool from the federal government. But the "carrot" or positive incentives to expand Medicaid remained. The first and major carrot was that the federal government would pay 100 percent of the state expansion costs beginning in 2014. By 2016, that payment, the FMAP discussed above, would remain at the 90 percent level. This is a much higher FMAP than the federal government would pay for normal Medicaid. Any state that adopted Medicaid later than 2016 would be compensated at the 90 percent level.

Additionally, proponents of expansion argued that expansion was a really good deal for the states. For example, in the 2015–2019 period, those states that expanded Medicaid (see below) spent more on Medicaid, but that spending for those who were on traditional Medicaid (the non-expansion part) either stayed the same or decreased by over 4 percent (Coleman 2020). The reason is that states moved some of their Medicaid recipients to the expansion category. These states were spending 10 percent of Medicaid funding rather than 25–50 percent for each person in traditional Medicaid (Coleman 2020). Because of the differences in federal support between traditional and expansion Medicaid, states saved, depending on what their FMAP was, between 15 and 40 cents for each dollar transferred to the expansion category. There were also a greater set of benefits, for the most part, for those in the expansion category than those in traditional Medicaid.

Further, the expansion reduced the number of people receiving uncompensated care and also reduced spending for some other non-ACA programs such as substance use disorder and mental health. Even those in jails and prisons might benefit as the expansion covered some of them, again reducing state spending (Coleman 2023).

Ward (2020) points out, and we shall look at this in more detail below, that on the surface, state budgets will increase to fund the expansion (the 10 percent states have to pay), about $7 billion in 2020. Ward (2020) argues that there are three reasons why this "sticker price" is misleading. First, the expansion can lead to cuts in other parts of Medicaid as people are moved into the expansion program. Second, as discussed in the previous paragraph, the expansion can lead to cuts in other parts of a state's budget. Third, Medicaid expansion can lead to increased revenues.

This third way of state savings needs some explanation. There are three ways that states could enhance taxes. Some states had provider fees or taxes that grew as expansion grew. Some states imposed new taxes to cover costs, for example, on cigarettes or alcohol. Arkansas enacted a tax cut that was funded by savings from Medicaid expansion (Ward 2020).

The additional federal funding, what might be called a "spigot," can increase economic activity and result in new jobs. And that additional economic activity results in additional state revenues (Ward 2020).

Some states have sought to impose premiums and/or cost-sharing on those in the expansion program as a way of paying for the additional expenditures. This may seem to raise more money for states to pay their 10 percent share, but it actually deters people from enrolling and increases the costs of administering the program. As a result, the effects mentioned above are lessened (Ward 2020).

Given these advantages of expansion, which seem almost miraculous, we would expect states to rush in and adopt expansion. But as Table 5.16 shows, that is not the case. Table 5.16 presents several important pieces of information.

First, the table shows who adopted and did not adopt Medicaid expansion. As can be seen in the table, all the blue states have adopted the expanded Medicaid program. Of the 24 red states, 15 have adopted Medicaid expansion and nine have not.

A second piece of information is when states adopted the expansion. The table shows that most of the blue states adopted expansion at the earliest point, in 2014. The exceptions are Pennsylvania, which adopted in 2015, and Maine, which adopted in 2019. The red states are all over the place in terms of adoption. Five red states adopted in 2014, two in 2015, two in 2016, two in 2020, two in 2021, and two in 2023. This suggests reluctance on the part of some red states, especially those that adopted in 2020 and after.

There is a third important piece of information the table gives us. This has to do with the process by which states adopted Medicaid expansion. There are four approaches states could take to approve expansion (Antonisse and Rudowitz 2019). The first approach is through the passage of legislation. The state passes a law that marks the approval. This usually requires that a state governor and legislature support the change, though

TABLE 5.16 Expansion and Non-Expansion States (2023)

Red States	Implemented	Year	Adoption Process	Blue States	Implemented	Year	Adoption Process
Alabama	No			California	Yes	2014	Leg?
Alaska	Yes	2015	Executive Order	Connecticut	Yes	2014	Legislation
Arizona	Yes	2014	1115 Waiver	Delaware	Yes	2014	
Arkansas	Yes	2014	1115 Waiver	Hawaii	Yes	2014	
Georgia	No			Illinois	Yes	2014	Legislation
Idaho	Yes	2020	Ballot Initiative	Maine	Yes	2019	Ballot Initiative
Indiana	Yes	2015	1115 Waiver	Maryland	Yes	2014	
Kansas	No			Massachusetts	Yes	2014	
Kentucky	Yes	2014	Executive Order	Michigan	Yes	2014	1115 Waiver
Louisiana	Yes	2016	Executive Order	New Jersey	Yes	2014	
Mississippi	No			New Mexico	Yes	2014	
Missouri	Yes	2021	Ballot Initiative	New York	Yes	2014	
Montana	Yes	2016	1115 Waiver	Oregon	Yes	2014	
Nebraska	yes	2020	Ballot Initiative	Pennsylvania	Yes	2015	1115 Waiver/traditional
North Carolina	Yes	2023		Rhode Island	Yes	2014	
North Dakota	Yes	2014	Legislation	Vermont	Yes	2014	
Oklahoma	Yes	2021	Ballot Initiative	Washington	Yes	2014	
South Carolina	No						
South Dakota	Yes	2023	Ballot Initiative				
Tennessee	No						
Texas	No						
Utah	Yes	2020	Ballot Initiative				
West Virginia	Yes	2014	Executive Order				
Wyoming	No						

Adapted from: Coleman and Federman (2022). Online at www.commonwealthfund.org and Kaiser Family Foundation (2023c). Online at www.kff.org.

in some cases the governor supported the change and lobbied the legislature to make the change. North Dakota, Illinois, and Connecticut are examples of states that took this approach.

A second approach is approval of expansion via executive order of the state governor. Several states, such as Alaska, Kentucky, and Louisiana, are examples of this. This approach is used when the governor supports expansion, but the legislature does not. Kentucky is an excellent example of this. In these cases, the governor is generally a Democrat, and the state legislature is generally controlled by Republicans (Antonisse and Rudowitz 2019).

A third approach involves the use of section 1115 waivers. In this approach, expansion is adopted with conditions contained in the waiver. The waiver may make use of Medicaid as premium assistance to purchase private policies, including those available through the ACA exchanges. Some states considered waivers to impose work requirements on Medicaid recipients (see below). Pennsylvania and Michigan were the two blue states that made use of the 1115 Section waivers. Arizona, Arkansas, Indiana, and Montana are the red states that used this approach (Antonisse and Rudowitz 2019). Kansas Governor Laura Kelly proposed a work requirement in December 2023 as a means of attracting Republican state legislatures to approve Medicaid expansion (Shorman and Ritter 2023). In South Dakota, where voters approved a Medicaid expansion initiative, two Republican legislators offered a bill that would add work requirements to the expansion (Todd 2023).

The last approach is perhaps the most interesting, the ballot initiative. In this approach, a petition process is used to obtain a sufficient number of registered voters (which varies depending on the state) to put a ballot proposal up for vote. This usually takes place when neither the state legislature nor the governor supports expansion. This usually means that both branches of state government are controlled by Republicans. The initiative process is used mostly by states in the western portion of the country and has resulted in things like legalization of medical and/or recreational marijuana and approval of abortion rights at the state level (see Chapter 7). In this case, the procedure has been used to approve Medicaid expansion (Antonisse and Rudowitz 2019). Table 5.16 shows that Maine was the only blue state to use this process, whereas six red states used this process. Perhaps the most interesting of the states was Missouri.

Missouri has shown much resistance to the ACA over the years. As we saw in Chapter 4, Missouri did not set up its own insurance exchanges, relying instead on federally run markets. Further, the state legislature passed a law that included a provision forbidding any state money to be used to pay navigators, people who help others find the best plans for them on the exchanges. It should not be surprising, therefore, that the state did not embrace Medicaid expansion. Missouri, prior to expansion, had one of the most restrictive Medicaid income eligibility policies in the country. A family of three with an income more than 21 percent of the FPL would not qualify for Medicaid. And childless adults were not eligible for Medicaid no matter how low their income (Sullivan 2021). Medicaid expansion would make a big difference if adopted.

But, as noted, Missouri was one of several states that voted on whether to expand Medicaid. As with all the other ballot initiatives, in August 2020, Missouri voters approved an amendment to the Missouri Constitution, with 53 percent of voters favoring expansion. However, the state legislature refused to appropriate money to run the program. In May of 2021, the Missouri Governor, Mike Pence, stated that because the legislature had not approved funding, Medicaid expansion would not be implemented in Missouri (Sullivan 2021). However, two court decisions moved Missouri closer to expansion. In July 2021, the state Supreme Court ruled that those who enrolled through the expanded program must be considered in the same pool as those in traditional Medicare and thus funded (Rosenbaum 2021). And a circuit court ruling in August 2021 required the state to implement the expansion (Weinberg 2021).

But this is not the whole story. Missouri continued to resist aggressively implementing Medicaid expansion. States that expanded Medicaid in recent years (see Table 5.16) saw massive signups for the expanded program. For example, the neighboring state of Oklahoma saw an increased enrollment of 200,000 early in the enrollment period, compared to about one-tenth of that amount in Missouri. The difference is that the Oklahoma legislature quickly appropriated the needed funds and then engaged in an extensive outreach program to those who might be eligible. In North Carolina, applications to the expansion program began in December 2023. Approximately 280,000 people enrolled by the middle of the month with another 56,000 more applications. North Carolina was enthusiastic in its outreach program to gain new enrollees, especially with marginal populations (Guinassi 2023).

In the case of Missouri, the state was slow in processing applications, and publicity about the program was limited to several postings on social media. This has changed, and by the beginning of 2023, over 300,000 people were enrolled in the expanded program (Norris 2023).

One question that can be asked is why red states were hesitant to expand Medicaid. After all, several studies plus the experiences of expansion states showed the benefits of expansion beyond just covering more people. There are a number of explanations for this hesitancy. First, Republicans unanimously opposed the ACA, as we discussed in Chapter 4. No

TABLE 5.17 Work Requirement Waivers

Red States		Blue States	
Alabama	Pending	California	
Alaska	Approved	Connecticut	
Arizona	Approved	Delaware	
Arkansas	Approved	Hawaii	
Georgia	Approved	Illinois	
Idaho	Pending	Maine	
Indiana	Approved	Maryland	Approved
Kansas	Pending	Massachusetts	
Kentucky	Approved	Michigan	Approved
Louisiana		New Jersey	
Mississippi	Pending	New Mexico	
Missouri		New York	
Montana	Pending	Oregon	
Nebraska	Approved	Pennsylvania	
North Carolina		Rhode Island	
North Dakota		Vermont	
Oklahoma	Pending	Washington	
South Carolina	Approved		
South Dakota	Pending		
Tennessee	Pending		
Texas			
Utah	Approved		
West Virginia			
Wyoming			

Adapted from: Kaiser Family Foundation (2023e). Online at www.kff.org.

Republicans in Congress voted for the proposal in 2010. A second reason is that state legislators did not want to pay the extra money for the program, despite the larger FMAP for the expansion and thus the smaller amount needed to pay. A third explanation is that Republicans did not trust that the federal government would keep its end of the deal, despite the 55 years of experience with federal funding. State Republican lawmakers have also argued that the expansion "oversteps" federal authority with the amount of money being spent on the program. Instead, advocates of this position argue that more effort should be directed toward private insurers and private markets (Neukam 2023).

Another argument against Medicaid expansion is that it takes the focus away from the most needy, such as the elderly and the disabled. Instead, it brings in childless adults at a higher rate than traditional Medicaid (Plescia 2023). There is also the argument that expansion, adding more people to Medicaid, would result in longer waiting times to see a doctor. This is partially because the number of doctors remains the same. More people, the same number of doctors = longer waiting times (Plescia 2023). Part of the reason is that Medicaid pays providers at a lower rate than either Medicare or private insurance and doctors can refuse to see Medicaid patients. Another part of the refusal to take Medicaid patients is that Medicaid denials are higher than for either Medicare or privately insured patients (Dunn et al. 2023).

Apart from the Medicaid expansion that was part of the 2010 ACA legislation, the Biden administration added an additional incentive. In response to the COVID-19 pandemic (see Chapter 7), Congress passed the American Rescue Act of 2021. Under the provisions of the law, states that had not expanded would be given an additional 5 percent increase in the FMAP if they expanded. The additional money for states newly approving expansion would be high enough that states would get a benefit of almost $10 billion over the two-year period of the increase (Rudowitz and Corallo 2021).

Medicaid expansion has had positive effects, despite what critics have maintained. One such effect is that it increases access to care (Advocacy Research Center 2020). This included an increase in the number of people in the expansion states who had regular access to care, such as those with chronic conditions. There was also an increase in preventive care visits in expansion states, whereas there was no such increase in non-expansion states. Perhaps most importantly, there was a decrease in the use of emergency services in expansion states.

A second positive outcome, in this case a very obvious one, was a decrease in the number and percentage of people uninsured (Advocacy Research Center 2020). A third positive outcome has to do with work. Studies have shown that almost two-thirds of those who got Medicaid because of expansion were in families where someone was working. And having Medicaid through expansion made it easier for recipients to get jobs, especially with small employers who are unlikely to offer health insurance as a benefit. Additionally, a study in California found a correlational effect with payday loans. The effect was that the use of payday loans decreased after expansion (Advocacy Resource Center 2020). We discuss work requirements and Medicaid in the next section.

A fourth, related, benefit of Medicaid expansion was that there was a decrease in delaying care because of cost and less trouble in paying bills (Advocacy Research Center 2020). This follows from more people having a regular source of care and decreases in the usage of emergency services.

One of the criticisms about Medicaid and expansion is that its impact on the health of recipients seems to be low, an argument we mentioned above. But studies, again, have shown this to not be the case. There was a decrease in death rates among low-income adults in expansion states.

There was a decrease in the number of uninsured low-income people diagnosed with cancer (Advocacy Research Center 2020). The following quote captures much of the direction of the research:

> Longitudinal research has found that individuals eligible for Medicaid since childhood had better health outcomes, and less hospitalizations and emergency room visits in adulthood than their non-eligible peers.
> (Advocacy Research Center 2020, 3)

In addition to the health effects discussed in the previous paragraphs, Medicaid has also had economic effects. Expansion can lead to new jobs and more funds for providers. The Advocacy Research Center (2020) of the AMA cites a study by the Urban Institute that estimates that in the period from 2017 to 2026, each dollar spent on expansion by states leads to receiving $7–$8 from the federal government. Expansion states experienced more job growth because of expansion than non-expansion states. One of the more interesting effects of expansion is on hospital revenues. Hospitals often have to absorb the cost of care for people who lack insurance and do not have the funds to pay for hospital stays. Hospitals in expansion states experienced a decrease in this charitable spending because more patients were covered by the Medicaid expansion. This was especially true for rural hospitals. Such hospitals, for a variety of reasons, experience fiscal distress leading to a decrease in services and, sometimes, hospital closures (see, for example, Carroll et al. 2023). Medicaid expansion has improved the financial situation of rural hospitals and makes it less likely that such hospitals would close (Advocacy Resource Center 2020).

Expansion has also helped the larger healthcare system. Premiums for ACA marketplace plans were lower in expansion states than in non-expansion states. Those eligible for coverage in expansion states spent less on healthcare than those in non-expansion states (Advocacy Resource Center).

Finally, if the states that had not expanded Medicaid did so, over three million more people could be covered by Medicaid and receive the benefits discussed in the previous paragraphs (Buettgens and Ramchandami 2022; Mitchell 2021). This gap became critical when the COVID-19 pandemic began in 2019 (see below and Chapter 7).

Work Requirements

Earlier we mentioned Section 1115 waiver provisions that are part of the Social Security Act. States can and have used the provision to make changes in their Medicaid programs. There are a wide variety of requests that have been made, resulting in another way in which state Medicaid programs differ from each other. The federal government must approve the requests and there are time limits on the waivers. The following paragraph provides a brief description of the kinds of changes requested through the Section 1115 waiver provisions.

> Key themes in current approved and pending waivers include targeted eligibility expansions, benefit expansions (particularly in the area of behavioral health, such as coverage of services provided in IMDs), and provisions related to social determinants of health. States may obtain "comprehensive" Section 1115 waivers that make broad changes in Medicaid eligibility, benefits, provider payments, and other rules across their programs; other waivers may be more narrow and address specific populations or benefits.
> *(Kaiser Family Foundation 2023d)*

Federal administrations differed in what kinds of waivers they would support. The Obama administration used waivers as a substitute for Medicaid expansion. States that did not expand Medicaid by statute, executive order, or ballot initiatives could still expand through these waivers. Those states that used the waiver procedure to expand coverage, as opposed to adopting it, saw decreases in uninsurance rates similar to what expansion states experienced. On the other hand, waiver expansion was sometimes restrictive by states either requiring contributions from beneficiaries or through work requirements (see below) (Guth, Garfield, and Rudowitz 2020).

The Trump administration (2017–2021) had different priorities. It focused on work requirements and approved work requirement waivers in 13 states. Those waivers were withdrawn by the Biden administration, which focused on using waivers to expand Medicaid coverage, particularly in areas such as social determinants of health (Kaiser Family Foundation 2023e).

Work requirements were an important response on the part of mostly red states to Medicaid expansion. Medicaid is a means-tested program, similar to the Temporary Assistance for Needy Families and the SNAP. Both programs have work requirements (Bauer and East 2023; Guth and Musumeci 2022) The idea behind work requirements is that if there is an adult, especially an able-bodied adult without dependents (abbreviated as ABAWDS), he or she should be engaged in some work-related activity. This could be a job, training, or education (Bauer and East 2023). The requirement, generally favored by Republicans, is that the country does not support those not willing to work. But Medicaid did not contain such a provision (Guth and Musumeci 2022).

The Trump administration encouraged states to utilize Section 1115 waivers to include a work requirement in their Medicaid programs. And some states would only expand Medicaid if a work requirement was included. The arguments in favor of work requirements in Medicaid include that it would give Medicaid recipients "skin in the game" (Musumeci 2017), it would prepare recipients for work, it would end dependence on government handouts, and that expansion to able-bodied adults is a disincentive to work. Such a view sees Medicaid as akin to TANF or SNAP, which are cash-based welfare programs, rather than health insurance (Musumeci 2017).

The arguments against work requirements in Medicaid are numerous. First, TANF has as one of its goals to promote independence, work, and marriage. But Medicaid has never had such a purpose, nor does the ACA. Rather, the purpose of both programs is to provide health insurance for those who cannot get it on their own. A second argument is that Medicaid actually supports work in several ways. Not all jobs provide health insurance. Those who work and become sick and have health insurance can get healthcare and keep their jobs (Guth and Musumeci 2022).

Another problem is administrative. Applying for Medicaid is a complex process, though somewhat simplified by the ACA. Medicaid recipients are required to periodically file paperwork showing any changes to their income situation and their work compliance. If the paperwork is not filed in a timely fashion or is incomplete or incorrect in some way, then the recipient may lose his or her Medicaid eligibility (Guth and Musumeci 2022).

As Table 5.17 shows, the Trump administration approved nine work requirement waivers in red states and two in blue states. An additional seven red state proposals were pending as of 2021. Two blue states had approved work requirement waivers. Sixteen red states had either approved waivers or pending waivers. Just under 12 percent of blue states had approved waivers.

Despite these approvals, very little of the work requirements were actually implemented. Arkansas had the most experience with such requirements but about one-quarter of those who might be required to work lost coverage. Guth and Musumeci (2022) point out that there were numerous reasons why people might lose coverage because of work requirements. These included attempts to report disabilities and the lack of internet access and computer literacy. It was difficult for these Medicaid recipients to report their activities and they were often confused or unaware of new requirements. In any event, after seven months of implementing work requirements in the Arkansas program, a federal court dismissed the program because the impact on coverage was not considered. For similar reasons, the Kentucky work requirements waiver was also rejected by the courts (Guth and Musumeci 2022).

TABLE 5.18 Structure of Medicaid Population and Expenditures

	Percent of Medicaid Population	Percent of Total Expenditures by Group
Children	40	17
Expansion Adults	22	17
Other Adults	17	10
Disabled Individuals	11	34
Individuals Based on Age	10	21

Adapted from: Rudowitz et al. (2023). Online at www.kff.org.

The Biden administration, as mentioned above, opposed the work requirements. In 2021, the Centers for Medicare and Medicaid Services withdrew all approvals for work requirement waivers and the U.S. Supreme Court dismissed all cases challenging the withdrawals in 2022 (Guth and Musumeci 2022). Of course, a future administration might favor such requirements and approve waiver requests.

There is one other thing that explains why work requirements were unlikely to be successful: the nature of the Medicaid population. Table 5.18 presents the data. The table shows national data, but percentages are pretty much the same in the states. The table shows that the largest portion of the Medicaid population are children. Adults make up about 39 percent of the Medicaid population. Those with disabilities make up 11 percent of the population and the aged make up 10 percent. If we look at expenditures, we find that the disabled and the elderly account for 55 percent of expenditures, the most of any of the groups. Children account for 17 percent (Rudowitz et al. 2023). So the first thing this tells us is that we are looking at what can be called the "concentration of healthcare spending" in the Medicaid population. To really save money, which is a high priority of the red states, one would look at the groups that account for the most. But the elderly, the disabled, and children, understandably, were not subject to work requirements.

A related point is that much of the Medicaid population that would have come under the work requirement were already in families where someone worked or was ineligible to work for various reasons. Sixty percent of eligible recipients were already working. There were several reasons why people did not work. Thirty-six percent were ill or disabled. Another 30 percent were taking care of their family. Fifteen percent were in school. Nine percent were retired (2018 data) (Luhby 2018; see also Guth et al. 2023 and Garfield, Rudowitz, and Damico 2018).

The attempt to add work requirements to Medicaid reappeared briefly in the spring of 2023. Republicans had regained control of the U.S. House of Representatives in the 2022 mid-term elections, albeit with a small majority of four votes. A small portion (about 50 members) of the Republican caucus formed what is known as the "Freedom Caucus," the most conservative of an already conservative House Majority ("What is the House Freedom Caucus?" 2023).

One of the important tasks of Congress is to deal with federal budget issues. And the Constitution states that all revenue bills begin in the House. Whether Democratically- or Republican-controlled, Congress has not done a very good job in fulfilling its budget task, rarely passing most of its 12 appropriations bills (see, for example, Burman 2020). What Congress usually winds up doing is passing continuing resolutions that allow the federal government to function for a period of time. Eventually, through something called a reconciliation act, Congress may fund the government through the rest of the fiscal year. Failure to pass any of these pieces of legislation would lead to a partial shutdown of the government. The continual resolutions and reconciliation acts provide an opportunity to add provisions that may or may not be related to the legislation itself.

The same is true of the debt ceiling (see, for example, Neuman, Ahn, and Horsley 2023). The United States needs to borrow money to pay its bills. The yearly budget deficits add to the budget debt. Congress, by law, sets a ceiling on how much the federal government can owe. In 2023, the government had a debt of over $33 trillion. Raising the debt ceiling allows the government to keep borrowing money and spending it and paying interest on the debt. Conservatives, among others, criticize this very large debt and the large interest payments that accompany it. The debt ceiling, like the budget-related bills, provides an opportunity to tack on legislation that may or may not be related to debt. The Freedom Caucus used this opportunity in the spring of 2023 to add a work requirement to Medicaid.

The work requirement bill, similar to the Section 1115 waivers discussed above, would require certain Medicaid recipients to work for a minimum of eighty hours a week or training or community service (Giled and Dong 2023). The bill was very specific as to who was targeted for the work requirements:

> The requirements would apply to enrollees who do not have dependents and who are 19 to 55 years old, physically and mentally fit for employment, not pregnant, not enrolled in an education program, and not participating in a drug or alcohol treatment and rehabilitation program.
>
> (Giled and Dong 2023)

One estimate, based on 2019 data, was that as much as 14 million Medicaid recipients (roughly 20 percent of all Medicaid recipients) would fit this definition of eligible people. That same estimate suggested that, given reasons for not participating in work, only about 1.7 million (a little more than 12 percent of the original 14 million and about 1 percent of the total Medicaid population) would be required to work (authors' calculations from Giled and Dong 2023). Medicaid recipients would have to prove that they are exempt from the work requirements and failure to do so could result in their loss of Medicaid coverage. This was the experience in Arkansas mentioned above.

All told, work requirements, whether in TANF or SNAP or Medicaid, have had limited effect, though red states tend to support them (Guth and Musumeci 2022).

Churning and the Great Unwinding

Churning

As mentioned at the beginning of this chapter, Medicaid and Medicare, both publicly supported healthcare insurance programs, were enacted in 1965. A major difference between them focuses on eligibility for the programs. For Medicare, eligibility is based on age (65+) or disability. The paperwork requirement to get on Medicare is relatively simple, especially if one is eligible because of age, where enrollment in Part A is automatic.

Medicaid is a whole other matter. The focus is on those who meet income eligibility requirements, as discussed earlier in the chapter. There is nothing automatic about getting on Medicaid. One must meet the income requirements (this is oversimplifying a bit) by providing proof of income and assets. And states require that recipients demonstrate eligibility at least once a year or lose their coverage. Prior to policies adopted because of the COVID-19 pandemic, eligibility checks could come monthly (Goldman and Sommers 2020). The process of getting on Medicaid and regaining Medicaid coverage is difficult involving much paperwork. Sometimes errors occur, denying some coverage who are eligible (Ruff and Fishman 2019).

The basic idea is that if a recipient or family becomes ineligible, then they should not be covered by a program that costs taxpayer money. Prior to the COVID-19 pandemic (see below and Chapter 7), about 25 percent of beneficiaries lost coverage and then regained coverage, a process known as churning (Sugar et al. 2021). There are a number of reasons why a beneficiary might lose coverage. An important one is a change in income, also known as income volatility (Wagner and Solomon 2021). Perhaps a beneficiary who is working gets a pay raise which makes her ineligible for coverage in her state. Maybe the beneficiary gets a temporary job, say during the Christmas shopping season when stores hire people to help customers. Or, given that the authors live in southwest Missouri, the head of the family might get a job in Branson, a vacation resort open mostly in the spring and summer. This might lead to an increase in income enough to make the person/family ineligible for Medicaid. Once the temporary job ends, the person/family would become eligible again. But regaining eligibility takes time and results in a gap in coverage (Wagner and Solomon 2021). Medicaid beneficiaries are, on average, covered for ten months of the year (Sugar et al. 2021). Income volatility occurs for a significant portion of U.S. families. One estimate is that more than one-third of families will have such an experience (Pew Charitable Trusts 2017).

The gap could be more critical for women who have just given birth (here we are discussing the pre-COVID-19 period). Women on Medicaid are more likely to experience a gap in coverage (55 percent) compared to women with private health insurance (35 percent). As we discussed earlier, the postpartum (post-delivery period) is a vital one for the health of both the child and the mother. This gap in postpartum Medicaid care is larger for those for whom English is a second language and for those whose income does not fit in the required range (Sugar et al. 2021).

Other reasons for the existence of Medicaid churn include the end of pregnancy and state policies that make remaining on Medicaid difficult. Three of the red states, Missouri, Tennessee, and Arkansas, required that Medicaid recipients use either a phone or mail to help determine retention. Those three states did not allow beneficiaries to create an online account that could be used to help determine eligibility (Ruff and Fishman 2019). Calling on phones often requires long wait times. And recipients may have moved and thus not gotten the redetermination information and forms. The result is a significant drop in the number of renewals (Sugar et al. 2021; Wagner and Solomon 2021).

Churning can lead to disruption in care and increases in emergency department visits and hospitalizations (Goldman and Sommers 2020; Sugar et al. 2021). Churning can also result in changes in a patient's healthcare system, including providers and drug formularies (which drugs are available under a plan). This too leads to a discontinuity in care (Sugar et al. 2021).

Churning policies differed among the states. Table 5.19 gives us the first indicator of churn. In the period between 2017 and 2018, overall Medicaid enrollment declined by 2.2 percent. Red state Medicaid enrollment declined by a little more, 2.3 percent. There was an overall decline in blue state enrollment as well, but only by 1.7 percent. The largest declines came

TABLE 5.19 Medicaid Enrollment Changes (2017–2018)

Red States	Percentage Change	Blue States	Percentage Change
Tennessee	-9.7	Illinois	-7.0
Arkansas	-7.3	Massachusetts	-5.4
Missouri	-7.2	Hawaii	-4.5
Wyoming	-5.9	New Jersey	-2.5
Idaho	-5.4	California	-2.3
Utah	-4.9	New Mexico	-2.1
Mississippi	-4.8	Vermont	-2.1
Kentucky	-4.0	Washington	-2.0
Texas	-3.7	Maine	-1.6
West Virginia	-3.2	Michigan	-1.1
North Dakota	-3.1	Pennsylvania	-1.1
Indiana	-1.8	Rhode Island	-0.7
South Dakota	-1.5	Maryland	-0.4
Arizona	-0.9	Oregon	0.2
Oklahoma	-0.7	Delaware	0.4
Louisiana	-0.4	New York	0.8
North Carolina	-0.4	Connecticut	2.3
Kansas	0.0		
Nebraska	0.1		
Georgia	0.4		
Alabama	0.7		
South Carolina	1.2		
Montana	1.8		
Alaska	5.9		
Average Red States	-2.3	Average Blue States	-1.7
U.S. Average	-2.2		

Adapted with permission from: Ruff and Fishman (2019). Online at www.familiesusa.org.

in the red states of Alaska, Arkansas, Idaho, Mississippi, Missouri, North Dakota, Tennessee, Texas, Utah, West Virginia, and Wyoming. Among the blue states, Hawaii, Illinois, and Massachusetts had high enrollment declines. Sugar et al. (2021) argue that it was differences in state policies that resulted in differences in enrollment declines. They also asserted that a major reason for moving people off Medicaid was faulty processes that created difficult barriers, some of which were discussed above. As one example, some states sent letters to beneficiaries asking for more information and gave them ten days to respond. But sometimes, it took more than ten days for the letters to reach the beneficiaries, resulting in loss of eligibility

TABLE 5.20 Continuous Eligibility Policies (2019)

Red States		Blue States	
Alabama	Yes	California	Yes
Alaska	Yes	Connecticut	No
Arizona	No	Delaware	No
Arkansas	No	Hawaii	No
Georgia	No	Illinois	Yes
Idaho	Yes	Maine	Yes
Indiana	No	Maryland	Yes
Kansas	Yes	Massachusetts	No
Kentucky	No	Michigan	Yes
Louisiana	Yes	New Jersey	Yes
Mississippi	Yes	New Mexico	Yes
Missouri	No	New York	Yes
Montana	Yes	Oregon	Yes
Nebraska	No	Pennsylvania	No
North Carolina	Yes	Rhode Island	No
North Dakota	Yes	Vermont	No
Oklahoma	No	Washington	Yes
South Carolina	Yes		
South Dakota	No		
Tennessee	No		
Texas	No		
Utah	No		
West Virginia	Yes		
Wyoming	Yes		

Adapted from: Brooks, Roygardner, and Artiga (2019). Online at www.kff.org.

(Sugar et al. 2021). Missouri stopped automatically using data from TANF or SNAP, thus requiring beneficiaries to provide information already provided to those programs (Ruff and Fishman 2019).

One way of reducing churn is to have continuous eligibility for a year. Even if a person or a family became temporarily ineligible, they would be able to stay on Medicaid for a year. Table 5.20 presents the data. Eleven of our 24 red states or about 46 percent had such policies. Nine out of 17 blue states, nearly 53 percent, had such policies (Brooks, Roygardner, and Artiga 2019). Additionally, and in line with previous paragraphs, there is some evidence that churn was reduced for low-income adults in states that expanded Medicaid as compared to states that did not expand (Goldman and Sommers 2020).

The federal government has offered policies to reduce churning (Sugar et al. 2021). These included encouraging non-expansion states to adopt expansion, offering higher FMAP payments, continuous coverage policies, continuous eligibility policies, and extending postpartum coverage to 12 months, among others (Sugar et al. 2021).

The Great Unwinding

We now turn to what we are going to call "the great unwinding." The issue is the beginning and ending of the COVID-19 pandemic public health emergency, which we discuss in Chapter 7. As the pandemic grew in the United States in 2020 and 2021, hospitals were finding themselves overflowing with COVID-19 patients. And many of the patients did not have health insurance. Here is where the federal government stepped in, especially during the Biden administration.

In March 2020, during the Trump administration, Congress passed legislation requiring states to keep recipients on Medicaid until the end of the COVID-19 pandemic, even if their income increased and exceeded state eligibility standards. The legislation also contained a provision increasing states' FMAP by 6.2% for all states (Congressional Research Service 2023). The purpose of the legislation was to cut down on churn and ensure that people would be insured during the pandemic (Erzouki 2023). The result was that Medicaid enrollment drastically increased by about 23 million, reaching an estimated 95 million people by early 2023. The state of the economy during the pandemic, which weakened, and expansion by several states during this time also contributed to the massive Medicaid enrollment increase (Tolbert and Ammula 2023). Uninsurance rates declined.

Legislation passed at the end of 2022 ended the continuous eligibility program as of March 31, 2023. The March 2020 legislation linked continuous coverage to the COVID-19 public health emergency. The 2022 legislation uncoupled that link. Beginning on April 1, 2023, states could unenroll recipients from Medicaid (Wikle, Wagner, and Erzouki 2023).

Estimates of how many people would lose Medicaid eligibility from the unwinding varied from eight million to 24 million people (Tolbert and Ammula 2023). One reason for losing Medicaid eligibility is that a person's/family's income might have been too high prior to the 2020 legislation. Another major reason is what has been called procedural or administrative barriers: not filling out paperwork, not getting in touch with agencies, administrative barriers such as inability to get through to a call center, and so forth (Erzouki 2023).

The unwinding created an enormous task for states. States had to set dates for beginning the terminations, some as early as April 1, 2023. The federal government gave states up to a year to begin the renewal process

TABLE 5.21 Medicaid Renewal Timetable (2023)

Red States			Blue States		
	First Month Unwinding Related Renewals are Initiated	Effective Date for First Anticipated Terminations for Procedural Reasons		First Month Unwinding Related Renewals are Initiated	Effective Date for First Anticipated Terminations for Procedural Reasons
Alabama	April	June	California	April	July
Alaska	April	June	Connecticut	March	May
Arizona	February	April	Delaware	April	July
Arkansas	February	April	Hawaii	April	June
Georgia	April	June	Illinois	April	July
Idaho	February	April	Maine	April	June
Indiana	March	May	Maryland	April	June
Kansas	March	May	Massachusetts	April	June
Kentucky	April	June	Michigan	April	June
Louisiana	April	July	New Jersey	April	June
Mississippi	March	June	New Mexico	March	May
Missouri	April	July	New York	March	July
Montana	April	June	Oregon	April	October
Nebraska	March	May	Pennsylvania	March	May
North Carolina	April	July	Rhode Island	April	June
North Dakota	April	June	Vermont	April	June
Oklahoma	March	May	Washington	April	June
South Carolina	April	June			
South Dakota	February	April			
Tennessee	March	June			
Texas	April	June			
Utah	March	May			
West Virginia	April	June			
Wyoming	March	May			

Adapted from: Centers for Medicaid and Medicare Services (2023). Online at www.cms.gov.

and 14 months to complete it (Wikle, Wagner, and Erzouki 2023). Table 5.21 shows which dates states picked to begin the renewal process and to make their first terminations. As the table shows, four of our blue states chose a date to begin the process prior to April 2023. That is about 23.5 percent of blue states. For red states, 12 of the 24 states, 50 percent of red states, chose an early start. Red states seemed to be more committed to reducing their Medicaid caseload than blue states.

This is reflected in different policies choices states made as to how to conduct the renewals and unwinding (Tolbert, Moreno, and Rudowitz 2023). Table 5.22 lists nine metrics that states might follow in their

TABLE 5.22 Unwinding Metrics

Renewal Policies

- State will take 12–14 months to complete all renewals
- State follows up on returned mail
- State follows up with enrollees who have not responded to a renewal request before terminating coverage

System Capacity Measures

- Processing of renewals is mostly automated
- 50% or more of renewals are completed on an *ex parte* basis
- State has taken steps to improve *ex parte* renewal rates

Eligibility Policies

- State has adopted the Medicaid expansion
- State has adopted 12-month postpartum coverage
- State has adopted 12-month continuous eligibility for all children in Medicaid and CHIP

Adapted from: Tolbert, Moreno, and Rudowitz (2023). Online at www.kff.org.

processes of determining whether someone will be removed from Medicaid.

Table 5.23 presents the data by state. Before we continue, one element of the table needs to be explained, the *ex parte* phrase. *Ex parte*, in this case, refers to renewing eligibility based on data that agencies have on hand (Tolbert, Moreno, and Rudowitz 2023). In the absence of such a process, agencies request information from Medicaid recipients. Obviously, the *ex parte* renewal process is quicker than requests, requires less agency staff, and requires less of recipients (Tolbert, Moreno, and Rudowitz 2023).

The fundamental idea behind Table 5.24 is that states have choices as to how they implement the unwinding. Those that have more of the metrics shown in Table 5.23 are likely to remove fewer Medicaid recipients than those that adopted fewer of the metrics. As the table shows, blue states have adopted more of these nine metrics, on average, than red states. The differences are relatively larger for the third set of metrics which deal with eligibility. The results follow from some of the tables discussed earlier in this chapter. For example, states differ on whether they expanded Medicaid and whether they expanded postpartum care to a year (Tolbert, Moreno, and Rudowitz 2023).

Using these metrics creates one way of looking at the capacity of states to determine continued eligibility during the unwinding process. States will

TABLE 5.23 States' Use of Unwinding Metrics

Red States	All Metrics	Renewal Policies	System Capacity	Eligibility Policies	Blue States	All Metrics	Renewal Policies	System Capacity	Eligibility Policies
Alabama	7	3	2	2	California	7	3	1	3
Alaska	5	3	0	2	Connecticut	7	2	3	2
Arizona	6	2	2	2	Delaware	6	3	1	2
Arkansas	3	2	0	1	Hawaii	5	2	1	2
Georgia	5	3	1	1	Illinois	8	3	2	2
Idaho	7	3	2	2	Maine	6	2	1	3
Indiana	8	3	3	2	Maryland	7	3	2	2
Kansas	5	2	1	2	Massachusetts	8	3	3	2
Kentucky	7	3	2	2	Michigan	8	3	3	2
Louisiana	7	2	2	3	New Jersey	6	3	1	2
Mississippi	6	3	1	2	New Mexico	8	2	3	3
Missouri	4	2	1	1	New York	7	3	1	3
Montana	7	2	2	3	Oregon	7	2	2	3
Nebraska	3	2	0	1	Pennsylvania	6	3	1	2
North Carolina	8	3	2	3	Rhode Island	6	3	1	2
North Dakota	7	3	1	3	Vermont	6	3	1	2
Oklahoma	4	0	2	2	Washington	8	3	2	3
South Carolina	6	3	1	2					
South Dakota	3	2	0	1					
Tennessee	6	3	2	1					
Texas									
Utah	5	3	1	1					
West Virginia	6	1	2	3					
Wyoming	4	2	0	2					
Average	5.6	2.4	1.3	1.9		6.8	2.7	1.6	2.4

Adapted from: Tolbert, Moreno, and Rudowitz (2023). Online at www.kff.org.

TABLE 5.24 Disenrollment and Renewal Rates (December 2023)

Red States	Disenrollment Rate (Percent)	Renewal Rate (Percent)	Blue States	Disenrollment Rate (Percent)	Renewal Rate (Percent)
Alabama	33	67	California	27	73
Alaska	53	47	Connecticut	23	77
Arizona	25	75	Delaware	29	71
Arkansas	59	41	Hawaii	26	74
Georgia	56	44	Illinois	10	90
Idaho	60	40	Maine	10	90
Indiana	35	65	Maryland	18	82
Kansas	41	59	Massachusetts		
Kentucky	32	68	Michigan	36	64
Louisiana	36	64	New Jersey	41	59
Mississippi	35	65	New Mexico	33	67
Missouri	30	70	New York	31	69
Montana	58	42	Oregon	13	87
Nebraska	31	69	Pennsylvania	35	65
North Carolina	20	80	Rhode Island	36	64
North Dakota	41	59	Vermont	34	66
Oklahoma	52	48	Washington	36	64
South Carolina	43	57			
South Dakota	58	42			
Tennessee	33	67			
Texas	64	36			
Utah	58	42			
West Virginia	47	53			
Wyoming	28	72			
Average	42.8	57.2		27.4	72.6

Adapted from: Kaiser Family Foundation (2023f). Online at www.kff.org.

also differ on staff capability and capacity, their outreach system for communicating with recipients, and so forth (Tolbert, Moreno, and Rudowitz 2023).

One of the problems that the great unwinding created was that in states that did not expand Medicaid, there were some recipients who would not be able to get back on Medicaid. These include children who have aged out of Medicaid, low-income parents whose children no longer live at home, and women who have given birth and have passed their state's post-birth coverage. Their income might be too low to qualify for subsidies on the

ACA marketplaces, thus creating a coverage gap (Wikle, Wagner, and Erzouki 2023).

By July 2023, almost four million people had been disenrolled from Medicaid (Coleman 2023). By December 2023, the number had risen to around 12.5 million people removed from the Medicaid rolls (Covert 2023). Some of those disenrolled may be able to enroll in the ACA marketplaces with subsidies. Some may be able to reenroll in Medicaid because they were eligible but lost eligibility for administrative reasons (known as administrative or procedural terminations). Most of the terminations were for procedural reasons, about 71 percent. Others may remain uninsured (Coleman 2023; Covert 2023).

Table 5.24 shows the differences in the unwinding between the red and blue states. The red states' disenrollment rate was 59 percent higher than the blue states' disenrollment rate. The renewal rates (someone taken off the rolls then allowed back on) were higher by 28 percent for the blue states over the red states.

We previously discussed terminations because of procedural reasons. Table 5.25 shows that red states were more likely than blue states to terminate Medicaid recipients' eligibility for administrative reasons. The red state rate was a little more than 16 percent higher than the blue state rate. Recall that administrative terminations are not based on income but on failure to meet all the procedures and timetables. The administrative problems can also affect those on programs such as SNAP (Houghton, Pradhan, and Liss 2023). Many states make use of the same workers and computer systems for Medicaid and other public assistance programs. The Medicaid unwinding has created problems for such states in terms of increased waiting times at call centers and there are limits to in-person opportunities to file paperwork and get questions answered. Call centers may drop phone calls after long periods of waiting. This is a particular problem for red states such as Montana and Missouri (Houghton, Pradhan, and Liss 2023).

An example of these kinds of problems can be seen in Kentucky (Pradhan 2023). Beverly Likens was on Medicaid because of her being on SSI. While in the emergency room one day she found out that she was no longer on Medicaid because her assets were greater than the SSI limits. The Kentucky agency that oversees Medicaid sent her a notice that she no longer qualified for Medicaid because of this and that she would no longer be on Medicaid. Likens has multiple health issues and would likely have qualified under a different category. But the state agency did not check whether this was the case and told her she should reapply for Medicaid coverage. This violated federal regulations. After some delays, she was reinstated because her income was within Kentucky guidelines. The story is an indication of problems recipients faced during the unwinding.

TABLE 5.25 Reasons for Terminations

Red States	Percent Terminated for Procedural Reasons	Percent Determined Ineligible	Blue States	Percent Terminated for Procedural Reasons	Percent Determined Ineligible
Alabama	87	13	California	88	12
Alaska	70	30	Connecticut	78	22
Arizona	72	28	Delaware	57	43
Arkansas	77	23	Hawaii	86	14
Georgia	86	14	Illinois	14	86
Idaho	72	28	Maine	30	70
Indiana	85	15	Maryland	49	51
Kansas	80	20	Massachusetts	65	35
Kentucky	58	42	Michigan	83	17
Louisiana	75	25	New Jersey	76	24
Mississippi	78	22	New Mexico	95	5
Missouri	79	21	New York	49	51
Montana	76	24	Oregon	33	67
Nebraska	47	53	Pennsylvania	45	55
North Carolina	88	12	Rhode Island	83	17
North Dakota	71	29	Vermont	73	27
Oklahoma	76	24	Washington	87	13
South Carolina	77	23			
South Dakota	54	46			
Tennessee	74	26			
Texas	68	32			
Utah	94	6			
West Virginia	72	28			
Wyoming	71	29			
Average	74.5	25.5		64.2	35.8

Adapted from: Kaiser Family Foundation (2023f). Online at www.kff.org.

A related point is that a significant number of children were wrongly removed from the Medicaid rolls during the unwinding because computer systems were improperly programmed and did not look at whether individual family members might still be eligible. This is a problem that has affected a number of states (Goldstein 2023).

Rural areas were of particular concern during the unwinding (Rodriguez 2023). Rural residents, including children, depend more on Medicaid than urban residents. Red states are more rural than blue states (see Chapter 2). Rural residents face enhanced barriers to access because there are fewer medical services in rural areas than in more populated communities; rural residents have less internet access than people in metropolitan communities (and thus less access to the appropriate agencies), and longer distances to get to those agencies. This includes less access to navigators who can help people find their way through the complex Medicaid (and other public assistance) agencies and procedures. The state of Montana has six navigators for the entire state (Rodriguez 2023).

The result of all this is that a significant number of people were wrongly removed from the Medicaid rolls, many of them children (Weiland 2023a, 2023b). Errors were discovered and by September 2023 about 500,000 people were able to keep their CHIP and Medicaid eligibility. Thirty states had computer systems that were vetted incorrectly. Mail delays were also a problem. Both the states and the federal government were slow to pick this up. Children made up a large percentage of those removed from Medicaid and a large percentage of those whose eligibility was restored.

Texas is an exemplar of states removing recipients from Medicaid. Almost 1.7 million Texans lost coverage, mostly for procedural reasons. There were backlogs for those reapplying, very limited use of automated systems to determine eligibility, and so forth. While the state is hiring more people to address the backlog, the numbers of people thrown off of Medicaid make this a slow process (Bohra 2023).

Polarization and the Politics of Medicaid

Unlike Medicare, there is no such thing as a single Medicaid healthcare system (this is less true lately of Medicare as well). Rather, there are 56 different Medicaid systems if we count the 50 states, the District of Columbia, and the five U.S. territories (American Samoa, the Commonwealth of the Northern Mariana Islands, Guam, Puerto Rico, and the U.S. Virgin Islands). In this chapter, we have focused on a subset of these Medicaid healthcare systems: red states and blue states. No two state systems, even in our subset of states, are the same. But there are some commonalities, and it is not wrong to say that Medicaid systems differ between our two groups of states.

As a summary statement, Table 5.26 makes this perfectly clear. The table (McCann 2021) uses three sets of metrics to compare Medicaid coverage. The first metric is spending, the second metric is quality, and the third metric is enrollment and eligibility. Totaling up the metrics' rating gives us a total score as presented in the table. The top nine states are all blue states. Louisiana is the tenth state, the highest rated red state. The bottom 11 states are all red states, with Maine being the lowest rated blue state. This is consistent with the discussion in this chapter. Looking at the overall

TABLE 5.26 Rating State Medicaid Programs

Red States	Rank	Blue States	Rank
Louisiana	10	Massachusetts	1
Alaska	11	Rhode Island	2
Kentucky	18	Vermont	3
Arizona	20	Pennsylvania	4
West Virginia	21	Connecticut	5
Indiana	24	Washington	6
Montana	30	California	7
Utah	31	New York	8
North Dakota	33	Oregon	9
Texas	34	New Jersey	12
Kansas	36	Delaware	14
Arkansas	37	Hawaii	22
North Carolina	38	Michigan	23
Missouri	40	New Mexico	27
Idaho	41	Illinois	28
South Carolina	42	Maryland	35
Nebraska	43	Maine	39
Alabama	44		
Mississippi	45		
South Dakota	46		
Wyoming	47		
Tennessee	48		
Oklahoma	49		
Georgia	50		
Average Rank	34.9		14.4

Adapted with permission from: McCann (2021). Online at https://wallethub.com/edu/states-with-the-most-and-least-medicaid-coverage/71573.

rankings in Table 5.26, the average ranking of blue states was 14.4 and the average ranking of red states was 34.9.

While there are several explanations for these results, such as the differences in state economies, racial makeups, and percentage of the state population in poverty, the political polarization explanation seems to be among the strongest if not the strongest.

As we have discussed in this chapter, states have had the ability to create their own version of Medicaid from the very beginning. They could decide what non-mandatory services to include in the program. They could decide what non-mandatory populations to serve. They could decide, within limits, income eligibility levels (percent of FPL) to determine whether someone qualified for Medicaid. They could decide to expand Medicaid in the wake of the passage of the ACA or they could decide not to expand Medicaid. They could decide how long to cover postpartum women. They could decide how quickly to remove people from the rolls after the COVID-19 public health emergency was declared over. They could decide what process to use in making those decisions. They could decide whether to impose work requirements on Medicaid recipients.

All of these are policy decisions. But the policy decisions worked through a partisan lens. Red states were less willing to help their poorer citizens than blue states. The polarization obvious at the national level is also apparent at the state level.

Bibliography

Advocacy Resource Center. 2020. *The Evidence on Medicaid Expansion*. Chicago: American Medical Association.

Antonisse, Larisa, and Robin Rudowitz. 2019. *An Overview of State Approaches to Adopting the Medicaid Expansion*. Menlo Park, CA: Kaiser Family Foundation.

Bauer, Lauren, and Chloe East. 2023. *A Primer on Snap Work Requirements*. Washington, DC: Hamilton Project, The Brookings Institution.

Brecher, Charles, and Shanna Rose. 2013. "Medicaid's Next Metamorphosis." *Public Administration Review* 73, no. 5 (September/October): S60–S68.

Bohra, Neelan. 2023. "Nearly 1.7 MillionBoh Texas Lose Medicaid as State Nears End of 'Unwinding'." *Texas Tribune* (December 14)

Brooks, Tricia, et al. 2018. *Medicaid and CHIP Eligibility, Enrollment, Renewal, and Cost Sharing Policies As of 2018: Findings From a 50-State Survey*. Menlo Park, CA: Kaiser Family Foundation.

Brooks, Tricia, Lauren Roygardner, and Samantha Artiga. 2019. *Medicaid and CHIP Eligibility, Enrollment, and Cost Sharing Policies As of January 2019: Findings from a 50-State Survey*. Menlo Park, CA: Kaiser Family Foundation.

Buettgens, Matthew, and Urmi Ramchandami. 2022. *3.7 Million People Would Gain Coverage in 2023 If the Remaining 12 States Were to Expand Medicaid Eligibility*. Washington, DC: The Urban Institute.

Burman, Leonard E. 2020. *It's Not News That Congress's Budget Process Is a Mess, but It Should be*. Washington, DC: Tax Policy Center. Online at https://www.economist.com/the-economist-explains/2023/01/09/what-is-the-house-freedom-caucus

Carroll, Caitlin, et al. 2023. "Hospital Survival in Rural Markets: Closures, Mergers, and Profitability." *Health Affairs* 42, no. 4 (April): 498–507.

Centers for Medicare and Medicaid Services. n.d.-a *Medicaid.Gov: Mandatory and Optional Medicaid Benefits*. Woodlawn, MD: Centers for Medicare and Medicaid Services. Online at www.cms.gov

Centers for Medicare and Medicaid Services. n.d.-b *Medicaid.Gov: Medicaid Per Capita Expenditures*. Woodlawn, MD: Centers for Medicare and Medicaid Services. Online at www.cms.gov

Centers for Medicare and Medicaid Statistics. 2010. *2010 CMS Statistics*. Woodlawn, MD: Centers for Medicare and Medicaid Services.
Centers for Medicare and Medicaid Services. 2022. *Medicaid.Gov: Medicaid, Children's Health Insurance Program, & Basic Health Program Eligibility Levels*. Woodlawn, MD: Centers for Medicare and Medicaid Services.
Centers for Medicare and Medicaid Services. 2023. *Anticipated 2023 State Timelines for Initiating Unwinding-Related Renewals*. Woodlawn, MD: Centers for Medicare and Medicaid Services. (February 24, 2023).
Clark, Maggie. 2020. *Medicaid and CHIP Coverage for Pregnant Women: Federal Requirements, State Options*. Washington, DC: Georgetown University Health Policy Institute, Center for Children and Families.
Clark, Maggie. 2023. *State Trends to Leverage Medicaid Extended Postpartum Coverage, Benefits and Payment Policies to Improve Maternal Health*. Washington, DC: Georgetown University Health Policy Institute, Center for Children and Families.
Coleman, Akeiisa. 2020. *Coverage Expansion Leads to Savings in Medicaid and Beyond*. New York: The Commonwealth Fund.
Coleman, Akeiisa. 2023. *Almost 3.8 Million People Have Lost Their Medicaid Coverage Since the End of the COVID-19 Public Health Emergency*. New York: The Commonwealth Fund.
Coleman, Akeiisa, and Sara Federman. 2022. *Where Do the States Stand on Medicaid Expansion?* New York: The Commonwealth Fund.
Congressional Research Service. 2023. *Temporary Federal Medical Assistance Percentage (FMAP) Increase for Title IV-E Foster Care and Permanency Payments*. Washington, DC: Congressional Research Service.
Corallo, Bradley, and Sophia Moreno. 2023. *Analysis of National Trends in Medicaid and CHIP Enrollment during the Covid-19 Pandemic*. Menlo Park, CA: Kaiser Family Foundation.
Covert, Bryce. 2023. "What Happened to My Heath Insurance?" *The New York Times* (December 20).
Dunn, Abe, et al. 2023. *A Denial a Day Keeps the Doctor Away*. Cambridge, MA: National Bureau of Economic Research.
Einav, Liran, and Amy Finkelstein. 2023. *We've Got You Covered: Rebooting American Health Care*. New York: PenguinRandomHouse.
Erzouki, Farah. 2023. *States Must Act to Preserve Medicaid Coverage as End of Continuous Coverage Requirement Nears*. Washington, DC: Center on Budget and Policy Priorities.
Garfield, Rachel, Robin Rudowitz, and Anthony Damico. 2018. *Understanding the Intersection of Medicaid and Work*. Menlo Park, CA: Kaiser Family Foundation.
Giled, Sherry A., and Dong Ding. 2023. *Medicaid Work Requirements Wouldn't Increase Employment and Could Imperil Future Labor Market Participation*.
Goldman, Anna L., and Benjamin D. Sommers. 2020. "Among Low-Income Adults Enrolled in Medicaid, Churning Decreased After the Affordable Care Act." *Health Affairs* 39, no. 1 (January): 85–93.
Goldstein, Amy. 2023. "Kids In Many States Wrongly Removed from Medicaid, U.S. Officials Say." *The Washington Post* (August 2023).

Guinassi, Luciana Perez Uribe. 2023. "Thousands Enrolled in Medicaid in NC's First 12 Days of Expansion. Here's the New Data." *Charlotte News & Observer* (December 19).

Guth, Madeline, Rachel Garfield, and Robin Rudowitz. 2020. *The Effects of Medicaid Expansion Under the ACA: Studies From January 2014 to January 2020.* Menlo Park, CA: Kaiser Family Foundation.

Guth, Madeline, and Mary Beth Musumeci. 2022. *An Overview of Medicaid Work Requirements: What Happened Under the Trump and Biden Administrations?* Menlo Park, CA: Kaiser Family Foundation.

Guth, Madeline, et al. 2023. *Understanding the Intersection of Medicaid & Work: A Look at What the Data Say.* Menlo Park, CA: Kaiser Family Foundation.

HealthCare.Gov. 2023. "Federal Poverty Level." Online at https://www.healthcare.gov/glossary/federal-poverty-level-fpl/

Hinton, Elizabeth, and Jada Raphael. 2023. *10 Things to Know About Medicaid Managed Care.* Menlo Park, CA: Kaiser Family Foundation.

Houghton, Katheryn, Rachana Pradhan, and Samantha Liss. 2023. "Medicaid 'Unwinding' Makes Other Public Assistance Harder to Get." *KFF Health News* (November 29).

Jones, Elaine C. 2013. "Supreme Court Decides on the Affordable Care Act." *Neurology Clinical Practice* 3, no, 1 (February): 61–66.

Kaiser Family Foundation. 2023a. *State Health Facts; Medicaid Income Eligibility Limits for Adults as a Percent of the Federal Poverty Level.* Menlo Park, CA: Kaiser Family Foundation.

Kaiser Family Foundation. 2023b. *Medicaid State Fact Sheets.* Menlo Park, CA: Kaiser Family Foundation.

Kaiser Family Foundation. 2023c. *Status of State Medicaid Expansion Decisions: Interactive Map.* Menlo Park, CA: Kaiser Family Foundation.

Kaiser Family Foundation. 2023d. *Medicaid Waiver: Approved and Pending Section 1115 Waivers by State.* Menlo Park, CA: Kaiser Family Foundation.

Kaiser Family Foundation. 2023e. *Medicaid Waiver Tracker: Approved and Pending Section 1115 Waivers by State.* Menlo Park, CA: Kaiser Family Foundation.

Kaiser Family Foundation. 2023f. *Medicaid Enrollment and Unwinding Tracker.* Menlo Park, CA: Kaiser Family Foundation.

Kaiser Family Foundation. 2023g. *Health Coverage & Uninsured.* Menlo Park, CA: Kaiser Family Foundation.

Karpman, Michael. 2023. *Medicaid Work Requirements Would Do Little or Nothing to Increase Employment, But Would Harm People's Health.* Washington, DC: The Urban Institute.

Luhby, Tami. 2018. "Millions of Medicaid Recipients Already Work." *CNN Business* (January 10). Online at https://money.cnn.com/2018/01/10/news/economy/medicaid-work-requirement/index.html

March of Dimes. 2020. "Medicaid Coverage of Births United States (2020)." Online at https://www.marchofdimes.org/peristats/data?reg=99&top=11&stop=154&lev=1&slev=1&obj=18

McCann, Adam. 2021. *State with the Most and Least Medicaid Coverage.* Wallethub. Online at https://wallethub.com/edu/states-with-the-most-and-least-medicaid-coverage/71573

Medicaid and CHIP Payment and Access Commission (MACPAC). 2021. *Report to Congress on Medicaid and CHIP*. Washington, DC: Medicaid and CHIP Payment and Access Commission.

Medicaid and CHIP Payment and Access Commission (MACPAC). 2022. *MACStats: Medicaid and CHIP Data Book*. Washington, DC: Medicaid and CHIP Payment and Access Commission.

Mitchell, Alison. 2021. *Overview of ACA Medicaid Expansion*. Washington, DC: Congressional Research Service.

Mitchell, Alison. 2023. *Medicaid: An Overview*. Washington, DC: Congressional Research Service.

Musumeci, MaryBeth. 2017. *Medicaid and Work Requirements*. Menlo Park, CA: Kaiser Family Foundation.

National Academy for State Health Policy. 2023. *State Efforts to Extend Medicaid Postpartum Coverage*. Washington, DC: National Academy of State Health Policy.

Neukam, Stephen. 2023. "These 10 States Have Not Expanded Medicaid." *The Hill* (March 23). Online at https://thehill.com/homenews/state-watch/3914916-these-10-states-have-not-expanded-medicaid/

Neuman, Scott, Ashley Ahn, and Scott Horsley. 2023. "The Fight Over the Debt Ceiling Could Sink the Economy. This Is How We Got There." *NPR* (May 2). Online at https://www.npr.org/2023/03/23/1163448930/what-is-the-debt-ceiling-explanation

Norris, Louise. 2023. "Medicaid Eligibility and Enrollment in Missouri." Health Insurance.org (November 3). Online at https://www.healthinsurance.org/medicaid/missouri/

Ochieng, Nancy, et al. 2023. *Medicare Advantage in 2023: Enrollment Update and Key Trends*. Menlo Park, CA: Kaiser Family Foundation.

Olson, Laura Katz. 2010. *The Politics of Medicaid*. New York: Columbia University Press.

Park, Edwin, et al. 2023. *Consolidated Appropriations Act, 2023: Medicaid and CHIP Provisions Explained*. Washington, DC: Center for Children and Families, Georgetown University

Patel, Kant, and Mark Rushefsky. 2020. *Healthcare Politics and Policy in America*. New York: Routledge.

Pew Charitable Trusts. 2017. *How Income Volatility Interact with American Families' Financial Security*. Washington, DC: Pew Charitable Trusts. Online at https://www.pewtrusts.org/en/research-and-analysis/issue-briefs/2017/03/how-income-volatility-interacts-with-american-families-financial-security

Philips, Alexander P., Eli Y. Adashi, and MaryBeth Musumeci. 2023. "Medicaid Section 1115 Waivers: From Work Requirements to Social Determinants of Health." *Health Affairs* (April 20).

Plescia, Marissa. 2023. "Is Medicaid Expansion Still a Political Wedge Issue?" *MedCityNews* (September 14). Online at https://medcitynews.com/2023/09/medicaid-expansion-political-democrats-republicans/

Pradhan, Rachana. 2023. "Lost in the Mix of Medicaid 'Unwinding': Kentucky Cut Off Her Healthcare Over a Clerical Error." *Kaiser Health News* (November 21).

Ranji, Usha, et al. 2022. *Medicaid Coverage of Pregnancy-Related Services: Findings from a 2021 State Survey*. Menlo Park, CA: Kaiser Family Foundation.
Rodriguez, Jaxmin Orozco. 2023. "How Will Rural Americans Fare During Medicaid Unwinding? Experts Fear They're on Their Own." *Kaiser Health News* (September 20).
Rosenbaum, Jason. 2021. "Voters Prevail In Missouri: 275,000 To Gain Access to Health Care." *NPR* (July). Online at https://www.npr.org/2021/07/22/1019401988/voters-prevail-in-missouri-275-000-to-gain-access-to-health-care
Rudowitz, Robin, and Bradley Corallo. 2021. "*New Incentives for States to Adopt the Medicaid Expansion: Implications for State Spending.*" Menlo Park, CA: Kaiser Family Foundation.
Rudowitz, Robin, et al. 2023. "*10 Things to Know About Medicaid.*" Menlo Park, CA: Kaiser Family Foundation.
Ruff, Emmett, and Eliot Fishman. 2019. "*The Return of Churn: State Paperwork Barriers Caused More Than 1.5 Million Low-Income People to Lose Their Medicaid Coverage in 2018.*" Washington, DC: Families USA.
Sable-Smith, Bram. 2021. "A Tale of Two Medicaid Expansions: Oklahoma Jumps In, While Missouri Lags." *KFF Health News* (December 3). Online at https://www.usnews.com/news/best-states/articles/2021-12-03/missouris-slow-moving-medicaid-expansion-sparks-criticism
Shorman, Jonathan, and Sarah Ritter. 2023. "Kansas Gov. Kelly Floats Work Requirements for Medicaid Expansion in Bid to Win GOP Support." *Kansas City Star* (December 14).
Smith, David G., and Judith D. Moore. 2008. *Medicaid Politics and Policy*, 2nd ed. New Brunswick, NJ: Transaction Publishers.
Starr, Paul. 1982. *The Social Transformation of American Medicine*. New York: Basic Books.
Sugar, Sarah, et al. 2021. *Medicaid Churning and Continuity of Care: Evidence and Policy Considerations Before and After the COVID-19 Pandemic*. Washington, DC: Office of Health Policy, Assistant Secretary for Planning and Evaluation, U.S. Department of Health and Human Services.
Sullivan, Becky. 2021. "Missouri Will Not Expand Medicaid Despite Voter Wishes, Governor Says." *NPR* (May 13). Online at https://www.npr.org/2021/05/13/996611586/missouri-will-not-expand-medicaid-despite-voters-wishes-governor-says
Taylor, Jamila, et al. 2022. *The Worsening U.S. Maternal Health Crisis in Three Graphs*. Washington, DC: The Century Foundation. Online at https://tcf.org/content/commentary/worsening-u-s-maternal-health-crisis-three-graphs/?gclid=CjwKCAjwyY6pBhA9EiwAMzmfwXEPecHw9xKEqFZm1Og-H5ofnnU10B3GDFE-VK_ZkdXVTTPnhCTgRxoCnzsQAvD_BwE
Thompson, Frank J. 2012. *Medicaid Politics: Federalism, Policy Durability, and Health Reform*. Washington, DC: Georgetown University Press.
Tolbert, Jennifer, and Meghana Ammula. 2023). *10 Things to Know about the Unwinding of the Medicaid Continuous Enrollment Provision*. Menlo Park, CA: Kaiser Family Foundation.
Tolbert, Jennifer, Sophia Moreno, and Robin Rudowitz. 2023. *State Policy Choices Are Likely to Affect the Extent of Medicaid Enrollment Declines During the Unwinding Period*. Menlo Park, CA: Kaiser Family Foundation.

Todd, Annie. 2023. "South Dakota Lawmakers Are Bringing Back a Medicaid Work Requirement Resolution in 2024." *Sioux Falls Argus Leader* (December 15).

Wagner, Jennifer, Judith Solomon. 2021. *Continuous Eligibility Keeps People Insured and Reduces Costs*. Washington, DC: Center for Budget and Policy Priorities. Menlo Park, CA: Kaiser Family Foundation.

Ward, Bryce. 2020. *The Impact of Medicaid Expansion on States' Budgets*. New York: The Commonwealth Fund.

Weiland, Noah. 2023a. "Nearly 500,000 in U.S. Will Regain Health insurance After State Errors." *The New York Times* (September 21).

Weiland, Noah. 2023b. "At Least 2 Million Children Have Lost Medicaid Insurance This Year." *The New York Times* (November 9).

Weinberg, Tessa. 2021. "Judge Orders State to Immediately Allow Missourians to Enroll in Expanded Medicaid." *Missouri Independent* (August 10).

"What is the House Freedom Caucus?" 2023. *The Economist*. Online at https://www.economist.com/the-economist-explains/2023/01/09/what-is-the-house-freedom-caucus

Wikle, Suzanne, Jennifer Wagner, and Farah Erzouki. 2023. *Unwinding the Medicaid Continuous Coverage: Frequently Asked Questions*. Washington, DC: Center on Budget and Policy Priorities.

6
REPRODUCTIVE RIGHTS IN RED AND BLUE STATES

Abortion rights are advancing across the globe. Countries across all continents have expanded abortion rights. Over the last three decades, over 60 countries have liberalized their abortion laws. Some have done so incrementally. Today, according to the Center for Reproductive Rights (2023), at least 75 countries allow abortion on request with varying gestational limits. Thirteen countries or territories allow abortion under a broad range of circumstances. Almost 50 countries or territories allow abortion for health or therapeutic reasons while 42 countries or territories allow abortion to save a pregnant woman's life. The trend toward liberalization of abortion laws has accelerated in the last five years. Between 2019 and 2023, 21 countries liberalized their abortion laws.

The liberalization of abortion laws and expansion of abortion rights have happened across a wide range of countries from the continent of Africa to the Middle East to Latin America and the Caribbean to Asia and the Pacific to Europe. In some countries, it has happened via court decisions while in others it has been done through legislative action.

Two major court rulings in Columbia and Mexico decriminalized abortion. In 2021, Columbia and Mexico liberalized abortion laws. In Columbia, the Constitutional Court voted to legalize abortion before 24 weeks of pregnancy. In Mexico, the Supreme Court voted to dismiss a federal law that punished women with jail time for having an abortion. In 2023, the Mexican Supreme Court reaffirmed an earlier decision that laws criminalizing abortion were unconstitutional. Before the ruling, 20 of the country's 32 states had laws criminalizing abortion. The ruling means that individuals nationwide will be able to access abortion care at federal health

DOI: 10.4324/9781032671147-6

facilities, even in states with laws banning the abortion procedure. About 70 percent of Mexico's population is subscribed to the federal health system. Nearly 80 percent of Mexico's population are Catholics. In fact, in a national survey conducted in 2021 by the Mexican newspaper *El Fianciero*, 45 percent of respondents favored legalized abortion while 53 percent objected (Ramirez 2023; Cunningham 2022). In September of 2023, Brazil's highest court opened its session that will decide whether abortion up to the 12th week of pregnancy will be decriminalized nationwide (Savarese 2023).

The Supreme Court of India in 2022 ruled that under India's Medical Termination of Pregnancies Act (MTP Act) and its related rules, all women are entitled to safe and legal abortion, regardless of their marital status and the distinction between married and unmarried women under the MTP Act was arbitrary and all women have the autonomy to exercise their rights to abortion up to 24 weeks of gestation (Center for Reproductive Rights 2022a).

In most countries where abortion is legal, it is regulated through legislation. The laws permitting abortion vary widely in what they allow and at what stages of pregnancy. In Europe, abortion is generally legal on request on broad social grounds. In 2018, in Ireland, the public voted to overturn a longtime constitutional ban on abortion (Cunningham 2022). Today, 60 percent of women worldwide live where abortion is broadly legal while 40 percent live under restrictive abortion laws (Center for Reproductive Rights 2023).

Despite global progress in abortion rights, about 91 million women of reproductive age live in 24 countries that prohibit abortion under all circumstances. Countries that ban abortion under all circumstances include Nicaragua, Honduras, Malta, the Dominican Republic, Egypt, the Philippines, Senegal, and Madagascar, to name a few (Laurin-Whitney 2022).

Since 1994, only four countries have rolled back abortion rights – El Salvador, Nicaragua, Poland, and the United States. El Salvadore has some of the strictest abortion laws in the world. Nicaragua in 2006 implemented a total abortion ban. Nicaragua has banned abortion since 1985 and hardened abortion laws in 2021 to make it difficult to change the abortion ban. In 2020, Poland's Constitutional Tribunal effectively ended legal abortion in the country. Since then, the Polish government has aggressively repressed the country's reproductive rights movement, including surveillance of women suspected of terminating their pregnancies. Poland, which is a majority Catholic, already has one of Europe's most stringent abortion laws on the books and began implementing a near-total ban on abortion in 2021 (Adams 2023; Westfall 2021; Parker 2021). The issue of reproductive and abortion rights has become a point of contention between Poland

and the European Union. Soon after Poland began implementing its near-total ban on abortion, the Belgium government announced that it would provide funding for women in Poland to access abortions abroad and a donation of $12,000 to Abortions Without Borders. The Polish government has tacitly allowed women to leave the country to obtain abortions (Parker 2021).

In the United States, in *Roe v. Wade*, the United Supreme Court in 1973 ruled that abortion was a constitutionally guaranteed right under the U.S. Constitution. For almost 50 years, women nationwide enjoyed a constitutional right to abortion with some restrictions. However, in June of 2022, a conservative majority on the U.S. Supreme Court overturned the *Roe v. Wade* decision stating that the U.S. Constitution does not guarantee women the right to abortion. The ruling effectively left it up to each state to determine abortion policy and regulation of abortion practices. Consequently, the battle for reproductive rights and abortion has shifted from federal courts to state legislatures, executive mansions, and state courts. Several red states immediately proceeded to ban abortion altogether or impose severe restrictions. Clinics in several states with less restrictive laws have become overburdened with people requesting appointments for abortion leading to delays. Just one week after the Supreme Court overturned *Roe v. Wade*, MSI Reproductive Choices, an international reproductive health non-profit organization, announced a plan to open an abortion clinic in Cancun and opened an abortion clinic in Tijuana close to the border with California. According to Mexican nongovernmental organizations, they are increasingly hearing from U.S. women traveling to Mexico for abortion care after the two countries reversed their long-standing abortion policies (Goldhill 2023a). Concerned over developments in the United States, women in France clamored to further protect their abortion rights. In response, President Emmanuel Macron proposed a language for a constitutional amendment that would make France the first country to enshrine the right to abortion in its Constitution (Adam 2023). In March 2024, France became the first country to explicitly enshrine abortion rights in its constitution when a specially convened session of lawmakers at Versailles, France endorsed the amendment referring to abortion as a "guaranteed freedom" (Adams 2023; Adam 2024).

The Context of Debate and Action Over Reproductive Rights

To understand the politics and policies of reproductive rights and abortion in the United States, it is important to first understand the context in which the debate and actions over these rights take place.

Reproductive Rights

Reproductive rights involve more than just abortion rights. The three primary principles involving the debate about reproductive rights include the right to have a child, the right not to have a child, and the right to parent children in a safe and healthy environment. Regulations that restrict the reproductive rights of women are often framed as a matter of finding a balance between the rights of individual women against the state's interest in protecting public safety, and health, and promoting social or common good. Thus, the debate over reproductive rights includes more than just pro-choice and pro-life debates. However, it is understandable that abortion rights are one of the most explored and debated areas of reproductive rights (Howard 2020).

Use and Misuse of Language

The debate about abortion rights over the years has involved constantly changing language to influence public perception and social conception of abortion. Before the Roe v. Wade ruling in 1973, prominent arguments made by reformers to advocate for abortion rights involved the risks of illegal abortions and how prohibiting abortion increased the risks. They focused on the suffering of women in need of medical care, and pregnant women dying each year from illegal and unsafe abortions. There was no mention of "privacy" or the right to privacy. The Roe v. Wade decision transformed how Americans talked about abortion giving rise to the "politics of rights." The proponents of abortion started to talk about "a woman's right to freedom of choice" and "a woman's right to personal privacy." The nature of public advocacy shifted the center of the debate to abortion as a constitutional right. Proponents called their support for abortion rights pro-choice, i.e., giving women the right to choose to have an abortion or not while labeling opponents of abortion as anti-choice. The opponents of abortion rights called their position pro-life implying that those who support abortion rights are anti-life. They emphasized the interests of the unborn and taking an innocent life as a matter of ethics and faith (Vecera 2014; Zeigler 2009).

Congressional law banning partial-birth abortion and upholding the law by the U.S. Supreme Court demonstrated the misuse of language surrounding the highly unusual procedure. The term "partial-birth" does not refer to a medical procedure. It was a political construct and the term "partial-birth abortion" was designed to resonate with the wider public. The term is not found in any medical dictionaries. Language is an important tool in framing and debating any policy issue. The challenge is to frame the debate in a way that resonates with the societal culture (Armitage 2010). After the overturning of the Roe v. Wade decision, the Republican Party and conservatives have tested different talking points and messages on abortion to make their anti-abortion policies sound less extreme. For example, there has been discussion about abandoning the term "ban" when speaking about anti-abortion legislation since an overwhelming majority of Americans opposed strict abortion bans. There is an effort to use "life-affirming" language. The hope is that changing the way Americans talk about abortion, might help change the way Americans feel about abortion from a "pro-choice" to a "pro-life" position (Valenti 2023).

American Federalism and States' Rights

Under the American federal system, states enjoy a considerable amount of freedom and autonomy to act in various policy areas within the constraints imposed by the U.S. Constitution. The Tenth Amendment reserves all powers not given to the national government nor denied to the states and its people. In addition, state governments also enjoy a considerable amount of discretion in how they go about implementing/enforcing federal policies. In overturning the Roe v. Wade decision, the Supreme Court in the Dobbs ruling essentially took away the constitutionally based national right to abortion and returned the power to ban, limit, and regulate abortion to individual states, i.e., state legislatures. In Dobbs, the court expressed federalism concerns when Justice Alito, writing for the majority, concluded that it was time to return the issue of abortion to the people's elected representatives in the state legislatures. On the issue of abortion policy, like a pendulum, American federalism has oscillated between national/federal and state powers (Hodge, Jr; Ghaith; and Krumholz 2022). At the state level, there has also been a strong trend away from divided governments to unified governments whereby one party controls both the executive and legislative branches of government. Republicans and conservatives have achieved some institutional advantage due to the recent ideological shift in the federal judiciary, especially the U.S. Supreme Court, and the Republican dominance of state legislatures (Konisky and Nolette 2022).

This has led to a profusion of varying policies ranging from a near-total ban to the least restrictive across 50 states governing abortion rights. Republic-led red states have either imposed bans or very restrictive policies while the blue states have moved to protect and expand abortion rights. State governments have indeed become a laboratory for experimentation. Some can argue that this is a good thing because the federal system allows state legislatures to follow and make abortion policy that reflects the wishes of its citizens. Others can argue such a policy variation creates inequities and injustices because it makes what reproductive rights women enjoy a function of which state they reside in.

Public Opinion and Reproductive Rights

One can argue that in a representative democracy, public policies should reflect the will of the people. It has been suggested that the aggregate state policy tends to be quite responsive to aggregate state public opinion. In other words, states with liberal populations produce liberal policies, and states with conservative populations produce conservative policies (Camobreco and Barnello 2008). Is this always the case? The answer is not necessarily. Often, a variety of factors such as constitutional arrangements, institutional structures, powerful interest groups, and such can thwart the will of the majority creating a disconnect between policy elites, i.e., policymakers and people's policy preferences.

At the national level, public opinion polls and surveys have consistently shown that a majority of Americans support women's right to an abortion with some limits and have expressed support for the *Roe v. Wade* decision. A Pew Research Center Report published in July 2022 found that many Americans disagreed with the U.S. Supreme Court's decision to overturn Roe v. Wade, with 62 percent saying that abortion should be legal in all or most states (Pew Research Center 2022). A Gallup poll released in June of 2023 showed that 69 percent of Americans believe abortion should be legal in the first three months of pregnancy. This is the highest number Gallup has found since 1996 (Reston and LeVine 2023).

At the state level, policies governing reproductive rights and abortion reflect congruency as well as a lack of congruency, i.e., a disconnect between policy elites' and voters' public policy preferences. In the blue states, there is more policy congruency between the state policymakers and citizens' policy preferences. States with liberal populations have adopted liberal reproductive rights policies. Also, states with higher percentages of Democratic legislatures and women, and pro-choice governors are associated with more liberal abortion policies (Camobreco and Barnello 2008). For example, since the Dobbs decisions, blue states such as California, Michigan, and Vermont voters have voted to enshrine women's right to abortion into the state constitutions (Reilly 2022).

The same cannot be said about the red states. In some red states, there is a disconnect between Republican state policymakers and their voters. In states such as Montana, Kansas, and Kentucky, voters through ballot initiatives have rejected efforts by state legislatures to ban or impose severe restrictions on abortion rights. On November 7, 2023, Ohio voters resoundingly approved a ballot measure enshrining a right to abortion in the state constitution despite the Republican Governor and Republican-controlled state legislature that wanted to impose severe restrictions on abortion rights (Zernike 2023).

Morality Politics and Policies

In policy areas such as climate change, voter ID laws, immigration, firearms restriction, and the like, states have indeed acted as laboratories for innovation and policy experiments (Tyler and Gerken 2022). There has been a great deal of policy diffusion as well as diversity among states especially over policies that can be described as "morality policies." Morality policies often involve conflicts over core values. These policies include abortion, same-sex marriage, LGBTQ rights, sex education, pornography, physician assisted suicide, among others. Morality policies have high public salience and can generate a high level of citizen interest and participation (Mooney 2000). Morality policies involve conflict over deeply held fundamental beliefs about right and wrong (Camobreco and Barnello 2008). By the 1990s reproductive rights and abortion had become one of the major morality policies involving conflict over core political and religious values.

Partisan and Religious Divide

Today, abortion has become a very partisan issue. This was not the case for almost two decades following the legalization of abortion by the U.S. Supreme Court in the 1973 Roe v. Wade decision. The Democratic and Republican national party platforms were not distinct on the issue of abortion. However, by the end of the 1980s and early 1990s, more than 80 percent of Democrats were in favor of abortion rights while 80 percent of Republicans opposed abortion rights. By 1980s both political parties had developed contrasting positions on the issue of abortion on their national platforms (Kreitzer 2015). Numerous studies of Congress have also documented that since the early 1980s Congressional parties became more cohesive and more differentiated ideologically, especially on abortion-related policies (Jaenicke 2002).

These developments coincided with the U.S. Supreme Court, beginning in the late 1980s, granting states more discretion in regulating abortion during the first trimester of pregnancy. Partisan control of state legislative and executive branches of government began to play a significant role in shaping abortion policy (Kreitzer 2015). Consequently, states' political context has become important in understanding abortion policy at the state level.

Abortion-related issues also reflected an emerging cultural-religious divide. The abortion issue is intertwined with morality politics. Morality policies are often defined as those issues in which at least one side of the debate frames the issue in terms of morality or sin and public policies seek to validate a set of values at the expense of others (Kreitzer 2015). A coalition of social and religious conservatives, often referred to as the Christian right, prioritized cultural-religious issues for political battle. Reproductive rights and abortion have become the most visible and contentious issues surrounding morality politics. The strongest opposition to abortion rights has come from conservative religious groups such as Catholics and evangelical Christians while support for abortion rights has come from secular and liberal religious groups. The debate surrounding abortion rights generates a great deal of passion on both sides because it raises some profound questions about when life begins and what constitutes a "person." Efforts to make laws and policies governing such questions inevitably lead to a clash between science, religion, and politics (Varney 2022).

Abortion Laws: Legality Vs. Access

One final word of caution that is warranted when discussing abortion is the difference between the legal availability of abortion and access to abortion. Liberal abortion laws do not always mean that abortions are easily available. Even in countries that permit abortion, access to abortion can be limited due to restrictive regulations such as mandatory waiting periods, requirements for counseling and/or parental consent, availability of abortion providers, and the like. For example, in Germany, a woman is required to get counseling and wait for three days to get an abortion. In the Netherlands, the waiting period is five days. Access to abortion also depends on the cost of abortion services. Another example is Italy where abortion is legal. However, access to abortion is limited because 70 percent of gynecologists are registered as conscientious objectors which allows them to refuse abortion due to moral or religious beliefs (Santamarina et al. 2022).

Certain Facts About Abortion in the United States

Abortion is a medical termination of a pregnancy. Primary methods used to terminate a pregnancy include medical procedures and medication. Today, most of the abortions performed in the United States include medication abortion. Both methods are very safe. Yet abortion remains a highly regulated medical service and depending on the state varies from a total ban to abortion restrictions involving mandatory counseling, waiting period, ultrasound, parental notification and consent, and gestational age limit, resulting in delays in provisions of service (Ranji, Diep, and Salganicoff 2023).

For several decades, there was a studied decline in abortion rates nationally but has increased slightly in recent years. Long-term decline in abortion rates can be attributed to more effective methods of contraception and reduced access in several states. At the state level, states with total bans or severe restrictions have seen a decline while states that have expanded abortion rights have experienced an increase in abortion rates. Thus, abortion rates vary widely between states. Almost 92 percent of abortions in the United States occur during the first trimester of pregnancy. In 2020, 96 percent of abortions were provided at clinics and 4 percent were provided in doctors' offices or hospitals. Abortions performed using a medical procedure must be provided in a clinical setting while medication abortion can be provided in a clinical setting or via telehealth. The median cost of abortion services is around $500. The cost increases if the woman seeking an abortion must travel long distances to seek abortion services due to state bans or the absence of service providers in the area. Insurance coverage for abortion services is often restricted in certain private insurance plans and public programs like Medicaid (Ranji, Diep, and Salganicoff 2023).

The Struggle for Reproductive Rights in America

Nineteenth Century

In the eighteenth and early nineteenth centuries, abortion was legal before "quickening" a point at which a woman could feel her fetus move and abortion after that was considered a common-law misdemeanor. During the 1820s and 1830s, women often used abortifacient herbs and fungi for abortion which often led to their deaths. As a result, states began to pass laws to control or ban the use of such substances. In 1821 Connecticut passed the first statutory abortion regulation in the United States banning the use of poison to induce abortion after quickening. Punishment for violation of the law was a life sentence (Kennedy 2023; Larson 2017).

In 1857 the newly formed American Medical Association (AMA) started a campaign to criminalize abortion. The group's 1959 report on "Clinical Abortion" proclaimed physicians to be the "guardians of women." Two of the purposes behind the campaign were to put midwives and homeopaths out of business since they were viewed by the AMA as competitors and to bolster the Anglo-Protestant birth rate in the face of immigration (Boodman 2023). In 1869, the Catholic Church's Pope Pius IX declared abortion at any stage of pregnancy punishable by excommunication. In March 1873, the U.S. Congress passed the Comstock Act. The law made selling or distributing contraception through the mail or across state lines a federal crime. The legislation was drafted by Anthony Comstock, a devout Christian well-known for his crusade against prostitution, pornography, and birth control. Following the federal Comstock Act, 24 states passed their own laws to restrict access to contraception at the state level. By the 1880s, all states had laws criminalizing abortion (Kennedy 2023; Larson 2017).

During the entire period from the mid to late 1800s to 1973, when abortion was illegal, it was common to link the words abortion and crime together. For example, abortion was a felony crime in Texas since 1856. During the nineteenth century and most of the twentieth century, women in Texas who were believed to have had abortions were frequently called to testify in criminal trials. Women themselves were seldom prosecuted but they were pressured to testify against doctors and others who were believed to have been involved in arranging the procedure. Prosecutors portrayed women as the victims and the abortion ban was defended as a necessary part of protecting pregnant women from being exploited (Miller and Pitcher 2022).

According to Reagan (1997), even though abortion was illegal, it was widely available. Abortion providers often practiced openly and safely and numerous physicians performed abortions despite state prohibition. However, doctors and patients were under constant threat of prosecution, public humiliation, and loss of privacy. Inferior medical care was also a concern.

Twentieth Century

On October 16, 1916, Margaret Sanger opened the nation's first birth control clinic in Brooklyn, New York. The police shut down the clinic after nine days and arrested Sanger, her sister, a registered nurse, and an interpreter. After serving 30 days in prison, Sanger launched the Birth Control Clinical Research Bureau in New York and the American Birth Control League which later merged to form Planned Parenthood. In December 1936, in *United States V. One Package*, a U.S. Circuit Court of Appeals ruled in favor of an amendment to the Comstock Act making it legal for doctors to distribute contraceptives across state lines. The ruling paved the way for new advances in contraception. On May 9, 1960, the Federal Food and Drug Administration (FDA) approved Envoid, known as "The Pill," the country's first oral contraceptive. In 1968 FDA granted similar approval to the IUD. This represented advances in birth-controlled methods available to women (Kennedy 2023; Larson 2017).

In 1967, Colorado became the first state to loosen abortion restrictions allowing abortion in cases of rape, incest, fetal defect, or if a woman's physical or mental health was at risk. In 1970 Hawaii became the first state to legalize abortion followed by Alaska, New York, and Washington.

The Supreme Court and Reproductive Rights, 1960S–1980S

Beginning in the 1960s the federal courts and specifically the U.S. Supreme Court became involved in issues surrounding contraception, family planning, abortion, and reproductive rights ("Reproductive Rights and the Supreme Court" n.d.; Harvey 2023; Kennedy 2023; Larson 2017).

In *Griswold v. Connecticut*, the Supreme Court in 1965 struck down state law prohibiting married couples from using birth control. In a 7-2 decision, the court ruled that the law infringed on the rights of married couples' privacy rights established by the Bill of Rights. In 1972, in the case of *Eisenstadt v. Baird*, the Supreme Court in a 6-1 decision ruled that unmarried individuals have the same right as married couples to obtain birth control.

In the case of *Roe v. Wade*, on January 22, 1973, the United States Supreme Court by a vote of 7-2 handed down a landmark decision ruling that women in the United States have a fundamental right to choose whether to have an abortion without excessive government restrictions. The court struck down Texas' ban on abortion as unconstitutional. The decision was issued together with a decision in a companion case, *Doe v. Bolton*, which involved a similar challenge to Georgia's abortion ban. The court declared that a woman's right to an abortion was implicit in the right to privacy protected by the 14th Amendment. The net effect of the ruling was to legalize abortion nationwide. In delivering the majority opinion of the court, Justice Harry Blackmun wrote,

> This right of privacy, whether it be founded in the Fourteenth Amendment's concept of personal liberty and restriction upon state action, as we feel it is, as the District Court determined, in the Ninth Amendment's reservation of rights to the people, is broad enough to encompass a woman's decision whether or not to terminate her pregnancy.... We, therefore, conclude that the right to personal liberty includes the abortion decision but that the right is not unqualified and must be considered against important state interests in regulation.
>
> Jane Roe et al., Appellants v. Henry Wade, 410 U.S. 113; p. 154.
> https://www.supremecourt.gov

The court divided pregnancy into three trimesters and declared that the choice to end pregnancy in the first trimester was solely up to the woman. Thus, the right to abortion is almost absolute during the first trimester. In the second trimester, the government could regulate abortion, but not ban it, to protect the mother's health. However, a state's regulation of abortion must pass "strict scrutiny" by demonstrating the state's "compelling interest" in protecting a mother's health. In the trimester, the state could prohibit abortion to protect a fetus that could survive on its own outside the womb, except when a woman's health was in danger. The state's interest in protecting prenatal life becomes compelling (Thakker 2017).

Post Roe V. Wade Developments

In 1976, Congress passed the bipartisan Hyde Amendment prohibiting the use of federal Medicaid dollars for abortion except in the cases of rape, incest, or to protect a woman's health (Adashi 2017). In 1980, the Supreme Court, in *Harris v. McRae*, upheld the Constitutionality of the Hyde Amendment and ruled that withholding Medicaid coverage for abortion was constitutional even when abortion was needed to protect a woman's health. Beginning in the 1990s, the U.S. Supreme Court began to make concessions to the states by allowing them more leeway to regulate abortion practices ("Reproductive Rights and the Supreme Court" n.d.; Harvey 2023; Kennedy 2023; Larson 2017).

The Supreme Court and Reproductive Rights – 1990S–2020S

Starting in 1989 the Supreme Court indicated a willingness to allow state legislatures to expand abortion regulations. In 1989, the Supreme Court, in the case of *Webster v. Reproductive Health Services*, upheld a Missouri regulation that required physicians to conduct viability tests before performing an abortion (Medoff 2002).

In 1992, in the case of *Planned Parenthood of Southeastern PA v. Casey*, the Supreme Court reaffirmed the essential holding of *Roe v. Wade* but ruled that states may regulate some aspects of abortions. This paved the way for states to impose waiting periods to get an abortion and require that abortion providers explain the risks of abortion. The court also established a "viability" standard prohibiting abortion once the fetus can survive outside the womb. The court ruled that laws regulating abortions must not impose an "undue burden" on women seeking abortion. In so ruling, the court rejected the rigid trimester framework established in *Roe v. Wade* and moved away from the "strict scrutiny" standard used to decide the constitutionality of laws regulating abortion and replaced it with an ambiguous "undue burden" standard (Thakker 2017). The decision had the effect of weakening Roe's ruling and eroding abortion rights. The ruling in this case opened a floodgate of abortion restriction at the state level (Hooton and Schvey 2014).

In 2000, the U.S. Supreme Court *in Stenberg v. Carhart* by a vote of 5-4 struck down Nebraska's partial-birth abortion ban because it placed an undue burden on a women's right to abortion and it did not allow an exception to preserve a woman's health. However, in 2007 in *Gonzales v. Planned Parenthood Federation of America* and *Gonzales v. Carhart*, the Supreme Court reversed its decision in Gonzales v. Carhart and ruled that the Partial-Birth Abortion Ban Act passed by Congress in 2003 was constitutional.

In 2014, in the case of *Burwell v. Hobby Lobby*, in a 5-4 decision the Supreme Court ruled that Hobby Lobby and other "closely held" corporations should be exempted from covering birth control as required by the Affordable Care Act passed by Congress in 2010 if it is against their religious beliefs. In 2016 in *Zubik v. Burwell*, the Supreme Court clarified its earlier ruling in *Burwell v. Hobby Lobby* that employers must provide coverage for contraceptives either through their health insurance coverage plans or through a third party in the case of a religious exemption.

Partisan Divide Over Reproductive Rights and Abortion: Red v. Blue States

As noted earlier in the chapter, reproductive rights and abortion rights were a non-partisan topic during much of the 1970s and 1980s. For example, the 1976 Hyde Amendment was approved by Congress on a bipartisan basis. During much of the 1970s and 1980s, there was no significant distinction on the topic of abortion in the Democratic and Republican national party platforms.

However, by the late 1980s and early 1990s, at the national level, sharp partisan differences had emerged with more than 80 percent of Democrats favoring abortion rights while 80 percent of Republicans opposing abortion rights. Both political parties' national party platforms also had undertaken contrasting positions on the issue of abortion (Kreitzer 2015). By the early 1980s, Congressional parties had become ideologically more cohesive and differentiated, especially on abortion-related policies (Jaenicke 2002).

The election of George W. Bush, a Republican, to the presidency in the 2000 election brought about a major conservative shift in reproductive health politics. The Bush Administration used four strategies to restrict access to reproductive rights. First, the administration significantly increased federal support for promoting an abstinence-only agenda in public education. Second, the administration leaned heavily on the FDA first to deny and then delay a decision on the over-the-counter (OTC) availability of Plan B, a brand name for the most common form of emergency contraceptive. Third, the administration and the Republican Party leaders publicly expressed their opposition to the 1973 *Roe v. Wade* ruling legalizing abortion nationwide. Congress passed and President Bush signed into law the Partial-Birth Abortion Ban Act in 2003. Fourth, the administration along with Republican Congressional lawmakers and leaders of the religious right launched a campaign using partial or misleading information about the effectiveness of contraceptives/condoms (Kulczycki 2007).

A seismic shift in favor of the anti-abortion policy agenda came about because of the 2010 midterm election results, particularly at the state level. Republicans swept into federal and state offices throughout the country. Before 2010, Democrats were at the peak of their political power. They held 59 seats in the U.S. Senate and 257 seats in the House. They held the governorship in 26 states and 55 percent of seats in state legislatures and controlled most of the state legislative chambers. In the 2010 elections, Republicans benefited from the emergence of the Tea Party movement driven by cultural wars and an aggressive effort to win control of state legislatures. Democrats suffered massive losses both at the national and state levels. They lost 63 seats in the House and lost their majority and they also lost six Senate seats. Even more dramatic losses for Democrats occurred at the state level. Republicans made a net gain of six governorship, Democrats lost 720 state legislative seats, and Republicans gained control of the 26 state legislatures (Greenfield 2021).

Republicans-led red states successfully used the watered-down "Undue burden" standard established in *Planned Parenthood of Southeastern PA v. Casey* to chip away at abortion rights by passing increased regulation of abortion practices. Reproductive healthcare providers also became targets of harassment, burdensome regulations, and occasional violence (Hooton and Schvey 2014). After the 2010 elections, the anti abortion movement picked up steam, and by June 2011, the number of abortion restrictions introduced in state legislatures had surpassed the number introduced in any year since the early 1990s (O'Connor 2019).

Even before the 2010 mid-term elections, between 2000 and 2010, several red states had passed "targeted restrictions on abortion providers" known as TARP laws. By 2017, 25 states had enacted TARP laws (Harrington and Gould 2017). Such laws restricted aspects of abortion clinics such as the size of their hallways; requiring doctors who provide abortions to have admitting privileges at nearby hospitals; requiring doctors to read an anti-abortion script to patients seeking an abortion; and mandating abortion providers to perform ultrasound and play ultrasound of the fetus's heartbeat for the patient before an abortion. One of the consequences of such regulations was a decline in the number of abortion clinics and healthcare facilities (abortion clinics, hospitals, doctor's offices, etc.) that provide abortion services.

Abortion Clinics/Facilities and Access to Abortion

In 2008, 851 clinics provided abortions nationwide. By 2014, their number had dropped to 788, a 7 percent decrease. In Texas alone, after the TARP law went into effect in 2013, the number of clinics providing abortions dropped from 41 to 22. Texas law required abortion clinics in Texas to meet strict standards ranging from the exact size of the examination room to doctors performing abortions to have admission privileges at a nearby hospital. In 2015, in *Whole Woman's Health v. Hellerstedt*, the U.S. Supreme Court by a 5-4 decision ruled that such requirements posed a substantial undue burden on women seeking abortion. Yer similar laws were in effect in almost half of the states in the country (Harrington and Gould 2017). By 2020, the number of active abortion clinics nationwide had dropped to 706. The same year Missouri became the first abortion-free state with no active abortion clinic (Sullenger 2021).

In 2011 the United States had around 1,720 facilities (including clinics, hospitals, doctors' offices, etc.) that provided abortion services, but by 2017 the number of such facilities had declined to 1,587, and six states were left with only one abortion clinic (O'Connor 2019). More than half of women in 25 states lived in a county without an abortion provider (Pettway 2017). Table 6.1 provides data on the number of abortion clinics in red and blue states and changes between 2017 and 2020.

Several observations stand out. First, red states have much fewer abortion facilities than blue states. The average number of abortion facilities in red states is five per state while for the blue states, the average is 32 per state. Second, the decline in the number of abortion facilities in red states is much more pronounced than in blue states. Of the 24 red states, seven states experienced an average decline of 27 percent. Among the blue states, nine experienced an average decline of 17 percent. Third, among the red states, 12 states experienced no change while only four saw an increase. Among the blue states, three states saw no change while five states saw an increase.

The decline in the number of abortion providers impacts access to abortion services. Table 6.2 provides data about the percentage of women aged 15 to 44 who lived in counties without an abortion provider in 2019.

In 2019, 39 percent of reproductive-aged women in the United States lived in counties that did not have an abortion provider (Welsh 2021).

TABLE 6.1 Number of Abortion Clinics by State 2017–2020

Red States	# of Abortion Clinics 2020	Change in # of Abortion Clinics 2017–2020	Abortion Clinics % Change in 2017–2020	Blue States	# of Abortion Clinics 2020	Change in # of Abortion Clinics 2017–2020	% Change in Abortion Clinics 2017–2020
Texas	24	3	14%	California	173	12	7%
North Carolina	16	2	14%	New York	104	-9	-8%
Georgia	14	-1	-7%	New Jersey	37	-4	-10%
Arizona	9	0	0%	Washington	37	-3	-8%
Indiana	7	1	7%	Illinois	30	5	20%
Tennessee	7	-1	-12%	Michigan	24	3	14%
Montana	6	-1	-20%	Maryland	23	-2	-8%
Alabama	5	0	0%	Connecticut	20	-6	-23%
Oklahoma	5	1	25%	Maine	17	1	6%
Alaska	4	0	0%	Massachusetts	17	-2	-11%
Kansas	4	0	0%	Oregon	17	1	6%
Idaho	3	-1	-25%	Pennsylvania	17	-1	-6%
Louisiana	3	0	0%	New Mexico	6	0	0%
Nebraska	3	-1	-25%	Vermont	6	0	0%
South Carolina	3	-1	-33%	Hawaii	4	0	0%
Arkansas	2	1	100%	Delaware	3	-1	-25%
Kentucky	2	0	0%	Rhode Island	1	-1	-50%
Utah	2	0	0%				
Wyoming	2	0	0%				
Mississippi	1	0	0%				
Missouri	1	-2	-67%				
North Dakota	1	0	0%				
South Dakota	1	0	0%				
West Virginia	1	0	0%				
Average	5				32		

Adapted from: "Number of Abortion Clinics by State, 2017–2020." 2021. Online at https://data.guttmacher.org/.

Note: Abortion Clinics are healthcare facilities other than hospitals and physicians' offices that provide abortions. Physicians' offices that provide 400 or more abortions in a calendar year are counted as clinics.

TABLE 6.2 Percent of Women Ages 15–44 who live in Counties without an Abortion Provider 2019

Red States		Blue States	
Wyoming	96%	New Mexico	48%
Missouri	94%	Pennsylvania	39%
West Virginia	90%	Vermont	38%
Mississippi	88%	Rhode Island	36%
Arkansas	86%	Michigan	34%
Kentucky	82%	Illinois	32%
South Dakota	76%	Maryland	25%
Louisiana	75%	Oregon	22%
North Dakota	72%	Delaware	18%
South Carolina	71%	Hawaii	18%
Idaho	67%	New Jersey	15%
Indiana	66%	Massachusetts	13%
Georgia	64%	Washington	10%
Utah	63%	New York	7%
Oklahoma	62%	Connecticut	4%
Kansas	61%	California	3%
Tennessee	61%	Maine	1%
Alabama	59%		
North Carolina	53%		
Montana	48%		
Texas	46%		
Nebraska	40%		
Alaska	32%		
Arizona	18%		
Average	65%		21%

Adapted from: Jennifer Welsh. 2021. "A Verywell Report: Abortion Access Ranked by State." 2021. Online at https://verywell health.com.

Note: Population data are five-year estimates. Abortion provider data are approximation of women who may seek abortion care.

However, when the data is broken down by red and blue states, a sharp contrast emerges between the two. Among the red states, in 19 out of 24 states, over 50 percent of women aged 15–44 live in counties without an abortion provider. Among the 17 blue states, only in one state – New Mexico – 48 percent of women lived in counties without an abortion provider. The top five worst states for access to abortion are all red states of Wyoming, Missouri, West Virginia, Mississippi, and Arkansas, with the percentage of 14–55 aged women living in counties without an abortion provider ranging from 82 to 96 percent. West Virginia had only one abortion provider in the entire state made up of 55 counties. Similarly, Missouri had only one abortion provider among its 116 counties (Welsh 2021). In contrast, the top five states for providing easy access to abortion services are all blue states of Maine, California, Connecticut, New York, and Washington with the percentage of women aged 15–44 living in counties without an abortion provider ranging from a low of 1 percent in Maine to 10 percent in Washington. Overall, among all the red states, on average, 65 percent of women lived in counties without an abortion provider compared to 21 percent among all blue states.

The lack of abortion providers at the county or state level means that women seeking an abortion must travel to other counties in the state or out of state to get an abortion. This increases the cost of getting an abortion by adding travel, food, and lodging expenses to the cost of the abortion procedure itself. This has a disproportionately negative impact on poor women who may not be able to afford the cost and thus are denied access to abortion services. Table 6.3 provides data on the percentage of legal abortions obtained by out-of-state residents in individual states.

Even before the *Roe v. Wade decision* was overturned in June of 2022, almost 10 percent of patients seeking abortion nationwide traveled out of state to get an abortion (Seshadri 2023). Residents of a state where abortion is banned or strictly restricted are likely to travel to neighboring states or other states where abortion is permitted or have fewer restrictions making it easier to get an abortion. For example, in 2020, Kansas led all states in the percentage of legal abortions obtained by out-of-state residents. Fifty-two percent of all legal abortions performed in Kansas were obtained by out-of-state residents. A major reason for this is the fact that in May 2019 Missouri passed a law known as HB 126 or the Missouri Stands for the Unborn Act that prohibited abortion after eight weeks of pregnancy, i.e., after a heartbeat is detected, the law was scheduled to go into effect on August 28 but was blocked by a court and consequently enforcement of the law delayed due to court appeals. However, Missouri already had some of the strictest abortion restrictions in the country. (Keller 2021; Andone 2019; North 2019). In sharp contrast, in April 2019, the Kansas State Supreme Court ruled that the Kansas constitution protects a woman's right to an abortion and the state may infringe on this right only if the state can demonstrate that it has a compelling interest (Margolies and Llopis-Jepsen 2019).

In 2020, Missouri also had only one abortion clinic and had the highest rate of residents leaving the state to get an abortion elsewhere. Consequently, only 1 percent of Missouri residents obtained an abortion in the state. Thus, it is not surprising that Missouri residents seeking abortion fled to neighboring states like Kansas and Illinois where abortion was

TABLE 6.3 Percentage of Legal Abortions Obtained by Out-of-State Residents, 2020

Red States	Percent	Blue States	Percent
Kansas	52%	New Mexico	30%
North Dakota	29%	Illinois	21%
Wyoming	24%	Vermont	17%
Missouri	20%	Rhode Island	16%
Georgia	17%	Delaware	12%
North Carolina	17%	Oregon	10%
Louisiana	17%	New Jersey	7%
Nebraska	16%	Pennsylvania	7%
Oklahoma	16%	New York	6%
Alabama	15%	Maine	6%
South Dakota	15%	Michigan	6%
West Virginia	15%	Connecticut	5%
Kentucky	15%	Washington	5%
Arkansas	12%	Massachusetts	4%
Montana	11%	Hawaii	2%
Mississippi	10%		
Idaho	6%		
South Carolina	5%		
Indiana	5%		
Utah	5%		
Texas	2%		
Alaska	1%		
Arizona	1%		
Average	14.0%		9.0%
Tennessee	NR	California	NR
		Maryland	NR

Adapted from: "Percentage of Legal Abortions Obtained by Out of State Residents." 2021. Online at https://www.kff.org/.

Notes: California, Maryland, and Tennessee did not report or did not meet reporting standards.

Data includes those reported by hospitals and licensed ambulatory facilities only.

NR = Not Reported or state did not report the data.

legal. In 2020, more than 10,000 pregnant women traveled to Illinois for an abortion which made up about 21 percent of all abortions performed in the state. Most of them came from Missouri with others coming from Indiana and Wisconsin ("Which States are People Traveling to For Abortion?" 2022).

After Kansas, New Mexico had the second-highest rate of (30 percent) legal abortions obtained by out-of-state residents. Largely because it is sandwiched between Arizona and Texas which have some of the country's most restrictive abortion laws. Similarly, more than 6,400 out-of-state residents got abortions in Georgia in 2020, about 17 percent of all abortions in the state. Most of these people traveled from South Carolina, Tennessee, and Alabama ("Which States are People Traveling to For Abortion?" 2022).

Abortion Restrictions, Bans, and Trigger Laws

According to the Guttmacher Institute, since the 1973 *Roe v. Wade* decision, states have passed more than 1,000 restrictions on abortion access with more than a quarter of them being enacted between 2010 and 2016 concerning medication abortion, private insurance coverage, parental involvement, counseling, and the like. By 1916, 11 states had imposed restrictions on private insurance plans' coverage of abortion services, in over 40 states individual or institutional healthcare providers could refuse to provide abortion services, and 27 states had imposed mandatory waiting periods (Pettway 2017).

The election of Republican Donald J. Trump to the presidency after the 2016 election harmed reproductive rights – from contraceptives to abortion – in the United States (Daniel 2022; Chuang and Weisman 2019; Pocan 2017). Reproductive rights advocacy became more difficult. Most importantly, President Trump had an opportunity to appoint three conservative justices to the United States Supreme Court creating a 6-3 conservative majority on the court. In addition, Trump nominated and the Republican-controlled Senate confirmed more than 220 judges on the lower federal courts throughout the country (Greenberger 2021). This further fueled the abortion debate in many states as anti-abortion groups used their political clout to push for restrictive abortion policies in state legislatures and courts.

Red state legislatures opposed to abortion rights pursued a variety of different strategies such as requiring that an abortion be performed by a licensed physician, restricting coverage of abortions in private health insurance plans, counseling, parental consent, and prohibiting abortion after a certain number of months of pregnancy ranging from six weeks to 18 weeks (Kitchener 2022a). Republican-led Kentucky legislature overrode Democratic governor Andy Beshear's veto and passed a law banning abortion after 15 weeks (Kitchener 2022b). Similarly, Arizona passed a 15-week abortion ban. Several states such as Idaho and Oklahoma passed laws based on Texas' 2021 fetal heartbeat law which prohibited abortion when a fetal heartbeat is detected ("Which States Passed New Abortion Laws in 2022" 2022). According to the Guttmacher Institute, between January 1 and March 15, 2022, 519 abortion restriction bills were introduced in 41 states (Rovner 2022).

As red states began to dismantle abortion laws, blue states started to strengthen their abortion laws. Blue states like Illinois, Maine, New York, and Rhode Island led the charge to enshrine abortion rights at the state level. By the year 2022, 16 states had codified the right to have an abortion in their state (Gonzalez, 2022; Luhby 2019; Vestal 2019). States such as New Jersey, Washington, Maryland, and Connecticut expanded abortion rights in their states ("Which States Passed New Abortion Laws in 2022." 2022)

The new state abortion laws further deepened the political divide between the red and blue states. Many red states passed laws restricting reproductive rights while many blue states have led the charge to enshrine abortion rights into the state laws or the state constitutions (Vestal 2019; Luhby 2019). States began to divide rapidly into two camps. Many red states banned almost all or most abortions and blue states codified reproductive rights (Karmarck 2022).

Table 6.4 illustrates how between 2017 and 2020 red and blue states were moving in opposite directions concerning the number of abortions, abortion rates, and trends.

In 2017 alone, the U.S. abortion rate dropped to 13.5 abortions per 1,000 women aged 15–44. Increased abortion restrictions were more pronounced in the Midwest and South (Jones, Witwer, and Jerman 2017). This trend continued between 2017 and 2020. As can be seen from the data in Table 6.4, some of the states with the most restrictive abortion laws saw a significant decline in abortion rates per 1,000 women aged 15 to 44 between 2017 and 2020. The most dramatic decline occurred in the red states of Missouri, South Dakota, Wyoming, West Virginia, and Louisiana ranging from 98 percent in Missouri to 25 percent in Louisiana. Among these five states, the average decline in abortion rate was 51.6 percent. Only two blue states – Oregon and Massachusetts – experienced double-digit declines in abortion rates – 13 and 10 percent drops, respectively. Some of the red and blue states experienced an increase in abortion rates due to easier access to abortion and out-of-state residents from neighboring states with abortion bans or restrictions traveling to get an abortion. By 2020, there was a considerable variation across states concerning abortion rates as can be seen from Table 6.5.

The difference between the red and blue states stands in sharp contrast. In 2020, the average abortion rate per 1,000 women aged 15 to 44, among the 24 red states, was 7.3 compared to 16.3 among the 17 blue states. Among the red states, only in four states out of 24 – Oklahoma, Kansas,

TABLE 6.4 Percent Change in Abortion Rate by State 2017–2020

Red States	% Change in Abortion Rate 2017–2020	Blue States	% Change in Abortion Rate 2017–2020
Missouri	−98.0%	Illinois	28.0%
South Dakota	−74.0%	New Mexico	26.0%
Wyoming	−31.0%	Rhode Island	20.0%
West Virginia	−30.0%	Michigan	18.0%
Louisiana	−25.0%	California	17.0%
Tennessee	−12.0%	Maine	15.0%
Montana	−1.0%	New York	10.0%
North Dakota	−1.0%	Maryland	4.0%
Alaska	0.0%	New Jersey	4.0%
South Carolina	0.0%	Pennsylvania	4.0%
Utah	0.0%	Hawaii	1.0%
Arizona	1.0%	Washington	−3.0%
Texas	1.0%	Delaware	−5.0%
Arkansas	2.0%	Connecticut	−6.0%
Indiana	2.0%	Vermont	−6.0%
North Carolina	5.0%	Massachusetts	−10.0%
Alabama	6.0%	Oregon	−13.0%
Nebraska	7.0%		
Georgia	12.0%		
Kansas	19.0%		
Idaho	23.0%		
Kentucky	26.0%		
Mississippi	42.0%		
Oklahoma	100.0%		

Adapted from: "Percent Change in Abortion Rate by State, 2017–2020." 2021. Online at https://data.guttmacher.org.

Note: Abortion rate is per 1,000 for women aged 15 to 44.

North Carolina, and Georgia – abortion rates reached double digits. In contrast, in all 17 blue states, abortion rates were in double digits varying from 10 per 1,000 in Delaware to 29 per 1,000 in New Jersey. The top five red states with the lowest abortion rates were Missouri, South Dakota, Wyoming, West Virginia, and Utah. The top five blue states with the highest abortion rates were New Jersey, New York, Maryland, Illinois, and California.

By the early 2020s, on the issue of abortion, and the broader issue of reproductive rights, America's red-and-blue divide had gotten starker

TABLE 6.5 Abortion per 1,000 Women Aged 15 to 44 by State: July 1, 2020

Red States	Rate per 1,000	Blue States	Rate per 1,000
Missouri	0.1	Delaware	10.0
South Dakota	0.8	Maine	10.1
Wyoming	0.9	Oregon	10.3
West Virginia	3.1	Vermont	10.7
Utah	4.4	Washington	11.7
Idaho	4.8	Hawaii	12.1
Kentucky	4.8	Massachusetts	12.2
South Carolina	5.3	Rhode Island	13.3
Arkansas	5.6	Pennsylvania	13.6
Nebraska	5.9	New Mexico	14.7
Alabama	6.0	Connecticut	16.7
Indiana	6.0	Michigan	16.8
Mississippi	6.1	California	19.2
North Dakota	7.8	Illinois	21.3
Louisiana	8.0	Maryland	25.9
Tennessee	8.1	New York	28.8
Montana	8.2	New Jersey	29.2
Alaska	8.6		
Arizona	9.3		
Texas	9.5		
Oklahoma	12.4		
Kansas	14.5		
North Carolina	15.3		
Georgia	18.9		
Average	7.3		16.3

Adapted from: Ranji, Usha; Karen Diep; and Alina Salganicoff. 2023. "Key Facts on Abortion in the United States." Online at https://www.kff.org.

creating a great chasm between the red and the blue America (Duggan 2022). Red and blue states had turned into mutually hostile legal territories with red states banning or severely restricting abortions and blue states becoming sanctuaries for women seeking abortion (Stancil 2022).

Tables 6.6 and 6.7 compare red and blue states' ranking and grades concerning reproductive rights in 2015 and 2022, respectively. The Institute for Women's Policy Research calculated each state's reproductive rights total score based on eight indicators that included state requirements for parental consent/notification for minors, waiting period, public insurance coverage for abortion, the share of women living in counties with at

TABLE 6.6 States' Reproductive Rights: Index Score, Ranking, and Grade 2015

Red States	Total Score	National Rank	Overall Grade	Blue States	Total Score	National Rank	Overall Grade
South Dakota	0.23	51	F	Michigan	1.66	45	D
Nebraska	0.59	50	F	Pennsylvania	2.53	31	C
Kansas	0.76	49	F	Maine	3.53	23	C+
Idaho	0.81	48	F	Delaware	3.82	20	C+
Tennessee	1.42	47	D-	Rhode Island	4.63	15	B+
Louisiana	1.62	46	D	Massachusetts	4.74	14	B+
Missouri	1.68	44	D	Illinois	4.78	13	B+
Arkansas	1.72	43	D	New Mexico	5.02	12	B+
Indiana	1.89	42	D+	Washington	5.20	10	B+
Alabama	1.91	40	D+	California	5.24	9	B+
Oklahoma	1.95	39	D+	New York	5.59	7	A-
Mississippi	2.09	38	C-	Connecticut	5.95	6	A-
Utah	2.16	37	C-	Hawaii	6.00	5	A-
Texas	2.19	36	C-	New Jersey	6.08	4	A-
Wyoming	2.21	35	C-	Maryland	6.14	3	A-
North Dakota	2.27	33	C-	Vermont	6.15	2	A-
Kentucky	2.43	32	C	Oregon	6.28	1	A-
Alaska	2.83	29	C				
Georgia	2.85	28	C				
North Carolina	3.01	26	C				
South Carolina	3.07	25	C+				
Arizona	3.36	24	C+				
West Virginia	4.35	18	B				
Montana	5.04	11	B+				
Average	2.19	36			3.50	13	
Washington DC	5.50	8	A-				

Adapted from: Institute for Women's Policy Research. 2015. Chapter 5: "Reproductive Rights," pp. 167–193 in The Status of Women in the States, 2015 Report. Online at https://statusofwomendata.org/.

Notes:

(1) Washington, D.C. which ranked eighth is excluded from analysis for our purpose.

(2) The total score on the Reproductive Rights index is based on eight indicators. They include parental consent/notice for minors; waiting period, public insurance coverage for abortion; share of women living in counties with at least one abortion provider; state governors and state legislature fully opposed to reproductive freedoms; expanded access to Medicaid Family Planning services; coverage of infertility treatments; and mandatory, high quality sex education in public school.

least one abortion provider, governor and state legislature fully opposed to reproductive freedoms, expanded access to Medicaid family planning services, coverage of infertility treatment, and mandatory, high-quality sex education in public schools. Each state's national ranking and grades are

TABLE 6.7 States' Reproductive Rights Index: Index Score, Ranking, and Grade 2022

Red States	Total Score	National Rank	Overall Grade	Blue States	Total Score	National Rank	Overall Grade
Missouri	0.22	50	F	Michigan	1.65	34	D+
Idaho	0.33	51	F	Pennsylvania	2.52	25	C+
Nebraska	0.60	49	F	Delaware	3.32	19	C+
Arkansas	0.73	48	F	Massachusetts	3.87	16	B-
South Dakota	0.74	47	F	Illinois	4.13	13	B
North Dakota	0.78	46	F	Rhode Island	4.78	12	B
Arizona	0.82	45	F	Hawaii	4.95	11	B+
West Virginia	1.10	44	D-	New Mexico	5.02	10	B+
Louisiana	1.28	43	D-	Vermont	5.12	9	B+
Indiana	1.30	42	D	Maryland	5.21	8	B+
Utah	1.37	41	D	Maine	5.26	7	B+
Alabama	1.41	40	D	New York	5.42	6	B+
Oklahoma	1.47	37	D	Connecticut	5.45	5	B+
Wyoming	1.54	36	D+	Oregon	5.77	4	A-
Mississippi	1.59	35	D+	Washington	5.90	3	A-
Kentucky	1.68	33	D+	California	6.22	2	A-
South Carolina	1.79	32	C--	New Jersey	6.24	1	A-
Tennessee	1.87	31	C-				
Kansas	1.89	30	C-				
Georgia	1.95	29	C-				
Texas	2.32	26	C				
Alaska	2.68	24	C+				
North Carolina	2.97	21	C+				
Montana	3.94	14	B-				
Average	1.60	39			4.75	11	
Washington DC	3.50	17	B-				

Adapted from: Manson, Nicole C. et al. 2022 "IWPR Reproductive Rights Index: A State-by-State Analysis and Ranking." Online at https://iwpr.org/.

Notes:

(1) Washington, DC which ranked 17th is excluded from analysis for our purpose.
(2) The total score on the Reproductive Rights index is based on eight indicators. They include parental consent/notice for minors; waiting period, public insurance coverage for abortion; share of women living in counties with at least one abortion provider; state governors and state legislature fully opposed to reproductive freedoms; expanded access to Medicaid Family Planning services; coverage of infertility treatments; and mandatory, high quality sex education in public School.

based on the reproductive rights scores (Institute for Women's Policy Research 2015; Mason et al. 2022).

As can be seen from the data in Table 6.6, in 2015, the five worst states for women's reproductive rights were red states of South Dakota, Nebraska, Kansas, Idaho, and Tennessee while the five best states were blue states of Oregon, Vermont, Maryland, New Jersey, and Hawaii. Of the 24 red states, 11 (46 percent) received a grade of D or F and only two states (8 percent) – Montana and West Virginia – received a grade of B. In sharp contrast, of the 17 blue states, 13 (76 percent) received a grade of B+ or better. Among the blue states, only Michigan received a grade of D and none received a grade of F.

Table 6.7 reflects some of the changes in states' reproductive rights ranking and grades that took place between 2015 and 2022. The number of states receiving failing grades increased between 2015 and 2022. Overall, red states had gotten worse while blue states had gotten better concerning reproductive rights. The five worst states for reproductive rights in 2022 were the red states of Missouri, Idaho, Nebraska, Arkansas, and South Dakota. There are states that imposed the most severe restrictions or limitations on access to reproductive healthcare, including abortion during this period. Of the 24 red states, 16 states (66 percent) received a grade of F or D. An increase of 20 percent from 46 percent in 2015 to 66 percent in 2022. Only one red state, Montana, received a grade of B–. Among the blue states, the five best states for reproductive rights were New Jersey, California, Washington, Oregon, and Connecticut. Of the best five states in 2015, the states of Hawaii, Maryland, and Vermont dropped out of the top five in 2022 and were replaced by states of California, Washington, and Connecticut. Of the 17 blue states, 13 (76 percent) received a grade of B or A. Only three blue states (18 percent) – that of Delaware, Pennsylvania, and Michigan – received a grade of C+ or D+.

The World Population Institute (2022) issued a report card on states' grades on reproductive health and rights in 2022 using a different number and set of criteria in determining each state composite index than had been used by the Institute for Women's Policy Research. It used 11 criteria that focused on three broad indicators – prevention, affordability, and access. The 11 criteria included were: state effort in promoting comprehensive sex education in schools (15 points maximum); whether nurses are authorized to dispense medication (5 points maximum); emergency contraception mandated in an emergency room (5 points maximum); minors' access to contraceptive services (10 points maximum); Medicaid expansion under ACA (15 points maximum); a Medicaid "waiver" for expanding eligibility for family planning services (10 points maximum); insurance coverage of abortion services (5 points maximum); an absence of burdensome abortion restrictions (10 points maximum); an absence of TARP laws (5 points maximum); abortion policy in absence of Roe (10 points maximum); and county level access to family planning and abortion services (10 points maximum). Table 6.8 reports the institute's measurement of total scores and assignment of grades.

TABLE 6.8 States' Grades on Reproductive Health and Rights 2022

Red States	Total Score[a]	Letter Grade[b]	Blue States	Total Score	Letter Grade[b]
South Dakota	9.0	F	Michigan	19.0	F
Mississippi	16.0	F	Pennsylvania	63.5	C
Kansas	19.0	F	Rhode Island	67.0	C
Alabama	21.0	F	Massachusetts	68.0	C
Louisiana	23.0	F	Delaware	69.0	C
Utah	24.0	F	Illinois	69.0	C
North Dakota	25.0	F	Connecticut	70.0	C
Oklahoma	28.0	F	Vermont	74.0	B
Kentucky	28.0	F	Hawaii	80.0	B
South Carolina	29.5	F	Maryland	83.0	B
Texas	30.5	F	New York	85.0	B
Indiana	31.0	F	Maine	88.0	A
Nebraska	32.0	F	New Jersey	88.0	A
Tennessee	33.0	F	New Mexico	93.0	A
Missouri	34.0	F	Oregon	93.0	A
Arizona	35.0	F	Washington	94.0	A
Arkansas	35.5	F	California	100.0	A
Georgia	37.0	F			
West Virginia	40.0	F			
Wyoming	44.0	F			
Idaho	44.0	F			
North Carolina	57.0	D			
Montana	63.0	C			
Alaska	65.0	C			
Average	33.5			76.6	

Adapted from: "The State of Reproductive Health and Rights: A 50-State Report Card." 2022. Online at https://www.populationinstitute.org/.

Notes:

[a] Eleven criteria were used in determining states' composite score.
[b] Grading system was based on 86–100 = A; 71–85.9 = B; 61–70.9 = C; 50–60.9 = D; <49.9 = F.

The five worst states for reproductive health and rights were the red states of South Dakota, Mississippi, Kansas, Alabama, and Louisiana while the five best states were the blue states of California, Washington, Oregon, New Mexico, and New Jersey. Among the 24 red states, 21 states (88 percent) received a grade of F. Among the blue states, only one state, Michigan, received an F grade. In sharp contrast, of the 17 blue states, 10 states (59 percent) received a grade of B or better.

What the above data illustrates is that red states have imposed more restrictive laws and regulations while the blue states have promoted and expanded reproductive rights, including abortion. Even before the Dobbs decision overturning *Roe v. Wade*, red and blue states were moving in opposite directions.

Dobbs V. Jackson Women's Health Organization 2022

Encouraged by the conservative majority on the Supreme Court, several red states passed extremely restrictive laws to get the issue to the U.S. Supreme Court in the hope that it would overturn the 1973 *Roe v. Wade* ruling that legalized abortion nationwide. In fact, by 2022, in anticipation of the Supreme Court overturning the Roe decision, 12 red states had passed "trigger laws" banning abortion altogether to go into effect or banning nearly all abortions except in most extreme cases. Some states like Florida and Arizona passed a 15-week ban on abortion modeled after Mississippi's Gestational Age Act of 2018 which bans abortion after 15 weeks ("Which States Passed New Abortion Laws in 2022" 2022). Also, in anticipation of the Supreme Court overturning Roe v. Wade and returning the issue to the states, several states proposed amendments to the state's constitutions seeking voter approval to ban abortion in the state or enshrine abortion rights into the state's constitutions. For example, red states like Kansas and Kentucky proposed amending the state constitution to ban abortion while blue states such as California and Vermont sought to enshrine abortion rights into their state's constitutions (Kindy 2022).

In March of 2018, Mississippi adopted the Gestational Age Act which prohibited almost all abortions after 15 weeks of pregnancy. Jackson Women's Health Organization, the only licensed clinic in the state, filed a lawsuit in the federal district court challenging the constitutionality of the law and requesting a temporary restraining order, which was issued. The district court also granted the clinic's motion for summary judgment and ruled that the state may not ban abortion before fetal viability which occurs around 24 weeks. The U.S. Court of Appeals of the Fifth Circuit upheld the district court's ruling. The state of Mississippi appealed the ruling to the U.S. Supreme Court which in May 2021 agreed to hear the case. The case was argued before the Supreme Court on December 1, 2021.

Jackson's Women's Health Organization argued that abortion is grounded in the 14th Amendment and physical autonomy and body injury are essential elements of "liberty" protected by the Due Process Clause of the 14th Amendment. The state of Mississippi argued that both the district court and the appeals court were wrong in finding a right to viability abortion in the U.S. Constitution since it does not mention abortion. Furthermore, the state argued that the word "liberty" as written in the 14th Amendment only involved fundamental rights that are deeply rooted in U.S. history and tradition. The state urged the court to overturn both *Roe v. Wade* and *Planned Parenthood of Southeastern PA v. Casey* decisions.

On May 2, 2022, Politico published a leaked draft opinion of the court which sent shockwaves across the country even though the overturning of Roe v. Wade was anticipated by many legal experts and analysts. The leaked initial draft opinion indicated that the Supreme Court intended to overturn *Roe V. Wade* (Gerstein and Ward 2022). Reactions to the leak among political leaders in the red and blue states provided insight into how the red-blue state divide would redefine reproductive rights after the end of the *Roe v. Wade* world (Kitchener and Roubein 2022). The draft opinion became a reality when on June 24, 2022, the U.S. Supreme Court issued its ruling in the case of *Dobbs v. Jackson Women's Health Organization* overturning the *Roe v. Wade* decision of 1973 by a vote of 6 to 3. Five conservative justices – Samuel Alito, Bret Cavanaugh, Neil Gorsuch, Clarence Thomas, and Amy Barrett – issued a majority opinion; the conservative chief justice John Roberts, Jr., issued a concurring opinion; and the three liberal justices – Stephen Bryer, Sonia Sotomayor, and Elena Kagan – issued a dissenting opinion. In delivering the majority opinion of the court, Justice Samuel Alito wrote,

> We hold that Roe and Casey must be overturned. The Constitution makes no reference to abortion, and no such right is implicitly protected by any constitutional provision, including the one on which the defenders of Roe and Casey now chiefly rely – the Due Process Clause of the Fourteenth Amendment. That provision has been held to guarantee some rights that are not mentioned in the Constitution, but any such rights must be "deeply rooted in this nation's history and tradition" and "implicit" in the concept of ordered liberty. The right to abortion does not fall within this category. ...The Constitution does not prohibit the citizens of each state from regulating or prohibiting abortion. Rose and Casey arrogated that authority. We now overrule those decisions and return that authority to the people and their elected representatives."
>
> *Dobbs v. Jackson Women's Health Organization,* 597 U.S. pp. 5–6; 79.
> https://www.supremecourt.gov

By overturning the Roe decision, the U.S. Supreme Court took away the nationally guaranteed right to abortion based on the U.S. Constitution. In *Roe v. Wade*, the U.S. Supreme Court in 1973 had recognized abortion as a liberty right under the 14th Amendment. In the Dobbs ruling, the U.S. Supreme Court dismantled 50 years of precedent protecting the national right to abortion by ruling that there is no constitutional right to an abortion agreeing with the state of Mississippi that both Roe and Casey cases were wrongly decided. It further argued that the right to abortion was not rooted in the nation's history and tradition. The ruling returned the issue of abortion to people and their elected representatives at the state level which meant that each state could set its abortion policy. The three liberal justices in their dissent argued that the majority had undermined women's personal autonomy and warned about total bans and severe restrictions states would be free to impose regarding abortion under the ruling.

The Dobbs decision also exemplified the pendulum feature of American federalism in which political power, over time, oscillates between federal and state governments. The court expressed federalism concern by noting that at the time of the *Roe v. Wade* ruling in 1973, 30 states prohibited abortion. In essence, by returning the power to make abortion policy to people and their elected representatives, the Supreme Court shifted power and authority back to the states and their legislative, electoral, and judicial processes (Hodge, Jr; Ghaith; and Krumholz 2022).

The ruling opened a new battleground in the abortion war – state legislatures/governors and state constitutions. This also meant, going forward, that state courts will also play a major role in deciding whether abortion is a fundamental right guaranteed in the state constitution and deciding the constitutionality of legislative actions dealing with abortion. The ruling also meant that 13 states that had passed trigger laws designed to go into effect as soon as Roe v. Wade was overturned would go into effect (Middleton 2022; Barnes, Marimow, and Wagner 2022; Kitchener et al. 2022; Lazzarini 2022).

The Dobbs decision was a major victory for the religious rights and Christian nationalists who had fought for 50 years to overturn Roe v. Wade (Stewart 2022a). It also meant that abortion rights groups would have to change their legal and political strategies to regain and protect abortion rights at the state level by filing lawsuits to prevent states from banning abortion, launching a political campaign to defeat ballot initiatives aimed at abolishing the constitutional right to abortion, and supporting ballot initiatives designed to enshrined abortion rights in the state constitutions where they can (Zernike 2022).

Post-Dobbs Decision: Reproductive Rights in Red and Blue States

The Dobbs ruling ushered in an era of uncertainty regarding abortion rights at the state level. Abortion rights supporters and foes started waging state-by-state battles on the battlefields of state legislatures, elections and ballot boxes, and the state courts. The worsening division and political divide between red and blue states concerning abortion rights are demonstrated in red states moving to ban or severely restrict abortion rights while the blue states moving to protect, expand, and enshrine abortion rights in the state constitutions (Weisman 2022).

The red and blue states moving in the opposite direction with more intensity is made possible by the significant increase in trifecta control of state government by one of the two political parties and a corresponding decline in divided governments. For example, in 1992, Republicans enjoyed trifecta control of government only in three states; today that number is up to 22 states. In 1992 Democrats enjoyed trifecta control of government in 16 states, and today they enjoy trifecta control in 17 states. Today, only 11 states have divided governments. Red states have become redder while blue states have become bluer (Kettl 2023). One of the primary causes for this development is the gerrymandering of legislative districts.

Legislative Actions

Soon after the Dobbs decision, the abortion landscape began to change dramatically as abortion was banned or severely restricted in many red states (Manzanetti 2022). Red states such as Missouri and Indiana pushed strident abortion bans while others imposed severe restrictions on abortion practices (Rovner 2022; Bacharier 2022; Phillips and Hamburger 2022). The Republican governors in blue states – Maryland, Massachusetts, New Hampshire, and Vermont – pledged to uphold abortion rights out of political necessity (Jeong and Bikales 2022) while Democratic governors of blue states promised to protect and strengthen abortion rights in their states. Red states restricted abortion rights by imposing pre-viability gestational bans, prohibiting specific methods of abortion care or procedures, targeting regulations of abortion providers, and requiring parental notifications and parental involvement. In 2022, Idaho and Oklahoma passed laws based on Texas' 2021 Fetal Heartbeat Law, which prohibits abortions if a fetal heartbeat is detected while Arizona and Kentucky passed a 15-week abortion ban. Florida, a state that is trending red, passed a law imposing a 6-week abortion ban (Rubin 2023; Parker 2023; Sarkissian 2023; "Which States Passed New Abortion Laws in 2022?" 2022).

In 12 state legislatures, Republican majorities passed 25 laws providing at least $250 million in taxpayer funds or tax credits for "crisis pregnancy centers" which are faith-based and aim to dissuade women from having abortions while in blue states Democratic governors and lawmakers cut funding to such centers and passed laws creating civil penalties for misleading women to stop them from seeking an abortion (Kindy 2023).

Blue states moved to strengthen and expand abortion rights by providing constitutional protection, increasing access to abortion services, increasing access and safety of abortion clinics, providing state public funding for medically necessary abortions, expanding abortion provider qualifications by allowing physician assistants and nurse practitioners to provide abortion care ("After Roe Fell: Abortion Laws by State" 2023; "State Pro-life and Pro-Abortion Laws and Initiatives" 2023). In Michigan, after gaining trifecta control of state government, Democratic governor Gretchen Whitmer signed a law repealing a 1931 near-total abortion ban. New York also passed a law ensuring all public colleges and universities offer medication abortion. Rhode Island passed a law letting state funds cover abortion in the Medicaid program and those on state employees' insurance plans (Rubin 2023).

By the end of 2023, the abortion landscape had changed significantly after the Supreme Court on June 24, 2022, in *Dobbs v. Jackson Women's Health Organization*, upended the nationally guaranteed right to abortion based on the U.S. Constitution by overturning *Roe V. Wade* decision of 1973 and returning the issue of abortion to the state legislatures and voters. Abortion was totally or almost totally banned in 14 red states. Nearly all states that ban abortion have imposed some form of criminal penalty on abortion providers. In several red state legislatures, "personhood bills" have been introduced that define life as beginning at fertilization or giving embryos legal rights. Blue states have taken actions to protect, expand, and codify abortion rights (Fernando 2023). Table 6.9 provides the current state of abortion laws in the red and blue states.

As can be observed from Table 6.9, there are dramatic differences between the red and blue states concerning abortion rights. Abortion is banned in 14 of the 24 red states. In the remaining 14 red states where abortion is legal, with few exceptions, it is severely restricted by gestational limits ranging from 6 weeks (Georgia and South Carolina) to 22 weeks. Alaska is the only red state that has no gestational limits. In Montana and Wyoming, abortion is legal until viability. Of the 14 states that ban abortion, nine do not even provide an exception for rape or incest, while others allow a very limited exception in medical emergencies like if the mother's life is in danger.

TABLE 6.9 Abortion Laws by State as of July 17, 2024

Red States	Abortion Law	Details
Alabama	Banned	No Exception for Rape or Incest
Alaska	Legal	No Gestational Limit
Arizona	Legal	15-Week Gestational Limit
Arkansas	Banned	No Exception for Rape or Incest
Georgia	Legal	6-Week Gestational Limit
Idaho	Banned	Near-Total Ban
Indiana	Banned	Limited Exceptions
Kansas	Legal	22 Weeks Gestational Limit
Kentucky	Banned	No Exception for Rape or Incest
Louisiana	Banned	No Exception for Rape or Incest
Mississippi	Banned	Exception for Rape but Not Incest
Missouri	Banned	No Exception for Rape or Incest
Montana	Legal	Legal Until Viability
Nebraska	Legal	12-Week Gestational Limit
North Carolina	Legal	12-Week Gestational Limit
North Dakota	Banned	Exception for rape and Incest
Oklahoma	Banned	No Exception for Rape or Incest
South Carolina	Legal	6 Weeks of Gestational Limit
South Dakota	Banned	No Exception for Rape or Incest
Tennessee	Banned	No Exception for Rape or Incest
Texas	Banned	No Exception for Rape or Incest
Utah	Legal	18-Week Gestational Limit
West Virginia	Banned	Near-Total Ban in Place
Wyoming	Legal	Until Viability

Blue States	Abortion Law	Details
California	Legal	Until Viability
Connecticut	Legal	Until Viability
Delaware	Legal	Until Viability
Hawaii	Legal	Until Viability
Illinois	Legal	Until Viability
Maine	Legal	Until Viability
Maryland	Legal	Until Viability
Massachusetts	Legal	Until 24 Weeks
Michigan	Legal	Enshrined in State Constitution
New Jersey	Legal	No Gestational Limit
New Mexico	Legal	No Gestational Limit
New York	Legal	Until Viability
Oregon	Legal	No Gestational Limit
Pennsylvania	Legal	Until 24 Weeks
Rhode Island	Legal	Until Viability
Vermont	Legal	No Gestational Limit
Washington	Legal	Until Viability

Adapted from: "Interactive Map: US Abortion Policies and Access After Roe." Online at https://states.guttmacher.org/policies.

In sharp contrast to the red states, abortion is legal in all 17 blue states. Ten states allow abortion until viability. In *Roe v. Wade*, the Supreme Court ruled that states could not ban abortions before fetal viability, i.e., the point at which the fetus can survive outside the womb. That was around 28 weeks at the time. Today, viability is around 23 weeks due to improvements in medical technology. Massachusetts and Pennsylvania viability is set at 24 weeks. Four states have no gestational limit.

Another way to analyze the status of abortion rights post-Dobbs decision is to compare red and blue states concerning how restrictive or supportive their abortion laws are. The Guttmacher Institute has categorized states along this dimension. They rated states' abortion policies using seven categories based on 20 types of abortion restrictions and 10 types of protective policies. Restrictions examined included factors such as a gestational age ban, a waiting period, a ban on insurance coverage, restrictions on medication abortions, and the like. Protective factors examined included state constitutional protection, funding for abortion, insurance coverage for abortion, protections for patients, abortion clinics, and abortion providers. States were assigned to one of the seven categories based on abortion policies in effect in December 2023 ("Interactive Map: US Abortion Policies and Access After Roe" 2023). Table 6.10 provides a listing of red and blue states by these categories.

Again, the sharp contrast between the red and blue states stands out. Fourteen states are categorized as the most restrictive, three states are considered very restrictive, while another three are considered restrictive. Three other states are categorized as having a mix of both restrictive and protective policies. Only one red state, Alaska, is categorized as protective.

In comparison, of the 17 blue states, one state – Oregon – is categorized as the most protective, six are categorized as very protective, eight states are categorized as protective of abortion rights, while one state, the state of Delaware, is categorized as having a mix of both restrictive and protective policies. Only one state – Pennsylvania – is rated as restrictive.

As mentioned above, two of the policies that tend to restrict abortion rights are the requirements of mandatory waiting periods and counseling before getting an abortion. Table 6.11 provides data on which states require or do not require mandatory waiting periods and/or mandatory in-person counseling.

Of the 24 red states, 21 require a mandatory waiting period ranging from 18 to 72 hours. Only three states – Alaska, Wyoming, and Montana – do not have a mandatory waiting period. In Montanan, it was a result of a court ruling. In contrast, among the 17 blue states, Michigan and Pennsylvania are

TABLE 6.10 Abortion Policies from Most Restrictive to Most Protective by State, as of December 20, 2023

Red States	Abortion Policies	Blue States	Abortion Policies
Alabama	Most Restrictive	California	Very Protective
Alaska	Protective	Connecticut	Protective
Arizona	Restrictive	Delaware	Restrictive/Protective
Arkansas	Most Restrictive	Hawaii	Protective
Georgia	Very Restrictive	Illinois	Protective
Idaho	Most Restrictive	Maine	Protective
Indiana	Most Restrictive	Maryland	Protective
Kansas	Restrictive	Massachusetts	Protective
Kentucky	Most Restrictive	Michigan	Protective*
Louisiana	Most Restrictive	New Jersey	Very Protective
Mississippi	Most Restrictive	New Mexico	Very Protective
Missouri	Most Restrictive	New York	Very Protective
Montana	Protective/Restrictive	Oregon	Most Protective
Nebraska	Very Restrictive	Pennsylvania	Restrictive
North Carolina	Very Restrictive	Rhode Island	Protective
North Dakota	Most Restrictive	Vermont	Very Protective
Oklahoma	Most Restrictive	Washington	Very Protective
South Carolina	Most Restrictive		
South Dakota	Most Restrictive		
Tennessee	Most Restrictive		
Texas	Most Restrictive		
Utah	Restrictive		
West Virginia	Restrictive/Protective		
Wyoming	Restrictive/Protective		

Adapted from: "Interactive map: US Abortion Policies and Access After Roe." 2023. Online at https://states.guttmacher.org/.

Note: The seven categories used are based on 20 types of abortion restrictions and 10 protective policies. Most restrictive = state bans abortion completely or has early gestational age ban along with other restrictions; very restrictive = state has multiple restrictions and early gestational age ban; restrictive = state has multiple restrictions and later gestational age ban; mix of restrictive/protective = state has a combination of restrictions and protections; protective = state has some protective policies; very protective = state has most of the protective policies; most protective = state has all or almost all the protective policies.

the only two states that have a mandatory 24-hour waiting period. The remainder of the 15 states do not have any waiting periods. Concerning mandatory counseling, 12 of the 24 states require in-person mandatory counseling while none of the blue states have such a requirement.

What is clear from the above discussion is that not only have the red and blue states moved further apart following the Dobbs ruling, but they have become hostile legal territories.

TABLE 6.11 Mandatory Waiting Periods and Counseling by State as of August 2023

Red States	Mandatory Waiting Period in Hours	Mandatory In-Person Counseling	Blue States	Mandatory Waiting Period in Hours	Mandatory In-Person Counseling
Alabama	48	No	California	No	No
Alaska	No	No	Connecticut	No	No
Arizona	24	Yes	Delaware	No	No
Arkansas	72	Yes	Hawaii	No	No
Georgia	24	No	Illinois	No	No
Idaho	24	No	Maine	No	No
Indiana	18	Yes	Maryland	No	No
Kansas	24	No	Massachusetts*	No	No
Kentucky	24	Yes	Michigan	24	No
Louisiana**	24	Yes	New Jersey	No	No
Mississippi	24	Yes	New Mexico	No	No
Missouri	72	Yes	New York	No	No
Montana*	No	No	Oregon	No	No
Nebraska	24	No	Pennsylvania	24	No
North Carolina	72	Yes	Rhode Island	No	No
North Dakota	24	No	Vermont	No	No
Oklahoma	72	No	Washington	No	No
South Carolina	24	No			
South Dakota	72	Yes			
Tennessee	48	Yes			
Texas	24	Yes			
Utah	72	Yes			
West Virginia	24	No			
Wyoming	No	No			
Total	21	12		2	0

Adapted from: "Counseling and Waiting Period for Abortion." 2023. Online at https://www.guttmacher.org/.

Notes:

* Permanently enjoined by Court
** Temporarily enjoyed by Court. Policy not in effect.

Abortion at the ballot box: elections and ballot initiatives

Justice Samuel Alito wrote in the Dobbs ruling overturning Roe v. Wade, "We do not pretend to know how our political system or society will respond." Eighteen months following the Dobbs decision, we have a pretty good idea of how the American voters have responded. In the USA TODAY/Suffolk University poll conducted of 1,000 registered voters in June 5–9, 2023, by almost a 2-1 margin – 58 to 30 percent – opposed the decision to overturn *Roe v. Wade*. One in four Americans stated that the state's efforts to impose strict limits on abortion access have made them more supportive of abortion rights. This included more women than men, more Democrats than Republicans, and more younger voters than seniors. Among women who identify themselves as politically independent, one of the most critical swing groups in elections, by a margin of 28 to 5 percent said that they had become more supportive of abortion rights. By a margin of 80 to 14 percent, those surveyed opposed the idea of enacting a federal law banning abortion nationwide pushed by anti-abortion activists. This included Democrats, Republicans, and Independents. In fact, by a margin of 53 to 39 percent, respondents supported a federal law ensuring access to abortion. The findings of this poll are consistent with other polls like the Gallup poll in May 2023, in which 69 percent of respondents stated that abortion should generally be legal in the first three months of pregnancy (Page, Locker, and Herszenhorn 2023). Polling suggested that a strong majority of Americans were opposed to the sweeping abortion bans that often failed to provide exceptions for rape and incest.

2022 Elections

American voters had a chance to express their displeasure about the Dobbs ruling and the resulting attacks on abortion rights at the ballot box in the 2022 November elections. While the Supreme Court justices were not on the ballot, the issue of abortion certainly was. The 2023 election is sometimes referred to as an "abortion election." Stakes were particularly high in states like Pennsylvania, Michigan, and Wisconsin where the legislature and governor's mansion were held by different political parties. In Pennsylvania, the Democratic governor who was term-limited had vetoed several bills passed by Republican-controlled legislature designed to restrict access to abortions. Similarly, in Michigan, the Democratic governor Gretchen Whitmer was engaged in a battle over abortion rights with the Republican-controlled legislature. In Wisconsin, the Democratic governor Tony Evers was also fighting with the Republican-led legislature over abortion rights (Ford 2022). Just hours after the Supreme Court ruling overturning Roe v. Wade, President Joe Biden in a defiant speech from the White House had declared "This fall, Roe is on the ballot."

American voters delivered their verdict on abortion rights on election night on November 8, 2022. Before the election, several polls and political experts had predicted a "red tsunami" or a "red wave" in favor of Republican candidates and the Democratic party suffering significant losses. Democrats had made protecting abortion rights a centerpiece of their campaign and it paid dividends. The red tsunami or the red wave failed to materialize and Democrats won major victories across the country. Access to abortion proved to be a powerful force in the mid-term elections and a significant surge in voter turnout due to the erosion of abortion rights carried Democrats to victory in races for the U.S. Senate, state governor, Attorney general, and state legislatures (Ewall-Wice and Huey-Burns 2022; Ford 2022).

In Pennsylvania, Democrat John Fetterman won the U.S. Senate flipping the U.S. Senate from Republicans to Democrats. Democrat Josh Shapiro won the governor's race by double-digits against Republican state senator, Doug Mastriano, who supported an abortion ban with no exception for rape or incest. Voters in Wisconsin reelected a pro-choice Democratic governor Tom Evers who defeated an anti-abortion Republican candidate. In the red state of Kansas, voters reelected a Democratic governor Laura Kelly who supported abortion rights. In Michigan, Democrats regained full (trifecta) control of state government for the first time in 40 years. In Arizona, Democrat Katie Hobbs defeated MAGA Republican Kari Lake. Democrats secured "trifectas" in several other competitive states and fended off Republican super majorities in others. The predicted red wave crashed into the wall of abortion rights (Ollstein and Messerly 2022; Whitehurst 2022; Ewall-Wice and Huey-Burns 2022; Hounsell 2022; "Abortion on the Ballot" 2022).

In addition to elections for public offices, in some red and blue states, the issue of abortion was directly on the ballot placed through ballot initiatives designed either to protect abortion rights or to ban abortion altogether by enshrining it into the state constitution. Voters again delivered a ringing endorsement of abortion rights on the mid-term ballot initiatives.

Kansas was the first state to vote on abortion rights since the Dobbs ruling. Even before the November mid-term elections in August of 2022, voters of the red state of Kansas decisively by a margin of 59 to 41 percent rejected a proposed amendment to the state constitution that would have stated that there was no right to an abortion in the state, even though registered Republicans far outnumbered Democrats in the state. The push for such an amendment was rooted in a 2019 ruling by the Kansas Supreme Court that had struck down some abortion restrictions and ruled that the right to an abortion was guaranteed by the state constitution. The supporters of the proposed amendment had argued that the Kansas Supreme Court had overreached in striking down the state's abortion restrictions. If the proposed amendment had passed, restrictions limiting abortion after 22 weeks of pregnancy and requiring an ultrasound before the procedure would have remained in effect. Supporters feared that the passage of the amendment would have led to a total or near-total ban on abortion (Smith and Glueck 2022; Lysen, Zeigler, and Mesa 2022).

In the November 2022 mid-term elections, five states – two red states of Kentucky and Montana and three blue states of California, Michigan, and Vermont – had ballot initiatives concerning abortion rights. Voters in all five states delivered a strong endorsement of abortion rights. In deeply red Kentucky, voters by a margin of 53 to 48 percent defeated a measure that would have amended the state constitution to say that nothing in the constitution should be construed to secure or protect a right to abortion or require funding for abortion. In Montana, a ballot measure would enact a law making any infant "born alive" at any gestational age a legal person. It would have made it a crime for healthcare providers not to make every effort to save the life of an infant born during an attempted abortion or after labor or C-section. Montana voters rejected the measure by a vote of 53 to 47 percent (Starcqualursi, Cole, and LeBlanc 2022; Reilly 2022; "Abortion on the Ballot" 2022).

California voters approved by a margin of 67 to 33 percent a measure that would amend the state constitution to enshrine a person's reproductive freedom including a right to abortion in the state constitution. Before that the state constitution guaranteed a right to privacy which the state Supreme Court had ruled included the right to have an abortion. In Vermont, voters by a margin of 77 to 23 percent approved a measure that would amend the state constitution to state that a person's reproductive autonomy is central to individual liberty and dignity and shall not be denied or infringed unless justified by compelling state interest using the least restrictive means. In Michigan, like in California, voters by a margin of 57 to 43 percent approved a measure to amend the constitution establishing a constitutional right to reproductive freedom, including all matters related to pregnancy such as abortion and contraceptives (Starcqualursi, Cole, and LeBlanc 2022; Reilly 2022; "Abortion on the Ballot" 2022).

Encouraged by victories in six out of six ballot initiatives, abortion rights activists are planning citizen-led ballot initiatives in future elections that would enshrine abortion rights in the state constitutions in several red states such as Arizona, Arkansas, Missouri, Nebraska, North Dakota, Oklahoma, and South Dakota, and Florida which has been trending red in recent years (Edelman 2022).

Republican Party which has supported abortion restrictions and bans suffered one of the worst mid-term performances in the 2022 mid-term elections. A Republican National Committee poll published in September of 2022 was a warning sign of what was to come. In this poll, 80 percent of voters polled said that they were unhappy with the Supreme Court's Dobbs decision. After the brutal defeat in the 2022 mid-term elections, some Republicans wondered about the need to rethink the party's abortion strategy and messaging while other Republicans and anti-abortion advocates pointed to Republican governors who had taken restrictive abortion positions getting reelected in states like Texas, Ohio, and Florida as a sign of success (Manchester 2022).

2023 Elections

In the 2023 elections, voters again showed support for protecting abortion rights. In the red state of Kentucky, a trigger law immediately took effect after the Dobbs decision banning abortion in almost all circumstances except to save the life of a woman or to prevent a serious injury. Efforts by abortion providers to block the ban in courts had failed. The Democratic governor Andy Beshear won re-election improving on his performance from four years ago. In one of his campaign ads, a young woman, Hadley Duvall, tells voters how when she was 12 years old, she was sexually assaulted by her stepfather and criticized Beshear's Republican opponent who supported Kentucky's abortion ban without exceptions for rape or incest. In his campaign, Governor Beshear emphasized his support for abortion rights (Greenblatt 2023; Knowles and Kitchener 2023; Lerer and Goldmacher 2023).

In Virginia, the Republican governor Glenn Youngkin had advocated a 15-week ban on abortion with exceptions for rape, incest, and the life of a mother as a reasonable and moderate position and tried to portray Democrats as extremists on abortion. He also hoped to regain control of the state Senate controlled by the Democrats while retaining Republican control of the state house. On election day, Democrats not only retained their control of the state Senate but also regained control of the state house halting the governor's conservative legislative agenda including abortion (Greenblatt 2023; Knowles and Kitchener 2023; Lerer and Goldmacher 2023).

In Pennsylvania, Democrats maintained their majority on the state Supreme Court. A state Supreme Court race drew more than $17 million in TV ad spending with many of them touching on abortion rights. In the April 2023 special election, Janet Protasiewicz, a Democrat who on the issue of abortion had stated that women have a right to choose, won the hotly contested race for the Wisconsin Supreme Court flipping the control of the Supreme Court to liberals for the first time in 15 years (Johnson 2023). This gave abortion rights advocates hope that the Supreme Court would hear and overturn Wisconsin's pre-Civil War ban on abortion. Wisconsin has stopped offering abortion following the Dobbs decision largely because of the long-dormant pre-Civil War ban on abortion. Wisconsin's Democratic Attorney General Josh Kaul sued days after *Roe's* overturn to block prosecutions of abortions under the law. The case is currently going through the court process and is likely to end up in the state Supreme Court (Greenblatt 2023; Knowles and Kitchener 2023; Lerer and Goldmacher 2023).

In the state of Ohio, a state in which Republicans enjoy a trifecta control of government, voters resoundingly approved (57 percent) a ballot initiative measure enshrining a right to abortion in the state constitution. The measure amends that state's constitution to say that individuals have the right to make their own reproductive decisions, including on abortion. This was the first time that voters in a state trending Republican were asked to affirmatively vote yes on a constitutional amendment establishing a right to abortion. Before the November vote, to forestall the voter approval, the republican state legislature had moved to change the rule at the last minute by calling for a special election on a constitutional amendment that would have raised the required number of signatures to put the issue on a ballot from each of Ohio's 88 counties and raised the required vote to pass a ballot initiative from a simple majority to 60 percent. On August 8, 2023, Ohio voters rejected the proposed change (Zernike 2023; Zernike and Lerer 2023; Berman 2023; Williamson and Grofman 2023).

Republicans in Ohio who control both the governor's mansion and both chambers of state legislatures used all their levers of power to defeat the ballot measure and failed. Exit polls showed strong support for the ballot measure across all age groups except for older Americans, all race groups, suburban voters, and voters who identify themselves as moderates. The success of the ballot initiative to protect abortion rights in Ohio demonstrates how much the debate and dynamics surrounding abortion have changed since the Dobbs decision.

With a string of losses in 2022 and 2023 on the issue of abortion, Republicans are struggling to find a winning strategy on abortion. However, these losses have not led Republicans and anti-abortion activists to moderate their position on abortion rights. Some Republicans have argued the problem is simply messaging or due to tactical campaign errors. Others have argued for a more aggressive strategy to pursue their anti-abortion agenda (Levine 2023). Still, others have responded by trying to keep the abortion issue off the ballot. For example, Republican-controlled legislatures in four red states – North Dakota, Arkansas, Kansas, and Missouri – are leading an effort to make it very difficult for citizen-led ballot initiatives to succeed by raising the threshold for the number of signatures required to place an issue on the ballot as well for the passage of the ballot measures (Zernike and Wines 2023). Few others have argued that Republicans and anti-abortion advocates need to show more support and sensitivity for provisions that provide exceptions for rape and incest in restricting abortion rights (Levine 2023).

Eighteen months following Dabbs's decision, American voters have answered Justice Alito's musing about how the American political system or society will respond to Doob's ruling overturning Roe v. Wade – they do not like the Doob's decision and they strongly support abortion rights.

Will Abortion Be on the Ballot in 2024 Elections?

The simple answer to this question is, yes. The 2024 election could turn out to be very pivotal not only because control of the White House, the U.S. Senate, and the U.S. House will be at stake at the national level but also because at the state level about a dozen states could decide the fate of abortion rights with citizen-led ballot initiatives. In as many as 12 states, voters could be voting on abortion-related ballot measures in the 2024 elections. Ballot initiatives in blue states such as Maryland and New York would enshrine abortion rights into the state constitutions. Similar efforts are underway in red states such as Arizona, Montana, Nebraska, Missouri, Arkansas, and South Dakota and in purple states like Nevada, Iowa, Colorado, and Florida. As we have noted before, over the last several elections, Colorado has been trending blue while Florida has been trending red (Sable-Smith 2023; Kochi, 2023; Wang and Caldwell 2023; Mazzei 2023).

The results of the 2022 and 2023 elections suggest that the issue of abortion rights galvanizes voter turnout and plays a major role in electing candidates who support access to abortion services. Currently, the wind is at the back of abortion rights advocates because the issue transcends partisan lines.

Ballot initiatives in ten states were approved for placement on the ballot in the November 2024 elections to protect abortion rights in state constitutions. This includes the red states of South Dakota, Arizona, Missouri, and Montana and Nebraska; the blue states of Maryland and New York; and the purple states of Nevada, Colorado, and Florida (Hanson 2024; Melton 2024; Lieb 2024; Zernike 2024; Edelman and Pipia 2024). In a strange twist, the Arizona Supreme Court in August 2024 ruled that a fetus can be referred to as an "unborn human being" in pamphlets for voters dealing with the ballot initiative about the constitutional right to an abortion. Arizona for Abortion Access, the coalition of advocacy groups supporting the amendment, expressed disappointment with the court's ruling (Singh 2024).

In Arkansas, election officials rejected the proposed abortion ballot measure on the flimsy excuse that ballot initiative organizers failed to provide the required paperwork which the abortion rights group has disputed. In August 2024, the Arkansas Supreme Court upheld the rejection of petitions by state officials dashing the hopes of the pro-abortion organizers of getting the abortion rights ballot initiative on the ballot in the 2024 elections (Demillo 2024). According to polls, Arkansas is one of the few states where only a minority of individuals believe that abortion should be legal in all or most cases (Axe 2024; Cochrane 2024).

Ultimately, of the abortion ballot initiatives in ten states, in seven states – Arizona, Missouri, Montana, Nevada, Maryland, New York, and Colorado – voters approved the constitutional right to an abortion while three states – Florida, Nebraska, and South Dakota – rejected it.

Abortion rights have won when it is on the ballot. However, it is important to note that 25 states do not allow citizen ballot initiatives or constitutional amendments on statewide ballots allowing citizens to circumvent their state legislature to preserve abortion rights (Kruesi, Fernando, and Willingham 2024). In several red states, where citizen-initiated ballot initiatives are available, Republican-controlled legislatures have imposed restrictions and erected barriers to make them more difficult to approve.

State Constitutions and Court Challenges

According to the Center for Reproductive Rights (2022b), at the time of the overturning of *Roe v. Wade* state Supreme courts in ten states recognized that their state constitutions protected abortion rights independent from the federal constitution. These states included four red states of Alaska, Arizona, Kansas, and Montana and four blue states of California, Massachusetts, New Jersey, and New Mexico. The other two states were the purple states of Florida and Minnesota. The highest courts in Alaska, Montana, Florida, and Minnesota couched abortion rights in the right to privacy. The Kansas Supreme Court held that "natural rights" protect personal autonomy including a right to abortion while the New Mexico Supreme Court interpreted the state's Equal Rights Amendment to find that abortion restrictions discriminated against women relative to men. The Alaska Supreme Court ruled that the law must treat minors and low-income people who want to continue a pregnancy equally to those who seek abortion care. The Florida Supreme Court recognized that the right to privacy in the state constitution protects the right to an abortion. Each state has a unique constitution and the highest courts in each of these states use a variety of novel legal theories to protect abortion rights.

However, following the Dobbs decision, abortion rights supporters and opponents have been waging a state-by-state fight to protect or restrict abortion rights. Abortion rights advocates have filed dozens of lawsuits arguing that many state abortion bans are illegal (Times Editorial Board 2023). Consequently, litigation over abortion restrictions is currently unfolding in several states, and court cases have frozen abortion bans in states like Wyoming, Montana, and Wisconsin and remain in flux (Sherman 2023; Sherman and Witherspoon 2023). Thus, the future of abortion bans in several states remains uncertain. In Iowa, conservatives were able to reverse a state Supreme Court precedent like Montana's after more Republican-appointed justices joined the bench. Abortion remains legal in the conservative stronghold of Montana because of a 25-year-old Supreme Court ruling that protects abortion grounded in the right to privacy included in the state's constitution. To outlaw abortion in Montana, voters would need to amend the state constitution or elect Supreme Court Justices willing to reverse the precedent. While a Republican state, Montana has a libertarian streak. Two Supreme Court open seats are up for election in the November 2024 elections. Montana is a sandwich between Idaho and Dakotas, which severely restricts abortions (Zionts 2024).

These lawsuits may force some states to clarify further exceptions when abortions are permitted in medical emergencies. For example, on December 29, 2023, an Idaho court ruled that a lawsuit seeking to clarify when physicians may perform abortion legally can move forward (Blanchard 2023). In January 2024, the U.S. Supreme Court let Idaho enforce its near-total abortion ban while legal procedures continue and agreed to hear the case involving whether the Biden administration under the Emergency Medical Treatment and Labor Act (EMTALA) can require hospitals in states that ban abortion to perform the procedure on pregnant patients whose lives are at risk (Quinn 2024). A ruling in favor of Idaho by the Supreme Court and against the Bident administration would have encouraged red states to impose more restrictions on abortion access (Goldhill and Merelli 2024). However, in June 2024, the U.S. Supreme Court dismissed the Idaho case because the court hearing was improvidently granted. This temporarily cleared the way for women in the state to receive an abortion when their health is at risk. The ruling, for the time being, reinstated a lower court ruling that had halted Idaho's near-total ban on abortion and permitted emergency abortion at hospitals to protect the health of the mother while the case is making its way its way through the lower courts (VanSickle 2024a). A federal appeals court in January 2024 had ruled that the federal guidance does not require emergency room doctors in Texas to provide emergency abortions and the Texas abortion law does not violate EMTALA. Thus, Texas can ban emergency abortions despite federal guidance (Jimenez 2024).

A recent case in Texas has received national publicity. Texas abortion laws are among the most restrictive in the country, outlawing all abortions except those that put a mother's life at risk. Under the law, doctors who perform abortions could be sentenced to five to more years in prison. Kate Cox, a pregnant woman whose fetus had a fatal diagnosis, sought permission from a court to get an abortion. Cox's doctor had told her that if the baby's heartbeat were to stop, inducing labor would carry a risk of a uterine rupture since she had prior cesarian sections. Another C-section at full term would endanger her ability to carry another child. On December 7, 2023, a Travis County district court judge, Maya Guerra Gamble (an elected Democrat), granted Cox permission to get an abortion. Texas Republican Attorney General Ken Paxton argued that Cox did not meet the criteria for a medical exception and threatened legal consequences if her physician provided abortion and appealed to the state Supreme Court. The Texas Supreme Court, made up of all nine Republican judges, on December 9, 2023, temporarily blocked a lower court ruling and the following week issued a final ruling against Kate Cox. She had left the state to get an abortion in another state before the final ruling. Another abortion-related case, Zurawski v. Texas, is currently pending before the State Supreme Court. The case is filed by two doctors and 20 women who were denied an abortion during severe pregnancy complications, including some women whose babies, like Cox, were diagnosed with fetal conditions (Vazquez 2023; Kitchener and Vazquez 2023; Wagner 2023; Weber 2023).

Over the first six months of 2023, there were 34 legal abortions recorded in Texas categorized as both "medical emergencies" and to "preserve the health of the woman." According to physicians and researchers, the number is far below the number of patients who would need an abortion to protect the health of a mother forcing many women to continue their pregnancy or travel out of state to get an abortion. In contrast, in the neighboring state of Oklahoma, in 2021, 324 abortions were performed because of risk to the mother's health, 59 of which were considered necessary to avert the death of the mother. Given the fact that Texas' population is seven times larger, the number of women facing death who needed abortion would have exceeded 400 a year while close to 2,400 women would have faced physical health risks (Goldhill 2023b). Texas, in fact, has three separate overlapping and vague abortion laws in the book making it nearly impossible to get an early abortion (Elliot 2023). Texas' anti-abortion extremism is hurting businesses in the state. According to a coalition of Texas businesses, ambiguity over the abortion ban is making recruiting harder and makes the state less appealing to families considering relocating to the state (Henderson 2023; "Texas Companies Say Republicans are Ruining Their Business" 2023).

Abortion rights activists have argued that the Texas case shows that abortion ban exceptions are a sham. Right-wing politicians who support them rather inflict unnecessary suffering on women than relax even a little bit of control over medical decisions. Anti-abortion activists have argued that pro-abortion groups are spreading false and exaggerated claims to discredit the laws (Goldberg 2023).

Abortion numbers by state: pre- and post-dobbs decision

Eighteen months after the Dobbs ruling, the full impact of its decision remains unclear and in flux. In some states, the implementation of abortion bans and restrictions has been delayed or blocked temporarily by courts due to lawsuits challenging their constitutionality. Some states have expanded abortion rights while others have restricted it. The increase in criminal prosecution that abortion rights advocates had feared, thus far, failed to materialize. Almost a year after the Dobbs decision, by June 2023, 17.5 million women (a quarter) of reproductive age lived where abortion was banned or almost banned (Kitchener et al. 2023). The number of legal abortions has dropped dramatically in states that have banned or almost banned abortions while it has increased significantly in states where abortion is legal. According to an analysis by the Institute of Labor Economics, births increased in every state with a ban following Dobbs decision. The birth rate increased, on average, in states with bans relative to states where abortion remained legal. The analysis also found that in the first six months of 2023, between one-fifth and one-fourth of women living in states with abortion bans who may have otherwise sought an abortion did not get one (Dench, Pineda-Torres; and Myers 2023; Sanger-Katz and Miller 2023; McPhillips 2023). However, there is a great deal of variability among states concerning the number of abortions performed due to variability in states' abortion laws. What do the data show about abortion before and after the Dobbs decision? Table 6.12 provides the number of monthly abortions performed by states in April 2022 (a month before the Dobbs ruling) and June 2023 (a year after the Dobbs ruling).

Several observations stand out. There is a dramatic difference in the number of abortions performed between the red and blue states. In 16 of the 24 red states, the number of abortions performed declined. In seven states, the number increased while in one state, Wyoming, there was no change. Among the states that saw an increase, three states – Kansas, North Carolina, and South Carolina – had an increase of 72, 44.6, and 34.8 percent, respectively, due to out-of-state residents seeking abortion, while the other three states saw a modest increase. Of the 14 red states that have imposed a total or near-total abortion ban, in 13 states the number of abortions performed declined 100 percent while in Texas it declined 99.7 percent. In April of 2022, before the Dobbs decision, there were a total of 21,840 monthly abortions performed. By June of 2023, the number of monthly abortions performed had dropped to 12,380.

TABLE 6.12 Monthly Abortions by State April 2022 and June 2023

Red States	Pre-Dobbs Monthly Abortions April 2022	Pot-Dobbs Monthly Abortions June 2023	% Change	Blue States	Pre-Dobbs Monthly Abortions April 2022	Pot-Dobbs Monthly Abortions June 2023	% Change
Georgia	4,260	2,340	-45.1%	California	12,980	14,440	11.2%
North Carolina	3,250	4,700	44.6%	New York	8,780	9,770	11.3%
Texas	3,190	10	-99.7%	Illinois	5,530	8,040	45.4%
West Virginia	2,040	0	-100.0%	New Jersey	3,840	4,730	23.2%
Arizona	1,330	1,080	-18.8%	Pennsylvania	2,910	3,850	4.8%
Tennessee	1,190	0	-100.0%	Michigan	2,680	3,080	14.9%
Kansas	970	1,670	72.0%	Maryland	2,630	3,620	37.6%
Indiana	940	700	-25.5%	Washington	1,760	1,980	12.5%
Louisiana	760	0	-100.0%	Massachusetts	1,590	1,730	8.8%
South Carolina	690	930	34.8%	New Mexico	1,200	2,140	78.3%
Alabama	650	0	-100.0%	Connecticut	890	1,210	36.0%
Oklahoma	480	0	-100.0%	Oregon	840	1,120	33.3%
Mississippi	350	0	-100.0%	Rhode Island	310	210	-32.3%

Reproductive Rights in Red and Blue States

Utah	320	330	3.2%	Hawaii	240	260	8.3%
Kentucky	310	0	-100.0%	Delaware	190	270	42.0%
Arkansas	290	0	-100.0%	Maine	190	250	31.6%
Nebraska	200	240	20.0%	Vermont	100	110	10.0%
Idaho	170	0	-100.0%				
Montana	170	200	17.6%				
Alaska	120	140	16.7%				
North Dakota	90	0	-100.0%				
Wyoming	40	40	0.0%				
South Dakota	20	0	-100.0%				
Missouri	10	0	-100.0%				
Totals	21,840	12,380			46,660	56,810	
Average	910	515			2,744	3,341	

Adapted from: "Change in Number of Abortions by State." 2023. Online at https://societyfp.org/research/wecount/.

In contrast, among the 17 blue states, 16 saw an increase in the number of abortions performed between April 2022 and June 2023. Only one state, Rhode Island saw a decline of 32.3 percent. The state of New Mexico witnessed the highest increase of 78.3 percent largely due to the influx of residents from Texas and Oklahoma, where abortion is banned, seeking abortion. Aside from New Mexico and Illinois, some of the other blue states like Illinois, Delaware, Connecticut, Maryland, Maine, and Oregon, witnessed an increase ranging from 31 percent to 45 percent. Illinois saw the second highest increase of 45.4 percent due to residents from neighboring states like Missouri and Indiana where abortion is banned traveling to Illinois to get an abortion. Overall, the total number of monthly abortions performed among the 17 blue states increased from 46,660 in April of 2022 to 56,810 in June of 2023.

Overall, abortions increased in states that protected abortion rights, states that border states where abortion is banned, while abortion decreased in states that have imposed severe restrictions or banned abortion ("Guttmacher Launches New Research Initiative to Track Monthly State Abortion Occurrences in the United States" 2023). According to a study by the Guttmacher Institute, national abortion rates have not meaningfully fallen since 2020. In fact, they have gone up a bit following the Dobbs ruling. Several factors may account for the increase including an increase in medication abortions and more women traveling to abortion-friendly states to get an abortion ("Monthly Abortion Provision Study" 2023). Another report by the Society of Family Planning showed that an increase in abortions in states that allow the procedure more than offset the post-Dobbs drop-off in states that banned/restricted abortions and closed abortion clinics ("WeCount Report Shows Major Disruption in Abortion Care One Year After Dobbs" 2023).

Abortion Providers/Clinics And Out-of-State Travel for Abortion

What impact the Dobbs decision have on abortion clinics/providers and women's access to abortion services given the fact that many red states have banned or severely restricted abortion services while most blue states have expanded them? Statistical data on abortion providers is difficult because no one organization has compiled a single list of what has happened to abortion providers in states and communities where abortion is banned or severely restricted (Bahr 2023). Thus, systematic state-level data for all states is still unavailable but some anecdotal evidence provides some answers. Hence, the numbers reported often vary depending on how the data is collected. It is worth noting that underneath the top trend lines, a large amount of variation by state exists.

A month after the fall of Roe, 11 states in the South had imposed either a total abortion ban or implemented a ban on abortion after six weeks of pregnancy. The states were Alabama, Arkansas, Mississippi, Missouri, Oklahoma, South Dakota, and Texas (total ban); Georgia, South Carolina, Tennessee, and Ohio (ban after six weeks of pregnancy). Of the 11 states, ten were red states and one was Republican-leading, Ohio. According to the Guttmacher Institute, before the Supreme Court's Dobbs decision, 11 states in the South had a total of 71 clinics that provided abortion services. Thirty days after the fall of Roe on June 24, 2022, there were only 28 clinics still offering abortions by July 2022 (Kirstein, Jones and Philbin 2022b; Christensen and Sneed 2022). A hundred days after the Dobbs decision, at least 66 clinics across 15 U.S. states had stopped offering abortion care. Of the 66 clinics, 40 were still offering services other than abortion while 26 had shut down entirely (Kirstein et al. 2022a; McShane 2022). An analysis by the New York Times in June of 2023, a year after the Dobbs decision, found that 61 abortion providers were no longer offering abortion services in 20 states that had banned or restricted abortion. Some of the clinics relocated, some remained open to provide other services, while many simply closed. Some of the blue states such as Oregon, California, New Mexico, Illinois, Delaware, and New Jersey added more abortion providers to meet increased demand for abortion services from residents from neighboring states where abortions were banned or restricted (McCann and Walker 2023; Bahr 2023). Twenty-two states, bordering states where abortion is banned, including 18 blue states implemented shield laws to protect healthcare professionals providing abortion services from legal or professional consequences enforced by states banning abortion (Forouzan and Guarnieri 2023). Abortion shield laws have become a new war between the red and blue states. Doctors in a handful of blue states are using the shield laws to mail abortion pills to women in red states (Belluck 2024a, 2024b).

Total abortion bans or severe restrictions on abortion imposed by many states also meant that residents of those states who wanted abortion had to travel to states where abortion is legal and/or has fewer restrictions. Even before the Dobbs decision, almost 10 percent of patients seeking abortion traveled out of state (McCammon 2023a; Maddow-Zimet and Kost 2022). In the state of Texas, after the Texas Senate Bill 8 (SB 8) – when one of the most restrictive abortion laws went into effect on September 1, 2021 – out-of-state abortions obtained by Texas residents increased from 514 (Pre-SB 8) between September and December 2019 to 5,574 (post-SB 8) between September and December 2021 (White et al. 2022).

Since the Dobbs decision, abortion providers in "sanctuary" states where access to abortion is protected have seen a dramatic increase in demand for abortion from out-of-state residents where abortion is banned or very restricted. For example, in abortion clinics in Illinois, abortions provided to out-of-state residents have increased six times, from about 5 percent to 30 percent. Most of them come from neighboring states like Missouri, Kentucky, and Tennessee where abortion is banned. Similarly, surrounded by the states of Arizona, Oklahoma, and Texas where abortion is banned, New Mexico has experienced a dramatic increase in out-of-state residents seeking abortion services in the state (Seshadri, 2023).

Data from the Guttmacher Institute shows widespread travel for abortion services and interstate travel for abortion care in the United States has doubled since 2020 with blue states like Illinois, New Mexico, and Washington experiencing increased demand. Even red states like North Carolina, which restricts abortion after 12 weeks of pregnancy, have experienced an increase in out-of-state demand because of bordering state Georgia in which a six-week abortion ban is in effect. Interstate travel for abortion in the United States has doubled from 1 in 10 in 2020 to 1 in 5 in the first half of 2023 (Maddow-Zimet et al. 2023; Forouzan, Friedrich, and Maddow-Zimet 2023; El-Bawab 2023). Table 6.13 provides an estimate of the number and percent of abortions provided by states to out-of-state residents.

As the data shows, among the red states, out of 24, 11 states provided abortion services to out-of-state residents. Kansas recorded the highest percentage (65 percent) of abortions provided to out-of-state residents. In 13 other red states, abortion is banned. In contrast, all 17 blue states provided abortion services to out-of-state residents with New Mexico providing the highest percentage (74 percent) of abortion to out-of-state residents.

One of the consequences of traveling out of state to get an abortion is the increase in cost involved for those seeking abortion which disproportionately adversely impact women with low income.

Medication Abortion

A medication abortion also known as medical abortion or abortion with pills involves taking two different drugs that can be safely used up to the first 10 weeks of pregnancy. The most common medication abortion regimen in the United States involves the use of two different medications. A patient takes a drug called mifepristone followed by a second drug called misoprostol, also known as RU-486, to end her pregnancy rather than having a surgical procedure. In the United States, it is sold under the brand name Mifeprex. FDA has found medication abortion to be safe and very effective. Self-managed abortion, also called "self-induced" or "at-home" abortion, is when a person ends a pregnancy outside the medical care setting ("The Availability and Use of Medication Abortion" 2023).

TABLE 6.13 Estimated Number and Percent of Abortion Provided to Out-of-State Residents

Red States*	# of Abortions Provided to Out-of-State Residents	% of Abortions Provided to Out-of-state Residents	Blue States	# of Abortions Provided to Out-of-State Residents	% of Abortions Provided to Out-of-state Residents
Kansas	5,780	65%	New Mexico	8,230	74%
South Carolina	2,490	42%	Illinois	18,870	42%
North Carolina	8,920	36%	Vermont	210	26%
Georgia	4,370	28%	Maryland	4,400	18%
Indiana	840	22%	Rhode Island	190	12%
Nebraska	260	20%	Oregon	670	11%
Montana	110	11%	New Jersey	3,040	10%
Wyoming	20	10%	Washington	1,210	10%
Utah	140	7%	Delaware	130	7%
Alaska	30	3%	Hawaii	140	7%
Arizona	180	3%	Maine	90	7%
Alabama*			Michigan	1,270	7%
Arkansas*			Pennsylvania	1,140	6%
Idaho*			Connecticut	400	5%
Kentucky			Massachusetts	580	5%
Louisiana*			New York	3,700	5%
Mississippi*			California	3,630	4%
Missouri*					
North Dakota*					
Oklahoma*					
South Dakota*					
Tennessee *					
Texas*					
West Virginia*					

Adapted from: "Monthly Abortion Provision Study." 2023. Online at https://www.guttmacher.org/

Note:

* Thirteen red states performed zero to few abortions due to state ban on abortion. Wisconsin is not included in the analysis.

In 1988, Mifepristone was approved for use up to seven weeks of pregnancy in France. In June 1989, the United States banned the import of mifepristone. During the 1990s, it became available in parts of Europe and China (Hawkins 2023). In the summer of 1992, in a test case, Leona Benton who was six and a half weeks pregnant flew from London to New York with abortion pills she wanted to use to end her pregnancy. The U.S.

Customs officials seized the abortion pills. She took her case to the U.S. Supreme Court but lost the case 7-2 to regain her pills. She chose to get a surgical abortion. However, she helped galvanize a movement to overturn the FDA's ban on abortion pills (Bella 2023).

In 2000, the Federal Drug Administration approved Mifeprex for use in the United States. The President of Planned Parenthood described this development as the most significant advance in women's reproductive health since the birth control pill (Bella 2023). Until 2019, mifepristone was only sold under the brand name Mifeprex. In 2019 the FDA approved a generic version of mifepristone. Getting a prescription for the medication required an in-person visit to a healthcare setting by a patient. In December 2021, the FDA removed the in-person dispensing requirement for mifepristone and allowed its distribution by pharmacies, in addition to certified clinicians. This put pharmacies in a legal gray area in red states that had the most restrictive abortion laws. Can state laws prevent people from accessing a drug approved by the FDA? For example, Republican attorney generals in 20 states sent Walgreens Company a letter warning that it could face legal consequences if it sold abortion medication in those states. In response, Walgreens decided not to sell abortion pills, by mail or in stores, where abortion is illegal (Atkins and Burke 2023; Sellers and Roubein 2023; Owermohle 2023a). Prescribers are still required to be certified by the drug manufacturers. The FDA removing the in-person dispensing requirement for abortion pills also expanded the opportunity for telehealth or telemedicine to dispense abortion pills in states where abortion is legal. In July 2023, the FDA also for the first time approved the counter birth control pill, Opill (Lupkin 2023; McGinley; Roubein; and Johnson 2023; Silverman 2023).

The use of medication abortion has grown significantly since its approval by the FDA in 2000. One year after the FDA's approval, medication abortions in 2001 accounted for 6 percent of all abortions in the United States (Jones et al. 2022). By 2019 medication abortion accounted for approximately 42 percent of all abortions performed in the United States (Staman and Shimabukuro 2022). Medication abortions have increased steadily over the last 15 years, and by 2022 medication abortion accounted for 53 percent of all non-hospital abortion settings (Jones et al. 2022; "The Availability and Use of Medication Abortion" 2023). Blue states like New York and Vermont passed shield laws providing legal protection to prescribe and send abortion pills to patients in states with abortion bans (Rubin 2023). The surge of overseas abortion pills ordered online also helps blunt the effects of abortion bans adopted by several states (Bhatia, Miller, and Sanger-Katz 2022).

After the June 2022 Dobbs decision overturning *Roe W. Wade*, requests for abortion pills increased significantly in 30 states. The main reasons cited by applicants for abortion pills included abortion bans and restrictions imposed by several red states and the cost of out-of-state travel to get an abortion. States with the largest increase in the number of requests per week per 100,000 women were those that had enacted total abortion bans like Alabama, Arkansas, Louisiana, and Mississippi (Aiken et al. 2022). Unfortunately, websites selling unapproved abortion pills without prescription also soared (Mosbergen and Agrawal 2022). As abortion pills and medication abortions took off, many states moved to curb their use (Vestal 2022).

Medication abortion is legal in 36 states and Washington, D.C., but in 15 of those states, it must be prescribed by a doctor, not other clinicians. The red and blue states are moving in opposite directions concerning medication abortions. Of the 24 red states, 14 states have banned medication abortions. They are the same red states that have imposed a total or near-total ban on abortions. In 11 red states where medication abortion is legal, it is very restricted because in these states only physicians can prescribe abortion pills. In addition, five states – Arizona, Indiana, Nebraska, North Carolina, and South Carolina – require an in-person visit to a healthcare facility by a patient adding additional obstacles to accessing abortion pills. Only in two red states – Montana and Wyoming – a clinician can prescribe abortion pills. In contrast, medication abortion is legal in all 17 blue states, and in 15 of those states, a clinician can prescribe abortion pills. In Michigan and Pennsylvania, only a physician can prescribe abortion pills (Cui and Jefferies 2024).

Court Challenges: Abortion Pill, Birth Control Pill, and IVF

Abortion Pill

According to one study of 30 states that examined requests for self-managed abortion using online telemedicine increased significantly both after the leak of the Dobbs decision and after the decision was formally announced. Every state showed a higher request regardless of the state's abortion policy (Aiken et al. 2022). Aid Access, the telemedicine service, reported that average requests per day for abortion pills increased from 83 in months preceding a leaked draft of the Supreme Court's Dobbs decision to 218 from June through September 2022 after the formal decision was announced (Bazelon 2022). Another study found that the outcomes of medication abortion through telemedicine compared to standard medication abortion at four Planned Parenthood Health Centers in four states were similar (Kohn et al. 2019). Yet utilizing telemedicine to expand abortion access continues to present many challenges (Hunt 2023).

In November 2022, Alliance Defending Freedom, a Christian legal advocacy organization, sued in federal court in Amarillo, Texas on behalf of several anti-abortion groups and doctors to reverse the FDA's approval of mifepristone. The group argued that the FDA lacked the authority to approve the drug. It also alleged that the FDA had failed to adequately study the drug (Hawkins 2023). On April 7, 2023, U.S. District Judge Matthew Kacsmaryk, who had long-held anti-abortion views and was appointed by President Trump, sided with the anti-abortion group. He ruled that both the initial approval of the pill in 2000 and the later decision by the FDA to allow abortion pills to be prescribed via telemedicine, sent by mail, and dispensed by local pharmacies are unlawful. The judge, in effect, issued a preliminary injunction invalidating the FDA's 23-year-old approval of mifepristone and virtually banned the sale of the pills across the country. Judge Kacsmaryk's life was shaped by conservative causes. In the fall of 2022, he had ruled that the Biden administration's guidelines protecting L.G.B.T.Q. workers went too far. In another case, he had also ruled that the federal program aimed at giving teenagers access to confidential contraception violated the U.S. Constitution and state law (Belluck 2023; Ollstein 2023; Marimow et al. 2023; VanSickle 2023; Shaw 2023). Ironically, on the same day, a U.S. District Court judge Thomas O. Rice in Washington state, who was appointed by President Obama, in a separate case involving mifepristone, ruled the drug was safe and effective and ordered the FDA to preserve the status quo and maintain access to the drug in 17 states and Washington, D.C. (Marimow et al. 2023).

The U.S. Justice Department immediately appealed Judge Matthew Kacsmaryk's ruling to the conservative-leaning 5th U.S., Circuit Court of Appeals (Ollstein 2023). On April 13, 2023, the court's three-judge panel ruled 2-1 that the abortion pill can remain on the market but only under conditions that prohibit its use beyond seven weeks of pregnancy and bar its distribution by mail. The ruling temporarily blocked several of the FDA's previous decisions like expanding the availability of mifepristone until the 10th week of pregnancy, authorizing retail pharmacies to dispense the drug, eliminating in-person office visit requirement to obtain a prescription, allowing physicians to prescribe the pill via telemedicine, and allowing non-physicians to prescribe the drug. The ruling essentially allowed the pill to remain on the market but limited its access (Cheney; Gerstein and Ollstein 2023).

The U.S. Justice Department on April 14, 2023, asked the U.S. Supreme Court to temporarily allow full access to the pill and urged the court not to second guess the expertise of the FDA which had relied on scientific data from dozens of clinical trials when it approved the drug in 2000 (Barnes and Marimow 2023). On the same day, the Supreme Court temporarily paused the mifepristone restrictions blocking a judge's ruling that would have completely invalidated the FDA's approval of the drug, maintaining the status quo while it weighs the appeal (Fritze and Fernando 2023). On December 13, 2023, the Supreme Court agreed to review the case and heard oral arguments in March 2024 (Owermohle 2024; Owermohle 2023b; Hurley 2023). In June of 2024, the Supreme Court in a unanimous decision upheld broad access to abortion pills on the ground that the plaintiffs lacked standing to challenge the FDA's actions because they had failed to demonstrate the harm caused to them by the FDA's mifepristone policies since they did not prescribe or use the pill (Howe 2024; VanSickle 2024b). However, if future plaintiffs with legal standing sue to ban the abortion pill, the case will likely return to the Supreme Court. The future ruling in the case will have serious repercussions for abortion rights (Lopez and Castronuovo 2024; Richards 2024). Meanwhile, CVS and Walgreens announced that they will start selling abortion pills beginning in March 2024 (Luthra 2024).

The Supreme Court probably had little choice but to hear the case given the various litigations involving the abortion pill and contrary rulings issued by courts in different states. In June 2023, a judge in Wyoming blocked the state's first-in-the-nation law banning abortion pills from going into effect on July 1 ("Judge Blocks Wyoming's 1st-in-the-nation Abortion Pill Ban" 2023). In August 2023, the 5th Circuit Court of Appeals in New Orleans ruled that the two abortion pills used in medication abortion should not be prescribed past seven weeks of pregnancy or via telemedicine (Simmons-Duffin and Webber 2023). In October 2023, a Kansas judge ruled that Kansas could not enforce a new law restricting abortion pills and forced patients to wait 24 hours before ending their pregnancies (Hanna 2023). The uncertainty surrounding access to abortion pills has caused several blue states like Massachusetts, Washington, New York, and Maryland to stockpile the drug (LeBlanc 2023; McCammon 2023b; Yang 2023).

In May 2024, Louisiana's Republican governor signed into law passed by the state legislature that designated the two primary drugs used in medication abortion – mifepristone and misoprostol – as controlled dangerous substances placing them in Schedule IV drugs putting them on par with potentially addictive prescription drugs. Louisiana became the first state to establish criminal penalties for anyone who prescribes or dispenses either of the two medications without proper authorization including jail time. The law is to take effect on October 1, 2024 (LaRose 2024). A Supreme

Court decision in June 2024 to preserve mail-order prescriptions to the widely used abortion pill mifepristone will still prevent women in Louisiana from accessing the drug for abortions. Louisiana's near-total abortion ban makes it illegal to use mifepristone to terminate a pregnancy and illegal to secure the medicine through the mail (Hilburn 2024).

Over-the-Counter Birth Control Pill

The first birth control pill that people could buy without a prescription will be available starting in March 2024. The pill called Opill made by *Perrigo*, the Ireland-based company, will be available for purchase at retail pharmacies and online. CVS has announced that it will stock the pill in its more than 7,500 stores nationwide. The U.S. FDA approved the over-the-counter pill in the Summer of 2023. Opill is up to 98 percent effective in preventing pregnancy (Park 2024).

Ironically, one month after the Supreme Court's decision overturning *Roe v. Wade in June 2022*, fearing access to contraception could be at risk, Democrats who controlled the U.S. House at the time pushed a bill aimed to ensure access to contraception nationwide. All but eight Republicans, 195 House Republicans voted against the Right to Contraception Act demonstrating the partisan polarization in Congress. The bill failed to receive the support of enough Republicans in the Senate to meet the 60-vote threshold. President Biden issued an executive order to strengthen access to affordable, high-quality contraception and family planning services (Karni 2024; "Fact Sheet: President Biden Issues Executive Order on Strengthening Access to Contraception" 2023).

According to a poll conducted in February 2024, by Americans for contraception, three out of five voters living in states where abortion has been banned or restricted expressed concern that contraception could be next. A majority of voters support the Right to Contraception Act with 94 percent of Democrats and 68 percent of Republican voters supporting it. Eighty percent of voters across the political spectrum believed that their access to birth control was at risk following the Dobbs decision. This again reveals a disconnect between Republican voters and Republicans in Congress (Karni 2024).

In Vitro Fertilization

In vitro fertilization (IVF) is a treatment for infertility in which a woman cannot get pregnant after at least one year of trying. It is also used to prevent passing on genetic problems to a child. IVF is also a reproductive option for same-sex couples or for people who want to have a child without a partner. IVF in a literal sense creates life. IVF involves a complex series of procedures in which medication is used to enhance egg production. Once the eggs are matured, they are collected from the ovary using a medical procedure, and then in the laboratory eggs are combined with the sperm collected from a partner or a donor allowing fertilization to occur outside of the body. After fertilization, embryos (fertilized eggs) are transferred into the woman's uterus in the hope that it will result in pregnancy.

The first baby was born through IVF in 1978. From the very beginning, the Roman Catholic Church opposed the procedure due to the freezing and destruction of excess embryos and because it interfered with marital sex for procreation. Evangelicals were ambivalent while secular people embraced it. Over the years, IVF grew in popularity, and today the procedure accounts for 2 percent of births nationally. One in six families in the United States grapple with infertility.

The Supreme Court of the State of Alabama sent shockwaves across the country when on February 16, 2024, by a vote of 8-1 it ruled that frozen embryos are children. The court held that a fertilized egg in a fertility clinic freezer should be treated as the legal equivalent of an existent child or a fetus gestating in a womb, i.e., unborn children are children and individuals can be held liable for destroying them. The court ruled that the 1872 statute allowing parents to sue over the wrongful death of a minor child applies to "unborn children." The case was originally brought by couples whose embryos were destroyed in 2020 when a hospital worker removed the frozen embryos from tanks of liquid nitrogen and dropped them on the floor leading to their destruction. Scientists in the field of reproductive medicine criticized the ruling as a medically and scientifically unfounded decision. The court's chief justice, Tom Parker, invoked God in deciding the case by stating that human life cannot be destroyed without incurring the wrath of God. The decision led many fertility clinics to suspend their operation for fear of being criminally prosecuted. Following the ruling, even in red states religious, conservative women rose up in revolt against the decision and galvanized to defend IVF. Several days following the court decision, the office of the state's Attorney General announced that it had no intention of using the state Supreme Court decision to prosecute IVF families or providers (Rabin and Ghorayshi 2024; Hennessy-Fiske and Craig 2024; Hennessy-Fiske 2024; Rojas 2024). In early March, the state's governor, Kay Ivey, signed a bill into law providing legal immunity to doctors and patients undergoing IVF treatment. Soon after, fertility clinics announced plans to resume IVF treatments. However, the new law failed to address the court's ruling that frozen embryos are considered children (Yurkanin 2024).

The Alabama Supreme Court's IVF ruling has opened a new front in the battle over reproductive rights in the election year. The Alabama Supreme Court decision created a new political landmine for Republican politicians. While several Republican governors and lawmakers disavowed the decision, many Republican legislators in conservative red states have pushed bills that would declare that life begins at conception. If such bills become laws, it would have serious legal consequences for fertility treatments. At the national level, more than 120 Republican members of the House of Representatives have signed on as co-sponsors of the Life at Conception Act. Among them is the Republican speaker of the house, Mike Johnson, and an evangelical Christian who has called abortion "an American Holocaust." In the U.S. Senate, a Republican, Cindy Hyde-Smith of Mississippi, blocked legislation that would protect in IVF and other assisted reproductive technologies. The Democrats promised to make the court decision and reproductive rights a major campaign issue in the 2024 elections. The whole issue of reproductive rights has become embroiled in religion. Like the Alabama Supreme Court's IVF decision, the religious doctrine was prominent at the center of Justice Samuel Alito's majority opinion in Dobbs v. Jackson Women's Health Organization ruling overturning the 50-year precedent established in Roe v. Wade in 1973 (Lerer, Dias, and Karni 2024; Ables 2024; Greenhouse 2024). One of the long-standing goals of conservative Republicans has been the recognition of fetal personhood from the moment of conception. The pro-life movement has aimed to codify legal protections for human life at every reproductive stage. However, it puts them at odds with IVF which is designed to create life (Bazelon 2024). In June 2024, the Southern Baptists, the country's largest Protestant denomination, voted to oppose the use of in IVF indicating that evangelicals are open to equating embryos with human life and "fetal personhood" may become the next frontier for the anti-abortion movement (Graham 2024).

Conservative Republican policymakers' position that life begins at conception puts them at odds with a majority of American voters including many Republican voters. An Axios/Ipsos poll conducted in February following the Alabama Supreme Court's IVF decision found that 66 percent of respondents opposed the idea that embryos are children and those who destroy them should be held legally liable. The Republicans were split evenly 49 percent to 49 percent on the issue (Bettelheim 2024). In another Economist/YouGov poll, also conducted in February 2024, respondents by a margin of 50 to 21 percent said that embryos were not children. Republicans were about evenly split with 31 percent saying embryos were children while 32 percent saying that embryos were not children. Sixty-seven percent said that IVF should be legal, including 58 percent of Republicans (Blake 2024).

Religious Divide Over Abortion

In a Washington Post-ABC News poll conducted over the telephone between April 28 and May 3, 3023, of a random national sample of 1,006 adults, 66 percent of respondents stated that mifepristone should remain on the market while 24 percent said that it should be taken off the market. The poll also found that white evangelical Protestants were most supportive of Supreme Court decisions in Dobbs v. Mississippi Women's Health Organization with 58 percent in favor of the decision and 41 percent also saying that mifepristone should be taken off the market (Guskin 2023).

According to the Pew Research Center survey conducted from March to April 2023, 53 percent of Americans expressed the view that medication abortion should be legal in their state while only 22 percent said that it should be illegal. However, the was a sharp partisan divide with 73 percent of Democrats and Democratic-leaning independents saying abortion should be legal in their state compared to 35 percent of Republicans and Republican-leaning independents. The survey also found a major divide by religion. White evangelical Protestants are about twice as likely – 53 percent – to say it should be illegal compared to 23 percent of Protestants overall. Also, 46 percent of Catholics expressed the opinion that medication abortion should be legal in their state compared to 26 percent who said it should be illegal. Seventy-four percent of religiously unaffiliated adults said it should be legal (Hartig 2023).

Individuals and groups have often used courts to achieve social change when they have failed to achieve the same via policymaking institutions like Congress and state legislatures. In the early 1970s, reproductive rights advocates turned to federal courts and succeeded in securing constitutionally based abortion rights nationwide in the Supreme Court's ruling 1973 in *Roe v. Wade*. Some scholars have argued that the decision provoked a backlash from anti-abortion advocates. Others have criticized the backlash theory arguing that the anti-abortion movement predates the Roe decision and political polarization on the issue of abortion emerged not from a negative reaction to the Roe ruling but rather from the calculated efforts by the Republican Party strategists to appeal to the social conservatives and peel away working-class white voters from the Democratic Party (Price and Keck 2015). It should be noted that Christian nationalists often have claimed that their movement got its start as a grassroots reaction to the *Roe v. Wade* decision in 1973 (Stewart 2022b). The Republican Party's anti-abortion stance coincided with the "culture wars" and the rise of the Christian Right, a loose alliance of conservative evangelical Protestants and Catholics (Hymel 2018). Challenging the legality of *Roe v. Wade* became the central goal of the conservative movement (Parinandi 2023).

Anti-abortion organizations emphasize the interests of the unborn and protecting the right to life. They also began to refute the reasoning behind the Roe decision and criticized the decision holding that the fetus was not a person and that women had a right to abortion. Many right-wing organizations such as the American Conservative Union and John Birch Society became prominent critics of legalized abortion (Ziegler 2009). The Christian Right became the primary carrier of cultural-religious conservatism. This distinguishes it from the old right that had emphasized economic conservatism. The Christian right also became a core constituency of the Republican Party at national, state, and local levels. Abortion became a hot-button issue motivating the Christian Right activists. It brought about partisan, ideological, and religious polarization concerning the issue of abortion (Jaenicke 2002). Religious influence on attitudes toward abortion is shaped by religious identities, affiliation, and participation and they are critical indicators of individuals' cultural orientation and value commitment (Woodrum and Davison 2023).

In 1989, the U.S. Supreme Court in *Weber v. Missouri Reproductive Services* signaled its willingness to consider restrictions on abortion rights contained in *the Roe v. Wade* decision and in 1992 in Planned Parenthood of Southeastern Pennsylvania v. Casey opened the gates for states to regulate and impose abortion restrictions on legal abortions. This effectively moved the abortion issue into the realm of state legislative and electoral politics. This allowed religious groups to influence the political process. The Catholic Church with its "pro-life" position had already been very active in many states in efforts to mold legislation restriction access to abortion (Cook, Jelen, and Wilcox 1993).

Religious groups have long been involved with abortion politics. For example, after the *Roe v. Wade* decision, representatives of the Roman Catholic Church and the United Methodist Church appeared before the Congressional Committee hearing on a proposed constitutional amendment to overturn the Roe decision. The Roman Catholic Church had led the effort to keep abortion illegal while the United Methodist Church was instrumental in founding a coalition of mainline Protestant denominations to defend the Roe decision and to keep abortion legal. Evangelical and Catholic organizations have been active in the "pro-life" side of the debate. Attitudes about abortion have become also polarized along the religious dimension. Polarization has increased between mainline and evangelical Protestants as well as between black Protestants and both Catholics and white evangelicals (Evans 2002).

Increased religious polarization within the American public has occurred over politicized moral issues and the issue of abortion has become the lightning rod in the cultural wars. Cultural wars represent conflict over issues that are viewed by opposite sides as non-negotiable on cultural and moral grounds (Mouw and Sobel 2001). They are often referred to as morality policies and they tend to generate a higher level of citizen participation due to emotional commitment to core values and beliefs (Patton 2007). Titles of several books published in the 1990s demonstrate such irreconcilable viewpoints on abortion: *The Abortion: The Clash of Absolutes* (Tribe 1992); *Between Two Absolutes: Public Opinion and the Politics of Abortion* (Cook, Gelen, and Wilcox 1992); *No Neutral Ground: Abortion Politics in the Age of Absolutes* (O'Connor 1996). Abortion turned out to be a critical unifying issue for conservative Catholics and conservative Protestant evangelicals and motivated them to pursue an anti-abortion agenda at the executive, legislative, and judicial branches of government at all levels.

Religious traditions have continued to play an important role in the abortion debate. Conservative religious groups have adopted pro-life language and positions while liberal religious groups and religiously non-affiliated individuals have adopted a pro-choice position (Hoffman and Johnson 2005). The Christian Right has become a significant political force in the Republican Party (Skidmore (2023) warns about the rise of reactionary theocracy in America and argues that Protestant fundamentalists and Catholics have captured the Republican Party. Paradoxically Americans have grown more secular over the years, and their attitudes about morality are now at odds with the teachings of major churches (Dombrink 2005). This perhaps explains the disconnect between Republican policymakers' efforts to ban or restrict abortion access and American voters' rejection of abortion bans and restrictions and support for protecting and expanding the rights as demonstrated by successful ballot initiatives in both the blue and red states.

The irony surrounding abortion policy is that while medicine can answer the question of when a biological organism ceases to exist, it cannot answer the question of when a person begins or ends since they involve philosophical issues and are not easy to resolve because we have come to live in a "sound-bite" that can inflame passions and emotions and undermine genuine, rational debate over abortion policy. The political polarization has only become shriller over the years making it almost impossible to achieve any national consensus over abortion policy even though a solid majority of Americans support abortion rights (Varney 2022; Mouw and Sobel 2001).

Political Polarization and Abortion Policy

Abortion policy in the United States has come full circle. From the mid to late 1800s to 1973, when abortion was illegal, it was common to link the words abortion and crime together. However, women who got abortions were rarely prosecuted and they were often portrayed as victims; prosecution was focused on doctors and others who helped women get an abortion. Despite this, abortion was available because many doctors were willing to perform abortions. After a hard-fought struggle for abortion rights, Americans in 1973 won a national right to abortion when the Supreme Court in *Roe v. Wade* declared that a woman's right to an abortion was implicit in the right to privacy protected by the 14th Amendment. For almost 50 years, women enjoyed the unfettered right to abortion. Until the 1990s, abortion remained a non-artisan issue.

However, in 1992, in the case of *Planned Parenthood of Southeastern PA v. Casey*, the Supreme Court reaffirmed the essential holding of *Roe v. Wade*; it also held that states may regulate some aspects of abortions. This paved the way for states to impose restrictions on abortion access and practices. In the 1990s, abortion became a partisan and ideological issue with Republicans and social conservatives pushing for restricting abortion access while Democrats and liberals supported protection and expansion of abortion rights. The issue became politically polarized. As the number of unified governments increased at the state level where one party controlled all the levers of political powers, it became easier for states to adopt and implement their abortion policy agenda. Many red states with Republican trifecta control imposed more restrictions on abortion rights while blue states with Democratic trifecta control moved to protect abortion rights. Red and blue states were already moving in opposite directions even before the Dobbs decision.

On June 24, 2022, the U.S. Supreme Court issued its ruling in the case of *Dobbs v. Jackson Women's Health Organization* overturning the *Roe v. Wade* decision of 1973. It upended 50 years of the national right to abortion guaranteed through the U.S. Constitution and returned the issue back to the states to decide on abortion policy. This further intensified political polarization as many red states imposed total or near-total abortion bans and others imposed severe restrictions to limit access to abortion. In contrast, blue states moved to protect, expand, and enshrine abortion rights in the state constitutions. American voters showed their displeasure with efforts to restrict abortion access in the elections in 2022 and special elections in 2023. Abortion policy in the United States has come full circle. In sharp contrast to the expansion of abortion rights worldwide over the last 50 years, United States became one of the four countries in the world to have rolled back abortion rights since 1994 – El Salvador, Nicaragua, Poland, and the United States.

The topic of abortion has become one of the most inflammatory and polarizing issues of our times. The American federal system has become the battleground over cultural wars as the future of abortion policy hangs in balance in American states. Varying, vague, and conflicting abortion policies among states have also put physicians at the center of controversy whereby science and medical advice and decisions often become entangled in the politics of abortion. Women's reproductive rights now depend on where they live since millions of reproductive-age women live in states where abortion is banned and there are few, if any, abortion providers left.

In an ironic twist of fate, back in the 1990s impressed by the success of abortion rights advocates, advocates of physician assisted death went to the Supreme Court in the hope of establishing a national right to die, i.e., physician assisted death rooted in the U.S. Constitution. In 1997, in two related cases, *Washington v. Glucksberg* and *Vacco v. Quill*, the Supreme Court ruled that assisted suicide is not a fundamental right guaranteed in the U.S. Constitution. Writing for the majority, Chief Justice William Rehnquist wrote that assisted suicide is not a "fundamental liberty interest" protected by the Due Process Clause of the 14th Amendment and states have an unqualified interest in protecting human life. Justice Samuel Alito writing for the majority in *Dobbs v. Jackson Women's Health Organization* overturning *Roe v. Wade* wrote that the Constitution does not refer to abortion and no such right is implicitly protected by any constitutional provisions, including the Due Process Clause of the 14th Amendment. Ironically, Justice Alito applied the ruling in Glucksberg as the main precedent for striking down Roe (Smith 2023).

Bibliography

Ables, Kelsey. 2024. "Senate Republican Blocks Bill to Protect IVF After Alabama Ruling." https://www.washingtonpost.com/

"Abortion on the Ballot." 2022 December 20. https://www.nytimes.com/

Adam, Karla. 2024. "France Becomes the First Country to Explicitly Enshrine Abortion Rights in Constitution." https://www.washingtonposty.com/

Adam, Karla. 2023. "French Senate Votes to Enshrine Abortion in Constitution, A World First." https://www.washingtonpost.com/

Adam, Karla. 2023. "Macron Moves to Add Abortion to France's Constitution, Reacting to U.S." https://www.washingtonpost.com/

Adams, Patrick. 2023. "In Poland, Testing Women for Abortion Drugs Is a Reality. It Could Happen Here." https://www.nytimes.com/

Adashi, Eli Y. 2017. "The Hyde Amendment at 40 Years and Reproductive Rights in the United States." *Journal of American Medical Association* 317, no. 15 (April): 1523–1524.

"After Roe Fell: Abortion Laws by State." 2023. https://reproductiverights.org/

Aiken, Abigail; Jennifer E. Starling; James G. Scott, and Rebecca Gomperts. 2022. "Requests for Self-Managed Medication Abortion Provided Using Online Telemedicine in 30 States Before and After the Dobbs v. Jackson Women's Health Organization Decision." *Journal of American Medical Association* 328, no. 17 (November): 1768–1770.

Andone, Dakin. 2019. "Missouri Governor Signs Bill that bans Abortion after 9 Weeks." https://www.cnn.cpm/

Armitage, Hannah. 2010. "Political Language: Uses and Abuses: How the Term 'Partial Birth' Changed the Abortion Debate in the United States." *Australasian Journal of American Studies* 29, no. 1 (July): 15–35.

Atkins, Chole, and Minyvonne Burke. 2023. "Walgreens will not sell Abortion Pills in 20 GOP States." https://www.nbcnews.com/

Axe, Joseph. 2024. "Arkansas Election Officials Reject Proposed Abortion Ballot Measure." https://www.reuters.com/

Bacharier, Galen. 2022. "Missouri Bans Abortion with 'Trigger Law' After U.S. Supreme Court Overturns Roe v. Wade." https://www.news-leader.com/

Bettelheim, Adriel. 2024. "Frozen Embryos Should Not be Considered People, Two-Thirds of Americans Say." https://www.axios.com/

Bazelon, Emily. 2022. "The New Abortion Landscape." https://www.nytimes.com/

Bahr, Sarah 2023. "Tracking What Happened to Abortion Providers After the Dobbs Decision." https://www.nytimes.com/

Barnes, Robert, and Anne E. Marimow. 2023. "Justice Department Asks Supreme Court to Restore Access to Abortion Pill." https://www.washingtonpost.com/

Barnes, Robert; Ann E. Marimow; and John Wagner. 2022. "Court Strikes Down Roe V. Wade, Ending Constitutional Protection for Abortion." https://www.washingtonpost.org/

Bazelon, Emily. 2024. "Why 'Fetal Personhood' is Roiling the Right." https://www.nytimes.com/

Bella, Timothy. 2023. "The Abortion Pill's 1992 Supreme Court battle and the Woman Who Started it." https://www.washingtonpost.com/

Belluck, Pam. 2024a. "Abortion Shield Laws: A New War Between the States." https://www.nytimes.com/

Belluck, Pam. 2024b. "A New Abortion Access Strategy." https://www.nytimes.com/

Belluck, Pam. 2023. "Judge Invalidates F.D.A. Approval of the Abortion Pill Mifepristone." https://www.nytimes.com/

Berman, Russell. 2023. "The Next Big Abortion Fight." https://www.theatlantic.com/

Bhatia, Aatish; Clare Miller; and Margot Sanger-Katz. 2022. "A Surge of Overseas Abortion Pills Blunted the Effects of State Abortion Bans." https://www.nytimes.com/

Blake, Aron. 2024. "New Polls Spotlight GOP's IVF Dilemma." https://www.washingtonpost.com/

Blanchard, Nicole. 2023. "Idaho Asked Court to Dismiss Lawsuit Over Abortion Laws, here is what a Juge Decided." https://www.msn.com/

Boodman, Eric. 2023. "How a Conservative, Gun-Toting Doctor Defended Abortion Access in Appalachia." https://www.statnews.com/

Burns, Alexander. 2022. "States that Ban Abortion Risk Losing Business." https://www.nytimes.com/

Camobreco, John F., and Michelle A. Barnello. 2008. "Democratic Responsiveness and Policy Shock: The Case of State Abortion Policy." *State Politics & Policy Quarterly* 8, no.1 (Spring): 48–65.

Center for Reproductive Rights. 2023. "The World's Abortion Laws." https://reproductiveirghts.org/

Center for Reproductive Rights. 2022a. "With Recent Ruling, India Follows Global Trend of Liberalizing Abortion Laws." https://reproductiveirghts.org/

Center for Reproductive Rights. 2022b. "State Constitutions and Abortion Rights: Building Protections for Reproductive Autonomy." https://reproductiveirghts.org/

"Changes in Number of Abortions by State." 2023. https://societyfp.org/resarch/wecount/

Christensen, Jen, and Tierney Sneed. 2022. "At Least 43 Abortion Clinics Shut in Month After Supreme Court Overturned Roe, Research Says, with More Likely to Close." https://www.cnn.com/

Chuang, Cynthia H., and Carol S. Weisman 2019. "Aiming at Contraceptive Coverage – The Trump Administration's Attack on Reproductive Rights." *New England Journal of Medicine* 380, no. 11 (March): 993–995.

Cheney, Kyle; Josh Gerstein; and Alice M. Ollstein. 2023. "Appeal Court Keeps Abortion Pill on the Market but Limits Access." https://www.politico.com/

Choi, Annette, and Devan Cole. 2023. "See Where Abortions Are Banned and Legal – And Where it's Still in Limbo." https://cnn.com/

Cochrane, Emily. 2024. "Abortion Rights Supporters Puts a Winning Strategy to the Test in Arkansas." https://www.nytimes.com/

Cook, Elizabeth; Ted G. Jelen, and Clyde Wilcox. 1993. "Catholicism and Abortion Attitudes in the American States: A Contextual Analysis." *Journal for the Scientific Study of Religion* 32, no. 3 (September): 223–230.

Cook, Elizabeth; Ted G. Gelen; and Clyde Wilcox. 1992. *Between Two Absolutes: Public Opinion and the Politics of Abortion.* Boulder, CO: Westview Press Inc.

"Counseling and Waiting Period for Abortions." 2023. https://guttmacher.org/

Cui, Jasmine, and Danica Jefferies. 2024. "Map: Where Medication Abortion is and Isn't Legal." https://www.nbcnews.com/

Cunningham, Erin. 2022. "In Many Countries, Abortion is Protected by Law, Not Court Decision." https://www.washingtonpost.org/

Daniel, Clare. 2022. "Compromising Justice: Reproductive Rights Advocacy in the Time of Trump." *Journal of Women Studies* 43, no. 1: 68–92.

Demillo, Andrew. 2024. "Arkansas Supreme Court Upholds Rejection of Petitions to Let Voters Decide on Abortion Access." https://apnews.com/

Dench, Daniel; Mayra Pineda-Torres; and Caitlin Myers. 2023. "The Effects of the Dobbs Decision on Fertility." *Institute of Labor Economics.* November. https://docs.iza.org/

Dombrink, John. 2005. "Red, Blue, and Purple: Americans Views on Personal Morality and the Law." https://www.dissentmagazine.org/

Duggan, Laurel. 2022. "Two Americas: Chasm Grows Between Red and Bue States on Hot-Button Social Issues." https://dailycaller.com/

Edelman, Adam. 2022. "Abortion Rights Groups Look to Build on Their Victories with New Ballot Measures." https://www.nbcnews.com/

Edelman, Adam, and Lindsey Pipia. 2024. "Abortion Rights Amendments Qualify for the ballot in Colorado and South Dakota." https://www.nytimes.com/

Elliot, Philip. 2023. "That Texas Abortion Case is Even Worse than You Think." https://times.com

El-Bawab, Nadine. 2023. "1 in 5 Patients Travel to Other States for Abortion Care, According to New Data." https://abcnews.go.com/

Evans, John H. 2002. "Polarization in Abortion Attitudes in U.S. Religious Traditions, 1972-1998." *Sociological Forum* 17, no. 3 (September): 397–422.

Ewall-Wice, Sarah, and Caitlin Huey-Burns. 2022. "Abortion Access Proved to be a Powerful Force in 2022 Midterm Elections." https://www.cbsnews.com/

"Fact Sheet: President Biden Issues Executive Order on Strengthening Access to Contraception." 2023. https://www.whitehouse.gov/

Fernando, Christine. 2023. "5 Ways the Landscape has Changed Since the End of Rose V. Wade "upended" Abortion Access." https://www.usatoday.com/

Ford, Matt. 2022. "The Abortion Election." *New Republic*. (September): 28–29.

Forouzan, Kimya; Amy Friedrich-Karnik; and Isaac Maddow-Zimet. 2023. "The High Toll of US Abortion Bans: Nearly One in Five Patients Traveling Our of State for Abortion Care." https://www.guttmacher.org/

Forouzan, Kimya, and Isabel Guarnieri. 2023. "State Policy Trends 2023: In the First Full Year Since Roe Fell, A Tumultuous Year After Abortion and Other Reproductive Health Care." https://www.guttmacher.org/

Fritze, John, and Chrstine Fernando. 2023. "Abortion Pill: Justice Alito Pauses Mifepristone Restrictions as Supreme Court Weighs Appeal." https://www.usatoday.com/

Gerstein, Josh, and Alexander Ward. 2022. "Supreme Court has Voted to Overturn Abortion Rights, Draft Opinion Shows." https://www.politico.com/

Goldberg, Michelle. 2023. "A Texas Case Shows that Abortion Ban Exceptions are a Sham." https://www.nytimes.com/

Goldhill, Olivia. 2023a. "Cancun Abortion Clinic Will Give Americans a New Reason to Visit the Mexican Resort." https://www.statnews.com/

Goldhill, Olivia. 2023b. "Kate Cox is One of Hundreds in Texas Denied Abortions Despite Serious Health Risks, Data Shows." https://www.statnews.com/

Goldhill, Olivia, and Annalisa Merelli. 2024. "Advocates Expect Supreme Court Idaho Abortion Decision to Fuel Further Efforts to Restrict Access." https://www.statnews.com/

Gonzalez, Oriana. 2022. "Blue States Move to Protect Abortion Access Without Roe." https://www.axios.com/

Graham, Ruth. 2024. "Southern Baptists Vote to Oppose Use of I.V.F." https://www.nytimes.ocm/

Greenberger, Scott S. 2021. "Trump-Appointed Judges Fuel Abortion Debate in the States." https://pewtrusts.org/

Greenfield, Jeff. 2021. "We're Still Feeling the Aftershocks of the 2010 Midterm Elections." https://www.washingtonpost.com/

Greenhouse, Linda. 2024. "Let's Thank the Alabama Supreme Court." https://www.nytimes.com/

"Guttmacher Launches New Research Initiative to Track Monthly State Abortion Occurrences in the United States." 2023. Https://www.guttmacher.org/

Guskin, Emily. 2023. "Most U.S. Adults Say the Abortion Pill Mifepristone Should Stay on the Market, Post-ABC Poll Finds." https://www.washingtonpost.com/

Hanna, John. 2023. "Kansas Can't Enforce New Law on Abortion Pills or Make Patients Wait 24 Hours, Judge Rules." https://apnews.com/

Hanson, Beth. 2024. "Montana Becomes Eighth State that Will Have Abortion Rights on the Ballot in November." https://time.com/

Harrington, Rebecca, and Skye Gould. 2017. "The Number of Abortion Clinics in the US has Plunged in the Last Decade – Here's How Many Are in Each State." https://www.businessinsider.com/

Hartig, Hannah. 2023. "By More than Two-to-One, Americans Say Medication Abortion Should be Legal in their State." https://www.pewresearch.org/

Harvey, Eric. 2023. "Reproductive e Rights: U.S. Supreme Court Cases." https://www.findlaw.com/

Hawkins, Derek. 2023. "For Abortion Pill Mifepristone, a Political Battle is Nothing New." https://www.washingtonpost.com/

Henderson, Alex. 2023. "Texas Businesses are Rebelling Against Draconian GOP Rule." https://www.msn.com/

Hennessy-Fiske, Molly. 2024. "Religious Red-State Women are Rising Up and Speaking Out for IVF." https://www.washingtonpost.com/

Hennessy-Fiske, Molly, and Tim Craig. 2024 "With Alabama's IVF Court Ruling, a Scary Future for Women's Health Care." https://www.washingtonpost.com/

Hilburn, Greg. 2024. "Will Supreme Court abortion pill decision change access to mifepristone in Louisiana?" https://www.shreveporttimes.com/

Hodge, James G, Jr.; Summer Ghaith; and Lauren Krumholz. 2022. "Federalism's Fallacy at the Forefront of Public Health Law." *Journal of Law, Medicine & Ethics* 50, no. 4 (Winter): 848–851.

Hoffman, John P., and Sherrie M. Johnson. 2005. "Attitudes Toward Religions Traditions in the United States: Change or Continuity?" *Sociology of Religion* 66, no. 2 (Summer): 161–182.

Hooton, Angela, and Aram Schvey. 2014. "50 States of Denial: States Deny Women Reproductive Rights." *Human Rights* 40, no. 2 (July): 15–18.

Hounsell, Balke. 2022. "In States, Democrats all but Run Table." https://www.nytimes.com/

Howard, Grace. 2020. "The Pregnancy Police: Surveillance, Regulation, and Control." *Harvard Law & Policy Review* 14, no. 2 (September): 347–363.

Howe, Amy. 2024. "Supreme Court Preserves Access to Abortion Pill." https://www.scotusbog.com/

Hunt, Samantha A. 2023. "Call Me, Beep Me, If You Want to Reach Me: Utilizing Telemedicine to Expand Abortion Access." *Vanderbilt Law Review* 76, no. 1 (January): 323–359.

Hurley, Lawrence. 2023. "Supreme Court Discuss Whether to Hear Abortion Pill Showdown." https://www.nbcnews.com/

Hymel, Caroline. 2018. "Louisiana's Abortion Wars: Periodizing the Anti-Abortion Movement's Assault on Women's Reproductive Rights: 1973-2016." *Louisiana History* 59, no. 1 (Winter): 67–105.

Institute for Women's Policy Research. 2015. Chapter 5: "Reproductive Rights," pp. 167–193 in *The Status of Women in the States, 2015 Report*. https://statusofwomendata.org/

"Interactive Map: US Abortion Policies and Access After Roe." 2023. https://states.guttmaher.org/

Jaenicke, Douglas W. 2002. "Abortion and Partisanship in the US Congress, 1976-2000: Increasing Partisan Cohesion and Differentiation." *Journal of American Studies* 36, no. 1 (April): 1–22.

Jeong, Andrew, and James Bikales. 2022. "GOP Governors in Four Blue States Pledged to Uphold Right to Seek Abortion." https://www.washingtonpost.com/

Jimenez, Jesus. 2024. "Court Rules Texas Can Ban Emergency Abortions Despite Federal Guidelines." https://www.nytimes.com/

Johnson, Shawn. 2023. "For the First Time in 15 Years, Liberals in Control of the Wisconsin Supreme Court." https://www.npr.org

Jones, Rachel K; Elizabeth Nash; Lauren Cross; Jesse Philbin; and Marielle Kirstein. 2022. "Medication Abortion Now Accounts for More than Half of All US Abortions." https://www.guttmacher.org/

Jones, Rachel K; Elizabeth Witwer; and Jenna Jerman. 2017. "Abortion Incidence and Service Availability in the United States, 2017." https://www.guttmacher.org/

"Judge Block's Wyoming's 1st-in-the-NationAbortion Pill Ban." 2023. https://www.nbcnews.com/

Karmarck, Elaine. 2022. "America After Roe v. Wade." https://www.brookings.edu/

Karni, Annie. 2024. "Republican Opposition to Birth Control Bill Could Alienate Voters, Poll Finds." https://www.nytimes.com/

Keller, Rudi. 2021. "Missouri's 8-Week Abortion Ban Will Get Another Look from the Federal Appeals Court." https://www.kcur.org/

Kennedy, Lesley. 2023. "Reproductive Rights in the US: Timeline." https://www.history.com/

Kettl, Donald F. 2023. "State vs. Locals: The Neer Ending Conflict." https://www.governing.com/

Kindy, Kimberly. 2023. "Partisan Battle Grows Over State Funding for Antiabortion Centers." https://www.washingtonpost.com/

Kindy, Kimberly. 2022. "State Constitutions Loom as the Next Front in Abortion Battle." https://www.washingtonpost.com/

Kirstein, Marielle; Joerg Dreweke; Rachel Jones; and Jesse Philbin. 2022a. "100 Days Post-Roe: At Least 66 Clinics Across 15 US States Have Stopped Offering Abortion Care." https://www.guttmacher.org/

Kirstein, Marielle; Rachel Jones; and Jesse Philbin. 2022b. "One Month Post-Roe: At least 43 Abortion Clinics Across 11 States have Stopped Offering Abortion Care." https://www.guttmacher.org/

Kitchener, Caroline. 2022a. "Ky. Republicans Override Veto, Impose Sweeping Abortion Restrictions." https://www.washingtonpost.com/

Kitchener, Caroline. 2022b. "Republicans Enacting a Wave of New Abortion Restrictions." https://www.washingtonpost.com/

Kitchener, Caroline, and Rachel Roubein. 2022. "Draft Opinion Jolts Abortion Clinics, Lawmakers to Prepare for the End of Roe." https://www.washingtonpost.com/

Kitchener, Caroline; Kevin Schaul; N. Kirkpatrick; Daniela Santamarina; and Lauren Tierney. 2022. "Abortion will Soon be Banned in 13 States, Here's Which Could be Next." https://www.washingtonpost.com/

Kitchener, Caroline, and Maegan Vazquez. 2023. "Texas Supreme Court Rules Against Woman at Center of Abortion Battle." https://www.washingtonpost.com/

Kitchener, Caroline; Rachel Roubein; Andrew Ba Tran; Caitlin Gilbert; and Hanna Dormido. 2023. "A Fragile New Phase of Abortion in America." https://www.washingtonpost.com/

Kochi, Sudiksha. 2023. "What's Next After Ohio? Here are the States Looking to Enshrine Abortion Protections In 2024." https://www.usatoday.com/

Kohn, Julia E.; Jennifer L. Snow; Hannah R. Simmons, Jane W. Seymour; Terri A. Thompson; and Daniel Grossman. 2019. "Medication Abortion Provided Through Telemedicine in Four U.S. States." *Obstetrics & Gynecology* 134, no. 2 (August): 343–350.

Konisky, David M., and Paul Nolette. 2022. "The State of American Federalism 2021-2022: Federal Courts, State Legislatures, and the Conservative Turn in the Law." *Publius* 52, no. 3 (Summer): 353–381.

Kreitzer, Rebecca J. 2015. "Politics and Morality in State Abortion Policy." *State Politics & Policy Quarterly* 15, no. 1 (March): 41–66.

Kruesi, Kimberlee; Christine Fernando; and Leah Willingham. 2024. "Abortion Access has Won When It's on the ballot. That's not an Option in Half the States." https://www.yahoo.com/

Kulczycki, Andrzej. 2007. "Ethics, Ideology, and Reproductive Health Policy in the United States." *Studies in Family Planning* 38, no. 4 (December): 333–351.

Larson, Jordan. 2017. "The 200-Year Fight for Abortion Access." https://www.thecut.com/

Laurin-Whitney, Gottbrath. 2022. "U.S. Joins only 3 Other Countries that have Rolled Back Abortion Rights Since 1994." https://www.axios.com/

Lazzarini, Zita. 2022. "The End of Roe W. Wade – States' Power Over Health and Well-Being." *New England Journal of Medicine* 387, no. 5 (August): 390–393.

LeBlanc, Steve. 2023. "Concerned US States Start Stockpiling Abortion Drug After Court Ruling." https://apnews.com/

Lerer, Lisa; Elizabeth Dias; and Annie Karni. 2024. "Alabama IVF Ruling Opens New Front in Election-Year Abortion Battle." https://www.nytimes.ecom/

Lerer, Lisa, and Shane Goldmacher. 2023. "Will Abortion Dominate the 2024 Elections Tuesday will Offer Clues." https://www.newyroktimes.com/

Levine, Marianne. 2023. "Republicans Still Struggle to Find a Winning Strategy on Abortion." https://www.washingtonpost.com/

Lieb, David A. 2024. "Initiative to Enshrine Abortion Rights in Missouri Constitution Qualifies for November Ballot." https://abcnews.go.com/

Lopez, Ian, and Celine Castronuovo. 2024. "Democratic Governors Brace for Supreme Court Abortion Pill Ruling." https://news.bloomberglaw.com/

Luhby, Tami. 2019. "These States are Strengthening Abortion Laws Even as Others Dismantle Them." https://www.cnn.com/

Luthra, Shefali. 2024. "CVS and Walgreens Will Start Selling Abortion Pills This Month." https://www.cbsnews.com/

Lysen, Dylan; Laura Zeigler; and Blaise Mesa. 2022. "Voters in Kansas Decide to Keep Abortion Legal in the States, Rejecting an Amendment." https://www.npr.org/

Lupkin, Sidney. 2023. "The FDA Approves the First Over-the-Counter Birth Control Pill, Opill." https://www.npr.org/

Maddow-Zimet, Isaac; Kelly Baden; Rachel Jones; Isabel DoCampo; and Jesse Philbin. 2023. "New State Abortion Data Indicate Widespread Travel for Care." https://www.guttmacher.org/

Manchester, Julia. 2022. "Republicans Rethink Strategy After Brusing Mid-Terms." https://thehill.com/

Manzanetti, Zoe. 2022. "Abortion Map 2022: US State Laws After Overturning Roe." https://www.governing.com/

Margolies, Dan, and Celia Llopis-Jepsen. 2019. "Kansas Supreme Court Rules State Constitution Protects Right to Abortion." https://www.npr.org/

Mason, Nicole C.; Kate Ryan; Olivia Starz; Georgia Poyatzis; and Ariane Hegewisch. 2022. "IWPR Reproductive Rights Index: A State-by-State Analysis and Ranking." *Institute for Women's Policy Research*, (July): 1–16. https://iwpr.org/

Maddow-Zimet, Isaac, and Kathryn Kost. 2022. "Even Before Roe was Overturned, Nearly One in 10 People Obtaining an Abortion Traveled Across State Lines for Care." https://www.guttmacher.org/

Marimow, Anne E; Caroline Kitchener; Perry Stein; and Robert Barnes. 2023. "Texas Judge Suspends FDA Approval of Abortion Pill; Second Judge Protects Access." https://www.Washingtonpost.com/

Mazzei, Patricia. 2023. "Ohio Voted to Protect Abortion Rights. Could Florida be Next?" https://www.nytimes.com/

McCammon, Sarah. 2023a. "Even Before the Dobbs Ruling, More Americans were Traveling for Abortion." https://www.npr.org/

McCammon, Sarah. 2023b. "With Abortion Pill Access Uncertain, States Strike Deal to Stock Up." https://www.npr.org/

McCann, Allison, and Amy Walker. 2023. "One Year; 61 Clinics: How Dobbs Changed the Abortion Landscape." https://www.nytimes.com/

McGinley, Lauri; Rachel Roubein; and Akilah Johnson. 2023. "Birth Control Pills aren't Available Over the Counter in U.S That Could Change." https://www.Washingtonpost.com/

McPhillips, Deidre. 2023. "Births have Increased in States with Abortion Bans, Research Finds." https://www.cnn.com/

McShane, Julianne. 2022. "At Least 66 Clinics in 15 States Have Stopped Providing Abortions Since Dobbs, Analysis Finds." https://www.nbcnews.com/

Medoff, Marshall H. 2002. "The Determinant and Impact of State Abortion Restrictions." *American Journal of Economics and Sociology* 61, no. 2 (April): 481–493.

Melton, Brittney. 2024. "These States will Vote on Abortion in 2024." https://www.npr/org/

Middleton, Chris. 2022. "America After Roe v. Wade." https://www.eurekastreet.com.au/

Miller, Justin, and Michelle Pitcher. 2022. "Before 'Roe' – And After." https://www.texasobserver.org/

"Monthly Abortion Provision Study." 2023. https://www.guttmacher.org

Mooney, Christopher Z. 2000. "The Decline of Federalism and the Rise of Morality-Policy Conflict in the United States." *Publius* 30, no. 1 (Winter): 171–188.

Mosbergen, Dominique, and Vibhuti Agrawal. 2022. "Websites Selling Unapproved Abortion Pills are Booming." https://www.wsj.com/

Mouw, Ted, and Michael E. Sobel. 2001. "Cultural Wars and Opinion Polarization: The Case of Abortion." *American Journal of Sociology* 106, no. 4 (January): 913–943.

North, Anna. 2019. "Missouri's 8-Week Abortion Ban Blocked by Court: The Restrictive Law will not Go into Effect, for Now." https://www.vox.com/

"Number of Abortion Clinics by State, 2017–2020." 2021. https://data.guttmacher.org/

O'Connor, Ema. 2019. "The Last Decade was Disastrous for Abortion Rights. Advocates are Trying to Figure Out What's Next." https://www.buzfeednews.com/

O'Connor, Karen. 1996. *No Neutral Ground: Abortion Politics in the Age of Absolutes*. Boulder, CO: Westview Press.

Ollstein, Alice M. 2023. "Texas Judge Halts FDA Approval of Abortion Pill." https://www.politico.com/

Ollstein, Alice M., and Megan Messerly. 2022. "A Predicted 'Red Wave' Crashed into Wall of Abortion Rights Support on Tuesday." https://www.politico.com/

Owermohle, Sarah. 2024. "Supreme Court Slates Abortion Pill Case for March." https://www.statnews.com/

Owermohle, Sarah. 2023a. "'Hot Mess': Abortion Pills at Pharmacies Could Face Legal Quagmire, Especially in Restrictive States." https://www.statnews.com/

Owermohle, Sarah. 2023b. "Supreme Court will Decide Abortion Pill Access." https://statnews.com/

Page, Susan; Rachel Locker; and Miles J. Herszenhorn 2023. "Exclusive: Support for Legal Abortion Rises a Year After Roe v. Wade Overturned—Poll." https://www.usatoday.com/

Park, Alice. 2024. "The First Over-The-Counter Birth Control Pill is Here." https://time.com/

Parker, Claire. 2021. "Belgium to help Fund Abortion for Women Who Can't Get Them in Poland." https://www.washingtonpost.com/

Parker, Kathleen. 2023. "In Post-Roe America, Weird Changes Might be Coming to Abortion Laws." https://www.washingtonpost.com/

Parinandi, Srinivas C. 2023. *Following in Footstep or Marching Alone? How Institutional Differences Influence Renewable Energy Policy*. Chicago: University of Chicago Press.

Patton, Dana. 2007. "The Supreme Court and Morality Policy Adoption in the American States: The Impact of Constitutional Context." *Political Research Quarterly* 60, no. 3 (September): 468–488.

"Percent Change in Abortion Rate by State (2017–2020)." 2021. https://data.guttmacher.org/

"Percentage of Legal Abortions Obtained by Out of State Residents, 2020." 2021. https://www.kff.org/

Pettway, Alice. 2017. "The Fight for Reproductive Rights: New Threats, New Activism." *The Progressive* 81, no. 4 (April-May): 16–18.

Pew Research Center. 2022. "Majority of Public Disapproves of Supreme Court's Decision to Overturn Roe v. Wade." https://www.pewresearch.org/

Phillips, Amber, and Tom Hamburger. 2022. "Abortion Law in Indiana Leads to Fallout for State, Politics." https://www.washingtonpost.com/

Pocan, Mark. 2017. "Resisting and Persisting in the Age of Trump." *Progressive* 81, no. 4 (April-May): 19–20.

Price, Richard S., and Thomas M. Keck. 2015. "Movement Litigation and Unilateral Disarmament: Abortion and the Right to Die." *Law & Social Inquiry* 40, no. 4 (Fall); 880–907.

Quinn, Melissa. 2024. "Supreme Court Lets Idaho Enforce Abortion Ban for Now and Agrees to Hear the Case." https://www.cbsnews.com/

Rabin, Roni C., and Azeen Ghorayshi. 2024. "Alabama Rules Frozen Embryos are Children, Raising Questions About Fertility Care." https://www.nytimes.com/

Ramirez, Marc. 2023. "The US Supreme Court Took Away Abortion Rights. Mexico's Highest Court Just Did the Opposite." https://www.usatoday.com

Ranji, Usha; Karen Diep; and Alina Salganicoff. 2023. "Key Facts on Abortion in the United States." https://www.kff.org/

Reagan, Leslie A. 1997. *When Abortion was a Crime: Women, Medicine, and Law in the United States, 1867–1973*. Berkley: University of California Press.

Reilly, Katie. 2022. "These are the States that Voted to Protect Abortion Rights in the Midterms." https://time.com/

"Reproductive Rights and the Supreme Court." n.d. https://www.ncjw.org/

Reston, Maeve, and Marianne LeVine. 2023. "GOP 2024 Hopeful Court Evangelicals as They Struggle Over Abortion." https://www.washingtonpost.com/

Richards, Cecile. 2024. "How Louisiana Has Become a Microcosm of the Abortion Access Fight." https://time.com/

Rojas, Rick. 2024. "The Alabama Chief Justice Who Invoked God in Deciding the Embryo Case." https://www.nytimes.com/

Rovner, Julie. 2022. "As Red States Push Strident Abortion Bans, Other Restrictions Suddenly Look Less Extreme." https://kffhealthnews.org/

Rubin, Lisa. 2023. "Idaho's Newest Abortion Law Could End Up in the Supreme Court." https://www.msnbce.com/

Sable-Smith, Bram. 2023. "Ohio Voted on Abortion. Next Year 11 More States Might, Too." https://kffhealthnews.org/

Sanger-Katz, Margot, and Claire Cain Miller. 2023. "How Many Abortions Did the Post-Roe Bans Prevent?" https://www.nytimes.com/

Santamarina, Daniela; Youjin Shin; Sammy Westfall; and Ruby Mellen. 2022. "How Abortion Laws in the U.S. Compare with Those in Other Countries." https://www.washingtonpost.com/

Sarkissian, Arek. 2023. "DeSantis Signs Florida's 6-Week Abortion Ban into Law." https://www.politico.com/

Savarese, Mauricio. 2023. "Brazil's to Court Opens Vote on Decriminalizing Abortion Up to 12th Weeks of Pregnancy." https://www.msn.com

Sellers, Frances S., and Rachel Roubein. 2023. "FDA to Permit Some Retail Pharmacies to Dispense Abortion Pills." https://www.washingtonpost.com/

Seshadri, Malika. 2023. "Out-of-Staters are Flocking to Places where Abortions are Easier to Get." https://www.npr.org/

Shaw, Kate. 2023. "The Abortion Pill Ruling is Bad Law, and the Biden Administration Should Fight It." https://www.nytimes.com/

Sherman, Carter. 2023. "The Fight for Abortion Rights: What to Know Going into 2024." https://www.thegaurdian.com/

Sherman, Carter, and Andrew Witherspoon. 2023. "Abortion Rights Across the US: We Track Where Laws Stand in Every State." https://www.thegaurdian.com/

Simmons-Duffin, Selena, and Diane Webber. 2023. "Ruling Deals Blow to Access to Abortion Pill Mifepristone – but Nothing Changes Yet." https://www.npr.org/

Silverman, Ed. 2023. "FDA Panel Votes in Favor of the First Over-the-Counter Birth Control Pill." https://www.statnews.com/

Singh, Kanishka. 2024. "Arizona Supreme Court: Fetus can be Called 'Unborn Human'." https://www.reuters.com/

Skidmore, Max. 2023. "Abortion—Reactionary theocracy rises in America, while declining elsewhere." *P&P: Politics and Policy* 51, no. 3: 437–457.

Smith, Mitch, and Katie Glueck. 2022. "Kansas Voters to Preserve Abortion Rights Protections in Its Constitution." https://www.nytimes.com/

Smith, Wesley J. 2023. "How Assisted Suicide Advocacy Overturned Roe v. Wade." *Journal of Human Life Review* 49, no. 1 (Winter): 53–59.

Staman, Jennifer A., and Jon A. Shimabukuro. 2022. "Medication Abortion: A Changing Legal Landscape." https://crsreports.congress.gov/

Stancil, Kenny. 2022. "Expert Warn GOP War on Abortion will Turn Red and Blue States into 'Mutually Hostile Legal Territories.'" https://www.commondreams.org

"State Pro-life and Pro-Abortion Laws and Initiatives." 2023. https://nrlc.org/

Stewart, Katherine. 2022a. "Christian Nationalists are Excited About What's Next." https://www.nytimes.com/

Stewart, Katherine. 2022b. "How the Christian Right Took Over the Judiciary and Changed America." https://www.theguardian.com/

Starcqualursi, Veronica; Devan Cole; and Paul LeBlanc. 2022. "Voters Deliver Ringing Endorsement of Abortion Rights on Midterm Ballot Initiatives Across the US." https://www.cnn.com/

Sullenger, Cheryl. 2021. "The Status of American Abortion Facilities in 2020: The First Abortion—Free State." https://www.operationrescue.org/

"Texas Companies Say Republicans are Ruining Their Business." 2023. https://www.newsweek.com/

Thakker, Niraj. 2017. "Undue Burden with a Bite: Shielding Reproductive Rights from the Jaws of Politics." *University of Florida's Journal of Law and Public Policy* 28, no. 3: 431–474.

"The State of Reproductive Health and Rights: A 50-State Report Card." 2022. https://www.populationinstitute.org/

Times Editorial Board. 2023. "The Fight Over Reproductive Rights Will Play Out in States and Courts in 2023." https://www.latimes.com/

Tribe, Lawrence H. 1992. *The Abortion: The Clash of Absolutes*. New York: W. W. Norton & Company.

Valenti, Jessica. 2023. "Abortion Bans by Any Other Name are Still Abortion Bans." https://www.nytimes.com/

VanSickle, Abbie. 2024a. "The Supreme Court Allows, for Now, Emergency Abortion in Idaho." https://www.nytimes.com/

VanSickle, Abbie. 2024b. "Supreme Court Maintains Broad Access to Abortion Pill." https://www.nytimes.com/

VanSickle, Abbie. 2023. "For Texas Judge I Abortion Case, a Life Shaped by Conservative Causes." https://www.nytimes.com/

Varney, Sarah. 2022. "When Does Life Begin? As State Laws Define It, Science, Politics, and Religion Clash." https://kffhealthnews.org

Vazquez, Maegan. 2023. "Texas Supreme Court Temporarily Halts Order that Allowed Pregnant Woman to Have Abortion." https://washingtonpost.com/

Vecera, Vincent. 2014. "The Supreme Court and the Social Conception of Abortion." *Law & Society Review* 48, no. 2 (June): 345–375.

Vestal, Christine. 2022. "As Abortion Pills Take Off, Some States Move to Curb Them." https://stateline.org/

Vestal, Christine. 2019. "New Laws Deepen State Differences Over Abortion." https://stateline.org/

Wagner, Bayliss. 2023. "Here's what the Texas Supreme Court's Ruling Against Kate Cox Means for Abortions." https://www.stateman.com/

Wang, Amy B., and Leigh Ann Caldwell. 2023. "12 States Where the Fate of Abortion Rights Could be on the 2024 Ballot." https://washingtonpost.com/

Weber, Paul J. 2023. "A Texas Judge Grants a Pregnant Woman Permission to Get an Abortion Despite the State's Ban." http://apnews.com/

"WeCount Report Shows Major Disruption in Abortion Care One Year After Dobbs." 2023. https://societyfp.org/

"Which States are People Traveling to For Abortion?" 2022. https://usafacts.org/

"Which States Passed New Abortion Laws in 2022." 2022. https://usafacts.org/

White, Kari; Asha Dane'el; Elsa Vizcarra; Laura Dixon; Klaire Lerma; Anitra Beasley; Joseph Potter; and Tony Ogburn. 2022. "Out-Of-State Travel for Abortion Following Implementation of Texas Senate Bill 8." https://sites.utexas.edu/

Welsh, Jennifer. 2021. "A Verywell Report: Abortion Access Ranked by State." https://www.verywellhealth.com/

Weisman, Jonathan. 2022. "Divided on Abortion, Guns, and More." https://www.nytimes.com/

Westfall, Sammy. 2021. "Poland's Abortion Law Under Scrutiny After Pregnant Woman Dies in Hospital." https://www.washingtonpost.com/

Williamson, Vanessa, and Itai Grofman. 2023. "Ohio Voters Reject Issue 1 – Here's What That Means for Democracy." https://www.brookings.edu/

Woodrum, Eric, and Beth L. Davison. 2023. "Reexamination of Religious Influences on Abortion Attitudes." *Review of Religious Research* 33, no. 3 (March): 229–243.

Yang, Maya. 2023. "Democratic States Stockpile Abortion Pills as Legal Fights for Access Looms." https://www.theguardian.com/

Yurkanin, Amy. 2024. "Treatment Resume After Alabama Governor Signs IVF Protection Bill." https://www.governing.com/

Zernike, Kate. 2024. "Arizona will Vote on Abortion in November: Could that Give Democrats an Edge?" https://www.nytimes.com/

Zernike, Kate. 2023. "Ohio Votes to Establish Right to Abortion." https://www.nytimes.com/

Zernike, Kate. 2022. "Strategic Shift in Bid to Regain Abortion Rights." https://www.nytimes.com/

Zernike, Kate, and Lisa Lerer. 2023. "Why the Abortion Ballot Question in Ohio is Confusing Voters." https://www.washingtonpost.com/

Zernike, Kate, and Michael Wines. 2023. "Losing Ballot Issues on Abortion, G.O.P. Now tries to Keep Them off the Ballot." https://nytimes.com/

Ziegler, Mary. 2009. "The Framing of a Right to Choose: Roe v. Wade and the Changing Debate on Abortion Law." *Law & History Review* 27, no. 2 (Summer): 281–330.

Zionts, Arielle. 2024. "Montana May Not Remain an Island of Abortion Access." https://www/governing.com/

7
RED AND BLUE STATES' RESPONSE TO THE COVID-19 PANDEMIC

Mankind has been plagued by plagues for millenniums. Plagues are a major cause of deaths in humans. COVID-19 is just the most recent of a long list of plagues.

The deadliest plague was the Black Death, which lasted from approximately 1334 to approximately 1353. It began in China and then spread eastward through Europe, killing almost half of the population. The cause was rats carrying infectious fleas on ships. The estimated number of people who died was 75–200 million people at a time when the earth's human population was much smaller than it is now (Prabhu and Gergen 2021).

Number two on the list was what has been called the Spanish flu. It lasted from 1918 to 1920 and is related to World War I. The flu killed, in its two-year run, an estimated 50–100 million people (LePan 2020; Prabhu and Gergen 2021).

The third most deadly plague was the New World Smallpox. It lasted from approximately 1520 to the early 1600s. It resulted in the deaths of approximately 25–56 million people. Smallpox was a continuing issue in Europe and European explorers brought the plague to the western hemisphere. It was so deadly to the indigenous people, Native Americans, because they had no immunity from the disease. An estimated 90 percent of the indigenous population died from smallpox (Prabhu and Gergen 2021).

Number four on the list was the Plague of Justinian, which lasted from approximately 541 to 549. It resulted in the deaths of approximately 30 to 50 million people. The plague, most likely bubonic plague, began in Constantinople, which was the home of the Byzantine Empire. It spread to other continents controlled by the empire. At one point, in Constantinople,

DOI: 10.4324/9781032671147-7

some 10,000 people a day died from the disease (Prabhu and Gergen 2021).

Number six on the list is HIV/AIDS (acquired immunodeficiency syndrome), which began in 1981 and continues to this day. An estimated 27–47 million have died from AIDS across several continents, including North America. There is no cure for the virus (HIV), but there have been medications developed that allow those infected to live a full life (Prabhu and Gergen 2021).

The last plague on the list of top seven plagues is COVID-19, which began in 2019–2020 and continues to this day, though it is no longer a pandemic. Nearly seven million people had died from COVID-19 as of January 2024 (Worldometer 2024a).

COVID-19 was categorized as a pandemic from 2020 to 2023. A pandemic is a fast-growing infection that rapidly affects many people in a large geographical area, usually over more than a single continent (Morgan 2023). COVID-19 certainly meets this definition.

The official name of the coronavirus is SARS-CoV-2 (World Health Organization 2023a). There was a SARS-CoV-1 virus that caused an epidemic in 2002–2004 (The Covid Crisis Group 2023). It is part of a family of viruses that includes SARS and MERS (Middle East Respiratory Syndrome). These kinds of viruses often originate in animals, such as camels and bats, and can cross over to humans. SARS began in China in 2002 and spread to over 24 countries. Coronaviruses have spikes on their surface and cause respiratory disease, some of which can be fatal (see below). COVID-19 is the disease caused by the coronavirus and is short for coronavirus diseases 2019. The virus is sometimes referred to as the novel (or new) coronavirus (Auwaerter 2023; National Foundation for Infectious Diseases 2023).

There have also been variants of the original coronavirus, which has produced waves or surges of illness. An early wave occurred in the 2020–2021 winter season. This was due to winter travel for the holidays. A July 2021 wave was largely due to a new variant, delta, combined with less concern about staying home and decreases in immunity (Maragakis 2021).

All viruses mutate; that is, their genetic makeup changes. The delta variant mentioned above is one example. Another variant is the omicron. The omicron variant is interesting for three reasons. First, it is more transmissible (picked up by others) than previous versions of the virus. Second, while all the variants have subvariants, the omicron variant was immediately accompanied by over 50 subvariants. The BA.2 variant is very contagious. Third, though omicron may cause more cases, it does not cause more serious illnesses, focusing more on the upper respiratory as opposed to the lower respiratory area, which is more characteristic of the original version of the virus (Maragakis et al. 2022).

As of this writing, the latest subvariant observed beginning in September 2023 was JN.1, based on the omicron variant. By January 2024 it was the dominant variant in terms of causing new cases. While it is causing more disease, it does not appear to be causing more serious diseases (Appleby 2024; Tin 2024). The problem of dealing with the pandemic was political. Red states and blue states addressed the disease and its impacts, on the health of the population, issues with the healthcare system, and the economy.

Much of the discussion, outside scientific circles, about the pandemic became politicized in ways that recall the other issues discussed in this book. What was the origin of the pandemic? How serious was the pandemic? What measures should we take to reduce the impact of the virus? Who should make decisions as to how to respond?

Politics and polarization were not the only factors in how the pandemic was handled, but they were very important ones. It could be said that in this period of time, 2000–2024, the United States faced two plagues: the novel coronavirus and partisanship.

The Impact of the Pandemic

Since the beginning of the pandemic in late 2019 through January 2024, there have been approximately 702.5 million cases of the coronavirus worldwide. During this same period, there have been 6,974,391 deaths due to the coronavirus worldwide. Table 7.1 presents data comparing total figures with the United States.

The coronavirus data shown in the table is cumulative through January 2024.

Let us begin by comparing the U.S. population to the world population. The United States has the third largest population in the world, behind only China and India. The U.S. population is about 4.1 percent of the

TABLE 7.1 Total Coronavirus Cases (January 2024)

	Total Cases (in millions)	Total Deaths (in millions)	Total Cases per 1 mil pop	Total Deaths per 1 mil Pop	Population (in millions)
World	702.5	6,974	90,120	897.4	8,087.8
USA	110.8	1,193	3,30,859	3,566	334.8

Adapted from: Worldometer (2024b). Online at https://www.worldometers.info/coronavirus/.

world's population. Of the total cumulative coronavirus cases, the United States accounts for nearly 16 percent of all cases. Of total cumulative deaths, the United States accounts for just over 17 percent of all cases. If we look at rates, total cases per million population, and total deaths per million population, we can see that the United States far surpasses the world rates. The total cases per million and total deaths per million in the United States are almost four times as high as the total cases for the world. It is clear that the coronavirus pandemic had a much more devastating effect in the United States than in most other countries in the world. It is also likely that the actual number of deaths from COVID-19 is higher than the official count, perhaps as much as 16 percent higher than the official count. That is because some deaths were attributed to other causes, such as overdoses, rather than to COVID-19 (Schreiber 2024). And we would argue that the larger number for the United States was a function of the response to the pandemic colored by partisan disagreement.

Figures 7.1 and 7.2 give us a picture of the impact of the COVID-19 pandemic and the different waves of the pandemic in the United States. Figure 7.1, which displays new hospitalizations on a weekly basis, shows five peaks from September 2020, the first full year of the pandemic, through the middle of June 2023. Especially in the early years of the pandemic, the surge in cases placed a great strain on the healthcare system, particularly hospitals. Part of the problem was the intensity of care that some of the patients needed, especially those who needed ventilators to help them breath. But the sheer number of patients overwhelmed hospitals and their

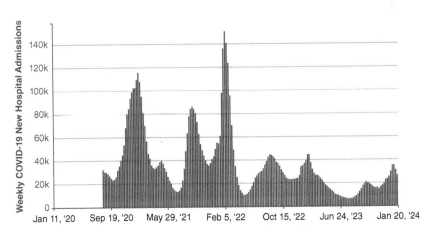

FIGURE 7.1 New Covid Hospital Admissions by Week. From Centers for Disease Control and Prevention (2023a). Online at https://covid.cdc.gov/covid-data-tracker.

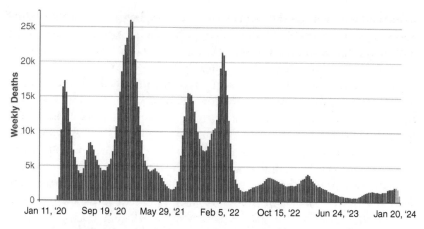

FIGURE 7.2   COVID-19 Deaths by Week. From Centers for Disease Control and Prevention (2023a). Online at https://covid.cdc.gov/covid-data-tracker.

staff. Hospitals had to devote significant portions of their capacity to COVID-19 patients resulting, in some case, in hospital capacity exceeding 100% (Grimm 2021).

Figure 7.2 displays COVID-related deaths. It also shows the waves and surges. The highest number of deaths came in the October/November 2020 period when more than 25,000 people died each week. Other major surges came in the later part of 2021 and in early 2022. This is despite the availability of vaccines, when shots were first available in April 2021.

Part of the problem was that hospitals did not have sufficient staff with experience in dealing with the complex cases the COVID-19 patients posed. Another problem was that hospitals needed to isolate COVID-19 patients from their other patients so that the virus would not spread. There were also delays in discharging patients to other facilities, such as rehab hospitals and nursing homes (Grimm 2021).

A related problem was that COVID-19 patients were taking up so much hospital space and workforce attention that other potential patients found that they had to delay care. This, of course, could lead to worsening conditions for those patients (Grimm 2021). Non-COVID-19-related hospital admissions declined, particularly in 2020 (Birkmeyer et al. 2020).

Another aspect of the impact of the pandemic on hospitals occurred in rural areas. As we have seen in Chapter 3, some rural areas lack hospitals. Even in rural areas that do have hospitals, the hospitals tend to be small and have fewer specialized providers than hospitals in suburban or urban areas (National Rural Health Association 2023). The result is that healthcare for people in rural areas often requires either foregoing such care or traveling, perhaps long distances, to obtain care. For someone with a COVID-19 virus, that would be difficult.

Yet another impact of the pandemic is on the healthcare workforce. The workforce, physicians, nurses, physician assistants, etc., were greatly stressed by the pandemic and the patients in the hospital. The stress included increased workloads and dealing with seriously ill people who might die. This caused trauma and burnout among staff, high turnover, and staff shortages. That in turn caused quality of care and patient safety issues. Hospitals experienced shortages of PPE (personal protective equipment), such as masks and gloves, to protect providers from contracting the disease from their patients (Grimm 2021).

Hospitals also experienced financial issues. For example, because of shortages, hospitals had to pay higher costs for staff and PPE. Patients might be enrolled in Medicaid, which pays less than privately insured or Medicare patients. Patients, especially in rural areas. might not be insured or were under-insured (Grimm 2021).

COVID-19 also has implications for other diseases. For example, because COVID patients took up so much hospital space and health professional's time, other illnesses that might otherwise have been detected were not. A recent study (Burus et al. 2024) estimated that as many as 135,000 cancer cases were undiagnosed. COVID-19 may also be implicated in a surge in heart disease fatalities (Gale 2024).

One of the things that the COVID-19 pandemic did was to underscore inequities that existed in the American healthcare system (see Ndugga, Hill, and Artiga 2022; Oladele et al. 2022; Patel and Rushefsky 2008; Tolchin et al. 2021). Cases, hospitalizations, and deaths were higher among people of color than among whites during the first two years of the pandemic. It was not until 2022 that the rates of the two sets of groups became similar.

There were also issues associated with the lockdowns. Groups and businesses were hurt economically. Schools moved to online teaching and educational learning declined (Nocera and McLean 2023; "The Damaging Legacy of COVID School Closures" 2024).

Responding to the pandemic required the use of policies or a toolkit that could help alleviate the impacts of the pandemic (The Covid Crisis Group 2023). These policies or tools include lockdowns, social distancing, medications, masking, and vaccinations. The country was not well prepared for the pandemic (Nocera and Mclean 2023a; The Covid Crisis Group 2023). This was true of the underfunded and neglected public health system as well as the larger political system.

Partisan Controversy Over the Origin of the Pandemic

The pandemic has its roots in China, particularly in the city of Wuhan in Hubei province in 2019 (The COVID Crisis Group 2023). One aspect of this story is the origin of the virus in humans and the politically divided debate over what is a scientific issue. Whatever the origin, it appears that travelers who had contracted the virus brought it to the United States and other countries.

There is a lot of controversy surrounding the pandemic and the responses to it. The perspectives on what the problems were and how to deal with them were colored by differences between red and blue states, Republicans and Democrats. Understanding the origin of the pandemic is an appropriate place to begin our examination of the relationship between partisanship and the pandemic.

It is fitting that one of the controversies has to do with the origin of the pandemic. There is little question that the coronavirus began in Wuhan, People's Republic of China (PRC). There are two major theories as to how the virus was passed on to humans (The COVID Crisis Group 2023). The first theory is the open market theory. The City of Wuhan is near wilderness areas and the Chinese cuisine includes wild animals, such as raccoon dog and Malayan porcupine (Quammen 2023). Wild animals have within their bodies several different viruses that may at some point infect humans. AIDS first infected a human in Africa (Quammen 2023). And there is genetic evidence suggesting the animal-to-human transference of the COVID-19 virus (The COVID Crisis Group 2023).

The other origin theory is that the transference was the result of a leak (intentional or not) from a laboratory in Wuhan (The COVID Crisis Group 2023). This theory, which suggests a lab leak from the Wuhan Institute of Virology, argues that the leak infected someone at the institute who then infected others and thus the virus spread. The theory seemed to gain support in 2023, especially with a statement from the head of the FBI that the lab-leak theory is the most likely one ("Covid Origin: Why Wuhan Lab-Leak Theory Is So Disputed" 2023). The U.S. Department of Energy came to its own conclusion that there is a "low probability" that the pandemic originated in a lab-leak (Doucleff 2023).

Part of the problem in establishing which of the theories is correct is that the Chinese government was not especially cooperative at first in letting other countries know about the COVID-19 outbreak in China. While there has been some cooperation between Chinese scientists and American scientists, especially concerning the genomic structure of the virus (Cohen 2020), the lack of complete information makes it difficult to fully test the theories.

There are multiple reasons for understanding the origin of the pandemic. If it were indeed due to lab-leak, then this might affect relations between the United States and China. There certainly is concern that in the very early stages of the pandemic in China, China was withholding critical information about the disease. If it is the animal-to-human origin, then care needs to be taken about contact with wild animals and concern that food products might be contaminated ("Covid Origin: Why Wuhan Lab-Leak Theory Is So Disputed" 2023). And most importantly, knowing the origin of the pandemic may help prevent such pandemics in the future.

There is very much a partisan dimension to the debate over the coronavirus origin. Stolberg and Mueller (2023) write that the origin story "is also about politics and how both Democrats and Republicans have filtered the available evidence through their partisan lenses." The lab-leak theory seems to be supported by Republicans. President Trump immediately accepted the lab-leak theory which led to a virtually automatic view against the theory by Democrats (Stolberg and Mueller 2023).

An example of this is a congressional hearing on the subject. The House Select Subcommittee on the Coronavirus Pandemic held a hearing on the origin of the pandemic in 2023 (Select Subcommittee on the Coronavirus Pandemic 2023a; Select Subcommittee on the Coronavirus Pandemic 2023b). The testimony taken by the committee seemed to conclude that the origin was a lab-leak. It should be noted that the U.S. House of Representatives in 2023 was controlled by Republicans. The Trump administration supported this theory (Banco and Lippman 2023). The Biden administration was more skeptical of the lab-leak theory and ordered the declassification of intelligence on the issue and more study of it. Ultimately, the administration said that there was insufficient evidence to determine conclusively which theory was correct (see, for example, Barnes 2023a, 2023b).

The public view ultimately fell along partisan lines. A Pew Research Survey in 2020 found a split in support of the theories by party. Forty-three percent of those surveyed said they thought the pandemic came about naturally (the animal-to-human transfer); about 29 percent of those surveyed thought the pandemic originated in a lab leak. The partisan difference was clear: Republicans, especially conservative Republicans, were more likely to pick the lab-leak theory, and Democrats were more likely to pick the animal origin theory. Conservative Republicans were the largest group, at 39 percent, that supported the lab-leak theory, while 64 percent of liberal Democrats in the survey supported the animal origin theory (Schaeffer 2020).

By 2023, the public's views on this question had changed considerably (Quammen 2023, Quamman 2023; Sforza 2023). Forty-four percent of those surveyed supported the lab-leak theory, while only 26 percent supported the animal-to-human transfer theory. Sixty-seven percent of Republicans supported the lab-leak theory while 39 percent of Democrats supported the animal-to-human theory. Thirty-two percent of Democrats supported the lab-leak theory.

Public opinion surveys by *The Economist* and YouGov show the partisan divide from 2020 to 2023. In May of 2020, 72 percent of Republicans believed that the lab-leak theory was either definitely true or probably true. Forty-nine percent of Democrats held the same belief. By March of 2023, 68 percent of Republicans held this belief versus 66 percent of Democrats (Sanders and Frankovic 2023). So, while the partisan divide is evident, a sizable majority support the lab-leak theory. Some of the evidence by 2023 went in the opposite direction, suggesting that the human-transference theory was the stronger one (Stolberg and Mueller 2023).

Interestingly, The COVID Crisis Group (2023) ultimately concluded that there is insufficient evidence to conclusively support either side. But they also note that it does not matter which theory is correct. Rather, they argue that the outbreak provides lessons for how to prepare for another outbreak and what worked and what did not.

Federalism and the Pandemic

Chapter 2 took a detailed look at the history of federalism and the combined impact of federalism and deep partisan splits between red and blue states. The burden of federalism, multiple layers of government, is that responsibility for dealing with public issues is split among the federal, state, and local governments.

Chapter 2 noted that academics have used various phrases to characterize periods of federalism, focusing on the relationship between the federal government and state governments. Three new phrases characterize federalism relationships during the COVID-19 pandemic.

The first phrase is "kaleidoscopic" federalism (Birkland et al. 2021). This term conceives federalism as fragmented and polarized, where state and local governments are on their own to deal with crises and emergencies. A second phrase is "fractured" federalism, which is characterized by states being pretty much left alone to deal with crises and emergencies (Birkland et al. 2021). A third term is "variable speed" federalism, which suggests that different states will go in their own direction; that is, there are variations in response to crises. In addition, the level of cooperation between the federal government and a state is affected by polarization and whether a state has the same partisan coloration as the federal government (Birkland et al., 2021).

Crises such as the September 11, 2001 (i.e., 9/11) attacks on the United States, Hurricane Katrina in 2005, the H5N1 avian flu outbreak in southeast Asia which began in 1996 and reached pandemic proportions beginning in 2002 during the George W. Bush administration, and the 2009 H1N1 (swine flu pandemic) during the Obama administration led to a ramping up of federal organizations to address these issues. The establishment of the Department of Homeland Security in response to the 9/11 attacks is one example of this. Legislation was passed to put Homeland Security in charge of the federal response to emergencies (the Federal Emergency Management Agency (FEMA) is part of Homeland Security) and other legislation that shields pharmaceutical companies from liabilities for drugs aimed at new (novel) viruses (Birkland et al. 2021). The response and responsibility for crises changed between Katrina and COVID-19:

> In contrast to the Katrina case, this accretion of federal power and leadership is not what has happened in the COVID-19 pandemic, both because federal leadership and inducements were often absent or confusing, and because the sorting of states into "red" and "blue" states with strong ideological commitments meant that response to the pandemic was remarkably divergent.
>
> (Birkland et al, 657)

In the case of the pandemic, early on in 2020, the Trump administration decided that the states had the major responsibility for seeing to the health of their citizens. The federal role would be limited to providing guidance and help either directly to citizens (testing, keeping people on Medicaid) or to businesses and their employees. The Biden administration continued this emphasis.

Leaving states with the major responsibility for the health of their residents meant that there would be differences in how states responded to the threat posed by the coronavirus. And the responses differed significantly between red and blue states. Most of the policies listed in Table 7.2 were ones that the states could carry out. The federal government played mostly a supportive role (Birkland et al. 2021). Leaving the states essentially in charge meant that the response to the pandemic was fragmented.

The Policy Toolkit and Partisanship

The responses to the pandemic can be divided into four categories. The first one is mitigation. Mitigation is the reduction of the impact of the

TABLE 7.2 Percentage Supporting Policies to Control the Spread of the Coronavirus by Party

	Republicans	Democrats
Staying Home and Avoiding Gatherings	72	96
Closing Most Businesses	40	78
Canceling Major Sporting and Entertainment Events	65	90
Limiting Businesses to Carry-Out	56	89
Restricting International Travel to the United States	85	92
Restricting Travel within the United States	57	82
Prohibit K-12 Schools from Teaching in Person	48	85
Average	60.4	87.4

Adapted with permission from Baum et al. (2020). Online at https://www.covidstates.org/reports/public-support-for-covid-19-measures

emergency on the public. It is an attempt to reduce the spread of the disease, in this case COVID-19. Policies under mitigation (not all of which are successful) included lockdowns, social distancing, and masking. The 1918–1919 flu pandemic (Spanish Flu) made much use of social distancing, quarantining those infected, and lockdowns (Tomes 2010).

Lockdowns, whether small or large scale, can include closing businesses, schools, events, and so forth. The point of lockdowns is to stem the spread of a disease by keeping people away from other people, some of whom may be infected, especially those who are asymptomatic, that is, show no symptoms even though they could spread the disease.

Social distancing serves a similar purpose. It keeps people apart so as not to spread the disease. Stores, schools, bars, businesses, etc. would be open but people were supposed to keep three to six feet away from other people. COVID-19 is spread from person to person by droplets in the air. The infected person needs to be reasonably close to somebody else to infect. Infection can occur via sneezing, speaking, breathing, etc. Areas with little ventilation and/or crowding (think rock concerts or football games) are perfect places for the spread of the virus (World Health Organization 2021).

Masking is another mitigation tool. Its purpose, again, is to keep the disease from spreading by covering the mouths of people in schools, businesses, sporting events, etc. Masks work by covering the mouths and noses of everybody, some of whom may be infected with COVID-19. Thus, lockdowns, social distancing, and masking can, in theory, make the transmission of the virus from one person to another more difficult and thus slow the spread of the disease.

Testing, a second category in the policy toolkit, is a bit different because it is designed to understand the extent to which a virus, in this case, is infecting the population. The field of epidemiology is at the heart of testing and the tactics discussed below. Testing works in conjunction with reports from healthcare facilities, such as emergency rooms. Testing is done on an individual basis using a test kit. Much of the testing was done at home; not all the results of individual testing were reported to public health authorities.

Another example of testing is analyzing wastewater from sewer systems. The advantage of such testing is that it does not require individuals to do anything, and it can track communities within a city. Wastewater testing can detect whether the virus is in a community, what the variant is, and what the trend of the number of cases is (National Institutes of Health 2023).

A third category of policy tools is reporting. Here agencies at the local, state, and federal levels gather information about the course of the pandemic. Reporting looks at the number of coronavirus cases, emergency room visits because of the virus, hospitalizations, and deaths, all over a period of time. The number of cases is likely the most difficult because, as we saw above, individuals can test themselves at home and may not report the results. It is likely that the number of cases over a period of time is understated. Deaths may also be underreported because it is not always clear that the virus was the cause of death.

The fourth category of policies is vaccinations. Ultimately, developing a vaccine against a disease is the best way to stop an epidemic or pandemic. We shall have more to say about vaccines below. One can argue that the possible policies, the policy toolkit, had one major purpose:

> Every mitigation measure that public health officials had urged since the start of the pandemic pointed toward one goal: keep people as far from each as possible until an effective vaccine could be developed.
>
> (Nocera and McLean 2023a, 259)

The Policy Toolkit and Public Opinion

The policy toolkit also became subject to differences based on partisanship and polarization. Public opinion is a good place to demonstrate this.

The COVID States Project is a consortium of four universities that conducted a series of public opinion surveys on issues related to the pandemic. The November 2020 report (Baum et al. 2020) asked respondents to look at seven policies that the government at all levels might take to constrict the spread of the COVID-19 virus. Table 7.2 lists the seven policies and approval of them by political party. A majority of Democrats supported all of the seven policies. A majority of Republicans supported five of the seven. The exceptions were requiring most businesses to close and closing elementary and secondary schools to in-person teaching. In all cases, Democrats were more supportive of the policies than Republicans (Baum et al. 2020).

Apart from public opinion surveys, one can get a sense of the public's views on social media, in this case what has been called "chatter" (Jiang et al. 2020). Using Twitter (now X) as the source of data, there was clearly a split in policy and political positions between red and blue states (2020 data). Red states were more supportive of President Trump than blue states. Jiang et al. (2020) note that in the early stages of the pandemic, blue states, such as New York and California, were more likely to take actions to slow down the pandemic than red states. This is because blue states tended to be west coast or east coast states and the virus was originally transmitted by those returning from overseas, including China. Thus, the conversations on Twitter in this early period reflected both the partisan divide that we have discussed in this book and also the impact the virus was having on these coastal states (Jiang et al. 2020).

Social networks like Twitter were also instrumental in spreading conspiracy theories (Jiang et al. 2020). Interestingly, those holding right-wing views and supporting conspiracy theories were less like than others to promote prevention, more likely to discount the seriousness of the pandemic, and less likely to adhere to orders to stay at home and to take other preventive measures. The authors of the study also state that elected officials have the ability to "shape public opinion"
(Jiang et al. 2020, 209)

Presidential Administrations Address the Pandemic

The Trump Administration (a Republican Response)

Birkland et al. (2021) argue that the federal government response, from a leadership perspective, was incoherent (see also Nocera and McLean 2023a and The Covid Crisis Group 2023). The organizing principle of the Trump administration seems to have been loyalty to the president. The administration cut the number of public health officials in China before the pandemic began. This made it more difficult to get a handle on possible diseases.

Birkland et al. (2021, 658) cite Ross Baker's (2020) discussion of an administration that wanted "total authority paired with total abdication of responsibility." The Covid Crisis Group (2023) referred to this as an abandonment of crisis management, leaving responsibility for the difficult decisions to the states.

The federal government did take some action and did have some tools to deal with the problems created by the pandemic. In March of 2020, Congress passed the CARES Act (the Coronavirus Aid, Relief and Economic Security Act). The Covid Crisis Group (2023) argues that the legislation gave out money to help with the economic distress caused by the pandemic. But there was no planning involved, just giving out money.

A second piece of legislation, already on the books, was the Defense Production Act (DPA). Passed in 1950, the DPA gives the president authority to command industrial facilities to produce needed supplies in the event of an emergency. It is run through the FEMA. The related Robert T. Stafford Disaster Relief and Emergency Assistance Act (known as the Stafford Act), passed in 1988, gives the president the power to declare national emergencies and to gain use of funds to deal with the emergency (Federal Emergency Management Agency n.d.; "The Stafford Act Explained" n.d.). For example, the DPA could have been used to produce more of the highly needed personal protective equipment (PPE) that would have been particularly useful to hospital nurses and doctors dealing with COVID-19 patients. But it was not. The president did invoke the Stafford Act in March 2020 which included a short national lockdown and limiting travel (Covid Crisis Group 2023). The president also issued a couple of travel bans, the first on those coming from China, with the idea that people, including Americans, coming into the United States from other countries might bring in the virus. He also set up a task force to deal with the problem, though it had limited success (Covid Crisis Group 2023).

Trump also issued several emergency declarations related to the pandemic. In March 2020, the president declared a public health emergency (PHE) which freed up federal resources to help deal with the virus (Yeung et al. 2020).

Part of the response (Birkland et al. 2021; Covid Crisis Group (2023) was due to the position of President Trump. The president knew that the virus' impact on the country would be enormous, but he insisted that he did not want to panic the country (Covid Crisis Group 2023). Publicly he downplayed the pandemic, stating at different times that it was under control. He also limited attempts by others to maintain the pandemic was indeed a national emergency that required emergency actions. He refused to wear a mask and he urged the reopening of various facilities.

At one point, the president stated in March 2020 that "Nobody knew that there would be a pandemic or an epidemic of this proportion. Nobody's ever seen anything like this before" (quoted in Parker and Stern 2022. 617).

The president also downplayed the importance of testing (Birkland et al. 2021). One of his more interesting comments, which he later claimed was his just being sarcastic, was "If we stopped testing, we'd have very few cases, if any" (Luthra 2020). Vice President Mike Pence suggested to Republican governors that they use this argument to alleviate public concern about the pandemic (Luthra 2020). The idea of less testing seemed to have been part of President Trump's election campaign. A smaller pandemic would be good, a larger one bad, and he would be blamed for it.

Of course, this is reminiscent of the puzzling question: If a tree falls in the forest and no one hears it, did it actually make a sound? The answer is yes. And so it was/is with COVID. Reducing testing does not reduce the number of those who test positive. It is just not noted, creating a false appearance of a less serious disease.

President Trump also made off-the-cuff suggestions about how to treat the disease. At one point, he suggested that people with COVID-19 could be injected with a disinfectant and suggested other unproven treatments, such as hydroxychloroquine, a medication to treat those who have contracted malaria or have an autoimmune disease (Clark 2020).

One thing that the Trump administration did that was necessary was to set up Operation Warp Speed to develop a vaccine. The vaccine became available in December 2020. Trump was unhappy that its unveiling came after the November 2020 presidential elections. We discuss the vaccines below.

The Biden Administration (a Democratic Response)

The Biden administration's attitude about the pandemic was considerably different from that of the Trump administration. On the day after Biden's inauguration, the administration released a national plan or strategy to address the pandemic. The administration faced a number of issues that the plan, the National Strategy for the COVID-19 Response, attempted to address (Simmons-Duffin and Huang 2022).

One goal was to restore trust in government agencies. For a variety of reasons, the administration was not terribly successful in this. We discuss trust issues below in the section on vaccines.

A second goal was to begin the vaccination process. As in other areas, such as PPE, there were originally supply and access issues affecting the vaccine. The administration handled these problems well and about 500 million doses were administered in 2021. The administration did face opposition to vaccination (Simmons-Duffin and Huang 2022) which we also discuss below.

A third goal focused on some of the policies/strategies mentioned above. The goal can be described as to "Mitigate spread through expanding masking, testing, treatment, data, workforce and clear public health standards" (Simmons-Duffin and Huang 2022). Here the administration did not make much progress. The Biden administration on several occasions sent free tests to households and made masks more available.

Goal 4 made use of the DPA and a new piece of congressional legislation, the American Rescue Plan. The latter made available almost $2 billion that included giving money to small businesses and families, allowing unemployment benefits to last longer, and increasing the child tax credit. The expanded credit expired at the end of 2021, when Congress, particularly Republicans, refused to continue despite the president's urging. An attempt to pass the legislation occurred in early 2024. It was part of a larger tax bill that passed the Senate, but Republicans in the House opposed the bill and it did not pass (Guo 2024). In addition, the Biden administration created an emergency rental assistance program to help renters who were having difficulty meeting their obligation because of the pandemic (Driessen, McCarty, and Perl 2023). Two pieces of legislation in 2021 provided almost $46 billion to help renters.

Other legislation passed during the Biden administration to address COVID-19 issues included the Inflation Reduction Act (2022) and the Consolidated Appropriations Act (2023) (Cubanski et al. 2023). These acts provided funds for dealing with various aspects of the pandemic and also gave the administration flexibility to take administrative actions to help stem the pandemic.

In addition, the Trump and Biden administrations issued some emergency declarations that allowed actions to be taken that might not otherwise happen. On January 31, 2020, the Department of Health and Human Services issued a PHE declaration, stating that COVID-19 constituted a public emergency. The declaration, which lasts 90 days, was renewed over the next three-plus years. The latest renewal came in February 2023 and expired on May 11, 2023. It is this last renewal that created what we called in Chapter 5 "the great unwinding," when a significant number of Medicaid recipients were taken off the Medicaid rolls because they no longer met eligibility requirements.

President Trump issued a national emergency declaration in March of 2020. The Trump declaration was supposed to promote the acquisition of PPE and enable laboratories to undertake faster diagnoses, among other things (Trump 2020).

Another important example of the use of emergency powers came in March 2020. The declaring agency was the Food and Drug Administration (FDA). The declaration, under the authority of the Federal Food, Drug, and Cosmetic Act, was an emergency use authorization (EUA). The FDA has authority over the development of pharmaceuticals, a process that normally can take five years. But the country did not have five years to wait for a vaccine to be approved that would protect against the novel coronavirus (Cubanski et al. 2023). As we shall see in the section below, the EUA allowed the FDA and pharmaceutical companies to develop, test, and make COVID vaccines available in a year.

The Importance of Partisanship

The Extent of Covid-19 and Its Impact on the Healthcare System

In this section, we look at data about the pandemic outbreak and how it differed between the red and blue states. Table 7.3 presents data on cases and deaths through May 2023. A couple of things need to be mentioned before we discuss the table. First, COVID-19 made its appearance in the United States in 2020 on the Atlantic and Pacific coasts, as previously mentioned. That is because the virus was transmitted by people coming from other countries. It is also a reason why the Trump administration, on January 31, 2020, issued a ban on people coming from China. The ban excluded U.S. residents and family members (A Timeline of the Trump Administration's Coronavirus Actions 2020). Because the ban did not apply to Americans, the virus was able to invade the United States. In 2021, the impact of COVID-19 had moved away from the coasts and 2021 data especially reflects this change. A third consideration is that the table is cumulative; it covers the period from the time the virus first appeared to May 2023. Fourth, it is likely that both the number of cases and hospitalizations understated the impact of the virus. For example, people who caught the virus but were asymptomatic might not report that they had contracted COVID-19. Finally, we should note that the death rates from COVID-19 exposure, both nationally (see U.S. average in Table 7.5) and for the red and blue states, was around one percent. That is, only about one percent of those contracting the virus died.

Having said all that, let us look at the data. The U.S. reported cases over these three-plus years were 31,524 cases per 100,000 people. As we have mentioned in other chapters, this is a rate and not the total number of cases. For the red states, the rate was 33,433 cases per 100,000 people. This is about six percent higher than the U.S. average. The average number of cases per 100,000 people for the blue states was 29,587, a little more than six percent lower than in blue states. The red state rate was almost 13 percent higher than the blue state rate.

TABLE 7.3 COVID-19 Metrics by State (through May 2023)

Red States	Total Reported Cases per 100k	Total Reported Deaths per 100k	Blue States	Total Reported Cases per 100k	Total Reported Deaths per 100k
Alabama	33,854	341	California	31,008	258
Alaska	40,679	201	Connecticut	27,553	346
Arkansas	32,972	435	Delaware	34,176	349
Arizona	33,992	460	Hawaii	26,433	131
Georgia	29,082	403	Illinois	32,645	331
Idaho	29,440	307	Maine	24,028	226
Indiana	30,817	392	Maryland	22,816	277
Kansas	32,469	351	Massachusetts	32,531	358
Kentucky	39,016	417	Michigan	31,105	429
Louisiana	34,431	408	New Jersey	34,623	407
Mississippi	33,588	453	New Mexico	32,489	440
Missouri	29,174	374	New York	35,154	398
Montana	31,247	348	Oregon	23,115	226
Nebraska	29,732	263	Pennsylvania	27,803	399
North Carolina	33,385	277	Rhode Island	41,660	370
North Dakota	38,198	330	Vermont	24,719	155
Oklahoma	33,014	403	Washington	25,707	213
South Carolina	35,971	387			
South Dakota	31,978	365			
Tennessee	37,208	432			
Texas	29,343	323			
Utah	34,232	167			
West Virginia	36,300	453			
Wyoming	32,279	351			
Average	33,433	360		29,857	313
Total U.S.	31,524	341			

Adapted with permissions from: "Tracking U.S. COVId-19 Cases, Deaths and Other Metrics by State." (2023). Online at https://www.washingtonpost.com/graphics/2020/national/coronavirus-us-cases-deaths/?itid=sn_coronavirus_1/&state=US.

Now we turn to deaths. The U.S. COVID death rate per 100,000 people was 341. The red state COVID death rate per 100,000 people was 360, almost six percent higher than the U.S. average. The blue state average per 100,000 people was 313, more than eight percent lower than the national average. The red state average per 100,000 was just over 15 percent higher than the blue state average. Red states were clearly more impacted by the COVID-19 virus than the blue states.

TABLE 7.4 Days of High ICU Stress Due to COVID-19 (2022)

Red States	Days	Rank	Blue States	Days	Rank
Wyoming	0	1	Illinois	0	1
Tennessee	4	6	Maine	0	1
Arizona	22	12	Connecticut	2	5
Utah	24	13	New Jersey	9	7
Montana	26	14	Maryland	11	8
South Dakota	28	15	Oregon	16	9
North Dakota	32	16	New York	18	10
West Virginia	48	19	Hawaii	31	16
Kansas	65	23	Washington	37	18
Indiana	87	24	Vermont	58	20
Louisiana	94	25	California	112	26
South Carolina	119	28	Massachusetts	139	32
Alaska	123	29	Pennsylvania	190	37
Nebraska	137	31	Michigan	234	40
Arkansas	144	33	Delaware	298	43
Idaho	170	36	New Mexico	310	46
Kentucky	216	39	Rhode Island	414	49
North Carolina	251	41			
Missouri	295	42			
Oklahoma	308	45			
Mississippi	323	47			
Georgia	375	48			
Alabama	517	50			
Texas	566	51			
Average	180	31		111	22
U.S. Average	112				

Adapted with permission from: Radley, Baumgartner, and Collins 2022. Online at https://www.commonwealthfund.org/sites/default/files/202206/Radley_2022_State_Scorecard_Appendices.pdf#page=24

Earlier we discussed the pandemic's impact on hospitals. During the surges (see Figures 7.1 and 7.2) hospital capacity was strained (Nocera and McLean 2023a; The Covid Crisis Group 2023). Now we look at measures of the strain and the relationship with state partisanship. Table 7.4 presents data about intensive care unit (ICU) stress due to COVID-19. The table shows the number of days in which ICUs in a state were over capacity.

We find the usual differences between red and blue states. The overall U.S. average was 112 days. For the red states, the average was 180 days, almost 61 percent more than the U.S. average. For the blue states, the

TABLE 7.5 Prevalence of Long Covid among Adults (2022)

Red States		Blue States	
Alabama	High	California	Medium
Alaska	Medium	Connecticut	Medium
Arizona	Medium	Delaware	Medium
Arkansas	Medium	Hawaii	Medium
Georgia	Medium	Illinois	Medium
Idaho	High	Maine	Low
Indiana	Medium	Maryland	Medium
Kansas	High	Massachusetts	Low
Kentucky	High	Michigan	Medium
Louisiana	High	New Jersey	Medium
Mississippi	High	New Mexico	Medium
Missouri	High	New York	Medium
Montana	High	Oregon	Low
Nebraska	Medium	Pennsylvania	Medium
North Carolina	Medium	Rhode Island	Medium
North Dakota	Medium	Vermont	Low
Oklahoma	High	Washington	Low
South Carolina	Medium		
South Dakota	High		
Tennessee	High		
Texas	Medium		
Utah	Medium		
West Virginia	High		
Wyoming	High		

Adapted from: Ford et al. (2024). Online at https://www.cdc.gov/mmwr/volumes/73/wr/mm7306a4.htm.

average was 111 days, almost identical to the U.S. average. The red state average was 62 percent higher than the blue state average.

Table 7.4 also presents a ranking of the states by this metric. As the table shows, the average blue state ranking was 22 and the average red state ranking was 31. The blue state ranking was about 41 percent higher than the red state ranking (this is mathematically wrong but illustrates the point of the differences). The story of the table is that the red states, again, did poorer during the pandemic than did the blue states.

Another measure of how the pandemic affected the states focuses on long-term COVID. Most people who have been infected by COVID-19 experience symptoms for a short period of time, such as a couple of days, or for a few weeks (Centers for Disease Control and Prevention 2023e).

Symptoms from COVID-19 that last longer than four weeks put the affected person into long COVID. Long COVID symptoms can last for some months or some years. Anyone who gets COVID-19 may experience long COVID and those who were unvaccinated when being infected with COVID-19 are more likely to get long COVID than those who were vaccinated (Centers for Disease Control and Prevention 2023e).

There are a variety of symptoms of long COVID, such as fatigue, breathing issues, chest pain, neurological symptoms such as headaches and depression, digestive symptoms, and joint or muscle pain (Centers for Disease Control and Prevention 2023e). And unfortunately, there is no cure for long COVID.

So how do red and blue states compare on long COVID? Table 7.5 presents the data. Rather than give numbers, the table shows whether the prevalence is high, medium, or low. For the red states, 13 of 24 states (54.2 percent) rated as high in prevalence of long COVID. The remaining 11 states rated medium (just under 46 percent). No red state was rated low in terms of long COVID prevalence. Of the 17 blue states, five states (29.4 percent) had a low prevalence rate, and the other 12 states had a medium prevalence rate (70.6 percent). No blue state had a high prevalence of long COVID.

A number of studies suggest the importance of the partisan divide in COVID-19 cases (we discuss partisanship and policies below). For example, as mentioned above, the blue states, especially coastal states, were hit the hardest at the beginning of the pandemic, in the first half of 2020. But by the summer, the virus had traveled across the country and, especially, impacted red states.

Again, as previously noted, President Trump downplayed the pandemic, often appearing at rallies during the 2020 presidential elections without wearing a mask. Data shows the movement from blue to red states (Frey 2020). In the first months of the pandemic, March and April 2020, new cases in blue states pretty much tripled that in red states. In the May–June 2020 period, blue states still had more new cases than red states, but the difference was much smaller than in the previous two months. By the July–August 2020 period, new cases in red states were nearly double that in blue states (Frey 2020). Of the states with a thousand or more new cases in this latter period, two were blue states and 13 were in red states (Frey 2020). New cases were higher in red states in both urban and rural areas (Frey 2020; Jones 2022). Toward the end of 2020 and the beginning of 2021, the differences between the red and blue states shrunk as the virus spread across the country (Frey 2021).

Tables 7.6 and 7.7 reinforce the impact of the pandemic. The tables have two parts.

TABLE 7.6 COVID-19 Impact on Health Care System (Red States) (2022)

	Days of Hospital Staff Shortages During Pandemic	Rank	Pandemic Hospital Admissions per 100,000 Population	Rank	Excess Deaths Associated with Pandemic per 100,000 Population	Rank
Alabama	516	50	1974	47	503	49
Alaska	60	29	920	8	330	24
Arizona	321	45	1670	36	494	47
Arkansas	148	35	1889	45	453	44
Georgia	312	44	1976	47	411	38
Idaho	0	1	1114	14	306	17
Indiana	19	21	1668	36	357	3
Kansas	44	25	1577	33	332	27
Kentucky	180	39	3010	50	423	39
Louisiana	158	36	1682	39	458	46
Mississippi	75	30	1559	31	596	50
Missouri	301	43	1598	34	353	29
Montana	50	26	2257	49	432	42
Nebraska	6	17	1236	18	251	8
North Carolina	0	1	1681	17	305	17
North Dakota	333	46	1538	30	336	28
Oklahoma	349	47	2564	50	428	40
South Carolina	487	50	1413	24	428	40
South Dakota	0	1	1687	39	358	32
Tennessee	85	31	1511	29	454	44
Texas	99	33	1693	41	386	36
Utah	0	1	1075	12	210	5
West Virginia	288	40	1723	42	585	50
Wyoming	262	40	1733	44	276	10
Average	170.5	30.5	1697.8	34.0	394.4	31.9
U.S. Average	50		1443		345	

Adapted with permission from: Radley et al. (2022). Online at https://www.commonwealthfund.org/sites/default/files/2022-06/Radley_2022_State_Scorecard_Appendices.pdf#page=24.

TABLE 7.7 COVID-19 Impact on Health Care System (Blue States) (2022)

	Days of Hospital Staff Shortages during Pandemic	Rank	Pandemic Hospital Admissions per 100,000 Population	Rank	Excess Deaths Associated with Pandemic per 100,000 Population	Rank
California	264	41	1087	13	289	15
Connecticut	0	1	1147	15	311	21
Delaware	0	1	1461	27	330	24
Hawaii	0	1	732	5	110	1
Illinois	0	1	1278	19	309	20
Maine	27	22	690	4	251	9
Maryland	0	1	1167	16	234	7
Massachusetts	12	20	930	9	204	4
Michigan	38	24	1440	26	380	45
New Jersey	0	1	1330	23	330	24
New Mexico	476	49	1461	27	494	48
New York	0	1	1308	21	386	36
Oregon	0	1	679	3	296	16
Pennsylvania	0	1	1422	25	327	22
Rhode Island	456	48	858	6	309	19
Vermont	174	38	564	1	327	22
Washington	0	1	656	2	194	3
Average	58.3	14.8	1071.2	14.2	298.9	19.8
U.S. Average	50		1443		345	

Adapted with permission from: Radley et al. (2022). Online at https://www.commonwealthfund.org/sites/default/files/2022-06/Radley_2022_State_Scorecard_Appendices.pdf#page=24

The first part of the two tables displays data related to the pandemic and hospitals. The last two columns of the two tables display data on excess deaths due to COVID and COVID deaths of nursing home residents. We begin with the impact on hospitals.

The first data column looks at how many days of hospital staff shortages there were in a state during the pandemic. We discussed the staff issue at the beginning of this chapter. The country as a whole averaged 50 days. For the blue states, the average number of staff shortage days was 58.3, almost 17 percent higher than the national average. For the red states, the average was 170.5 days, 241 percent higher than the national average. The red state levels were considerably higher than the blue state levels. This is reflected in the rankings of the two sets of states on hospital staff shortages The red states' average ranking was 30.5 and the blue states' ranking was 14.8. Obviously, the fact that many blue states did not have any staff shortages helped their ranking.

The second data column of the two tables focused on the rate of pandemic hospital admission per 100,000 people. States differ considerably in size, so calculating numbers per 100,000 adjusts for state size. For the red states, the average rate of pandemic admissions was almost 1,700 people. For the blue states, the average rate was just over 1071 people. The national average rate was 1443 per 100,000 people. The red state rate was almost 59 percent higher than the blue state rate and almost 17 percent higher than the national rate. The blue state rate was almost 26 percent lower than the national rate. The rankings on this variable reflect the numbers we just looked at. The average red state ranking was 34; the average blue state ranking was 14.2.

The last data column focuses on deaths. It presents data on excess deaths due to the pandemic per 100,000 population. The numbers in this data column in both tables reflect more than deaths directly linked to COVID-19. As we mentioned earlier, the stress that the pandemic placed on the American healthcare system meant that many people could not get the care they needed when they needed it. Recall the brief discussion of cancer. It was harder for a person who had cancer to get a cancer diagnosis because hospitals and other health facilities diverted their resources to the pandemic. Thus, such a cancer patient may have gotten a late diagnosis, too late for health providers to address the cancer issue. Excess deaths suggest that if care had come at an appropriate time, these people would not have died. The deaths were preventable (Radley, Baumgartner, and Collins 2022). The data in this column reflect this. We should also point out that the data in this column are estimates.

Apart from people dying because they could not get the care they needed, there are other reasons for excess deaths. One important reason was deaths due to drug overdoses, especially opioids (Meara 2022). So, some of the numbers in this last data column reflect this factor, especially for those in the 25–44 age group.

The U.S. average number of excess deaths was an estimated 345 per 100,000 people. For the red states, the average number of excess deaths was an estimated 394.4 per 100,000 people. The red state average was 14.3 percent higher than the overall average. For the blue states, the average number of excess deaths was an estimated 298.9 per 100,000 people. The blue state average was 13.3 percent lower than the U.S. average and was almost 32 percent lower than the red state average. Again, the rankings of states on this variable reflect the blue state advantage. The average red state ranking was 31.9 while the average blue state ranking was 19.8.

One interesting finding about excess deaths was that the number of such deaths in 2020 was not much different from excess deaths in 2021, when the vaccine became available in April. A second important finding is that in 2020 the deaths were concentrated in large urban areas. This is consistent with what we previously noted about coastal states having more deaths than more rural areas. But in 2022, the virus impacted more rural areas, especially in the south. The greater use of vaccines in urban areas than in rural partly accounts for this. The poorer health of rural residents compared to more urban residents and weaknesses in healthcare availability in rural areas may also have been a factor (Paglino et al. 2023).

Partisanship played a role in the differences between red and blue states. Consider the excess deaths discussion. A study of individuals in Ohio and Florida (neither state is considered blue or red by our accounting) over the 22 months between March 2020 and December 2021 found that the excess death rates were reasonably close together between Republican and Democratic voters. But when vaccines became available in 2021, excess death rates were considerably higher for registered Republicans than for registered Democrats. This was particularly true for voters in Ohio (Wallace, Goldsmith-Pinkham, and Schwartz 2023). We discuss vaccinations below, but it is important to note that, for whatever reason, political party affiliation (i.e., partisanship) has some relationship to COVID-19 outcomes.

Mitigation

As mentioned earlier, mitigation regarding the pandemic refers to a range of policies designed to slow the spread of COVID-19. Mitigation policies, what can be called non-pharmaceutical interventions or NPIs (Romano 2021), include lockdowns, social distancing, and masking. Containment includes testing and contact tracing. In some cases, containment may result in isolation of an infected individual (Pearson et al. 2020). In this section, we focus on mitigation policies.

We start by remembering that mitigation policies were the responsibility of state and (to a lesser extent) local governments. The federal government, including agencies such as the Centers for Disease Control and Prevention (CDC), made recommendations about whether masking and/or lockdowns should be promoted. Most of the policies that were implemented came in 2020, the first year of the pandemic and before vaccines were available. Of the mitigation policies, lockdowns were the most controversial.

The idea behind lockdowns was to keep all but essential workers and services in place so that the virus would not spread. Democratic governors were more likely to use lockdowns than Republican governors, while Republican governors were more likely to end lockdowns sooner (The COVID Crisis Group 2023).

What was clear was that there was a high price to pay for the lockdowns. Economic enterprises closed, especially small businesses, such as restaurants. Sports events were canceled or played before empty stadiums. For example, the National Basketball Association (NBA) played a small number of games to end their season and then playoff games with no fans present. Those who could work from home used computers. But the essential services, such as trash haulers, grocery stores, and so forth, could not be done from home or online and those who worked in those services, generally lower class, risked catching the disease at work (Nocera and McLean 2023a).

Schools were closed in spring 2020. During the 2021–2022 school year, schools were open but a significant number of students took their classes online. By the 2021–2022 school year, when schools were fully reopened, a significant number of children, especially from low-income and minority groups, had gone down in their learning and achievement. This was true for both math and reading based on the results of achievement tests. Further, test scores declined more for those in high-poverty families than for those at higher income levels (Kuhfeld, Soland, and Lewis 2022; see also Nocera and McLean 2023a).

Lockdowns also had devastating effects on the economy, though there were some mitigation policies put in place to limit them. Small businesses took a major hit, but larger companies were given federal assistance. Areas that saw major declines in revenue included local travel, dining and retail, recreation, and large in-person events. Loses in these areas cost the economy an estimated $14 trillion (Hlavka and Rose 2023).

While a number of countries had their own lockdowns (such as the PRC whose lockdowns were much more severe than in the United States), not all countries employed this tool. The major example of a country not engaging in a lockdown was Sweden. There were predictions that 46 million people worldwide would die from the pandemic and that in Sweden 96,000 people would die during the first nine months of the pandemic. But Sweden did not go into lockdown and 5,700 people died, a considerably smaller amount than predicted (Miltimore 2023).

Wallace-Wells (2023a), on the other hand, argues that Sweden's statistics were average among neighboring countries. He noted that those touting the Swedish example emphasized that the country did not engage in the kinds of mitigation efforts, such as lockdowns and masking, that other countries, including the United States, did. He provides figures showing lockdowns and masking had limited impacts on the pandemic. It was vaccinations that really turned things around. Wallace-Wells (2023a) also noted that the Swedish government recommended measures, rather than mandate them.

By September 2020 all states had reopened their economies. But having done so does not mean that states were prepared to deal with future surges. Lopez (2020), using data from both the *New York* Times and the CDC Coronavirus databases, provides a basis for comparing how well prepared red and blue states were in reopening their economies. Lopez (2020) used five measures or metrics showing state preparedness for a rise in COVID-19 cases. The five metrics are:

> They should see a two-week drop in coronavirus cases, indicating that the virus is actually abating. They should have fewer than four daily new cases per 100,000 people per day – to show that cases aren't just dropping but are also below dangerous levels. They need at least 150 new tests per 100,000 people per day, letting them quickly track and contain outbreaks. They need an overall positive rate for tests below 5 percent – another critical indicator for testing capacity. And states should have at least 40 percent of their ICU beds free to actually treat an influx of people stricken with Covid-19 should it be necessary.
>
> (Lopez 2020)

Overall, only four states met four of the five criteria: Colorado, Connecticut, New Jersey, and New York. Colorado is a purple state in our analysis; the other three states are blue states. No red state met this goal. Most of the states that met one or none of the criteria were red states (Lopez 2020). While almost all blue states measured high for testing capacity, red states were more mixed in such capacity. All blue states met the low positive test metric, whereas only four states met that metric (Lopez 2020).

A final consideration: A study of large states facing the pandemic in 2020 found that states with stricter NPIs had relatively fewer cases and less impact on the economy, as measured by gross domestic product (GDP), than did states with looser interventions. California did better than either Florida or Texas (Romano 2021).

Masking

Another mitigation policy or NPI was masking. Because COVID-19 is spread through droplets in the air (Centers for Disease Control and Prevention 2023f), putting distance or some kind of barrier between an infected and a non-infected person is one way to contain the pandemic. Social distancing is one policy under this category. Social distancing might include limiting the size of events or the number of people in a commercial store such as a restaurant. Or it might include staying a certain distance from another person. Grocery stores had distance reminders.

Another policy that might contain the spread is masking. Masks create a barrier between people that would keep the COVID-19 droplets from moving from one person to another. Masking could be voluntary, with public health officials or other officials recommending masking. Or it could be mandatory, requiring people to wear masks when they go outside their domicile. One of the reasons for recommending or mandating masks is that COVID-19 can be transmitted by asymptomatic people, that is, people who have COVID-19 but have no symptoms and thus do not know that they have COVID-19. In April of 2020, the CDC recommended that everyone wear masks if they would be in close contact with others (Lyu and Wehby 2020). Some of the recommendations were confusing. Anthony Fauci, the face of the federal government's response to the pandemic for a while, did not advocate masks. President Trump refused to wear masks in public (The Covid Crisis Group). Masking mandates became very controversial.

Research supports the influence of politics on activities such as wearing face masks. Ideology and political affiliation can provide a basis for deciding whether to wear a face mask (or engage in other protective behaviors, such as vaccines discussed below) (Howard 2022). An ideological view of masking is based on values, for example, the importance of individual freedom. Political affiliation provides values but also information that may differ between Republicans and Democrats. If Republicans primarily watch Fox News and Democrats MSNBC, members of the parties will get different information regarding the parties but also on policy issues such as masking and masking mandates. One study suggests that political affiliation has a stronger influence on behaviors such as masking than does ideology (though there is overlap) (Howard 2022). For example, Republicans may be exposed to information on the media that they view that masking is not particularly effective (efficacious) in preventing the spread of the coronavirus. Howard (2022, 157) writes: "Because face mask wearing more closely relates to shared political information, face masks should be seen as inextricably linked to political discourse."

Thirty-three states adopted statewide mask mandates (Adolph et al. 2022). States that did not impose a statewide mask mandate included (in 2020) Alaska, Arizona, Georgia, Idaho, Mississippi, Missouri, Nebraska, Oklahoma, South Carolina, Tennessee, Wyoming (Asmelash, McNabb, and Watts 2020), all red states.

Governors have influence on whether a state adopts a mask mandate. President Trump set the stage for states not issuing mask mandates by mocking those who wore masks as weak. Republican governors followed suit. States with more liberal citizens (i.e., blue states) were more likely to support state mask mandates than states with more conservative citizens (i.e., red states) (Adolph et al. 2022).

Partisanship is certainly related to how political units and states responded to the pandemic and to the adoption of a variety of policies designed to stem the pandemic. Research shows that the association between partisanship and mask wearing is strong (Milosh et al. 2020). One interesting finding focused on President Donald Trump. In July of 2020, President Trump became infected with the coronavirus and was hospitalized. His illness was quite serious and required the use of advanced anti-viral medications for his recovery. Later that month, Trump endorsed the use of masks (though not necessarily mask mandates) and that endorsement increased favorable views toward masks (Milosh et al. 2020).

Controversy over the use of masks and mandates continued in 2023. As a new spike and new subvariant (BA.2.86) were making their appearance in parts of the United States and in other countries, Republicans were concerned that some states or municipalities or schools might require the wearing of masks. It was clear that officials, such as Arkansas Governor Sarah Huckabee Sanders, would forbid mask mandates. Interestingly, Democrats, including President Joe Biden, stayed out of the fray, stating that using masks was a personal decision or a school decision. New York's governor was ready to send masks to students but did not require that they be used (Garrison et al. 2023). Hospitalizations and deaths from COVID-19 were rising in August of 2023, though not at the levels seen in 2020 and 2021.

It was clear that by 2023 the enthusiasm for mask wearing had greatly diminished. In 2020, some 60 percent of those polled said they wore masks when they went outside. An August 2023 poll showed that only 12 percent of those polled wore masks. Interestingly about 14 percent of those polled in August 2023 "said they 'think less' of those who wear masks."

The big question surrounding the use of masks and mask mandates is how effective were they in stemming the pandemic or bending the curve of cases. Like everything else, there is disagreement on this issue.

Some (for example, Miltimore 2020) pointed to a 2020 study in the *Annals of Internal Medicine* (Bae et al. 2020) that suggested that masks were not effective in controlling the spread of the coronavirus. Miltimore's ultimate point was that people should wear masks if they wanted to but should not be required to (mandates) nor be shamed for not doing so. Unfortunately for his argument about the effectiveness of masks, the article in the *Annals* was retracted a couple of months after it was published.

Another study in 2020 found that masking mandates were effective in saving lives and slowing the spread of the virus. States that issued a face mask mandate (wearing masks in public) showed "greater decline in daily COVID-19 growth rates after issuing these mandates compared with states that did not issue mandates" (Lyu and Wehby 2020, 1425).

Bollyky et al. (2023) provide a comprehensive analysis of factors related to differences in infections and deaths due to COVID-19. They point to various inequities that distinguished states, such as poverty rates, educational levels, and access to quality healthcare. Where does partisanship appear as a factor differentiating the states? The researchers wrote "that partisanship made a nuanced contribution to state differences in COVID-19 death rates" (Bollyky et al. 2023, 1355). They found that the party affiliation of the state governor made little difference in outcomes. However, they did find that voting behavior in the 2020 presidential elections was related to outcomes. States that voted for President Donald Trump, the Republican candidate, had more infections and deaths than those states voting for the Democratic candidate, Joe Biden.

They also found that partisanship related to personal behaviors (such as the use of masks and social distancing) and mandates designed to mitigate the spread of the virus. The key initial period was in April of 2020, when protests began against some of the mandates and the November elections got closer. Red states issued fewer mandates and kept what mandates were imposed for a shorter period than blue states. The researchers found that states that implemented more mandates (blue states), including vaccinations and masking, had lower rates of infections than those with fewer and shorter mandates (red states).

Similarly, another study found that there was an inverse relationship between mask mandates and death rates from COVID-19 (Lazar, Baum, and Qu 2023). Their argument was a response to a piece by *The New York Times* columnist Brett Stephens (Stephens 2023) citing a review by

Jefferson et al. (2023, aka the Cochrane Report). The researchers concluded that wearing masks had little impact on the spread of diseases such as COVID-19 compared to not wearing masks. This was the key finding of the research and the one that Stephens and others relied upon for their argument that masks, and thus mask mandates, make little difference. Stephens (2023) described the Jefferson et al. (2023) piece as "the most rigorous and comprehensive analysis of scientific studies conducted on the efficacy of masks for reducing the spread of respiratory illnesses." Stephens characterized the study as "unambiguous" (Stephens 2023). To Stephens, those pushing masks and mask mandates were undermining trust in science and institutions such as the CDC.

One important point that Stephens makes, but Jefferson et al. (2023) do not, is that it was unlikely that under any circumstances, there would be 100 percent compliance with mask mandates. Stephens (2023) continues by calling mask mandate "a fool's errand" creating a "false sense of security." To Stephens, the Jefferson et al. (2023) analysis should end all discussions about the efficacy of masks and mandates. It can be concluded, though Stephens does not say that, that red states were right in not imposing mandates.

But there are some problems with Stephens' and other attacks on mandates. Going back to the Cochrane report, the results were much more tentative than some have made them to be. The researchers noted that some of the studies they examined occurred during times when there was no epidemic of viral respiratory infections (many of the studies were of other respiratory infections in addition to COVID-19). The researchers also said that compliance with masking was often low, which by itself raises questions about drawing conclusions from this study. The researchers' language also suggests tentativeness, for example, that mask wearing "probably makes little or no difference ... compared to not wearing masks" (Jefferson et al. 2023, p. 2). They also wrote "Harms are rarely measured and poorly reported" (Jefferson et al. 2023, p. 2). And in the summary appears the following: "We are uncertain whether wearing masks or N95/P2 respirators helps to slow the spread of respiratory viruses based on the studies we assessed" (Jefferson et al. 2023, p. 3).

We return to the Lazar, Baum and Qu (2023) response to the Cochrane analysis. They ask two questions: "1. Did COVID-related death rates in states that had mask mandates differ from those in states that did not have mandates? 2. Is there a difference in death rates between states with higher and lower levels of mask wearing?"

Lazar, Baum, and Qu (2023) found that states without mandates, where just under two-thirds of the population wore masks, had about 30 percent higher death rates than states with mandates, where just over three-quarters of the population wore masks. The data for their analysis was from June 1, 2020 to December 31, 2020. This was a period of high surges and before vaccines were available. The authors noted that there were other policies ongoing during this time, such as social distancing and lockdowns, and that there are population differences between the states (see Chapters 2 and 3). Ten of the states that did not have mask mandates were red states.

The lead author of the Cochrane study, Tom Jefferson, made the claim that there is no evidence that masks make a difference. However, the editor-in-chief at Cochrane stated that such a claim is "inaccurate and misleading" (cited in Tufekci 2023). Perhaps the best conclusion from the Cochrane study is that if people do not wear masks, they will not work (Tufekci 2023; Wen 2023).

However, if mandates are complied with, then masking can be effective. In one study at Massachusetts General Brigham Hospital, infection rates among healthcare workers grew dramatically before mask mandates, doubling in a very short period of time. The rate of infection was over 20 percent. After the mask mandate at the hospital, the infection rate dropped by more than half. Masking in Germany in 2020 reduced the infection rate by nearly 50 percent, especially among the elderly (Tufekci 2023).

One estimate is that if 95 percent of the American population wore masks in public from September 2020 to February 2021, over 120,000 deaths would be prevented. If the percentage of the population wearing masks in public was lower, at 85 percent, then an estimated more than 95,000 deaths could be prevented (Hauck 2020).

Another study looked a data at the county level (Baird et al. 2024). The researchers looked at four policies: "bans on large gatherings, stay-at-home orders, mask mandates, and bar and restaurant closures" (Baird et al. 2024, 435). They found that all four policies were effective in slowing the spread of the virus (flattening the curve), but masks were the most effective. The key variables in the protection afforded by the policies were the dosage, the timing of the policy, and compliance, which from our standpoint may be the most important variable.

Nevertheless, for various reasons, some who have studied the issue (i.e., Wen 2023) have suggested that the decision to wear a mask should be an individual decision and not a mandated decision.

Mandates, like much of what happened during the pandemic, became extremely politicized. In the fall of 2023, with a rise in coronavirus infections, some schools and states moved toward mask mandates again. In one kindergarten class, masks were required for a short period of time after some students tested positive for the virus. The New York Governor distributed masks to schools, though she did not require them to be worn. In another school, masks were required for all who either worked or visited the school (Natanson, Nirappil, and Vazuez 2023).

The reaction to these actions on the part of conservatives was quick and harsh. Consider the following quote in response to these kinds of actions:

> Even though these campuses are the exception, as few schools require masks, lawmakers and presidential candidates have seized on the issue. A group of Senate Republicans unveiled legislation this week to prohibit federal mask mandates on domestic air travel, public transit and public schools through the end of 2024. On Wednesday, Sen. Ted Cruz (R-Tex.) shared a warning in response to the Maryland elementary school action: "If you want to voluntarily wear a mask, fine, but leave our kids the hell alone."
>
> (The school, Rosemary Hills in Silver Spring, boosted security and kept recess indoors because of online backlash earlier the same day)
>
> Former U.N. ambassador Nikki Haley, who was seeking the 2024 Republican presidential nomination, suggested in a Fox News interview Wednesday that mandated school mask-wearing is an attack on parental rights, and former president Donald Trump promised last month that, if reelected, he would "use every available authority to cut federal funding to any school" that imposed a mask rule.
>
> (Natanson, Nirappil, and Vazuez 2023)

In January 2024, mask mandates returned to hospitals in four blue states. The reason was the significant increase in COVID-19, as well as flu, cases. The mandates applied to patients and providers. CDC data showed a 16 percent increase in COVID-19 cases from one week to the next in December 2023. The four states were California, Illinois, Massachusetts, and New York, all blue states (Brooks 2024).

Mandates were imposed or attempted to be imposed by both the federal government and the states. In the case of the federal government, Joe Biden, the successful Democratic presidential candidate in 2020, stated during the campaign that he would require (mandate) people to wear masks in public (Wu 2020). In November 2020, after his election victory, Biden created a task force on the pandemic, and a website was set up stating a COVID-19 plan. Most of this involved bringing in state and local officials who have such authority. Biden, as president, did not have the authority to issue a nationwide mask mandate (Hauck 2020).

Lawsuits Over Federal Mandates

The Constitution and the American political system allow citizens, interest groups, and government officials to make use of the judicial system to challenge policies made by some level of government. During the pandemic, a number of lawsuits were filed by Republican state attorneys general against the Biden administration. Most of them involved mandates.

In February 2021, the Biden administration, through the CDC, issued a public health order requiring that those traveling between the states wear masks. The Transportation Security Administration (TSA) was one of the agencies enforcing the order. Airlines and Republicans opposed the order. A case was brought before a federal court, and in April 2022, a federal judge ruled that the CDC had overstepped its authority and had violated provisions of the Administrative Procedures Act. The Biden administration considered appealing but ultimately with the end of the PHE, wearing masks became moot and the appeal was dismissed in 2023 (Gershman 2022; Leff 2023; Sneed 2022).

More importantly, the administration sought to impose vaccine mandates. Two cases involved workplaces. In one case, the Occupational and Safety Administration (OSHA) issued an emergency rule requiring workers in companies with more than 100 employees to be vaccinated. If this rule were violated, then the workers would have to wear masks and be tested on a regular basis. Failure to follow the rule would result in fines (Marcus 2021).

The second case, brought by the Centers for Medicaid and Medicare Services (CMS), requires healthcare workers in facilities that participate in the two large federal programs, Medicaid and Medicare, to be vaccinated. The two cases raised issues of the broad powers of the administrative state and, also, the extent to which the federal government can act to protect the health and safety of the population (Marcus 2021).

In January 2022, the Supreme Court handed down its decisions in the two cases. In the large employer case, *National Federation of Independent Business et al. v. Department of Labor*, the Court held that the administration had gone too far in its use of the OSHA law and blocked the mandate. In the second case, *Missouri v. Biden*, the Court upheld the administration's rule that healthcare workers must be vaccinated. Lempert (2022) argues that both decisions are an indication of how polarization has affected the Court. Both sets of decisions take a somewhat narrow perspective on the power of administrative agencies (Lempert 2022). And, again, the cases were brought by Republican attorneys general as well as interest groups.

Vaccines

Earlier in this chapter we mentioned the idea of a policy toolkit to address the pandemic (The Covid Crisis Group 2023). These included lockdowns, social distancing, medications, masking, and vaccinations. Of these, the most important was vaccinations. And, as with the other components of the toolkit, vaccines were controversial, especially along partisan lines. We begin this section by looking at what vaccines are and what the origin of vaccines was.

Origin of Vaccines

A vaccine is defined by the CDC as

> A preparation that is used to stimulate the body's immune response against diseases. Vaccines are usually administered through needle injections, but some can be administered by mouth or sprayed into the nose.
> (National Center for Immunization and Respiratory Diseases 2021)

The basic idea is that the body's response to the vaccine will activate body cells that will then attack the threatening disease. The vaccine contains a remnant of the disease and when introduced to the body, the body creates what Dettmer (2021) calls memory cells. When the disease itself infects a person, the memory cells (white blood cells) attack the disease.

The first vaccine, though not as we think of them, occurred in medieval China and focused on smallpox (Dettmer 2021). Smallpox was a scourge of mankind, with about 30 percent of those infected dying from the disease. By contrast, SARS-CoV-2 has a death rate of about one percent.

The big smallpox vaccine breakthrough came in the eighteenth century. In 1796, Edward Jenner speculated that inoculating someone with cowpox would provide protection against smallpox ("Vaccine History Timeline" n.d.). Jenner turned out to be correct and this, along with other advances in biology and similar fields, eventually led to more immunizations.

Perhaps the largest vaccination experiment took place in the 1950s in the United States. In this case, the target was polio, which causes paralysis of the spinal cord, affecting the legs and sometimes the lungs, especially among children. The vaccine in this case was the Salk vaccine, developed by Jonas Salk. In 1954, the vaccine underwent a massive human trial with over one million children taking the vaccine (including one of the authors of this book). Between the Salk vaccine and the Sabin vaccine, polio has been nearly wiped out. In 1955, there were some 29,000 U.S. cases. By 1957, the number had dropped to less than 6,000 (Tan and Ponstein 2019). Vaccines have been widely used to limit or eliminate diseases from viruses and bacteria.

Vaccine development, under the supervision of the FDA, can take from five to ten years. There is first the development and then the testing of the vaccine. A first round of testing is done on animals to see if the vaccine is toxic and whether it produces the desired immunization effect. If the vaccine passes these trials, the next three stages are human trials. This is done with a relatively small number of test subjects and the goal is to see how the vaccine works in humans. This includes testing the vaccine at different dose levels. Of course, safety concerns and side effects are examined. The second phase of testing makes use of a larger number of test subjects and focuses on safety and immune response. The test subjects are more varied than in the Phase 1 trials, with different groups, such as children. Phase 3 trials are larger scale (more test subjects) and focus on safety and the immune response to the vaccine. Safety focuses on short-term and long-term effects. Participants do not know whether they have been given the test vaccine or a placebo (Coronavirus Resource Center n.d.).

The timeline can be shorted by conducting the clinical trials at the same time (i.e., simultaneously) rather than sequentially as is done with most vaccine development (Coronavirus Resource Center n.d.; see also Kesselheim et al. 2021) In the case of the coronavirus vaccine, because of the spread of the virus and the deaths that accompanied that spread, speed was of the essence. A vaccine can keep people from getting the disease, lessen the severity of the disease, or lessen the length of the infection. Vaccination can create immunity against the disease, though that varies from person to person. Vaccination is the most effective way of stopping the spread of a virus, as seen with smallpox and polio. But only if people take it.

Operation Warp Speed

It became apparent by March of 2020 that the SARS-CoV-2 presented a serious threat to the United States and elsewhere. That month the World Health Organization (WHO) declared COVID-19 a pandemic. Officials within the Trump administration began planning out what would be called Operation Warp Speed (Nocera and McLean 2023a, 2023b; Gottlieb 2021; Mango 2022; The COVID Crisis Group 2023). The purpose was to develop a vaccine in as short a period of time as possible. On May 15, 2020, President Trump announced the formation of the group and the target: "100 million vaccine doses available by November and 300 million by January 2021" (Nocera and McLean 2023b). The November target date was one that the President liked because it would come just before the November 2020 elections and Trump's (hopefully) reelection. But the goal was not met until January 2021.

The federal government's role in Operation Warp Speed was to enable private pharmaceutical companies, such as Pfizer, Moderna, Johnson & Johnson, Merck, and Novavax, to develop a vaccine in a short period of time by compressing the normal time period for developing drugs, as discussed above, to about a year. A second thing Operation Warp Speed did was to choose which drug companies would develop which type of drug. There were three possible paths to developing a COVID-19 vaccine, the most well-known of which was mRNA (Nocera and McLean 2023a, 2023b). The vaccine was developed based on the genetic structure of the virus. By January 2020, the genetic sequence had been fully developed. Clinical trials were conducted between March and December 2020 and the FDA granted EUA to the Moderna and Pfizer-BioNTech vaccines in December 2020 (National Institute of Allergy and Infectious Diseases n.d.). The first vaccinations took place in December 2020 for healthcare workers. The vaccines then became more widely available based on CDC guidelines in April of 2021.

The federal government also helped with the construction of manufacturing facilities. And, perhaps most important, the feds created a guaranteed market for pharmaceutical companies. It ordered millions of doses from different pharmaceutical companies and paid them upfront for the doses. This was because previous efforts to develop a vaccine for the Zika virus, for example, ended when the virus disappeared. The companies were then stuck with the costs for what they had developed and those unused doses (Nocera and McLean 2023a).

By March 2022, one could see the effectiveness of the vaccination program (National Institute of Allergy and Infectious Diseases n.d.). 577 million doses were administered. An estimated 2.3 million lives were saved, an estimated 17 million hospitalizations were prevented, and an estimated $900 billion in healthcare costs were averted.

Table 7.8 presents data about vaccination rates among the states. The table shows three types of vaccinations. The first data column for the red and blue states shows the percentage of the state's population that had at least one dose of a COVID-19 vaccine. The second data column shows the percentage of a state's population that has had all the recommended vaccinations. COVID-19 vaccine effectiveness declines over time, so booster shots are recommended. Additionally, there are new variants (i.e., delta and omicron) that might require a vaccine reformulation. This is similar to flu vaccines given every fall when the CDC and pharmaceutical companies

TABLE 7.8 State Vaccination Rates (2022)

Red States	% of Population with at Least One Dose	% Fully Vaccinated	% with Booster or at Least One Additional Dose	Blue States	% of Population with at Least One Dose	% Fully Vaccinated	% with Booster or at Least One Additional Dose
Alabama	64.3	52.5	20.1	California	85.2	74.2	41.5
Alaska	72.0	64.4	30.8	Connecticut	95.0	81.8	44.3
Arizona	76.4	63.8	29.4	Delaware	86.3	71.8	35.4
Arkansas	68.8	56.1	24.0	Hawaii	90.2	80.5	46.8
Georgia	67.3	56.4	23.6	Illinois	78.1	70.3	39.0
Idaho	63.0	55.7	26.0	Maine	94.6	82.1	48.6
Indiana	63.6	57.2	28.2	Maryland	90.0	78.3	43.1
Kansas	74.9	64.1	30.3	Massachusetts	95.0	82.2	44.8
Kentucky	67.9	58.9	27.7	Michigan	68.6	61.6	35.2
Louisiana	62.3	54.6	23.0	New Jersey	93.2	77.9	39.4
Mississippi	61.1	53.3	21.4	New Mexico	91.7	73.7	39.1
Missouri	68.2	58.0	26.5	New York	92.9	79.4	38.0
Montana	67.2	58.4	29.5	Oregon	80.2	71.3	40.6
Nebraska	72.3	65.3	35.2	Pennsylvania	88.5	71.5	32.6
North Carolina	89.2	65.0	19.5	Rhode Island	95.0	86.1	48.9
North Dakota	68.0	57.4	26.7	Vermont	95.0	83.9	54.0
Oklahoma	73.4	59.4	23.9	Washington	83.7	74.8	42.1
South Carolina	69.9	59.0	48.8	Nevada	77.6	62.6	26
South Dakota	81.0	64.4	29.0				
Tennessee	63.8	55.8	26.2				

(Continued)

TABLE 7.8 (Continued)

Red States	% of Population with at Least One Dose	% Fully Vaccinated	% with Booster or at Least One Additional Dose	Blue States	% of Population with at Least One Dose	% Fully Vaccinated	% with Booster or at Least One Additional Dose
Texas	75.0	62.4	23.5				
Utah	74.3	65.9	31.7				
West Virginia	55.7	59.1	28.6				
Wyoming	59.8	52.3	24.0				
Average	69.1	59.1	27.4		87.8	75.8	41.1
U.S. Average	78.3	67.8	35.1				

Adapted from: USAFacts (2024). Online at https://usafacts.org/visualizations/covid-vaccine-tracker-states/.

predict which versions of the flu will be prevalent. The third data column shows the percentage of the population that has at least one booster shot or an additional dose, for the reasons just mentioned. This was especially important in 2021 when the delta variant became the predominant variant. One dose of the vaccine provided significantly weaker protection against the variant than two doses (Keating et al. 2021).

The first observation is that moving from left to right in the data columns, the percentages decline. A majority of people in all states, blue, red (or purple), have had at least one dose of the vaccine. But the percentage of the population getting more than the first does declines significantly. Consider the U.S. average: the decline from one dose to fully vaccinated is a little over 13 percent. The decline from the first column to the third is almost 68 percent.

More importantly is the difference between the red and blue states. Clearly, the blue states have a higher vaccination rate than do the red states. If we look at the first data column for each set of states, the blue state rate is just over 21 percent higher than the red state rate. The red state rate is nearly 12 percent lower than the U.S. average, while the blue state rate is nearly 11 percent higher than the U.S. average. In the second data column, the blue state rate is 22 percent higher than the red state rate. The red state rate is nearly 13 percent lower than the U.S. average rate. The blue state rate is about 11 percent higher than the U.S. average rate. Finally, the blue state rate on the third data column (at least one additional vaccination) is 33 percent higher than the red state rate. The red state rate is about 22 percent lower than the U.S. average rate. The blue state rate is about 15 percent higher than the U.S. average rate.

We should also add that if we look at this table and Tables 7.6 and 7.7, we can see that the rates for hospitalizations and excess deaths show the same relationship between the blue and red states as do the vaccination rate tables. There is an inverse relationship between vaccinations and COVID-19 impacts. Higher rates of vaccinations are associated with fewer hospitalization rates and lower excess death rates due to the pandemic (blue states) and lower rates of vaccinations are associated with higher hospitalization rates and higher excess death rates due to the pandemic (red states). This inverse relationship also holds true within counties, regardless of whether a state is blue or red. Counties with high vaccination rates have lower COVID-19 hospitalization rates (see Keating et al. 2021).

With all this good news, there were still questions about vaccines. Why was there not more compliance with vaccinations? What was the basis for opposition to vaccines? Why were there excess deaths when vaccines were available? We turn to these questions next.

One of the objections to vaccinations is the fear that it may cause serious side-effects. For example, there were claims that the childhood vaccination MMR (measles, mumps, rubella) may cause autism. The normal side-effects of this combination of vaccines are "injection site soreness, lump or bump at the site, fatigue, fussiness, headache, decreased appetite, or low-grade fever" (LaGare 2022). As we have seen earlier and in other areas (such as whether opioids are addictive) (Patel and Rushefsky 2022), a 1998 study suggested a relationship between MMR vaccinations in children and the development of autism. However, the study was eventually retracted, and the author had used false information in his report. Subsequent studies showed no relationship between the vaccine and autism (LaGare 2022). But it does not stop people from making such claims, for example, about COVID-19 vaccines.

In the case of COVID-19 vaccines, a massive study reported in 2024 found that a side effect of the vaccine included some brain and heart disease. But those same diseases could come about from being infected by COVID-19. The study found that the vaccine effect was much smaller than the infection effect and thus it was better to get the vaccine than get infected (Johnson 2024). The same appears to be the case with autoimmune diseases. Getting the COVID-19 infection increases the likelihood of getting an autoimmune disease, and getting vaccinated against COVID reduces that risk (Cueto 2024).

Another source of reluctance came from members of the Black community. The hesitation was based on a combination of two series of events. One was the infamous Tuskegee experiments, officially known as "the Study of Untreated Syphilis in the Negro Male" by the U.S. Public Health Service (Elliott 2021). The purpose of the study was to examine the course of the disease. The participants were not told the purpose of the experiment and were offered meals and checkups to participate. At the beginning of the experiment, there was no known cure for syphilis. But the discovery of penicillin in 1928, the first of a long list of antibiotics (Gaynes 2017), and its massive use by the late 1940s created a cure for syphilis. However, the researchers never provided informed consent to the participants, nor did they notify the participants when a cure (penicillin) was available. The study lasted for 40 years, from 1932 to 1972 (Nix 2023).

But the legacy of the Tuskegee experiments in the Black community is only one, and possibly not the most important, reason for hesitancy. Perhaps more important is Black experiences with the healthcare system in present-day America. Surveys show that Blacks have less favorable experiences with and trust in the American healthcare system and its providers (see, for example, Ober 2022).

Misinformation and Anti-Vaxxers

An example of misinformation about vaccines came in 2023 (Kertscher 2023). An anti-vaxx activist posted on Facebook, which was then shared with other social media, that some 676,000 people died following vaccinations from anti-COVID shots. The Kaiser Family Foundation and PolitiFact found that the allegation was unfounded based on incomplete information.

One of the more interesting, what we will call, semi-anti-vaxxers was former president and 2024 Republican nominee Donald Trump. On the one hand, in 2020, the Trump administration pushed COVID-19 vaccine development through Operation Warp Speed. On the other hand, Trump said during the 2024 campaign that he was against mandates, whether masking or vaccine, and that any school that had such mandates would lose federal funding. Of course, all public schools in the United States have vaccine mandates for a range of illnesses, such as "measles, mumps, polio, tetanus, whooping cough and chickenpox" (Weixel 2024). And no schools, as of March 2024, had a COVID-19 vaccine or mask mandate. But such statements by a prominent politician create uneasiness within the public health community (Weixel 2024).

Table 7.9 presents a stark contrast between the red and blue states on two sets of strategies for addressing the pandemic. The table shows which states forbad or banned mandates for wearing masks and for COVID-19 vaccinations. The table shows that states that banned mask mandates also banned vaccination mandates. Of the blue states, only Michigan instituted mandate bans. Of the 24 red states, 16 states, two-thirds of red states, issued such bans.

Public Health and Partisanship

A related phenomenon focused on emergency powers of public health agencies. In the aftermath of the 9/11/2001 attack on the United States and the fear of possible biological and chemical weapons, public health agencies at all levels were given additional powers (Mello 2023). Those powers could infringe on personal rights, such as movement (Mello 2023). The lockdowns in the early years of the COVID-19 pandemic were a good example of this.

But the PHE orders resulted in changes in public sentiment. A series of court cases aimed at loosening or changing the orders were reasonably successful (about one-quarter of the time) (Parment and Khalik 2023). States also passed legislation limiting state and local public health agencies' power to issue regulations to address the pandemic. These included

TABLE 7.9 State Bans on School Mask and COVID-19 Vaccination Mandates

Red States	Mask Mandate Ban	COVID Vaccine Mandate Ban	Blue States	Mask Mandate Ban	COVID Vaccine Mandate Ban
Alabama	Yes	Yes	California		
Alaska			Connecticut		
Arizona	Yes	Yes	Delaware		
Arkansas	Yes	Yes	Hawaii		
Georgia	Yes	Yes	Illinois		
Idaho	Yes	Yes	Maine		
Indiana	Yes	Yes	Maryland		
Kansas	Yes	Yes	Massachusetts		
Kentucky			Michigan	Yes	Yes
Louisiana			New Jersey		
Mississippi	Yes	Yes	New Mexico		
Missouri			New York		
Montana	Yes	Yes	Oregon		
Nebraska			Pennsylvania		
North Carolina			Rhode Island		
North Dakota			Vermont		
Oklahoma	Yes	Yes	Washington		
South Carolina	Yes	Yes			
South Dakota	Yes	Yes			
Tennessee	Yes	Yes			
Texas	Yes	Yes			
Utah	Yes	Yes			
West Virginia	Yes	Yes			
Wyoming					

Adapted with Permission from: National Academy for State Health Policy (2024). Online at https://nashp.org/state-tracker/states-address-school-vaccine-mandates-and-mask-mandates/.

mandates, lockdowns, social distancing, and so forth (Hodges, Dunning, and Piatt 2023; Mello 2023). For example, in 2023, Texas banned private employers and public health agencies from mandating vaccinations (Texas State Law Library n.d.).

The legislation, mostly by red states, had its consequences. According to one study, states with Republican governors (mostly red states) had a 1.8 higher rate of deaths and cases in the June to December 2020 period than states with Democratic governors (mostly blue states) (Hodges, Dunning, and Piatt 2023; see also Neelon et al. 2021). Neelon et al. (2021, 118) conclude that "these findings suggest governor political party affiliation may differentially impact COVID-19 incidence and death rates. Attitudes toward the pandemic were highly polarized in 2020."

A major issue about vaccine hesitancy is the lack of trust in public health agencies (such as the CDC, the FDA, and state agencies) on the part of Republicans compared to Democrats. Democrats' views of public health agencies have remained pretty much stable since 2009, but Republican views of these agencies have declined (Findling, Blendon, and Benson 2022). Additionally, Democrats have a much more expansive view of the "role and responsibilities" of public health agencies compared to Republicans (Findling, Blendon, and Benson 2022).

Vaccines, Misinformation, and Partisanship

We can understand much of the reluctance of Blacks to get COVID-19 vaccine shots because of the Tuskegee Syphilis experiments and the way Blacks are often treated in the healthcare system (see, for example, Hostetter and Klein 2021; Yearly, Clark and Figueroa 2022). But much of the overall vaccine hesitancy was caused by anti-vaxxers and misinformation.

One of the prominent anti-vaxxers was Florida Governor Ron DeSantis (LaFraniere, Mazzei, and Sun 2023). DeSantis originally supported vaccinations, but by September 2020 he had decided that the pandemic had peaked in Florida and only supported vaccinations for seniors. DeSantis also expressed distrust of public health officials. The result, especially after the Delta variant created a new surge, was that deaths due to COVID-19 were higher in Florida than in almost any other state. About 39 percent of the people who died in the July through October 2021 period were under the age of 39. Most of them were unvaccinated or had not gotten a second vaccination. DeSantis opposed the mandate partially because it violated individual freedom, a common view among anti-vaxxers. He also opposed it because some proportion of people who had been vaccinated still caught the virus (LaFraniere, Mazzei, and Sun 2023). In January of 2024, DeSantis, during his abortive campaign for the 2024 Republican presidential nomination, told Republicans in New Hampshire that "Every booster you take, you're more likely to get COVID as a result of it" (quoted in Santhanam 2024).

The Governor also appointed Dr. Joseph Ladapo as the state's surgeon-general. Ladapo was opposed to mandates for masks and vaccines but went further than that. He said that the process of approving the mRNA vaccines was flawed and also made comments that the vaccine damaged DNA. He also spoke against the measles vaccine at a time when the disease was making its reappearance in the United States, largely because people refused to get the vaccine (see Anderson and Crowley 2024).

The kind of misinformation that takes place on social media and by influential public figures leads to a decrease in vaccinations. And that leads to more and more serious cases (Santhanam 2024). Some of this is due to the public being tired of the virus. Perhaps more important is a growing lack of trust in public health officials (Santhanam 2024).

A 2015 public opinion survey found that both Republicans and Democrats believed that childhood vaccines were safe and appropriate, with the favorability level in the high eighties. Another poll in 2021 found that only a small majority of Republicans had taken the COVID-19 vaccine compared to a much larger percentage of Democrats (Greenblatt 2021). Polls by the Kaiser Family Foundation (Kates, Tolbert, and Rouw 2022; Kirzinger et al. 2021) show the partisan divide regarding vaccinations. In April 2021, 43 percent of adults were unvaccinated. For Democrats, the unvaccinated percentage was 36 percent, and for Republicans 42 percent, a difference of six percent. By October 2021, 27 percent of adults were unvaccinated. For Democrats, the unvaccinated percentage was 17 percent, and for Republicans 60 percent, a difference of 43 percent (Kirzinger et al. 2021). The gap continued to increase into January 2022 (Kates, Tolbert, and Rouw 2022).

Another way of looking at vaccination levels is to consider them at the county level (Ivory, Leatherby, and Gebeloff 2021). Counties that voted for Donald Trump in 2020 had lower vaccination rates than counties that voted for Joe Biden. Ivory, Leatherby and Gebeloff (2021) spell out the differences between the two sets of counties:

> The relationship between vaccination and politics reflects demographics. Vaccine hesitancy is highest in counties that are rural and have lower income levels and college graduation rates – the same characteristics found in counties that were more likely to have supported Mr. Trump. In wealthier Trump-supporting counties with higher college graduation rates, the vaccination gap is smaller, the analysis found, but the partisan gap holds even after accounting for income, race and age demographics, population density, and a county's infection and death rate.

Polarization and the Politics of COVID-19

On March 11, 2020, the World Health Organization (WHO) declared that COVID was a global pandemic. In the early part of 2020, the Trump administration issued four emergency declarations regarding COVID-19. For example, on March 13, 2020, the President declared a national emergency via the National Emergencies Act of 1976 (National Conference of State

Legislatures 2020). WHO declared the emergency over in May 2023. On April 10, 2023, President Biden signed a bipartisan congressional resolution stating that the emergency was over (Associated Press 2023).

Thus, the emergency/pandemic ran for about three to four years. The United States was not prepared for the pandemic. An article in *Foreign Affairs* in 2005 (Osterholm 2005) examined where we were in terms of preparedness to address epidemics. He noted that infectious diseases are the most dangerous to humans. The author pointed out that since the 1917–1918 Spanish flu pandemic, the closest we have come to a pandemic was in 2003 caused by the SARS-CoV-1 virus, a precursor to SARS-CoV-2 that struck in 2019. Though the 2003 version had a smaller impact than the 2019 one and it was more of a problem in Asia than in the United States, there were lessons to be drawn from it. Osterholm (2005, 28) writes:

> In a recent analysis of the epidemic, the National Academy of Science's Institute of Medicine concluded: "The relatively high case-fatality rate, the identification of super-spreaders, the newness of the disease, the speed of its global spread, and public uncertainty about the ability to control its spread may have contributed to the public's alarm. This alarm, in turn, may have led to the behavior that exacerbated the economic blows to the travel and tourism industries of the countries with the highest number of cases."

The article concluded that the United States and the world would not be prepared for the next pandemic.

The United States had the highest death rate from COVID-19 of any nation. But more importantly, warnings such as Osterholm's did not anticipate that perhaps the biggest challenge was not the virus itself, but the reaction to policies designed to address the pandemic, at least in the United States. The United States faced shortages of vital PPE and hospital staff. The elderly, especially those in assisted living and nursing home facilities, suffered the most.

Partisanship and polarization made it more difficult to control the spread of the virus. There is little question that mistakes were made in attempting to deal with the virus. But beyond those, there was disagreement along party and ideological lines about almost every element of the pandemic.

Consider first, the question of the origin of the virus. Was it animal-to-human transmission or was it a leak from the laboratory in the PRC? There is still no, and may never be, a definitive answer to this question. But

Republicans tend to support the lab-leak theory and Democrats tend to support the animal-transmission theory.

One of the first policies that attempted to slow the spread of the virus (i.e., bend the curve) was the lockdowns. There is no question that the lockdowns had an adverse impact on the economy, on children's education, and on mental health. Democrats tended to support the lockdowns (though there was a hesitation there) and Republicans opposed them. Republican officials tended to be more hesitant to impose lockdowns and more eager to end them than Democratic officials.

Wearing masks and mandates (both lockdowns and masking) were another source of disagreement. Does masking work? Evidence suggests that they do if people wear masks. But Republican political leaders tended to downgrade masking (including President Trump) while Democrats tended to support it. There is a value judgment here as with other related policies. Mandates, such as required masking, lockdowns, and restrictions on public events, violate the notion of individual freedom. Public opinion polls show that masking was unpopular, particularly among Republican officials and public.

Finally, we come to vaccines. There is a long history of the development of vaccines dating back to the late eighteenth century and the smallpox vaccine. The major success of the fight against the pandemic was the development of COVID-19 vaccines in 2020. The Trump administration deserves credit for enabling the rapid development of the vaccines. But vaccines too became a victim of partisanship.

As we have noted, the percentage of those receiving the vaccine and getting booster shots was higher among Democrats than among Republicans. Again, there was opposition to vaccine mandates and opposition to requiring that companies mandate their workers to be vaccinated. Decisions by the courts, including the Supreme Court, reinforced this vaccine requirement.

One of the arguments against vaccination was again the personal freedom one. Another was to call into question the safety of the vaccine given the expedited process by which they were developed, reviewed, and approved by the FDA (months, not years). Public figures such as Florida Governor Ron DeSantis and his Surgeon-General cast doubt about the vaccine. Public figure Robert F. Kennedy, Jr., formerly an independent candidate for the presidency in 2024 and nominated by President Trump for his second term as president to become the Secretary of the Department of Health and Human Services, was another one. Misinformation and media, both cable and online, fed opposition to vaccines and misinformation.

The data are clear. Disease rates and deaths are higher among those who were unvaccinated than those who were. Think of auto accidents. Those not wearing seat belts will more likely get a serious injury in an accident, including brain trauma, than those who do wear seat belts. Vaccines are like seat belts. They do not provide complete protection (people who have gotten vaccinated can be diagnosed with the coronavirus) but it is much safer to wear a seat belt than not (those who were vaccinated and diagnosed with the coronavirus had less severe and shorter durations of the disease). There is a bigger issue here that goes beyond COVID-19: antivaxxers oppose a number of vaccines that have pretty much controlled the targeted disease. The measles outbreak in 2024 is at least partially the result of decreases in vaccinations.

One way of looking at this are studies that show that there were more excess (preventable) deaths in red states due to COVID-19 than in blue states (see, for example, Tayag 2022; Wallace, Goldsmith-Pinkham, and Schwartz 2023). A related point is that there was a partisan divide over reporting side effects from the COVID-19 vaccine. More such reports came from Republican states than from Democratic states (see Asch, Luo, and Chen 2024; Cooney 2024). One interesting perspective, which we discussed in Chapter 3, is that the disparities between red and blue states in healthcare preceded the pandemic. On a long list of health metrics, blue states do better than red states. The pandemic continued this trend (Tayag 2022).

Another consideration is the growing lack of trust in public institutions, particularly those devoted to public health. Again, the partisan divide is clear. Republicans tend to be less trusting of such institutions, especially, but not only at the federal level, than Democrats. This may mean that, as in 2005, we may not be prepared for the next epidemic or pandemic (Owens 2024).

We should add one other factor to the response of the public sector to the pandemic: federalism. Federalism means that different levels of government are responsible for different public needs and desires. The federal government, which has more resources for addressing public health emergencies than any other political entity, decided early in the pandemic, not necessarily incorrectly, that the states were responsible for seeing to the health of its residents. It was up to the 50 states, the District of Columbia, and six territories how to respond. Polarization meant the states would respond in different ways. Partisanship meant that there were some commonalities in response by red and blue states. Partisanship and federalism created the environment in which the country faced the pandemic. Of course, not all Republicans rejected vaccines or masks or social distancing. We are talking in terms of tendencies.

As we end this chapter, a couple of things need to be pointed out. First, while some may argue that the COVID-19 pandemic is over, the country returned to normalcy (a phrase used in the elections of 1920 by successful Republican candidate Warren G. Harding) in 2023. But the disease remains. In the winter of 2023–2024, the United States saw a new surge in COVID cases (the second highest since the pandemic began), powered by a new variant, JN.1, and the low level of vaccinations (Hohman 2024).

A second important point is that because of the controversy and polarization over various aspects of the pandemic and the response to it, the United States is likely not well prepared for the next epidemic. There is a low level of trust in public health institutions. States, mainly red ones, have limited the ability of public health officials to make use of the policy toolkit we have discussed (Baker and Ivory 2021; Gonzalez, 2021). Furthermore, funding for, and staffing of, public health agencies remains below what is necessary to meet the challenges that the United States will inevitably face.

The United States faced two major problems in the 2020–2024 period: partisanship and COVID-19. The difficulty was that there was a vaccine for only one of those problems. The title of an article by Alan Greenblatt (2021) summarizes our argument: "Partisanship = Death."

Bibliography

"A Time of the Trump Administration's Coronavirus Actions." 2020. *Al Jazeera* (April 23). Online at https://www.aljazeera.com/news/2020/4/23/a-timeline-of-the-trump-administrations-coronavirus-actions

Adolph, Christopher, et al. 2022. "Governor Partisanship Explains the Adoption of Statewide Mask Mandates in Response to COVID-19." *State Politics & Policy Quarterly* 22, no. 1 (March): 24–49.

Anderson, Zac, and Kinsey Crowley. 2024. "Florida Surgeon-General Dr. Ladapo Wants to Halt COVID mRNA Vaccines, Going Against FDA." *USA Today* January 4.

Appleby, Julie. 2024. "There's a New COVID-19 Variant and Cases Are Ticking Up. What Do You Need to Know?" *CBS News Health Watch* (January 8). Online at https://www.cbsnews.com/news/covid-19-variant-jn1-rsv-flu-cases-what-to-know/?ftag=YHF4eb9d17

Asch, David A., Chongliang Luo, and Yong Chen. 2024. "Reports of COVID-19 Vaccine Adverse Events in Predominantly Republican vs Democratic States." *JAMA Network Open* 7, no. 3: e.244177 (March 29). Online at www.jamanetwork.com

Asmelash, Leah, Nakia McNabb, and Amanda Watts. 2020. "Coronavirus: These Are the 13 States That Still Don't Require Face Masks." *The Mercury News* (November 18). Online at https://www.mercurynews.com/2020/11/18/these-are-the-13-states-that-still-don't-require-face-masks

Associated Press. 2023. "Biden End COVID National Emergency After Congress Acts." *NPR* (April 11). Online at https://www.npr.org/2023/04/11/1169191865/biden-ends-covid-national-emergency

Auwaerter, Paul. 2023. *Coronavirus*. Baltimore: Johns Hopkins University. Online at https://www.hopkinsguides.com/hopkins/view/Johns_Hopkins_ABX_Guide/540143/all/Coronavirus

Bae, Seongman, et al. 2020. "Effectiveness of Surgical and Cotton Masks in Blocking SAR-CoV-2: A Controlled Comparison in Four Patients." *Annals of Internal Medicine* 173, no. 1 (July 7): W22–W23.

Baird, Courtney E., et al. 2024. "County-Level Mandates Were Generally Effective At Slowing COVID-19 Transmission." *Health Affairs* 43, no. 3 (March): 433–442.

Baker, Mike, and Danielle Ivory. 2021. "Why Public Health Faces a Crisis Across the United States." *The New York Times* (October 18).

Banco, Erin, and Daniel Lippman. 2023. "Top Trump Officials Pushed the COVID-19 Lab-Leak Theory. Investigators Had Doubts." *Politico* (June 15). Online at https://www.politico.com/news/2021/06/15/wuhan-lab-trump-officials-covid-494700

Barnes, Julian E. 2023a. "U.S. Intelligence Report Finds No Clear Evidence of COVID Origins in Wuhan Lab." *The New York Times* (June 23). Online at https://www.nytimes.com/2023/06/23/us/politics/covid-lab-leak-wuhan-report.html

Barnes, Julian E. 2023b. "The Covid Origin Debate." *The New York Times* (July 26).

Baum, Matthew et al. 2020. "A 50-State COVID-19 Project Report #25: Public Support for Measures Aimed at Curbing COVID-19." From the COVID-19 Consortium for Understanding the Public's Policy Preferences Across States." Online at https://www.covidstates.org/reports/public-support-for-covid-19-measures

Birkland, Thomas A., et al. 2021. "Governing in a Polarized Era: Federalism and the Response of U.S. State and Federal Governments to the COVID-19 Pandemic." *Publius: The Journal of Federalism* 51, no. 4 (August): 650–672.

Birkmeyer, John D., et al. 2020. "The Impact of the COVID-19 Pandemic on Hospital Admissions in the United States." *Health Affairs* 39, no. 11 (November): 2010–2017.

Bollyky, Thomas J. et al. 2023. "Assessing COVID-19 Pandemic Policies and Behaviours and Their Economic and Educational Trade-Offs Across U.S. States from Jan 1, 2020, to July 2022: An Observational Analysis." *The Lancet* 401, no. 10385 (April 22): 1341–1360.

Brooks, Brad. 2024. "Mask Mandates Return at Some U.S. Hospitals as COVID, Flu Jump." *Reuters* (January 4).

Burus, Todd, et al. 2024. "Undiagnosed Cancer Cases in the US During the First 10 Months of the COVID-19 Pandemic." *JAMA Oncology* (February 22). Published online at https://jamanetwork.com/journals/jamaoncology/fullarticle/2815435?utm_campaign=articlePDF&utm_medium=articlePDFlink&utm_source=articlePDF&utm_content=jamaoncol.2023.6969

Centers for Disease Control and Prevention. 2022. "Wastewater Surveillance: New Frontier for Public Health." Online at https://www.cdc.gov/amd/whats-new/wastewater-surveillance.html

Centers for Disease Control and Prevention. 2023a. *CDC Museum COVID-19 Timeline*. Atlanta: David J. Spencer CDC Museum: In Association with the Smithsonian Institution. Online at https://www.cdc.gov/museum/timeline/covid19.html

Centers for Disease Control and Prevention. 2023d. *Long COVID or Post-COVID Conditions*. Atlanta: Centers for Disease Control and Prevention. Online at https://www.cdc.gov/coronavirus/2019-ncov/long-term-effects/index.html

Centers for Disease Control and Prevention. 2023e. *Long COVID or Post COVID Conditions*. Atlanta: Centers for Disease Control and Prevention. Online at https://www.cdc.gov/coronavirus/2019-ncov/long-term-effects/index.html#:~:text=Long%20COVID%20is%20broadly%20defined,after%20acute%20COVID%2D19%20infection

Centers for Disease Control and Prevention. 2023f. *About COVID-19*. (July 10). Atlanta: Centers for Disease Control and Prevention. Online at https://www.cdc.gov/coronavirus/2019-ncov/your-health/about-covid-19.html

Clark, Dartunorro. 2020. "Trump Suggests 'Injection' of Disinfectant to Beat Coronavirus and 'Clean' the Lungs." *NBC News* (April 23). Online at https://www.nbcnews.com/politics/donald-trump/trump-suggests-injection-disinfectant-beat-coronavirus-clean-lungs-n1191216

Cohen, Jon. 2020). "Chinese Researchers Reveal Draft Genome of Virus Implicated in Wuhan Pneumonia Outbreak." *Science* (January 11). Online at https://www.science.org/content/article/chinese-researchers-reveal-draft-genome-virus-implicated-wuhan-pneumonia-outbreak

Cooney, Elizabeth. 2024. "People in Republican-Voting States More Likely to Report COVID-19 Side-Effects, Study Says." *Statenews* (March 19). Online at www.statenews.com

Coronavirus Resource Center. n.d. *Vaccine Research Development*. Baltimore: Johns Hopkins University. Online at https://coronavirus.jhu.edu/vaccines/timeline

"COVID Origin: Why the Wuhan Lab-Leak Theory Is So Disputed." n.d. *BBC* (March 1). Online at https://www.bbc.com/news/world-asia-china-57268111

Cubanski, Juliette, et al. 2023. *What Happens When COVID-19 Emergency Declarations End? Implications for Coverage, Costs, and Access*. Menlo, CA: Kaiser Family Foundation. Online at https://www.kff.org/coronavirus-covid-19/issue-brief/what-happens-when-covid-19-emergency-declarations-end-implications-for-coverage-costs-and-access/

Cueto, Isabella. 2024. "Covid-19 Increases Risk of Developing Autoimmune Disease, But Vaccination Helps, Large Study Shows." *Statnews* (March 4). Online at https://www.statnews.com/2024/03/04/covid-19-south-korea-japan-study-lupus-sjogren-autoimmune-disease/

Dettmer, Phillip. 2021. *Immune: A Journey into the Mysterious System That Keeps You Alive*. New York: Random House.

Doucleff, Michaeleen. 2023. "What Does the Science Say about the Origin of the SARS-CoV-2 Pandemoc?" *NPR* (February 28). Online at https://www.npr.org/sections/goatsandsoda/2023/02/28/1160162845/what-does-the-science-say-about-the-origin-of-the-sars-cov-2-pandemic

Driessen, Grant A., Maggie McCarty, and Libby Perl. 2023. *Pandemic Relief: The Emergency Rental Assistance Program*. Washington, DC: Congressional Research Office.

Elliott, Debbie. 2021. "In Tuskegee, Painful History Shadows Efforts to Vaccinate African Americans." *NPR* (February 16). Online at https://www.npr.org/2021/02/16/967011614/in-tuskegee-painful-history-shadows-efforts-to-vaccinate-african-americans

Federal Emergency Management Agency. n.d. *Defense Production Act*. Washington, DC: Department of Homeland Security. Online at https://www.fema.gov/disaster/defense-production-act

Findling, Mary G., Robert J. Blendon, and John W. Benson. 2022. "Polarized Public Opinion about Public Health During the COVUD-19 Pandemic: Political Divides and Future Implications." *JAMA Health Forum* 3, no. 3. Online at https://jamanetwork.com/journals/jama-health-forum/fullarticle/2790248

Ford, Nicole, et al. (2024). "Long COVID Prevalence among Adults—United States, 2022." *Morbidity and Mortality Weekly Report* 73, no. 6 (February 15): 135–136.

Frey, William H. 2020. *COVID 19's Summer Surge Sets the Stage for November's Election*. (September 14) Washington, DC: The Brookings Institution. Online at https://www.brookings.edu/articles/covid-19s-summer-surge-into-red-america-sets-the-stage-for-novembers-election/

Frey, William H. 2021. *One year in, COVID-19's uneven spread across the US continues*. Washington, DC: The Brookings Institution. Online at https://www.brookings.edu/articles/one-year-in-covid-19s-uneven-spread-across-the-us-continues/

Gale, Jason. 2024. "A Spike in Heart Disease Since COVID Is Puzzling Scientists." *Bloomberg News* (February 26). Online at https://www.bloomberg.com/news/articles/2024-02-26/covid-made-heart-disease-deadlier-puzzling-scientists

Garrison, Joey, et al. 2023. "COVID Spike Has GOP Fighting Over Mask Mandates and Bans. The White House Wants No Part of it." *USA Today* (September 8). Online at https://www.usatoday.com/story/news/politics/2023/09/08/covid-spike-mask-mandates-bans/70784145007/

Gaynes, Robert. 2017. "The Discovery of Penicillin—New Insights After More than 75 Years of Clinical Use." *Emerging Infectious Diseases* 23, no. 5 (May): 849–853.

Gershman, Jacob. 2022. "States Challenge Biden Administration's Mask Mandate for Public Transportation." *Wall Street Journal* (March 29).

Gonzalez, Orlana. 2021. "Over 30 States Have Limited Officials' Public Health Powers." *Axios* (October 18). Online at https://www.axios.com/2021/10/18/32-states-limit-public-health-powers-covid

Gordon, Sarah H., Nicole Huberfeld, and David K. Jones. 2020. "What Federalism Means for the U.S. Response to Coronavirus Disease 2019." *JAMA Health Forum* (May 8). Online at https://jamanetwork.com

Gottlieb, Scott. 2021. *Uncontrolled Spread: Why COVID-19 Crushed Us and How We Can Defeat the Next Pandemic*. New York: HarperCollins.

Greenblatt, Alan. 2021. "Partisanship = Death: How Vaccines Became a Polarizing Issue." *Governing* (October 6). Online at https://www.governing.com/now/partisanship-death-how-vaccines-became-a-polarizing-issue

Guo, Kayla. 2024. "Bipartisan Tax Bill Is Stuck in Senate Limbo After Broad House Approval." *The New York Times* (March 13).

Grimm, Kristi A. 2021. *Hospitals Reported that the COVID-19 Pandemic Has Significantly Strained Health Care Delivery*. Washington, DC: Office of Inspector General, U.S. Department of Health and Human Services.

Hauck, Grace. 2020. "Biden Wants Mask Mandates Nationwide, But He Can't Actually Enforce Them. Here's What He Could Do Instead." *USA Today* (November 11).

Hlavka, Jakub, and Adam Rose. 2023. *COVID-19's Total Cost to the U.S. Economy Will Reach $14 Trillion by End of 2023*. Los Angeles: Center for Economic and Social Research, University of Southern California.

Hodge, James G., Lauren T. Dunning, and Jennifer L. Piatt. 2023. "Emergency Powers in Response to COVID-19." *American Journal of Public Health* 113, no. 3 (March): 275–279.

Hohman, Maura. 2024. "The US Is Starting 2024 in its Second Largest Surge Ever, Experts Say." *Today* (January 15). Online at https://news.yahoo.com/viral-social-media-post-claims-045511438.html

Hostetter, Martha, and Sarah Klein. 2021. *Understanding and Ameliorating Medical Mistrust among Black Americans*. New York: Commonwealth Fund. (January 14)

Howard, Matt C. 2022. "Are Face Masks a Partisan Issue During the COVID-19 Pandemic? Differentiating Political Ideology and Political Party Affiliation." *International Journal of Psychology* 57, no. 1 (January): 153–160.

Hubbard, Kaia. 2022. "These States Have COVID-19 Mask Mandates." *U.S. News & World Reports* (March 28). Online at https://www.usnews.com/news/best-states/articles/these-are-the-states-with-mask-mandates

Ivory, Danielle, Lauren Leatherby, and Robert Gebeloff. 2021. "Least Vaccinated U.S. Counties Have Something in Common: Trump Voters." *New York Times* (April 17).

Jefferson et al. 2023. "Physical Interventions to Interrupt or Reduce the Spread of Respiratory Viruses (Review)." *Cochrane Data Base of Systematic Reviews*. Issue no. 1

Jiang, Julie, et al. 2020. "Political Polarization Drives Online Conversation about COVID-19 in the United States." *Human Behavior & Emerging Technology* 2, no 3 (July): 200–211.

Johnson, Ariana. 2024. "Covid Vaccines Linked To Small Increase In Heart And Brain Disorders, Study Finds —But Risk From Infection Is Far Higher." *Forbes* (February 19). Online at https://www.forbes.com/sites/ariannajohnson/2024/02/19/covid-vaccines-linked-to-small-increase-in-heart-and-brain-disorders-study-finds-but-risk-from-infection-is-far-higher/?sh=782d082460ff

Jones, Bradley. 2022. *The Changing Political Geography of COVID-19 Over the Last Two Years*. Washington, DC: Pew Research Center. Online at https://www.pewresearch.org/politics/2022/03/03/the-changing-political-geography-of-covid-19-over-the-last-two-years/

Kates, Jennifer, Jennifer Tolbert, and Anna Rouw. 2022. *The Red/Blue Divide in COVID-19 Vaccination Rates: An Update*. Menlo Park, CA: Kaiser Family

Foundation. (January 19). Online at https://www.kff.org/policy-watch/the-red-blue-divide-in-covid-19-vaccination-rates-continues-an-update/

Keating, Dan, et al. 2021. "Coronavirus Infections Dropping Where People are Vaccinated, Rising Where They Are Not, Post Analysis Finds." *Washington Post* (June 14).

Kertscher, Tom. 2023. "Activist Misuses Federal Data to Make False Claim that COVID Vaccines Killed 676,000 People." *Kaiser Health News* (September 1). Online at https://kffhealthnews.org/news/article/activist-misuses-federal-data-to-make-false-claim-that-covid-vaccines-killed-676000/

Kesselheim, Aaron S., et al. 2021. "An Overview of Vaccine Development, Approval, and Regulatioxfn, with Implications for COVID-19." *Health Affairs* 40, no. 1 (January): 25–32.

Kettl, Donald F. 2021. "How American Federalism-Style Federalism Is Hazardous to Our Health." *Governing* (March 27). Online at https://www.governing.com/now/how-american-style-federalism-is-dangerous-to-our-health

Kirzinger, Ashley, et al. 2021. *KFF COVID-19 Vaccine Monitor: The Increasing Importance of Partisanship in Predicting COVID-19 Vaccination Status*. Menlo Park, CA: Kaiser Family Foundation. (November 16). Online at https://www.kff.org/coronavirus-covid-19/poll-finding/importance-of-partisanship-predicting-vaccination-status/

Kuhfeld, Megan, James Soland, and Karyn Lewis. 2022. *Test Score Patterns Across Three COVID-19-Impact School Years*. Providence, RI: Annenburg Institute at Brown University.

LaFraniere, Sharon, Patrcia Mazzei, and Albert Sun. 2023. "The Steep Cost of Ron DeSantis's Vaccine Turnabout." *The New York Times* (July 22).

LaGare, Jennifer. 2022. *Link Between Autism and Vaccination Debunked*. Rochester, MN: Mayo Clinic Health. Online at https://www.mayoclinichealthsystem.org/hometown-health/speaking-of-health/autism-vaccine-link-debunked

Lazar, David, Matthew Baum, and Hong Qu. 2023). "Did States with Mask Mandates Have Fewer Deaths From COVID?" COVID States Project (February 27). Online at https://www.covidstates.org/blog/did-mask-mandates-reduce-covid-deaths

Leff, Gary. 2023. "Court Rules on Biden Administration's Transportation Mask Mandate Appeal." *View from the Wing* (June 23). Online at https://viewfromthewing.com/court-rules-on-biden-administrations-transportation-mask-mandate-appeal/

Lempert, Richard. 2022. *The Vaccine Mandate Cases, Polarization, and Jurisprudential Norms*. (January 15) Washington, DC: The Brookings Institution.

LePan, Nicholas. 2020. "Visualizing the History of Pandemics." Visual Capitalist (March 14). Online at https://www.visualcapitalist.com/history-ofsevenDea-pandemics-deadliest/

Lieb, David A., Geoff Mulvihill, and Andrew DeMillo. 2021. "Lawsuits Over Workplace Vaccine Rule Focus on States' Rights." *AP* (November 5). Online at www.apnews.com

Lopez, German. 2020. "Just 4 States Meet These Basic Criteria to Reopen and Stay Safe." *Vox* (September 2). Online at https://www.vox.com/2020/5/28/21270515/coronavirus-covid-reopen-economy-social-distancing-states-map-data

Luthra, Shefali. 2020. "Trump's Take on COVID Testing Misses Public Health Realities." *KFF Health News* (June 17). Online at https://kffhealthnews.org/news/trumps-take-on-covid-testing-misses-public-health-realities/

Lyu, Wei, and George L. Wehby. 2020. "Community Use of Face Masks and COVID-19: Evidence From a Natural Experiment of State Mandates in the US." *Health Affairs* 39, no. 8 (August): 1419–1425.

Mango, Paul. 2022. *Warp Speed: Inside the Operation That Beat COVID, the Critics, and the Odds.* New York: Republic Book Publishers.

Maragakis, Lisa. 2021. *Coronavirus Second Wave, Third Wave and Beyond: What Causes a COVID Surge?* Baltimore: Johns Hopkins Medicine. Online at https://www.hopkinsmedicine.org/health/conditions-and-diseases/coronavirus/first-and-second-waves-of-coronavirus

Maragakis, Lisa, et al. 2022. *COVID Variants: What You Should Know?* Baltimore: Johns Hopkins Medicine. Online at https://www.hopkinsmedicine.org/health/conditions-and-diseases/coronavirus/a-new-strain-of-coronavirus-what-you-should-know

Marcus, Ruth. 2021. "Supreme Court Cases over Vaccine Mandates Are Really About Whether Government Can Protect Us." *The Washington Post* (December 23).

Meara, Ellen. 2022. "Excess Deaths In A Time Of Dual Public Health Crises: Parsing The Effects Of The Pandemic, Drug Overdoses, And Recession." *Health Affairs* 41, no. 11 (October); 1561–1595.

Mello, Michelle M. 2023. *Modernizing Public Health Emergency Powers Laws—Again.* Washington, DC: The Brookings Institute. Online at https://www.commonwealthfund.org/blog/2023/modernizing-public-health-emergency-powers-laws-again

Milosh, Maria, et al. 2020. *Unmasking Partisanship: Polarization Undermines Public Response to Collective Risk.* Chicago: Becker Friedman Institute, University of Chicago.

Miltimore, Jon. 2020. "New Study Casts More Doubt on the Effectiveness of Masks in Preventing COVID-19 Spread." Online at https://fee.org/articles/new-study-casts-more-doubt-on-effectiveness-of-masks-in-preventing-covid-19-spread/

Miltimore, Jon. 2023. "The New York Times' Stunning Confession on Sweden's Pandemic Response." (April 14) Online at https://fee.org/articles/the-new-york-times-stunning-confession-on-sweden-s-pandemic-response/

Natanson, Hannah, Fenit Nirappil, and Maegan Vazuez. 2023. "A Few Schools Mandated Masks. Conservatives Hit Back Hard." *The Washington Post* (September 7).

National Academy for State Health Policy. 2024. "States Address School Vaccine Mandates. (January 2). Online at https://nashp.org/state-tracker/states-address-school-vaccine-mandates-and-mask-mandates/

National Center for Immunizations and Respiratory Diseases. 2021. *Immunization: The Basics.* Atlanta: Centers for Disease Control and Prevention. Online at https://www.cdc.gov/vaccines/vac-gen/imz-basics.htm

National Conference of State Legislatures. 2020. "Trump Declares State of Emergency for COVID-19." Online at https://www.ncsl.org/state-federal/trump-declares-state-of-emergency-for-covid-19

National Foundation for Infectious Diseases. 2023. "Coronaviruses." Online at https://www.nfid.org/infectious-disease/coronaviruses/

National Institute of Allergy and Infectious Diseases. n.d. "COVID-19 MRNA Vaccines." Online at https://www.niaid.nih.gov/sites/default/files/mRNA%20Vaccine%20Development.pdf

National Institutes of Health. 2023. "Tracing COVID-19 Through Wastewater." (March 23). Online at https://covid19.nih.gov/news-and-stories/tracking-covid-19-through-wastewater-testing

National Rural Health Association. 2023. *About Rural Health Care*. Kansas City, MO: National Rural Health Association.

Ndugga, Nambi, Latoya Hill, and Samantha Artiga. 2022. *DOVID-19 Cases and Deaths, Vaccinations and Treatments by Race/Ethnicity as of Fall 2022*. Menlo Park, CA: Kaiser Family Foundation.

Neelon, Brian, et al. 2021. "Association Between Governor Political Affiliation and COVID-19 Cases, Deaths, and Testing in the U.S." *American Journal of Preventive Medicine* 61, no. 1 (March 9): 115–119.

Nix, Elizabeth. 2023. "Tuskegee Experiment: The Infamous Syphilis Study." *History.com* (June 13). Online at https://www.history.com/news/the-infamous-40-year-tuskegee-study

Nocera, Joe, and Bethany McLean. 2023a. *The Big Fail: What the Pandemic Revealed About Who America Protects and Who It Leaves Behind*. New York: Portfolio/Penguin.

Nocera, Joe, and Bethany McLean. 2023b. "Operation Warp Speed: The Untold Story of the COVID-19 Vaccine." *Vanity Fair* (October 12). Online at https://www.vanityfair.com/news/2023/10/operation-warp-speed-covid-19-vaccine

Oladele, Carol R., et al. 2022. *The State of Black America and COVID 19*. Washington, DC: Black Coalition Against COVID. Online at https://blackcoalitionagainstcovid.org/wp-content/uploads/2022/03/2022-Report-State-of-Black-America-and-COVID-19-A-Two-Year-Assessment-3292022.pdf

Osterholm, Michael T. 2005. "Preparing for the Next Pandemic." *Foreign Affairs* 84, no. 4 (July/August): 24–37.

Owens, Caitlin. 2024. "COVID Backlash Could Leave the U.S. Less Prepared for the Next Pandemic." *Axios* (March 16). Online at https://www.axios.com/2024/03/16/covid-political-vaccine-skepticism-misinformation

Paglino, Eugenio, et al. 2023. "Monthly excess mortality across counties in the United States during the COVID-19 pandemic, March 2020 to February 2022." *Science Advances* 9, no. 25 (September) Online at https://www.science.org/doi/10.1126/sciadv.adf9742

Parker, Charles F., and Eric K. Stern. 2022. "The Trump Administration and the COVID-19 Crisis: Exploring the Warning-Response Problems and Missed Opportunities of a Public Health Emergency." *Public Administration* 100, no. 3 (September): 616–632.

Parment, Wendy E., and Faith Khalik. 2023. "Judicial Review of Public Health powers Since the Start of the COVID-19 Pandemic: Trends and Implications." *American Journal of Public Health* 113, no. 3 (March): 241–287.

Patel, Kant, and Mark Rushefsky. 2008. *Health Care in America: Separate and Unequal*. M.E. Sharpe.

Patel, Kant, and Mark Rushefsky. 2022. *The Opioid Epidemic in the United States.* New York: Routledge.

Pearson, Mark, et al. 2020. *Flattening the COVID Peak: Containment and Mitigation Policies.* Paris: Organization for Economic Cooperation and Development. Online at https://www.oecd.org/coronavirus/policy-responses/flattening-the-covid-19-peak-containment-and-mitigation-policies-e96a4226/

Prabhu, Maya, and Jessica Gergen. 2021. "History's Seven Deadliest Plagues." *VaccinesWork* (November 15). Online at https://www.gavi.org/vaccineswork/historys-seven-deadliest-plagues

Quamman, David. 2023. "What Does the Science Say About the Origins of the SARS-COV-2 Pandemic?" *NPR* (February 28). Online at https://www.npr.org/sections/goatsandsoda/2023/02/28/1160162845/what-does-the-science-say-about-the-origin-of-the-sars-cov-2-pandemic

Quammen, David. 2023. "The Ongoing Mystery of Covid's Origins." *The New York Times* (July 25).

Radley, David C., Jesse C. Baumgartner, and Sara R. Collins. 2022. *2022 Scorecard on State Health System Performance: How Did States do During the COVID-19 Pandemic?* New York: The Commonwealth Fund. Online at https://www.commonwealthfund.org/sites/default/files/2022-06/Radley_2022_State_Scorecard_Appendices.pdf#page=24

Romano, Andrew. 2021. "'Lockdown' States Like California Did Better Economically than 'Looser' States Like Florida, New COVID Data Shows." *Yahoo News* (June 8). Online at https://news.yahoo.com/lockdown-states-like-california-did-better-economically-than-looser-states-like-florida-new-covid-data-shows-153025163.html

Sanders, Linley, and Kathy Frankovic. 2023. "Two-Thirds of Americans Believe That the COVID-19 Virus Originated from a Lab in China." *YouGov* (March 10). Online at https://today.yougov.com/politics/articles/45389-americans-believe-covid-origin-lab

Santhanam, Laura. 2024. "As COVID Cases Rise, Doctors Worry About the Consequences of Misinformation." *PBS News Hour* (January 18). Online at https://www.pbs.org/newshour/health/as-covid-cases-rise-doctors-worry-about-the-consequences-of-misinformation

Schaeffer, Katherine. 2020. "Nearly Three-in-Ten Americans Believe COVID-19 Was Made in a Lab." *Pew Research Center.* Online at https://www.pewresearch.org/short-reads/2020/04/08/nearly-three-in-ten-americans-believe-covid-19-was-made-in-a-lab/

Schreiber, Melody. 2024. "COVID Death Toll in US Likely 16% Higher than Official Tally, Study Says." *The Guardian* (February 21). Online at https://www.theguardian.com/world/2024/feb/21/us-covid-death-rate-testing-reporting

Select Subcommittee on the Coronavirus Pandemic. 2023a. *COVID Origins Hearings Wrap Up: Facts, Science, Evidence Point to a Wuhan Lab Leak.* Washington, DC: House Committee on Oversight and Accountability. Online at https://oversight.house.gov/release/covid-origins-hearing-wrap-up-facts-science-evidence-point-to-a-wuhan-lab-leak%EF%BF%BC/

Select Subcommittee on the Coronavirus Pandemic. 2023b. *COVID Origins Hearings Wrap Up: Intelligence Community Officials Provide Further Evidence That COVID-19 In a Wuhan Lab.* Washington, DC: House Committee on Oversight and Accountability. Online at https://oversight.house.gov/release/covid-origins-part-2-hearing-wrap-up-intelligence-community-officials-provide-further-evence-that-covid-19-originated-in-a-wuhan-lab/

Sforza, Lauren. 2023. "More Think COVID Came From Chinese Lab Than Occurred Naturally: Poll." *The Hill* (February 28). Online at https://thehill.com/blogs/blog-briefing-room/3877072-more-think-covid-came-from-chinese-lab-than-occurred-naturally-poll/

Simmons-Duffin, Selena, and Pien Huang. 2022. "A Year In, Experts Biden's Hits and Misses on Handling the Pandemic." *NPR* (January 18). Online at https://www.npr.org/sections/health-shots/2022/01/18/1073292913/a-year-in-experts-assess-bidens-hits-and-misses-on-handling-the-pandemic

Sneed, Tierney. 2022. "Inside the Ruling Striking Down the Mask Mandate and What Comes Next." *CNN* (April 19). Online at https://www.cnn.com/2022/04/19/politics/cdc-mask-ruling-legal-explainer/index.html

Stephens, Brett. 2023. "The Mask Mandates Did Nothing. Will Any Lessons Be Learned?" *The New York Times* (February 21).

Stolberg, Sheryl Gay, and Benjamin Mueller. 2023. "Lab Leak or Not? How Politics Shaped the Battle over COVID's Origin." *The New York Times* (March 23).

Tan, Siang, and Nate Ponstein. 2019). "Jonas Salk (1914–1995): A Vaccine Against Polio." *Singapore Medical Journal* 60, no. 1: 9–10.

Tayag, Yasmin. 2022. "How Many Republicans Died Because the GOP Turned Against Vaccines?" *The Atlantic* (December 23). Online at

The Covid Crisis Group. 2023. *Lessons from the Covid War: An Investigative Report*. New York: Public Affairs. Online at https://www.who.int/emergencies/diseases/novel-coronavirus-2019

Texas State Law Library. n.d. "COVID-19 & Texas Law." Online at https://guides.sll.texas.gov/

"The Damaging Legacy of COVID School Closures" 2024. *National Review* (March 20). Online at https://www.nationalreview.com/2024/03/the-damaging-legacy-of-covid-school-closures/

"The Stafford Act Explained." n.d. *Findlaw*. Online at https://www.findlaw.com/consumer/insurance/the-stafford-act-explained.html

Tin, Alexander. 2024. "COVID Variant JN.1 Is Not More Severe, Early CDC Data Suggests." *CBS News* (January 24). Online at https://www.cbsnews.com/news/covid-variant-jn-1-is-not-more-severe-early-cdc-data-suggests/

Tolchin, Benjamin, et al. 2021. "Racial Disparities in the SOFA Scores Among Patients Hospitalized with COVID-19." 16, no. 9 (September). Online at https://journals.plos.org/plosone/article?id=10.1371/journal.pone.0257608

Tomes, Nancy. 2010. "'Destroyer and Teacher': Managing the Masses During the 1918-1919 Influenza Pandemic." *Public Health Reports* 125, Supplement 3 (April 10): 48–62.

"Tracking U.S. COVId-19 Cases, Deaths and Other Metrics by State." 2023. *Washington Post* May 11). Online at https://www.washingtonpost.com/graphics/2020/national/coronavirus-us-cases-deaths/?itid=sn_coronavirus_1/&state=US

Trump, Donald J. 2020. "Declaring a National Emergency Concerning the Novel Coronavirus Disease (COVID-19) Outbreak." *Federal Register* (March 18). Washington, DC: Executive Office of the President.

Tufekci, Zeynep. 2023. "Here's Why the Science is Clear That Masks Work." *The New York Times* (March 10).

USAFacts. 2024. "US Coronavirus Vaccine Tracker." Online at https://usafacts.org/visualizations/covid-vaccine-tracker-states/

"Vaccine History Timeline". n.d. Online at https://www.immunize.org/vaccines/vaccine-timeline/

Wallace, Jacob, Paul Goldsmith-Pinkham, and Jason L. Schwartz. 2023. "Excess Death Rates for Republican and Democratic Registered Voters in Florida and Ohio During the COVID-19 Pandemic." *JAMA Internal Medicine* (July 24): E1–E8. Online at https://jamanetwork.com/journals/jamainternalmedicine/fullarticle/2807617

Wallace-Wells, David. 2023a. "How Did No-Mandate Sweden End Up with Such an Average Pandemic?" *The New York Times* (March 30).

Wallace-Wells, David. 2023b. "The Myth of Early Pandemic Polarization." *The New York Times* (June 28).

Weixel, Nathaniel. 2024. "Trump's Vaccine Rhetoric Sends Chills Through Public Health Circles." *The Hill* (March 9). Online at https://thehill.com/policy/healthcare/4517350-trump-vaccine-rhetoric-public-health/

Wen, Leana S. 2023. "The Checkup with Dr. Wen: Let's Talk about Masks (Again)." *The Washington Post* (September 7).

World Health Organization. 2021. *Coronavirus disease (COVID-19): How Is It Transmitted?* Geneva, Switzerland: World Health Organization. Online at https://www.who.int/news-room/questions-and-answers/item/coronavirus-disease-covid-19-how-is-it-transmitted

World Health Organization. 2023a. *Coronavirus Disease (Covid 19)*. Geneva, Switzerland: World Health Organization.

World Health Organization. 2023b. *COVID-19: Symptoms*. Geneva, Switzerland: World Health Organization. Online at https://www.who.int/westernpacific/emergencies/covid-19/information/asymptomatic-covid-19

Worldometer. 2024a "COVID-19 Coronavirus/Death Toll." Online at https://www.worldometers.info/coronavirus/coronavirus-death-toll/

Worldometer. 2024b. "COVID-19 Coronavirus Pandemic." Online at https://www.worldometers.info/coronavirus/#countries

Wu, Nicholas. 2020. "Joe Biden Says He Would Require Wearing Masks in Public to Prevent Coronavirus Spread." *USA Today* (June 26).

Yearly, Ruqaiijah, Brietta Clark, and Jose F. Figueroa. 2022. "Structural Racism in Historical and Modern US Health Care Policy." *Health Affairs* 41, no. 2 (February): 187–194.

Yeung, Jessie, et al. 2020. "March 13 Coronavirus News." *CNN* (March 13). Online at https://www.cnn.com/world/live-news/coronavirus-outbreak-03-13-20-intl-hnk/index.html

8
POLITICAL POLARIZATION AND AMERICA'S DIVIDED HEALTHCARE

On the presidential election night of 2000, as Americans turned on their televisions to watch the election results, they saw an American map made up of states won by the Democratic candidate Al Gore in color blue and states won by the Republican candidate George W. Bush in color red. This created a new political lexicon for discussing and debating American politics divided into "Red States" and "Blue States" (Atman and Rhodan 2015; Honoree, Terpstra, and Friedl 2014; Benson 2014; Saad 2013; Rugy 2011; Baumgartner et al. 2008; Doyle 2006; Cox 2005; Giroux 2004). Red states Bush won were clustered in the states of the Old Confederacy, states on the high plains and the Rocky Mountains, and some Midwestern states – more rural, culturally more conservative, and poorer. The blue states Gore won were clustered in the Northeast, the upper Midwest, and the Pacific – were more urban, culturally liberal, and more affluent (Cummings 2008). It was the red states, especially the conservative Evangelical Christians in those states, that helped George W. Bush in 2000 and Donald Trump in 2016 elect to the presidency (Denker 2019). In 2016, white Evangelical Christians united behind Trump and are doing so again in 2024 as he runs again for president. They are rabid partisans and cultural warriors who feel that their values and lifestyles are under attack (Perry 2024). This phenomenon of "Christian Nationalism" believes that the United States should be a Christian nation that preserves a conservative social order. Many Republicans and conservatives embrace the idea of Christian national origin (Gorski and Perry 2022; McDaniel, Nooruddin, and Shortle 2022; Whitehead and Perry 2020).

DOI: 10.4324/9781032671147-8

Political Polarization and the Crisis of American Democracy

This color divide has also become symbolic of the economic and cultural war that thrives on stereotypes of pickup-driving Republicans in red states who vote based on issues such as God, guns, and sexual orientation and blue-state Democratic elites who are out of touch with heartland values (Gelman 2010). Cummings (1998) divided America into two economic models originating in the economies of the Northeast and the South and argued that the liberal model of the Northeast was more successful than the conservative model of the South. The language of the red-blue color scheme has been extended to discuss cities and counties as red or blue cities/counties (Ambrosius 2016) and red and blue families in the analysis of American politics. Democrats and Republicans live apart from each other down to the neighborhoods divided by geography based on race, religion, politics, education, and income. They live in communities where they are less likely to encounter people with opposing political views (Badger, Quealy, and Katz 2021). The blue family paradigm is associated with equality and egalitarian gender roles while the red family paradigm is associated with the Bible Belt, the Mountain West, and rural America which rejects the notion of gender equality and emphasizes traditional family values and views the changing moral and sexual values as a crisis (Cahn 2011). Bishop (2008) has suggested that Americans have been sorting themselves into homogeneous communities divided politically and culturally not just by region but also by red and blue states, which is tearing America apart.

Partisan and Ideological Polarization

Political parties are more polarized today than at any other time since the Civil War. Today, Americans disagree ferociously over just about everything (Kinder and Kalmoe 2017). Now bipartisanship is viewed as a problem and political parties are taking increasingly inflexible and extreme positions on policy questions that have led to partisan warfare and legislative gridlock in Washington. At the same time, at the state level, an increase in the number of trifecta governments, where one party controls both the executive and legislative branches of government, has made it easier for the party in control to pass laws and policies and implement their own conservative or liberal policy agenda creating a dramatic rift between red and blue states. Party labels have become aligned with political ideology. The Republican Party label has become synonymous with conservative ideology and the Democratic Party label has become synonymous with liberal ideology (Rosenfield 2017).

Affective Polarization

Today, partisan polarization has moved beyond disagreements about matters of public policy. Americans are not only divided by politics but also the dividing lines between America's political parties have sharpened (Pacewicz 2016). One of the most defining features of American politics in the twenty-first century is the rise of affective polarization. Americans not only disagree with those from the "other" political party but dislike and distrust the "other" party (Levendusky 2023). Both political parties hold very unfavorable views of their opponents. In essence, Americans are effectively polarized (Levendusky and Stecula 2021). The affective polarization is social polarization and it is rooted in social identity and is growing. There is a growing political and social gulf across racial, religious, and cultural lines. Social identity has also become political identity where everything is viewed as "us" against "them," and political discourse has become uncivil. American politics has become more emotional with a visceral dislike of the opposition. The hate for the "out-group" has become embedded into American politics. Tribalism has become more intensified fueled by the contempt for the other side. The reported number of hate crimes – crimes motivated by bias against someone's race, color, religion, national origin, sexual orientation, and the like – increased by 7 percent between 2021 and 2022. Blacks and/or African Americans were the most frequent targets overall. Anti-transgender and religiously motivated hate crimes also increased by 35 and 27 percent, respectively ("Which Groups Have Experienced an Increase in Hate Crimes?" 2023). Conservative activists in states like Texas and Florida have set out to abolish diversity, equity, and inclusion programs from public colleges and universities on the claim that the drive to increase racial diversity has corrupted higher education (Confessore 2024). In 2016, Donald Trump's use of "us against them" rhetoric allowed him to tap into the anger and resentment felt by many voters (Mason 2018). The more inflammatory the rhetoric, the more it is likely that rage will turn into hate. The rhetoric and violence were on display on January 6, 2021, when insurrectionists carried wooden crosses and wooden gallows, Christian flags and Confederate flags, and carried signs like "Don't Tread on Me," as they entered the U.S. Capitol using force and violence (Achenbach 2024; Gorski and Perry 2022).

Ben Sasse (2019), former Republican Senator from Nebraska, has argued that the crisis of American democracy is not just about politics but also about the loneliness that many Americans experience in their lives and that isolation and loneliness often find their release in anger. Millions of people feel rootless because they do not feel connected to their neighbors and communities as many public places where people often congregate to feel connected like little leagues, and Rotary clubs, have disappeared and many Americans do not know their neighbors two doors down. Such isolation and loneliness lead many to hate and rally against perceived enemies. U.S. Surgeon General Vivek Murthy's (2023) latest report describes loneliness as America's national epidemic and concludes that nearly half of Americans experienced significant stretches of loneliness in their daily lives. Americans have lost a sense of community and the country has become lonelier and divided (Garcia-Navarro 2024). Oldenburg (1989) and Oldenburg and Christiansen (2023) have argued that the "third places" (home as the first and work as the second place) are public spaces where people can gather and simply hang out with others for good company and conversation. Such places are symbols of a community's social vitality and the grassroots of a democracy.

Robert Putnam (2000, 2001) has argued that Americans have become increasingly disconnected from one another as many public places such as PTA, community centers, bowling leagues, salons, and other such places have declined or disappeared due to changes in work, family structures, and gender roles, and these have caused people to become increasingly disconnected from family, friends, and neighbors. This contrasts with early American history when Americans were celebrated for their extroversion. Alexis de Tocqueville admirably wrote about Americans' ability to form social and political groups which imbued its citizens with a vibrant social metabolism of getting out and hanging out with fellow citizens. Since the 1970s, the decline in membership in social groups and attendance at social gatherings reflects the increased loneliness felt by many Americans. This in turn has created a crisis of social fitness, i.e., inability to fit into society. The decline in socializing among Americans has its roots in the rise of television, smartphones, modern-day hectic lifestyles, social mobility, and the erosion of America's social infrastructure (Thompson 2024). The existentialist philosopher Jean-Paul Satre's famous quote, "Hell is—other people" has almost become a truism in contemporary American society and politics.

The loneliness and solitude often lead to anxiety, dissatisfaction, and anger toward the "other." In politics, it translates to distrust and hatred of the "other" political party and those with different political views. Many Americans have lost the art of "tolerance" for multiculturalism and pluralism (Abernathy 2023). Hillary Clinton (1996) in her book, *It Takes a Village*, argued that American life had become too frantic, and fragmented, and social, economic, and technological changes were pulling Americans apart. Americans were becoming more isolated, lonely, and uprooted from traditional sources of meaning and social support. Americans' attitudes had shifted from "we are all in this together" to "you are on your own." Clinton (2023) further argues that there are groups in American society who would exploit Americans' social disconnectedness by weaponizing loneliness. The decline in civic engagement and social cohesion increases political polarization and animosity. Loneliness can generate anger, resentment, and paranoia making such individuals susceptible to conspiracy theories, misinformation, and propaganda. Such individuals also become susceptible to a would-be strongman and demagogue. (McQuade 2024b, 2024c) has argued that disinformation is tearing America apart because it inflames people's passion and demonizes political opponents whereby political discourse is confined to only two perspectives on an issue, i.e., "either-or fallacy" where one side is portrayed as good and the other as evil. In a healthy democracy, people need a shared set of facts as a basis for debating and making decisions that help support and advance collective interests. Without it, a democracy can experience death by disinformation. Sustained and successful democracy depends on access to credible information. Today, many Americans are experiencing a twin crisis of despair and misinformation created by the decline of newspapers and the proliferation of fake news sites funded by "dark money." This provides a fertile ground for the spread of misinformation and falsehood exacerbating political polarization and threatening American democracy (Graham 2024).

The advent of 24/7 cable news networks and the rapid spread of social media platforms such as Facebook, Instagram, X (former Twitter), and Tik-Tok since the 1990s offering partisan take has made it possible for people to live in their own "bubble" or "silos." Studies have shown that Americans who watch partisan media programs become more certain of their own beliefs and are less willing to consider the merits of opposing views or compromise (Levendusky 2013). Blatantly partisan news organizations such as Fox News have contributed to further political polarization in America. A former Fox News political editor has argued that new organizations have succumbed to the temptation of "rage revenue" through slanted news coverage that drives political divisions and rewards outrageous behavior. Rage-revenue news organizations are inflicted by groupthink, sensationalism, and partisan tribalism. Often, news organizations emphasize disagreements and conflicts in reporting because it is easy and profitable (Stirewalt 2022). Increased affective polarization, based on emotions and passions rather than reason and rational political discourse, fuels the anger, hate, and rage that ultimately leads to not only violent rhetoric but also actual violence.

Political Violence

The United States has a complicated relationship with the notion of political violence since the country was founded out of violent struggle. Many in the country give credence to Thomas Jefferson's maxim that "the tree of liberty must be refreshed from time to time with the blood of patriots and tyrants." The major expansion of civil rights, from emancipation to desegregation, happened under the threat of violence or actual state violence (Homans 2024). Thus, violence has been present throughout American history, and only the targets of violence and those who used violence have varied over time. In recent years, political polarization has further inflamed violent tendencies in the country whereby political candidates and elected officials often refer to their adversaries as enemies, traitors, and threats to America (Suri 2024). The attempted assassination of the former president and the republican nominee for president in the 2024 election, Donald Trump, in July 2024 underscores the continuing political divisions and polarization in the country (Greenblatt 2024).

Political violence is on the rise in America. January 6, 2021 insurrection is an example of how political rhetoric from political leaders inflames their followers who justify and engage in violence to achieve political goals that they could not achieve through the normal political and electoral processes (Kalmoe and Mason 2023). According to Kalmoe (2020), during the Civil War partisanship played a role in shaping the legacies of political parties. Partisan identities motivated mass violence by ordinary citizens when activated by political leaders and legitimized by the state. On September 29, 2019, President Donald Trump warned that his impeachment and removal from office would cause a Civil War-like fracture from which the country will not recover. In fact, since the 2020 election, state and local officials have faced a surge in not only violent threats and intimidation but also actual physical violence. According to a new report by the Brennan Center for Justice based on a series of national surveys, 20 percent of state officials and 40 percent of local officials said that they were less willing to work on controversial public policies such as gun control or reproductive rights due to harassment. Some officials are forced to spend their own money to provide extra security for themselves, their family members, and their staff. Public officials are facing a surge of threats ahead of the 2024 election (Ramachandran et al. 2024; Bergengruen 2024).

There is a rising tide of political violence in America. Attacks on political figures are on the rise. According to the Anti-Defamation League, there were ten times as many threats against members of Congress in 2021 as there were in 2016. In recent years, political violence has mostly been inflicted by the extreme right (Goldberg 2023). Polls find that one in ten Americans say violence is justified to advance important political objectives. This figure rises to one in five among Republican-voting men (Byman 2023). Violent political threats are increasing with the approaching November 2024 elections. Such threats can easily shift to actual physical violence. A vast majority of violent threats are coming from activists and others on the far right (Ellison, Sanchez, and Marley 2024; Byman 2023). Political violence is not new in America. Historian Joanne Freeman (2018) details the story of physical violence on the floor of the U.S. Congress decades before the Civil War. Legislative sessions were often interrupted by threats, canings, flipped desks, and slugfests. The United States has a long history of violence against racial/ethnic groups, religious institutions, and the like. However, the recent rise in political threats against election workers, judges, abortion clinics, and other citizens who hold different political views is a relatively new phenomenon. Terrorism is frequently defined as violence or threats of violence to achieve some political, social, or religious end. Domestic terrorism is evolving and poses a threat to American Democracy (Englund 2023).

The latest development law enforcement is facing is what is called swatting, i.e., sending armed police officers to someone's home on the ruse that violence is happening, thereby increasing the probability of violence resulting in tragic outcomes and fatalities. For example, Maine's secretary of state, Shenna Bellows, was victimized by swatting after she removed Donald Trump from the primary ballot in her state because he had engaged in insurrection under the Fourteenth Amendment to the U.S. Constitution. The recent uptake in swatting is attributed to the spread of misinformation, falsehoods, and demonizing of political opponents (McQuade 2024a). According to McQuade (2024b), disinformation – the deliberate spreading of lies disguised as truth – endangers American democracy. The advances in technology such as artificial intelligence are likely to make problems worse by amplifying falsehoods. The rule of law, the very foundation of American democracy, is under attack and American democracy is not only in crisis but on the verge of cracking. Political divisions in American politics have become calcified. The problem is compounded by the fact that many politicians gin up voters' anger and affective polarization creates a tribal community that encourages aggressive authoritarian personalities and violence directed against targeted groups (Balz 2023; Balz and Morse 2023; Picone 2023; Kleinfeld 2023; Levendusky et al. 2022).

The rise in political threats and violence has spurred discussion of whether America is on the verge of civil war. Political Scientist Barbara Walter (2022) argues that we are closer to civil war than we would like to believe because of the toxic mix of political extremism, polarization, social and cultural tribalism, the embrace of conspiracy theories by a sizable segment of the population, the proliferation of guns and militia groups, and erosion of faith in democratic institutions and Western democratic state. She further suggests that a civil war in America would not look like America in the 1860s. Rather, it will begin with sporadic violence and terror accelerated by social media and it would sneak up on us. Marche (2022) argues that a new American civil war is inevitable and the only question is not when but how it will happen because the United States is descending into sectarian conflict and the future collapse is unfolding before our eyes. Simon and Stevenson (2022) argue that the United States could easily tip into civil war because it is in a state of "unstable equilibrium" and the risk of violence could plunge the United States into chaos and disorder. Hoffman and Ware (2024) suggest that today the likelihood of a civil war like the one in 19860s is relatively low. Today, the United States faces a different kind of threat. Rather than organized separatism, the country is more likely to experience sustained forms of nationwide acts of far-right violence and domestic terrorism. Hass (2023) has raised the possibility of the United States facing long-lasting troubles like the three-decade-long struggle Northern Ireland faced starting in the late 1960s. According to him, the greatest threat to the United States is likely to come from within. He suggests that the antidote to disunity and threats to American democracy is to revise and expand the idea of citizenship by placing citizen obligations on the same footing as the Bill of Rights.

Divided We Fall?

American democracy is on the decline. The process of such decline starts from the slow erosion that is often incremental and episodic. Terms often used to describe democracies in decline are "democratic erosion," "democratic backsliding," "democratic regression," and "autocratization." Two major forms of democratic erosion in the United States include erosion in governing institutions and executive overreach. Examples include laws passed by many states intended to reduce voters' access to the ballot, the politicization of the administration of elections, the judiciary, the elimination of electoral competition via gerrymandering, and power grab by the executive branch without any meaningful oversight and constraints (Williamson 2023). In 2016, the Economist Intelligence Unit, the research and analysis division of the Economic Group, downgraded the United States from a "full democracy" to a "flawed democracy" ("Democracy Index" 2016). In its 2021 Democracy Index Report, the United States remained a "flawed democracy" (Democracy Index 2021). In 2021, the Freedom House, a non-profit organization that charts the health of democracies internationally, concluded that U.S. democracy had declined significantly (Repucci 2021).

As Richardson (2023) points out democracies often die through the ballot box rather than at gunpoint. The first term of the Trump presidency witnessed an unprecedented attack on American democracy (West 2019,

2022). Amid the sinking trust in democratic institutions and talk of civil war, millions of Trump supporters believe that the use of force is justified to prevent the prosecution of Donald Trump and return him to the White House (Knowles and Kornfield 2024). This is despite the fact he has been criminally charged in four cases involving 91 felony counts (Stableford 2023). An American Values Survey by the Public Religious Research Institute (2023) found an increasing acceptance of violence and conspiracy theories and nine out of ten respondents, including members of both political parties, expressed the belief that a victory by the other side in the 2024 election would pose a threat to American democracy ("Threat to American Democracy head of an Unprecedented Presidential Election." 2023; Smith 2023). The Washington, D.C., Federal District Court judge, Beryl Howell, who has presided over many cases involving individuals involved in the January 6th insurrection warned that the United States faces an "authoritarian" threat (Gerstein 2023). The upcoming 2024 presidential election is viewed by many as a referendum on American democracy, and whether American voters will be swayed by the seductive lure of authoritarianism, fascism, and autocracy against the backdrop of the erosion of American democracy (Maddow 2023; Rachman 2022; Ben-Ghiat 2021; Applebaum 2020). Some view the possible election of Donald Trump to the presidency in the 2024 election as a clear path to a dictatorship in the United States (Kagan 2024, 2023).

Today, there is little doubt that America is politically and culturally divided into two tribal nations. One nation is made up of red states, and the other is made up of blue states, polarized along partisan and ideological dimensions. The United States is less united than at any other time in our history since the Civil War. The only thing that the red and blue states have in common is their belief and conviction that their values and liberties are threatened by the other side. This polarized tribalism views dialogue and compromise as appeasement (French 2020). The result is a Republic that is fractured and in danger of a breakup. It is like a marriage that has run out of steam in which both sides conclude that they cannot stay together and it is time to untie the knot (Buckley 2020; French 2020; Levin 2017; Enriquez 2005). Marjorie Taylor Greene (R-Georgia), on President's Day, tweeted "We need a national divorce. We need to separate by red states and blue states and shrink the federal government…" While her comments were widely condemned, it does appear that there are two Americas, one red and one blue, driven by irreconcilable differences (Jenkinson 2023). As political strategist Michael Podhorzer has observed, the United States is more like a federated republic made up of red and blue nations. The other reality is that a national divorce would be a disaster for red states because it would create an economically affluent blue nation and an economically poor red nation (Reid 2023).

The decline in American democracy is part of a worldwide trend. Autocracies and strongmen are on the rise in different parts of the world. Right-wing politicians are making gains in political power structures via the ballot box. In recent years, many European governments, from France to Sweden, have seen gains made by right-wing political parties and candidates. In the Netherlands, Austria, Germany, and France, the far-right is attracting more support. Far-right is becoming mainstream in Europe. In Portugal, in the March 2024 elections, the far-right Chega Party doubled its vote from 9 percent in the previous election to 18 percent. The party's campaign drew inspiration from the likes of Donald Trump, Brazil's former president Jair Bolsonaro, and French nationalist Marine Le Pen. The Chega Party thrives on polarization, division, and misinformation (Faiola and Martins 2024a, 2024b; Faiola, Rauhala, and Morris 2023). If fascism were to come to America, what might it look like? According to a quote often attributed to novelist Sinclaire Lewis, if fascism were to come to America, it would come "wrapped in a flag carrying a cross." Or, as comedian George Carlin once stated, it would come not "with jackboots" but with Nike sneakers and smiley shirts (Poniewozik 2024)

American conservatives' infatuation with foreign dictators is not a new phenomenon. As Jacob Heilbrunn (2024) explains in his book, *America Last: The Right's Century-Long Romance with Foreign Dictators*, during the First World War, some American conservatives openly rooted for Kaiser Wilhelm II to defeat the forces of democracy. In the 1920s and 1930s, Hitler and Mussolini attracted various American admirers. Throughout the Cold War, the American Right showed a fondness for autocrats such as Francisco Franco and Augusto Pinochet. Donald Trump and many conservative Republicans' attraction to autocrats like Russia's Vladimir Putin, Hungary's Victor Orban, and North Korea's Kim Jung Un fits the same pattern. The American far right is drawn to foreign dictators because it sees them as models of how to fight against American liberalism and progressivism. A novel by Thomas Mullen (2024) describes how during the Great War, America was divided over whether to enter the war, isolationists opposed sacrificing American lives to save democracies of Western Europe, and thousands of Nazi sympathizers openly showed support for Hitler. Mullen's description of a divided, rumor-riddle country in the 1940s offers some parallels to today's America.

Since the 1980s, the world has witnessed globalization and the liberalization of world markets, the spread of liberal ideas, the explosion of information technology, and the democratization of politics. These developments have also produced a sizable segment of the population around the world that is left isolated, disconnected, alone, and insecure creating anger and resentment in them. This has resulted in not only a reaction against Western liberal ideas and values but also skepticism about liberal democracy itself. They are attracted to ideas of populism, nationalism, and authoritarianism and are exploited by the far-right for political gains (Zakaria 2024).

Liberal democracies have also often failed to deliver promised goods to their citizens. Liberal democracies tend to focus on procedural aspects of democracy such as the protection of basic freedoms, free and fair elections, the right to vote, adherence to the rule of law, an independent judiciary, and a strong civil society. However, citizens often judge liberal democracies not by their procedural system but by their outcomes. The financial crisis that started in 2008, not just in the United States but in Europe, the rising income inequality and the ever-widening gap between the haves and the have-nots, the economic decline of the working class, and failure to address the problem of immigration, along with other factors, have led to a breakdown in liberal consensus. When democracies fail to deliver sustained economic and social stability, voters become more susceptible to the appeal of a strongman who says, "I alone can fix the problems," and who is willing to bend and/or break the democratic rules and norms. Voters may choose to elect a strongman and vote away their freedoms. The question facing many liberal democracies is whether they can fight back ("Are We All Authoritarian at Heart?" 2023; Richardson 2023; Rachman 2022).

Are There Solutions to Political Polarization?

Many factors have contributed to partisan, ideological, electorate, political elite, and affective polarization. Are there ways in which political polarization can be reduced and unite the country as one nation? There is a consensus among scholars that factors such as our electoral system, legislative processes, and social media have played a critical role in contributing to political polarization in the country. Consequently, a variety of solutions have been proposed to reduce political polarization. They can be divided into four broad categories – electoral reforms, legislative reforms, regulation of social media, and social/psychological reforms.

Electoral Reform

Under this umbrella, reform proposals include eliminating the Electoral College, eliminating the primaries, or changing the way they are conducted, eliminating partisan redistricting and gerrymandering, instituting multi-member legislative districts with proportional representation, losing the hold of the two-party system by encouraging the development of a multiparty system, and ranked-choice voting (RCV).

Eliminating the Electoral College in Favor of the Popular Election of the President

Critics of the current system advocate abolishing the Electoral College in favor of a popular election of the president. Or, at a minimum, some advocate doing away with the winner-take-all system and replacing it with a proportional method for allocating state delegates to the Electoral College. According to critics, the Electoral College is unfair. Since each state is allocated electors equal to its representation in the House and the Senate, small states gain extra weight. For example, the people of Wyoming have nearly four times the power of the people of California. Thus, a small number of states exercised undue weight in the outcome of the presidential election through the Electoral College. In the past, the Electoral College tended to amplify the popular vote but lately that has not been the case. Since 2000, two times, in 2002 and 2016, Republican presidential candidates (George W. Bush and Donald J. Trump) who received less popular vote than Democratic candidates (Al Gore and Hillary Clinton) won the presidency by getting a majority in the Electoral College (Liasson 2021). Critics argue that the Electoral College distorts and mal-distributes political power with negative consequences. Furthermore, since states want to maximize their influence in electing the president, they have a strong incentive to use winner-take-all for awarding electors instead of a proportional system for allocating delegates which currently only two states do (Chafetz 2020; Wegman 2020). Using the Electoral College to elect a president is antithetical to the democratic principle of popular election of the president.

There is certainly strong support among the American public for abolishing the Electoral College in favor of the popular election of the president. In a PRRI/The Atlantic survey conducted between June 6 and June 18, 2018, 65 percent of the respondents stated that presidential elections should be decided by the popular vote while only 32 percent favored the Electoral College ("PRRI/The Atlantic 2018 Voter Engagement Survey" 2018). In a Pew Research Center poll conducted between July 10 and July 16, 2023, again 65 percent of respondents favored electing the president by popular vote compared to 33 percent who favored keeping the Electoral College. The opinions were divided along partisan lines, with 82 percent of Democrats supporting the popular vote to elect the president compared to only 47 percent of Republicans (Pew Research Center 2023).

As well-intentioned as the proposal to abolish the Electoral College in favor of the popular election of the president is, it is unlikely to happen soon, especially in the current polarized political climate. It will face a major constitutional obstacle. It will require both houses of Congress to pass a constitutional amendment with a two-thirds majority. Given the slim majority enjoyed by Republicans in the House and the Senate and the current toxic political environment in Congress, passing such an amendment with a two-thirds majority would be an impossible task. Even if by a miracle it were to pass Congress, it would require three-fourths of the states to ratify such an amendment which again would be next to impossible. Republican-led red states will surely oppose such an amendment which in effect would dilute their political power and influence in electing the president.

Another possible solution, without abolishing the Electoral College, is for states to sign a compact that guarantees their Electoral College vote goes to the winner of the popular vote nationwide regardless of the outcome in their individual states. Such a compact would work only once the number of states involved passes the 270 Electoral College vote threshold required to win the presidency. Today, such a pact has the support of some states, largely Democratic blue states, and Washington, D.C. It also creates a question of fairness. If a state allocates all its electoral votes to a candidate who won the national popular vote instead of the candidate who won the state's popular vote, voters of that state are likely to view this as very unfair (Parks 2019).

Replacing Partisan Primaries with Nonpartisan Primaries

Some view political party primaries as a major problem facing the American political system. Political party primaries are where voters decide who will run on the party's name for various national state and local elected offices. Primaries can be closed primaries in which only voters registered with a party affiliation can vote; in an open primary, voters do not have to be officially registered with a party to vote in its primacy or can declare a party affiliation at the poll on the day of the primary; hybrid primaries are those in which unaffiliated voters may participate in the partisan primaries of their choice. The method used by political parties to conduct their primaries varies among states.

Political party primaries in recent years have come under increased scrutiny for primarily two reasons. One problem is the fact that only a small minority of voters decide a significant majority of elections in partisan primaries resulting in the disenfranchisement of voters, distortion of representation, and fueling of political extremism. For example, despite a record voter turnout in the November 2020 election, only 10 percent of eligible voters nationwide voted in the primaries that effectively decided the outcome of more than 80 percent of U.S. House Elections (Troiano 2021). In essence, primary elections (especially closed primaries), not general elections, ultimately decide the winners. This is because partisan gerrymandering creates "safe districts" that are non-competitive, meaning one party dominates districts where the other party has very little chance of winning. Today, four in five, 80 percent of the U.S. House seats are in Republican or Democratic "safe districts" (Barton 2023a). Consequently, winning the party's primary pretty much ensures winning the general election. The general elections have become a rubber stamp.

According to the critics, the second problem associated with partisan primaries and safe districts created by gerrymandering is that it encourages more extreme candidates either of the right or the left of the ideological spectrum to run in the primary and challenge more moderate candidates or incumbents. One of the most important incentives that drive the incumbents is to win the party's next primary. A challenge in the primary by an ideologically more extreme candidate forces the incumbent to take a more extreme stand on policy questions to win the primary and thus the general election (Gehl 2021). Partisan primaries incentivize incumbents to appeal to the narrow and extreme slice of the electorate instead of governing in the public interest (Troiano 2021). The result is more partisan and ideological polarization and less emphasis on governing through bargaining, compromises, and building a consensus since it would be viewed as appeasement. Several reforms have been advocated by critics of the partisan primaries as antidotes to address the problem of political polarization (Persily 2015).

One of the most advocated reforms includes replacing separate partisan primaries with a single, nonpartisan primary. In such a system, all candidates, regardless of partisan affiliation, compete in one nonpartisan primary, and the top two candidates advance to the general election. Under such a system, the top two candidates who advance to the general election might be from the same political party. There can be variation in such a system whereby instead of the top two candidates, four or five candidates are allowed to advance to the general election. Critics argue that allowing only two candidates in the general election limits voter choice and benefits the established parties. In the case of multiple candidates advancing to the general election, RCV can be used to ensure that the ultimate winner receives more than 50 percent of the vote.

According to the advocates of a single, nonpartisan primary, it would encourage more moderate candidates since they would have to appeal to a broader swath of voters to win both the primacy and the general election. Alaska was the first state to adopt a nonpartisan primary with RCV in the general election. Alaska allows the top four vote-getters in the primary to advance to the general election. In the general election, voters have the option to rank them by preference (Troiano 2021). Currently three states – Alaska, California, and Washington – use nonpartisan primaries. The state of Louisiana is unique in that it did away with party primaries altogether in the 1970s. Louisiana differs from the other three states in that it holds only a nonpartisan general election featuring all candidates and requires a majority winner (Barton 2023a). Research suggests that eliminating partisan primaries has helped improve governance and reduced political polarization in the state. Louisiana legislature is ranked second or third least polarized in the country (Barton 2022).

Christian Grose (2020), who compared the election results of the U.S. House of Representatives members from Louisiana, California, and Washington, found that the nonpartisan primary system led to less extreme behavior by members of Congress from these three states. One example may help illustrate this point. Out of 40 Republican U.S. Senators who were planning to run for reelection in a future partisan primary, only two, Ben Sasse (R-Nebraska) and Mitt Romney (R-Utah), voted to convict former President Trump in his second impeachment trial. In contrast, out of four Republican Senators who hailed from states without partisan primaries, two – Alaska's Lisa Murkowski and Louisiana's Bill Cassidy – voted to impeach Trump (Barton 2023a).

How have California and Washington faired under a nonpartisan primary system? Both California and Washington use a top two nonpartisan primary system in which the top two vote-getters, regardless of their party affiliation, advance to the general election. Research suggests that California and Washington are politically less polarized compared to other Western states (Barton 2023a, 2023b). However, some other research casts some doubts on nonpartisan primaries' impact on reducing political polarization. Research by McGhee and Shor (2017) examined the impact of top two nonpartisan primaries in California and Washington and found that the post-reform moderating effect on legislators' behavior was stronger in California than in Washington. However, the stronger moderating effect in California might be the result of other contemporaneous reforms such as redistricting done by the Independent Redistricting Commission and changes in the term limits that were adopted at the same time.

Voters in a few other states have expressed an interest in switching to nonpartisan primaries. Advocates of nonpartisan primaries in Oregon succeeded in putting put a constitutional amendment on the 2024 ballot that, would have required the state to use nonpartisan primaries in almost all elections. It was defeated. Similar effort in Idaho was also defeated in, it would have created nonpartisan primaries and institute RCV in general elections. In Nevada, ballot measure in 2024, the state's constitution would require a single open primary for all candidates for federal and statewide legislative offices and RCV in general elections to determine the winner. Nevada voters also rejected this. Only time will tell if many states adopt nonpartisan primaries and whether it would reduce political polarization.

Ranked Choice Voting

RCV, also referred to as "instant run-off voting," is seen as a tool to give voters a more nuanced range of issue positions than choosing from simple extreme versus moderate issue positions and breaking the current stronghold of the two major political parties. Such a system of voting would provide alternatives to the two-party system by encouraging third-party and independent candidates to run for office and offer voters more diverse candidates to choose from. Advocates suggest that instead of races decided by a slim plurality, RCV guarantees that a winner in a crowded field receives the support of a majority of voters. It would also encourage more civil campaigns and political discourse. Critics further argue that the current plurality voting system is biased against moderation and compromise while RCV encourages cross-party cooperation. RCV system would incentivize politicians to find a middle ground in their district to win voters' second- and third-choice votes. This could lead to fewer ideologically extreme lawmakers (Fukuyama 2022; "How to Fix Polarization: Bold Solutions to America's Problems" 2019). In RCV, voters rank-order multiple candidates instead of making a single selection among candidates. If one candidate gets a majority of first-place votes, that candidate is declared the winner, and the election is over. If no candidate wins a majority outright, the candidate with the lowest number of votes is eliminated and his or her second-choice votes are redistributed among the remaining candidates. This process continues until a candidate reaches a majority.

In recent years, RCV has been gaining ground (DeSilver et al. 2021). However, at present only three states use RCV statewide. Alaska and Maine use RCV in federal and statewide elections while Hawaii uses RCV in certain statewide elections. RCV is more popular at local levels of government. By 2022, nationwide 62 jurisdictions had adopted RCV (Vasilogambros 2022). However, by January 2024, 25 localities had stopped using RCV in local elections. Some resumed their use later. Skeptics of the RCV worry that RCV can confuse voters and could harm marginalized communities. This could result in lower voter turnout. Thus, there is skepticism among some that RCV can bring about the transformational change promised by the advocates of RCV, and at present, there is little evidence to suggest that it leads to decreased polarization (Parks 2023). One of the reasons RCV is adopted by local communities is because it is relatively easy to implement on a small scale involving thousands of voters. On a large scale, i.e., state or national elections, involving millions of votes, determining the ultimate winner can become more cumbersome and may require a long time to determine the ultimate winner. As of January 2024, five states – Florida, Idaho, Montana, South Dakota, and Tennessee – have enacted laws that prohibit the use of RCV statewide ("Ranked-Choice Voting RCV" 2024). For RCV to make a significant impact in reducing national political polarization, it would require all or almost all states to adopt the RCV for national and statewide elections.

Replacing Single-Member Districts with Multi-Member Districts with Proportional Representation

In the United States, legislators at the national and state levels are elected using a single-member district with a winner-take-all system. For example, 435 U.S. House seats are divided into 435 Congressional districts with voters in each district electing one representative to represent them in Congress. A candidate who wins a majority of the vote is declared a winner. In case no candidate wins a majority, generally a run-off election is held between the top two vote-getters. In an overwhelming number of cases, the winner tends to be a Democratic or a Republican Party candidate since these two parties have dominated American politics for over a century. Political reform advocates argue that such a system has outlasted its effectiveness and it is time to break the stronghold of the two-party system.

Reformers advocate replacing the current system with a system that uses multi-member districts with proportional representation. Under this system, instead of electing one member per district, U.S. House districts could be divided into larger districts and voters elect multiple members from each district. Multiple seats would be parceled out among political parties in proportion to the actual percentage of popular vote each party receives. This means that minor parties have a shot at winning some seats based on the percentage of votes they get and do not have to win a majority of votes to get their candidate elected. Such a system would encourage the development of a multiparty democracy which would do a better job of representing diverse viewpoints and political ideologies. Critics argue that the current two-party domination of American politics has contributed to partisan and ideological polarization. The only way to make space for more parties is to end the current single-member district, winner-take-all. A multi-member, proportional representation system will help end the zero-sum nature of binary political conflict and drive the two major parties to the center of the political spectrum (Crosson and Tsebelis 2022;

Drutman 2020; "How to Fix Polarization: Bold Solutions to America's Problems" 2019; Lee-De-Wit, Linden, and Brick 2019). However, even the advocates of proportional representation acknowledge that such a reform taking place is a long shot (Berman 2023).

Reforming redistricting and gerrymandering

Another electoral reform advocated to reduce political polarization is to reform the redistricting process. Every ten years, after the new Census, U.S. House and state legislative district lines are redrawn to reflect the shift in population. In most cases, this is done by state legislatures. Thus, it becomes a partisan issue as the party in the majority tries to redraw the district lines in a way that would benefit the majority party while diluting the strength of the other party. Redistricting for purely political purposes is called gerrymandering. Reformers argue that gerrymandering has contributed to political polarization because both political parties have used it to create "safe districts" without any meaningful party competition. Gerrymandering creates districts so safe that incumbents win 98 percent of the time. Partisan gerrymandering has stifled political debate, made politics very toxic, and harmed American democracy (Kenny et al. 2023; DeSmith 2023; "How to Fix Polarization: Bold Solutions to America's Problems" 2019). The only recourse to challenge openly blatant and partisan gerrymandering is to challenge the redistricting done by a state legislature in courts. In 2019, in *Rucho v. Common Cause*, the U.S. Supreme Court closed the door to such challenges in the federal courts.

Reformers have argued for doing away with partisan gerrymandering and replacing it with a nonpartisan or bipartisan redistricting process. Several states have adopted reforms designed to address the problem. However, most of them rely on state-by-state solutions which are available in some but not all states (Wang, Ober, Jr., and Williams 2019). In response to the 2021 redistricting cycle, the *Gerrymandering Project* (2021) at Princeton University developed a report card to grade each state's newly drawn maps. Similarly, the nonpartisan nonprofit anticorruption organization *RepresentUs* also issues a Redistricting Report Card which rates the level of gerrymandering distortion of Congressional district maps within each state ("Redistricting: Proposed Reform in 2023" 2023).

Some states have established independent redistricting commissions while others have established redistricting advisory commissions. In 2021, five states – Iowa, Maine, New York, Utah, and Virginia, had established advisory commissions while Arizona, California, Colorado, and Michigan had established independent commissions. In 2020, in Nebraska, Oregon, and Oklahoma, there were ballot initiatives to vote on reform but the COVID-19 upended the efforts to get the issue on the ballot (Li 2021). In recent years, Montana, Idaho, Washington, and Vermont have also established independent redistricting commissions. In 2023, there were bills introduced to reform the redistricting process in several states such as Texas, Oregon, and the Carolinas but they failed to pass the state legislatures ("Redistricting: Proposed Reform in 2023" 2023).

How have redistricting reforms faired in reducing political polarization? The results are mixed but not very encouraging. In theory, the independent commissions were supposed to be insulated from politics. The experience suggests that such has not been the case. Given the importance of redistricting in determining who controls Congress for the next decade, both the Republican and Democratic parties have engaged in trench warfare over redistricting. In Virginia, commission meetings have often dissolved into shouting matches. In Ohio, Republican-controlled legislature simply ignored the state's redistricting commission and drew up the maps themselves. In Arizona and Michigan, independent commissions have been besieged with shadow campaign pressures from both parties. In some states, commissions were poorly designed structures that fell victim to the entrenched political divisions. In summary, the supposed fix has frequently fallen short (Corasaniti and Epstein 2021).

Legislative reforms

Some of the legislative reforms advocated to reduce hyper-partisanship and polarization includes things such as eliminating the filibuster in the Senate or at least requiring the filibuster to be "talking" filibusters; lowering barriers to policymaking by requiring a simple majority to pass major policy measures instead of a super-majority which allows a minority of Senators to thwart the will of the majority; requiring a super-majority instead of a simple majority to elect a speak of the House; and reducing transparency to allow for more room for negotiating, bargaining, and compromising (Berman 2016; Persily 2015). However, since partisan and ideological polarization has its roots in deeply held philosophical differences about the public sphere and the role of government, it is difficult to see how some of these proposals can help reduce polarization. Eliminating filibusters whereby a majority can impose its will on the minority that feels intensely about a policy issue can easily generate more hostility, can be counterproductive, and lead to more polarization.

Regulation of the mass media and social media platforms

Since both mass media and social media are often cited as contributing factors to political polarization in the United States and for inflaming tribalism, some reform advocates have called for more regulation of both. Critics have charged that mass and social media driven largely by "rage news" for profit has spawned affective polarization that undermines trust in democratic institutions and fellow citizens. It accelerates the movement of citizens into informational bubbles and "echo chambers" who are constantly exposed to inflammatory stories and videos, conspiracy theories, misinformation, half-truths, and falsehoods which have also contributed to a rise in depression and anxiety (Overgaard and Wooley 2022; Haidt 2019; Zittrain 2019; Foster 2018).

While laws against hate speech and deceptive advertising do exist, freedom of speech in the United States is considered inviolable and the Internet has given everyone a microphone. U.S.-based companies enjoy considerable leeway regarding what is allowed on their platform. Some of the reforms designed to regulate mass and social media platforms are focused on requiring companies to change their policies regarding content moderation. Content moderation can take three approaches. One is removing the offending content by removing individual posts, temporarily or permanently banning individuals who violate the company's terms of service and guidelines, or denying websites or entire platforms the assistance they need to reach large audiences. The second approach involves reducing the distribution of offensive content by reducing its visibility, downranking or demoting, and making use of warning labels. The third approach to content moderation is by influencing and shaping the dialogue by moderating debate and discussion, elevating trustworthy and positive content, providing reminders and warnings, turning off or hiding comments, incentivizing better behavior, and ending anonymity of postings and shaming users (Byman 2022; Overgaard and Wooley 2022).

How can the government tell private news organizations what they may or may not publish or ask a social media platform to remove a hateful and inflammatory posting or a false story? Under the First Amendment, media companies enjoy a considerable latitude to establish their own policies free of government interference and regulation. Any attempt at government regulation of the media is likely to be viewed by its critics as censorship.

The U.S. Supreme Court heard oral arguments in March 2024 in the case of Murthy V. Missouri concerning whether misinformation about COVID-19 on social media platforms is protected speech. During the COVID-19 pandemic, social media sites were flooded with misleading posts about vaccine safety, mask effectiveness, and COVID-19's origins and the

Biden administration officials urged these platforms to remove such posts. The lawsuit alleged that federal officials coerced social media platforms such as Facebook, Twitter, YouTube, and Google to remove or downgrade or remove posts that questioned vaccine safety and the origin of the pandemic. Critics argued that federal public health officials should not have tried to remove misleading posts while defenders of the government's action argued that the court limiting federal health agencies' communication with social media platforms could hamstring government agencies' ability to achieve higher vaccination rates and contain the pandemic. Furthermore, the Biden administration has argued that federal health officials requested but never forced social media companies to downgrade or remove misleading or false posts (Owermohle 2024). In June 2024, the U.S. Supreme Court by a 6-3 majority ruled that the Biden administration could not be sued for pressuring social media companies to remove misinformation about COVID-19 (Kern and Gerstein 2024).

The U.S. Supreme Court also heard oral arguments in March 2024 regarding the constitutionality of Texas and Florida's laws prohibiting social media platforms from suspending the accounts of political candidates or media publications. The Court had asked the Biden administration to weigh in on whether states can prohibit social media platforms from removing certain types of political speech (Barnes and Zakrzewski 2023). States have been increasingly eying social media bans (Hutton 2024). Some see states' attempts to regulate social media as misguided (Chemerinsky 2024). The Supreme Court in July of 2024 sent the case back to lower courts for further examination. The court ruling, however, left unanswered the broader question of whether Texas law is unconstitutional. The district courts in both Texas and Florida had issued orders temporarily banning states from enforcing their laws (Howe 2024). The ultimate resolution of the case will determine whether state governments or tech companies have the power to set rules governing what posts appear on popular social networks (Zakrzewski and Marimow 2024).

Social reforms

A host of proposed solutions in this category can be labeled as social/psychological solutions to the problem of polarization. While many of them are laudable, it is unclear how practical they are and whether they can reduce political polarization. One proposed solution is to reform public education by placing more emphasis on civic education since polls consistently have shown citizen's ignorance about governmental institutions and how they function. Such ignorance makes them susceptible or gullible to misinformation, falsehoods, and conspiracy theories (Jenkinson 2021).

Ironically, for over a hundred years the United States has used a civics test to screen for individuals from other countries who apply to become U.S. citizens. The idea behind the test is that to participate in American life, newcomers must demonstrate some knowledge of the values and operations of the American democracy. Yet no such test is required of individuals born in the United States (Pink 2024).

Mounk (2018) and Fukuyama (2018) have called for educating Americans about the Enlightenment values that guided the framing of the U.S. Constitution and replacing partisan, gender, racial, and religious tribalism with a renewed national identity that makes Americans feel like they are members of the same team. It is unclear how this takes place in a politically charged environment in which many red states are busy banning books from public libraries and public schools. However, others (Sides, Tesler, and Vavreck 2018) have argued that the persistent "national identity" framing is part of the problem and that the politics of national identity have made American politics more toxic because defining what it means to be an American itself has become a very divisive issue of our times. They argue that our efforts to find a shared American identity have left us more divided. Instead, they call for replacing the politics of national identity with a revived focus on local identity and reviving community public spaces with neighborhood block parties, co-ops, and mutual aid networks and organizing local festivals.

Along the same line, another reform advocated is to institute mandatory civilian or military service to bring people from different backgrounds together to work toward a common goal that can reduce intolerance (Mason and Liu 2019; Liu 2019). One of the ways to counter affective polarization and reduce partisan animosity is by stressing and focusing more on our common bonds and bringing ordinary Democrats and Republicans together for cross-party political discussion (Levendusky 2023; Levendusky and Stecula 2021). It is unclear how one accomplishes this when Democrats and Republicans have sorted themselves by geography not just at the state level but also at the city and county levels including by neighborhoods.

Polarization and divided state of american healthcare

Red and blue states represent different economies, socio-demographics, political ideologies, and cultural values. Blue states have industrial and technology-based economies and they are more affluent, while red states have agricultural-based economies and are less affluent. Red states' economies have been surging since the pandemic partly because of the migration of people and businesses from blue states to red states due to warmer climates, lower taxes, and lower cost of living. Blue states have more educated and urban populations while red states have less educated and more rural populations. Blue states are more secular while red states are more religious. Blue states have more immigrant and racially diverse populations compared to red states. Blue states promote citizen participation in politics and support democratic values while red states engage in opposite practices. Blue states are politically and culturally liberal while red states are politically and culturally conservative.

The partisan and ideological divide can undermine America's health. Research shows that political affiliation is one of the factors shaping the lifespan across the United States. There is a growing life expectancy gap between blue and red counties. People in Republican counties are more likely to die prematurely than Democratic leading counties. This holds when adjusting for age and urban-rural divide. Political polarization has created gridlock and Congress has been unable to act on major public policies. Consequently, policymaking has shifted to state governments, where the trifecta control of state government has led red and blue states to pass not only different but diametrically opposite health policies resulting in a greater divide in health outcomes (Martinez and Aubrey 2022; Weber, Diamond, and Keating 2023). Red states have passed more conservative health policies while the blue states have passed more liberal health policies. For example, red states that pushed back on COVID-19 vaccination and enforcement of public health policies experienced much higher death rates than the blue states that implemented a proactive approach (Metropoulos 2022). At a local level, counties with a higher percentage of White Evangelicals, who tend to be Republican-leaning and very conservative, have higher mortality rates and more individuals with fair/poor health (Kindig, Ariffin, and Olson-Williams 2024). Red and blue states have been moving further apart on health policy for quite a while (Armour 2018).

Even the healthcare profiles of red and blue states vary considerably. Red states spend less money per capita on healthcare, have a lower life expectancy, higher rates of uninsured people, higher death rates from major causes of death, higher rates of obesity, smoking, mental illness, suicide, maternal mortality, teen birth rates, and a higher percentage of low-weight babies compared to blue states.

Given the fact that the red and blue states differ from one another concerning their economics, politics, and culture, it is perhaps not too surprising that they also differ considerably concerning public policies ranging from environment and climate change to education to gun control to immigration, and civil rights and voting rights. Perhaps in no other policy area, the sharp divide between the red and blue states is more evident than in the field of healthcare policy. Red and blue states are moving in opposite directions when it comes to public policies involving the Affordable Care Act, Medicaid, reproductive rights, physician assisted suicide, and their response to the COVID-19 pandemic.

At the national level, Republicans in Congress opposed the Patient Protection and Affordable Care Act, in short the Affordable Care Act (ACA), also known as Obamacare. Not a single Republican in Congress voted for the passage of the ACA. After the passage of the Act, they tried many times to repeal and/or defund the program over the years. Red states launched several lawsuits challenging the constitutionality of the law itself or its various provisions which led to some important changes in the law. Red states particularly opposed the insurance mandate and many red states initially failed to set up their own insurance exchange markets under the ACA and relied instead on federal exchanges. They also placed various barriers making it difficult for individuals to enroll in the exchanges. Consequently, uninsurance rates in red states declined less than in the blue states. In sharp contrast, blue states welcomed the implementation of the ACA in their states, set up their insurance exchanges, and made it easier for citizens of their states to enroll in the insurance exchanges. In sum, the Republicans and the red states waged a ten-year war on the ACA (Oberlander 2020). Ironically, the public opinion polls suggest that a majority of Americans today have a favorable view of the ACA. A poll conducted by the Kaiser Family Foundation in May of 2023 found that 59 percent held a favorable opinion of ACA compared to 41 percent who held an unfavorable opinion (Kirzinger et al. 2023). In 2024, a record number of Americans, 21.3 million, signed up for health insurance coverage, exceeding last year's record by five million people (Ortaliza, Cox, and Amin 2024). States with the largest increase in sign-ups included the red states of Louisiana, Indiana, Tennessee, Mississippi, Arkansas, Alabama, South Carolina, Georgia, Arizona, and Texas (Millman 2024).

The political divide between the red and blue states is also clear concerning the Medicaid program. Medicaid is a joint federal-state program that gives state governments considerable leeway when it comes to funding, establishing eligibility standards, and optional services covered under the program. Considerable policy differences can be seen between the red and blue states. For example, blue states have more generous eligibility standards, especially for pregnant women and children. They enroll a high percentage of their population in Medicaid providing healthcare coverage compared to red states. Blue states spend more money per beneficiary and they also spend a higher percentage of their own funds than do the red states. Blue states have expanded their eligibility standards to cover more individuals while the red states have been more reluctant to do so. Medicaid expansion in red states came about very slowly and gradually and not all red states have expanded Medicaid. Expansion of the Medicaid program in some red states came about due to citizen-driven ballot initiatives (for example, Missouri) and not due to legislative action by Republican-controlled state legislatures. Blue states have opposed work requirements while the red states have supported them. On measures of spending, enrollment, eligibility, and quality, blue states rank higher compared to red states. Historically, Social Security and Medicare are considered the "third rail" of American politics. Today, Medicaid covers more Americans (83.5 million) compared to 64.9 percent covered by Medicare. Medicaid probably has become as sacrosanct as Medicare and Social Security (Levitt 2022). More Americans are connected to the Medicaid program, support its expansion, and no longer view it as stigmatizing (Gorgan and Park 2017). During the pandemic, Medicaid came to be viewed as a safety net program. As a result, public support for the program increased. Medicaid program becomes less polarizing among Americans when it is viewed as a safety net program (Zhu et al. 2021).

The topic of reproductive rights, especially abortion, has become the most inflammatory and divisive issue of our times between the red and blue states. It has become a battleground for the "cultural wars." For 20 years after the Roe v. Wade ruling in 1973 legalizing abortion, abortion remained a bipartisan issue. However, after the U.S. Supreme Court in the case of *Planned Parenthood of Southeastern PA v. Casey* gave states more discretion to regulate abortion practices, partisan and ideological divisions emerged with red and blue states moving in different directions. The red states began to impose a variety of restrictions on abortion rights including regulation of abortion clinics, imposing waiting periods, requiring parental consent, and mandatory counseling, while the blue states moved to protect abortion rights. The fight over abortion rights intensified when the U.S. Supreme Court in 2022 in *Dobbs v. Jackson Mississippi Women's Health Organization* overturned *Roe. V. Wade* and returned the abortion policy-making to the states. Many red states quickly moved to impose a total or near-total ban on abortions while blue states moved to enshrine abortion rights in their state constitutions and expand abortion rights. The result of political polarization on the issue of abortion is that reproductive rights now depend on where one lives. Abortion bans in many red states have also produced several negative consequences. For example, residents in states with abortion bans experienced significantly increased anxiety and depression symptoms compared to residents in states without abortion bans (Thornberg et al. 2024). One study estimated that more than 65,000 pregnancies have resulted from rape in states that have banned abortions (Dickman, White, and Himelstein 2024). Women in states with abortion bans are forced to flee under the cover of darkness to other states to get an emergency abortion (Tirrell and Bonifield 2024). In Ohio, a woman was charged with a felony after a miscarriage at home. She was charged with abuse of a corpse, a charge that was ultimately dismissed when a grand jury refused to indict her (Duncan et al. 2024). This has happened despite the fact a strong majority of Americans support abortion rights and oppose the Dobbs decision.

The red and blue states have responded very differently to the COVID-19 pandemic. Red states opposed lockdowns, social distancing, vaccines, and mask-wearing while the blue states embraced these measures. Not surprisingly, vaccination rates were much lower in red states compared to blue states. Consequently, red states experienced a higher rate of hospitalization and deaths compared to blue states. Red states placed more emphasis on keeping the state economy going while the blue states put more emphasis on saving lives. During the pandemic, blue states suffered more economically than the red states. It also took a longer time for blue states' economies to recover from the pandemic compared to red states. During the pandemic, there was also a great deal of misleading and false information regarding the vaccine on the Internet and various social media platforms. One of the casualties is Americans' declining trust in science and scientists. The number of Americans who say that science has had a mostly positive effect on society has declined from 67 percent in 2016 to 57 percent in 2023. There are also significant differences between Republicans and Democrats in their confidence in scientists. In 2023, 86 percent of Democrats and 61 percent of Republicans expressed confidence in scientists to act in the best interest of the public. Only 13 percent of Democrats compared to 38 percent of Republicans expressed not much or no confidence at all in scientists to act in the best interest of the public (Kennedy and Tyson 2023). In addition, the public's attitudes about the virus were shaped by polarized messages they received from Republican and Democratic party leaders (Sides, Tausanovitch, and Vavreck 2020). Partisan affiliation is one of the strongest predictors of behavior and Americans' attitudes toward COVID-19 (Rothwell and Makridis 2020).

Red and blue states are moving in different directions when it comes to American healthcare. Public option polls have consistently demonstrated that a majority of Americans support the Affordable HealthCare Act, Medicaid, reproductive rights and abortion, and medical aid in dying. Yet, in the red states, there is a disconnect between public opinion and Republican political elites who have become captured by political and socially conservative elements of their party. Citizens of blue states enjoy better healthcare, better healthcare quality and outcomes, broader and more generous health insurance coverage via ACA and Medicaid, reproductive rights, and freedom to seek medical aid in dying. In red states where

Republicans enjoy trifecta control of the government, they have used their political power and authority to pursue policies designed to limit their citizens' access to healthcare, and health benefits, and limit women's freedom to control their bodies (Bouie 2023). In the divided state of American healthcare, red states are left to sing the blues.

Concluding thoughts

American politics has become a zero-some game in which "compromise" and "consensus" necessary to govern a nation have become dirty words. There is shrinking ground for compromises as exemplified by recent backlash against the proposed bipartisan border deal to address the migration problem at the southern border (Karni 2024). Winning at any cost and taking no prisoners have become the battle cry in political and cultural warfare. All the electoral reforms proposed to reduce political polarization, well-intentioned as they are, are unlikely to be adopted and implemented. Political polarization in the United States is increasing, not abating. The warning signs are everywhere. According to the Federal Bureau of Investigation (FBI), hate crimes at schools and colleges are on the rise ("Reported Hate Crimes at Schools: 2018–2022" 2024). Twenty-three states, mostly red states, have enacted laws/policies limiting access to gender-affirming care ("Policy Tracker: Youth Access to Gender Affirming Care and State Policy Restrictions" 2024). In states with laws targeting LGBTQ issues, school hate crimes have quadrupled (Meckler, Natanson, and Harden 2024).

New waves of legislation in many red state legislatures are banning books in public schools and libraries. In 2024 alone, 13 states introduced legislation designed to censor library material dealing with topics such as race, gender identity, or sexual orientation (Kottke 2024). In Florida, where Republicans enjoy a trifecta control of state government, Escambia County School District pulled 1,600 books from its shelf, including the Merriam-Webster Dictionary (Heubeck 2024). Public libraries have become a new frontier in cultural wars (Mumma 2023; Gowen 2022).

Public colleges and universities have also become battlegrounds in the cultural wars. Florida also removed a sociology core course option from public colleges on the claim that sociology had been hijacked by left-wing activists (Somasundaram and Natanson 2024). In Texas, the State Board of Education put a break on the proposed American Indian/Native Studies course (Lee 2024). Red states are targeting black history lessons while blue states are embracing them (Natanson 2023; Meckler and Natanson 2023).

As citizens have acted to counter and defeat trends in red states to restrict reproductive freedoms and refuse to expand Medicaid programs by ballot initiatives, lawmakers in many states are trying to override ballot initiatives and to make ballot initiatives difficult to succeed or to simply ignore them. Citizen-driven lawmaking has come under increasing attack (Whitesell 2024; Milchen 2023; Greenblatt 2019, 2017).

Texas Governor Abbott has floated the idea that Texas can ditch its ties to the United States and has argued that the state is under invasion from migrants and has a right to self-defense, even if it means defying federal authority. Other Republican leaders, including Nikki Haley, the Republican candidate for the presidency, have suggested that states have a right to decide if they want to succeed from the Union. Even after the Supreme Court sided with the federal government on a border dispute with Texas, some Republican lawmakers suggested that it was OK to ignore and disregard the Supreme Court ruling (Elliot 2024; Bouie 2024; Blake 2024; Hernandez 2024). More than a dozen red state governors have sent state National Guard units to the Texas border since 2021(Coronado 2024; Hernandez and Allam 2024). Twenty-five states with Republican governors (24 red states and Florida) signed a letter supporting Texas in a border fight with the federal government even though only three red states – Texas, New Mexico, and Arizona – share a border with Mexico (Crowley and Gore 2024). There has been an overall increased confrontation between the red states and the federal government over other issues as well.

There are threats to the security of the 2024 elections. According to experts, there is an equal risk of domestic disruption and interference from foreign actors in the 2024 elections. The risk of misinformation is heightened due to advances in artificial intelligence (Smith 2024). Federal law enforcement and cyber security officials have warned secretaries of state and state election officials about possible cyberattacks, targeting of voter databases via phishing and ransomware, as well as possible threats to the personal safety of election officials and workers (Vasilogambros 2024).

Political polarization has divided the country into red and blue nations. American political system has become dysfunctional. In a CBNS News poll, 61 percent of Americans described the state of the American Union as divided (De Pinto 2024). Most Americans show a lack of trust in major institutions of government. In a Marquette Law School national survey, 10 percent expressed a great deal or a lot of confidence in Congress, 25 percent in the presidency, and 25 percent in the U.S. Supreme Court (Franklin 2024). In a USA Today poll, seven out of 10 Americans agreed with the statement that American democracy is in peril (Bailey and Collins 2023). A Fox News poll found that 30 percent of Americans, including 56 percent of Republicans, still think that President Biden was not legitimately elected. Government institutions are not likely to be the protectors of American Democracy (Bump 2024). Nor are the politicians since there are very few profiles in courage. Americans are losing faith in American democracy and democratic institutions. The answers to protecting democracy and addressing the problem of political polarization ultimately lie with the American voters. America is divided into red and blue nations by race, gender, geography, religion, education, and partisanship. Is it possible to bridge this divide?

American voters were confronted with two major choices in the November 2024 elections. The first choice was whether they wanted to continue political polarization by electing or reelecting extremist candidates who inflame division and discord or do they want to end the cycle of polarization and tribalism by electing cross-party consensus builders? The second choice confronting American voters was whether they wanted the United States to continue to slide toward autocracy. By reelecting Donald Trump to the presidency, Americans opted for continued polarization and further erosion of democratic institutions, rules, and norms. The next four years will determine whether America becomes more polarized and how far down the country slides toward autocracy.

Bibliography

Abernathy, Gary. 2023. "Americans Need to Rediscover the Lost Art of Tolerance." https://www.washingtonpost.com/

Achenbach, Joel. 2024. "Science is Revealing Why American Politics are so Intensely Polarized." https://www.washingtonpost.com/

Atman, Alex, and Maya Rhodan. 2015. "Blue States Make Voting Easier as Red States Add Restrictions." https://time.com/

Ambrosius, Joshua. 2016. "Blue City...Red City? A Comparison of Competing Theories of Core County Outcomes in U.S. presidential Elections, 2000–2012." *Journal of Urban Affairs* 38, no. 2 (May): 169–195.

Applebaum, Anne. 2020. *Twilight of Democracy: The Seductive Lure of Authoritarianism.* New York: Doubleday.

"Are We All Authoritarian at Heart?" 2023. Transcript of podcast Hosted by Michelle Cottle, Ross Douthat, Carlos Lozada, and Lydia Polgreen. https://www.nytimes.com/

Armour, Stephanie. 2018. "Red and Blue States Move Further Apart on Health Policy." https://www.wsj.com/

Badger, Emily; Kevin Quealy; and Josh Katz. 2021. "A Close-Up Picture of Partisan Segregation, Among 180 Million Voters." https://nytimes.com/

Bailey, Phillip M., and Terry Collins. 2023. "What is the State of American Democracy? As July 4th nears, Poll Shows Voters are Worried." https://www.usatoday.com/

Balz, Dan. 2023. "A Dizzying Divisive Week in Politics Spotlights America's Raging Battle." https://www.Washingtonpost.com/

Balz, Dan, and Clara E. Morse. 2023. "American Democracy is Cracking. These Forces Help Explain Why." https://www.washingtonpost.com/

Barnes, Robert, and Cat Zakrzewski. 2023. "Supreme Court Asks Biden Administration to Weigh in on Social Media Case." https://www.washingtonpost.com/

Barton, Richard. 2023a. "An Antidote to Our-Polarized Politics." https://www.governing.com/

Barton, Richard. 2023b. "The Good Things California's 'Top Two' Elections Have Wrought." https://www.governing.com/

Barton, Richard. 2022. "Louisiana's Long-Term Election Experiment: How Eliminating Partisan Primaries Improved Governance and Reduced Polarization." https://www.uniteamericainstitute.org/

Baumgartner, Jody; Peter L. Francia; Jonathan S. Morris; and Carmine P. Scavo. 2008. "Is it Really Red Versus Blue? Politics, Religion, and the Culture War Within." *American Review of Politics* 29, no. 1–2 (Spring): 1–18.

Ben-Ghiat, Ruth. 2021. *Strongmen: How They Rise, Why They Succeed, How They Fall.* London: Profile Books.

Benson, John E. 2014. "Red—Blue? Left-Right?" *Dialog* 53, no. 1 (Spring): 2–5.

Bergengruen, Vera. 2024. "Public Officials Face Surge of Threats Ahead of 2024 Election." https://time/com/

Berman, Russell. 2023. "A Radical Idea for Fixing Polarization: Can Proportional Representation Save American Democracy?" https://www.theatlantic.com/

Berman, Russell. 2016. "What's the Answer to Political Polarization in the U.S.?" https://www.theatlantic.com/

Bishop, Bill. 2008. *The Big Sort: Why the Clustering of Like-Minded America is Tearing US Apart.* New York: Houghton Mifflin Harcourt.

Blake, Aaron. 2024. "Republicans Now Say It Might be Okay to Ignore the Supreme Court." https://www.washingtonpost.com/

Bouie, Jamelle. 2024. "No, Nikki Haley, the Constitution Does not Say That." https://www.nytimes.com/

Bouie, Jamelle. 2023. "Red States and Blue States are Becoming Different Countries." https://www.nytimes.com/

Buckley, Frank H. 2020. *American Succession: The Looming Threat of a National Breakup.* New York: Encounter Books.

Bump, Philip. 2024. "The Institutions of Government Aren't Going to Protect Democracy." https://www.washingtonpost.com/

Byman, Daniel L. 2023. "The Risk of Election Violence in the United States in 2024." https://www.brookings.edu/

Byman, Daniel L. 2022. "Content Moderation Tools to Stop Extremism." https://www.lawfaremedia.org/

Cahn, Naomi. 2011. *Red Families v. Blue Families: Legal Polarization and the Creation of Culture.* New York: Oxford University Press.

Chafetz, Josh. 2020. "Why We Should Abolish the Electoral College." https://www.nytimes.com/

Chemerinsky, Erwin. 2024. "States' Misguided Attempts to Regulate Social Media." https://www.governing.com/

Clinton, Hillary R. 2023. "The Weaponization of Loneliness." https://www.theatlantic.com/

Clinton, Hillary R. 1996. *It Takes a Village.* New York: Simon and Schuster.

Confessore, Nicholas. 2024. "America is Under Attack: Inside the Anti-D.E.I. Crusade." https://www.nytimes.com/

Corasaniti, Nick, and Reid J. Epstein. 2021. "How A Cure for Gerrymandering Left U.S. Politics Ailing in New Ways." https://www.nytimes.com/

Coronado, Acacia. 2024. "What to Know as Republicans Governors Consider Sending More National Guard to Texas Border." https://apnews.com/

Cox, Stanley E. 2005. "Red States, Blue States, Marriage Debates." *Ave Maria Law Review* 3, no. 2 (Summer): 1–20.

Crosson, Jesse M., and George Tsebelis. 2022. "Multiple Vote Electoral System: A Remedy for Political Polarization." *Journal of European Public Policy* 29, no. 6 (June): 932–952.

Crowley, Kinsey, and Hogan Gore. 2024. "25 States with Republican Governors Sign Letter Supporting Texas in Border Control Fight: What to Know." https://www.usatoday.com/

Cummings, Stephen D. 2008. *Red States, Blue States, and the Coming Sharecropper Society*. New York: Algora Publishing.

Cummings, Stephen D. 1998. *The Dixification of America: The American Odyssey into the Conservative Economic Trap*. Westport, CT: Praeger Publishers.

"Democracy Index 2016." 2016. https://www.eiu.com/

"Democracy Index 2021." 2021. https://www.eiu.com/

Denker, Angela. 2019. *Red State Christians: Understanding the Voters Who Elected Donald Trump*. Minneapolis: MN. Fortress Press.

De Pinto, Jennifer. 2024. "CBS NEWS Poll Finds Most Americans See "State of Union' as Divided, but Their Economic Outlook Has Been Improving"." https://www.cbsnews.com/

DeSilver, Drew; Carrie Blazina; Janakee Chavda; and Rebecca Leppert. 2021. "More U.S. Locations are Experimenting with Alternative Voting Systems." https://www.pewresearch.org/

DeSmith, Christy. 2023. "Biggest Problem with gerrymandering." https://news.harvard.edu/

Dickman, Samuel L.; Kari White, and David U. Himelstein. 2024. "Rape-Related Pregnancies in the 14 US States with Total Abortion Bans." *JAMA Internal Medicine*. Published online on January 24th. https://jamanetwork.com/

Doyle, Roger. 2006. "Myth: Red-Blue States." *Scientific American* 295, no. 5 (November): 38.

Drutman, Lee. 2020. *Breaking the Two-Party Doom Loop: The Case for Multiparty Democracy in America*. New York: Oxford University Press.

Duncan, Jericka; Rachel Bailey; Cassandra Gauthier; and Hillar Cook. 2024. "Brittany Watts, Ohio Woman Charged with Felony After Miscarriage at Home. Describes Shock of Her Arrest." https://www.cbsnews.com/

Elliott, Philip. 2024. "No, Texas Can't Secede, and the Border Fight is About Politics More than Policy." https://time.com/

Ellison, Sarah; Yvonne Sanchez; and Patrick Marley. 2024. "Violent Political Threats Surge as 2024 Begins, Haunting American Democracy." https://www.washingtonpost.com/

Englund, Scott. 2023. "Domestic Terrorism is Evolving. It Needs Imaginative Counterterrorism." https://www.brookings.edu/

Enriquez, Juan. 2005. *The United States of America: Polarization, Fracturing, and Our Future*. New York: Crown Publishing Group.

Faiola, Anthony, and Catarina Martins. 2024a. "Cool to be Far Right? Young Europeans are Stirring a Political Youthquake." https://www.washingtonpost.com/

Faiola, Anthony, and Catarina Martins. 2024b. "Socialist Conceding in Portuguese Election Seen as Bellwether for Europe." https://www.washingtonpost.com/

Faiola, Anthony; Emily Rauhala; and Loveday Morris. 2023. "Dutch Election Shows Far Right Rising and Reshaping Europe." https://www.washingtonpost.com/

Foster, David. 2018. "Potential Solutions to the Polarization Problem." https://knowthesystem.org/

Franklin, Charles. 2024. "Mew Marquette Law School National Poll Finds Approval of U.S. Supreme Court at 40%, Public Split on Removal of Trump from Ballot." https://law.marquette.edu/

French, David. 2020. *Divided We Fall: America's Secession Threat and How to Restore Our Nation.* New York: St. Martin's Press.

Freeman, Joanne B. 2018. *The Field of Blood: Violence in Congress and the Road to Civil War.* New York: Farrar, Straus, and Giroux.

Fukuyama, Francis. 2022. "Paths to Depolarization." https://www.persuasion.community/

Fukuyama, Francis. 2018. *Identity: The Demand for Dignity and the Politics of Resentment.* New York: Farrar, Straus, and Giroux.

Garcia-Navarro, Lulu. 2024. "Robert Putnam Knows Why You're Lonely." https://www.nytimes.com/

Gehl, Katherine M. 2021. "It's Time to Get Rid of Party Primaries." https://www.cnn.com/

Gelman, Andrew. 2010. *Red State, Blue State, Rich State, Poor State: Why Americans Vote the Way They Do.* Princeton, NJ: Princeton University Press.

"Gerrymandering Project." 2021. https://gerrymander.princeton.edu/

Gerstein, Josh. 2023. "Judge Key to Jan. 6 Case Warns US Faces 'Authoritarian' Threat." https://www.politico.com/

Giroux, Gregory L. 2004. "Red States, Blue States – Or Shades of Violet?" *Congressional Quarterly Weekly* 62, no. 46 (November): 2775–2777.

Goldberg, Nicholas. 2023. "Don't Turn Away from the Rising Tide of Political Violence in America." https://www.governing.com/

Gorski, Philip S., and Samuel L. Perry. 2022. *The Flag and the Cross. The White Christian Nationalism and the Threat to American Democracy.* New York: Oxford University Press.

Gorgan, Colleen M., and Sunggeun Park. 2017. "The Politics of Medicaid: Most Americans are Connected to the Program, Support Its Expansion, and Do Not View It as Stigmatizing." *Milbank Quarterly* 94, no. 4 (December): 749–782.

Gowen, Annie. 2022. "The Culture Wars Next Frontier: Public Libraries." https://www.washingtonpost.com/

Graham, Carol. 2024. "Our Twin Crises of Despair and Misinformation." https://www.brookings.ecu/

Greenblatt, Alan. 2024. "Attempted Trump Assassination Exposes Continuing Divisions in the Country." https://www.governing.com/

Greenblatt, Alan. 2019. "Lawmakers Eye Changes to Ballot Measures – Passed and Future." https://www.governing.com/

Greenblatt, Alan. 2017. "Don't Like the Ballot Measure Voters Approved? Just Ignore It, Some Lawmakers Say." https://www.govering.com/

Grose, Christian R. 2020. "Reducing Legislative Polarization: Top-Two and Open Primaries Are Associated with More Moderate Legislators", *Journal of Political Institutions and Political Economy* 1, no. 2 (June): 267–287.

Haidt, Jonathan. 2019. "More Social Media Regulation," in "How to Fix Polarization: Bold Solutions to America's Problems." 2019. https://www.politico.com/

Hass, Richard. 2023. *The Bill of Obligations: The Ten Habits of Good Citizens.* New York: Penguin Books.

Heilbrunn, Jacob. 2024. *America Last: The Right's Century-Long Romance with Foreign Dictators.* New York: Liveright Publishing Company.

Hernandez, Arelis R. 2024. "Texas Border City on Edge as Gov. Abbott Dials Up Battle with Biden." https://www.washingtonpost.com/

Hernandez, Arelis R., and Hannah Allam. 2024. "Texas Border Showdown is Far-Right Magnet, Hate Trackers Warn." https://www.washingtonpost.com/

Heubeck, Elizabeth. 2024. "Florida County Removed Dictionary and 1,600 Other Books." https://www.governing.com/

Hoffman, Bruce, and Jacon Ware. 2024. *God, Guns, and Sedition: Far-Right Terrorism in America.* New York: Columbia University Press.

Homans, Charles. 2024. "How Americans Justify Political Violence." https://www.nytimes.com/

Honoree, Andre L; David Terpstra; and John Friedl. 2014. "Red v. Blue States: Case of Employment Discrimination Influenced by Geography." *International Journal of Business and Social Research* 4, no. 3 (March): 1–11.

Howe, Amy. 2024. "Court Sends Media Moderation Cases Back to Lower Courts." https://www.scotusblog.com/

Hutton, Zina. 2024. "States Eye Social Media Bans Despite Legal Roadblocks." https://www.governing.com/

Jenkinson, Clay S. 2023. "What Would a National Divorce Look Like?" https://www.governing.com/

Jenkinson, Clay S. 2021. "Looking for Leverage: Moving America Forward." https://www.governing.com/

Kagan, Robert. 2024. *How Authoritarianism is Tearing America Apart—Again.* New York: Knopf Doubleday Publishing Group.

Kagan, Robert, 2023. "Opinion: A Trump Dictatorship is increasingly Inevitable. We Should Stop Pretending." https://www.Washingtonpost.com/

Kalmoe, Nathan P. 2020. *With Ballots and Bullets: Partisanship and Violence in the American Civil War.* Cambridge: Cambridge University Press.

Kalmoe, Nathan P., and Lilliana Mason. 2023. *Radical American Partisanship: Mapping Violent Hostility, Its Causes, and the Consequences for Democracy.* Chicago: University of Chicago Press.

Karni, Annie. 2024. "G.O.P. Backlash to Border Deal Reflects Vanishing Ground for a Compromise." https://www.nytimes.com/

Kennedy, Brian, and Alec Tyson. 2023. "Americans' Trust in Scientists, Positive Views of Science Continue to Decline." https://www.pewresearch.org/

Kenny, Christopher T; Cory McCartan; Tyler Simko; and Kosuke Imai. 2023. "Widespread Partisan Gerrymandering Mostly Cancels Nationally, but Reduces Electoral Competition." *Proceedings of the National Academy of Sciences* 120, no. 25 (June): 1–7.

Kern, Rebecca, and Josh Gerstein. 2024. "Biden Admin Can't be Sued for Pressuring Social Media Companies to Remove Misinformation, Supreme Court Rules." https://www.politico.com/

Kinder, Donald R., and Nathan P. Kalmoe. 2017. *Neither Liberal nor Conservative: Ideological Innocence in the American Public.* Chicago: University of Chicago Press.

Kindig, David A; Yasmin Mohd Ariffin; and Hannah Olson-Williams. 2024. "Is White Evangelical Antistructural Theology Related to Poor Health Outcomes?" *Milbank Quarterly* 102, no 2 (January);1–14.

Kirzinger, Ashely; Alex Montero; Liz Hamel; and Mollyann Brodie. 2023. "5 Charts About Public Opinion on the Affordable Care Act." https://www.kff.org/

Kleinfeld, Rachel. 2023. "Polarization, Democracy, and Political Violence in the United States: What the Research Says." https://carnegieendowment.org/

Knowles, Hanah, and Meryl Kornfield. 2024. "Loyalty, Long Lines, 'Civil War' Talk: A Raging Movement Propels Trump." https://www.washingtonpost.com/

Kottke, Joe. 2024. "New Wave of Bills Targeting Libraries is a Threat to Our Democracy, American Library Association Warns." https://www.nbcnews.com/

Lee-De-Wit; Sanders Van Der Linden; and Cameron Brick. 2019. "What are the Solutions to Political Polarization?" https://greatergood.berkeley.edu/

Lee, Josephine. 2024. "Abbott Appointee Slams Brakes on American Indian/Native Studies Course." https://www.texasobserver.org/

Levendusky, Matthew. 2023. *Our Common Bonds: Using What Americans Share to Help Bridge the Partisan Divide.* Chicago: University of Chicago Press.

Levendusky, Matthew. 2013. *How Partisan Media Polarizes America.* Chicago: University of Chicago Press.

Levendusky, Matthew, and Dominik A. Stecula. 2021. *We Need to Talk.* New Edition. Cambridge, MA: Cambridge University Press.

Levendusky, Matthew; Hosh Pasek; R. Lance Horbert; Bruce Hardy; Kate Kenski; Yotam Ophir; Andrew Renninger; Dan Romer; Dror Walter; and Kathleen Hall Jamieson. 2022. *Democracy Amid Crises: Polarization, Pandemic, Protests and Persuasion.* New York: Oxford University Press.

Levitt, Larry. 2022. "Medicaid as a Potential Third Rail of US Politics." *Journal of American Medical Association* 3, no. 12 (December): 1–3.

Liu, Eric. 2019. *Becoming America: Civic Sermons on Love, Responsibility, and Democracy.* Seattle: Sasquatch Books.

Levin, Yuval. 2017. *The Fractured Republic: Renewing America's Social Contract in the Age of Individualism.* New York: Basic Books.

Li, Michael. 2021. "The Redistricting Landscape, 2021–2022." https://www.brennancenter.org/

Liasson, Mara. 2021. "A Growing Number of Critics Raise Alarms About the Electoral College." https://www.npr.org/

Maddow, Rachel. 2023. *Prequel: An American Fight Against Fascism.* New York: Crown Publishing Group.

Marche, Stephen. 2022. *The Next Civil War: Dispatches from the American Future.* New York: Avid Reader Press.

Martinez, A., and Allison Aubrey. 2022. "The Partisan Divide Can Undermine Americans' Health, Research Say." https://www.npr.org/

Mason, Lilliana. 2018. *Uncivil Agreement: How Politics Became Our Identity.* Chicago: University of Chicago Press.

Mason, Lilliana, and Eric Liu. 2019. "Mandatory National Service." in "How to Fix Polarization: Bold Solutions to America's Polarization." https://www.politico.com/

McDaniel, Eric L.; Arfan Nooruddin; and Allyson F. Shortle. 2022. *Everyday Crusade: Christian Nationalism in American Politics.* New York: Cambridge University Press.

McGhee, Erick, and Boris Shor. 2017. "Has the Top Two Primary Elected more Moderates?" *Perspectives on Politics* 15, no. 4 (December): 1053–1066.

McQuade, Barbara. 2024a. "Swatting and the Dangerous Risk of Political Violence." https://www.nytimes.com/

McQuade, Barbara. 2024b. *Attack from Within: How Disinformation is Sabotaging America.* New York: Seven Stories Press.

McQuade, Barbara. 2024c. "Disinformation is Tearing America Apart." https://time.com/

Meckler, Laura, and Hannah Natanson. 2023. "More States Scrutinizing AP Black Studies After Florida Complaints." https://www.washingtonpost.com/

Meckler, Laura; Hannah Natanson; and John D. Harden. 2024. "In States with Laws Targeting LGBTQ Issues, School Hate Crimes Quadrupled." https://www.washingtonpost.com/

Metropoulos, Arielle. 2022. "For Red and Bue America, A Glaring Divide in COVID-19 Death Rates Persists Two Years Later." https://abcnews.go.com/

Milchen, Jeff. 2023. "The Escalating Attacks on Citizen Lawmaking." https://www.governing.com/

Millman, Jason. 2024. "ACA Enrollment Surged in Red States this Year." https://www.axios.com/

Mounk, Yascha. 2018. *The People Vs. Democracy: Why Our Freedom is in Danger and How to Save it.* Cambridge, MA: Harvard University Press.

Mullen, Thomas. 2024. *The Rumor Game: A Novel.* New York: Minotaur Books.

Mumma, Kristen S. 2023. "Politics and School Libraries: What Shapes Students' Access to Controversial Content." https://www.brookinmgs.edu/

Murthy, Vivek. 2023. *Our Epidemic of Loneliness and Isolation: The U.S. Surgeon General's Advisory on the Healing Effects of Social Connection and Community.* Washington, DC: Office of the U.S. Surgeon General.

Natanson, Hannah. 2023. "As Red States Target Black History Lessons, Blue States Embrace Them." https://www.washingtonpost.com/

Oberlander, Jonathan. 2020. "The Ten Years' War: Politics, Partisanship, and the ACA." *Health Affairs* 39, no. 3 (March): 471–478.

Oldenburg, Ray. 1989. *The Good Places. Cafes, coffee shops, Community Centers, General Stores, Bars, Hangouts, and How They Get Through the Day.* 1st edition. New Yorker: Paragon Press.

Oldenburg, Ray, and Karen Christiansen. 2023. *The Great Good Place: Cafes, Coffee Shops, Bookstores, Bars, Hairr Salons, and Other Hangouts at the Heart of a Community*. Great Barrington, MA: Berkshire Publishing Group, LLC.

Ortaliza, Jared; Cynthia Cox, and Krutika Amin. 2024. "Another Year of Record ACAN Marketplace Signups, riven in Part by Medicaid Unwinding and Enhanced Subsidies." https://www.kff.org/

Overgaard, Christian Staal Bruun, and Samuel Wooley. 2022. "How Social Media Platforms Can Reduce Polarization." https://www.brookings.edu/

Owermohle, Sarah. 2024. "Supreme Court to Weigh Whether COVID Misinformation is Protected Speech." https://www.statnews.com/

Pacewicz, John. 2016. *Partisans and Partners: The Politics of the Post-Keynesian Society*. Chicago: University of Chicago Press.

Park, Miles. 2023. "Ranked Choice is 'the Hot reform' in Democracy. Here is What You Should Know About it." https://www.npr.org/

Parks, Miles. 2019. "Abolishing the Electoral College Would be More Complicated Than It May Seem" https://www.npr.org/

Perry, Samuel L. 2024. "Why Evangelicals Went All in on Trump, Again." https://time.com/

Persily, Nathaniel. Editor. 2015. *Solutions to Political Polarization in America*. New York: Cambridge University Press.

Pew Research Center. 2023. "Majority of Americans Continue to Favor Moving Away from Electoral College." https://www.pewresearch.org/

Picone, Paul. 2023. *Italian Marxism*. Oakland: University of California Press.

Pink, Daniel. 2024. "Why Not Require a Civic Test as a Rite of Passage for All Americans?" https://www.washingtonpost.com/

"Policy Tracker: Youth Access to Gender Affirming Care and State Policy Restrictions." 2024. https://www.kff.org/

Poniewozik, James. 2024. "How Does Democracy Die? Maybe by Laser Vision." https://www.nytimes.com/

"PRRI/The Atlantic 2018 Voter Engagement Survey." 2018. https://www.prri.org/

Putnam, Robert D. 2001. *Bowling Alone: Revised and Updated: The Collapse and Revival of American Communities*. New York: Simon and Schuster.

Putnam, Robert D. 2000. *Bowling Alone*. New York: Simon and Schuster.

Rachman, Gideon. 2022. *The Age of Strongman: How the Cult of the Leader Threatens Democracy Around the World*. New York: Oher Press Publisher.

Ramachandran, Gowri; Chisun Lee; Kimberly Peeler-Allen; Ruby Edlin; Julia Fishman; Jiyoon Park; and Grady Y. Short. 2024. *Intimidation of State and Local Officials: Left Unchecked, Abuse Harms Not Only Elected Officials but the Public They Serve*. Washington, DC: Brennan Center for Social Justice.

"Ranked-Choice Voting RCV." 2024. https://ballotpedia.org/

"Redistricting: Proposed Reforms in 2023." 2023. https://represent.us/

Reid, Jo-Ann. 2023. "A 'National Divorce' Would Destroy Red States. Let's Count the Ways." https://www.msnbc.com/

"Reported Hate Crimes at Schools: 2018–2022." 2024. Federal Bureau of Investigation, U.S. Department of Justice. https://cde.ucr.cjis.gov/

Repucci, Sarah. 2021. "From Crisis to Reform: A Call to Strengthened America's Battered Democracy." Special Report, 2021. https://freedomhouse.org/

Richardson, Heather Cox. 2023. *Democracy Awakening: Notes on the State of America*. New York: Viking Press.
Rosenfield, Sam. 2017. *The Polarizers: Postwar Architects of Our Partisan Era*. Chicago: University of Chicago Press.
Rothwell, Jonathan, and Christos Makridis. 2020. "Politics is Wrecking America's Pandemic Response." https://www.brookings.edu/
Rugy, Veronique de. 2011. "The Red/Blue Paradox." *Reason* 43, no. 4 (Aug/Sept): 18–19.
Saad, Lydia. 2013. "In the U.S., Blue States Outnumber Red States, 20 to 12." https://news.gallup.com/
Sasse, Ben. 2019. *Them: Why We Hate Each Other—and How to Heal*. New York: St. Partin's Press.
Sides, John; Chris Tausanovitch; and Lynn Vavreck. 2020. "The Politics of COVID-19: Partisan Polarization About the Pandemic has Increased, but Support for Health Care Reform Hasn't Moved at All." *Harvard Data Science Review*. Special Issue 1. Published online on November 30. https://hdsr.mitpress.mit.edu/
Sides, John; Michael Tesler; and Lynn Vavreck. 2018. *Identity Crisis: The 2016 Presidential Campaign and the Battle for the Meaning of America*. Princeton, NJ: Princeton University Press.
Simon, Steven, and Jonathan Stevenson. 2022. "These Disunited States." https://www.nybooks.com/
Smith, Carl. 2024. "Domestic Disruptions are Equal Risk to Foreign Interference in 2024 Elections, Expert Say." https://www.governing.com/
Smith, Carl. 2023. "Taking Temperature of American Democracy." https://www.governing.com/
Somasundaram, Praveena, and Hannah Natanson. 2024. "Florida Removes Sociology as Core Course Option for Public Colleges." https://www.washingtonpost.com/
Stableford, Dylan. 2023. "Trump Criminal Charges: Here are 91 Felony Counts Against the Former President Across 4 Cases." https://news.yahoo.com/
Stirewalt, Chris. 2022. *Broken News: Why the Media Rage Machines Divides America and How to Fight it Back*. New York: Hachette Book Group, Inc.
Suri, Jeremi. 2024. "How the Attempted Assassination of Donald Trump Fits into America's Violence History." https://time.com/
Thompson, Derek. 2024. "Why Americans Suddenly Stopped Hanging Out." https://www.Atlantic.com/
Tirrell, Meg, and John Bonifield. 2024. "Fleeing Under the Cover of Darkness: How Idaho's Abortion Ban is Changing Pregnancy in the States." https://www.cnn.com/
Thornberg, Benjamin; Arlene Kennedy-Hendricks; Joanne D. Rosen; and Matthew D. Eisenberg. 2024. "Anxiety and Depression Symptoms After Dobbs Abortion Decision." *Journal of American Medical Association* 331, no 4 (January): 294–301.
"Threat to American Democracy Head of an Unprecedented Presidential Election." 2023. https://www.prri.org/
Troiano, Nick. 2021. "Party Primaries Must Go." https://www.theatlantic.com/

Vasilogambros, Matt. 2024. "Feds Deliver Stark Warning to State Election Officials Ahead of November." https://www.governing.com/
Vasilogambros, Matt. 2022. "Don't Vote for Just One: Raked-Choice Voting is Gaining Ground." https://www.governing.org/
Walter, Barbara F. 2022. *How Civil War Start: And How to Stop Them*. New York: Crown Publishing Group.
Wang, Samuel S.; Richard F. Ober, Jr; and Ben Williams. 2019. "Laboratories of Democracy Reform: State Constitutions and Partisan Gerrymandering." *University of Pennsylvania Journal of Constitutional Law* 22, no. 1 (November); 219–290.
Weber, Lauren; Dan Diamond; and Dan Keating. 2023. "How Red-State Politics are Shaving Years off American Lives." https://www.waashingtonpost.com/
Wegman, Jesse. 2020. *Let the People Pick President: The Case for Abolishing the Electoral College*. New York: St. Martin's Press.
West, Darrell M. 2022. *Power Politics: Trump and the Assault on American Democracy*. Washington, DC: Brookings Institution Press.
West, Darrell M. 2019. "It's Time to Abolish the Electoral College." https://www.brookings.edu/
"Which Groups Have Experienced an Increase in Hate Crimes?" 2023. https://usafacts.org/
Whitesell, Anne. 2024. "The Increasing Trend of Lawmakers Overriding Ballot Initiatives." https://www.governing.com/
Whitehead, Andrew L., and Samuel L. Perry. 2020. *Taking America Back for God: Christian Nationalism in the United States*. New York: Oxford University Press.
Williamson, Vanessa. 2023. "Understanding the Democratic Decline in the United States." https://www.brookings.edu/
Zakaria, Fareed. 2024. *Age of Revolution: Progress and Backlash From 1600 to the Present*. New York: W. W. Norton & Company.
Zakrzewski, Cat, and Ann E. Marimow. 2024. "Supreme Court to Decide if States Can Control Fate of Social Media." https://www.washingtonpost.com/
Zhu, Jane M; Sarah Gollust; Yuan-Chi Yang; Abeed Sker; and David Grande. 2021. "Public and Political Opinion on Medicaid." https://ldi.upenn.edu/
Zittrain, Jonathan. 2019. Rethink Social Media So It Doesn't Encourage Conflict." in "How to Fix Polarization: Bold Solutions to America's Problems." 2019. https://www.politico.com/

INDEX

Pages in **bold** refer to tables.

Abbott, Greg 98, 486
Abortion legality versus access 332
Administrative Procedures Act (APA) 433
Affordable Care Act (ACA), red and blue state divide: court cases 233–240; divide over adoption 223–229; Medicaid expansion 292–296; partisan divide 229; polarization and ACA 261–265; states' rights 328–329; Trump administration 231–233
American democracy in decline 466–468
American federalism 63–69, 447; benefits of 65–66; dangers of 66–67; evolution of 63–64; fractured 408; kaleidoscopic 408; politics of 67–69; variable speed 408
American Medical Association (AMA) 332
Anti-Defamation League 464
attack on Affordable Care Act 231

Biden Administration 433, 445; American Rescue Plan 415; Consolidated Appropriations Act (2023) 415; emergency rental assistance program 415; Inflation Reduction Act (2022) 415; National Strategy for the COVID-19 Response 414–415; mandates 433; Medicaid work requirements 303
Biden, Joseph 142–148, 445
Broderick, John T. 1
Brody, David 24
Brooks, David 94–97

causes of political polarization: divided government 30; Electoral College 31; mass media 32–35, 463; primaries 32; redistricting/gerrymandering 31
Centers for Disease Control and Prevention (CDC) 174–176, 425, 427–433
Centers for Medicaid and Medicare Services (CMS) 433
China 401, 406, 434
Christian right 384–385
Clinton, Hillary 462–463
Commonwealth Fund 201–202, 213–215
Comstock Act 333
consequences of political polarization 38–42; negative consequences 38–40; positive consequences 40–41

Coronavirus Aid, Relief and Economic Security Act (CARES Act) 413
court cases: *Braidwood Management, Inc. v. Becerra* 239–240; *Burrell v. Hobby Lobby Stores* 234–236, 336; *California v. Texas* 238–239; *Citizens United* 21; *Dobbs v. Jackson's Women Health Organization* 22, 189–190, 351–353, 386; *Doe v. Bolton* 334; *Gonzalez v. Carhart* 336; *Gonzales v. Planned Parenthood Federation of America* 336; *Griswold v. Connecticut* 334; *Harris v. McRae* 335; *King v. Burrell* 236–237; *McCutcheon v. FEC* 21; *Missouri v. Biden* 433; *Moore v. Harper* 21; *National Federation of Independent Businesses v. Sebelius* 233–234; *National Federation of Independent Businesses et al v. Department of Labor* 433; *Planned Parenthood of Southeastern PA v. Casey* 335–336; *Roe v. Wade* 22, 334–336, 341, 343, 351–353, 386; *Shelby County v. Holder* 21; *Stenberg v. Carhart* 336; *United States v. One Package* 333; *Vacco v. Quill* 387; *Washington v. Gluckberg* 387; *Webster v. Reproductive Health Services* 335; *Whole Woman's Health v. Hellerstedt* 338; *Zubik v. Burwell* 336
COVID-19: and cases 402–403, 416–417; and rural areas 404–405; and social networks 412; and workforce 405; deaths from 401–403, 417–418; impact on hospitals 404–405, 418–419; long COVID 419–420; state and local government responsibility 425; variants 401–402, 448
COVID Crisis Group 408, 413
COVID States Project 411–412

debate over reproductive rights 316–328
Defense Production Act (1950) 413
DeSantis, Ron 443
differences between Medicaid and Medicare 271
divided government 4, 30

emergency declarations 413, 415–416
Emergency Medical Treatment and Labor Act (EMTALA) 367
emergency powers/declarations 415–416
emergency use authorization 416
evolution of political polarization 6–14; nativism 11–14; sectarianism 8–10; tribalism 7–8

facts about abortion in the United States 331–332
Federal Bureau of Investigation (FBI) 485
Federal Emergency Management Agency 409, 413
Federal Food, Drug, and Cosmetic Act 415–416
Food and Drug Administration (FDA) 415–416, 435
federalism 447; fractured 408; kaleidoscopic 408; variable speed 408
Food and Drug Administration (FDA) 173, 333, 337, 376, 378–380, 415

Gallup Organization 260
George W. Bush administration 409
Gestational Age Act 351
great replacement theory 12
Greenblat, Alan 7–8, 448
Guttmacher Institute 357–372, 374

Haas, Richard 466
Harding, Warren G. 448
Health and Human Services, Department of 4
history of plagues: black death 400; HIV/AIDS 401; plague of Justinian 400; Spanish flu 400, 443; smallpox 400, 434
Homeland Security, Department of 409
House Select Subcommittee on the Coronavirus Pandemic 407
Huckabee, Sarah 98

implementation of Affordable Care Act 240–256
Institute for Women's Policy Research 346, 349
Institute of Labor Economics 369
insurance: uninsurance 253–254

Jefferson, et al 430
Jefferson, Tom 431
Jenner, Edward 434
Johnson & Johnson 436

Kennedy, Robert F., Jr. 44
Kornacki, Steve 6

Ladapo, Joseph 443
Lazar, Baum, and Qu 430–431

mask mandates 429–432
McQuade, Barbara 465
Measles 447
Medicaid 191–192
Medicaid and CHIP eligibility 275–281; children 278; population covered by Medicaid 280–281; pregnancy or pregnant women 278–279
Medicaid expansion 292–300; reasons for and against 299–300
Medicaid financing 284–289
Medicaid work requirements 300–305
Merck 436
Middle East Respiratory Syndrome (MERS) 41
Moderna 436
morality politics and policies 330
mRNA 436
Murthy, Vivek 462

National Basketball Association (NBA) 425
National Emergencies Act (1976) 444
non-pharmaceutical interventions (NPI) 424–425
Novavax 436

Obama administration 409
Occupational Safety and Health Administration (OSHA) 433
Operation Warp Speed 414, 435–436
origin of pandemic 406, 429–430, 445–446; lab leak theory 406, 446; open market theory 406, 446
origins of Medicaid 270–271
origins of political polarization 4–6
Osterholm, Michael T. 445

partial birth abortion 327
Partial Birth Abortion Ban Act 337

partisan and religious divide over abortion 330–333, 353
partisan divide over abortion in red and blue stats 336–351; abortion clinics/facilities and access to abortion 338–343; abortion restrictions, bans, and trigger laws 343–351
partisan divide over COVID-19 pandemic: in COVID cases and deaths 420–424; over masking 427–428
partisan divide over public health 442–443
Pew Research Center 329
Pfizer 436
polarization and healthcare policy 215–216
polarization of the American electorate 24–29; affective polarization 27–29; ideological polarization 26–27; partisan polarization 24–25; public opinion 29–30
policy toolkit: analyzing wastewater 411; lockdowns 405, 410, 425–427, 446; masking 410, 427–433, 446; mitigation 409–410, 419, 424–426; public opinion 412; reporting 411; social distancing 410; testing 410–411, 414; vaccines 411, 414, 434
political discourse 2
political polarization: affective 3, 27–29, 461–463; asymmetric polarization 17; definition 3; elite polarization 3–4, 14–18; ideological 3, 26–27, 460; mass polarization 3–4; partisan 3, 24–25, 460
political polarization and abortion policy 386–387
political polarization and public policy 41–42; national level 41–42; state level 42
political polarization and states health policy 480–485
political polarization and the presidential election of 2020 138–148; demographic divide 146–147; economic divide 145–146; geographic divide 142–145; religious divide 147–148

political polarization of the elite
14–18; elite ideological polarization
16–18; elite partisan polarization
14–16
political polarization of the judiciary
18–24; federal judiciary 19–24;
state judiciary 19
political rhetoric-violence-Civil War
35–38, 463–466; Civil War 37;
public opinion and hate speech 36;
public opinion and violence 37–38
public opinion: and Affordable Care
Act 227, 256–261; and American
democracy 38–39, 486–487; and *in
vitro fertilization* 382; and masking
429; and pandemic 407–408; and
policy toolkit 411–412; and
reproductive rights 329–330,
359–360, 362–363; and the
Supreme Court 23–24; and trust in
government 39
public health: preparedness for
pandemic 405; lack of trust 443,
447–448
Putnam, Robert 462

red and blue state politics 112–127;
ease or difficulty of voting 123–125;
gender, racial, and ethnic
composition of state legislatures
113–117; gender, racial, and ethnic
composition of state supreme courts
117; political ideology 125–127;
registration and voter turnout
117–123
red and blue states demographics
70–74; age and gender 84–87;
immigration 76–79; racial and
ethnic diversity 79–84
red and blue states economic indicators
99–112; cost of living 106–107;
dependence on federal government
109–111; fiscal stability 111–112;
income 99–102; poverty 102–104;
productivity 107–109; taxes
105–106; unemployment 102
red and blue states education 87–99;
educational achievement 91–93;
public school expenditures 98–91;
quality of public education 94–99
red and blue states health care
financing 160–165

red and blue states health care
indicators 200–221
red and blue states health status
indicators 165–177; causes of death
167–177; children 191–200; guns
and homicides 185–188; life
expectancy 165–167; mental health
177–185; maternal health 188–191
red and blue states Medicaid divide:
enrollment and disenrollment
289–292, 305–316; expansion **295**,
296–300; financing 285–289; rating
of Medicaid programs 316–318
red and blue states vaccination rates
436, **437**
red states and blue states and public
policy 43
religion and politics: cultural wars
127–138; religious divide in the
2020 presidential election 147–148;
religious divide over abortion 381,
383–385; religion and *in vitro
fertilization* 381–382
reproductive rights around the world
324–326
reproductive rights in red and blue
states after *Dobbs* ruling 354–360;
abortion, elections, and ballot
initiatives 360–366; abortion
numbers by state—pre and post-
Dobbs decision 369, 372; abortion
providers/clinics and out-of-state
travel for abortion 372–374; court
challenges over abortion pill
377–380; court challenges over
birth control pill 380; court
challenges over *in vitro fertilization*
380–382; legislative actions
354–359; medication abortion
374–377; religious divide over
abortion 383–385; state
constitutions and court challenges
383–385
rise of right-wing authoritarianism
468–469
Robert T. Stafford Disaster Relief and
Emergency Assistance Act (Stafford
Act) 413
Roper Center 259–261

SARS-CoV-2 401; *see also* COVID-19
Sasse, Ben 461–462

Index **501**

schools 425
Solutions to political polarization: electoral reforms 469–477; legislative reforms 477; regulation of mass media 478–479; social reforms 479–480
State Children's Health Insurance Program (SCHIP) 273; eligibility 277
Stephens, Bret 429–430
structure of Medicaid: benefits 275; coverage 278
Sullivan, Andrew 7–8
Sweden 426

target restrictions on abortion providers 337–338
Tomasky, Michael 5
transformation of Medicaid 271–273; and Affordable Care Act 272–273
Transportation Security Administration (TSA) 433
Trump administration: emergency declarations 415–416; Medicaid work requirements 301–305; pandemic 407, 409, 412–414, 416, 446

Trump, Donald 12–13, 21, 35–37, 142–148, 343, 407, 413–416, 420, 427–428, 435–436, 444, 446, 461, 464, 487
typology of red, blue, and purple states 43–46

U.S. Department of Health and Human Services (HHS) 174
U.S. Supreme Court and reproductive rights 327–328
Urban Institute 254–256
use and misuse of language about abortion 327–328

vaccines 414, 446–448; mandates 433; misinformation 443–444; objections to 440–441; polio 434; Sabin vaccine 434–435; Salk vaccine 434–435; side effects 440; Tuskegee experiments and the Black community 440, 443; vaccine development 435
Vance, J. D. 98

Walters, Barbara 465–466
World Health Organization (WHO) 435, 444–445